Using Political Ideas

Fourth Edition

Barbara Goodwin

University of East Anglia, Norwich

JOHN WILEY & SONS

Chichester · New York · Weinheim · Brisbane · Singapore · Toronto

First Edition 1982
Second Edition 1987
Copyright © 1982, 1987 by John Wiley & Sons Ltd,
                        Baffins Lane, Chichester,
                        West Sussex PO19 1UD, England

                        National   01243 779777
                        International (+44) 1243 779777
                        e-mail (for orders and customer service enquiries):
                        cs-books@Wiley.co.uk
                        Visit our Home Page on http://www.wiley.co.uk
                                            or http://www.wiley.com

Third Edition © 1992 by Barbara Goodwin   ·
Fourth Edition © 1997 by Barbara Goodwin

Reprinted October 1998

Other Wiley Editorial Offices

John Wiley & Sons, Inc., 605 Third Avenue,
New York, NY 10158-0012, USA

WILEY-VCH Verlag GmbH, Pappelallee 3,
D-69469 Weinheim, Germany

Jacaranda Wiley Ltd, 33 Park Road, Milton,
Queensland 4064, Australia

John Wiley & Sons (Asia) Pte Ltd, 2 Clementi Loop #02-01,
Jin Xing Distripark, Singapore 129809

John Wiley & Sons (Canada) Ltd, 22 Worcester Road,
Rexdale, Ontario M9W 1L1, Canada

Library of Congress Cataloging-in-Publication Data

Goodwin, Barbara.
    Using political ideas / Barbara Goodwin. — 4th ed.
        p.   cm.
    Includes bibliographic references and index.
    ISBN 0-471-97343-2 (paper)
    1. Political science.   2. Ideology.   I. Title.
    JA71.G66   1997
    320.5—dc21   97-26643
                                                 CIP

British Library Cataloguing in Publication Data

A catalogue record for this book is available from the British Library

ISBN 0-471-97343-2

Typeset in 10/12pt Times from the author's disks by Dobbie Typesetting Ltd, Tavistock, Devon
Printed and bound in Great Britain by Redwood Books, Trowbridge, Wiltshire
This book is printed on acid-free paper responsibly manufactured from sustainable forestation,
for which at least two trees are planted for each one used for paper production.

Contents

Preface to the Fourth Edition

This new edition of *Using Political Ideas* contains two new chapters, one on feminism and one on Green ideologies. These additions reflect the constant transformation of political debate by new discourses and ideologies—political ideas are not static. The rest of the book has also been revised and updated to reflect the changing political scene and to take into account new arguments. Despite the demise of communism in the Soviet Union and Eastern Europe, there is still a chapter on Marxism because Marxist thought continues to challenge to liberal-democratic ideas in important ways and to offer an alternative perspective on our social and economic system.

My sincere thanks go to all those who have commented on the third edition of the book, including many students; in particular, I am grateful to the colleagues who commented on parts of the new edition, especially John Greenaway and Kate Nash at the University of East Anglia, and Nick Rankin of the BBC World Service. Above all, I would like to thank my husband Michael Miller, whose computer expertise has been invaluable in ensuring the smooth production of the new book, for his generous help, support and kindness.

BARBARA GOODWIN
School of Economic and Social Studies,
University of East Anglia, Norwich

_____ Part One

Introduction

Chapter 1

What is Political Theory?

This chapter sets out to define terms such as political theory, political philosophy and ideology, and to clarify the meaning of various specialist terms used by political theorists. It offers examples of contentious or fallacious arguments to illustrate the fact that any political argument advanced can be contested from a different ideological perspective and to demonstrate the importance of political theory for evaluating the validity of ideological arguments.

Should people be more equal? Is the state more important than the individual? Can a socialist society be free? Is political violence ever justified? Must we tolerate the intolerant? Can the majority dictate to the minority? Is it right that the rich should also be powerful? Such questions are the concerns of political theory. Although they sound deceptively simple, susceptible to 'Yes' or 'No' answers, when we try to answer them it becomes evident that each conceals a wealth of disputable assumptions and that the meaning of its key words is also disputable. Furthermore, the answers inevitably express opinions on *what ought to be the case*, rather than describing *what is the case*. Political values and ideals are at stake here, and choices between ideals must be made. *I* may give priority to freedom rather than equality because I think it more vital to human happiness, *you* may judge the opposite. Most of us are influenced by political ideology, whether we knowingly subscribe to it or unconsciously absorb it as part of received opinion, so not only do the answers to political questions vary according to individual opinion, they also differ with the individual's ideological position.

The practice of political theory helps us to set about answering such questions logically, and to criticize the answers which others give, by dealing with political matters at a more abstract and general level than does political science. Take the question 'Is political violence ever justified?' The constitutional theorist's answer would be an emphatic negative since violence is outlawed both legally and constitutionally. But political theory asks if justification might not be advanced according to circumstance. Does not an oppressed minority, denied the freedom to state its case, have a justification for using violence? Does not the validity of that justification further depend on what sort of violence and against whom it is directed? And so on. The usefulness of political theory is that it allows us to consider such problems without always returning to the factual replies of the constitutionalist or lawyer. It frees us to think critically, speculatively or idealistically, instead of being trapped into describing what exists as if it could never be changed. A critical approach rests on the ability to escape from the existent.

At first it appears that most 'great' political theorists are engaged not in criticism but in a permanent struggle to legitimize rulers or governments and to justify the phenomenon of power. Plato looked to absolute justice to justify his Guardians as rightful rulers, Christian theologians of the middle ages looked to God's intentions to sanction the rule of kings, while contract theorists such as Hobbes and Locke saw government as founded on the people's rational choice. But Plato, Hobbes and Locke were also among the foremost critics of the politics of their own societies and voiced this opposition in their descriptions of government *as it should be*, ideal government. Naturally, there have also been theoretical apologists for most existing regimes, but propagandists are intrinsically less interesting except to the social historian, and rarely end up on political theory syllabuses. Political theory is a technique of analysis which can be used to overturn, as well as to uphold. Departing from fact and detail, it describes and explains politics in abstract and general terms, which allow scope for the critical imagination.

Political theory may therefore be defined as the discipline which aims to explain, justify or criticize the disposition of power in society. It delineates the balance of power between states, groups and individuals. 'Power' is used broadly here: even *obedience* is an aspect of power, for it connotes deliberate self-restraint by citizens who might otherwise resist the government. Essentially, power lies where resources (personal, economic, moral, ideological, etc.) lie, and operates through inducements as much as through threats and through the withholding as well as the deployment of resources. Sociologists often analyse power in terms of individual interaction, as A's capacity to get B to comply with her (A's) desires; political theory sets these familiar, everyday machinations in a formal power structure. However, even theorists observing the same phenomena may conceptualize the power structure differently (where liberals saw equality and social harmony, Marx saw conflict and oppression). Different conclusions result: for example, a constitutionalist who views politics in terms of institutions might consider that unions should not be politically active, while someone viewing politics as pressure group activity would think it inevitable that they should be. Diverse conceptualizations of power therefore generate diverse political ideals and problems.

The reader new to political theory might raise the following objection to the subject: surely it would be better to study political institutions rather than abstract concepts, since ideas must be incarnated in institutions if they are to have any meaning. We can best discover the meaning of 'democracy', it might be thought, by examining the institutions of our own and other democratic countries and extrapolating their crucial features, rather than by reading Plato *et al*. This raises a fundamental problem which haunts all social science subjects: which comes first, concept or fact, theory or reality? Is there an *essence* of democracy, or is it constituted by a configuration of the institutions observed in Western-style democracies? This is a modern reiteration of the most ancient philosophical controversy: does reality reflect ideas, or vice versa?

This perennial question cannot be answered satisfactorily here, but it provides an opportunity to define some of the mysterious labels which are tied to various arguments in political theory. Plato's view, also associated with Descartes and others, that reality approximates to unchanging transcendental ideas, is labelled *idealist* (not to be confused with the more familiar 'idealistic' which means 'promoting ideals or values'). In social science, an idealist approach means that ideas and theory precede factual observation. The opposing view, originally associated with Locke, that concepts derive from our observation of physical or material reality, is generally called *materialist* (again, differing from 'materialistic', which means 'concerned with material wealth or goods').

A materialist outlook is often associated with the *empirical* and *inductive* scientific method, although not invariably. *Empiricism* requires that the natural or social scientist should first observe reality and then induce a general theory based on a large number of instances or facts. It is associated with *positivism*, which insists that the only meaningful statements are those which are verifiable by reference to the real world; moral, religious and metaphysical statements are, as a consequence, held to be meaningless and empty. Empiricism is the dominant scientific method in the Anglo-Saxon world. The Greek root of 'empirical' means 'trial', which suggests that the empiricist lacks preconceptions and is a naïve observer who makes discoveries through experiment: this contrasts with the procedure of the *rationalist*, who starts with a theory. The conflict between the empiricist and rationalist viewpoints is one of *epistemology*—that is, it is concerned with the criteria by which knowledge can be established and so with truth, falsehood and proof. This debate, although philosophical, is closely related to issues in political theory, as we shall see.

Meanwhile, the objector who wants to define democracy by observing democratic states still awaits an answer. She is evidently advocating an empirical approach which would supply the general principles of democracy by investigating its organizational features. The obvious drawback is that to analyse the idea by examining countries or institutions which are reputedly democratic leaves us with no independent criterion to judge whether they are so or not. And how would this approach cope with non-Western, self-proclaimedly democratic countries which seem authoritarian to the Western observer, such as Singapore and Tanzania? It has no obvious justification for excluding them from its analysis. To define 'democracy' through a study of existing, so-called democracies begs the question of what democracy means. A theory so formed can only mirror observed phenomena, whereas a theory which is to have critical power needs to make reference to the ideal composition of democracy.

The case against the empirical or 'concrete' approach to political concepts was well put by Marcuse. He contended that our political vocabulary has become increasingly 'closed', with key words being defined in concrete, factual terms (for example, 'democracy means one-man-one-vote, the secret ballot, equal constitu-encies . . . ') so that critical usages have become impossible.

> Such nouns as 'freedom', 'equality', 'democracy', and 'peace' imply, analytically, a
> specific set of attributes which occur invariably when the noun is spoken or
> written. . . . The ritualized concept is made immune against contradiction.[1]

In other words, political concepts have become like the minor characters in Dickens' novels, each with his or her distinguishing trait. We cannot imagine freedom without consumer choice any more than we can picture Mrs Gamp without a gin bottle, hence we have a 'one-dimensional' view of freedom. Marcuse cited research about factory workers' grievances in which the researchers made the complaints concrete, transforming vague grumbles about conditions and pay into specific complaints about dirty washrooms or the financial problems of particular workers. By such devices (which employers also use), heartfelt alienation is dissolved into concrete trivia and the critical element of the grievances is banished. Marcuse's general thesis was that the concrete approach to political matters deliberately precludes the proper use of abstract concepts as open-ended tools for criticism and protest. Even if Marcuse's attack on capitalism is rejected, his point, that the critical dimension is essential to thought and argument, is indisputable.

The term 'criticism' is frequently given a pejorative undertone, but in defining criticism as the central task of political theory, I view it in the neutral sense in which Enlightenment philosophers saw it, as the tool by which our reason appraises the social order. Only by taking an abstract, conceptual approach, starting from ideals or theory, can we achieve an appraisal which is *detached* from existing society, even if it cannot be entirely impartial. Political science and political sociology often lack detachment; political theory is important because it can offer this perspective.

Such arguments may convince the sceptic that political theory is indeed worthwhile, but she may still doubt its relevance to real life. Is it not an ivory-tower subject of no interest to ordinary citizens, a subject whose detached approach prevents it from influencing the world below? The next few pages are intended to show not only that political theory can sharply analyse current political controversies, but also that even the crudest political argument relies on the fundamental concepts and ideals supplied by theory. Often these are unvoiced, but their role in determining the forms which political argument and *Realpolitik* take is crucial. Consequently, the political theorist has the important task of exposing these hidden mechanisms.

The debate about workers' participation in management, alias 'industrial democracy', appears to concern industrial relations but is really a contemporary rehearsal of age-old arguments as to the best form of government. The advocates of workers' management (including some employers) see participation as a positive good. It increases the number of viewpoints considered, gives the workers the sense that they are controlling their own destinies, increases the acceptability

---

1. H. Marcuse, *One Dimensional Man*, Sphere, 1968, pp. 79–80.

of decisions and emphasizes workers' responsibility to follow management policies. (The idea of workers' representatives on Boards of Directors could in this sense be said to draw implicitly on Hobbes's view that the elector has a duty to abide by what his/her representative decides.[2]) Against this, opponents assert the value of specialist and expert management, reflecting the justification of elite government which, since Plato's time, has often rested implicitly on an assumed division between mental and manual labour. In the context of this argument, workers are said to be preoccupied with their own short-term wellbeing, and unable to make the strategic industrial choices which require economic know-how and managerial experience. By contrast, a board of experts, managers, and informed outsiders would supposedly make un-self-interested decisions benefiting both firm and employees.[3]

The two underlying principles in this debate were familiar even in classical times, when both government by experts and participation by the people were tried in the Greek *polis* or city-state of ancient Athens. The former emphasizes the benefits that knowledge and wisdom bring to mankind, while the more egalitarian principle spells out the subjective importance for individuals of having a voice in public affairs. Expertise and efficiency or participation and greater satisfaction? These rival values are incommensurable, and cannot be simultaneously realized; a choice about worker participation (or, more generally, about good governance) requires an ordering of priorities. A change of priorities, or values, changes the social institutions which embody the values, so the ability to identify and evaluate the old and new values is important for participants in such political debate.

I now turn to a set of arguments based on less reputable principles. It is often argued that immigrants in Britain have no right to be here, even 'third-generation immigrants', and that they consume resources to which indigenous British people are entitled. Underpinning this assertion is a view of *'natural' justice*, which deems that being born in a country gives one a special right to its resources, including a right to welfare and a right to work. This is an instinctive or 'gut' conception of justice, hence the epithet 'natural', a term often invoked when rationality offers no support to an argument.

In times when there was little transport or mobility and people lived in village economies which were locally self-sufficient, there was some basis for the view that they had a primary claim to the local resources which they themselves processed and relied on (although there were also traditions of generosity between communities in hard times.) Now that migration is common and mobility almost universal, at least in the West, and economies are not local or national, but international, how could we substantiate such a claim to natural entitlement? Anyone who maintained that only native Mancunians had the right to work in Manchester or consume its precious manufactures would rightly be found guilty of absurdity. But this patently absurd argument differs only in degree from the claim that immigrants should not live or work here. The controversy over the

2. T. Hobbes, in *Leviathan*, (Ed. C. B. Macpherson), Penguin, 1968, pp. 218–19.
3. M. Kiloh, 'Industrial democracy' in D. Held & C. Pollitt (Eds.), *New Forms of Democracy*, Sage, 1986.

notion of patriality in the 1971 Act restricting immigration (further complicated by the Acts of 1981 and 1988) made plain the incongruity of the idea of natural entitlement. In what sense is a 'patrial', someone with at least one British grandparent, *entitled* to come to Britain and work? Grandpaternity may be a natural relationship, but it is also arbitrarily chosen—why not cousinhood, or aunthood?—and bears a tenuous link to the right or need to immigrate.

If, on the other hand, there *is* a principle of natural justice, it might equally support immigration. Most immigration since the Second World War has been a consequence of the colonization which created the British Empire: the extension of British nationality to inhabitants of the colonies gave them a right, and an incentive, to migrate to Britain. Our present wealth, it could be argued, is substantially derived from our use of those colonies' resources, to which the forebears of today's immigrants may have considered that *they* had a natural entitlement. Does not natural justice therefore decree that their grandchildren should come and share our prosperity? This argument may be as poor as the opposing one, but it shows that citing natural justice to substantiate a non-legal claim against someone is a double-edged process, because the notion of entitlement by birth, geography or similar accident can usually be countered by another, equally 'natural', claim. There may be pragmatic and tactical reasons for limiting immigration, but we should refrain from thinking that such a limitation is necessarily based on justice.

The emotional and intuitive appeal of claims to natural justice is evidently strong, but the concept collapses under scrutiny. Bentham argued in the eighteenth century that 'natural rights' are nonsense, the only rights being those established in positive law. He would have said that the same goes for natural justice. Malthus wrote of the pauper, 'At Nature's mighty feast there is no vacant cover for him. She tells him to begone.' In one respect, Malthus was right: in no sense does the world 'naturally' owe us a living, even less does a particular corner of the world owe some people, rather than others, a livelihood. The fact that such claims have been established by social and legal convention does not make them naturally just. There is no justice in nature, although we have contended against the intractability of the natural world and its imperviousness to our needs by creating the idea of human rights and, more recently, those of 'welfare rights' and the 'social minimum'. But crucial to the idea of human rights is their *universality*, i.e. *every* individual's claim to life and livelihood—a claim which 'natural justice' arguments often reject.

Prominent among contemporary political movements are nationalism, separatism, regionalism and devolutionism. Kurds, Armenians, Kashmiris, Scottish nationalists, the IRA and many other minority groups demand, or fight for, autonomy, and recently many such groups in the former USSR and Eastern Europe have succeeded, such as the peoples of Lithuania, Latvia and Estonia and the Croatians. The justifications for these demands and struggles all rest on an ideal of self-determination, supported by a notion of the 'natural' geographical, racial or cultural unit. The axiom 'what is natural is good' prevails. When we consider how arbitrarily and for what Machiavellian reasons many national boundaries were drawn, especially in colonial Africa or post-1918 and post-1945 Europe, it is small wonder that internecine wars and separatism are now rife. At first, the idea of the natural social unit seems valid, because members of racial or language groups, for example, clearly have salient cultural characteristics which unite them and differentiate them from others. But it is not easy to devise a general political principle on this basis of natural affinity. 'The people's right to self-determination' which created free Balkan states in 1919 also provided justification for Hitler's march into Austria and his invasions of Czechoslovakia and Poland to 'protect' German-speaking citizens. Similar problems have arisen again in Eastern Europe, where each country contains minorities whose ethnic allegiance is to a neighbouring state. The most aggressive forms of nationalism are often based on a dogmatic assertion of the naturalness of the national unit. Certainly, many nations today suffer from unsuitable or inconvenient boundaries, or are unhappy agglomerates of different cultural groups (as was the former Yugoslavia), yet the destruction of their territorial integrity might have worse consequences for everybody, separatists included. In the face of such intractable problems, political theory can at least analyse the arguments about 'natural units', to see whether they are well founded or universally applicable. It can also offer alternative ways of conceptualizing such situations, which may be more appropriate or fruitful. Nationalism is discussed further in Chapter 11.

The goodness of what is natural is an adage which has not lost its appeal in our highly artificial civilization. In politics, it is used to sanction gut convictions and propositions for which no evidence can readily be advanced. But the implication that society is as natural as trees and rocks is totally misleading. Certainly, human beings are part of nature, subject to the same needs and aging processes as other mammals, but society is an artificial environment *not* subject to inexorable natural laws: we *can* manipulate and change society. However fond some politicians may be of the analogy of the Body Politic, society does not function like a living organism. So claims about what is natural in society are misleading. Equally, it is wrong to cite nature as the moral yardstick by which to measure our social arrangements: there is no morality in nature, and not much that is natural in society.

One of the tasks of political theory must be to dispel popular delusions of the kinds just described and to expose misleading ideas. In this connection, it is relevant to consider briefly the other misleading idea so often accorded final authority in political arguments, *human nature*. Often, in debate, an insubstantiable hypothesis about human nature is invoked to refute a theory or ideology. (How often was it said that socialism is impossible because people are greedy by nature?) In common with other social science subjects, political theory itself must make suppositions about people's character or motivation, or, at least, minimal assumptions about regularities in their behaviour. This is necessary for a consistent explanation of political life. But such assumptions, whether covert or explicit, hypothetical or well grounded in fact, determine from the start which form a theory will take.

Mediaeval Christian theorists, convinced of mankind's original sin and depraved, bestial nature, saw the power hierarchy as the curse of imperfect humanity: heaven would need no politics. Hobbes, believing in people's natural aggressiveness, depicted political institutions as barriers against a flood tide of violence. But optimists of the Enlightenment and after, among them Rousseau, the utopian socialists and various anarchists, viewed the individual as a *tabula rasa* (blank sheet) at birth, innocent of evil and only corrupted later, by invidious social institutions. In consequence, they imagined ideal societies resting on the natural faculty of reasoning and requiring no political or legal control. Some even believed that in ideal circumstances people could become morally perfect: hence they were labelled 'perfectibilists' or 'optimists' by contrast with the pessimists who thought humankind irredeemably corrupt.

By contrast with these moralistic accounts of human nature, the fundamental liberal assumption that our natural inclination is to maximize our own wellbeing seems morally neutral, until we recognize that the scarcity of resources may mean that one person's maximization is necessarily another's minimization. This unpalatable implication is often ignored, although many liberals contend that it is inevitable anyway because people are 'naturally competitive'. The evidence offered is that they compete in competitive situations, which is hardly conclusive. (An interesting twist has been given to the human nature argument by some feminists who argue that politics is virtually an all-male activity and political theory nearly an all-male subject because men, the dominant partners in society since time immemorial, have shaped both in the image of their own salient characteristic: aggressiveness. Hence the emphasis on power, competition, assertiveness, and domination, with the correlative, despised 'female' counterparts of obedience, conciliation, and acquiescence. Negotiation and peaceful compromise are regarded as loss of face in politics and political language reflects this contempt.)

Arguments from behaviour do not constitute evidence for there being an *innate* human nature and individuals are surely moulded by institutions, rather than vice versa. Most theorists derive their generalizations about human nature from how people currently behave in society: this is by definition socially determined behaviour, so it does not necessarily reflect a fundamental 'human essence'. Vandalism and violence are not proof of original sin—or are they? This debate is a species of the more general controversy as to whether we are formed by heredity or environment, nature or nurture. Different political consequences stem from whichever assumption is made. My own preference is for the environmental explanation, partly because of the scientific evidence supporting it, partly because of the impossibility of even conceiving of a human being *outside* society who could serve as an exemplar of untainted human nature, and partly because it has positive implications for social amelioration. We can change and improve our environment more easily than our genes. Indeed, the most radical and revolutionary socio-political theories date from Locke's promotion of the *tabula rasa* concept, which implies that individuals will improve if their environment is improved. For similar reasons, Marxist theorists say that it is reactionary to claim that human nature is fixed; they argue that the individual is formed by socio-economic factors and can change or be changed. As this brief account of the 'human nature' debate suggests, we should beware when confident claims are made about what people are 'really' like, and should carefully scrutinize any political argument or work of political theory for concealed assumptions of this kind. Theorists as well as politicians must make some such assumptions, but at least we can uncover them and evaluate their validity, to some extent.

The arguments of the last few pages illustrate that political theories, ideologies, and opinions conceal a wealth of assumptions and arguments, not always well founded, which a student of political theory is better equipped to uncover than a bystander. In this respect, academic political theory is more a technique than an end in itself: it cuts sharply through the verbiage and factual confusions of political debate to the core of beliefs and prejudices, and raises such questions as 'Is this assumption tenable?' and 'Do these values really represent what is valuable?'

In common with other philosophical subjects, political theory has various inner logics which need to be exposed and a number of conventions must be inwardly digested before the subject can be fully intelligible and stimulating. Unfortunately, many writers use shorthand to denote familiar theoretical positions, which may confuse or annoy the uninitiated. References to idealism, naturalism, relativism, etc., which carry a wealth of connotations for the *habitué*, have zero, or negative, explanatory force for the newcomer. I shall try to demystify some of these obscure terms. Idealism, materialism, empiricism and rationalism have already been mentioned. Most such concepts come in contrasted pairs and supposedly exhaust the logical possibilities between them. One such pair is *descriptive* and *evaluative*, adjectives used of statements or theories. This distinction was implicit in earlier paragraphs of this chapter where political science, which *describes* reality and builds explanatory theories on the facts, was contrasted with political theory, which analyses and *evaluates* ideas by reference to other concepts and values. Similar to this is the *descriptive–normative* distinction, which may generate confusion for anyone familiar with the sociologist's use of 'normative' to mean 'conforming to a norm or average'. In political theory 'normative' simply means 'bearing or promoting norms (in the sense of 'values')', as opposed to 'descriptive'.

The opposition between the descriptive and evaluative approaches is mirrored in the distinction which is often made in political debate between *facts* and *values*. Facts which are established empirically are said to be beyond dispute—as if nobody knew how to lie with statistics, or present a one-sided case! Values, by contrast, are often considered insubstantial and unverifiable, mere opinion, and therefore inadmissible as evidence in debate; it follows that an evaluation is merely an expression of opinion. In social science, it is now more generally acknowledged that facts are not such innocent entities, since any framework of social investigation dictates *which* facts shall be singled out, and which ignored. Indeed, some philosophers would argue that the fact/value distinction has been conceptually dissolved. However, political polemics, both academic and popular, are frequently conducted as if facts were facts and values were values, and never the twain should meet.

The fact–value dispute relates back to the choice of methodology in social science: an empiricist approach naturally purports to deal in facts, whereas a theoretical method admits insubstantiable, even metaphysical, theses and values. (An empiricist approach could not have achieved the Copernican revolution). Two other terms which also relate to this fundamental methodological division are *appearance* and *essence*. These terms had strongly technical connotations for scholastic philosophers and others such as Kant, but in the present context they denote differing approaches to the analysis of a political idea. The imaginary objector who contended that democracy could be defined by studying the attributes of democratic countries was recommending an empirical examination of the *appearance*, the *contingent* or *accidental* characteristics, of democratic systems, such as the secret ballot, regular elections, and the existence of at least two parties. The alternative is to consider theoretically the *essence* of democracy, its *necessary* or *defining* characteristics (abstractly conceived) such as political equality and the responsiveness of government to the will of the people. In practice, one approach to political analysis needs correction by the other and the distinction between appearance and essence becomes blurred, but for the purposes of argument they are often presented as irreconcilable opposites, as are facts and values.

The meaning of *relativism* is further discussed in Chapter 2. Relativism is an epistemological position which repudiates the view that objective, universal or timeless knowledge is possible. It asserts that there are no absolute, indisputable criteria for truth, and hence for knowledge; such criteria are relative to time, place, and culture, and knowledge is only valid within the context which generates it. This doctrine undermines some of the distinctions already made—today's value may be tomorrow's fact. Relativism can be intellectually liberating, but it can also culminate in total uncertainty or unwillingness to adhere to any principle or position.

The distinction between *subjective* (personal, individual) and *objective* (impartial, impersonal) often plays a pivotal role in political theory, as when Rousseau argues that in an ideal democratic assembly men would put forward their *subjective* interests in discussion but vote according to the *objective* good of the community, thus becoming part of the General Will. Important parts of Marx's political argument turned on his assertion that the proletariat, *objectively* the most exploited class under capitalism, had no *subjective* awareness of its situation, and so had not yet become a revolutionary force. Political theory is usually concerned with the nature of the 'Good Society' and thus, directly or indirectly, with human happiness, and so the subjective aspects of life cannot be ignored by theorists, although they sometimes are by political scientists.

Political theory is a close relation of moral philosophy. Both are normative and evaluative and, although not all political values have moral origins (*tradition*, which Burke valued, and *efficiency* seem to be non-moral), they rely on moral language, since a value is something we would consider *good*, and would prefer to have more, rather than less, of. Although an ideal such as democracy is primarily political, its supporting values, freedom and equality, are as pervasive in moral as in political philosophizing. This shared area of concern and similarity of language is appropriate, since both moral and political philosophy attempt to define the Good Life, the first on an individual level, the second for the community at large. So the importation of moral terms into political theory is both permissible and necessary.

Is there also a necessary connection between political theory and ideology? Ideology, as will be argued, is crucial in forming the political theorist's own view of the world. It would be convenient if we could distinguish clearly between ideology and theory—if we could label theory 'ideological' whenever values and prescriptive or persuasive elements are visible. But many ideological influences affect theory invisibly, pre-selecting which data the theory will explain, and dictating its conceptual vocabulary from the start. Likewise, much theory contains ideological bias without having ideology's express aim of persuasion. So I shall assume that *all* political theory and theorizing, is susceptible to greater or lesser ideological bias, and that a necessary task for commentators and students is to identify and evaluate that bias—and, of course, their own bias. The next chapter of this book sets out to analyse the concept of ideology: Part II gives a critical account of the major political ideologies and the problems which they encounter.

Political theory is an umbrella term. It comprehends the persuasive and normative doctrines called ideologies; it also embraces the analytical activity known as *political philosophy*, which styles itself 'value-free'. Rather than propounding grandiose theses about the nature of political society and the Good Life, this examines the units of which political theory, including ideology, is composed, the *concepts*. Hence, it is sometimes called 'conceptual analysis'. It has been said that its main endeavour is to 'clear up confusions' which result from unclarity or inconsistency in the use of concepts such as freedom and equality by providing a clear and coherent account of their proper use.[4] This activity often employs the methods established by the school of philosophy called 'linguistic analysis' which flourished in the 1950s but is now, by and large, rejected as too narrow. The other task of political philosophy is said to be to provide generally acceptable definitions of central political terms. These self-ascribed functions also rest on the conviction that even value-laden concepts are capable of a constant and definite meaning. Formulae such as 'justice is giving every man his due' and 'democracy means "one man one vote"' summarize attempts at comprehensive, foolproof definitions which appear to be factual and to describe justice, democracy and so on in terms of behaviour or institutions. But these formulae can be shown to be disguisedly normative and therefore contentious. (The endeavour to provide such definitive analyses also falls foul of the linguistic philosophers who condemn *any* attempt to define *values* as ill-founded.) In recent decades some political philosophers have been sceptical about the search for fixed meanings and have argued that political concepts are 'essentially contested'—that is, that their meanings are necessarily disputed and vary according to the meaning of a cluster of related 'contextual' concepts, and are ineradicably dependent on values and ideologies.[5] If no final definitions are possible, it would seem that political philosophy has no useful role to play. But it can still be maintained that

---

4. A. Quinton (Ed.), *Political Philosophy*, Oxford U.P., 1967.
5. W. B. Gallie, in 'Essentially contested concepts', *Pro. Aristotelian Soc.*, **56**, 167–98, (1955–6). For a later exposition, see W. E. Connolly, *The Terms of Political Discourse*, Martin Robertson, Oxford, 1983, p. 225 ff.

the discipline deals with problems that are *in principle* open to theoretical solution, despite the contestability of the concepts which are its tools. In any case, the logical basis of the 'essential contestability thesis' has itself been called into question.[6] Part III of this book illustrates how such disputes may arise by showing the range of meanings which political ideas can have in different ideological contexts.

Newcomers to the subject deserve two cautions. The first concerns values and value-neutrality. Political philosophy sometimes appears unsatisfactory because it fails to deliver decisive answers to political questions. It can analyse the logic of liberalism and the concept of tolerance but cannot determine whether we should tolerate the intolerant because this requires an ordering of values, which is said to be the task of the committed, ethical individual. Political ideology is an artefact, in which priorities are ordered and values asserted, but political philosophy strives to be a neutral tool of analysis and appraisal—so argue its partisans, although opponents see this neutrality as mere pretence. The 'neutral' approach associated with liberalism leads to the unsatisfactorily inconclusive character of much of the political theory of the mid-twentieth century, and its concentration on the secondary or 'meta' level of debate and avoidance of substantive questions. However, not all political theorists seek to be neutral, and indeed the current fashion is for more committed theory which seeks to influence, stimulate and provoke.

The second caution concerns the idiosyncratic way in which political theorists argue. A case is stated and evidence offered, then various objections are raised and sustained with apparent conviction, only to be elegantly disposed of, whereupon the theorist reverts to a modified version of the original proposition. The process manifests a degree of showmanship, and the reader has the impression of receiving a guided tour of cul-de-sacs, followed by a smug arrival at a pre-determined destination. The reason for this form of argument is that political theory, like other philosophical subjects, originated in the oral, dialectical tradition whose essence was argument, objection, modification, restatement, and so on, and whose intent was to move rationally towards a final definition of a political idea such as justice.

Plato's *Republic*, of which Socrates is the intellectual hero, is one of the earliest examples of this approach, and the dialogue form was still employed in some philosophical writing as late as the eighteenth century, long after oral debate had been replaced by printed polemics. Today, the writer of theory, unlike Socrates, has no troublesome Thrasymachus to interrupt and contradict, and so she must anticipate, state and refute all likely objections to the theory. But the dialectical process, though circuitous, is essentially one of explanation and proof, rather than dogmatic assertion, and so these rehearsals of criticism and self-criticism are vital to political theorizing.

_____

6. E.g., J. Gray, 'Political power, social theory and essential contestability' in D. Miller and L. Siedentop (Eds.), *The Nature of Political Theory*, Oxford U.P., 1983 and K. Dowding, *Rational Choice and Political Power*, Edward Elgar, 1991, pp. 167–173.

I have suggested that the political theorist cannot be value free, and is not immune to ideological infection. Readers may therefore rightly wonder what the hidden values of this book will be, and where its bias lies. No doubt this becomes clear in the course of the book! I would, however, like to state one of my reasons for writing such a book, and to say where I believe its value lies. In my view, we in the West are all, as individuals, enmeshed in a complex socio-politico-economic-military network (which comprises states, superstate bodies and the global economy) against which there are few weapons except reason, information and intelligence. (The same is equally true of the citizens of the former communist countries and of Third-World countries, which are willy-nilly embroiled in international politics and finance capitalism.) Our progress to advanced industrialism has created a form of sociopolitical organization which is neither manipulable nor controllable by individuals or groups and has its own logic and momentum. However, our *compliance* is necessary for its continuance and success. Compliance is as much a mental as a physical act: the ideas supporting and validating advanced industrial society must be propagated and internalized. The study of political theory should make us more defensive and more sceptical of the justifications of the system which nourish our compliance, and more willing to contemplate alternative political and social forms. This book advocates a critical appraisal of political ideologies, concepts, habits of thought, and prejudices: this in turn may lead readers to consider critically the political behaviour which certain political ideas generate—and even to behave differently.

FURTHER READING

D. Held (Ed.), *Political Theory Today*, Polity Press, 1991.
K. Graham (Ed.), *Contemporary Political Philosophy*, Cambridge U.P., 1982. This collection contains essays which reflect the more committed approach of political philosophers in the 1970s and 1980s (cf. Partridge and Plamenatz in Quinton, Ed.).
P. Laslett *et al.* (Eds.) *Philosophy, Politics and Society*, Series 1–5, Blackwell, 1956–79. These volumes are a useful collection of classic articles on political theory in general, and on specific political concepts.
R. Plant, *Modern Political Thought*, Blackwell, 1991.
A. Quinton (Ed.), *Political Philosophy*, Oxford U.P., 1967. See especially the articles on political theory by P. H. Partridge and J. P. Plamenatz, which reflect the problems of the discipline at the time.
D. D. Raphael, *Problems of Political Philosophy*, 2nd edn, Macmillan, 1990.
L. Strauss, *What is Political Philosophy?* Greenwood Press, 1973. (Title essay.)
G. Tinder, *Political Thinking*, 6th edn, HarperCollins, 1995.
J. Wolff, *An Introduction to Political Philosophy*, Oxford U.P., 1996.

Ideology

'Ideology' must be the most overworked word in political debate. The word has been drained of most of its analytic content and has become a mere label to be tied on doctrines which we dislike. 'Ideological' is rarely used except pejoratively, as a synonym for 'doctrinaire' and 'dogmatic'. But the contention of this book is that all coherent political doctrines are ideological, as is our use of political ideas themselves: if this is accepted, the pejorative connotations of the term must be laid aside. This chapter examines the various concepts of ideology which have developed, and their significance for political theory.

MARX ON IDEOLOGY

The term 'ideology' literally means 'the science of ideas' but in the early nineteenth century a more critical usage was established: it came to mean an abstract, visionary or speculative way of thinking. While it was Marx who offered the first major analysis of ideology as such, the philosophical problem which gave rise to the notion had been widely debated during the Enlightenment. The problem is that of the status of knowledge. Many previous cultures had believed knowledge to be certain, absolute and objective: Plato thought that there existed in some metaphysical dimension Ideas or Forms, absolute truths which served as models which men should strive to realize in society. The knowledge of these Ideas (such as Justice and the Good) was absolute knowledge, attainable through philosophical contemplation. Despite its pre-Christian origins, Platonism later influenced the Christian view of knowledge and truth. Mediaeval Christian theology held that truth was God-given and absolute, reflecting the divinely ordained and fixed order of the world. The chief source of such knowledge was the scriptures, although during the Renaissance the experimental, scientific method of gaining knowledge was reconciled with Christian precepts. According to both Platonic and Christian views, knowledge 'exists' independently or emanates from a non-human source, and so is objectively established. Knowledge is to be discovered, not created, by human beings.

Enlightenment philosophers, many of whom were atheists, used *reason* as an implement for destroying the prejudices and mysteries of Christianity, arguing that the world was in principle explicable scientifically. A new conception of knowledge resulted: the thinking being was seen as the *creator* of knowledge. Kant and Hegel developed theories of knowledge, epistemologies, on the basis of this insight, which abolished the polarity between the individual as a thinking *subject*, passively absorbing objective knowledge, and the external world, the source and *object* of knowledge. The new theories emphasized the *subjective* aspect of knowledge: the thinker inevitably intrudes herself into her perception of the object which she is trying to know. This had been implicit in Locke's argument, a century before, that knowledge of the external world is gained through our senses and so is sense-dependent, and therefore subject-dependent: for example, given a different eye structure, the world would appear to us as black and white. Kant emphasized that knowledge results from an active process, not mere passive absorption of data, while Hegel's dialectical account of knowledge described the constant dialogue between the conscious subject and the object, each stage raising the subject to a higher form of knowledge.

Marx's achievement was to codify the ways in which the social identity of the 'knowing subject' altered her knowledge, and to describe the process of knowing in concrete terms. As a *materialist*, he believed that material causes could be found for all events and phenomena in the world: there were no mysterious or metaphysical events and everything was scientifically explicable, including humankind. All human thought, ideas, and theories (in general, 'consciousness') were determined by material factors and, more precisely, by social circumstances.

> Consciousness is, therefore, from the very beginning, a social product, and remains so as long as men exist at all.[1]

Marx considered that the economic structure of society determined all its other aspects, from social relations and political institutions to law, morality and knowledge itself. Each economic system gave rise to the existence of classes in society, and people's knowledge and beliefs were determined not only by the general social context but by their particular class position in society. In propounding this materialist theory of consciousness, Marx challenged the 'Young Hegelians' and, indirectly, Hegel himself, who were, by contrast, *idealists*. They believed that ideas had an autonomous existence and could act as independent causes of events in the material world: the intellect had priority over mere physical existence. Revolutions, even, were made by ideas. Hegel had seen history as the movement of 'Spirit' through the world, realizing itself in different social forms. Marx thought such idealism (not to be confused with 'idealism' in the sense of 'the pursuit of ideals', although the two meanings are related) illusory and philosophically false.

---

1. K. Marx and F. Engels, *The German Ideology*, in *Selected Works*, Vol. 1, Progress Publishers, 1969, p. 32.

Marx never set out his theory of ideology systematically in one text, but a coherent doctrine can be extrapolated from his works. Social reality itself is contradictory, Marx held: capitalism fosters two antagonistic classes, the bourgeoisie and the proletariat, whose interests are diametrically opposed, and which will finally come into direct conflict. Ideology is a resolution of these contradictions *in the mind*: thus, capitalist ideology may 'resolve' class conflict by emphasizing the common interests and harmony between the classes, or the 'organic' nature of society, but this cannot alter the *real* antagonism between the interests of those classes. Because ideology tries to resolve the irresoluble, it gives an inaccurate and distorted representation of material reality.

The elaboration of this general conception of ideology shows what Marx thought its social functions to be. An individual's consciousness is determined by his class position, his ownership or non-ownership of the means of production, and the social relationships into which he enters as a member of a certain class. Marx gave an account of the genesis of different class viewpoints in economic circumstances, showing how each point of view distorts reality according to its own interests. His dialectical view of social processes (discussed in Chapter 4) entailed that in every conflict the opposing classes or groups had their own *partial* understanding of the process: he described the production process from the viewpoint of the capitalist and from that of the labourer, showing the differences between these subjective, one-sided accounts of the same phenomenon.[2] Because such knowledge was bound up with the knower's class position, it was necessarily a partial and inaccurate representation of the world: hence, it was ideological. For Marx, the only escape route from ideology to accurate knowledge was via a synthetic account which comprehended both sides of the process, as did his own theory, which he designated 'scientific', in contradistinction to 'ideological' social theory.

Under capitalism, the bourgeoisie reinforces its dominant position in the economy by all possible social and political means, including the creation of the state. Ideology is viewed by Marx as a major instrument of repression in the hands of the ruling class, used to deceive subordinate classes about the true nature of capitalism and to perpetuate its own domination. The law, religion, morality, social theory, and philosophy all evolve or are refashioned so as to reflect the bourgeois standpoint, and they become part of the wider ideology, functioning to disguise the contradictions in society and the grievances and discontent of the proletariat. Although the worker's class position should give him a set of ideas which reflect his own reality, he may instead absorb the all-pervasive bourgeois ideology which misleads him as to his own (exploited) situation: then, he is said to be the victim of *false consciousness*, which makes him unlikely to rebel against his oppressed condition. The idea of 'inverted' or false consciousness attributed to Marx did not mean anything so simple as the direct deliberate deception of gullible proletarians by a malevolent bourgeoisie. Bourgeois ideology invades the consciousness of workers through the propagation of commonsensical, seemingly non-dogmatic ideas, such as 'Everyone should pay their way', which establish the

---

2. K. Marx, *The Grundrisse* (trans. D. McLellan), Harper & Row, 1972, p. 72ff.

work ethic, the consumption ethic, and the ideal of the 'self-made man', all of which are vital to capitalism. A doctrine of individualism likewise develops which teaches that we establish our personal identity via material possessions. This conveniently extends our desires and needs and thus maintains the level of demand necessary for capitalism to operate. Everyday wisdom dictates the behaviour which best supports the capitalist system. Established beliefs tell us that capitalism is the 'natural' form of society. Such doctrines permeate the workers' consciousness imperceptibly; also, the better off they become, the more inclined are they to identify with the bourgeoisie and accept its values and doctrines, thus extending their own false consciousness—Marxists call this process 'embourgeo-isement'. Thus, ideology is the gentlest method of oppression, but also the most invidious.

Marx did not consider that bourgeois ideology was always a deliberate distortion of reality: its distorting nature was sometimes merely a consequence of its class origin. The economic theories of Adam Smith, whom Marx admired, fell into this category. Although they were ideological, they were not intended as propaganda to foster bourgeois domination; they merely charted economic reality from the bourgeois standpoint. By contrast, Marx castigated Bentham as a mere apologist of capitalism, whose utilitarian doctrines presented a distorted view of reality intended to deceive and indoctrinate other classes. Most people latch on to the idea of deliberate distortion as the defining characteristic of ideology, but Marx often used it to mean simply an account of reality which is incomplete and partial and so, incidentally, tends to favour one class. The focus of Marx's theory was, of course, the proletarian revolution. The worker who shares the ideas of the capitalist about the sanctity of private property and the importance of individual rights has misidentified his true interests, so that, before a revolution is possible, workers must shed their false consciousness and develop a consciousness which accurately depicts their exploitation and oppression and shows them their real interests. When such consciousness becomes widespread, the workers constitute a 'class-for-themselves', a class aware of their true situation, primed to take political action. Marx's doctrines were themselves intended to form an important part of this new class consciousness.

Many sophisticated theories have been built upon Marx's account of ideology, and many controversies stem from it which cannot be examined here, but one question must be asked: was Marx's theory itself ideological? Critics of Marx hope to disprove his theory by showing that it fell into the very category of thought which he condemned. Briefly, Marx considered his own theory objective and scientific, believing it to give a complete, non-partial account of reality and its contradictions, but to some it appears ideological in that it espouses the proletarian viewpoint and attacks capitalism. Lenin argued that *all* class knowledge is ideological, yet he viewed Marxism as a science. Other Marxists do, however, concede that Marxism may be an ideology. The question cannot easily be resolved, because our own ideological convictions enter into the debate, but according to modern, non-Marxist definitions of ideology, Marxism is unquestionably one ideology among many—although left-wing thinkers might say that is nearer the truth than its rivals.

'IDEOLOGY' SINCE MARX

Marx's theory was one expression of the conviction widely held from the Enlightenment onwards, that knowledge is relative to the time, place, and thinker, or to a combination of all three. This relativism dispelled the hope that absolute truth could be established in any field, except perhaps that of pure science. Mannheim offered an influential account of ideology based on Marx's ideas, although he rejected Marx's political conclusions. Mannheim believed in the relativity of *all* knowledge which, he thought, always originated in the lives of groups or classes, within which certain climates of ideas develop. He defined ideology as an idea or ideas 'incongruent with reality', which have the effect of protecting a contradictory reality, and supporting the status quo.[3] The precise meaning of 'incongruent with reality' is unclear, however, and any attempt to clarify it would have to answer the perennial question of how ideas relate to material reality. Mannheim contrasted ideologies with 'utopias', sets of ideas which were also incongruent with reality but which, if translated into action, would have the effect of overthrowing an existing system. His definition can, I believe, be disputed, since at the heart of any ideology we find a set of utopian ideas which prescribe how society should, ideally, be organized. However, in normal circumstances, the utopia contained within a dominant ideology will tend to support the status quo.

Mannheim distinguished the *particular conception of ideology* from the *total conception of ideology*. The former refers to a set of ideas particular to a group's special interests, which promotes these interests and deceives other groups. The ideological weapons used by the bourgeoisie exemplify this. Total ideology is a way of thinking common to a whole society or a particular historical period, a 'world-view' (*Weltanschauung*) from which individuals cannot escape unless they migrate to another culture—where they will find a different total ideology. The classification of various epochs as 'The Age of Belief', 'The Age of Reason', and so on, reflects this idea of a total ideology or world-view which goes beyond class interests and establishes the form in which all thought, including particular ideology, must present itself. We might, for example, characterize the world-view of our own time by saying that this is the Age of Technology, when people and institutions are dominated by the technological ethos. To count as knowledge, something must be proved by scientific procedures. New doctrines and policies are evaluated according to strictly technical, not moral, criteria.

Mannheim has been criticized for his acceptance that all knowledge is relative and ideological in one sense or the other (including, logically, his own theory, which is relative to an age of relativism . . .), an admission which blunts the critical edge of the concept of ideology. If everything is ideological, how can we judge between or criticize doctrines? Even if we eradicate particular ideologies, our thoughts are still trapped inside the total ideology. Mannheim hoped that 'classless' intellectuals would produce a synthesis of non-ideological knowledge,

---

3. K. Mannheim, *Ideology and Utopia* (trans. E. Shils), Routledge & Kegan Paul, 1936, pp. 49–53.

but this aspiration has been generally derided, given the clear allegiance of most intellectuals to one class or another. Undoubtedly we cannot escape from the dominant ideas or the ethos of our own time and culture, but this fact does not diminish the force of Mannheim's critique of partial ideology, which can, he says, be recognized and eradicated. Since Mannheim, many Western political thinkers who reject Marxism have nevertheless turned their attention to ideology. Ironically, whereas Marx and Mannheim both defined ideology as a reactionary phenomenon, such thinkers condemn it for its *radical* tendencies! Foremost among the ideologies which they criticize is, of course, Marxism itself, while liberal-democratic ideas are considered not ideological, but true. Arendt emphasized the deceptive explanatory nature of ideology and its one-dimensionality. 'Ideologies are *isms* which to the satisfaction of their adherents can explain every occurrence by deducing it from a single premise'.[4] Putnam, a political scientist, defined it more loosely and less critically as 'a lifeguiding system of beliefs, values and goals affecting political style and action'.[5] Other definitions include 'a specific mixture of Mosaic myth, with argument and purported evidence' (Feuer) and 'a coherent value-laden mode of understanding the totality of phenomena' (Ruddock). Larrain's analysis emphasizes Marx's original view that ideology conceals contradictions and promotes class interests, Seliger's 'inclusive definition' makes all political thought—and all politics—inseparable from ideology, because they are goal-directed, while Adams describes it broadly and simply as 'a form of moral understanding built upon conceptions of human nature'.[6]

From these modern non-Marxist analyses a number of defining characteristics of ideology can be deduced, which are as follows:

(a) Ideology presents ideas and knowledge in a way which entails certain kinds of beliefs and actions.
(b) Ideology purports to have explanatory power, to make the world comprehensible to its believers, although in fact it distorts the truth by selection, interpretation or plain falsification.
(c) Ideology has persuasive force; its precepts often appear as moral imperatives. It tries to harness the emotions by evoking common prejudices and deep-rooted fears.
(d) Modern ideology often claims to be scientific, based on patterns of argument like those of science, or invokes pseudo-scientific evidence, as the Nazis did in trying to prove Aryan superiority. This helps to give it explanatory force. (Mannheim would say here that particular ideology necessarily conforms to the total, scientific, ideology.) Such ideology also manifests a spurious

4. H. Arendt, *The Origins of Totalitarianism*, revised edn, Allen & Unwin, 1967, p. 468 and Chap. 13 generally.
5. R. D. Putnam, *The Beliefs of Politicians*, Yale U.P., 1973.
6. L. S. Feuer, *Ideology and the Ideologists*, Blackwell, 1975, p. 183; R. Ruddock, *Ideology*, Manchester Monographs, 15, 1981, p. 12; J. Larrain, *The Concept of Ideology*, Hutchinson, 1979, p. 210; M. Seliger, *Ideology and Politics*, Allen & Unwin, 1976, pp. 119–20; I. Adams, *The Logic of Political Belief*, Harvester Wheatsheaf, 1989, p. xiii.

coherence and logicality and substitutes itself for superstition, religion and tradition.

(e) Despite (d), ideology is frequently irrational and illogical, when analysed. It reconciles within itself incompatible elements by changing the meaning of words or distorting the facts, so as to present itself as an apparently self-consistent, logical whole.

Evidently, characteristics (b)–(e) were not specified by any friend of ideology. They suggest that it beguiles us away from clear, discoverable political truths. But the existence of such objective truths, especially in politics and social life, is to be doubted according to any relativist conception of knowledge. The pejorative account of ideology which derives from those characteristics need not, in fact, be accepted. But it is not surprising that writers within the dominant ideology of liberal democracy (which denies its own ideological status) should give a derogatory account of the nature of other doctrines, *qua* ideologies.

The conception of ideology rests on prevailing views of the nature of knowledge. The stronger the doctrine of empiricism, which stipulates that knowledge is constructed on the basis of *data*, the more critical the conception of ideology, which connotes a departure from empirical truth into the realm of theoretical abstraction and distortion. However, in the 1960s, some of the more radical philosophers and social scientists in the West advanced the view that the social and even the natural sciences were 'theory-laden' and not purely empirical and objective:[7] in a parallel development, a number of political theorists acknowledged and analysed the evaluative and ideological dimensions of all political thinking.[8] Since then, many theorists have tried to deal with ideology, not by searching for the 'pure truths' from which ideology deviates, but by analysing the functions and limits of ideology. This leads to a sociological, rather than a philosophical, account of ideology. A number of rival theories have emerged:

(a) Some theorists retain a Marxian view of ideology as an instrument of class rule which vindicates, persuades, and deceives, but use this to criticize communist regimes.

(b) Ideology is seen as a remedy for 'stress': it compensates for the psychological inadequacies experienced by individuals because of social maladjustment, alienation, and personal problems. Thus it is seen as a necessary evil. This *functionalist* account, which explains adherence to ideology because of its usefulness to individuals, does not distinguish between ideologies: all

---

7. An important milestone in the rethinking of the basis of the natural sciences, which greatly influenced social-scientific thinking, was Thomas Kuhn's *The Structure of Scientific Revolutions* (1962), 2nd edn, Chicago U.P., 1970.
8. Early indications of this new approach are found in P. H. Partridge, 'Politics, philosophy and ideology', in *Political Philosophy* (Ed. A. Quinton), Oxford U.P., 1967, and C. Taylor, 'Neutrality in political science', in *The Philosophy of Social Explanation* (Ed. A. Ryan), Oxford U.P., 1973. The changing nature of political theory was documented in R. J. Bernstein, *The Restructuring of Social and Political Theory*, Blackwell, 1976.

ideologies are distortions, and any ideological commitment is a sign of malfunctioning which, presumably, could be eradicated in a healthy society.[9]

(c) Ideology is explained by its general social functions. It provides solidarity for communities and a basis for authority in newly emergent nations; it can also provide a role for young people in search of identity. Whereas traditional societies bound their members together in other ways, ideology is an important factor in social cohesion in modern, atomistic, fissiparous society.[10]

(d) Ideology, like myth, may perform symbolic functions, reconciling the irreconcilable. (This reflects Marx's view that ideology conceals contradictions, although denying that capitalism suffers such contradictions.) Marcuse described the role of Marxism in the USSR as a ritualized language with a magical quality which obliterated the split between reality and illusion.[11] Geertz argues that ideology can symbolically formulate scientifically unformulable realities and render incomprehensible social situations meaningful.[12] (We should note that *meaningfulness* may have little to do with *truth*.)

Thus, many twentieth-century thinkers have conceded that ideology need not be dismissed outright as distortion and deception, but can be explained within a functionalist model of society. This approach wrongly implies that ideologies are clearly recognizable, self-contained doctrines, espoused by those with special needs and eschewed by the well-adjusted mass of adults in the West: in other words, these definitions are so contrived as to exclude liberal democracy from the category of ideology and to present other ideologies as temporary, functionally useful addictions which would vanish from mature, Western-style societies.

The exclusion of liberal democracy from the category deserves closer scrutiny. The academic onslaught on ideology emanated from the USA in the 1950s. Ideology was viewed as a root cause of the Nazi and Stalinist phenomena and a contributory cause of the Second World War. The anti-Communist 'purges' associated with Senator McCarthy removed many left-wing figures from public office in the United States, and the postwar lull and increasing prosperity made a consensual, bipartisan approach to politics possible there. Political discussion turned on technical, rather than moral, issues. Intellectually, the dissemination of logical positivist philosophy (which had started in the 1920s in Europe) with its ruling that moral statements and value-judgements were unverifiable, led to a rejection of normative social science in favour of positivist, empirical studies. It was felt that the dangerous 'rule of ideas' was coming to an end, and intellectuals would henceforth participate in government and administration on the basis of their neutral, scientific skills. In the mid-fifties, the doctrine of 'the end of

9. C. Geertz, 'Ideology as a cultural system', in *Ideology and Discontent* (Ed. D. Apter), Free Press, 1964, pp. 47–76.
10. D. Apter, 'Ideology and discontent', in *Ideology and Discontent* (Ed. D. Apter), Free Press, 1964, pp. 18–30; P. Ricoeur, *Hermeneutics and the Human Sciences*, Ed. J. B. Thompson, Cambridge U.P., 1984, p. 223; D. Manning, *Liberalism*, Dent, 1976, p. 154.
11. H. Marcuse, *Soviet Marxism*, Columbia U.P., 1958, pp. 88,159.
12. C. Geertz, 'Ideology as a cultural system', p. 58ff.

ideology' ('endism') was put forward by Bell and others and became a symbol of the intellectual climate of the time, which rejected ideological commitment and dispute.

Bell wrote, of the preceding, turbulent thirty years,

> But out of all this history, one simple fact emerges: for the radical intelligentsia, the old ideologies have lost their 'truth' and their power to persuade . . . . In the Western world, therefore, there is today a rough consensus among intellectuals on political issues.

The issues were the welfare state, decentralized power, the mixed economy and political pluralism. Bell concluded that, while developing countries were manufacturing new ideologies such as industrialization and Pan-Arabism, in the West 'the ideological age has ended'.[13] Ideology had, in short, been superseded politically by consensus, and academically by the scientific method. As a result, the study of politics was transformed: political theorists adopted methods of 'linguistic analysis' then popular among philosophers, and argued that the subject should not promote values or ideologies but should analyse the *uses*, and hence the meanings, of political terms, neutrally. Sociologists and political scientists meanwhile adopted functionalist and consensus models of analysis, applying both in ways which validated the American political and social system.

The result was that values went underground: covertly, 'objective' analyses upheld the liberal way of thinking. The political scientist Sartori, for example, published in 1966 an influential study of various democratic states which showed the high incidence of conflict in states with a multiplicity of parties with strong ideological commitments.[14] He concluded that ideological politics were inimical to democracy and that a two-party system was best. Many other political scientists came to similarly 'neutral' conclusions. The value-free 'post-ideological' approach led political theory into an impasse, since analysing and criticizing values had been its traditional function. For a time the discipline was almost in abeyance, with political science being sucked in to fill the vacuum. But the Civil Rights, Black Power, Women's Liberation, Student Power, and Anti-Vietnam movements of the 1960s and 1970s in the USA showed that ideology and conflict could not be excluded from American politics for ever. Left-wing thinkers such as Marcuse and Wolff sought to expose the covert ideological premises of liberal-democratic thought and institutions and others, such as Feyerabend, demonstrated that most empirical studies were in fact guided by theoretical presuppositions which could not themselves be empirically established, but were *assumed*;[15] such covert values

---

13. D. Bell, *The End of Ideology*, (1968), new edn, Harvard U.P., 1988. In this reissue with an 'afterword', Bell argues, not entirely convincingly, that the committed radicalism of the 1960s did not disprove his thesis. See too C. Waxman (Ed.), *The End of Ideology Debate*, Funk & Wagnalls, 1968.
14. G. Sartori, 'European political parties: the case of polarised pluralism', in *Political Parties and Political Development* (Eds. J. Lapalombara and M. Wiener), Princeton U.P., 1966, pp. 137–176.
15. See especially R. P. Wolff, H. Marcuse and B. Moore, *A Critique of Pure Tolerance*, Beacon Press, 1965 and R. P. Wolff, *The Poverty of Liberalism*, Beacon Press, 1969; also, P. Feyerabend, 'How to be a good empiricist', in *The Philosophy of Science*, Oxford U.P., 1968 (Ed. P. Nidditch), and P. Feyerabend, *Problems of Empiricism*, Cambridge U.P., 1981.

pervaded political science in particular, with its supposedly neutral, 'quantitative' definitions of concepts like consensus, political system, and elite. As the 'end of ideology' vogue itself ended in response to political circumstance, and the 'theoretical' (as opposed to empirical) and ideological nature of social and political studies was acknowledged, there was a resurgence of controversy and commitment in political theory and the subject was restored to health. More recently, the various world recessions of the 1970s and 1980s produced a polarization between left and right in the USA, Britain and many West European countries. This encouraged many political theorists to engage in advocacy as well as analysis: both political and moral philosophy became more committed and tendentious, applying themselves to problems such as world poverty, pollution and the arms race. This ideological involvement created a more lively, if more acerbic, climate for political philosophy. It remains to be seen whether the rejection of Marxist doctrine by the former communist countries will lead to a new consensus based on the apparent victory of liberal ideas and values, and a second 'end of ideology'. Fukuyama has asserted that these events constitute 'the end of history',[16] with liberal democracy triumphant, but other ideological divisions in the world are already asserting themselves, especially that between Islam and the West.

A divergent analysis of ideology from that proposed by English and American thinkers appears in the work of such philosophers as Foucault, whose analysis focuses on the 'discourse' of politics; in his view, ideology is an outcome of power and domination, which determine the construction and use of language and creates a discourse which validates its own usages.[17] Ideas such as rationality are criticized because they are created within an ideological discourse of logic. The problem, as always with such relativist analyses, is how the thinker can claim a status above and beyond ideology for his own analysis of the situation, and whether he can acknowledge that any particular discourse is more 'true' than another—indeed, for Foucault, truth itself is only created *within* a discourse. This problem has bedevilled the analysts of ideology since Marx himself.[18]

CONCEPTUAL PROBLEMS

The readiness with which non-Marxist thinkers borrowed the concept of ideology and adapted it as a critique of radical theories suggests that such a concept is indispensable to political analysis, whether Marxist or not. But the precise scope and meaning of the term is often unclear and non-Marxists do not employ it in the same sense as Marxists. The relativist approach casts doubt on all knowledge,

---

16. F. Fukuyama, *The End of History and the Last Man*, Hamish Hamilton, 1992. This book fails as political theory, but reasserts the 'end of ideology' thesis in the circumstances of the early 1990s.
17. M. Foucault, 'Truth and power', *Power/Knowledge: Selected Interviews and Other Writings*, Harvester, 1980.
18. An interesting exchange on this topic appears in *Politics*; see R. Gann, 'The limits of textbook ideology', *Politics* (1995), 15(2), pp. 127–133 and A. Vincent, 'The ambiguity of ideology', *Politics* (1996), 16(1), pp. 47–52.

including the status of any theory of ideology and of the discipline which Mannheim inaugurated, the 'sociology of knowledge'. Marx's contention that consciousness, and hence knowledge, is historically produced, determined by material conditions, suggests that, while all knowledge is relative in this respect, it need not be ideological: a class may obtain accurate knowledge which appropriately reflects its circumstances and is a guide to political action and truth. On this account, Marxism itself would not count as an ideology, but as true knowledge. But on the other hand, according to Mannheim, objective truth is to be found only in mathematics and perhaps in the natural sciences. Otherwise, all our ideas are to some extent incongruent with reality, and either tend to uphold the existing system (as ideologies do) or to destroy or 'transcend' it (as utopias do). No political ideas merely reflect reality objectively. A different view is held by Western thinkers working within the empiricist tradition who, while conceding the functional uses of ideology, criticize its distortion of 'objective' fact and its secretion of values, which cause people to deviate from the direct, empirical path to knowledge.

In each of these three critiques of ideology, there is an implicit standard of truth against which it is measured: for Marx, true ideas are those which acknowledge contradictions and accurately reflect the class position of the knower. Mannheim refers to 'reality' as some kind of standard; ideas congruent with it would be true, neither utopian nor ideological. For the empiricist, knowledge based on the accumulation of data and induction of general principles without the intrusion of values is true and objective. Marx and Mannheim would acknowledge that truth is relative to time and place, while the empiricist approach seems to imply the possibility of permanent truths.

This book is based on my conviction that in thinking about politics (and studying social science) it is impossible to think non-ideologically or in a 'value-free' way. The relation between ideology and values needs some explication here. Since Weber's influential pronouncements on the social science method,[19] practitioners have felt duty-bound to strive for value-free social science, although Weber himself thought that since this was almost unattainable, social scientists should, rather, seek to make their values explicit and justify them. The suspicion of value judgements engendered by logical positivist philosophy, on account of their unverifiability, gave social science a new impetus towards neutrality. However, while admitting their own susceptibility to value judgements, Western social scientists had to deny that such judgements were ideological, having already defined ideology pejoratively. The implication was that values were plucked out of a vacuum and could, as easily, be banished from social science. But clearly all values emanate from some ideological outlook, which need not be narrowly political but offers an interpretation of social life and action and a standard for judging good and bad. Values are symptoms of ideology, including value judgements about epistemology and scientific method. In general, the empirical method in scientific studies is connected both historically and doctrinally with

_____

19. M. Weber, *The Methodology of the Social Sciences*, Macmillan, 1950.

liberal ideology, while what empiricists think of as the ill-founded 'theoretical' (theory-informed) approach to social science has affinities with Marxism and some kinds of feminism.

Someone who denies political commitment in arguing the virtues of empirical social science is nevertheless maintaining a value found in the liberal world-view, and empirical studies tend to support the existing form of society because they have no critical dimension. Likewise someone who claims not to have an ideology but strongly advocates the freedom of the individual is voicing a part of liberal ideology, even if unwittingly. People may adopt the values embedded in an ideology without knowing or understanding it as a comprehensive doctrine, especially in societies where the existence of ideologies is not officially acknowledged and isolated beliefs appear in everyday political argument without the supporting justifications which an ideology provides—a procedure which does not facilitate the understanding of politics. While someone who only holds some isolated beliefs cannot be said to be an adherent of an ideology, such beliefs *are* ideologically determined, and we can only escape from one ideology into another. This is another reason why liberals deny that their own beliefs are ideological and deplore the espousal of ideology by others: it damages their conception of the individual as a free and rational being, who chooses objectively between political doctrines on the basis of their manifest truth and rightness.

A major purpose of this book is to show, by exposing the logic and preconceptions of each political ideology, which particular ideas and values (which may appear in isolation in the context of political argument) derive from which particular ideology, so that in political debate the critical listener will see the further implications of each apparently autonomous, non-doctrinaire idea. Since we cannot expel ideological elements from political thought and practice, and since the results would prove disastrous if we tried—all sorts of clandestinely ideological concepts like 'efficiency' and 'consensus' might be sucked in to fill the vacuum—what we should do is acknowledge and try to understand rival ideologies and their component values and then choose between them. In reply to the objection that adherence to any ideal or ideology must be arbitrary, given their unverifiable nature, it can be argued that, different though facts are from values, the former can assist us to make rational choices between doctrines. For example, the incontrovertible *fact* that a large part of the world's population suffers poverty and malnourishment might cause one to espouse some form of internationalist socialism, which advocated world-wide redistribution on the basis of material need, rather than an ideology which commended distributions based on merit or legal entitlement. However, facts are not themselves neutral, but are usually selected—or constructed—on the basis of pre-existing, ideological, values. So facts can only give qualified guidance in choosing or justifying political positions, and are not themselves absolute truths. The relation between facts, values, and ideology is complex and much debated. That they are all interconnected is clear: it is less clear whether one causes the others, or vice versa, or whether there may not be a constant process of mutual adaptation going on between them. The arguments which follow assume that ideology conditions values and our selection and presentation of facts—although the 'brute facts' of the world around us may well, in turn, condition our selection of an ideology.

Since this book treats as ideologies some doctrines which would deny having ideological status, such as liberalism and conservatism, some account of the conception of ideology on which the analysis is based is called for. I would argue that an ideology is a doctrine about the right way, or the ideal way, of organizing society and conducting politics, based on wider considerations about the nature of human life and knowledge. The 'action-guiding' aspect of such doctrines derives from the fact that they claim to establish what is politically true and right, and so give rise to imperatives which are essentially moral. They inevitably include the recommendation that their ideals should be realized, or should continue to be realized. I do not argue that ideologies are bad, or that politics should be conducted on the basis of 'fact' or 'truth', because such facts and truths, uncontaminated by values, do not exist in most areas of human thought and discourse. It is a necessary consequence of the relativity of knowledge that different political doctrines will conceptualize society differently according to when, where and from what group they emanate. Certainly, ideologies are, in Mannheim's phrase, 'incongruent with reality', but although we are unlikely ever to perceive the nature of reality in a neutral, objective way (this is ruled out by the relativity of personal perceptions and analysis to the situation and personality of the knower), we may at least be able to gauge that some doctrines are less incongruent than others, and thus to criticize and choose between ideologies, with the help of facts. The real deceiver is not ideology, but the idea that there could be a single explanation or one set of truths about something as complex and heterogeneous as society.

The inclusive approach to ideology taken here does not imply that we should abandon the quest for political ideals, or adopt ideologies arbitrarily, unthinkingly. Quite the contrary. The more aware someone is of the ideological nature of her own thought, and the more explicit about her values, the better will she be able to identify and criticize those of others and to promote her own. Most important of all, understanding the pervasive nature of ideology helps us to expose and scrutinize the hidden premises and values which are treated as established facts in a particular society.

Ideology determines the use of political concepts and language, and even the form of logic used to prove political points: the liberal equates rational argument with formal logic, while Marxists use dialectical reason, which they consider scientific, and many right-wing thinkers are prone to argue by analogy (which does not formally constitute proof) or to invoke symbols or myths. The forms of reasoning typical of each ideology are discussed in Part II. Part III is an analysis of political ideas and ideals in the light of the discussion of the main ideologies. There is no pretence at 'objective' conceptual analysis leading to definitive, neutral definitions such as linguistic philosophers commended to political philosophers in the recent past. But the intention has been to set out as objectively as possible different ideological conceptions of ideas such as liberty, obligation, and the state and to assess them critically—such assessment still being, inevitably, an ideological process.

This approach bears out the argument of those who have argued that the major political ideas are 'essentially contested concepts', meaning that no single, final definition of such terms can be established which will not itself be contested sooner or later. This view is sometimes used to justify intellectual quietism: 'all knowledge is relative, all ideas are ideological, all concepts are contested' may lead to the conclusion that political beliefs should never be challenged—*de gustibus non est disputandum* (there's no accounting for tastes). Some disciples of logical positivism even recommended an end to political argument about values, since nobody could ever convince anyone else of the rightness of his own values, these being unverifiable. Weldon, a champion of this view, asserted that all rival political arguments should be reduced to statements of fact which could then be compared and found to correspond with reality, or not, resolving the dispute. He suggested a similar factual 'unpacking' process for finding the meaning of political concepts.[20] As has been suggested above, the assumption that such facts are neutral cannot be accepted. The facts do not speak for themselves, we speak for them. Anyone embarking on political theory—or practice—must remember that facts are largely 'constructed' on the basis of ideological commitment, and that argument must therefore take place principally at this level.

We live in an age of relativism which creates painful uncertainties. Postmodernist theory in particular has called all values and all 'discourse' into question—these, and even language itself, are said to be replete with ideological content[21] (however, postmodernists reject any standard of truth against which to measure ideology, thus falling into total relativism). Studies of the philosophy and method of the social sciences have also made us aware of the limitations of our knowledge. 'Pure knowledge'—that elusive ideal—is so vitiated by its relation to place and time, by the subjectivity of the thinker and by her culture, let alone her ideological commitments, that we must wonder whether such an ideal standard is not illusory. All four factors circumscribe and direct the form and content of our social and political knowledge and beliefs. We can make allowances for time, place, subjectivity, and culture-specificity when evaluating arguments and theories, in an attempt to come nearer to objective knowledge even though we cannot attain it (indeed, many contemporary philosophers argue that objectivity is impossible). Furthermore, we do not *choose* our ideologies as rational consumers choose the best detergent—to a large extent the ideologies choose us, given that we are socialized into a particular world-view (as Mannheim would say) and our room for intellectual manoeuvre is limited. The best we can hope for is not to achieve complete objectivity, but to achieve the most comprehensive understanding possible of a social phenomenon, which encompasses it in all its heterogeneity. This book, then, is intended to show what sort of allowances must be made for ideological bias in the study of politics, and how we might proceed to a more comprehensive understanding of political life.

---

20. T. Weldon, *The Vocabulary of Politics*, Penguin, 1953.
21. T. Eagleton, *Ideology: An Introduction*, Verso, 1991.

FURTHER READING

I. Adams, *The Logic of Political Belief*, Harvester Wheatsheaf, 1989.

R. Boudon, *The Analysis of Ideology*, Trans. M. Slater, Chicago U.P., 1989.

T. Eagleton, *Ideology: An Introduction*, Verso, 1991.

M. Freeden, *Ideologies and Political Theory: A Conceptual Approach*, Oxford U.P., 1996.

J. Larrain, *The Concept of Ideology*, Hutchinson, 1979.

J. Larrain, *Ideology and Cultural Identity*, Polity Press, 1994.

D. McLellan, *Ideology*, 2nd edn, Open University Press, 1995.

K. Minogue, *Alien Powers: The Pure Theory of Ideology*, Allen & Unwin, 1986.

N. O'Sullivan, *The Structure of Modern Ideology*, Edward Elgar, 1989.

B. Parekh, *Marx's Theory of Ideology*, Croom Helm, 1982.

J. P. Plamenatz, *Ideology*, Macmillan, 1970.

M. Rosen, *On Voluntary Servitude: False Consciousness and the Theory of Ideology*, Polity Press, 1996.

J. B. Thompson, *Studies in the Theory of Ideology*, Polity Press, 1985.

H. Williams, *Concepts of Ideology*, Wheatsheaf, 1988.

Part II

Ideologies

Chapter 3

Liberalism

The description of what Marxists would call the 'dominant ideology' is a difficult task. In Britain we imbibe liberal ideas effortlessly from an early age, with the result that liberalism appears as a necessary truth, the basis of reality, rather than as one political ideology among many. One feature of liberal thought which seems to support this view is that it has no ideological bible available for exegesis, revision, and faith. The growth of liberal doctrine is more akin to the growth of the shell of an ancient tortoise, and the slow development and accumulation of its principles promotes the view that there is something natural about liberalism.

The development of liberal thought in England began in the seventeenth century. For many centuries before the Renaissance, political institutions had been subordinated to, or amalgamated with, the religious establishment; kings claimed to rule by divine sanction so that, for their subjects, obedience was a religious duty. The Reformation reversed the balance of power, subjecting the Church to the monarch, but in the seventeenth century divine right was still often cited as the basis of monarchy. The need for a novel, secular theory of monarchy was manifest during the English Civil War and Commonwealth, and Hobbes justified authority on the grounds of a social contract in *Leviathan* (1651), but nevertheless advocated undivided, unlimited sovereignty. But at the time of the Glorious Revolution of 1688 and the establishment of William and Mary on the throne with a parliamentary constitution, Locke encapsulated the contemporary anti-authoritarian, secular idea of politics in his justification of constitutional monarchy, which is often perceived as the beginning of liberal theory. His approach also reflected the effects of a period of rapid social change: as traditional, hierarchical social forms disappeared, so did the strict subordination of some people to others, creating a need for a theory of social order in which all owed allegiance to a central authority on an equal footing. The hypothesis of the social contract provided such a theory.

A systematic, but controversial, account of the origins of liberal thought has been given by Macpherson, who correlates the theories of Hobbes and Locke with the growth of the commercial middle classes, and with innovatory patterns of wealth accumulation and consumption accompanied by a new, individualistic morality. He sees such writers as the chroniclers and champions of the development of bourgeois society.[1] A major problem with Macpherson's reading is that England in the seventeenth century was by no stretch of the imagination a 'bourgeois' society in any accepted sense of the word. Yet his account of liberalism as 'possessive individualism' is a catalyst to understanding the ideology: it reminds us that both Hobbes and Locke start by describing *individuals* in the state of nature, and that both consider the individual and his needs the basic explanatory unit of a systematic analysis of political society. Although individualism as we now understand it is merely embryonic in such theories, the basis for the egoistic economics and utilitarian morality of later liberalism is already present. Whatever dispute there may be about the details of Macpherson's interpretation, he is undoubtedly right in emphasizing the intimate connection of liberalism with capitalism. The similarity of the premises and the structure of liberal political theory and 'classical' economics shows how close knit are the various strands of the ideology.

The hallmark of the liberal is a concern with the limits of authority, and opposition to state interference with individual activities. The corollary of this is an emphasis on the importance of the individual and the promotion of human rights and liberties which serve to delimit the area within which the state is entitled to act. Liberal thought evolved at a time when the favoured scientific method was to decompose objects and substances into their smallest parts and to examine how these combined to form the whole, a method which Hobbes claimed to adopt in *Leviathan*. He and other more liberal theorists take the individual as the basic unit of society and view the latter as no more than an aggregate of individuals—an approach which leaves various 'holistic' social phenomena unexplained. There is, of course, perpetual controversy among theorists as to how we should conceptualize society. Just as a jar of pickle could be viewed as a compilation of the listed ingredients, or else as a distinct and different substance, society can be viewed as a combination of individual parts or as a qualitatively different whole. The liberal preference for the former conception, although modified by 'social liberals' like J. S. Mill and Hobhouse, has important consequences for the liberal view of political and social being.

THE INGREDIENTS OF LIBERALISM

Liberalism is better understood through an examination of the elements which go to make up the liberal model of society than through a historical survey of liberal authors, so many and varied were these. This section therefore sets out the main elements of the ideology, proceeding from the basic unit, the individual, to the resulting conception of society and the political ideals which follow from this. The initial focus will be the ideas of classical liberalism as it developed from the

1. C. B. Macpherson, *The Political Theory of Possessive Individualism*, Oxford U.P., 1962.

seventeenth century onwards, but we shall also consider the more socially orientated ideas of social liberals in the last two centuries, and some of the late-twentieth-century revisions made by neo-liberals and their communitarian critics.

The Individual

The preservation of the individual and the attainment of individual happiness are the supreme goals of a liberal political system, at least in theory. The individual person is to be regarded as inviolable, and all human life as sacrosanct; violence is therefore prohibited except in a war to preserve liberal society itself. This individualism is based on a morality which commands equal respect for all persons as moral beings with equal sensitivity. Individualism can take many forms,[2] and can rest on a more or a less elevated view of human beings, but its general consequence is to diminish the importance of the social whole, which is viewed as no more than the sum of its parts, and so cannot have a 'public interest' of its own, or any rights against the individual. This outlook can be called *atomistic*. It hindered orthodox liberals from giving a satisfactory account of the ways in which the individual atoms interact, or of the meta-individual structures such as groups and institutions which develop in reality. But then, liberal theory had historically to distinguish its conception of society from the feudal view of society as a hierarchical, coherent whole which it had displaced: individualism was instrumental in this. From the moral idealization of the individual stems the political necessity of liberty and also various cultural values which embody the notions of individuality, originality, and self-distinction.

The form which individualistic political theory takes depends on how human nature is conceived. Liberalism assumes the individual to be essentially rational— a necessary premise if the individual is to be the prime source of value, for it would be hard to value highly an irrational creature, who would be no more than a beast. The assumption of rationality also determines the form of political organization chosen, justifying participatory, rather than authoritarian, government. The individual is also credited with knowledge of his own best interests and the ability to pursue them rationally. Rational economic man, according to classical economists, maximizes profits; political man maximizes his utilities through judicious participation and choice. Liberal thinkers achieved what seemed impossible in the Christian middle ages: they made a virtue of selfishness. From Hobbes and Locke onwards, the pursuit of *self-interest* was accepted as man's proper motivation. Locke said that the 'laws of nature' gave man the right 'to preserve his property—that is, his life, liberty and estate',[3] and that the task of government was to help him in so doing. Bentham's utilitarianism elevated 'enlightened' self-interest to the status of morality and became widely accepted despite protests against this vindication of selfishness such as Dickens' satirization

---

2. The varieties of individualism are discussed in S. Lukes, *Individualism*, Blackwell, 1974.
3. J. Locke, *An Essay Concerning the True Original, Extent and End of Civil Government*, Dent, 1924, p. 159. Referred to hereafter as *Essay*.

of the self-made man, the objectionable and lying Bounderby, in *Hard Times*. Hence Macpherson's more recent characterization of the individual of classical liberal theory as possessive and infinitely acquisitive. So much for the materialistic side of human nature.

Man's spiritual side was acknowledged in the assumption that he is a free, rational, self-improving being. Locke considered man's natural state to be that of freedom; the duty of government was to provide the conditions for him to enjoy the maximum possible freedom within a framework of law. The conception of man as a free being led liberals to condemn any social arrangements which put him in a state of dependence, such as slavery or indentured labour. Locke disapproved of the practice of servants of binding themselves to their masters, and thought that they should not have voting rights because they had forgone their freedom. Since man is a free being who knows his own interests best, authoritarian or paternalistic government is against human nature. The problems which liberals encounter in reconciling this premise with the modern, interventionist, welfare state are discussed later. As for the human capacity for self-improvement, this was largely ignored in early liberal theory. Bentham maintained that 'lower' and 'higher' pleasures were qualitatively the same in any utility calculation: it would be paternalistic of any government to try to elevate people's tastes. Although later liberals did not go as far as Enlightenment Utopians, who considered human beings to be *perfectible*, J. S. Mill emphasized 'man's interests as a progressive being' and recommended intellectual pursuits and self-improvement through education and political activity. This—although Mill hesitated to acknowledge it and opposed state education—implied an eventual extension of government activity to make the opportunities for self-development available.

Finally, what of man as a social creature? Hobbes's state of nature, with men engaged in a constant struggle for power and scarce resources, suggested innate anti-social tendencies which only an authoritarian sovereign could hold in check. Liberal theorists (of whom Hobbes was a forerunner in some other respects) rejected this conclusion, but did not, however, assume natural sociability. The assumption is rather that men are 'mutually indifferent' because of their free, independent nature. The pursuit of self-interest can lead to co-operation or to competitive and aggressive behaviour. Competition should only arise when a shortage of resources prevents everyone's being satisfied; likewise, co-operation should occur when it is in people's interests. Locke envisaged the social contract being made co-operatively when it was seen to be for everyone's benefit. It is not true that liberal theory assumes that man is *naturally* competitive, although many adherents of liberalism take that as a necessary truth; liberal contract theorists such as Locke, and Rawls in this century, emphasize the voluntary and consensual basis of society. Nevertheless, the counterpart of the strong conception of the individual is a weak conception of the nature and purpose of society and in particular of government, which is seen as a device for performing the residual tasks which individual self-interest leaves undone. This means that liberal theorists are unwilling to invoke concepts such as the common good or the public interest, which are predicated of society as a whole, and would circumscribe their use in justifying state intervention. The only common good which classical liberals would recognize is the maximization of the aggregate of individual benefits.

What of the role of *woman* in all this? Perhaps it is not surprising that liberal thinkers during the past three centuries did not take her into account. However, as Pateman has argued in *The Sexual Contract*, the liberal view looks rather different from a feminist perspective.[4] The neglect of one half of the human race in a theory of the individual must give rise to doubts about its adequacy. This is discussed further in Chapter 9.

Contract and Consent

A central political axiom deriving from the idealization of individual freedom and rationality is that government should be based on the consent of the people, which legitimizes it. This forms the basis of the affinity between liberalism and democracy although they are in some respects incompatible. The idea of consent first appeared in the guise of contract theory. Locke imagined a peaceful, sociable state of nature with many of the characteristics of established society; men would own property in such a state. The problem would be that in the case of a dispute no impartial judge existed to arbitrate. The inconvenience of this would cause men voluntarily to contract to form a society 'for their comfortable, safe and peaceable living . . . in secure enjoyment of their properties'. Thus, a community would be formed and a government would be constituted by majority decision. Each individual gives up his natural rights of self-protection and the right to punish transgressors, and the government takes on the duty of protecting its subjects' rights.[5] A consequence of Locke's social contract (though not of Hobbes's) is that governments hold power on trust and in extreme cases the people may resist or overthrow a government which betrays this trust. Locke elaborated the government actions which would be a breach of trust: it may not destroy, enslave or impoverish its subjects, nor rule by arbitrary decrees, nor transfer its own powers to others, nor take a man's property without his consent. The last prohibition, popularized in the slogan 'no taxation without representation', was a powerful weapon in the arsenal of the American revolutionaries demanding independence from England and was also proclaimed by taxpaying suffragettes.

Locke's contract was not a guess at pre-history but a hypothetical explanation of the origin of government in consent. Later generations consented 'tacitly' to government, Locke considered, when they inherited property under its laws or enjoyed their protection. Most eighteenth-century liberals rejected the social contract because of its mythical nature, and emphasized the role of consent in legitimizing government, but a contemporary theorist John Rawls has used the idea of a hypothetical contract as the basis of his theory of justice and the good (liberal) society. The contract has always played a central role in liberal thinking about politics because it is the paradigm way in which free, rational, knowledgeable individuals would deal with each other. But critics of liberalism

4. C. Pateman, *The Sexual Contract*, Polity Press, 1988.
5. Locke, *Essay*, Chaps VIII–IX.

point out that many of the real or hypothetical contracts referred to in liberal theory are not made under the paradigm, fair conditions which make contracts just and binding.

As the franchise in Britain was extended and finally made universal, it became increasingly realistic to pin 'the consent of the governed' on the act of voting. This is still the major liberal justification of political obligation and gives rise to the claim that the elected government has a mandate to act—ideas which will be discussed further in Chapter 12 and 15. The usual assumption is that government based on consent must be democratic, so that consent is renewed or refused at regular intervals, However, it would not be illogical for a liberal to consent permanently to a different form of government which he trusted to oversee his interests.[6] Liberalism does not entail democracy, but democracy is probably the best guarantee for liberalism.

Constitutionalism and the Law

Although democracy is not essential to liberalism, some form of constitution which limits the powers of government is. Locke rejected Hobbes's view that sovereignty must be undivided as potentially tyrannical, and sketched an ideal division and balance of powers to counteract usurpation and tyranny, emphasizing that the legislative power, the power of lawmaking, was supreme, and that this belonged to the people or their representatives.[7] He foreshadowed the limitations placed on the constitutional monarchy established after the 1688 revolution: a century later, his ideas were made concrete in the checks and balances of the US constitution. When Locke wrote the English parliament was highly unrepresentative, being elected on a narrow property franchise, of which he approved. His contribution to the liberal theory of government was not the idea of representative democracy, but the theory of the separation of powers, which had the same ultimate aim of safeguarding people's rights from tyrannical encroachment. The English constitution which resulted from the 1688 revolution became an object of admiration for the French philosopher Montesquieu, whose *Spirit of the Laws* (1748) reasserted the need for legality and constitutionalism and in turn influenced the American revolutionaries.

The constitution and the law have parallel roles in liberal theory: the constitution, a form of higher law, prevents the government from transgressing against individuals while the law prevents individuals from transgressing against each other. From Locke onwards, liberals emphasized the role of law in ensuring individual liberty. He had argued that liberty without law was mere licence, and that

> freedom of men under government is to have a standing rule to live by, common to every one of that society and made by the legislative power erected in it.[8]

---

6. I. Berlin, 'Two concepts of liberty', in *Political Philosophy* (Ed. A. Quinton), Oxford U.P., 1967, p. 148.
7. Locke, *Essay*, Chap. XIII.
8. Locke, *Essay*, p. 127.

Law is the paradigm method of solving conflicts: 'force is to be opposed to nothing but to unjust and unlawful force'. Yet, although liberalism is highly legalistic, the closely associated ideas of individual liberty and *laissez-faire* in economics dictated, for classical liberals, that only a small nucleus of regulatory laws should be enacted and that interventionist or paternalistic government should be avoided. Nowadays this stipulation has to be regarded as precept rather than reality. The idea of 'due process' underlies liberal considerations on government. If proper procedures for making and executing laws can be devised and enforced constitutionally, the risk of arbitrary or tyrannical rule is minimized. The establishment of *procedures* which will best advance the goals of individual freedom and happiness is thus the first aim of a liberal system.

Freedom as Choice

Freedom is the primary value in the liberal creed, being the means whereby the rational individual pursues her own interests. Viewed thus, freedom is an instrumental value which helps people to get what they want. But liberals have always associated freedom closely with the 'human essence', so that political, economic and social freedom is seen as a human necessity, and a good in itself, rather than merely as a means to an end. The liberal conception of freedom has been widely identified with material choice and the right to spend one's money (if any) as one wishes. In Britain in the 1980s, this was advanced by the neo-liberal Conservative government as the justification for lowering direct taxation, for extending the fee-paying school sector and encouraging private health care. Such a view of freedom is closely connected with the doctrine of *laissez-faire* which advocated minimum regulation and maximum freedom of action for the entrepreneur. The conception of freedom as choice makes implicit reference to the economic model: 'sociopolitical man', the consumer and voter, is viewed as a maximizer in the social market place.

The more ennobling aspects of freedom were emphasized by Mill in the nineteenth century; according to Macpherson, the shortcomings of liberalism based on classical economics were then becoming clear and Mill and others introduced humanitarian elements into the ideology, dwelling on people's *capacities* and *powers*, rather than on their utility-maximizing, consumption role.[9] Mill advocated freedom of speech, thought, and religion as the right of every rational adult (male or female), to be curtailed only where their exercise threatens direct material harm to others. Realization of the freedoms of speech and choice in the political sphere requires that citizens should be able to choose between a variety of doctrines: one-party elections are a deprivation of freedom. A pluralist democracy is thus the political outcome of the liberal ideal of freedom. (A pluralist society is one where there is a multiplicity of interest groups and associations and a variety of political doctrines. The concept of pluralism is discussed in Chapter 12.) British governments of all persuasions have usually upheld the Millean notion of the freedom of the individual against the state and

---

9. C. B. Macpherson, *Democratic Theory*, Oxford U.P., 1973, pp. 3–23.

against the tyranny of public opinion, but contemporary threats to individual freedom come not so much from visible centres of power such as parliament as from diverse power structures such as the bureaucracy, quangos and the 'military-industrial complex'. These threaten individual freedom by propagating of their own institutional values (efficiency, security and so on) and by self-serving activity; their lack of public accountability precludes any possibility of individual intervention and control. Such threats are harder to conceptualise and cope with, theoretically and practically, than the deliberate power-seeking which may threaten freedom overtly in the political sphere. Today, liberal theory and the idea of freedom need updating to comprehend these kinds of dangers. Chapter 14 discusses these problems in greater detail.

Equality of Opportunity

Liberalism evolved in conjunction with capitalism, an economic system which operates on the basis of great inequalities of wealth and income. Substantive equality has been conspicuously absent from liberal society, particularly in the nineteenth century. Liberal theorists had to reconcile these 'natural' inequalities of capitalism with their egalitarian view of human beings in the abstract. They therefore attributed various abstract, formal equalities to the citizen and the private individual, such as equal rationality, equal self-interest, equal voting rights, and equal rights before the law. By doing this, liberal theory *formally* equalizes individuals although real individuals have differential levels of wealth, competence, and intelligence. These abstract equalities support the fiction that everybody starts the race of life equal, and this takes the sting out of competition, which classical liberals assumed to be a perennial feature of human life. Competition would, of course, be an invidious basis for social organization if it were admitted that the odds were fixed against some individuals from the start. Therefore, liberals wish to prove that competition takes place in a context of *equality of opportunity* which guarantees a fair outcome, with the most meritorious individuals gaining the rewards. The equality of opportunity which liberals advocate is the contrary of substantive equality, for it denotes the opportunity to differentiate oneself from others by becoming unequal, and better. But even if the 'equalizing' social services, such as state education or health services worked perfectly, which they evidently do not, the natural inequalities of talent and energy would make equality of opportunity a myth. But this myth is important to liberal ideology, which can claim that, unlike conservatism, it is not an inegalitarian doctrine but one based on fundamental human equalities, out of which emerges differentiation based on the just reward of merit.

Social Justice Based on Merit

Gallie characterized the liberal theory of social justice as *commutative*, based, like capitalism, on exchange.[10] Individuals are said to gain rewards in proportion to

---

10. W. B. Gallie, 'Liberal morality and socialist morality' in *Philosophy, Politics and Society* (Ed. P. Laslett), Blackwell, 1956.

their talents and merits and in exchange for their contribution to society: contribution is assumed to be an approximate measure of talent. The argument asserts that the system is organized so as to reward the most deserving, therefore those who gain most have deserved most. This theory of justice appears as an afterthought attached to liberalism, rather than an analytical theory. It offers justification after the event, allowing the liberal to argue that the rich are rich because they have merited it, and thus preventing us from further questioning their deserts or their entitlement to their wealth. Classical economic theory was instrumental in the creation of this notion of social justice, which is reminiscent of the 'just price' for a commodity which results from the interplay of market forces, but in no way necessarily reflects the intrinsic worth of the commodity. But even Hayek, champion of the market system, concedes that the rewards which it delivers do not bear any close relation to subjective merit and are in no sense socially just; the market can only guarantee fair rules, and not just outcomes.[11] However, liberal ideology vindicates the system by arguing that, given equality of opportunity, free enterprise and competition produce a just distribution of income and other goods. (This is sometimes called a 'meritocratic' system, but the term 'meritocracy' refers more properly to the rule of the most talented, a doctrine consonant with the liberal outlook and one dear to the two Mills, but one which has been overshadowed by the general commitment of liberals to democracy.) Without the constraint of equality of opportunity (often absent in real life), the liberal theory of social justice would resemble the puzzling biblical parable of the talents.

> For unto every one that hath shall be given, and he shall have abundance: but from him that hath not shall be taken away even that which he hath.[12]

Liberals see social justice in terms of specifiable, just procedures, rather than in terms of predictable outcomes. The recent major contribution to liberal thinking on justice, that of Rawls, is discussed in Chapter 14, and his theory too is deliberately 'procedural': it specifies the rules which should govern a just society, but not the social outcomes which should be aimed at. This procedural emphasis is a result of the liberal conviction that each person knows her own interests best: a system of justice must therefore not dictate a specific distribution of goods, but should establish rules by which people can *fairly* pursue their desires. Although all ideologies claim to promulgate justice, in liberalism justice is seen as the result of the pursuit of other ideals rather than as a separately definable principle, and indeed in early utilitarianism (the moral theory which developed at the same time as many liberal political ideas) justice was explicitly subordinated to considerations of utility, and was only valued for its contribution to utility.

---

11. F. Hayek, 'The principles of a liberal social order', in *Ideologies of Politics*, (Eds. A. Crespigny and J. Cronin), Oxford U.P., 1975, pp. 67–9; *Law, Legislation and Liberty*, Routledge & Kegan Paul, 1982 (one-volume edn), II, pp. 70, 126–8.
12. *Matthew* 25:29.

Tolerance

Tolerance originated as an instrumental or secondary ideal, related to freedom, which facilitates the pursuit of individual interest. However, today it is often given the status of a good in itself. Liberal society prides itself on its tolerance and passes unfavourable judgements on societies which suppress dissidence and nonconformist views. The classic argument for religious tolerance was put forward in Locke's *Letter Concerning Toleration* (1689), at the end of a century fraught with religious struggles in England. Locke argued that the government's task is the preservation of peace, while morality is the business of priests, thus delimiting the role of government rather more strictly than is sometimes done today. Civil rights belong to men *qua* human beings and cannot be removed on the grounds of religious nonconformity. (It should be noted, however, that Locke did not extend tolerance to Roman Catholicism, for reasons explicable in terms of the events of his own time.) Despite Locke, various prohibitions against dissenters, Catholics and Jews remained in force in Britain until the nineteenth century, but his *Letter* initiated the idea that society should accept a variety of religious, moral and political opinions, and that human and civil rights belong to all by virtue of their humanity.

Another argument for tolerance was advanced by Mill: 'we can never be sure that the opinion we are endeavouring to stifle is a false opinion.'[13] His argument can be summarized as follows: (1) all views contain, or may contain, some grain of truth and only 'the collision of adverse opinions' can lead us to truth; (2) intolerance is an assumption of infallibility by the intolerant; (3) received opinion, even if true, will become mere irrational prejudice or habit if uncontested; and (4) an unchallenged doctrine will gradually lose its power to affect people's conduct.[14] For Mill, tolerance directs us towards the truth. The empiricist epistemology to which he subscribed dictates that we can never know a truth *finally*, and so can never categorically define what is in people's best interests: this determines the open-endedness of the liberal approach to political theory and practice. From the ideal of tolerance derives the conviction that a pluralist society which accommodates a multiplicity of beliefs is necessary to the search for human good. These arguments are considered further in Chapter 14.

Private and Public Life

As a result of other liberal ideals, the value and importance of private (economic and social) life is enhanced at the expense of public or political life. The distinction can be traced back to Locke, who separated the formation of *society* from the appointment of *government*. His theory of resistance suggests that he thought that society could still function in the absence of government. This conception departed from Hobbes's view that government and society are co-extensive: if one is overthrown, the other disintegrates, since only government can create the order which makes society possible. Locke's view has the clear implication that

13. J. S. Mill, *On Liberty*, Collins, 1962, p. 143.
14. Mill, *On Liberty*, Chap. 2.

government should not pervade every area of social life, which is a separate sphere. Locke thus provided the foundation for the modern liberal view of *civil society*—that is, the sphere of autonomous social institutions which are protected by the rule of law but should be immune from state interference. Similarly, Mill's conception of individual liberty and the restrictions which he places on government action would, if realized, entail a very large sphere of privacy within which the individual could act without interference. A strict distinction is drawn between the private and the public, the former being seen as the focus of interest and satisfaction for individuals, by contrast with the classical Greek view of politics as the sphere in which the citizen realizes himself most fully. *Laissez-faire* economists like Cobden advanced the view that the state's role was merely that of an arbiter between conflicting interests, a regulatory rather than a constructive role. This view permeated liberal theory, as the inactivity of English governments in the early nineteenth century bears witness: Lord Palmerston, when Prime Minister, said 'We cannot go on legislating for ever'. This limited view of government's functions gave rise to a certain distaste for the business of politics, an outlook which is explicitly opposed to anything approaching compulsion in political participation. A major liberal criticism of the former totalitarian communist states concerned the obligatory nature of political activity there, and the extension of politics into spheres which liberals consider private. For this reason, most liberals oppose a compulsory voting system, even though there are compelling reasons for trying to find out the opinion of the whole population in a true democracy. Yet such a system operates in Australia without detriment to liberal democracy.

The consequence of this outlook, in conjunction with representative democratic practice, is the removal of most political power, except the power of withholding acquiescence, from the people. Most liberal democracies have developed elite systems of government in which politicians pursue what they take to be in the people's interest—or act in their own interests—and are only weakly responsible to their constituents. This is especially true of Britain, where the tradition of parliamentary sovereignty and the independence of representatives is always cited in rejection of pleas for referenda, or attempts to render MPs more directly accountable. Justifications of elite governments within liberal democracy are discussed in Chapter 12. The remoteness of government from the people has been perceived as a danger in the latter part of this century: even in the 1960s the (then) Liberal Party in Britain became a strong advocate of regionalism, devolution, and other devices to extend popular control over politicians and administrators. The problem is that, by enlarging our conception of the private sphere and emphasizing the individual's right to opt out of politics, liberalism has opened the path to an imposition of elite institutions against which people would, *in extremis*, find that they had no protection. Intimations of this could be seen in the 1985 trial of a British civil servant, Clive Ponting, for passing a classified document about the Falklands War to an MP. Mr Ponting argued that it was in the public interest for the truth to be revealed, but the judge asserted that 'the interests of the state' meant, simply, the policies of the current government.

The risk of a 'government against the people' situation has led to the development of theories of participation which are, in effect, applications of basic democratic theory.[15] Advocates of participation could draw on Mill's arguments in favour of popular political participation and the extension of the franchise. In contrast to the prevailing *laissez-faire* view of the virtues of minimal government (a view which the excesses of popular sovereignty during the French Revolution had powerfully reinforced), he argued that participation is educational and improving and that the calibre of a people can be gauged by its level of political activity.[16] Such arguments contrast with his views on liberty, which would tend to support the individual's right to withdraw into his private life, and the tension between these two components of liberal democracy remains unresolved.

THE LIBERAL MODEL: PERPETUAL MOTION?

When the elements of liberal thought summarized above are combined they constitute a coherent, self-consistent model of society. This is, of course, highly abstract, as the essence of model-making is to extract the fundamental characteristics of a situation and to discard the details which locate it in time and space. However, political theorists can use such a model to expose more clearly the bare bones of an ideology and the basic assumptions which conditioned its development. Many liberal theorists write as if the value of the individual, and of liberty, is neither time-bound nor culture-bound, but a universal necessity, and as if the model will operate for ever. This is indeed Fukuyama's claim in *The End of History and the Last Man* (1992), which argued in the aftermath of communism that liberal ideas and the market economy had successfully seen off their rivals and had put an end to History. Perhaps every dominant ideology necessarily represents itself as immortal. Because of this, the liberal model tends to be ahistorical, lacking any theory of past history or future development, although endorsing a cautiously optimistic view of human progress, which differentiates it from conservative doctrines. Classical liberal ideology views society as a voluntarily and rationally constituted aggregate of self-interested individuals. The model is set in motion *spontaneously* by their desires and interests; because human nature is thought to be the same at all times and in all places, this guarantees the possibility of perpetual motion, and the fact that the system operates on the basis of natural desires makes it ideal.

In 1985 the neo-liberal Prime Minister Thatcher stated that there was no such thing as society, there were only individuals and families. She echoed the classical view that society is no more than the vehicle whereby we pursue our interests and has no independent existence or value over and above that of individuals. Self-interest is regulated by contracts enforced by law, the ideal means by which free and equal individuals deal with each other. Society itself is founded on a contract, or on consent, a weaker form of contract; viewed like this, it resembles a private

---

15. See, e.g., C. Pateman, *Participation and Democratic Theory*, Cambridge U.P., 1970.
16. J. S. Mill, *Considerations on Representative Government*, Oxford U.P., 1912, Chap. II.

club whose limited rules the members accept because they benefit by them, and wish to belong to the club. The most important human activities are deemed to take place in the economic and social spheres, which are self-regulating. Politics is the circumscribed area where interests are furthered by political means, mainly because conflicts have to be mediated there, or because individuals will not agree to co-operate to provide some social necessity, such as a defence system, because the costs would be too unevenly divided. Politics is a means, not an end, so it is small wonder that the individual's loyalty to the system is contingent upon its furthering her private interests.

The conception of the individual's duty to society is strictly limited and the idea of the 'common good' is, by and large, discounted except by social liberals such as T. H. Green who had a moral conception of individuals' duties to each other as members of that shared enterprise, society.[17] Green's philosophy was influenced by Hegelian idealism: he saw individuals as socially formed beings. For him, freedom was not merely the absence of legal restraint but the presence of opportunities for self-development. Government has a duty to create these and to legislate for the common good. The community, as well as individuals, has rights. Liberals with a more atomistic view of society hold that the concept of the common good is itself philosophically fallacious.[18] The substance and joy of life is to be found in the private, not in the public sphere, and the virtue of the system is that it allows individuals the chance to satisfy themselves as they please within the limits of law. In this respect, liberalism represents a utopian ideal although, as Mannheim points out, a realized utopia is no longer utopia. Certainly, liberal practice differs greatly from the model. But the purpose of models is to provide political guidance. Although the model purports to be descriptive, to describe schematically how society works, its main function is a normative and justificatory one. It can be invoked to justify or criticize political practice in liberal society, and elsewhere.

The liberal model of society, as was mentioned, has analogies with the free enterprise system idealized by early economists. The free market was seen as a collection of independent individuals producing, buying and selling in order to maximize their utilities, without government interference. Adam Smith introduced the notion of the Invisible Hand, which supposedly guaranteed that this multiplicity of self-interested transactions would lead to the greatest possible national prosperity spontaneously, without any individual actually intending this.[19] Earlier, Mandeville's *Fable of the Bees* (1714) had shown allegorically how general prosperity is produced via the pursuit of private interests—unity through diversity, 'private vices, public benefits'. The invisible hand idea has re-emerged in Nozick's advocacy of a minimal state within which a multiplicity of free associations can operate, each motivated by self-interest.[20] The virtue of such

---

17. T. H. Green, *Lectures on the Principles of Political Obligation*, Longmans Green & Co., 1901, pp. 123–6.
18. J. P. Plamenatz, *Consent, Freedom and Political Obligation*, 2nd edn, Oxford U.P., 1968, Chap. 3.
19. A. Smith, *The Wealth of Nations*, London, 1776, Bk IV, Chap. 2.
20. R. Nozick, *Anarchy, State and Utopia*, Blackwell, 1974.

theories is that they do not seek to change people and make them act altruistically or virtuously. But their shortcomings are manifested in real life, where the universal pursuit of self-interest does not lead to universal fulfilment or happiness: government intervention and some concept of the general good is needed to protect those individuals who fail to prosper. While some orthodox liberal thinkers such as Malthus and Spencer thought that the poor and inadequate should be left to perish, to enhance the health of society at large, later, more humanitarian liberals such as Hobhouse accepted the need for government intervention to ensure some level of wellbeing for all.

Both the economic and political theories of liberalism assume, in different ways, the possibility of a harmony of private interests which ensures the good of all, if not the 'common good', but there is no evidence that this harmony will occur or that conflicting interests will produce overall prosperity. Indeed, the assumption of scarcity which underlies the idea of competition strongly suggests that conflict, rather than harmony, will prevail in liberal systems. (A situation of scarcity is likely to lead to what rational choice theorists call a 'zero-sum game', where one person's gain is another's loss.) Yet, as Macpherson observes, liberal democrats implicitly hope for harmony or equilibrium, since 'equilibrium is a nice tune for whistling in the dark'.[21] In recent political science, the notion of harmony has reappeared in the guise of *consensus*. This is measured in various ways (a 70% agreement is often taken to constitute consensus on some issue) and its existence is seen as a manifestation of the good health of liberal-democratic society. For Marxists, the concepts of harmony and consensus are mere delusions, ideological defences against a highly inegalitarian and conflictual reality. However, some such concept is evidently vital to an ideology which advocates human diversity and self-interest. In classical economics, harmony reigns, thanks to the invisible hand; in liberal political thought, it is achieved through the pluralistic democratic process via consensus and tolerance. And in utilitarianism, the idea of 'the greatest happiness of the greatest number' implies that a harmonious aggregation can be achieved, even though little evidence is offered for this.

Utilitarianism has already been cited as the moral theory with the strongest links with liberalism. The theory was given its first definitive formulation by Bentham in the late eighteenth century, although some of its assumptions were implicit in Hume's writings. As a moral system based on a calculus of pain and pleasure, it justifies morally the self-seeking activities of the individual who first appeared in Hobbes's state of nature. Its radicalism lay in its secularization of morality and its vindication of 'enlightened' self-interest. Yet as a social and political philosophy, aggregating individual interests to calculate and achieve the greatest happiness of the greatest number, it could logically offer no protection for individuals or minorities if the wellbeing of the majority required their suppression. By contrast, the liberal formula aims to protect the rights of each individual, which constitute a limitation on the government's power to promote the good of the majority. Liberalism, utilitarianism, and classical economics were

---

21. Macpherson, *Democratic Theory*, p. 192.

all part of a homogeneous intellectual world-view which developed at the time of the Enlightenment. The liberal's 'political man' who knows his own interests and follows them is none other than the utilitarian moralist who calculates the utility of his actions; his *alter ego* is 'economic man', who maximizes his profits and miraculously benefits society as a whole. All three theories, because of their individualistic basis, suffer problems of aggregation: they cannot cope with the development of cartels and monopolies at the practical level, nor with the theoretical claim that society has political or moral rights. In reality the inevitable tensions between the individual and the social whole require that these ideas should be modified. While social liberals such as Mill and Hobhouse modified the theories accordingly, their amendments could not wholly abolish these internal tensions.

Liberal theory is, then, a political doctrine which exalts the individual at the expense of the state and the social whole, and sees freedom as a condition for human happiness. As the long-dominant ideology in Britain, the USA, and parts of Europe, it has been assailed from both left and right. The criticisms which socialists, Marxists and others have made will be considered in later chapters. But liberalism cannot solve all the internal problems which it harbours, and the following sections will highlight some of these. The permanent problem which liberals face is to find an appropriate division of powers between the individual and society: this changes over time, as social conditions alter. Mill's assertion that 'over himself, over his own body and mind, the individual is sovereign',[22] together with his formula that government interference is only warranted to prevent material harm to others, provides us with a yardstick by which to measure liberty. But it does not offer a ready solution to complex problems such as whether emergency laws against terrorism should be enacted if they also threaten the rights of innocent members of the population.

The real problem is that political theorists have to assume that the chain of causality in social life *ends* somewhere—like economists, they must add a *ceteris paribus* clause and ignore some remote possible repercussions of political action— but in reality the effects of government and individual action are too unpredictable and extensive to be comprehended by such simple, formal principles as that of Mill. An 'enabling law', like that which gives strikers the right to picket, may turn out, paradoxically, to curtail the freedom of the whole non-striking population. (In 1985, the British National Council for Civil Liberties [now called Liberty] nearly split over arguments as to whether the right to work of non-striking miners deserved equal protection with the rights of strikers.) Today, some of the most serious disputes arise over the freedoms granted to certain sections of the population which may detract from those of other groups; positive discrimination policies in educational institutions gives rise to such disputes. Some of these issues are elaborated in Chapter 14. Here, I shall consider the value of the individual, her interests, and her relationship to the welfare state, as they appear in liberal ideology, along with associated problems.

---

22. Mill, *On Liberty*, p. 135.

WHY DOES THE LIBERAL VALUE THE INDIVIDUAL SO HIGHLY?

The ideas of the autonomy, the dignity, and the unique value of the individual are relatively recent acquisitions and have given rise to an ethical system and a political ideology widely different from those of the ancient Greeks and of Christian theology. Plato's organic view of society dealt with the (male) individual only in terms of his social function and measured his virtue and value according to his conduct as a citizen: such a view leaves no room for the cult of individuality. Political theology during the middle ages allocated a similarly insignificant place to the individual, accepting the necessity of a hierarchical society, where the individual was defined by position or class. But, curiously, the seeds of modern individualism were also present in Christianity: the tenet that all souls are equally precious in the eyes of God provided grounds for a notion of human equality and dignity, although on an abstract plane. Early liberals like Locke built on this, contending that men's intrinsic equality must be reflected in the impartial, equal treatment of individuals by the legal system.

The birth of liberal individualism occurred in the period which saw the final disappearance of feudal remnants from England, as the spread of commerce and then of industrialization created new roles and new fortunes. Rapid social mobility gave rise to the idea of an individual (still male) who individuated himself by his achievements and his resulting possessions. Classical liberals viewed individuals, theoretically, as bundles of interests and desires which, left to themselves, they would satisfy. During the eighteenth-century revolutionary era, the individual was depicted as the bearer of political rights. Meanwhile, liberal economists assumed individuals to be the free, independent vendors of their own talents and labour power, operating in the free market. The idea of the individual's powers or capacities formed the basis of nineteenth-century accounts of democracy, which assumed political rationality on the part of the individual.[23]

These forms of individualism emphasized the characteristics common to all men. While Mill made similar assumptions in his writings on liberty and government, he also praised *individuality*, which rests on the individual's desire to differentiate himself from others, often through competition—a characteristic essential to the innovatory phase of early capitalism. Mill and Humboldt valued individual originality, creativity, and spontaneity which would, they hoped, motivate progress to a better society.[24] In this century, Ortega y Gasset and other critics of 'mass society' have again praised individuality as a defence against the conformism and mediocrity of modern society.[25] In the mid-twentieth century some social liberals and liberal socialists once again envisaged the individual as a bundle of desires—to be satisfied by the welfare state. This passive individual living in a modern land of Cockayne where all his needs are met may have been

23. See again Lukes, *Individualism*.
24. Mill, *On Liberty*, Chap. 3, and W. Humboldt, *The Sphere and Duties of Government* (trans. J. Courtland), London, 1854.
25. J. Ortega y Gasset, *The Revolt of the Masses*, Unwin, 1961.

the logical conclusion of a theory which dwells on individual interests, but was a far cry from the active self-seeking individual depicted by Locke, Bentham, Mill, and Spencer. Neo-liberalism in the 1980s and 1990s again emphasized self-help and independence to combat what was perceived as welfare dependence.

A historical account of the rise of individualism leaves unanswered the philosophical question of how the liberal justifies placing the highest political value on the individual, as he does by asserting the sanctity of human life and the right to happiness, viewed as the pursuit of self-interest. The strongest justification for giving human life and happiness a special value is based on the view that egoism and self-love are natural. Human desires are therefore the foremost criterion for deciding human good, according to a naturalistic ethic. Any political value which makes reference to the social whole is suspect as society is itself an artificial aggregate, and because such a value may depart from and contravene individual interests. Hobbes, who is sometimes called a 'psychological hedonist', argued that 'of the voluntary acts of every man, the object is some *Good to himself*'.[26] Locke's account of the state of nature likewise assumed self-preservation and the protection of his interests ('life, liberty and estate') as man's primary motives. Later, Hume, entering the current controversy as to whether men are ruled by reason or passion (that is, self-interest), came down firmly on the side of passion. Reason is a poor guide to action: 'It is not contrary to reason to prefer the destruction of the whole world to the scratching of my little finger.'[27] His contemporary, Bishop Butler, argued that even altruistic actions are ultimately attributable to self-love. Among the other multifarious apostles of self-interest in the eighteenth century was the Marquis de Sade, who believed that anyone had the right to use any other individual as he or she liked, for sexual pleasure, since it was wrong to break the laws of desire, Nature's laws. The crucial difference between Sade's view and that of liberals is that he denied the existence of the inviolable personal rights which would prevent self-interest leading to a riot of mutual destruction.

The egoistic individual received his apotheosis in utilitarianism. For Bentham, the utility principle was a first principle, which needed no proof because it was rooted in human psychology. Actions were to be morally judged according to their tendency to augment or diminish an individual's pleasure. Like Butler, he argued that no action was entirely disinterested, for even sympathy rests basically on self-interest: it pleases us to be thought compassionate. However, when Bentham extended the utility principle to society as a whole, he could not resolve the problem of reconciling the individual's right to happiness with the good of the greatest number when these came into conflict. The majority principle threatened the individual rights which liberals considered inviolable.

The focus on the individual as a creature of the senses, rather than a soul, leads directly to liberalism's central value, the pursuit of self-interest, for which the sanctity of human life is a necessary precondition. In secular moral theory, the individual must be the final arbiter of what is good. If she is but a bundle of

---

26. T. Hobbes, *Leviathan* (Ed. C. B. Macpherson), Penguin, 1968, p. 192.
27. D. Hume, *Treatise of Human Nature*, Fontana, 1972, Bk II, p. 157.

appetites, the definition of 'good' will centre on what satisfies her. Hence, the fallacious equation of what is *desired* with what is *desirable* (i.e. good) of which Mill is accused. The resulting reduction of human values to matters of pain and pleasure or approval and disapproval, is what is known as *subjectivist ethics*. But if our definitions of good and evil are rooted in individual desires, and if people desire different objects, there is no appropriate way of judging between their definitions of the good: differences of morals must therefore be tolerated. So the liberal doctrines of freedom and tolerance are closely connected with their moral outlook—an outlook which liberated them from Christian morality, with its disapproval of self-love and self-interest. But if the new morality was liberating for liberals, it also liberated their opponents. If it is my subjective moral conviction that all capitalists should be bloodily exterminated, who shall gainsay it? Liberalism relies on a close coincidence of individuals' intuitions on such matters, which allows a consensual ordering of political and moral priorities, but it cannot with consistency condemn a situation where diverging moral views and political opinions threaten to disrupt society.

The liberal belief in the absolute sanctity of life needs further examination. Life is clearly a precondition for happiness, but it may not be a good in itself. Should a badly deformed baby be kept alive, when it has no chance of a happy life? The idea of a 'right to life' is itself curious, although the right to a *decent* life, once one is alive, and the right not to be used instrumentally by others, are easier to justify. The American Declaration of Independence held it to be 'self-evident' that men are endowed by their Creator with an inalienable right to 'life, liberty and the pursuit of happiness'. Other liberal professions of faith may not invoke a Creator, but they still assert the value of life as self-evident. Is it? This, surely, depends on the quality of life, and while liberalism guarantees the right to life, it offers fewer sureties about quality.

However, self-preservation seems to be an instinctive principle. The isolated individual of the liberal model, seen abstractly, has no attachment to wider groupings or to society itself and so, logically, no duties or values such as altruism and patriotism: his only duty is to himself. In such a case, since men are mortal and since the individual can only fulfil himself through the subjective experiences he gains through living, he must instinctively value the prolongation of his own life above everything. Yet real people often sacrifice themselves for others, or gladly accept death as the gateway to an afterlife, as did teenage Iranian soldiers in the Iran–Iraq war and as do suicide bombers fighting the Palestinian cause. We could say that in such cases religious and patriotic doctrines outweigh the individual's fundamental prejudice in favour of himself. But perhaps, alternatively, self-love is merely the product of an individualistic and egoistic ideology—liberalism—and is no more *natural* than the self-effacing love of family, nation or God. If so, the sanctity of human life is not self-evidently the highest human value. However, in setting up the individual as the supreme source of value, the liberal rejects religious and supra-individual moralities and captures something of the agonizing predicament of the secular individual. Like other metaphysical positions, the liberal view of the status of life cannot be substantiated, but many would adhere to it intuitively.

DO I KNOW MY OWN INTERESTS?

This question challenges the assumption which provides the dynamic of the liberal political model, that of rational self-interest. At the heart of the theory is an individual with personal interests which she somehow 'knows' and unerringly pursues. Her account of her interests, wants, and needs is held to be authoritative. All are said to be equally deserving of respect, so all should have an equal opportunity to realize these interests. So far so good. But such simple assumptions invite many objections and questions. First, must I know my interest *consciously*? There may be things which would promote my wellbeing of which I am ignorant. But because the individual is assumed to be rational, conversant with her needs and omniscient with regard to the available opportunities, it follows from the unrefined notion of interest just described that if she does not consciously want something it is not in her interests. However, an impartial observer could tell me that some things which I hate would be in my interests, such as a daily work-out. Should I therefore call these my interests? Other things which I *do* want, such as cigarettes and alcohol, are clearly *not* in my interest: these might be called 'perverse wants', but should they be called 'my interests'?

The problems for a political theory based on subjective interest are: (1) whether to take only people's apparent, felt or expressed interests into account; (2) whether to ignore their 'perverse wants'; and (3) whether to modify (1) by imposing a category of 'real' interests, whose realization would benefit people even if they do not consciously want, or would reject, them. Liberalism has always repudiated the idea of 'real' interests, arguing that that way lie paternalism and even totalitarianism. This means that only subjectively felt or expressed interests can count. Liberals also reject the Marxist contention that people *en masse* can be deluded about their interests and suffer widespread false consciousness, since this erodes the concept of rationality.

When it comes to the political application of the principle of subjective interests, because it is impossible to ascertain what interests every individual has, it is *expressed interests* that are taken into account. Economics operates with a similar concept, that of *revealed preferences*, stipulating that people's true preferences can be deduced from what they choose and ignoring financial constraints on their choice. Likewise, the political opinions that people express in voting are assumed to express their interests. This is a wickedly simplifying assumption, since people can only manifest their interests through politics in certain, formalized ways; they are given a pre-selected set of options, which may exclude their real political preferences. The party manifesto system gives voters a 'take it or leave it' menu and electors have to vote for policies which they do not want, along with those that they do: interests expressed in such ways are only the most approximate guide to what people want. To interpret votes under these circumstances as free, rational choices made in pursuit of self-interest ignores the large number of constraints which make that untrue. But, for the liberal, expressed preferences are an important part of the practice of freedom as choice.

One liberal attempt to escape from the problems of subjectivity surrounding interests takes the form of specifying 'proper' interests for mankind. Mill's reference to 'the permanent interests of man as a progressive being' and his contention that intellectual pleasures are more valuable than those of the senses, lead in this direction. Others, such as Green, substituted ideas of self-realization and self-mastery for the more instinctual idea of pursuing one's interests, and virtually introduced the notion of a higher ethical self, which Berlin maintains is an illiberal idea.[28] This account of interests closely approaches the idea of 'real' interests which liberals have so often branded as totalitarian. But it is difficult to divorce the idea of interests from the paternalistic impulse to make people better by telling them what they should want.

A logical solution to this problem is offered by Barry. He enumerates five ways in which 'X is in A's interests' can differ from 'A wants X', and shows how men can mistake their interests in various ways. He then provides a new definition of 'interest' which overcomes such anomalies.

> To say, therefore, that an action or policy is in somebody's interests is not actually to say that it satisfies his immediate wants at all; it is rather to say that *it puts him in a better position to satisfy his wants.*[29]

Such a definition could justify handing over the individual's interests in part to the care of politicians who will help people satisfy their wants, perceived and unperceived. Something like Barry's definition is needed to propel liberalism towards progress, for if we equated wants with interests, and interests with expressed interests, in a situation of limited choice, little social progress would be likely.

The answer to the original question, then, is that I cannot know my interests in the immediate, rational, omniscient way that liberal theory sometimes implies, and that in various circumstances I have to be helped to 'know' them. Government policies in apparent opposition to people's wishes must therefore sometimes be sanctioned, and in all societies some decisions must be taken paternalistically, with reference to people's 'real' interests. The theory of interests therefore needs to be modified to mould it to reality and to justify judicious government intervention. First, individuals are said to know their immediate interests better than their long-term interests, which they tend to ignore. The mature collective wisdom of the community, embodied in the state, brings our long-term interests to our notice, as, for example, in the establishment of a compulsory pension scheme which many young people would opt out of if it were voluntary. The provision of collective defence is a similar case, where people's more remote interests are taken care of by the government. Second, individuals' private interests will inevitably sometimes run counter to those of their fellows, or of society as a whole. Early writers in the tradition soft-pedalled this possibility, optimistically hoping for a harmony of interests. Later, Mill introduced the notion of 'material harm' to demarcate such clashes of interest. Most liberals

---

28. Berlin, 'Two concepts of liberty', in *Political Philosophy*.
29. B. Barry, *Political Argument*, Harvester, 1990, p. 183. Emphasis added.

would concede the need for government intervention to protect the majority's interest where individual or group interests threaten it. Government intervention when strikers threaten vital services falls into this category. Liberals do not abandon their individualism in making such concessions, but in practice they accept the likelihood of conflict and the need for majority rule in such extremities. This constitutes an acknowledgement that not all individual interests can be pursued simultaneously, but this is a fact of life, and the justification for the existence of government.

Another problem which vexes the liberal account of interests is that of the 'free-rider'. This maverick is someone who decides that it is in his interests not to contribute to a collective enterprise because he knows that he will get the benefits irrespective of his contribution. The concept of the free-rider originated in economic theories dealing with the financing of collective and public goods,[30] but it can equally be applied to joint political activity. The tax-evader who saves his money while enjoying the same amenities as other citizens is a free-rider. It could also be said that those who do not bother to vote are riding on the backs of those voters who fulfil their citizenly duties and contribute to the stability of democracy. Liberalism has to make special theoretical provision to exclude the interests of free-riders from counting as 'proper interests'—ironically, for the free-rider is the rational, self-interested individual *par excellence*. Since many liberals would not wish to make out a strong case for social duty, they can only argue that a contribution to some collective effort is ultimately more in the free-rider's interests than evasion, which it would be difficult to prove, and which could be seen as a covert assertion of 'real' interests. The case of the free-rider suggests that there is something special about the public sphere and that the provision of collective amenities cannot be satisfactorily left to individual initiatives and voluntary cooperation, as classical liberals and libertarians would recommend. Different forces operate, different rules must apply. Problems such as these raise in turn the question of what the liberal's attitude should be towards interventionist and/or paternalistic government and, particularly, towards the welfare state.

LIBERALS AND WELFARE STATES

> Freeland was a welfare state. If a citizen wanted anything from a load of bone meal to a sexual partner some department was ready to offer effective aid. The threat implicit in this enveloping benevolence stifled the concept of rebellion.
>
> William Burroughs, *The Naked Lunch*

The liberal case against state interference with individual freedom, and against paternalistic legislation, has already been reviewed. Here I shall examine how it applies to welfare states, which exemplify both these 'sins' against individual freedom. The welfare state is defined here as an interventionist state which goes beyond the minimal state functions of providing defence and security of property,

---

30. M. Olson, *The Logic of Collective Action*, Harvard U.P., 1971.

and legislates to improve people's well-being, to a greater or lesser extent. The liberal, unlike Burroughs, is not so much worried that rebellion will be stifled but that the very concept of the free, independent individual will disappear as the state grows. The case against welfare states can be viewed in several ways: first, they can be seen as straightforward interference with individual freedom. Individuals are forced to contribute to the maintenance of health, education and social services whether they wish to or not. Furthermore, before they can benefit from the services for which they have paid, they have to provide the state with personal information and submit to various intrusive procedures. Second, welfare measures can be viewed as tantamount to interfering with individuals for their own good, sometimes in defiance of their express wishes.

These arguments are familiar, but a third line of attack illustrates the harshness with which hard-line classical individuals might condemn the welfare state. In 1803, Malthus wrote

> A man who is born into a world already possessed (i.e. under ownership), if he cannot get subsistence from his parents, on whom he has a just demand, and if society do not want his labour, has no claim or *right* to the smallest portion of food, and, in fact, has no business to be where he is. At nature's mighty feast there is no vacant cover for him. She tells him to begone . . .[31]

We can correlate this with a remark of Spencer's, made eighty years later, when Gladstone's reforming Liberal ministry was introducing considerable reforms, which Spencer regarded as too paternalistic.

> The command 'if any would not work neither should he eat', is simply a Christian enumeration of that universal law of Nature under which life has reached its present height—the law that a creature not energetic enough to maintain itself must die.[32]

Spencer developed a theory of evolution some years before Darwin, which turned on the vision of a war of all against all: intra-, rather than inter-, species competition. His book *The Man versus the State* champions *laissez-faire*, 'survival of the fittest' liberalism against Liberal reformers. He, like Malthus, thought that the 'deserving poor', the concern of so many Victorian philanthropists, were poor because they were *undeserving* and should not receive government aid. He fiercely opposed 'meddling legislation' designed to mitigate the harsh conditions of life for the inadequate. Such views were underpinned by his hypothesis that evolution operated within society, eliminating inferior strains and promoting the eventual physical and moral perfection of the race.

While he held many liberal convictions, such as the belief in *laissez-faire* and the need to limit the state's functions, Spencer was clearly not a typical liberal, for he dismisses the importance of individual life and substitutes a supra-individual value, that of the long-term improvement of society and the species. But his theory suggests what might have become of liberal ideology if, instead of being tempered by humane values, the 'ethical liberalism' attributed to Mill, it had

31. T. Malthus, *Essay on the Principles of Population*, 2nd edn, London, 1803. This passage was removed from subsequent editions.
32. H. Spencer, *The Man versus the State*, Penguin, 1969, p. 83.

become fused with less humanitarian doctrines such as Social Darwinism. Another part of Spencer's argument is the anti-paternalist point that government aid weakens the individual and atrophies his capacity for independent action—a view in which some modern liberals might concur.

Against Malthus we can assert the right of the living to a decent life, a claim made in liberal declarations of human rights, while the argument against Spencer is that his analogy is misapplied: evolution does not operate in society as he hypothesized, and the survival of the less adequate members of society does not weaken the structure or health of the 'social whole' (which is, in any case, a concept repudiated by many liberals). It could be added that, when it is a question of life or death, subsistence or starvation, the *deserts* of the pauper should not be taken into account, but only his right to life. But the antipaternalistic argument is harder to refute: no doubt, to some extent, Freeland-style welfare services sap the independence of the individual and her free, rational status, which must be surrendered in part to the state. The loss of independence—hard as it is to measure—should be counted as a cost against the benefits offered by welfare measures, and policies should be evaluated accordingly. One instance where social policy has been explicitly changed in order to avoid sapping the independence of individuals and to enhance their freedom, is in the treatment of the mentally ill who are now, wherever possible, rehabilitated in the community, to give them more normal lives and to avoid both the ill-effects and the public costs of institutionalization.

Mill conceded the need for some measures to increase welfare, despite his express objections to state interference, but the landmark in the adaptation of liberal thought to the growth of the welfare state was Hobhouse's book *Liberalism* (1911). The welfare measures of Lloyd George's reforming budget of 1909, which created a contributory pension scheme and sickness and unemployment benefits for the lowest-paid workers, had to be reconciled with the liberal creed, since they represented intervention in the market system and, further, interfered paternalistically with individual freedom. Hobhouse, who reiterated some of Green's views, argued that modern liberals could justify the extension of public control on humane grounds. The doctrine of liberty should not prevent the general will from acting, where it must, for the common good. He emphasized the contribution which welfare measures make to the realization of that essential liberal value, equality of opportunity. This argument could be interpreted as a claim that such intervention is not made paternalistically but, rather, in the interests of maintaining the preconditions of liberal society. Hobhouse also criticized the extreme *laissez-faire* view of the state as umpire and argued the necessity for intervention where appropriate. Hobhouse's argument about equality of opportunity had been foreshadowed by many socialists, who pointed out that the conditions for a liberal society did not really exist. Thus, paradoxically, what seemed at first to be a concession on a matter of principle ultimately strengthened liberal theory by ushering in a period of social liberalism.

Modern liberal-democratic governments are bound to intervene to some extent to promote their subjects' welfare, and while this is *prima facie* irreconcilable with classical liberal beliefs, it can be shown to operate in the spirit of the liberal model and, by guaranteeing minimum subsistence to the worst-off members of society, to enhance equality of opportunity and so make competition fairer. Particular welfare policies will always present a problem for liberals because the harm they do to individual freedom is incommensurable with the material or other benefits which they bring, so that it is never easy to decide whether, on the whole, they are warranted. (For example, the proactive policy of some social work teams suspecting child abuse has seriously infringed the freedom of both children and parents.) It is also true that liberals may differ among themselves over the priority to be observed between freedom and other goods.

Today, the role of government in the economy presents liberals with problems parallel to those of the welfare state. Ignoring the obvious divergences of advanced capitalism from the capitalism of early liberal society, Hayek developed an economic model for modern Western society similar to that of classical liberalism: his ideas have had considerable influence, monetarism being one of their offshoots and neo-liberal politics another. Hayek claims that liberalism 'derives from the discovery of a self-generating or spontaneous order in social affairs'. The ideal model for the economy and the polity is what he calls the 'catallaxy', a spontaneous organization resembling the free market, which generates a plurality of values. Social and interpersonal transactions would be modelled on market exchanges, while the government's role would be strictly limited to keeping order and providing some public services which do not spontaneously emerge because of the huge capital outlays required.[33] Objections to Hayek are similar to those raised to early, *laissez-faire* liberalism. The market system which, if perfect, should supply all human needs, did not and cannot adequately supply them, because of its many imperfections; hence the need for state intervention and, if necessary, a welfare state to help those whom the market system neglects because their demands are not backed by cash.

In order to criticize Hayek's attempts at ideological regression further, we can look to Western economists who have applied themselves to the problem of the provision of public goods, that is, shared amenities such as roads, hospitals, the legal system, and education. Arrow showed that individual preferences cannot be aggregated to provide the best possible social welfare provision: in the important field of the provision of major amenities and large-scale investment, there is no way in which individual choices will sanction such provision. Arrow concludes '... the only methods of passing from individual tastes to social preferences which will be satisfactory ... are either imposed or dictatorial'.[34] The provision of public goods will be necessarily 'undemocratic', that is, not based on expressed preferences, and often 'illiberal', in that such provision may override many individuals' interests. The majority of taxpayers, for example, might not choose to finance new motorways, and such decisions have to be imposed by government.

Arrow's theory should be taken in conjunction with Olson's account of 'the logic of collective action', where the problem of the free-rider is elaborated. Olson's conclusion is that coercion is needed to make everyone contribute fairly to

33. Hayek, 'The principles of a liberal social order', pp. 58–61 especially.
34. K. Arrow, *Social Choice and Individual Values*, 2nd edn, Yale U.P., 1963, pp. 59–60.

the cost of public or collective goods.[35] These theories together can be construed as an account of the impasse to which individualism leads, when taken as the fundamental principle of liberal theory and social policy. Where market forces and enlightened self-interest will not serve to obtain what many individuals want (but what many others would refuse to contribute to voluntarily), government must intervene. This suggests that a new line should be drawn, which permits government intervention to promote the provision of such 'public goods'. However, there is no self-evident limitation to the concept of public goods: many things that we now consider a matter for individual provision could come within the compass of an interventionist government, as in Burroughs's Freeland. Conversely, eighteen years of neo-liberal Conservative government in Britain so radically altered the perception of public goods that, for many people, the first question is now, 'Why shouldn't private enterprise provide this service, rather than the state?' This approach led to the privatization of utilities such as water, which had been regarded as a matter for public provision for over a century. So liberals must ask, of each new measure concerned with public goods provision, 'Is this public good really necessary?' and 'Could it be privately provided?' and answers will doubtless differ. Arrow and Olson do not solve the problems of liberalism by demarcating the area of public goods (and indeed later theorists have argued against them that there is nothing distinctive about public goods[36]), but they suggest that some liberal assumptions about the virtues of the free market and individual choice are untenable. How, then, can a liberal-democratic government act to promote individual wishes and social goods simultaneously? Here lies the permanent dilemma of liberalism.

LIBERALISM TODAY

This century has seen the development of three contemporary doctrines with apparent affinities to liberalism which also challenge it in various ways. *Libertarianism* is an anti-state ideology which takes liberalism to its logical extreme, although libertarians sometimes form part of the conservative 'radical right', as in the United States. The fundamental belief of libertarians is Lockean: the right to life, liberty and property. This requires 'elimination of coercive intervention by the state, the foremost violator of liberty'. The state is to be reduced to a mere 'protection agency', as recommended in Nozick's *Anarchy, State and Utopia*, a book which, together with Hayek's works, has become a chapter in the scriptures of libertarianism. Libertarian arguments have two targets: they pillory socialist ideas and the extension of the state which would be required to create greater equality, and they also attack liberal governments for incursions into individual freedom. The political demands of libertarians—such as the Libertarian Alliance in Britain—typically include the abolition of taxation

---

35. Olson, *The Logic of Collective Action*.
36. See, for example, J. Malkin & A. Wildavsky, 'Why the traditional distinction between public and private goods should be abandoned', *Journal of Theoretical Politics* 3(4), 1991: pp. 355–78.

('taxation is theft'), of the welfare state, of government economic intervention, of immigration controls and of 'victimless crimes' such as drug-taking and prostitution. On the positive side, they advocate free speech, no censorship and total *laissez-faire*. The supposition is that all necessary goods and services will better be provided voluntarily, via the cash nexus which gives the parties to a transaction equal status and dignity.[37] The arguments against early and Spencerian liberalism, that such a society would result in deprivation or death for many people, apply equally to libertarianism, but are dismissed by libertarians because they, quite simply, value individual liberty above everything. There is, of course, some incoherence in arguing for a 'minimal' state which is still strong enough to guarantee and enforce the many freedoms which libertarianism demands. Libertarians cannot be labelled simply as extreme right-wingers, for many of their demands (e.g. no censorship of pornography, free sexual relations and, in Britain, repeal of the Official Secrets Act) would be anathema to conservatives. This suggests the difficulty of locating libertarianism on the ideological continuum, and the one-dimensional over-simple nature of that continuum itself: there are elements of liberalism, conservatism and anarchism in libertarian ideas, although not of socialism, to which they are implacably opposed. Obviously libertarianism has been produced by the hypertrophy of the modern state and the covertly socialist elements which even the most capitalist states harbour, but whether it presents a coherent or feasible remedy is questionable. The ideals of libertarianism are best understood with reference to anarchism, which is discussed in Chapter 6.

It is curious, but significant that liberalism, although individualistic, focuses on *man*: 'woman' rarely, if ever, appears in the work of liberal thinkers before J. S. Mill. For some, this absence indicates that liberalism has nothing to offer the feminist movement, yet *feminism* is seen by others as the logically and practically necessary extension of the liberal ideal of equal rights to the other half of the human race. Certainly, Mill's *The Subjection of Women* was written from this standpoint and some recent feminist causes, such as campaigns for equal pay, have been presented in this light to gain greater acceptance. But, as Pateman and others have shown,[38] most liberal writers from Locke onwards consistently neglected the issue and accepted patriarchal society and the propriety of the subordination of women. Therefore it is certainly wrong to regard feminism as merely seeking to tie up the loose ends of liberalism and make it self-consistent. Feminists offer a new and radical critique of liberalism, as Chapter 9 demonstrates.

Nationalism too has been associated with liberalism. In nineteenth-century Europe, when nationalism became a major cause, progressive liberals supported nationalist movements and revolutions against oppressive regimes because of

---

37. The principle of free transaction is extolled in a typical libertarian text, W. Block's *Defending the Undefendable*, Fleet Press, 1976. Block defends, among others 'the pimp, the drug pusher, the blackmailer'.
38. C. Pateman, 'Feminism and Democracy', in *Democratic Theory and Practice*, Ed. G. Duncan, Cambridge U.P., 1983, and C. Pateman, *The Sexual Contract*. See too S. Okin, *Women in Western Political Thought*, Virago, 1980, Pt. IV.

their inhumanity; also, because the territorial settlements made at the 1815 Treaty of Vienna signally ignored the wishes of indigenous peoples. At that time, the concepts of individual liberty and nationhood were thought to be indissolubly linked. However, in this century, nationalist movements have been conjoined with socialism, communism and, often, racism. Thus, as Kedourie argues, 'it is a misunderstanding to ask whether nationalism is politics of the right or left'. The nationalist movements in Asia and Africa showed that nationalism and liberalism 'far from being twins are really antagonistic principles'.[39] The same can be said of the various nationalist movements in Eastern Europe and the former USSR, where the rights claimed by one nationality seem frequently to entail the suppression of another national group's aspirations. So nationalism, like libertarianism and feminism, challenges the certainties of liberalism on many points. The status of nationalism as an independent doctrine is discussed at length in Chapter 11.

Mainstream liberalism, refined to take into account historical changes, continues to be the dominant ideology in the West. It provides the paradigms within which much academic work on politics is conceived. Most recent major revisions of liberalism appear not as political polemics but as contributions to academic debate. Rawls's liberal theory of justice, which blossoms out into a full account of the Good Life, is one such text, as is Nozick's anarchist utopianism, mentioned above. Another influential development of liberalism is the theory of pluralism: pluralist society is composed of many different interest and opinion groups who are obliged to co-operate and compromise in order to promote their own interests. In a sense, this is liberalism writ large. The self-interested individual has been replaced by the self-interest group. It is a descriptive theory of how American politics works, rather than an ideal, but many theorists, notably Dahl, propose pluralism as a normative theory which resolves various problems of liberalism such as its over-individualistic basis and its inability to cope with group phenomena or to analyse institutions properly. Pluralist theory retains the methodological individualist approach, but explains these features of society more satisfactorily. More will be said about this in Chapter 12. Many other books of political science written in this century have aimed at reconciling liberal theory with political fact. While still professing methodological individualism, theorists have concentrated on larger units of analysis, submerging the individual in the interest group or party or even in 'the system'. The fact-gathering of modern political scientists has also produced results which are discrepant with liberal assumptions about individual rationality and capability and these, too, have been instrumental in producing modifications of the theory of liberal democracy.

Theories have been advanced to vindicate the elite nature of politics in representative liberal democracy, and to explain how the system can survive and flourish when so many people are the exact opposite of that hero of liberal-

39. E. Kedourie, *Nationalism*, 3rd edn, Hutchinson, 1966, pp.89, 109. See also A. D. Smith, *Nationalism in the Twentieth Century*, Martin Robertson, 1979.

democratic theory, the free and rational individual.[40] Exchange and transaction analyses of politics have also been developed, both suggesting that all human interaction is conducted on the basis of profitable exchange.[41] Such theories illustrate the continuing intimacy between liberal political thought and the economic theory which upholds capitalism. Whether such analyses will survive as amendments to liberal theory or will pass away as academic ephemera, time will tell. They exemplify an interesting fact: each major ideology needs a large body of academics to service and maintain it, smoothing out anomalies and explaining new developments in terms of the doctrine. Or, as Marx said, every ideology needs its apologists. Ideologies may derive from a few basic texts, but there will always be a role for ideologues.

An important development affecting liberal theory since the 1980s has been the espousal of *communitarianism* by a number of left-of-centre philosophers within the liberal tradition, including Barber, Sandel and Walzer. They have advanced communitarian theories, the departure point of which is the judgement that the free, autonomous, unattached individual of liberal theory is an impoverished being, lacking true identity. Communitarian philosophers challenge the universalizing claims of liberalism, and argue that self-identity and human values must be located in a cultural and historical context. A satisfying moral identity can only be achieved through a sense of, and attachment to, community. A renewed sense of community, social responsibility and citizenship would reactivate democratic politics, which has been etiolated by extreme liberal individualism, and would diminish the invidious distinction between the public and private spheres.[42] The continuing dialogue provoked by these arguments has helped to reclaim liberalism from the excesses of neo-liberalism and libertarianism. In many ways, liberals and communitarians are fighting on the same side. However, communitarians have a problem with cultural relativism: in a multicultural society, must the values of each minority culture be upheld, even when these conflict with the beliefs of the wider community? More generally, must any set of values and any kind of moral identity be accepted as valid because they are 'local' and emerge from a specific cultural and historical context? Liberals would find this too dangerous a conclusion.

In Western society, the association of liberalism with *democracy* is usually taken for granted, and one term is understood to embrace the other. Logically, liberalism is separable from democracy, as has been intimated, for the liberal ideal entails no particular form of government, as long as that government does not encroach upon individual rights. There are risks of liberal and democratic ideals conflicting in liberal democracy, which hinge on the potential conflict

---

40. A survey of such theories is offered in P. Bachrach, *The Theory of Democratic Elitism*, London U.P., 1968.
41. These are discussed in S. Waldman, *The Foundations of Political Action*, Little, Brown & Co., 1972.
42. See C. E. Cochran, 'The thin theory of community: the communitarians and their critics', *Political Studies*, Vol. XXXVII, 3 (1989); M. Sandel, *Liberalism and the Limits of Justice*, Cambridge U.P., 1982, is a major text in the debate.

between individual and majority interests: these flashpoints will be discussed in Chapter 12.

Liberalism in practice is less clear cut, more diffuse, than the ideology as it has been described here. The schematic presentation has been intended to expose the internal logic and the consistency, or otherwise, of the ideology which underpins our own form of society, and to suggest the reasons for its continuing force and appeal. The 'pure' theory is modified by the details of each major text—Mill's chapter on 'Applications' almost annuls the principles which he advances in the first part of *On Liberty*—and even more by practice. Social liberalism softened the extreme individualism of classical liberalism and recently communitarian ideas have modified the atomistic assumptions of neo-liberalism: liberalism continues to develop. Liberalism is a versatile and adaptable ideology; it has presided over what were arguably three of the most progressive and liberating centuries of human history. It should therefore be credited with many of the advances of this era, even if it is also rightly blamed for many of our endemic social problems.

FURTHER READING

R. J. Arneson (Ed.), *Liberalism*, Edward Elgar, 1992.
N. Barry, *On Classical Liberalism and Libertarianism*, Macmillan, 1987.
R. Bellamy, *Liberalism and Modern Society*, Polity Press, 1992.
R. Eccleshall, *British Liberalism*, Longman, 1986.
M. Freeden, *The New Liberalism*, Clarendon Press, 1978.
G. Himmelfarb, *Liberty and Liberalism*, Knopf, 1974.
J. Gray, *Liberalism*, Open University Press, 1986.
J. Gray, *Post-liberalism*, Routledge, 1996.
C. B. Macpherson, *The Life and Times of Liberal Democracy*, Oxford U.P., 1977.
S. Mendus, *Toleration and the Limits of Liberalism*, Macmillan, 1989.
S. Mulhall and A. Swift, *Liberals and Communitarians*, 2nd edn, Blackwell, 1996.
M. Sandel (Ed.), *Liberalism and its Critics*, Blackwell, 1984.

Chapter 4

Marxism

The spectacular collapse of communism is now history. In 1989 most of the communist governments of Eastern Europe were overthrown by popular movements although by contrast, in the same year, students challenged the legitimacy of the communist government of the People's Republic of China and were mercilessly crushed in Tiananmen Square. In 1991 the reforming government of President Gorbachev in the Soviet Union was challenged by a hard-line communist coup, which failed. Gorbachev then repudiated the Communist Party, but his progress towards pluralist democracy was overtaken by events—by the nationalist separatist movements of the Baltic states, which triggered secessionist movements among a number of other Soviet Republics. In 1992 the Republics, spearheaded by Russia under the leadership of Boris Yeltsin, announced the dissolution of the USSR and the formation of the Commonwealth of Independent States (CIS), a federation in which the Communist Party had no role. Thus ended three-quarters of a century of communist rule in the first country to attempt to put the principles of Marxism into practice.

In these circumstances, you might ask why anyone should bother to study Marxism as an ideology. There are, I believe, good reasons for including the doctrines of Marx and subsequent Marxists in this book. The first is that the ideas of Marx were wide-ranging and subtle; the fact that purportedly Marxist governments have been overthrown does not necessarily invalidate all his ideas. Indeed, it can be contended that the former communist countries were better described as 'state capitalist' societies, and never sought to implement many of the features of socialist society which Marx himself advocated. A second reason is that Marxism continues to offer an important alternative perspective to that of liberalism. As J. S. Mill stated, an unchallenged doctrine becomes mere habit; the idea that the sudden triumph of capitalist liberalism in the strongholds of its former enemies should leave it as an unchallengeable victor is contrary to the whole history of ideas. Whether future challenges to liberalism will come from the Marxist or socialist left, or from some quite different source such as the Green movement or Islamic fundamentalism, is a matter for speculation. It is important still to study Marxist and socialist ideas, because they present alternative utopias to the liberal capitalist utopia of individual liberty and consumerism with its apparently inevitable concomitant of inequalities of material wealth. More importantly, perhaps, the criticisms of capitalism made by Marx provided may still provide us with tools of critical analysis to understand the shortcomings or failures of Western society. The third reason is that only by understanding what Marx said, and what communism meant, can we fully understand some of the driving forces and momentous events of the twentieth century, such as the division of the world into the 'Eastern bloc' and 'the West', the Cold war, the Korean and Vietnamese wars and the arms race.

To give an account of the whole of Marxism in one chapter is an impossible undertaking. Changing circumstances have produced many different theoretical currents within the ideology during the last hundred years, with many subtle divergences from Marx's own text. Since subsequent Marxist thinkers explicitly located themselves in relation to Marx, however, the most important thing is to understand the principles of his own theory. These will be examined in this chapter, which will also give a brief account of later developments of Marxist theory.

PROBLEMS IN READING MARX

Several obstacles face anyone who tries to learn about Marxism from reading Marx's own works. The first is the remarkable breadth of topics and disciplines which they span. In 1840 the death of the Prussian king Frederick William III resulted in the lifting of strict censorship, which had limited freedom of expression in Prussia for a long time. Karl Marx, previously a doctoral student, was able to begin a career as a political journalist—but two years later censorship was re-imposed and he moved to Paris, where he met Engels. His activities in France and Prussia during the 1848 revolutions caused him to be expelled and he went to live in England, ending his days in Highgate Cemetery. During this exile, he was involved in the International Working Men's Association (the 'International') from 1864 until 1872, when he quarrelled with Bakunin and the movement split. Marx was therefore exposed to a wide variety of European cultures, historical dramas, and political activities, so that much of his theory appears as commentary on recent events, such as the coup of Louis Bonaparte, the 1870 Paris Commune and the formation of the German SPD. This makes it less accessible to the student searching for a compact, definitive version of the theory.

Another difficulty is that much of Marx's theory grew out of polemics against contemporary thinkers, some of whose views have long been forgotten. At first, he engaged battle with the 'Young Hegelians', who were obsessed with the obscure idea of 'absolute negation' and whom Marx condemned as 'idealist' because of their faith in the power of ideas. In particular, he rejected Bauer's simplistic view of revolution: 'once the kingdom of ideas is revolutionized, reality cannot hold out'. The early 'Paris manuscripts' of 1844 contained Marx's criticism of Hegel and of the liberal economists Smith, Say, and Ricardo, who nevertheless influenced his own economic ideas. Politically, Marx counterposed his own 'scientific' socialism to the 'utopian' socialism which was then prevalent, another idealist doctrine which he feared would produce political quietism and forestall revolutionary activity. To understand Marx fully, then, one needs an acquaintance with the many authors with whom he takes issue—or at least some idea of their theories.

A further complication is the controversy about the 'two Marxes'. In the 1960s and 1970s, influential Western commentators hypothesized a split between the work of the young and the older Marx, following the belated publication in translation of some of his early writings, which seem to soften the impersonal economic theory of *Capital*. His writings were said to fall into two periods, the crucial transitional link being his *Introduction to the Critique of Political Economy* (The *Grundrisse*), written 1857–58 but unpublished until 1953, which was heralded as a bridging work which combines ethics and humanism with economic theory. Commentators such as McLellan acclaimed the young, 'humanist' Marx who discussed alienation, human nature, and morality and seemed less distant from the concerns of liberal individualism than his later self.[1] But orthodox communists such as Althusser discounted the early works as juvenilia, denied the presence of humanism in Marx's works, and maintained that only the later economic texts such as *Capital* were important for Marxist science. In part this controversy rests on the facile, perhaps fallacious, assumption that great thinkers should manifest consistency—or at least a linear progression—throughout their thinking life. But anyone approaching Marxism should know of the existence of this controversy, for otherwise these diametrically opposed interpretations of Marx are confusing. One further complication is the collaboration of Marx with Engels. In the exposition which follows, Engels's views are not treated separately from those of Marx, although in his writings after Marx's death he departed in some respects from Marx's views.

THE VOCABULARY OF THE DIALECTIC

Despite his many disagreements with Hegel, Marx employed a version of Hegel's dialectic. This form of argument often mystifies readers who are accustomed to the empiricist way of thinking based on inductive reasoning and formal, deductive logic, and this section is intended as a guide for those wishing to read Marx's own writings. The dialectic is claimed to be a form of argument which can explain developmental processes and the oppositions which exist in the phenomenal world. Formal logic, which is based on the laws of identity and non-contradiction, is said by Marxists to be static, unable to explain change or contradiction, whereas the dialectic can encompass historical developments, and shows

---

1. See McLellan's introduction to his translation of Marx's *Grundrisse*, Harper and Row, 1971, pp. 1–15 and his introduction to Marx's *Early Texts*, Blackwell, 1972, pp. ix–xliii.

contradictions to be progressive.[2] Hegel viewed history as a dialectical progression, where unstable, seemingly contradiction-ridden stages of society resolved themselves into higher sociopolitical forms, which still preserved elements of the earlier stages. Any historical process is said by Hegel to consist of 'moments', or temporary states, which contain contradictory elements. Each moment is succeeded by a new moment which *negates* it, *transcends* it (that is, progresses beyond it) and yet *conserves* its particular characteristics. Thus there is a constant historical progression towards a more sophisticated reality. Hegel used the verb *aufheben* to connote this complex process of transcendence, and the illustration often given is that of the process of a bud, which becomes a flower, which becomes the fruit, each stage of its life going beyond the previous stage, yet in a sense conserving it.

Marx used the dialectic less technically and insistently than Hegel, but it forms the basis of his conception of capitalism as 'contradictory' and ridden with class conflict. If we focus on the composition of a particular state of affairs, it will consist of two opposed elements, and the situation can be examined from the point of view of each element. You can examine the process of capitalist production from the viewpoint of *labour*, one factor of production, or from that of *capital*, the other factor in a simplified model. Labour (the worker) sees itself as a subject, and sees capital as an object, something outside itself and set apart from itself, despite the fact that capital is created by labour. Likewise, capital sees labour as an opposing, separate force, although it could not function without labour. As each is essential to the other in the economic process, the polarity which both perceive is false, and appears as a result of looking at the process from only one side. Because labour and capital have a symbiotic relationship, Marx said that the bourgeoisie, by creating a class of wage labourers to work with their capital, called into existence their own gravediggers. All the social and political divisions of capitalist society result from this labour–capital polarity but the socialist revolution, Marx predicted, would abolish this opposition and transcend it, bringing about a classless society, which would conserve the previous elements, since industrial production would continue under socialism.

A warning should be added against any attempt to anglicize the dialectic by paraphrasing it in terms of thesis, antithesis, and synthesis, as does Berlin:[3] this formulation fails to capture the subtlety of the dialectical process of *Aufhebung* or the co-existence of contradictory elements in a state of affairs, and suggests that the whole can be seen as analogous to an argument in formal logic, which Marx would have denied strenuously. The consequence of Marx's utilization of the dialectic is his conclusion that there is a causal, predictable process at work in human history, of a dialectical kind.

Some of the other terms and definitions which Marx used need clarification. *Capital*, which he also referred to as *private property*, was wealth used productively, to produce more wealth, which is then reinvested in more capital

2. G. Novack, *The Logic of Marxism*, Pathfinder Press, 1971. See too J. Zeleny, *The Logic of Marx* (trans. T. Carver), Blackwell, 1980.
3. I. Berlin, *Karl Marx*, Home University Library, 1939.

goods. In pre-capitalist societies, wealth was generally used for immediate consumption purposes, or merely hoarded, and so did not become capital. *Labour* can be productive, in the sense that it produces capital, or unproductive. Marx gives the example of the piano maker, who is productive, and the pianist, who creates no new wealth, but merely exchanges his services for money. The terms *subjective* and *objective* are also often contrasted by Marx. The working class is objectively the revolutionary class, although subjectively it is not so. That is, seen from the viewpoint of history, the proletariat is the class which has the potential for making the revolution, although it may not *feel* itself to be revolutionary, or have any self-awareness, alias class-consciousness. A class's subjective viewpoint can differ from its objective reality because, being within a contradictory situation, it has only a partial view of the totality. A scientific theory, as Marx believed his was, which takes account of the whole, can explain that class's objective position. Western commentators who accuse Marx of forgetting the psychological aspects of human life should perhaps see his acknowledgement of subjective viewpoints as a gesture in this direction. Two other key terms in Marx's analysis are *appropriation* and *expropriation*. From the viewpoint of the capitalist, who is engaged in accumulating profits, he is appropriating this private property, setting it aside for himself. But from the labourer's point of view, the capitalist is expropriating him, seizing the goods which he has produced and depriving him of a proper reward for his labour.

Marx borrowed the term *objectification* (which some translators render as 'reification') from Hegel, for whom it was part of the dialectical movement of individual consciousness. The dialectic begins with a thinking subject, and objectification means that something which is really part of the subject itself is placed outside itself in its mind, and regarded as an object, which results in a distortion of the subject's view of the situation. For Marx, one of the prime causes of the worker's alienation under capitalism is that he is forced to objectify his own creations, the products which he makes, and he then sees them as no longer part of himself, or as not belonging to him, so that his products appear as alien, hostile objects, appropriated by the capitalist. Here, Marx may mistake what is the aftermath of any kind of creative activity for a specific property of capitalist production. But the account of alienation is important for his general criticism of the capitalist way of life.

Marx's way of thinking is often referred to as *dialectical materialism*, a term which needs some explanation. Materialism is a philosophical position based on the axiom that all events in the phenomenal world can be explained adequately in terms of other events, or causes, in the world. A major influence in the development of materialism was Locke's view that all our ideas are caused by the perceptions of the external world which reach us via our five senses, and by our reflections on these. In asserting this, he was rebutting Descartes' claim that people were born with innate ideas of God and other absolute truths, such as those of geometry, from which their knowledge was constructed. For Marx, as for Locke, ideas can have no existence without prior causes in the external world, but while Locke was asserting this doctrine against those who maintained that knowledge was ultimately produced by divine intervention or other metaphysical (literally 'beyond the physical') influences, Marx used it against the eighteenth-century philosophers who had used such fictions as 'human nature' and 'pure reason' in their explanations of society. Most of all, he disputed the German idealists' claim that ideas can arise independently of social context and act as causes within society. He held that all social phenomena and human consciousness itself are produced by material causes, and that these causes lie finally in the economic arrangements of society, which he called *the mode of production*. 'Man', his thoughts and his activities, are therefore determined by society—an axiom which deliberately strikes at the liberal assumption of individual autonomy and free will. 'My own existence is a social activity', Marx said and 'activity and mind are social in their context as well as in their origin; they are *social* activity and *social* mind'.[4]

Relating this general insight to his economic theory, he also asserted that 'what [individuals] are coincides with their production, both with *what* they produce and with *how* they produce'.[5] It is, of course, possible to espouse materialism without agreeing with Marx that the ultimate causes of social events are economic, and Enlightenment philosophers such as Helvetius had already argued that individuals were determined by the social environment without adding this hypothesis. Marx was not so much original in adopting the materialist epistemology as in postulating that economic activity was its basis (which, however, some early socialists also posited) and systematically building on it a coherent theory of social and political relations and ideology. But his materialism and his claim that people are formed by society does *not* imply that we are passively determined creatures and can never bring about social change. However, Marx asserted that such changes will not come about through the force of ideas conceived *in vacuo*, as the utopians had hoped, or through sheer willpower, but via ideas and circumstances arising in the material, social world.

MARX'S ECONOMICS

The early manuscripts which Marx wrote in 1844, which were only published in this century, explain the distinctive nature of human life and its basis in economic activity. Man, he says, differs from other animals which merely produce to satisfy their immediate needs, even when, like beavers, they appear to work in a systematic, quasi-human fashion. Man produces things according to pre-conceived plans: the architect's construction is planned, whereas that of the bee merely follows an instinctive pattern—we might now say that it was genetically programmed. Furthermore, man 'produces free from physical need and only truly produces when he is thus free'.[6] Liberated from the stark physical necessities which motivate other animals, man can work creatively and make things according to canons of beauty. In fashioning the natural world consciously, man

---

4. The major discussion of the material causes of consciousness appears in K. Marx and F. Engels, *The German Ideology* in *Selected Works*, Progress Publishers, 1969, Vol. 1.
5. Marx and Engels, *The German Ideology*, p. 20.
6. Marx, *Early Texts*, p. 140.

'affirms himself as species-being'. That is, the essential characteristic which differentiates the human species and gives it a generic identity is man's productive activity. In making these claims, Marx comes near to idealism, in that he seems to be describing a universal human essence despite his scorn for other thinkers who posit such an abstraction, but he would no doubt have argued that there was nothing mysterious or non-material about this 'essence' since it emanates from man's biological and intellectual constitution, and has no teleological connotations.

From the centrality of economic activity to mankind, Marx infers that the way in which that activity is organized determines all other aspects of social life. The mode of production, together with the form of distribution, constitutes the economic structure, and determines the superstructure. The 'relations of production' determine the social relations on which the political system and all other features of social organization base themselves. As is well known, Marx had an elaborate theory of history, which is discussed below, and he applied his analysis to earlier modes of production, but the focus of all his work was the capitalist mode, and this was crucial to his political theory, so only his account of capitalism will be detailed here. The capitalist economy rests on a fundamental dichotomy between capital and labour, the two sides of the 'contradiction' of capitalism, and this is transmuted at the level of social relations into the opposed and potentially antagonistic relations between the bourgeoisie and the proletariat.

First, Marx defines productive labour as having the unique quality of being able to create new values. Labour is the ultimate source of all value (this statement entails a simplifying assumption about natural resources, which most people would call valuable in themselves, and which Marx discusses further in *Capital*), and capital is merely accumulated, or 'objectified' labour—the result of the exploitation of past generations—in the form of machinery, factories, and other apparatus which contributes to the productive process. Capitalist manufacture is based on private property, accumulated capital, which, concentrated in the hands of the capitalist, enable him to hire 'living labour'—the wage labourer, whose position in the economic process is defined as someone who does not own the means of production. It is in the productive process that the contradiction between capital and labour becomes manifest. Marx assumes, like other economists of the time, that labourers are paid subsistence wages. The commodities which they produce have a certain *exchange value*, measurable in money terms, which is determined by the amount of labour which they embody, and can also vary with the state of the market. For example, the labourer works, say, ten hours per day. In six hours he produces goods whose *exchange value* (price) is equal to the wages that he earns in a day. Marx calls this six hours 'necessary labour', the labour necessary for the labourer and his family, the next generation of labourers, to survive. But he is not paid for the remaining four hours that he works, and their value is expropriated by the capitalist. This Marx calls *surplus value*, and this is the yardstick of the exploitation of the worker. The residue of surplus value, after rent, dividends, and other costs have been paid, becomes the capitalist's profits, which Marx assumes to be reinvested in further production. Each new injection of capital increases the capitalist's power to hire ('appropriate') more labour, and so to expand his business.

> The past appropriation of alien labour is thus the simple condition for fresh appropriation of alien labour.[7]

The process is thus a dynamic, continuing one for each individual capitalist and is sure to continue because of its own momentum unless the capitalist's incentive, the *rate of profit*, is reduced. (A simplified definition of the rate of profit is that it is the ratio of wages paid to surplus value produced.) And what is true of individual firms is true of capitalism as a whole: it must expand to survive. But, as capitalism thrives on competition, Marx thought that the less successful capitalists would be driven out of business, and he predicted the rise of monopolies and the cartelization which has led to today's giant corporations.

Marx shows that capitalism is endangered by various processes which threaten to reduce the rate of profit. First, there is an internal contradiction in the productive process. As expansion and reinvestment continue, the proportion of machines ('constant capital') to workers ('variable capital') will increase, assuming that machinery becomes more sophisticated. In other words, industries will become more capital-intensive. But since it is only the labour component that creates surplus value, the more machines and the fewer men used, the lower the surplus value and the lower the rate of profit. Marx assumes that the capitalist's motivation is to maintain his rate of profit at all costs, although modern economists suggest that as long as the business expands fast enough for turnover and the *amount* of profit to remain constant, or grow, the actual *rate* of profit is not crucial. But in terms of Marx's analysis, if the rate of profit falls, the capitalist's reaction will be to cut wages to restore surplus value, and his profits. This will impoverish the working class, especially as the presence of a 'pool of unemployment' will ensure that workers have to take what is offered, and wages will therefore not rise above subsistence level. We should note that Marx's preliminary analysis omits factors like unionization, which might prevent wage-cutting. But he is specifically analysing the idealized free market situation of the classical economists, in which individual employers and workers negotiate in a state of 'perfect competition'.

Other, external factors may cause the rate of profit to fall. Unionization has the effect of forcing up wages and lowering profits. If prices in the market fall because of a glut or a drop in demand, the worker takes longer to earn his wages (in terms of the price of the goods he produces) and so, again, surplus value is squeezed. There was also the possibility that markets would be permanently satiated, with similar results. When employers *en masse* cut wages, a depression ensues. Marx expected the trade cycle of booms and slumps to oscillate ever more violently until the severity of a depression brought about a revolution.

The causal mechanism was the pauperization of the proletariat; workers would become aware of their oppressed and exploited condition and their common predicament as a class and begin to engage in political activity to remedy it,

---

7. Marx, *Grundrisse*, p. 140.

invading the political sphere, which had hitherto safeguarded the interests of the capitalists. The major contradiction of capitalism is thus that as it expands its tendency to collapse increases.

This, then, is Marx's economic model, much simplified. But *Capital* and his other works are rich in insights as to how economic organization affects the whole of social life. Two apparent paradoxes result from the nature of capitalism. First, that capitalism can flourish only through the creation of extremes of wealth and poverty. The capitalist grows richer while 'only the growing impoverishment of living labour is its own'. The early socialists observed this too, and remarked on the anomaly that labourers could not afford to buy the luxuries that they produced for others. Second, and more dialectically, capitalists and the workers, antagonistic though their interests might be, cannot survive without each other. 'Proletariat and wealth are opposites; as such they form a single whole.'[8] This Hegelian formulation bears out the optimistic intuition of classical economists that the pursuit of individual interests leads to the benefit of all, although Marx gave the doctrine a pessimistic twist because he was convinced that capitalism's contradictions would lead to its demise.

The market system which endows manufactured objects with exchange value perverts our perception of them, which should be based on their *use value*, that is, on their usefulness to human beings. 'I speak of this as the *fetishistic character* which attaches to the products of labour, as soon as they are produced in the form of commodities.'[9] Since social relations reflect the relations prevailing in the economic sphere, other things begin to be regarded as mere commodities, in particular the labourer himself. What we now call 'instrumental relationships' pervade society: the bourgeois man regards his wife and children as forms of private property, a fact on which Marx and Engels based their critique of the bourgeois family. In the free market, *money* assumes a dominant role as the chief means of exchange. 'The more production is shaped in such a way that every producer depends on the exchange value of his commodities, the more must *money relationships* develop.'[10] Money becomes omnipotent and its power distorts all human qualities.

> What I have thanks to money . . . that is what I, the possessor of the money, am myself . . . I am ugly, but I can buy myself the most beautiful women. Consequently I am not ugly . . . (Money) changes fidelity into infidelity, love into hate, hate into love, virtue into vice.[11]

Individuals and relationships are thus perverted by the 'almighty being', money, and this contributes to the alienation of those living under capitalism. While analysing and deploring these distortions, Marx chiefly condemns the capitalist system for being exploitative, first of all because of the extraction of surplus value from the labourer who is not justly rewarded for the values which he creates, and also because of the manipulation of people's needs by the capitalist (who has to

---

8. Marx and Engels, *The Holy Family*, Progress Publishers, 1956, p. 51.
9. Marx, *Capital* (trans. G. D. H. Cole), Dent, 1972, pp. 45–6.
10. Marx, *Grundrisse*, p. 60
11. Marx, *Early Texts*, p. 180.

ensure his market) which has the paradoxical result that 'the growth of needs and of the means to satisfy them results in a lack of needs and of means.'[12]

> Labour produces works of wonder for the rich, but nakedness for the worker. It produces palaces, but only hovels for the worker; it produces beauty, but cripples the worker . . . It produces culture, but also imbecility and cretinism for the worker.[13]

Marx's economic analysis was, of course, based on his observations of the English system where capitalism was relatively advanced, but he considered it applicable to all capitalist countries. The causal links between the economic and the political make it important to understand Marx's economics in order to understand his theory of revolution.

THE SOCIAL CONSEQUENCES

Marx's political writings employ a different terminology from his economic works. The *bourgeoisie* is the class embodiment of capital and the *proletariat*, the propertyless class, that of labour. Class is, for Marx, fundamentally an economic category, determined by an individual's relation to the means of production. His class position determines his ideas and his possibility of action. The *Communist Manifesto* gives a historical account of the emergence of the two classes out of the dying feudal system. The 'elements' of the bourgeoisie were to be found in the burgesses of mediaeval towns, and the modern bourgeoisie 'is itself the product of a long course of development'. As technology advanced and the mode of production changed through the industrial revolution, the bourgeoisie 'called into existence' the proletariat, whose members can only live as long as they sell their labour. As industrialization spread, social relations were brought into harmony with the new state of economic relations. Such changes are not sudden: the bourgeoisie was 'involved in a constant battle', at first with the aristocracy, then within itself because of competition, and then with the bourgeoisie of foreign countries. The motive force of capitalism, competition, actually divides the bourgeoisie internally. 'The separate individuals form a class only in so far as they have to carry on a common battle against another class.'[14] So, in relation to the proletariat, the bourgeoisie becomes the dominant class by virtue of its dominant position in the economic process. Like all dominant classes, it gradually creates society in its image, establishing a political and legal system which supports its hegemony. Laws for the maintenance of private property are established, which treat all social relationships as if they were money relationships. Politically, the bourgeoisie becomes the ruling class: 'the executive of the modern State is but a committee for managing the common affairs of the whole bourgeoisie.'[15] Because

12. The paradoxes of capitalism are set out in the *Early Texts*, pp. 134–7. Needs are discussed in *German Ideology*, pp. 30–31.
13. Marx, *Early Texts*, p. 136.
14. Marx and Engels, *German Ideology*, p. 65.
15. Marx and Engels, *The Manifesto of the Communist Party* in *Selected Works*, Vol. I, pp. 110–11. Referred to hereafter as *Communist Manifesto*.

of the class antagonisms which are implicit in capitalist society, even when they are not expressed, the state develops as an apparatus for the oppression of the proletariat, with its panoply of weapons—the police, the army, and a judicial system devoted to upholding property laws. Again, Marx based his social analysis on the empirical evidence which he gathered in England. How then did he square the fact that England had a democratic form of government with his description of the repressive functions of the state? His view was that democracy purports to reconcile class interests, to create the illusory impression that a parliamentary assembly embodies the will of the people, as if such a unity could exist among irreconcilably opposed interests. The rights which the liberal state bestows on its citizens were all dismissed by Marx as a thinly disguised assertion of bourgeois individualism, egoism, and property rights. His criticisms will be discussed further in the chapter on liberty and rights (Chapter 14).

Not only does the bourgeoisie control all social relationships, it also dominates society at the level of thought. Bourgeois ideology reflects the ascendancy of the bourgeoisie and vindicates capitalism. Marx gave the examples of classical economic theory, with its justification of *laissez-faire* and competition, and the utilitarian ethic which exonerates self-interest as the basis of all action and reflects the profit-maximizing activity of the capitalist. He also considered that Christianity, with its doctrines of humility, earthly poverty, and its assertion of the necessity of social hierarchy, served the interests of the bourgeoisie—although religion had always been 'the opium of the people'. Marx's view of how ideology arises, discussed in Chapter 2, need not be recapitulated here. But it must be emphasized that in describing the creation of bourgeois ideology and the bourgeois state, Marx was not putting forward a conspiracy theory, as some critics suggest. Ideas and institutions are produced by the fundamental economic arrangements in society, without anyone necessarily *willing* their appearance. For this reason, Marx did not morally condemn the bourgeoisie or the individual members of that class. His is intended as a non-moral, scientific analysis, and even the *Communist Manifesto*, where his indignation at the capitalist system is most forcefully expressed, admits that the bourgeoisie had made important innovations, and a valuable contribution in dispelling the remnants of feudalism. 'The bourgeoisie, historically, has played a most revolutionary part.' It was simply that its course was run. This is not to say that Marx did not deplore the cruelties and social injustice which resulted from the capitalist system, but he did not blame particular individuals for this, because it would have been in contradiction to his materialist account of the formation of individuals by social conditions to hold them responsible for being born into a certain class or for acting according to the dictates of their position and ideology.

Marx's condemnation of capitalism rested on the bad effects that it had on people—not only on members of the proletariat but also on the bourgeoisie. The impoverishment of workers and the atrocious conditions under which many of them laboured was the cardinal indictment of the system. So also was the perversion of social relations through the prevalence of money relationships and commodity fetishism. In some respects, Marx thought that mankind was worse off under capitalism than it had been under feudalism, despite technological advances. This is made clear in his early writings on *alienation*, in which he comes closest to Hegel. (Although psychologists and sociologists today make liberal use of the idea of alienation, Marx's discussion, like Hegel's, is philosophical, rather than an attempt to psychologize.) In ideal circumstances, creative man, the worker, 'appropriates' the external world by his labour, making raw materials into artefacts which are his own. But under capitalism his product, the commodity, is instead appropriated by the capitalist.

> The worker relates to the product of his labour as to an alien object . . . The worker puts his life into the object and this means that it no longer belongs to him but to the object.[16]

And the object belongs to his employer. As a result, the worker is alienated—from himself, from his product, from his fellow men, and from his 'species-being'.[17] But the capitalist suffers as well, for he too has a less than ideal relation to the material world and to his fellows. This echoes the famous 'master and slave' dialectic in Hegel's *Phenomenology of Spirit*, which demonstrates that the master gains no true satisfaction from dominating the slave, his inferior, and has a flawed relationship with other people and with nature. In this way also, capitalism benefits nobody: spiritually, it impoverishes even the rich. Alienation is thus a major reason for the moral condemnation of capitalism.

HISTORY AND REVOLUTION

> Every change in the social order, every revolution in property relations is the essential result of the creation of new productive forces which no longer correspond to the old property relations.[18]

Marx's conviction that revolution would occur in capitalist countries, and that a socialist society would result, is bound up with his theory of history. The *Manifesto* states that 'the history of all hitherto existing society is the history of class struggles' and supports this generalization by delineating the triumph of capitalism over feudalism as the most recent example of full-scale change. The originator of all historical change is economic and technical innovation which changes the mode of production and creates new economic relations: social relations have to adapt to these, more slowly, and this entails a transformation of the sociopolitical superstructure. Thus, the hierarchical feudal system was dismantled and gradually replaced by the bourgeois nation-state. History is a dialectical process, in that it proceeds through contradictions: the contradiction between economic and social relations, and the antagonisms between the two major classes which develop in each new historical period. The new form of society which emerges negates and transcends the previous one, while conserving many of its elements.

---

16. Marx, *Early Texts*, p. 135.
17. Marx, *Early Texts*, pp. 137–41.
18. The materialist view of history is discussed in Marx's *Contribution to the Critique of Political Economy* and in *German Ideology*.

This is the skeleton of Marx's doctrine, often referred to as 'historical materialism' or 'historical determinism'. Marx was not alone in propounding a theory of history: in the eighteenth and nineteenth centuries such theories abounded and most had the tendentious aim of showing that mankind was progressing to ever higher levels. Many of these theories were teleological and conjectured about the final, perfect state of society; for Hegel, this was marked by the self-realization of 'Absolute Spirit' through society. Fourier and Saint-Simon also used theories of history to prove that their versions of socialism constituted higher stages of social development, and the latter influenced Marx considerably despite his repudiation of utopian socialism. But Marx differed from other philosophers of history in several ways. First, he rejected the idea of progress as being an idealist notion. As we have seen, he thought that society could progress materially while it regressed spiritually, so there was no inevitability about humanity's advance towards perfection or happiness. He also abstained from teleology in his account of history, refusing to postulate a final goal: this was in keeping with his dialectical view of society. If every society develops contradictions which must be transcended, there is no end to the process, and to hypothesize that history will one day come to an end and that change will cease is another idealist notion, belied by man's creative nature, which constantly transforms his surroundings. Although Marx did not speculate on what kind of society would supersede socialism, he would not have denied that it, too, would eventually be transcended. Marx regarded his own theory of history as scientific in a way which rival theories were not, because it was founded on the postulate that real, economic changes produced advancement in all other spheres of life in a determinate, predictable way. He accused other philosophers of failing to offer material causes to explain the movement from one stage of society to the next. But while abjuring any idealist content, he profited from locating his political ideal, communism, at the next, higher stage in what was undeniably a progressive theory of history. It is, after all, good propaganda to assert that the form of society which you advocate will emerge inevitably, and this is the rallying cry of his *Manifesto*.

Revolution is the dynamo of history in Marx's account, and his doctrine of the socialist revolution gave rise to more hopes and fears, perhaps, than any other political theory. We have already seen the economic determinants of revolution: internal and external contradictions in capitalism lead to ever greater pauperization of the workers, which necessitates increasingly severe oppression to stifle their discontent. At the social level, Marx thought that successive crises would polarize the two major classes, displacing other, subsidiary classes and forcing them into the proletariat, which would absorb the 'petty bourgeoisie' (small businessmen) and failed capitalists who had been squeezed out by competition. The intelligentsia would, he hoped, side with the proletariat as polarization occurred. These new recruits would increase the degree of self-awareness and solidarity among the proletariat. Thus, the subjective feelings of workers would at last catch up with their objective situation and they would become, subjectively as well as objectively, 'the most revolutionary class'.

Marx did not commit himself to predicting the precise nature of the proletarian revolution or the exact means which would be used to overthrow the bourgeoisie.

He countenanced violence, but did not justify or glorify bloodletting and revenge. Rather, violence might be a necessary instrument because the bourgeoisie would not relinquish its privileges without a struggle. On the other hand, he speculated that the transition to socialism might come about peacefully in England, the most advanced capitalist country, given that workers already had representation in parliament. Marx's dicta about the time, place and manner of revolution are statements of tendencies, not prophecy. The gloating of opponents over Marx's unfulfilled 'predictions' is therefore misdirected. What Marx *did* predict was the necessary steps which the victorious proletariat would take. The first would be to establish a democracy which would automatically raise the workers, who form the majority, to the status of the ruling class. And then

> the proletariat will use its political supremacy to wrest, by degrees, all capital from the bourgeoisie, to centralize all instruments of production in the hands of the State, *i.e.* of the proletariat organized as the ruling class.[19]

The immediate measures which Marx thought would be 'generally applicable' after such a revolution are worth quoting at length:[20]

(1) Abolition of property in land and application of all rents of land to public purposes.
(2) A heavy progressive or graduated income tax.
(3) Abolition of all right of inheritance.
(4) Confiscation of the property of all emigrants and rebels.
(5) Centralization of credit in the hands of the State, by means of a national bank with State capital and an exclusive monopoly.
(6) Centralization of the means of communication and transport in the hands of the state.
(7) Extension of factories and instruments of production owned by the State . . . .
(8) Equal liability of all to labour. Establishment of industrial armies, especially for agriculture.
(9) Combination of agriculture with manufacturing industries . . . .
(10) Free education for all children in public schools . . . .

What is noteworthy here (but is often ignored) is that, although Marx saw the abolition of private property (capital) as the aim and precondition of socialism, this programme does not recommend *instant* expropriation of all capitalists, but suggests a progression towards collective ownership of the means of production which would extend over time and be achieved by high income tax and the extension of state ownership. Such a programme could even be implemented by democratic means in a country with universal suffrage, without violent revolution. The gradualist intention is emphasized when Marx continues:

---

19. Marx and Engels, *Communist Manifesto*, p. 126.
20. Marx and Engels, *Communist Manifesto*, pp. 126–7.

> When, *in the course of development*, class distinctions have disappeared . . . the public power will lose its political character. Political power . . . is merely the organized power of one class for oppressing another.[21]

This is another formulation of Marx's belief that the state would 'wither away'. Clearly, then, any account of Marx's view of revolution as violent and immediate radical change misrepresents his actual recommendations to the point of travesty.

What would happen to the state after the revolution was made clearer in Marx's criticisms of the programme put forward in 1875 by German socialists. Because they planned to take over the state without radically transforming it, he accused them of treating it 'as an independent entity that possesses its own intellectual, ethical and libertarian bases' (an excusable mistake for those brought up on a diet of Hegel!) and he re-emphasized the oppressive, class nature of the state. A successful revolution would entail 'a political transition period in which the state can be nothing but the revolutionary dictatorship of the proletariat'.[22] However, the state could not merely change hands but must ultimately be destroyed. Marx saw the oppressive nature of the state as a barrier to the gradual assumption of power by social-democratic parties, and so he scorned the hopes of social-democratic parties of gradual assuming power within the existing system. But he failed to distinguish adequately between the state as a revolutionary dictatorship and the bourgeois state. This is perhaps the major area where Marx erred by giving too little analysis. The dangers of merely capturing and using the repressive state apparatus were made manifest in the Russian revolution.

It is now possible to consider some of the problems of Marx's historical and revolutionary theory, and various criticisms. A major question is how the deterministic and voluntaristic elements of the theory are to be reconciled. A possible consequence of maintaining that the revolution would be brought about by economic factors was political quietism, and in fact a section of the Second International maintained that socialists had only to wait for capitalism to collapse of its own accord. Engels outlived Marx and was drawn into this debate after his death. He strove to rebut the charge that Marx was an economic determinist who thought that revolution would arrive automatically, while himself upholding the doctrine that certain objective economic and political conditions must be realized before the proletariat could create a revolution.

> Revolutions are not made deliberately and arbitrarily, but everywhere and at all times they were the essential outcome of circumstances quite independent of the will and the leadership of particular parties and entire classes.

When the circumstances are appropriate, revolution is a product of voluntary activity, of men's wills, but these wills are themselves shaped by the context. 'Men make their history themselves, only they do so in a given environment' and often 'what emerges is something that no-one willed'.[23] Engels, elaborating Marx's view,

---

21. Marx and Engels, *Communist Manifesto*, p. 127. Emphasis added.
22. Marx, *Critique of the Gotha Programme* in *Marx and Engels: Basic Writings* (Ed. L. Feuer), Doubleday-Anchor, 1959, p. 127.
23. Engels, *Letters*, in Feuer (Ed.), pp. 411, 399.

preserved an important place for individual will and action in the revolution without allowing that revolutions and their outcomes could be attributed to the initiatives of individual heroes. Seen thus, Marx's theory is not so deterministic as to enable us to predict when revolution will arrive, although it enables us to recognize when the conditions for revolution do not exist.

Marx and Engels were often accused of subordinating all aspects of society to the economic in a way which falsified the real workings of society. Engels denied this, maintaining that they held that economic elements were the *ultimate*, but not the *sole*, determinants of history.

> The economic situation is the basis, but the various elements of the superstructure (constitutions, legal forms, philosophical theories, etc.) also exercise their influence upon the course of the historical struggles and in many cases preponderate in determining their *form* .... We make our history ourselves, but, in the first place, under very definite assumptions and conditions. Among these the economic ones are decisive.[24]

So, although primary causes are economic, elements of the superstructure interact, setting up other causal networks and can even, Engels admitted, react on the economic base and produce changes there. Those who called Marx an economic determinist were not altogether mistaken, because he emphasized the economic at the expense of the social so as to make his theory more rigorously scientific—political economy being the first major social science. But 'economic determinism' is an emphasis rather than a dogma, for Marx did not ignore the complex interactions of the other parts of society.

Various other criticisms can be offered of this aspect of Marx's theory. The socialist revolution is not strictly analogous to the bourgeois revolution which routed feudalism, because it is caused not by technological progress, but by the exhaustion of an existing economic system. And a socialist revolution will not actually transform the *mode* of production, since Marx envisaged that industrialism would continue, but will merely change the ownership of the means of production. So the socialist revolution does not exemplify the paradigm which Marx set up. He evades this objection by saying that distribution is a 'feature' of the mode of production: so socialist production is a different 'mode' from capitalist industrialism.

Some commentators find it curious that Marx thought that the proletariat, the most fragmented and alienated class, could be the bearer of revolution.[25] This is a practical rather than a theoretical objection, and indeed pessimism about the workers' capacity and inclination to make the revolution led to Lenin's theory of the vanguard party. Marx's argument was that, as the major oppressed class under capitalism, and half of the contradictory whole, the proletariat was objectively the revolutionary class, however far it might be, subjectively, from realizing this. Since Marx did not endorse the idea of a glorious revolution and heroic violence, or the role of charismatic individuals, the lack of political acumen or personal courage in the worker was irrelevant: the precondition of the

---

24. Engels, *Letters* in Feuer (Ed.), p. 398.
25. J. P. Plamenatz, *Karl Marx's Philosophy of Man*, Clarendon Press, 1975, p. 13.

revolution was his desperation, not his daring. Of course, Marx expected leaders to arise, despite the downtrodden state of the majority of workers. His description of the general condition of the class does not entail that each of its members is equally ignorant and oppressed—as those who level this criticism imply. The other major objection to Marx, that his theory has been disproved by the failure of his predictions, is discussed in a later section.

COMMUNIST SOCIETY

Since Marx criticized the utopian socialists for providing blueprints for the future society, an endeavour which he considered idealist in the worst sense, he was reluctant to offer any detailed picture of the communist utopia. But the formal characteristics of communist society are made clear in his works, as are the particular principles on which it would operate. Essentially, communism connotes the abolition of private property, the capitalist mode of production and alienated labour. It establishes the appropriation of nature *for man* by contrast with the appropriation of human life by the capitalist. After the exacerbation of class conflict had produced a proletarian revolution, and the revolutionary dictatorship of the proletariat had been established, Marx predicted that communism would develop in two stages. In the first stage, under the revolutionary dictatorship, when the state retains its oppressive nature but is turned against bourgeois counter-revolutionaries, there are still classes and there is still wage labour and a division of labour. But capital will be collectively owned, which changes the mode of production, and a new principle of distribution operates, 'to each according to his contribution'. But, 'in spite of this advance, this *equal right* is still constantly stigmatized by a bourgeois limitation' because workers have different skills and talents. So, even when they are paid in proportion to the value of their labour, without exploitation, inequalities occur.[26] But payment will reflect labour time, with small deductions for public facilities and welfare programmes. No surplus value will be extracted.

The second stage, 'higher communism', also referred to by Marx as 'true socialism', is the classless society. Here, the division between mental and physical labour has vanished and nobody has one exclusive sphere of activity: anybody can become skilled at whatever work he or she wishes.

> Labour has become not only a means of life but life's prime want . . . the springs of co-operative wealth flow more abundantly—only then can the narrow horizon of bourgeois right be crossed in its entirety and society inscribe on its banners: 'From each according to his ability, to each according to his needs'.[27]

Marx's suggestion that after the division of labour had ended man could be a hunter, fisherman, shepherd, and critic all in the same day[28] (often considered ironic) is curious, because it seems to idealize non-industrial work while elsewhere

---

26. Marx, *Critique of the Gotha Programme*, pp. 118–19.
27. Marx, *Critique of the Gotha Programme*, p. 119.
28. Marx and Engels, *The German Ideology*, p. 36.

he suggests that industrial labour will be the basis of communism. In fact in *Grundrisse* he argues that capitalism has provided the conditions for widespread leisure in socialist society because it maximizes surplus value which could then be restored to the labourer.

> What is new in capital is that it also increases the surplus labour time of the masses by all artistic and scientific means possible . . . Thus, despite itself, it is instrumental in creating the means of social disposable time, and so in reducing working time for the whole of society to a minimum and thus making everyone's time free for their own development.[29]

So, while communism transcends capitalism, it still preserves valuable capitalist innovations.

Under higher communism the state, representing oppressive, 'political' power, would wither away, although government would continue to be necessary. What form Marx envisaged this would take may perhaps be deduced from his essay on the Paris Commune of 1870, where he praises the organization set up by the communards. The governing commune was formed of municipal councillors, mainly from the working class, chosen by universal suffrage, responsible to their electors and subject to rapid recall if they displeased them. The commune was both executive and legislative: the protective liberal separation of powers is unnecessary in a truly representative and responsive democracy. Like the councillors, police and other officials were responsible and revocable delegates of the commune, and all received workers' wages, which prevented the development of any hierarchy with vested interests. Marx called the commune an 'expansive' or non-repressive form of government and he doubtless expected some similar embodiment of popular sovereignty to emerge in a communist society.

> Its true secret was this. It was essentially a working-class government, the produce of the struggle of the producing against the appropriating class, the political form . . . under which to work out the economic emancipation of labour.[30]

The Marxist ideal of popular sovereignty is often likened to Rousseau's vision of direct democracy. Liberals see both as potentially totalitarian because of the absence of limitations on the government's powers. Marx's reply would be that the 'checks and balances' of representative democracy are unnecessary where accountability is strong and representatives have no special privileges or status. Furthermore, in the classless society of higher communism there would be no conflicting wills which needed to be reconciled by a division of sovereignty: the people would have a unified will.

How ideal would a communist society be for its inhabitants? What would they be like? Marx talks of fulfilment rather than of happiness or utility. Man under communism is a fully developed individual, enjoying many forms of activity, rather than being 'the mere bearer of a particular social function', a specialized worker. He experiences the true freedom only available in a co-operative,

---

29. Marx, *Grundrisse*, p. 144.
30. Marx, *The Civil War in France*, in *Selected Works*, Vol. II, p. 223.

communist society. Using Hegelian terms, Marx said that communism accomplishes the appropriation of the human essence by man for man, that it emancipates all man's qualities and senses, and that it achieves the union of man with nature. Man reassumes his species-being as a creative worker in co-operation with his fellows. Alienation disappears as the proper relationship is restored between the worker and what he produces: although his products are still for the use of others, as they must be with any division of labour, he feels his labour to be socially necessary and valuable in satisfying the needs of others. Like other socialists who believed in co-operation, Marx assumed (tacitly) that it would fuse the egoistic and altruistic impulses. Since he did not believe in any human nature other than that determined by a particular form of society, he expected—logically enough—that the communist form of organization would eventually produce 'co-operative man', hardly recognizable as the descendant of competitive, utility-maximizing capitalist man. The dispute between Marxists and those who believe human nature to be irreducibly competitive and greedy cannot be resolved scientifically but the general acceptance today that environment largely determines character offers some support for Marx's optimism.

CRITICIZING MARX

Arguments between liberals and Marxists are ultimately sterile because their world-views are antagonistic at every point. This is no accident, since Marx saw capitalism as a coherent whole, in terms of the intimate relations between all the elements of the structure and superstructure: his doctrine therefore necessarily denied the validity of capitalist economics *and* of capitalist morality, ideology, and politics. The antagonisms between the two ideologies are, briefly, as follows: liberal ideology presupposes ultimately harmonizing individual interests, independent and mutually indifferent individuals, the supremacy of the individual, government based on consent; it advocates maximum privacy, minimal government and the impartial rule of law. Marx would retort that capitalist society rests on irreconcilably antagonistic interests, that men are, even if unwillingly, interdependent and exploiting or exploited, that class is more important politically than the individual and that government is based on force and domination, while all aspects of life are in fact pervaded by politics and ideology. Thus Marx gives a conflictual account of bourgeois society while liberals have a consent or consensus model. Marx's materialism, in particular the doctrine that man is determined by society and his class position, threatened the fundamental liberal tenet that man is free and rational, able to choose his goals and activities in private isolation. Marx's views on ideology, discussed in Chapter 2, challenge both this and the bourgeois belief that capitalism is a natural, rational, and permanent system. His theory of ideology, which anticipatorily refutes any criticism by claiming to be scientific itself, brands the whole of liberal democracy as ideology.

   Liberalism is based on the empirical method, which claims to attain knowledge through an accumulation of data. The empiricist demands visible proof and immediacy in any hypothesis, and rejects Marxism as being 'theoretical', based on *a priori* assumptions about such matters as surplus value, which cannot be empirically verified. Marxists in turn accuse empiricists of working on the basis of a covert theoretical framework which validates and supports capitalism—of having a surrogate metaphysic.[31] There seems to be no satisfactory way of choosing between these rival theories of knowledge according to their view of what makes a doctrine scientific, for each invalidates the other, just as the Marxist view of politics invalidates the liberal view, and vice versa. Empiricists consider their own system to be open to refutation and say that Marxism is a self-enclosed, self-validating system like some theologies. Certainly, Marxism represents itself as a privileged philosophy, since it can both account for the existence of rival philosophies and refute them. Without a 'higher' theory of knowledge which can comprehend both Marxism and empiricism and measure them against a yardstick of validity outside them both, there seems to be no philosophical way of justifying adherence to one rather than the other: personal preference must operate. But it might be argued that whichever theory can explain most and has the more universal scope should be preferred. These remarks are meant to alert the reader to the insoluble contradictions between opposed ideologies, rather than attempt to resolve them.

However, we may ask why Marx considered his own theory to be scientific, and whether it succeeds according to his own criteria for science. Marx defined his doctrine as scientific socialism by contrast with utopian socialism, which he thought was a rationalist attempt to impose the utopians' brainchildren on the world. Fourier, Owen, and Saint-Simon, he said, had rashly *invented* 'social laws' to explain the necessity of socialism before the 'material conditions for the emancipation of the proletariat had arisen'.[32] They were before their time, and had therefore misunderstood the true nature of class: they dreamt of class unity rather than of the abolition of classes. Marx criticized the utopians for being belated Enlightenment idealists who thought that their blueprints could simply be imposed on the world. He also condemned them politically for hampering working-class action by their illusory theories. At the same time, he and Engels admired their critiques of early capitalism and agreed with many of the ideals which they invoked, such as co-operation and distribution according to need.

It was not Marx's view of socialism that differed widely from that of the utopians so much as his conception of how it would come about. He gave a materialist, and therefore 'scientific', account of the transition, while the utopians imagined that socialism could be suddenly inscribed on society, as if on a blank sheet. This is why theory and practice must be seen in relation to each other, in order to check such utopian idealism. In his acknowledgement of the need for a transitional period, Marx anticipated Popper's criticism that he, like Plato and

31. See, e.g., R. Blackburn (Ed.), *Ideology in Social Science*, Fontana/Collins, 1972, and P. Feyerabend, 'How to be a good empiricist', in *The Philosophy of Science* (Ed. P. Nidditch), Oxford U.P., 1968.
32. Marx and Engels, *Communist Manifesto*, pp. 134–6.

other enemies of the 'open society', required a clean canvas which would entail the purging, banishment or murder of those adhering to the old way of life.[33] The transitional period would be one of gradual habituation to the new way of life: the ideal society was not to be achieved at one violent stroke. In relation to liberalism, Marx maintained that his own theory was more scientific since it gave an accurate account of the economic and social relations of which liberal theory gave a distorted, one-sided picture. It was also more scientific because he provided a theory of history which liberals could not give, since they regarded capitalism as a realized utopia, the culmination of historical progress, a self-perpetuating system. So it is on the basis of his theory's scientific nature and its comprehension of the whole dialectical movement of society and history that Marx asserted its truth against its rival.

The validity of scientific theories is generally held to lie in the success of their predictions. Marx's theory, and his claims for it, are vulnerable in this respect, because his predictions about the collapse of capitalism failed and many of his hypotheses now appear inapplicable to contemporary circumstances. Responses to this vary: some liberals are simply relieved that history has 'disproved' Marx. More philosophically, Karl Popper asserted that Marx's theory is not scientific because it has been reinterpreted to explain falsified predictions: a theory which can be stretched to explain *anything* has no explanatory power, the criterion of good science. Popper argued that since Marxism is not falsifiable in principle it could not be scientific. By contrast, Marxists have constantly revised Marx's theory to take account of the changing circumstances which have defeated his predictions, and would still consider it scientific. Some of their revisions are examined in the final part of this chapter. What, then, were the predictions which have failed, and should such failures count as refutations of Marx's theory?

The fact is that capitalism has not yet collapsed even in the countries of Europe which Marx thought most likely to succumb to a proletarian revolution. Paradoxically, most communist revolutions occurred in countries which were not industrialized and where the peasantry, which Marx did not see as a revolutionary class, preponderated: Russia, China, Cuba, and Indochina. Furthermore, capitalism, in moving towards monopoly capitalism as he predicted, has raised the standard of living of workers in a way which he did not envisage. Despite world recession in the late twentieth century, the degree of affluence achieved in the West since the Second World War has been unprecedented. Does this constitute a refutation of Marx's predictions, and hence of his whole theory? First, it must be remembered that Marx set no time limit to his predictions, even though he worked for their fulfilment in his own lifetime; also, that he spoke of tendencies rather than laws.

It could be argued that a prediction not yet fulfilled is different from a prediction refuted, and Marxists might say that the preconditions for revolution do not yet obtain in the capitalist world, although there are increasing indications

33. K. Popper, *The Open Society and Its Enemies*, Routledge & Kegan Paul, 1962, Vol. 1, pp. 157–68.

of a general crisis. Marx himself refined his basic theory in many ways, enumerating the exogenous factors which might postpone the final crisis. The danger of saturated markets, for example, could be staved off as capitalism created new needs and hence new markets. The bourgeoisie was renowned for its inventiveness, and would create new industries with higher rates of profit as old industries declined. The meteoric rise of computer and other high-technology industries, simultaneous with the decline of heavy industries like steel and coal, provide a recent example. On the other hand, the ability of highly automated industries to produce high rates of profit calls into question his stipulation that surplus value is only created by labour, which entails that capital-intensive industries would have low rates of profit.

The nature of the ownership of capital has changed in ways which seem to undermine Marx's basic assumptions. On one hand, huge amounts of capital are concentrated into conglomerated corporations; on the other hand, the ownership of smaller quantities of shares is far more widespread than it was a century ago. Indeed, one of Mrs Thatcher's ambitions as Prime Minister was to make Britain a nation of small shareholders. The demise of the individual capitalist entrepreneur, who risks his all and profits richly if successful, has been followed by the rise of a managerial class whose members stake less, if anything, yet who earn handsome remuneration before the shareholders' dividends are paid. 'Who are the capitalists now?' we might ask. Is a managing director a capitalist or a worker? If workers own shares, or participate in profit-sharing schemes, can the class distinction between capitalist and worker be maintained? From a purist viewpoint it can, since the profit-sharing worker still does not *own* the means of production: her bonus could be regarded as a hostage given to fortune by the capitalists, as can other features of modern society which mitigate the exploitation of the proletariat, such as the welfare state. What Marxists have to admit, however, is that the new, paternalistic capitalism, together with ideological and superstructural elements, have prevented impoverishment and the sharp polarization of classes which Marx predicted. (More correctly, certain sections of the population are sometimes impoverished but the majority pays them benefits, which prevents polarization. In Britain after eighteen years of Conservative government, everyone who had a job was better off than in 1979; however, two million or more people were also unemployed.) But the non-fulfilment of Marx's prediction is explicable in Marxist terms and is not an outright indictment of his theory. There is also the possibility that Marxism is a self-defeating theory, since capitalists have recognized their enemy and taken steps to protect themselves: many social theories run this risk. Undoubtedly, had Marx lived for another hundred years, he would have refined his own theory in many respects to explain modern developments. Perhaps the ruling class's ideological strength and capitalism's capacity for innovation will enable it to postpone a socialist revolution indefinitely, so that social change will eventually take an entirely different form. Those who pin their hopes for the demise of capitalism on the exhaustion of natural resources may well be misled, since that would probably cause a universal calamity, leading to a quite different kind of revolution.

The judgement that Marx's theory is scientific, then, is best seen as a claim made at a time when most social theories were not scientific, and made partly with the tactical aim of gaining more credence for it. While much of his theory of history is as idealist as the rival theories which Marx rejected, his materialism and the sophistication of his economic theory give him a claim to be as scientific a political economist as any, given that social science can never attain to the certainty and universality of the natural sciences. His theory of politics and revolution is more of an optimistic codicil, tacked on to the theory of history which makes many valid points about conflict and change in society, but which is less scientific than his economics. As a political theorist, Marx deserves respect for the precision of his analysis, which makes his theory systematic if not *per se* scientific. Many English readers find Marx indigestible in translation, but this is partly because he used terms in a precise, technical way and coined new words which have a strange ring to us. An example is his use of the word 'class' to describe categories of people according to their role in the productive process. Our uses of the word today are many and diverse: it can signify status, prestige, income group or occupation group, and sociologists use the term in a way which cuts across economic categories. Someone who is in Marx's sense a worker, might still have a high status and income, identify with bourgeois values, and even vote Conservative, as do more than a third of the British working population. Marx would say that such a person was still exploited, however much this was alleviated by superstructural elements. His idea of class must not therefore be assimilated to our own.

Ultimately, the force of Marx's theory rests on the precision of his theoretical terms, which is why one must adopt his language to represent his theory adequately. Attempts to paraphrase Marx usually end in disaster. If we summarized his theory as 'Marx said that history was a series of struggles between the oppressors and the oppressed', we lose the sense of a *class* struggle which relates social conflict to the economic basis, and end up with something like Bakunin's theory which was based on sentiment, on his identification with the oppressed, rather than on analysis. Marx's claim to be objective, to describe the dialectics of society from a position outside the two major classes, also bolsters his claim to be scientific, although this claim is the easiest point of attack for his critics. If Marx's ideas, like everyone else's, were determined by his class position, how could he be objective? This apparent inconsistency probably did not escape Marx himself. As was said earlier, his hypothesis that men are determined by their class position does not mean that they are *fully* determined. Different experiences and, in the case of intellectuals like Marx, social mobility and freedom to criticize, as well as natural differences of intelligence, allow individuals to produce theories which transcend ideology and class position.

Marx's scientificity or otherwise is part of a wider controversy about the nature of social science: even the certainty and objectivity of the natural sciences is often questioned today. Therefore no conclusive answer as to whether he was scientific is likely to be forthcoming, although dogmatic Marxists still make 'Marxism' and 'science' synonymous. It is more rational to adhere to Marxism because it coincides with one's convictions, or because of its potential for bringing about social change, than because of its scientific standing.

THE EVOLUTION OF MARXISM

Many major modifications have taken place to adapt Marx's theory to historical change and to non-European countries. Some of these are intellectually directed; also, as soon as a theory is adopted by a movement, it begins to change. While the First International was dominated by Marx himself and racked by the quarrels between his supporters and those of Bakunin, the Second International (1889–1914) consisted of European socialists who were often backed by working-class movements and were beginning to win seats in parliaments, especially those of France and Germany. The residual anarchists were soon expelled and the remaining groups, dominated by the German SPD, confronted questions such as whether it was permissible to co-operate with bourgeois parties and accept ministerial positions. These dilemmas are discussed in Chapter 5.

Lenin's major contributions to Marxist theory were made in the context of these quarrels of the Second International and the objective unreadiness of Russia for a socialist revolution. In reply to socialists who advocated an 'evolutionary' approach towards socialism, notably Bernstein, Lenin emphasized the need for an act of will to create the revolution, for voluntarism rather than determinism. He argued that in the absence of a politically aware proletariat a revolutionary vanguard party was needed, with a proper understanding of theory, to initiate a revolution and, in Russia's case, to lead what was only an embryonic working class. He advocated a small, secret party of professional revolutionaries: secrecy was essential in the Russian police state. Lukács characterized Leninism as a 'double break' with the mechanistic theory of revolution espoused by some Marxists. Revolution was no longer seen as an automatic outcome of economic events, and workers' consciousness was not expected to arise spontaneously: the party must engineer this. This was, of course, Lenin's own achievement as leader of the Bolshevik party. This enhancement of the role of the vanguard party was strongly condemned by the German Socialist, Rosa Luxemburg. She believed that direct, independent action by the mass was a necessary part of the class struggle: she rightly anticipated and criticized the centralism and elitism which Leninism brought about in the USSR. Certainly, the domineering role of the Communist Party in the Soviet Union can be traced back to Lenin's idea of the elite revolutionary party, even though the blame for many abuses must be laid at Stalin's door.

Lenin also allocated a revolutionary role to the peasantry, which Marx had believed to be an essentially conservative class, a remnant of feudalism irrelevant to the socialist struggle, despite its exploitation by landlords. Lenin's espousal of the Russian peasants appears to be opportunistic rather than the result of a theoretical revelation about their importance; in the event, the peasants rapidly defected from the Bolshevik cause when their demands for land had been met. Lenin restated the importance of the state, transformed into a revolutionary dictatorship, in the first stage of communism when it would become an instrument for the oppression of the ex-bourgeoisie, but he also issued prophetic warnings about the perennial need for some form of state. Dreams of abolishing management are utopian, and 'serve only to postpone the socialist revolution . . . until people are different', whereas, 'we want the socialist revolution with people as they are now, with people who cannot dispense with subordination, control and "foremen and accountants" '.[34] Lenin did not believe that the state, or some similar apparatus, could wither away entirely.

Most of Lenin's additions to Marxism were the results of adapting theory to circumstance, and his theoretical account of imperialism was no exception. Imperialism, 'the highest form of capitalism', was a new form of monopoly capitalism in which the advanced countries plundered the less developed by exporting capital and setting up industries, usually for the extraction of natural resources, which yielded superprofits.

> Out of such *superprofits* . . . it is possible to bribe the labour leaders (at home) and the upper stratum of the labour aristocracy.[35]

Capitalist countries had developed unevenly, some industrializing faster than others, and these variations were intensified by colonization. Lenin was clearly thinking of the 'race for Africa'. Hence, he argued that imperialist wars for the redistribution of the spoils would occur, rendering the system highly unstable, and eventually destroying it. Since he wrote *Imperialism* in the middle of the First World War, these observations could be regarded as political commentary rather than theory, but it adds an important international dimension to Marxist thought.

Other leading Bolsheviks shared Lenin's view on the interdependence of capitalist countries, which led to the cheering conclusion that when the system began to collapse, revolution would be universal. Even in 1906, Trotsky was arguing that the Russian proletariat would carry revolution into Europe, first to Germany and Poland. But in 1924, in the face of the failure of the German workers' uprising of 1919 and the retrenchment and opposition of capitalist countries to the USSR, Stalin propounded the doctrine of 'socialism in one country', to explain and justify Russia's position as a communist enclave in a hostile world. This in effect denied the necessity of world revolution and asserted that a self-sufficient communist country could still develop satisfactorily. Trotsky refuted Stalin's argument in *Permanent Revolution*, which reasserted the inevitability of world revolution. He said that there were three senses in which the revolution must be 'permanent'. First, the proletariat, once in power, could not stop after a bourgeois democratic revolution had given workers a majority voice—here, he referred to the liberal regime set up in Russia after the first revolution of 1917—but must in turn destroy this illusion of democracy.

---

34. V. I. Lenin, *The State and Revolution*, Progress Publishers, 1972, p. 46.
35. Lenin, *Imperialism, The Highest Stage of Capitalism*, in *Collected Works*, Progress Publishers, 1960–70, Vol. 22, p. 281.

[The proletariat] must adopt the tactics of *permanent revolution*, i.e., must destroy the barriers between the minimum and maximum programme of Social Democracy, go over to more and more radical reforms and seek direct and immediate support in revolution in Western Europe.[36]

Backward countries, Trotsky added, would achieve socialism via dictatorship, circumventing the bourgeois democratic revolution. Second, revolution must become world-wide. For an isolated country such as Russia

the way out lies only in the victory of the proletariat of the advanced countries . . . a national revolution is not a self-contained whole, only a link in the international chain.[37]

This *ad hominem* contention did not endear Trotsky to Stalin. Finally, socialist society must be self-revolutionizing, and initiate technical and social innovations: communism was not to be regarded as the terminus of history. Society constantly changes its skin, 'therein lies the permanent character of the socialist revolution as such'.

This assertion, directed against the ossification of the Bolshevik regime under Stalin, could well be cited as a justification of Mao Tse Tung's 'cultural revolution' which was aimed against the entrenchment of the party bureaucracy. Trotsky claimed to have been aware of the dangers of bureaucracy from the very start of the Bolshevik revolution, and in *The Revolution Betrayed* (1937), he criticized the hierarchical structure of the party and the 'caste system' established by Stalin which was antithetical to egalitarian socialism. He characterized the Soviet system as 'state capitalism'. 'State capitalism' signifies an exploitative mode of production in which surplus value is still taken from workers by the state, which becomes increasingly unlikely to wither away because of its dominant role in the economy. Marx had acknowledged that collective ownership of the means of production would entail some centralization, but had never conceived of the state as becoming the new exploiter, as it did in the Soviet Union.

In the second half of the twentieth century, what Trotsky himself referred to as the 'sin of Trotskyism' gained many left-wing adherents in Europe. The main reason for the revival of Trotskyism was that many Marxists, who felt that the established communist parties were discredited by their implication in Russia's invasion of Hungary in 1956, turned to Trotskyist groups, as did those who eschewed the sin of Stalinism; the Soviet interference with Czech liberalization in the 'Prague Spring' of 1968 led to further disenchantment with orthodox Communist Parties. It is not altogether clear what latter-day Trotskyism represents to its diverse supporters, beyond a rejection of Soviet-style state capitalism and bureaucracy, and a commitment to international revolution. Among the various fringe groups still operating in Europe, some are intellectual and elitist, others are 'workerist', dedicated to involving workers in the economic and political struggle, while others engage in 'entryism', the infiltration of social-

---

36. L. Trotsky, *Results and Prospects* and *Permanent Revolution*, Pathfinder Press, 1969. Introduction to first Russian edn.
37. Trotsky, *Results and Prospects* and *Permanent Revolution*. See Engels's earlier statement of the need for world revolution in *Principles of Communism*, in *Selected Works*, Vol. I, pp. 92–3.

democratic parties (such as Militant Tendency members attempted in the British Labour Party in the 1970s and 1980s. They were later expelled by the leadership.) What is clear is that Trotskyism had a strong appeal for left-wingers critical of the USSR, but had no single identifiable theoretical position, except its critique of that system as a deviation from true socialism.

The problem for Marxists in the West in this century has been to modify the theory to explain the continued strength of capitalism and the lack of revolutionary enthusiasm among the working classes. Symptomatic of this is the predominance of social-democratic parties which generally uphold the capitalist system. Many theories about this have been developed, of which only a few can be mentioned here. In the 1960s the then theoretician of the French Communist Party, Althusser, offered an account of 'ideological state apparatuses' which develop their own independent momentum and uphold the system; these include trades unions.[38] This helps explain the persistence of the system even in bad times. Philosophers of the Frankfurt School, which developed in the 1930s in Germany, a dangerous climate for Marxists, also offered subtle analyses of advanced monopoly capitalism. Habermas advanced an influential theory of the interrelation between knowledge and power under capitalism, and illustrated how knowledge is 'manufactured' to support the system.[39] Among the Frankfurt School, the best-known philosopher was probably Marcuse. As a response to 'embourgeoisement', the assimilation of workers to the bourgeois system and their adoption of bourgeois values in a time of affluence, his theory discarded the working class as a revolutionary force and looked to a 'New Opposition', oppressed people everywhere. These include students, intellectuals, oppressed ethnic groups, and the inhabitants of the Third World. The puzzle is how such diverse groups could develop sufficient sense of solidarity to become a revolutionary force. It is certainly true that the interests of the Western proletariat are permanently opposed to those of workers in the Third World, since their affluence depends in part on the latters' poverty, a view which has led some Marxists to see exploitation as a global phenomenon, existing between countries as well as between classes. Marcuse analysed the superstructural mechanisms whereby advanced capitalism defends itself, including 'repressive tolerance' and perversion of language to prevent the development of criticism. He advocated the 'Great Refusal', the destruction of all the institutions of repressive society.[40] Marcuse's use of Hegelian and Freudian ideas made him a highly unorthodox Marxist, but one who achieved widespread popularity after the revolutionary events of 1968 in France, especially among students. For such Marxists as Marcuse, the problem is that the objective conditions for revolution have failed to materialize and so therefore has the subjective condition, the development of class

---

38. L. Althusser, *Lenin and Philosophy* (trans. B. Brewster), New Left Books, 1977, pp. 122–73. See too his *Essays on Ideology*, Verso, 1984.
39. J. Habermas, *Knowledge and Human Interests* (trans. J. Shapiro), Heinemann, 1972. See too W. Outhwaite, *Habermas*, Polity Press, 1986.
40. H. Marcuse, *An Essay on Liberation*, Penguin, 1969.

consciousness. The proposed solution is a return to theory and a drive to win intellectual converts from all classes.

A further problem for Western Communists was the tyrannical behaviour of the Soviet Union in Hungary (1956), Czechoslovakia (1968) and its interventions in Poland to ensure the suppression of the free trade union, Solidarity (1980–81). Such events caused the Communist Parties in Europe to try to dissociate themselves from such activities, and to free themselves of Moscow's domination. The idea of Eurocommunism was promulgated in the late 1960s and early 1970s. Its most prominent champion, the Italian Communist, Berlinguer, drew on Gramsci's idea of 'hegemony' or leadership.[41] The Leninist notion of the dictatorship of the proletariat was supplanted by the notion that a broadly based, popular majority (including members of the bourgeoisie) should exploit the current contradictions of capitalism, starkly outlined by the 1970s recession, under the leadership (but not dictatorship) of the proletariat. This strategy was compatible with the preservation of democratic rights and a 'parliamentary road to socialism'. As with so many other developments in Marxism, it is debatable whether 'Eurocommunism' was a tactical decision or a genuine theoretical innovation, and it certainly achieved little electorally except in France where the Communists, by forming a united front with the Socialist Party (PS), briefly gained a share of ministerial power in the early 1980s.

The problems facing Marxists in the Third World are altogether different. Marxist parties have everywhere been associated with nationalism and the struggle against colonialism. Sometimes, when independence has been achieved, the revolutionary party is revealed to be more nationalist than Marxist. Revolutionary theories have been developed to direct these endeavours. In most such countries the proletariat is small or non-existent and peasants constitute the main oppressed class. They have two enemies, the capitalist countries and the 'national bourgeoisie', the indigenous ally of the imperialists which advances its own interests by fostering neo-colonialism, a form of capitalism which rests on the export of capital, often disguised as 'aid' to developing countries. This gave rise to new 'theories' which, when analysed, appear short on theory but long on pragmatism. In *The Wretched of the Earth* (1961) Frantz Fanon, moved by the problems afflicting the French colony Algeria, developed a theory of revolution resting on the peasants and the *lumpenproletariat* (the 'dregs of society'); he also, unlike Marx, emphasized the need for violence, which would enable the colonized peoples to purge themselves of the humiliation of their experience.[42] At the same period, in Latin America, 'Ché' Guevara wrote *Guerrilla Warfare*, drawing on the experience of the Cuban revolution in the late 1950s. Later, Debray used Guevara's experiences of guerrilla war in Bolivia in the 1960s to adapt Marxism to the Latin American situation where there was no direct colonization and the oppressors were and still are the native military and, indirectly, the USA. Debray

---

41. For a useful bibliography of material on Eurocommunism, see O. A. Narkiewicz, *Eurocommunism, 1968–1986. A Select Bibliography*, Mansell Publishing, 1987. Gramsci's concept of hegemony is discussed in R. Simon, *Gramsci's Political Thought*, Lawrence & Wishart, 1983.
42. F. Fanon, *The Wretched of the Earth* (trans. C. Farrington), Penguin, 1967, p. 74.

also saw the peasants as the potentially revolutionary class, and recommended guerrilla tactics. The revolutionary vanguard should consist of guerrillas operating from the countryside, winning over the peasants to their cause and acting independently of political parties. Debray indicted the established, urban communist parties which hindered rather than aided the efforts of Guevara.[43] Again, this seems like a guerrilla's manual rather than a political theory. The way that communism has been viewed in Third-World countries varies considerably. In Africa, leading socialists have disputed the relevance of Marxism and the European experience to the creation of socialism on the African continent. However, some of them have turned to China for aid and advice, feeling the Chinese version of socialism to be nearer to their own than that of the Soviets.

Mao Tse Tung, who died in 1976, is inseparably associated with the success of the Chinese Communist revolution in 1949, even if many of his achievements have been undone and his memory effaced. His voluminous writings offer both tactical advice and theoretical innovations but here we need only note the main points of his revolutionary theory. Mao's own revolution was anti-colonial and nationalistic; he viewed it as a class struggle with the peasants as the revolutionary class. In the absence of an industrial proletariat and of the economic conditions which Marx saw as essential to revolution, Mao expounded a doctrine of revolution which was emphatically voluntaristic, writing that 'the people of China are poor and blank' but have the will to make a revolution. It is the man who *wills*, rather than the man who *knows*, who is the true revolutionary. Mao's party therefore differed greatly from Lenin's group of informed theoreticians and he strove to prevent an entrenchment of the Chinese Communist Party like that in the USSR. At the time of the Cultural Revolution (1965 onwards), he divorced himself from the party apparatus and appealed over the head of the party directly to the people. The Cultural Revolution was intended to remove stratification in society by destroying respect for the standing of party members and for intellectuals, for Mao maintained that political authority lay in the mass.[44] Evidently, this was a very different form of socialism from that practised in the former USSR, despite their common theoretical origins. Chinese communism underwent many changes and policy reversals after Mao's death including a move towards markets and enterprise; but the abuses and social disturbances brought about by the Cultural Revolution remain fresh in the memories of the older leaders of the Chinese Communist Party, which may help to explain why they so ruthlessly suppressed the students who demonstrated in favour of democracy in 1989. It seems that the Confucian idea of stability has been fused with the Marxism of Mao.

In general, the nationalist emphasis of Third-World communism and the non-capitalist conditions in which it was created differentiate these varieties of communism from that proposed by Marx. Their nationalism needs not conflict with the internationalist aspirations of Marxism, but it does entail a view of the

---

43. R. Debray, *Revolution in the Revolution?* (trans. B. Ortiz), Monthly Review Press, 1967.
44. S. Schram, *The Political Thought of Mao Tse Tung*, Penguin, 1969, gives a useful selection of Mao's texts.

revolution analogous to that of Stalin: 'socialism in one country'. Likewise, the achievement of communism in a predominantly peasant country entails a different socialist mode of production from that which industrialized socialist countries would establish, such as the system of agricultural communes in China. The opportunities for leisure and self-development which, according to Marx, capitalism establishes do not yet exist in such countries, where communism has often meant the chance to share poverty more equally, and an end to quasi-feudal oppression.

REVISIONISM AND RECANTATION

The Marxists whose emendations of Marx's theory have just been discussed were, essentially, commenting on the conditions which they faced at particular times— so was Marx. This in itself suggests that his theory, however self-sufficient, scientific, and universal he claimed it to be, should not be treated as an authoritative text, any revision of which constitutes heresy. This in turn suggests that a would-be Marxist is not obliged to adopt Marx's theory in its entirety, but may adapt or omit aspects of it without rendering what she does accept false because of its incompleteness. No doubt the suggestion that we can accept Marxism partially would be anathema any remaining orthodox communist theorists who see themselves as the self-appointed guardians of 'pure' Marxism– Leninism. But it would be sheer dogmatism to claim that a theory which boasts of its basis in material circumstances should not adapt to changing material conditions. What seems to have underlain the ceaseless disputes during this century about the purity of Marxism is a feeling that 'mine are revisions, yours are heresies'—an authoritarian attitude to be avoided if Marxism is to survive as a living political theory. Perhaps Marx himself should have the last word on this: 'All I know is that I am not a Marxist.'[45]

If they accept that revision does not constitute an abandonment or a diminution of the central truths of Marx's theory, Marxists will be spared a lot of agonizing about what is the proper course of action in certain cases. (For example, this would put an end to the obsolete controversy in the Third World as to whether *all* countries must undergo a bourgeois-democratic revolution before a communist revolution is possible, this being the historical sequence which Marx described with England, France, and Germany in mind, or whether communism can be achieved in a peasant society). If Marx's theory is regarded as a set of extrapolations from recent history rather than as a series of necessary truths, such controversies can be avoided and anomalous events need not be reinterpreted to fit his categories. If it were accepted by Marxists themselves that Marxism does not constitute a watertight, self-sufficient doctrine, eternally opposed to every point of liberal ideology, their chance of convincing others that it contains both insight and truth might be enhanced.

45. Engels, *Letters*, in Feuer (Ed.), p. 396.

Today the controversy about revisionism seems rather outdated. The question for the future is rather whether Marxist doctrines can survive at all, given the rejection of communism by the East European states and the former Soviet Republics. However, it can be argued that what the people of these countries were rejecting was not Marxism itself, but the travesty of Marx's ideas represented by Leninist doctrines and Stalinist practices. There was little attempt to realize Marx's socialist ideals in the state-capitalist Soviet Union. There were also, certainly, reasons why the kind of socialism which Marx envisaged could not be easily achieved; at the time when the Tsarist empire fell, Russia was barely industrialized, and lacked the capitalist base out of which Marx believed communism would grow. We should also remember that the Soviet Union was an *empire*, although this sometimes escaped notice, and that the events there in the early 1990s signified a centrifugal, anti-imperialist movement among the Republics as much as an ideological shift. The ending of communism in that part of the world and the current experiments with free-market systems and liberal democracy may in turn be followed by a return to socialist ideals, if capitalism fails to 'deliver the goods' in economic terms, or even by a move to authoritarian or military states. Certainly, the communist vote has been substantial in elections in many formerly communist states, and there is some nostalgia among their populations for the security and certainties of the old system. As a consequence of the collapse of communism, West European Communist Parties have experienced internal crises and have adopted new names and new policies; many such parties may even disappear.[46] However, we should remember that more than a billion Chinese still live under communism and that despite the conflicts of 1989 it is by no means certain that the majority of Chinese have rejected communism. Callinicos argues that 'as long as capitalism continues on its unjust and destructive path, it is likely to find Marxism, in some form or other, confronting it'.[47] The story of Marxism is still being written, and it is probably too early for liberals to write it off as a spent force.

FURTHER READING

It is important to read Marx's own texts: in particular, *Early Writings*, *The German Ideology*, *The Communist Manifesto*, *The Critique of the Gotha Programme* and *Contribution to the Critique of Political Economy*. There is no shortage of secondary works, although significantly less has been published on Marx and Marxism since 1989. The following are recommended:

P. Anderson, *Considerations on Western Marxism*, New Left Books, 4th edn, Verso, 1984.
S. Avineri, *The Social and Political Thought of Karl Marx*, Cambridge U.P., 1970.
T. Carver, *Marx's Social Theory*, Oxford U.P., 1982

---

46. See M. J. Bull, 'A new era for the non-rulers too: West European Communist Parties, *perestroika* and the revolution in Eastern Europe', *Politics*, Vol. 11, No. 1 (1990).
47. A. Callinicos, 'Premature obituaries: a comment on O'Sullivan, Minogue and Marquand', *Political Studies*, XLI, Special Issue 1993, p. 65.

J. Elster, *An Introduction to Karl Marx*, Cambridge U.P., 1986.

J. Femia, *Marxism and Democracy*, Oxford U.P., 1993.

D. McLellan, *The Thought of Karl Marx*, 2nd edn, Macmillan, 1980; *Marx: The First Hundred Years*, Oxford U.P., 1983.

P. Singer, *Marx*, Oxford U.P., 1980

J. D. White, *Karl Marx and the Intellectual Origins of Dialectical Materialism*, Macmillan, 1996.

Chapter 5

Socialism

Socialism, Marxism and communism are not synonymous. To treat them as such is to ignore their theoretical differences and the disputes within 'the left'. Socialism is in fact the theoretical genus of which Marxism is a species and anarchism another; communism is best viewed as political practice, rather than as an ideology. As the title of Engels's *Socialism: Utopian and Scientific* implies, he and Marx were aware that they formed part of a wider movement whose origins could be traced back to the French Revolution and the utopian ideas which it seeded. English socialists are apt to trace their lineage even further back, to the Levellers of the Civil War period.[1] Ethically, some forms of socialism sprang from a Christian impulse, others from atheistic humanism. So, even more than liberalism, socialism is an amalgam of philosophies emerging from diverse social movements which, consequently, presents certain difficulties of definition.

Despite this, attempts have been made to define the 'essence' of socialism. The penalty of such attempts is to reduce its contours to a single dimension. In *The Left in Europe*, Caute argued that popular sovereignty (rule by the people) is the doctrine which most typifies the left. 'The notion of self-government is a single manifestation, albeit a primary one, of a wider, egalitarian impulse'.[2] However, liberals have also advocated self-government in varying degrees. Durkheim offered what became a classic definition of socialist doctrines as those which 'demand the connection of economic functions . . . to the directing and conscious centres of society'—that is, doctrines advocating a planned economy.[3] This definition seems to mistake a *means* of achieving socialism for its goal, and it ignores the advocacy by some socialists, past and present, of decentralization. These accounts fail to indicate the breadth and coherence of the socialist ideal, because they search for a defining characteristic. By contrast, Berki proposed a

1. A. Benn, in *Arguments for Socialism* (Ed. C. Mullins), Cape, 1979, pp. 29–32.
2. D. Caute, *The Left in Europe*, Weidenfeld & Nicolson, 1966, p. 33.
3. E. Durkheim, *Socialism and Saint-Simon* (trans. C. Sattler), Antioch Press, 1958, p. 19.

pluralist approach. He found four basic 'tendencies' in socialist ideology: egalitarianism, moralism, rationalism and libertarianism.[4] According to which tendency is uppermost, socialist doctrine varies in its choice of methods. Berki identified each tendency with a major strand of modern socialism. Western social democracy rests heavily on moralism, communism in the Eastern bloc emphasized rationalism, Third-World socialists pin their hopes on egalitarianism, while the New Left is libertarian. While Berki's approach is helpful in accounting for the differences between socialist practices, it does not illustrate the inner coherence of the ideology. Crick argues for a more universal and coherent conception of socialism, seeing it as 'a special form of democracy' and as a moral doctrine based on the cluster of values first promoted by the French revolutionaries, liberty, equality and fraternity.[5] Perhaps, as the lifelong socialist G. D. H. Cole said of socialism, 'the most that can be attempted . . . is the discovery of a central core of meaning'.[6] I shall analyse the ideas which compose this core, and try to show their coherence.

THE NUCLEUS OF SOCIALISM

> It really is impossible to understand either the French revolution or the early socialists unless one possesses some awareness of the challenge which the new liberal individualism represented to older ways of life.[7]
>
> *(George Lichtheim)*

> Socialism began as a revolt against capitalism and its conception of man and society was initially developed as an alternative to the one which in the socialist view underlay and reinforced capitalist society.[8]
>
> *(Bhikhu Parekh)*

As these quotations suggest, socialist doctrine in the West must always be examined with liberalism and capitalism in mind, although Third-World socialism has developed differently, having different antecedents and different forces with which to contend. In the account of socialism which follows, I shall show that one socialist ideal rests on another: taken together, they form a socialist philosophy, which will now be examined point by point.

(1) The Concern with Poverty

Poverty was seen by early socialists both as direct economic oppression and as the root cause of social oppression. The utopian Fourier, in an analysis admired by Engels,[9] proclaimed 'Poverty is the principal cause of social disorders'. The paradox of capitalism was that workers could not afford to buy what they

---

4. R. N. Berki, *Socialism*, Dent, 1975.
5. B. Crick, *Socialism*, Open University Press, 1987, pp. 6, 79.
6. G. D. H. Cole, *Socialist Thought: The Forerunners*, Macmillan, 1958, p. 1.
7. G. Lichtheim, *The Origins of Socialism*, Weidenfeld & Nicolson, 1969, p. 11.
8. B. Parekh (Ed.), *The Concept of Socialism*, Croom Helm, 1975, p. 3.
9. F. Engels, *Socialism: Utopian and Scientific* in *Selected Works*, Vol. III, p. 122.

produced and that 'an excess of work brings them to poverty as does excessive idleness'.[10] Many others also blamed the industrial system for manufacturing poverty and demanded its abolition. In the nineteenth century, *absolute* deprivation was the worst evil, forcing people into crime, prostitution and the workhouse. In the Third World it is still absolute deprivation that fuels socialist aspirations. But with the recent, precarious affluence of the West, socialists have often focused their attention on *relative* deprivation.[11] That more than ten million people in Britain are on or below the 'absolute' poverty line is shocking, but it is also the great differentials of income and wealth that indicate the endemic injustice of our society. Five per cent of the population owns 95 per cent of the wealth—a statistic which has changed remarkably little since Marx wrote. Not everyone reacts to poverty in the same way. The almost fatalistic approach of earlier Christianity, which still seems to influence some conservatives, asserted that poverty provided the 'deserving poor' with the opportunity for virtue in adversity and the rich with the chance to do good works. Extreme liberals have taken another view: Spencer argued that the 'undeserving poor' should be winnowed out to purify society. The evils of poverty are not, then, self-evident, because certain thinkers view it as inevitable or as a useful social mechanism. Therefore, the socialist attack constitutes a distinctive starting point for a social theory. The attack is sometimes based on the humanitarian conviction that it is wrong that people should suffer misery, and sometimes on a view of social justice and human rights which dictates that people should be treated more equally. Either way, socialist indignation about poverty points inexorably to egalitarianism as the remedy.

(2) A Class Analysis of Society

The recognition of poverty as a social problem led many socialists to argue that society is divided into two classes, the 'haves' and the 'have-nots'. Socialists are themselves divided into two classes—those who see class as a structural consequence of capitalism (notably Marx) and those who see it as a passing—or past—phenomenon. Marx objected that the utopian socialists had not understood that class was economically determined and that classes with necessarily opposed interests were not reconcilable.[12] For almost a hundred years, European socialists, following Marx, accepted class struggle as a necessary element of socialist politics. Today, most social-democratic parties play down the importance of class and class struggle. Is this because the structure of capitalism has changed and classes no longer exist, or because the preferences of the electorate have moved towards the 'classless' centre of the political spectrum? Certainly, if one adopts it, a class analysis adds an extra dimension to socialist egalitarianism, since it requires the elimination of status and privilege as well as greater material equality.

---

10. J. Beecher and R. Bienvenu (Eds), *The Utopian Vision of Charles Fourier*, Cape, 1972, pp. 87, 124.
11. W. G. Runciman, *Relative Deprivation and Social Justice*, Penguin, 1972.
12. Marx & Engels, *Communist Manifesto, Selected Works*, Vol. I, pp. 134–5.

(3) Egalitarianism

This, in my view, is the central ideal of socialism. Socialists extend the notion of justice from the legal and political into the economic and social spheres. The socialist idea of what constitutes equality moved historically from Babeuf's assertion of the complete equality of human beings, which entailed uniform treatment, to the Saint-Simonian notion of equal but different treatment, 'from each according to his capacity, to each according to his works', then to the Marxist formulation, 'from each according to his ability, to each according to his needs'. Equality does not necessitate levelling down and uniformity, as critics often suggest. Utopian socialists such as Fourier, Saint-Simon and William Morris depicted ideal societies which accommodated differences of talent and temperament within an egalitarian framework: their ideal was *equality of treatment*, with equal opportunities, rather than absolute equality. Some predicted that industrialism, properly organized, would produce an abundance of goods, so that all genuine needs could be satisfied non-competitively. The abolition of class is a further necessary consequence of egalitarianism. As a result of the stress placed on equality, social justice is sometimes seen primarily as a matter of distribution and, especially in day-to-day politics, of redistribution. But, properly understood, the ideal also embraces the productive process and requires a fair contribution from each individual to society. The concept of equality, with its many variants, is discussed in more detail in Chapter 16.

(4) Communal Ownership of the Means of Production

Although earlier thinkers—Plato, More and Owen, for example—had attacked private property, Marx analysed the term most precisely. For him, it meant the means of production, ownership of which placed an individual in the bourgeois class and enabled him to employ workers and make profits. Equality could not come about without the abolition of private property, which was synonymous with the abolition of the bourgeoisie. In the past, many socialists demanded the abolition of private wealth. This demand, of course, referred to productive assets, rather than to everyone's favourite possessions, but misunderstandings on this score have always cost socialism dear in political and propaganda terms.

The corollary of eliminating private property would be the collective or communal ownership of the means of production—factories, land, machinery. The meaning of 'communal ownership' was the subject of fierce disagreement between Marxist and anarchist socialists in the First International. The latter feared that national institutions would be set up to administer it, and that the state would thus be reinstated. Anarcho-communists like Kropotkin advocated the ownership by each local village producer group of land and factories. Durkheim's description of socialism as 'the connection of all economic functions to the directing . . . centres of society' foreshadowed state capitalism such as existed in the USSR—a spectre which justified the anarchists' detestation of national 'collective' ownership.

In 1959–60 the British Labour Party was embroiled in a bitter, historic dispute as to whether to drop Clause 4, part 4 of its constitution, which read:

> To secure for the workers by hand or by brain the full fruits of their industry and the most equitable distribution thereof that may be possible upon the basis of the common ownership of the means of production, distribution and exchange, and the best obtainable system of popular administration and control of each industry or service.

The clause (which was not dropped until 1995) did not indicate what common ownership entails: a 1960 Party statement made it clear that a variety of devices were acceptable, including state-owned industries, producer and consumer co-operatives, municipal ownership and public participation in private concerns. The postwar Labour government in Britain believed that nationalization of strategic industries is a crucial step towards socialism, but later experience suggested that such half-measures do not produce greater equality of wealth and income, or make work less alienating for those in publicly owned enterprises. Many socialists would now prescribe a variety of forms of ownership within a mixed public/private sector economy as the best approximation to the ideal and such ideas have now been adopted by the 'new' Labour Party. Under Tony Blair's leadership, the party deleted the contentious Clause 4 in 1995, replacing it with a wider ranging statement of beliefs which are discussed later in this chapter.

Common ownership is not an end in itself, but a *means* for attaining greater equality and opinions can legitimately differ about the form it should take, as about other policies, as circumstances differ. In largely agricultural countries which espoused socialism, like Tanzania or Portugal, collective farms were established relatively free from statist overtones. But in the industrialized world it is hard to see how any socialist government could communalize the vast business conglomerates without resorting to state capitalism, with its attendant dangers. Furthermore, the growth of multinational companies makes it almost impossible for a socialist government in one country to nationalize any of their branches, for they will simply migrate elsewhere, taking jobs with them. These developments bear out the early socialist insight that international capitalism should be countered by world socialism, which is probably a vain hope. In Britain, the privatization policies of the Thatcher government were doubtless instrumental in persuading Labour party members to accept the abolition of Clause 4; ownership of the formerly nationalized industries is now dispersed between large company investors (both British and overseas) and a multitude of individual shareholders, and any attempt at renationalization would be dogged by insuperable difficulties. The Labour government has therefore chosen to promote competition and to regulate monopolies, rather than to expand public ownership, thus accepting explicitly the importance of entrepreneurialism and the market as the hallmark of the modern economy.

(5) Popular Sovereignty

This ideal derives from a belief in the equal ability of all human beings to govern themselves, a premise shared, in principle, by liberals. There is a divide between social democrats who find representative democracy acceptable and more radical socialists including some Marxists, who espouse the principle of direct democracy propounded by Rousseau. But Rousseau's idea of the General Will, which promoted the common good and which a group, or even an individual, might express, has also been invoked to justify Party dictatorship in the name of the people.[13] Rousseau himself specified carefully the conditions of social and economic equality necessary to the proper expression of the General Will, conditions which never obtained in most communist countries. However, the Workers' Soviets in the early days after the Russian revolution were perhaps an attempt to implement popular sovereignty on Rousseau's lines, albeit a short-lived one.

There are theoretical and practical reasons why democracy under ideal socialism would be different from liberal democracy. The expression of class interests would no longer be necessary, nor would so many competing economic pressure groups exist, so that parties representing such interests might cease to operate. If the possibility of a classless society is accepted, even a one-party state can still be considered democratic because everyone has similar interests, which the party represents.[14] The socialist ideal of popular sovereignty, which makes the people as a whole supreme, deliberately transcends liberal democracy, which withholds power from individuals via the representative system and rejects the notion of the people as a 'whole'. These differences are discussed in Chapter 12.

(6) Human Interdependence, alias 'Subordination of the Individual to Society'

Critics assert that socialist doctrine does not safeguard the free, independent individual of liberal theory, and would subsume individual interests under the 'general interest'. But, as Parekh states, people *are* 'necessarily interdependent not only in the obvious material sense but also in the cultural and spiritual sense . . . [man] is totally unintelligible outside of society'.[15] This conception of man-in-society derives from the definition of human beings as creatures formed by the environment. Within society, our fellow men and women constitute the greater part of our environment; our behaviour can only fully be explained, and our interests can only properly be consulted, with reference to them and thus to the social ensemble. This seems uncontroversial, but many critics suggest that this view gives the 'general interest' dangerous priority over individual interests, which become subordinate. Socialists might well conceptualize this supposed subordina-tion as Rousseau does: in making the social contract, the individual gives up most of her power over herself, but gains a fraction of power over every other citizen. If *all* are equally 'subordinate', tyranny is not a danger.[16] Rousseau was worried by the economic (and hence social) dependence of one individual upon another,

13. J.-J. Rousseau, *The Social Contract* (Trans, G. D. H. Cole), Dent, 1913, pp. 22–4, 85–7. See too B. Holden, *The Nature of Democracy*, Nelson, 1974, pp. 41–51, who shows the similarities between the Rousseauist and the Marxist theories of democracy.
14. This case is put for the developing countries by C. B. Macpherson in *The Real World of Democracy*, Clarendon Press, 1966, Chap. 3.
15. Parekh, *The Concept of Socialism*, pp. 4–5.
16. Rousseau, *The Social Contract*, p. 12.

which he thought degrading to the human spirit.[17] The utopian socialists followed him in arguing that, if *each* depended on *all*, debilitating personal dependence would be averted.

However, the dependence of each on the state, an elite organization with its own interests, is a very different proposition. The fear that this would be a likely outcome of socialist policies led some postwar socialists to combat state-dependency by schemes for greater voter and worker participation, or even to move towards anarchism.[18] The conceptualization of the individual as a fraction of the whole is a logical consequence of other socialist tenets, notably the commitment to popular sovereignty and the premise that human nature is eminently sociable, and formed by society. But this 'subordination' indicates a reordering of priorities in *theory*: in *practice* it need not entail the loss of human rights or the enforced uniformity which critics fear.

(7) Human Creativity and Sociability

At the heart of every ideology is a conception of human nature. Socialists typically assume that human beings are creative and can find pleasure and fulfilment in work. Marx was influenced by Hegel's thesis that man, in transforming nature, transforms himself, a process which makes the 'slave' superior in some ways to the 'master'.[19] Saint-Simon, too, spoke of the urge to control nature and to be creative: 'for man, being happy is to act, then to enjoy'. Socialists consider the pleasures of creation equal, if not superior, to those of acquisition and consumption, hence the importance of *work* in a socialist society. Whereas the Calvinist/capitalist work ethic applauds the moral virtue of hard work, idealistic socialists emphasize the *joy*. This vision of 'creative man', *Homo faber*, has consequences for their view of freedom, as (10) below suggests.

The socialist conception of human nature has other elements: natural sociability and goodwill between people are assumed. Socialist accounts are invariably optimistic, differing greatly from Hobbes's picture of mankind as an aggressive, greedy species, and dictating a social theory in which co-operation and collectivism, rather than competition and individualism, are uppermost. *Fraternity* and *community*, ideals in which interest has recently revived, are expressions of the socialist belief in our essential sociability and solidarity.[20] Crick argues that fraternity 'must involve, firstly, common tasks and activities, and secondly an exultant recognition of diversity of character'. Fraternity is not based on sameness, but on friendship and fellow-feeling between individuals.[21] Similarly, the idea of community goes beyond the liberal notion of society as an

---

17. Rousseau, 'A Discourse on the Origin and Foundations of the Inequality of Mankind', in *The Social Contract*, pp.189, 202.
18. See, e.g., E. Luard, *Socialism without the State*, Macmillan, 1970, Part II.
19. G. Hegel, *The Phenomenology of Spirit* (trans A. V. Miller), Oxford U.P., 1977, Section B.IV.B.
20. Fraternity is discussed in K. Dixon, *Freedom and Equality: The Moral Basis of Democratic Socialism*, Routledge & Kegan Paul, 1986. A useful list of works on community can be found in C. E. Cochran, 'The thin theory of community: the communitarians and their critics', *Political Studies*, Vol. XXXVII, 3 (1989).
21. B. Crick, *Socialism*, p.100.

agglomeration of individuals, and emphasizes the common interest of a group of people who have a sense of shared identity and common purpose. The communitarian arguments discussed in Chapter 3 are essentially not socialist but liberal arguments, but some aspects of their emphasis on community and critique of individualism would be accepted by socialist thinkers.

(8) The Virtues of Co-operation

If people are naturally sociable, co-operation is the natural form of social organization.[22] It works on society as a moral and galvanizing force and guarantees equality of benefits for the co-operators; it is the antithesis of the ethos of competition and individualism which vindicates capitalism. Early socialism developed in conjunction with co-operative movements for the production and distribution of goods. Robert Owen—who set up a producers' co-operative in London in 1832—saw co-operation as the moral basis of social life, as well as the only truly successful mode of production. Industrialization and the division of labour were irreversible: the task was to find a form of voluntary co-operation which differed from the enforced, dehumanizing co-operation experienced in factories.

For many modern socialists, co-operation is still both an ideal and a policy. The 'Co-op' today is indistinguishable from other stores, but the principle remains alive. Experimental producers' co-operatives are often set up even within capitalist societies and in many Third-World countries; they operate on the basis of equal revenue- or profit-sharing between the producers. The practical problem for socialists is whether this scale of co-operation can be enlarged beyond the local group with common interests, where it flourishes naturally, to become the basis of social organization, without losing its voluntary and ethical quality. If not, socialist theory would require revision since the implication would be that national units were too large for socialism—a point made by many early socialists and anarchists. In fact, new methods of involving workers in capitalist enterprises have recently been devised and advocated by social democratic parties, including profit-sharing, allocating shares to workers, and having workers' representatives on Boards of Directors. These may be a poor substitute for true co-operation but they are a realistic compromise in a world of mega-companies.

(9) Idealization of Work as Unalienated Labour

The socialist idealization of work contrasts with both the biblical stigmatization of toil as Adam's curse and the Calvinist identification of work with virtue. Human creativity makes it possible for the pleasures of work to exceed even those of consumption, as the utopian, Fourier, amply illustrates: in his ideal community, people would pursue eight different occupations during a long working day. His principle of 'attractive labour' dictated that everyone should work at what she enjoys most: the rose-lover grows roses, and so on. For Marx, it

---

22. P. Kropotkin, *Mutual Aid*, reprinted, New York U.P., 1972.

was less the content than the form of work which mattered. Working for a capitalist could never be satisfying because of the worker's alienated, exploited state, whereas (ideally) any work under socialism should be fulfilling because of its 'social' nature. William Morris made the same point in his socialist utopia, *News from Nowhere* (1891), when he introduced Boffin, an intelligent man who had chosen to be a dustman because he found the work socially worthwhile: dustmen, in this utopia, had as high a status as anyone else.

For nineteenth-century socialists, work appeared to be mankind's perpetual burden, but changing technology in the 1950s and 1960s led thinkers to speculate about the possibility of a leisure-based society. Marcuse argued the need to transform work into *play* when superautomation had superseded most manual work—an interesting instance of the adaptation of an idea to changing material circumstances.[23] Today, unfortunately, different circumstances dictate that socialists should concern themselves with the 'right to work' above all else. However, it is important that socialists should theoretically explore the role of leisure and recreation in socialist societies in order to flesh out an ideology which sometimes appears to look no further than the workplace in seeking the betterment of society.

(10) Freedom as Fulfilment

The consequence of the socialist view that people are formed by society is a redefinition of freedom compatible with this deterministic perspective and with the premise of human creativity. Socialist freedom is the freedom to unfold and develop one's potential, especially through unalienated work. Freedom is separated from its liberal synonym, choice: if, for example, someone has great mathematical talent, all that is necessary for her freedom is that a mathematical career should be open to her, rather than a range of inappropriate choices. The superfluity of consumer products which capitalism offers is also largely irrelevant to the socialist analysis of freedom—they offer the illusion of choice, yet they cannot enhance the development of the individual who is too poor to benefit from the consumer society. This is discussed again in Chapter 14.

(11) Internationalism

The international dimension common to most versions of socialism needs no further justification than the argument that, for the humanist, all humanity is one race. National boundaries cannot circumscribe universal political truths, nor limit universal human rights. In this respect, socialists are at one with liberals. The utopian socialists, writing during and after the protracted Napoleonic wars, were instinctively internationalist. Fourier planned a world confederation of communities: Saint-Simon wanted a federation of industrial countries—for which both have been accused of totalitarian inclinations. Marx and Engels promoted the International on the basis of their analysis of the economic interdependence of

---

23. Marcuse, *Eros and Civilisation*, Sphere, 1969, p. 151 ff.

capitalist countries and the common interests of workers everywhere. The socialist movement was self-proclaimedly internationalist until 1914, when the outbreak of war in Europe forced existing social-democratic parties to choose between patriotism and internationalism. The difficulties of the Second International in peacetime in coordinating socialist action in European countries (it even proved impossible to agree on concerted May Day demonstrations), and the experience of 1914, when the French and German socialist parties were forced to vote war credits or be denounced as traitors, left a lasting scar on the socialist parties of Europe.[24] Between the wars, the USSR posed grave problems for socialist parties which wished to be internationalist yet to avoid accusations of being pro-Moscow. Today, the Third-World dimension presents further problems: how can solidarity subsist between the proletariat of industrial countries and that of developing countries, when their standard of living is inversely related?

Recent history shows the evils of nationalism all too clearly: selfishness, belligerence, wasteful expenditure on armaments and tragic wars are the legacy of the cult of the nation-state. Internationalism is the highest ideal of socialist ideology, with its demand for worldwide equality and peace, yet the strength of nationalism and international capitalism—not to mention people's myopia where remote countries are concerned—make it the hardest ideal to pursue in practice.

These ideas constitute the 'common core' of socialism. Not all socialists subscribe to all of them. But anyone searching for an essentialist definition of socialism should, I think, take the notion of equality as the determining moral force on which other elements of the ideology rest. The presentation of the eleven key ideas here is intended to illustrate the logical connections between them and the way in which policies derive from philosophical assumptions, so as to demonstrate the force and coherence of the socialist ideal. These interconnections are set out schematically in the diagram below.

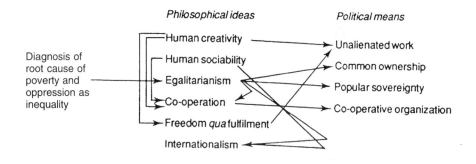

24. See J. Joll, *The Second International 1889–1914*, and Caute, *The Left in Europe*, pp. 219–20. For a British case study, see M. Winter, *Socialism and the Challenge of War*, Routledge & Kegan Paul, 1974.

THE CHANGING FACE OF SOCIALISM

In the West today (except in the United States), social-democratic parties provide the major opposition to liberal and conservative parties and often form governments. While their parliamentary role has been developing, socialist politicians, political commentators and academics have written countless volumes on the principles and practice of socialism; much of what is written is ephemeral, but some of it adds to the understanding of the meaning of socialism in contemporary contexts. There is no space here to survey all this literature but the section on further reading lists some survey works. Instead, I shall illustrate how socialism adapts its beliefs to time and place, using the examples of British and African socialist thinkers.

The term 'social democrat' needs some explanation. In the late nineteenth century, the term included both revolutionaries and parliamentarians: many members of the Russian Social Democratic Labour Party were revolutionaries. In 1918 the Bolshevik section of the RSDLP renamed itself the Communist Party of the Soviet Union. However, the term had already begun to change, even in the late nineteenth century, and began to denote someone who wished to implement socialism through existing or developing democratic institutions rather than by revolution. Social-democratic parties were formed in most European countries to field candidates in elections: they were especially successful in France and Germany. The debates of the Second International were preoccupied with the question of how far socialists could go down the parliamentary road without being compromised by co-operation with bourgeois parties. 'Social democrats' differed from 'revolutionary socialists' and 'anarchist socialists': all of them held socialist ideals, but they differed over the means by which socialism could be attained and over the form of social organization appropriate to a socialist society. Social-democratic parties were sometimes explicitly Marxist, like the German SPD in its early years, but most such parties repudiated the connection with Marxist ideas in the 1920s, or have done so since. The British Labour Party, therefore, in the original sense of the word, was a social-democratic party, being committed to working through parliament. Recent usage has given the term a different nuance: 'social democrat' today suggests someone whose priority is to give capitalism and liberal democracy an acceptable face by promoting a mixed economy and a welfare state, while 'democratic socialist' signifies a socialist who wants democratically organized socialism by contrast with, say, the bureaucratic socialism of communist countries. ('Social democratic' best describes the new Labour Party, although it still contains left-wing 'democratic socialists'.) The term 'socialist' has often evoked hostility, particularly in the USA, because of its association with Marxism and communism—hence the tendency to add qualifying adjectives or even to abbreviate the inflammatory name of socialist to 'social', as in 'social democrat'.

Britain's first major experience of socialist government was the postwar Attlee government of 1946–51, whose measures included nationalization of the mines, the steel industry and the setting up of the welfare state and the health service. Later Labour governments (1964–70, 1974–9) were markedly less doctrinaire in their measures although steel (denationalized by the Conservatives) was renationalized and secondary schools were made comprehensive in the pursuit of an egalitarian education system. Both of these governments could claim that their socialist programmes had had to be modified because of intolerable economic pressures, but the lack of strongly socialist measures reflected something more fundamental. Already, during the affluent late 1950s when the Labour Party, out of power, was trying to efface from its record the memory of postwar austerity over which it had presided, and trying to appear less dogmatically socialist, Crosland had written in *The Future of Socialism*:

> In my view Marx has little or nothing to offer the contemporary socialist, either in respect of practical policy, or of the correct analysis of our society, or even of the right conceptual tools or framework.[25]

Crosland's book was published in 1956, when many left-wing supporters were re-considering their position in the light of the Soviet invasion of Hungary, which had outraged the West. In preaching against Marxism to the Labour Party he was preaching to the already converted. However, in the same, highly influential book, he argued for 'revisionism', for the need to reformulate many cherished Labour Party doctrines and adapt them to modern capitalist society. Militant class struggle was no longer relevant; poverty had almost disappeared and capitalism could not be blamed for inefficiency since it had provided full employment. Co-operative aspirations had, Crosland thought, been partly fulfilled: society was less individualistic and competitive than previously. Crosland proposed retaining two socialist 'aspirations': social welfare ('an acceptance of collective responsibility and an extremely high priority for the relief of social distress or misfortune') and social equality and the 'classless society', an aspiration which he thought more applicable to the gap between rich and poor countries than to Britain's internal arrangements. Gaitskell, as leader of the Labour Party (1955–63) attempted without success to persuade the party to be revisionist—to endorse the mixed economy and repudiate the demand of some members for extensive nationaliza-tion. Despite his efforts, Clause 4 (communal ownership) remained part of the constitution. However, the Labour governments of the 1960s and 1970s progressed very little way towards realizing its recommendations, partly for economic reasons.

This failure (from the viewpoint of advocates of strongly socialist policies), together with a worsening economic situation in the 1970s, led to internal dissension in the Labour Party about the interpretation and the relevance of orthodox socialist principles and caused polarization between the right and left wings of the party. The rising level of unemployment led some Labour politicians to reject the Crosland/Gaitskell line and to reinvoke the class struggle. Their opponents, in turn, rejected 'strong socialism' because it seems to be anti-democratic. This dispute brought about the formation of the Social Democratic Party (SDP) in 1981. Among those who analysed the predicament of socialists in Britain at the time were the politicians Benn (Labour) and Luard and David

---

25. A. Crosland, *The Future of Socialism*, Cape, 1956, p. 2.

Owen (both SDP). Although their arguments were shaped by the British experience, many of them could be applied to socialism in other industrialized countries. Benn and Luard agreed that the mixed economy did not work: that we were no closer to securing for workers 'the full fruits of their industry and the equitable distribution thereof', nor to ending work alienation and dissatisfaction. Public ownership and government attempts to induce private investment in depressed areas had failed and, in Benn's words, 'we have come to the end of that road'.[26] His prescription was for a further extension of state ownership, increased industrial democracy, and greater public accountability of nationalized industries. But this is precisely what Luard feared, as the title of his book, *Socialism without the State*, indicates. He deplored the size and scale of organization in modern society and the ubiquitous presence of the state, and proposed 'grassroots socialism' with experiments in local producer groups and neighbourhood ownership.[27] Luard opposed the state in communist *and* capitalist societies because he had individualistic ideals and a dislike of uniformity shared by liberals such as Mill, rather than because he viewed the state as oppressor, as Marx did. The same theme is found in Owen's writing: he argued that 'the task for Social Democrats is to . . . build a fresh decentralized philosophy, and put forward a detailed programme of legislative and administrative reforms to diffuse power in Britain'.[28] This was necessary to counteract *corporatism*, which he defined as the attempt to control private industry through the state apparatus. In Britain, corporatism took the form of a tripartite negotiating mechanism in which employers, unions and state participated to a certain extent. This form of economic management, initiated by the Labour governments of the 1960s and 1970s, led to committee decision-making by consensus 'which erodes democra- tically elected and responsible decision-making'.[29] Owen's concern was for the creation of a participatory democracy, within a mixed economy; he stated that the Labour Party always lacked a theory about the proper distribution of power in a socialist society, and so opted for a form of socialism heavily dependent on bureaucracy and corporatism.

These debates between right- and left-wing socialists in Britain and elsewhere about the role of the state echo the anarchists' quarrels with Marx in the First International, but the exponential increase in the size and powers of states still makes the problem relevant for contemporary socialist theorists. The regular recurrence of this debate in socialist circles proves that conceptual, as well as contextual, issues are at stake. The question is one of means and ends, and their relation. Could a state-run socialist economy achieve the wider, non-material aims of socialism or would such a structure, by centralizing power in a way which was inevitably undemocratic, undermine the very principles of socialist equality and freedom? For the remaining Marxists, the issue is still clear: the state continues to be an instrument of bourgeois oppression even when it takes on the guise of

---

26. Benn, *Arguments for Socialism*, p. 52.
27. Luard, *Socialism without the State*, Chap. 9.
28. D. Owen, *Face the Future*, Oxford U.P., 1981, p. 27.
29. Owen, *Face the Future*, p. 32.

welfare state or state socialism. Earlier social democrats regarded the state less suspiciously (a fault for which Marx criticized the German SPD in 1875) and believed that it could be captured democratically and diverted to socialist uses. The unpromising results of periods of socialist government, together with the spectre of the authoritarian communist states, caused Owen, Luard and many others to seek to change the state (though not for Marx's reasons) and to seek alternative forms of socialist political organization. At the periphery, these alternatives merge with the demands of other political groups—ecologists, feminists and anarchists might agree with some of their decentralist propositions. Even Communists came to parallel conclusions, through observing the development of the USSR. In 1970, Garaudy, a French Communist, argued:

> The concept of State ownership is highly contradictory: State ownership connotes . . . the abolition of capitalist private ownership . . . but it is also a form of ownership which perpetuates the alienation of the means of production with respect to the worker by excluding him not only from decisions affecting production and the allocation of surplus-value but also from the general administration of the economy.[30]

Garaudy recommended an alternative similar to the workers' management system then operating in Yugoslavia.

The technologically advanced, bureaucratized state is bigger than any government whose life is democratically limited; likewise, international capitalism has proved impossible for socialist governments to control. The modern, interventionist state presents social democrats, committed to working through the existing apparatus, with formidable problems of theory and practice. Since communist countries were afflicted with 'statism' no less than capitalist countries, it seems that a radical new theory is needed to analyse and combat a form of state which is not so much the tool of the bourgeoisie but an independent and self-aggrandizing force, equipped with all the repressive technology that advanced capitalism can produce for its own self-defence and self-perpetuation. Many socialist thinkers appreciate this problem and propose solutions but the effect on socialist practice so far is negligible. Once in power, many socialists—for example, the former President Mitterrand in France—have found it expedient to increase the power of the state in order to implement economic measures.

In Britain in 1997 a Labour government was elected after 18 years of Conservative rule, in part as a result of modernization of the party's policies and doctrines. Many supporters of old, 'socialist' Labour criticized the doctrinal changes which Blair had wrought to create 'new' Labour. It is therefore instructive to ask whether the creed which replaced Clause 4 departs significantly from the ideals of socialism. The new clause reads:

> The Labour Party is a democratic socialist party. It believes that by the strength of our common endeavour we achieve more than we achieve alone, so as to create for each of us the means to realise our true potential and for all of us a community in

---

30. R. Garaudy, *The Turning Point of Socialism* (Trans. P. Ross and B. Ross), Fontana-Collins, 1970, pp. 180–1. The democratic nature of the Yugoslavian workers' management system is discussed in C. Pateman, *Participation and Democratic Theory*, Cambridge U.P., 1970.

which power, wealth and opportunity are in the hands of the many not the few, where the rights we enjoy reflect the duties we owe, and where we live together, freely, in a spirit of solidarity, tolerance and respect.

This declaration seems to offer, in modern and rather general terms, an acknowledgement of the value of co-operation, an account of freedom as the fulfilment of individual potential and a re-statement of the classic idea of equality—power, wealth and opportunity should be in the hands of the many, not the few. It also counters recent criticisms that the modern welfare state has produced a culture of rights demands which take no account of social duties, and it explicitly emphasizes the solidarity and tolerance needed for the wellbeing of a multicultural society (a phenomenon not considered in classical socialist texts). What is missing is the commitment to communal ownership—but new Labour might argue that this would now be an outmoded method of attaining the socialist aspiration of a more equal society. Wright describes the Blair revolution as 'converting socialism into "social-ism", and constructing a liberal communitarianism anchored in a broad intellectual inheritance of the left centre'.[31] For Wright, socialism had long suffered from a confusion between means and ends, and from its dogmatic commitment to outdated means (methods) such as communal ownership. The transformation of socialism into 'liberal communitarianism' may affront old-style socialists, but the Labour Party's re-location in centrist politics is a striking example of how ideologies change and adapt to circumstances. Extensive privatization was a phenomenon of the 1980s and 1990s, not just in Britain but also in would-be socialist countries like India, where the economy is being 'liberalized'—i.e. state enterprises are being privatized. After the Thatcherite reforms no party advocating extensive public ownership could have hoped to succeed: Thatcher moved the political spectrum to the right and the Labour Party adapted accordingly. Whether a Labour government elected on the new terms can realize any socialist ideals remains to be seen.

Socialism is not confined to the West, nor are its problems merely those of advanced capitalist societies. By contrast, I shall now look briefly at some early exponents of African socialism. These thinkers usually dismissed social democracy and Marxism as alien ideologies inappropriate to Africa's material conditions and predicament. President Nyerere of Tanzania wrote:

> These two revolutions (agrarian and industrial) planted the seeds of conflict within society, and not only was European socialism born of that conflict, but its apostles sanctified the conflict itself into a philosophy . . . The European socialist cannot think of his socialism without its father—capitalism! Brought up in tribal socialism, I must say I find this contradiction quite intolerable. It gives capitalism a philosophical status which capitalism neither claims nor deserves. For it virtually says 'Without capitalism . . . there can be no socialism'.[32]

Nyerere emphasized the contingency of the historical events out of which socialist ideology grew in Europe and, in defiance of Marx, rejected the 'necessary'

---

31. T. Wright, *Socialisms: Old and New*, Routledge, 1996, p. 135.
32. J. Nyerere, 'Ujamaa: the basis of African socialism', in *African Socialism* (Eds. W. H. Friedland and C. G. Rosberg), Stanford U.P., 1964, pp. 245–6.

dialectical connection between capitalism and socialism. He argued that 'tribal socialism', a qualitatively different social form from the European variety, had existed in the past in Africa, without any capitalist preconditions.

> We, in Africa, have no more need of being 'converted' to socialism than we have of being 'taught' democracy. Both are rooted in our own past—in the traditional society which produced us. Modern African Socialism can draw from its traditional heritage the recognition of 'society' as an extension of the basic family unit.[33]

Nyerere's socialism centred on the concept of *Ujamaa*—'familyhood' or 'brotherhood'—and is practised in Tanzania at village, not state, level. Despite various initial problems caused by the imposition of the socialist project from above, there are about 8000 collective villages, many implementing Ujamaa principles, run on the basis of common ownership of the means of production, especially land, co-operative production, participatory decision-making and total self-organization. These villages offer various social services and reinvest surpluses to increase production; the benefits or profits are shared as in a family. 'Self-reliance' (which implies hard work by each individual) is the watchword of Tanzanian co-operation.

Although some early observers saw Ujamaa merely as the rehabilitation of traditional co-operative forms, the emphasis on participation and socialist ideology was new, and manifested the principles of an alternative, African socialism. The stress—quite naturally, in an agrarian continent—was on production on the land and co-operative labour. The social obligation to work was proclaimed by Nyerere, who pointed out that in traditional society nobody was idle. African socialism concerns the joint *creation* of wealth rather than its *redistribution* (a major concern of European socialism). The traditional, extended family is to be further extended, in spirit at least, to embrace the whole village, for greater social cohesion. Although Nyerere used the phrase 'tribal socialism', perhaps to explain himself better to Westerners obsessed by African 'tribalism', the basic socialist unit is the village, which is viewed as an organic, familial entity.

Most exponents of indigenous African socialism asserted that it is a classless phenomenon. Ex-president Nkrumah of Ghana wrote in 1964 that Africa was by tradition a classless society and that the imperialists were the chief enemy.[34] (Later, in 1970, in *The Class Struggle in Africa*, he attempted to explain in Marxist terms how revolution could occur in predominantly peasant countries.) President Senghor of Senegal also characterized African society as classless because community-based, with a hierarchy founded on spiritual and democratic—not economic—values. The proclaimed classlessness of African society offers a theoretical justification for the popularity of one-party democracies in Africa, although the practical reason for such developments is undoubtedly the desire to modernize efficiently and rapidly. Typically, African socialism declares itself *evolutionary*, although the pressures of the struggle against colonialism and the growth of neo-colonialism (economic domination by Western countries) have

---

33. Nyerere, *Ujamaa*, p. 246. See also Nyerere's *Freedom and Socialism*, Oxford U.P., 1968, pp. 1–32.
34. K. Nkrumah, *Neo-Colonialism, the Last Stage of Imperialism* (1964), Panaf, 1971.

produced theories of revolution such as Nkrumah's. The hope during the decolonization of the 1950s and 1960s was that traditionally homogeneous African society would undergo a socialist metamorphosis painlessly and without revolution. But the emergence of a 'national bourgeoisie' (Westernized bureaucrats, professionals and businessmen) in most ex-colonial countries, and the accelerating dependence of African economies on the capitalist world economy make this appear over-optimistic.

African socialists also attack the alienation and spiritual poverty of Western life and emphasize spiritual values and freedom. Senghor wrote:

> Our socialism is not that of Europe . . . we are forced to seek our own original mode, a Negro-African mode, of attaining [maximum satisfaction of spiritual and material needs], paying special attention to the two elements I have just stressed: *economic democracy and spiritual freedom*.[35]

His emphasis on the spiritual complemented his concept of 'negritude', the assertion of the racial and intellectual uniqueness of the Africans. The freedom which such socialists demand is clearly not that of liberals, but is closer to Rousseau's ideal: freedom through one's development as a full member of society. The published writings of perhaps the most famous of African politicians, Nelson Mandela, contain little about African socialism but plenty about social justice.[36] For black South Africans living under apartheid, the class struggle was in fact a race struggle, concerning equal access to political power and to the natural wealth of Africa's most prosperous nation. Mandela's works are a humbling reminder that, from the perspective of the millions in South Africa who suffered racial oppression and degradation, the ideological controversies of the West were as irrelevant as the dispute in Swift's Lilliput between the Big-Endians and the Little-Endians.[37] But Mandela's pursuit of (racial) justice and equality is equally a part of the socialist endeavour.

Another aspect of African socialism was the Pan-Africanism promoted by Nkrumah and later by ex-President Amin of Uganda. Nkrumah worked for African unity, without much success; he argued that socialism should be pursued on an all-Africa scale. Pan-Africanism differed from the older socialist internationalism, being a doctrine which calls for the organization of the Third-World oppressed in a way which would inevitably set them against the proletariat of the capitalist world. Today the North/South gap is constantly widening. The socialist doctrines propounded when the world was regarded as consisting of Europe, America and a mass of subject peoples, are mutating to take account of conflicts (rich/poor, white/black) which cut right across the categories of the old analysis. Even when African socialists use similar concepts—co-operation, for example—interpretation and implementation differ greatly in European and African contexts. Although some of them have been influenced by Chinese communism, especially Maoism, most African socialists reject the European

---

35. L. Senghor, 'African-style socialism', in *African Socialism*, p. 264.
36. N. Mandela, *The Struggle is my Life*, IDAF Publications, 1990.
37. J. Swift, *Gulliver's Travels*, Part I, ch. 4.

experience and the logic and categories of Western socialism, while retaining the name of socialism for their own sets of values. As this shows, ideologies are inseparable from their social, political and economic context even when they share a name.

OBJECTIONS TO SOCIALISM

I now turn to some theoretical objections to the general principles of socialism. The socialist conception of human nature has often been challenged by liberals and conservatives. Why assume people to be naturally sociable, co-operative and creative rather than aggressive, competitive or idle? Casual observation and sociobiology, it is said, support the latter view.[38] Socialists may retort that we compete only because we are born into societies whose institutions are competitive—it is nurture not nature, conditioning not heredity. The long-standing controversy about the extent to which behaviour is inherited or conditioned shows no imminent sign of being resolved, and, failing strong evidence, the political thinker may make any assumption she likes about human nature. Socialists posit a kind of human nature which everyday behaviour in the West seems to belie, but they can still cite examples of co-operative societies and institutions to justify their argument that our naturally sociable inclinations are perverted by capitalist institutions. Ultimately, any conception of human nature is an act of faith, not a scientific fact, which means that no conception can be ruled out conclusively. Conceptions which diminish the role of self-interest are viewed with suspicion in capitalist culture, but socialists do not need to claim that we are all altruists to prove that socialist society is possible. It would be enough to show that co-operation creates greater abundance and wellbeing than competition, to show that even self-interest is served by 'sociable' behaviour: this is a line taken by early socialists. The 'People aren't like that' argument against socialist optimism is, in my view, a weak one, given the remarkable adaptability of human beings to a wide variety of social forms.

The charge most frequently made against socialism is that equality cannot be reconciled with liberty: a socialist society is necessarily unfree. In part, this is a factual argument based on the suppression of civil liberties in communist states, but it is backed by several conceptual arguments, which run as follows: given the natural inequality of talents and abilities, any egalitarian system will thwart some individuals and hamper the free development of their potential—a point often made about comprehensive schools. Likewise, a system of equal reward for work unfairly discourages the more able in their attempts to succeed (this of course has no bearing on *freedom* unless we define it to include the liberty to get ahead of others). It is also said that an egalitarian society prevents individuals from getting their just rewards. These arguments focus attention on the problems which an

---

38. From K. Lorenz's *On Aggression* (trans. M. Latzke), Methuen, 1966, to R. Dawkins's *The Selfish Gene*, Oxford U.P., 1976, the innate selfishness and aggressiveness of human nature has been a focus of sociobiology.

authentic socialist society would face in operation; they can all, I believe, be circumvented by the procedural concept of *equality of treatment*, which can take into account people's natural differences.

Hardest to answer is the accusation that any transition to socialism would destroy present liberties. Given existing financial and social inequalities, any move towards equality through redistribution would, it is said, necessarily make some people worse off, thus limiting their freedom. Liberty, choice, and money are closely associated in the liberal mind, hence this criticism. 'Levelling down' is a common accusation made against socialists, but the logic of it is only correct if the situation is static, like a game of Monopoly in which a limited quantity of money circulates, a typical zero-sum game where gains must equal losses. Since in times of world recession a fixed supply of prosperity is the most we can hope for, the introduction of socialism might indeed entail a temporary levelling down. Some socialist governments could even find themselves having to redistribute 'negative income', like the Labour government of 1974–9, which administered cuts in the real standard of living. But such circumstances are only contingent and may change. Utopian socialists answered the challenge by hypothesizing that their systems would produce ever-increasing abundance so that *everyone* could have more, yet inequalities would be reduced or eliminated. Whether redistribution deprives people of income and freedom therefore depends on what accompanying assumptions are made about the quantity of wealth available. It also depends partly on the degree of existing inequality: the greater that is, the more impossible 'levelling up' and the more likely that very rich people will be compulsorily deprived of their wealth. Critics of socialism assume that the rich would not voluntarily give up this wealth, which also constitutes their liberty, and that, in being coerced to do so, they would undergo a double encroachment on their freedom. A further elaboration of the criticism is that levelling up, if it were ever possible (as it has been in suddenly oil-rich countries with small populations like the Gulf States and Libya), would deprive the better-off of their relative privileges over others, entailing a loss of social status, so that it would still be unfair.

The fallacious assumption behind all such arguments is that there is some inherent *fairness* in the existing accidental distribution of goods. No convincing evidence is offered for this assumption: even a conservative liberal like Hayek admits that market mechanisms are not *just*. Furthermore, there is a degree of self-contradiction involved. If freedom equals choice, signified by money, and money is redistributed to worse-off people, they thereby receive greater freedom, simultaneously with the better-off losing some freedom. We thus move towards an equality of individual freedom, to which the liberal is also committed by other liberal ideals. As Hart argues, if there is any natural right, it is the equal right to be free.[39] How can those who maintain that money is an important component of freedom begrudge it to those who have less, or hold that existing income and wealth differentials promote maximum freedom?

---

39. H. L. A. Hart, 'Are there any natural rights?', in *Political Philosophy* (Ed. A. Quinton), Oxford U.P., 1967.

There is some inconsistency in liberal thinking about freedom in terms of civil liberties, allocated to everyone equally, and liberalism's practical equation of freedom with the choice which cash provides: the latter form of freedom, alias economic power, can destroy the value of the formal liberties.

Another part of the liberal's case rests on the prohibition made in utilitarianism of interpersonal comparisons of utility. We are not allowed to hypothesize that one unit of freedom redistributed from a free to an unfree person will cause her less pain than it gives the other pleasure. Yet this is clearly true at the margin and such comparisons must be made in politics. Carritt used an extreme example of this to show that equality is not only compatible with, but supportive of, liberty: he imagined an island where one man has the monopoly of the water supply, greatly incommoding the freedom of other inhabitants. If water ownership is then equalized, only the monopolist loses his liberty, while the others gain dramatically. Hence Carritt's conclusion, which vindicates socialist principles: 'To be forcibly deprived of superabundance or even of conveniences impairs liberty less than to be forcibly prevented from appropriating necessities.'[40] Greater equality should therefore conduce to a greater total sum of liberty and happiness except where the original inequalities were very slight. Here we must distinguish between particular liberties and general personal liberty to which income and other factors contribute. It would be wrong to redistribute someone's voting rights, since everyone has an equal, invariable amount of vote, but other freedoms are more divisible, and more easily redistributed.

What of the fear of coercion during the transition to socialist equality? Only by assuming that the rich would defend their wealth and would have to be coerced into parting with it can this transition be seen as a greater threat to liberty than other government measures involving sanctions. Since the rich are, by definition, in the minority, such a transition could be decided upon democratically. Progressive taxes, widely accepted in the West, are a means of effecting the move to a more equal society, and have not until recently been considered an infringement of liberty. The policy, pursued by Prime Minister Thatcher and President Reagan in the 1980s, of reducing income tax along with the public expenditure and welfare benefits was, however, an example of a regressive redistribution of income, and hence liberty, towards the *better-off*: they justified their measures precisely because greater disposable income would increase liberty for such people. Right-wing thinkers who accept that view must see that, logically, the reverse—Carritt's argument—is also true.

Socialists are concerned with the negative aspect of the cash–freedom nexus: poverty equals *unfreedom*. They resent not the fact that some have more, but the fact that some have less. But where relativities are concerned you cannot give someone more without giving someone *relatively* less (even if their total amount remains the same)—a problem which has haunted governments trying to help low-paid workers during periods of income restraint, when the better-off workers object to the erosion of pay differentials. But, as Carritt shows, any process which

---

40. E. F. Carritt, 'Liberty and equality', in Quinton (Ed.), *Political Philosophy*, pp. 138–9.

reduces relativities increases the total amount of liberty. Another reason why socialists deny the dichotomy between liberty and equality is that, as was said, they define freedom differently from liberals, as the opportunity to fulfil one's potential. To arrange appropriate opportunities for everybody would not require great discrepancies of wealth; it would merely require 'equal but different' treatment based on the principle 'to each according to his/her needs'. The appropriate definition of liberty for socialists might be stated as 'freedom from unsatisfied needs', which can be interpreted to include the need for self-realization. Certainly, this raises tricky philosophical questions about distinguishing between true, false, basic and acquired needs, and which needs should be allowed to count in social justice calculations, but these details could surely be worked out in policy terms. Thus, for socialists, the principles of freedom and equality are interlocking and complementary, equal articles of the socialist catechism.

THE CONTRADICTIONS OF SOCIAL DEMOCRACY

The failure of Western social-democratic parties in government to achieve socialism is usually explained historically. In Britain, for example, the Labour Party was often hampered in the past by its links with trades unions, which tend to be conservative and concerned with short-term economic gains. Another reason is the strength of world capitalism which makes 'socialism in one country' hard to achieve, except through self-imposed isolation. International financiers can hamstring a would-be socialist government; there are other organizations such as the CIA whose policy is to prevent socialist encroachments in friendly capitalist countries. Nationalism, and nationalist wars have forced social-democratic parties to place national interests before socialist principles on many occasions. But such explanations are based on historical contingency. More satisfying as a general explanation of this failure is an analytical approach which shows the incompatibility of social-democratic strategy with socialist goals. Today, social democrats often repudiate the class analysis of society and advocate parliamentary reconciliation of interests—which Marx, for one, considered impossible. If, when in government, they attempt redistributive measures, vested interests block or modify them, so that only minor reforms are achieved. By taking a democratic and parliamentary approach to socialist goals, the social-democratic movement has tried to make use of the bourgeois state and bourgeois techniques and values. Because these instruments were devised to protect the system and the rule of the bourgeoisie, they cannot be used successfully against capitalism. Social democrats, like liberals, often seem to assume that the state and the political system are neutral—mistakenly. In fact, the task of implementing socialism through the liberal-democratic apparatus, may well be structurally impossible.

A further reason for the failure is that socialism was primarily an intellectuals' movement, inspired by ideals which appeal to the impartial reasoner. When it becomes the doctrine of a mass party, the party must adapt these ideals to the demands of supporters who are often, by definition, the least favoured, least educated members of society. Since social democrats, unlike revolutionary socialists, operate through the democratic system, they can only gain power by appealing to this section of the electorate, their natural supporters, and so compromise is inevitable. Unreconstructed working-class electors will continue to vote to better their lot in the immediate future: if high socialist principles do not offer this prospect, they will take their custom elsewhere in most cases. Equality in its fullest sense is an ideal appealing to educated members of society, who infuse into the notion many liberal values, such as freedom and dignity: for most other people, perceived unfairness to self is the evil to be removed—an aspiration limited in scope and separable from equality. This mismatch between the perspectives of socialist politicians and ideologues and their voters is undoubtedly a reason why most socialist governments are less radical in deed than in word. Whether the answer is political education of the electorate to proselytize them, or whether socialist activists should accept their electors as a democratic drag-brake is another question.

A further problem of social democracy—and socialism in general—is the lack of a shared conception of what a socialist economy might be. The economic means which might lead to socialist ends are many and varied, and frequently debated: each has disadvantages, as Nove showed in *The Economics of Feasible Socialism*.[41] This in part explains the dissensions and rifts which occur within socialist parties: *methods* rather than principles are in dispute—but methods are all-important in real politics. There are many ingenious proposals for economic democracy[42], employee representation, worker participation and profit-sharing, and whether these would realize the ethical ideals of socialism remains a matter of speculation until they have been tried out systematically.

One practical problem in the dissemination of socialism, especially in Britain, is that it is not the dominant ideology—voting Labour is different from having socialist convictions—and that socialism is not the prevailing form of organization, despite our mixed economy, so that socialist values are always challenged from the stronghold of the liberal ideas which they contradict. The dominant ideology, however contestable, has the inestimable advantage of being transmitted explicitly or covertly in schools, through the media, and throughout the culture. A rival ideology therefore appears to threaten all that we have been taught to hold dear. The dominant ideology also has the privilege of setting the conditions for knowledge: that is, of excluding all doctrines which fail the tests set by its own epistemology. The liberal thinker, operating on an empirical and inductive method can thus dismiss Marxism because there is no 'conclusive' evidence of class conflict or because its predictions do not come true. Similarly, in many ways the non-Marxist socialist is ruled offside before she even starts to play because her premises do not coincide with the prevalent political preconceptions.

The history of social-democratic politics in Britain demonstrates how those social democrats who entered parliament were swiftly beguiled into believing

---

41. A. Nove, *The Economics of Feasible Socialism*, Allen & Unwin, 1983.
42. See R. Archer, *Economic Democracy: The Politics of Feasible Socialism*, Oxford U.P., 1995.

liberal doctrines about the supremacy of parliament and the virtues of the existing system.[43] Those who, like the Fabians, hoped to 'permeate' the system were themselves assimilated. Experience suggests, then, that Marx was right in thinking that the state, an epiphenomenon of capitalism, cannot be merely diverted to achieve socialism, and that some form of 'revolutionary socialism' is necessary for this goal—which does not, however, *entail* violence, although it may occur. The most that social democrats can hope to achieve, given their assumptions and chosen strategy, is to socialize and humanize the existing state—which is itself a worthy aim—but their collaboration with that state precludes the achievement of some of the central ideals of socialism.

In 1991, after the collapse of Soviet communism, André Gorz wrote:

> As a system, socialism is dead. As a movement and an organized political force, it is on its last legs. All the goals it once proclaimed are out of date.[44]

He argued that the industrial workforce had declined in numbers, so that the aspiration of socialists to represent the interests of the working class was outdated. Nevertheless, Gorz believed that some kind of re-defined socialism must be supported, as the only ideology which offered hope of something beyond capitalism. If liberalism and capitalism continue to occupy the high ground of the state, the continuing question for those on the left is what to do about it. Should the high ground be flattened, as anarchists recommend, or levelled and then reconstituted, as Marxists advocate? Or should the high ground merely be landscaped as social democrats seem to propose? This question is one of great theoretical and practical (i.e. tactical) interest to all socialists, but they have yet to find a satisfactory answer which commands agreement from all shades of opinion on the left.

FURTHER READING

R. Archer, *Economic Democracy*, Oxford U.P., 1995.
R. N. Berki, *Socialism*, Dent, 1975.
B. Crick, *Socialism*, Open University Press, 1987.
J. Dunn, *The Politics of Socialism*, Cambridge U.P., 1984.
G. Lichtheim, *A Short History of Socialism*, Fontana-Collins, 1975.
D. McLellan & S. Sayers (eds.), *Socialism and Democracy*, Macmillan, 1991.
R. Miliband, *Socialism for a Sceptical Age*, Polity Press, 1995.
B. Parekh (Ed.), *The Concept of Socialism*, Croom Helm, 1975.
C. Pierson, *Socialism after Communism*, Polity Press, 1995.
E. Shaw, *The Labour Party Since 1945*, Blackwell, 1997.
O. Sik (ed.), *Socialism Today*, Macmillan, 1991. This provides an East European perspective.
T. Wright, *Socialisms: Old and New*, Routledge, 1996.

---

43. R. Miliband, *Parliamentary Socialism*, Allen & Unwin, 1961.
44. A. Gorz, *Capitalism, Socialism, Ecology* (French edition, 1991), trans. C. Turner, Verso, 1994, p. vii.

_____ Chapter 6

Anarchism

Although I am a strong supporter of order, I am in the fullest sense of the term, an anarchist.

(*Michael Bakunin*)

He who says 'No' says 'Yes' by affirming values beyond the boundary.

(*Albert Camus*)

Anarchist doctrine has always been dogged by the vulgar interpretation of the word 'anarchism', which equates it with disorder and chaos, the fear of which plays a central role in Western political thought.[1] The word literally means the absence of authority, which expresses the central anarchist conviction that government is an absolute evil. It is no coincidence that anarchist theories originated after the triumph of secular and scientific thought in the Enlightenment, and were concurrent with the development of the modern state. And, although some, like Woodcock, have traced the ancestors of anarchism back to Muntzer and the anabaptists,[2] modern anarchism is transparently a political consequence of the *rejection* of Christianity. Both Proudhon and Bakunin equated the idea of God with that of authority:[3] from the notion of divine authority derived justifications of the oppressive domination of man over man, which is inimical to individual freedom and happiness. They concluded that once authority in all its forms had been abolished, in particular the legal-bureaucratic state, together with all the varieties of domination parasitic on economic inequalities, society could be re-fashioned on a new moral basis. Human nature, no longer degraded by subjection or corrupted by authority, could come to fruition. It must be understood that anarchists consider the state and society completely separable:

---

1. D. Hall, 'Irony and anarchy', in *Alternative Futures*, Vol. 2. No. 2. pp. 3–24.
2. G. Woodcock, *Anarchism*, Penguin, 1963, pp. 36–9.
3. M. Bakunin, 'Social and economic bases of anarchism', in *The Anarchists* (Ed.I. Horowitz), Dell, 1964, p. 133.

the former is an artificial, manipulative device, the latter a natural formation, so that the destruction of the state will not jeopardize society itself, nor civilization.

It is hard to generalize about anarchist thought because of the variety of doctrines to which the label has been attached, and the anarchists' congenital individualism, which makes them even less likely to agree than doctors. Broadly speaking, the nineteenth century produced a few anarchists who were emphatically individualistic, and a far greater number whose analysis of capitalism and the ideal society resembled that of socialism in many respects. The former group includes Godwin, Stirner, and Thoreau, while the latter encompasses Proudhon, Bakunin, Kropotkin, and Malatesta. While some twentieth-century thinkers have adapted the anarchist analysis to advanced industrial society, a lot of what passes for anarchism today is a crusade for escape from a society of total alienation, and for the salvation of the individual psyche. This chapter discusses the anarchist critique of capitalism, and then examines the form which an anarchist society might take; finally, it considers the ethics of violence, which some anarchists espoused as a means of political change. During the course of the argument, I hope to dispel three prevalent misconceptions about anarchism by showing that: (a) the anarchist is not just a nihilist who has no constructive ideas; (b) she is not merely a socialist who happens to dislike the state; and (c) she is not inevitably committed to terroristic violence, even though she may advocate it as the only way to social salvation.

Anarchist thinkers, like many socialists, feel moral indignation at the state of society; this is coupled with a perception of the individual as naturally 'good'—or at least, as not naturally bad. They then have to explain the paradox that, while people are good, society is bad. This leads to an analysis of the social evils which have turned some people into authoritarian monsters, others into mere subjects or slaves. Three major evils are identified: government, the law, and private property. The source of all these evils is seen to be the institution of authority.

THE CRITIQUE OF AUTHORITY

Whether it is embodied in the Church, the state or even in the schoolteacher, authority is seen as oppressive by anarchists since it brings about the suppression of the individual's beliefs or actions in deference to another and violates her freedom and equality. There is no good reason why one adult individual should exercise authority over another, even in her best interests, and power is generally used in the interests of whoever wields it. Wherever there is power, it is likely to be abused: the result is coercion and oppression. This is a practical observation *and* a theoretical axiom of anarchism. Unlike liberals, anarchists cannot accept the sufficiency of constitutional limits on the abuse of power, since constitutions and rights are established by the very institution against which they supposedly provide protection, and are therefore likely to prove illusory. Godwin called government 'regulated force', a definition curiously close to the sociologist Weber's 'neutral' definition of the state as having a monopoly of force. Bakunin perceived a categorical division between self-interested rulers and their oppressed subjects, and claimed that government is a permanent conspiracy against 'the drudge people'. The whole of world history could be analysed in terms of oppressors and oppressed. Bakunin's imprecise class analysis was disapproved of by his rival, Marx, but had considerable emotional appeal. Bakunin asserted, in effect, that authority is inimical to the very nature of mankind: even the ruling class does not *like* government, but needs the state for the purpose of exploiting, and thereby oppressing, the mass.

It follows that anarchists reject the conservative view that authority is sanctified, and its wisdom increased, by tradition. Likewise, they refute the liberal view of government as based on contract. They see the origins of society as a deception perpetrated by the rich or the strong against the poor or the weak: this makes government exploitative by definition. 'Conquest', wrote Bakunin, 'is also the basis of every state, . . . the organization guaranteeing the existence of this complex of historical iniquities (property, the Church, misery and ignorance)'.[4] Early anarchists attacked 'government' where modern anarchists might speak of 'the state', but their butt is essentially the same: the panoply of the modern state is a relatively recent outgrowth of government. Parallel with the attack on government is the attack on nationalism which is seen as a mode of territorial self-aggrandizement made inevitable by the predatory nature of governments. The nation is not a natural social unit and should be dismantled in favour of self-sufficient communities which, by definition, would have no territorial ambitions.[5] A contemporary critic might comment that this assertion seems to be flying in the face of nature, given the current strength and territorialism of nationalist movements.

The consequence of this condemnation of government is a repudiation of all political systems and political methods, a stance which differentiates anarchists from socialists and fosters the cliché that the anarchist is politically impotent, someone without a party. The anarchist's theoretical reasoning here is impeccably consistent: apart from the fact that politics is itself corrupting for individuals, if someone successfully campaigns for change by political means the result is that she herself ends up in power, and so the 'oppressors and oppressed' cycle recommences–a point often made about Lenin's revolution. Government and the state can only be abolished by non-political means, from the outside. (Of course, in the wider sense of 'political' current today, all actions with political intent are political, even though they may not be institutionally so.) This dictate of conscience led some anarchists into strategic backwaters, as they felt unable to join any form of organization and ended up in a state of apolitical paralysis. Proudhon, for example, refused leadership and support to the delegates of the International who called themselves Proudhonists. By contrast, Bakunin spent his life indefatigably organizing associations and meetings, with propagandistic and educative aims.

4. Bakunin, 'Social and economic bases of anarchism', pp. 142–4.
5. W. Godwin, *Enquiry Concerning Political Justice* (1793), (Ed. K. C. Carter), Oxford U.P., 1971, pp. 210–14. To be referred to as *Enquiry* hereafter.

The corollary of the attack on government is the rejection of *law* as the chief instrument of government. If government consists of a self-interested ruling class, its laws are inevitably biased in its favour. Anarchists from Godwin onwards accepted that the ultimate purpose of law was the protection of private property. The *form* of law, a class weapon, and its *content*, the protection of various class interests, are thus inseparable, and the whole legal system must therefore be abolished. Godwin refuted the theoretical basis of law and punishment, arguing that the law neither deters nor informs, as it purports to do, and that it inevitably denies justice by forcing particular acts into general categories of crime, inhumanely ignoring individual circumstances. The philosophical justifications of punishment are also fallacious because they are wrongly predicated on free will and responsibility. Since crime is socially determined, like all other actions, punishment is arbitrary and unjust: nor can it lead to individual or social improvement.[6] Although Godwin advanced his argument in the spirit of Enlightenment humanism, his logic reflected the new, 'scientific' social determinism too. A third reason for abolishing the legal system as an instrument of control, as both Godwin and Bakunin perceived, is that it abrogates the individual's rational moral judgement and so impairs her freedom: Bakunin defined freedom as following one's own reason and understanding justice.[7] Law is thus rejected by anarchists because it is a class weapon, it is based on a false conception of freewill, and it usurps individual reason and morality.

The anarchists perceived as clearly as the socialists the paradoxes of early capitalism: the co-existence of luxury and indigence, the fact that a diligent worker might nevertheless starve, and that he could not afford to buy what he produced. They too traced these evils to the institution of *private property*, alias capital accumulation, which enables the capitalist to exploit the worker. Proudhon's analysis of exploitation preceded that of Marx. He argued that the employer pays for individual workers' efforts, but pays nothing for the value of the collective effort of his workforce: it is this collective addition, created by the division of labour, that constitutes his surplus.[8] Accumulated capital should therefore be shared by all, Proudhon concluded, as nobody could claim exclusive ownership. Bakunin argued that *conquest* was the sole basis of the 'rights' of property and inheritance which permitted and legitimized the exploitation of the masses for the benefit of the few, and kept them in misery and ignorance.[9] For Kropotkin, the state, surplus value and wage labour constituted an invidious nexus which had to be totally destroyed. The adherence of most anarchists to a system of payment based on labour shows that their analysis of labour as the source of all value was close to that of Marx. Their conclusion was the same: expropriate the owners of capital.

---

6. Godwin, *Enquiry*, pp. 244–77. See also B. Goodwin, *Social Science and Utopia*, Harvester, 1978, pp. 93–110.
7. Bakunin, 'Social and economic bases of anarchism', p. 137.
8. P.-J. Proudhon, *Selected Writings* (trans. E. Fraser), Macmillan, 1970, pp. 42–7.
9. Bakunin, 'Social and economic bases of anarchism', p. 143.

The relation of the anarchists to Marx and other socialists in the International was complex and turbulent.[10] Bakunin's theoretical and tactical disagreements with Marx ended by splitting the movement. The struggle for the International was fundamentally one of libertarian versus authoritarian socialism. The anarchists, with their plurality of views, opposed the dogmatism of the Marxists; they were also against the capture and use of the state as advocated by the German SPD. The anarchists had a less rigid notion of class than Marx or Lenin and did not believe in the inevitability of class war—an idea which Proudhon considered merely wasteful. Bakunin's inclusion of the peasantry and lumpenproletariat in the revolutionary class antagonized Marx. To anarchists, the dictatorship of the proletariat signified the substitution of a new class of oppressors. As Sorel said, proletarian dictatorship merely meant a change of masters.[11] Furthermore, anarchists rightly doubted the state's capacity to 'wither away'.

So, while agreeing on the necessity for the revolution and the destruction of all capitalist institutions, anarchists disagreed with Marxists over the tactics by which this should be achieved, condemning the use of unions and political parties, and over what form the revolution would take. With regard to the organization of socialist society, the anarchists were deeply suspicious of Marx's proposed large-scale collectivism, fearing (again correctly) the emergence of what we now brand as state capitalism, and of nationalism. In their turn, the Marxists considered the anarchists romantic, anti-scientific and impractical, and condemned their dream of federations of small communities as obsolete. Evidently, the Marxists had the best of the argument, although anarchists might draw consolation from having been right.

While defining itself as distinct from socialism and opposed to liberalism, anarchism shares characteristics with both. The dislike of the state and love of individual liberty is also found in the works of liberals such as Mill. But there is a crucial difference: liberals accept the necessity of a state to act as arbiter between individuals, though they prefer it to be minimal, and deny the class nature of the state; they also believe that the state can protect the people against itself, by means of civil rights. The liberal gives an account of freedom in terms of unlimited choice (usually expressed in money terms) and analyses freedom abstractly, as if the individual acted in a vacuum. The anarchist defines freedom through an account of the individual's place in society; likewise, individualism is modified by the social context and in no way resembles the bourgeois 'egoism' which Marx decried, except in the doctrine of Stirner, who was in some ways a liberal extremist, rather than an anarchist. The resemblance of the two ideologies is therefore superficial at most. The tension between individual freedom and social needs is the focus of both theories, but in anarchism it is solved via a whole-hearted acknowledgement of the centrality of society to the being of each individual. While the liberal safeguards individual freedom with laws and rights,

10. These disputes are charted in Woodcock, *Anarchism*, Chap. 9.
11. G. Sorel, *Reflections on Violence* (trans. T. E. Hulme and J. Roth), Collier, 1961.

the anarchist solution rests on a faith in the natural unity of the individual's interests with those of her fellows, in the ideal society.

THE ANARCHIST ORDER

Contrary to the popular opinion that the anarchist's ideas go no further than destruction, and that she is committed to 'the permanence of a revolutionary state of flux and to the impermanence of all social order',[12] a clear account can be given of the principles on which anarchist society would be based, although the details remain hazy. Anarchist society would be a 'natural', stateless entity based on morality, reason, and unmediated relationships between human beings, free from contamination or distortion by the state, exploitation, and commerce. Despite the abolition of government and law, anarchist society is not a state of disorder or licence; order is produced by the internalization of moral values and norms, brought about by the development of the individual's moral faculty, and her reason. Self-control replaces control from above. Some anarchists hoped that social good behaviour could become completely instinctive and spontaneous.

Anarchism would be organized on the basis of small communities bound together in a loose federation, a social form which avoids the centralization and nationalism so hated by anarchists, and removes the necessity for any vestige of state authority. The proposed nature of the communities varies: Godwin's craft-based 'parishes' and Proudhon's peasant villages might well be self-sufficient, whereas the Russian 'anarcho-communists' envisaged the federated communities as productive units in an economy built on the specialization of functions, so that interdependence would be inevitable. The federal power (if any) would in all cases be kept to a minimum, strictly under the control of the community delegates. Some anarchists wish to eliminate industrial and urban life entirely: from Tolstoy to the advocates of alternative technology, they constitute the 'back to nature' strain of anarchism. But Kropotkin and others who accepted the irreversibility of industrialization also dreamed of re-integrating rural and urban life: Kropotkin's ideal model was the small communities of watchmakers in the Swiss Jura.

THE MORAL BASIS OF ANARCHIST SOCIETY

The real interest of anarchism lies not in the precise details of communal organization, but in the universal principles on which such communities would be based. The claim that society could be governed by morality alone rests on an optimistic view of the human capacity for sociable behaviour which contrasts vividly with the orthodox view of human beings as creatures whose sinfulness or rampant egoism necessitates authoritative government. We cannot understand the moral optimism of anarchism without some appreciation of certain Enlightenment ideas which also influenced the development of socialist thought. Both

---

12. Horowitz, 'Postscript' in *The Anarchists*, p. 590.

ideologies held it to be axiomatic that human nature and behaviour are determined by the social environment, a theory known as 'environmentalism'. In Bakunin's words,

> man is a social animal . . . he does not create society by means of a free agreement . . . society shapes and determines his human essence, man is dependent upon it as completely as upon physical nature . . . social solidarity is the first human law; freedom is the second law.[13]

It follows that by changing the circumstances you can change individuals for the better: here is the rationale for radical social and political reform. Several consequences for the conception of human nature follow from such determinism. First, egalitarianism becomes a factual premise, rather than a moral claim. Equally blank or malleable people are necessarily equal, and so have equal rights and duties.

Second, environmentalism (social determinism) opens the way for an optimistic account of human nature. Godwin deduced the possibility of human perfectibility from his environmentalist premise, and hoped for limitless progress. However, social determinism led most anarchists to adopt Rousseau's more modest supposition that natural man is essentially innocent, knowing neither virtue nor vice. Bakunin wrote that

> From his birth not a single human being is either bad or good . . . 'good', that is, the love of freedom, the consciousness of justice and solidarity, the cult of or rather the respect for truth, reason and labour can be developed in men only through upbringing and education.[14]

Hence, for the anarchist we all start out as blank sheets, innocent and morally neutral. By contrast with Christian or Hobbesian doctrines of man's evil nature, this innocence has a positive moral quality about it, being in effect an assertion of our *potential goodness*, and contradicting the dogma of original sin. In addition to innocence, the anarchists imputed various other qualities to mankind which were tantamount to the assertion that human goodness would be attained in the right social context. The anarchist's second major ethical premise is that we are all naturally sociable—parallel to Rousseau's assumption that we have natural compassion.

Such sweeping premises about the goodness of human nature inevitably raise the question, 'How did society reach such a deplorable state?', which cannot be satisfactorily answered on the basis of the anarchist's own assumptions. If people are potentially sociable and compassionate, how do we explain the eternal division into oppressors and oppressed?[15] If people are only corrupted by institutions, how do we explain the origin of evil institutions? Bakunin's suggestion that human misery is caused by a lack of hygiene and rational upbringing, by inequalities and ignorance, fails to explain how *these* arise. In fact,

---

13. Bakunin, 'Social and economic bases of anarchism', p. 135.
14. Bakunin, 'Social and economic bases of anarchism', p. 141.
15. This point is made in connection with the modern anarchist, Paul Goodman, in T. Roszak, *The Makings of a Counter Culture*, Faber, 1971, p. 195.

the major function of the premise of natural sociability and goodness in anarchist thinking is to refute Hobbesian or pessimistic accounts of human nature. Most anarchists would prefer to gloss over the contradictions which result from maintaining that human beings are good while society is bad.

Like most post-Enlightenment atheists, the early anarchists looked to 'Nature' as the source of moral values and other norms. Proudhon argued that social science has laws as natural and inexorable as those of physics: that societies are based on natural groups: that property (in the sense of *collective ownership*) and the division of labour are both natural, and that capitalist property is 'impossible', against nature. Society is created by the spontaneous development of man's nature. He also saw *rightness* as lying in an 'organic equilibrium' of which truth, beauty, and justice are manifestations. While Proudhon blandly asserts such analogies between nature and society without further justification, Kropotkin's *Mutual Aid* (1897) details the parallels between society and the animal world, which he had studied scientifically. He used evidence of co-operation between animals to attack Darwin's theory of 'the survival of the fittest' and to demonstrate that small communities were the natural form for human society, thus damning national boundaries and the centralized state as being *against Nature*. Bakunin maintained that whereas obedience to human authority was unacceptable, 'obedience' to natural social and economic laws constitutes freedom. Tolstoy displayed an instinctive 'naturalism' similar to Rousseau's when he extolled country life and decried the unnatural corruption of town and city. Even in the present century, Goodman has used 'natural society' as a measuring stick, while Read claimed that only anarchist society was 'natural'.

The appeal to Nature for the validation of political beliefs is open to many objections. Anarchists hold that there is a 'natural' form of society distinct from contemporary society which is 'unnatural': to prove the point, they cite primitive communities or animal groups as essentially natural. But in this realm of hypothesis, pre-history or natural history, it is anyone's guess what is the most natural form of society. Nature's book is open to too many readings. And the distinction which is drawn between the natural and the artificial will not stand up to scrutiny. (The most 'natural' human state might be that of the pre-linguistic, cave-dwelling hunter, but no anarchists propose reversion to that condition; they are no more primitivist than Rousseau. They wish to discard only those aspects of civilization which they choose to regard as unnatural.) A parallel problem of defining 'the natural' arises when freedom is equated with obedience to natural laws. Who identifies these? Who decides whether monogamy is more natural than polygamy, or vice versa? Natural laws are not self-evident, contrary to Bakunin's belief, nor is the form which a 'natural society' should take. At most, so-called natural laws reflect their discoverer's perception of human nature. Then again, it is not certain that if such natural principles could be unearthed they would necessarily promote happy and harmonious living among irreversibly *civilized* men and women. Similar objections can be made against the concept of 'authenticity' invoked by Goodman and other modern anarchists, which rests on an untenable distinction between man's 'authentic' essence and subsequent artifice, between Nature and nurture. Certainly, some of the anarchists' judgements based on the appeal to Nature seem intuitively right: small communities *are* preferable to large conurbations, but surely this is because of their manifest advantages, not their 'naturalness'. Evidently, the vindication of anarchist principles by the appeal to nature is challengeable in many respects. However, this does not impugn other anarchist values, or contradict the idea of society based on morality, for these ideas can be justified without any such appeal.

FREEDOM WITHIN SOCIETY

Anarchism's supreme political ideal is individual freedom: supporting ideals are equality, co-operation, and solidarity. Freedom is specified by contrast with authority. For Bakunin, the term denotes both freedom from oppression by the external world, attained via knowledge, and freedom to act in conformity with one's own judgements. Furthermore, individual freedom has a social dimension.

> Thus, too, *the freedom of all is essential to my freedom*. And it follows that it would be fallacious to maintain that the freedom of all constitutes a limitation upon my freedom for that would be tantamount to the denial of such freedom. On the contrary, universal freedom represents the necessary affirmation and the boundless expansion of individual freedom.[16]

For this reason, Bakunin says, even the master is in fact a slave in an oppressive society. The arch-egoist Stirner likewise maintained that to rule others destroys one's own independence. These views reflect Kantian morality (which enjoins us to treat everyone as an end in him/herself, and not as a means) and Hegel's insight that satisfaction is only afforded through recognition by one's equals. Thus, anarchists conclude that the abolition of authority will be as beneficial for the oppressors as for the oppressed.

Is individual freedom really connected analytically with the freedom of all? Given a certain conceptualization of the wide network of causal links operating in society, this could be shown to be theoretically true. However, in reality, many societies based on inequality and oppression seem to accord a remarkable degree of freedom to the elite. To equate personal freedom with freedom for all, therefore, either we must make it part of the definition that one cannot feel or be truly free while others are oppressed—and this is the upshot of the arguments of Hegel, Bakunin and others—or else we could use a philosophical argument like Hart's, that the very idea of freedom contains the notion of equality of freedom. He shows that a natural right to be free would entail a right to *equal* freedom.[17]

But the liberal's analytic argument for equal freedom contrasts with that of the anarchist because it rests on the premise of free will (Hart says 'the right is one which all men have if they are capable of choice'), which conflicts with the supposition of most anarchists that we are socially determined beings. Partial determinism is compatible with partial free will, of course, and this is the position

16. Bakunin, 'Social and economic bases of anarchism', pp. 136–7. Emphasis added.
17. H. L. A. Hart, 'Are there any natural rights?', in *Political Philosophy* (Ed. A. Quinton), p. 53.

that many thinkers today would accept, but Bakunin goes much further, demanding the negation of free will itself.

> [S]ince every human individual is but an involuntary product of natural and social environment . . .[t]he negation of freewill does not connote the negation of freedom. On the contrary, freedom represents the corollary, the direct result of natural and social necessity.[18]

Godwin undermined free will with philosophical arguments, showing that any action not fully determined by motives would not be free, but merely capricious. The freedom he most valued, private judgement, would in fact be freedom to operate in accordance with the dictates of reason.[19] By attacking free will in various ways, anarchists differentiated their idea of freedom from that of liberals, for whom free, abstract man performed his acts of choice in a vacuum created by theory. Anarchists advocate freedom, then, without subscribing to philosophical or religious notions of free will: it is *freedom from* the coercion and oppression typical of the modern state, and *from* inequalities and scarcity, and *freedom to* follow natural laws. In other words, it aims at the rectification of our present state. And in freeing one individual by abolishing oppressive institutions, the anarchist would necessarily free *all* individuals.

Freedom for one in this (negative) sense can thus be equated with freedom for all, but would the realization of more positive forms of individual freedom be limited in reality by the strongly collective nature of anarchist society? There seems to be a paradox here, and we must turn for a solution to the anarchist conception of the nature of society. Rousseau—who influenced many early anarchists—stipulated that in the creation of an ideal society man would surrender his natural freedom in exchange for a new moral persona, capable of far greater satisfaction and enrichment. Proudhon echoed this, arguing that the free individual is also an integral part of the collective existence and carries in himself a 'social' morality which serves the collectivity. Two hypotheses about social morality are possible. Either we could suppose that morality is the creation of society and hence necessarily social, or else that an instinctive altruism is to be found even in pre-social beings, which comes to fruition in the ideal society. These views are not, of course, incompatible and either would support the anarchist view of society as a collective moral entity greater than its individual parts.

From asserting the social nature of human beings and of morality, which is created by society and binds it together, it is a short step to deducing the necessarily integrated and coherent nature of society and the importance of solidarity. However, the anarchists' appeal to social solidarity often seems mystificatory. We can perhaps understand how solidarity might be manifested in the workplace, a limited context, but not how solidarity could exist in the community at large, where its scope and application would be unspecifiable and unlimited. Is there really any substantive content in Read's dictum, that 'subjective harmony would be reflected in personal integrity and social unity'?

---

18. Bakunin, 'Social and economic bases of anarchism', p. 134.
19. Godwin, *Enquiry*, Bk IV, Chap. 7.

Or are the ideas of solidarity, integration, and unity vague hopes which turn out to be analytically vacuous?

Whatever the answer, the anarchist still has to explain how the strong social integration that she wants, which would presumably require conformity and sacrifices of individual self-interest on behalf of the whole, can be made compatible with extensive individual freedom. Various solutions are offered. Godwin and Bakunin both define freedom primarily in terms of reason or opinion, rather than as the pursuit of interests.

> To be personally free means for every man living in a social milieu not to surrender his thought or will to any authority but his own reason and his own understanding of justice . . . not to submit to any other law but the one arrived at by his own conscience.[20]

For Godwin, 'private judgement' (reason) is the essence of freedom, but reason entails giving justifications for one's actions which will be publicly assessed and accepted as valid. Hence, there is already a social element built into private judgement. Since society makes people free and rational beings, the exercise of the individual's rational judgement should not run counter to society's interests—not, at least, in the anarchist utopia, where pure reason rules. Thus, when freedom is severed from self-interest and transformed into a quality of mind, the collective nature of freedom and the necessary connection between individual freedom and social unity, can be posited. Another possibility is to define freedom, as Bakunin sometimes does, as obedience to natural laws, which would favour society as a whole—but this sounds suspiciously like being free to do what we ought to want to do, and to the liberal way of thinking at least, freedom should include the chance to be bad, and to make mistakes. This is where the anarchists make an act of faith: they believe that a society could be created which was so harmonious and benign that everyone would freely wish to do what was good for society as a whole, and thereby for themselves.

ORDER WITHOUT DEPENDENCE

For a further understanding of the individual's relationship with her fellows in anarchist society, we must examine the concept of *dependence*. 'Dependence' may denote a loving, caring relationship, such as that of mother and child, but in anarchist argument it signifies dependence upon another's arbitrary whims or commands, a relation of inequality. The anarchists were strongly influenced in their condemnation of dependence by Rousseau. Analysing the origins of inequality, he asked 'What ties of dependence would there be among men without possession?' As property develops, so do inequalities and dependence, whose origins lie in both need and in power-seeking greed. Man becomes an extended being in the worst sense—'social man . . . only knows how to live in the opinion of others'—and so is corrupted. Paradoxically, though, dependence is also the only road to self-fulfilment since moral being presupposes society and society

_____
20. Bakunin, 'Social and economic bases of anarchism', p. 136.

presupposes interdependence. For Rousseau, dependence comes about because civilized man, unlike the savage, is not self-sufficient: the power of man over man is always degrading, because it detracts from his human essence, his free choice, and his natural independence. Rousseau therefore proposed in the *Social Contract* to substitute the law for the personal domination of powerful individuals, and proposed the General Will as a means whereby each should depend on all. However, some critics interpret this as requiring the complete subjugation of the individual to the whole.[21]

The nineteenth-century anarchists concurred with Rousseau on the corrupting influence of dependence and of man's authority over man, being witnesses to archaic feudal relationships in Russia, the domination of employer over employee in Europe, and the domination of oppressive governments everywhere. Dependence in social life and economic production they accepted as *natural*, but the dependence created by authority was not so, and ran counter to the proper equality of mankind. The dependence of one man on another because of his power was a degradation of his nature. Godwin's dislike of it led him to reject all forms of co-operation, even that of musicians playing in orchestras. Bakunin deplored the 'incessant mutual dependence' of individuals and of the masses, and demanded independence from the despotic acts of men. Such strictures are quite compatible with many anarchists' acceptance of our natural interdependence as social animals, which would form the basis of anarchist society. It was the elements of personal, irresponsible power, inequality, and coercion which made the prevalent forms of dependence so obnoxious. Like the utopian socialists, the anarchists proposed that *each* should depend on *all*. Such reciprocal dependence would not degrade human nature. How, then, would such a society, which eschewed political dependence and authority, function?

Rousseau's solution to the organizational problem by the impartial, truth-embodying General Will was not satisfactory for anarchists, since it would entail the perpetuation of the state. But since they accepted that order must somehow be maintained, other solutions had to be sought. Bakunin recommended obedience to natural laws, and independence from the commands of men, whether individual or collective. This typifies the anarchist idea of a self-regulating society in which individuals 'spontaneously' obey unwritten, unenforced laws through instinct, reason, morality or a combination of all three. Self-control is the watchword. Proudhon defined anarchy as the government of each by himself; order would be enforced by public and private consciousness. Godwin proposes that order should be maintained by self-control but also by mutual moral surveillance—he even argues that each man should appoint himself the moral inquisitor of his neighbour![22]

At this point, it becomes clear that *absolute* freedom is as much a chimera for the anarchist as for the liberal, even when the worst forms of dependence are abolished. Whether I am controlled by my neighbour's disapproval or my

---

21. For Rousseau's comments on dependence see his *Discourse . . . On Inequality*, Dent, 1913, pp. 189, 208.
22. Godwin, *Enquiry*, Vol.I, 1st edn, Dublin, 1793, pp. 106–7.

internalized moral precepts and conscience, I am not perfectly free: self-government by guilt and conscience may be more oppressive than government by law. My neighbour's interventions may not always be rational and benign, and even if I govern myself entirely, according to morality, someone else still has to inculcate the moral code, which suggests a relationship of domination. In any case, such self-control would only leave me free to do what I should do. These difficulties explain why anarchists tried to fuse the moral and rational with the *instinctual* and to prove that obedience to natural laws would be spontaneous, free of *any* control or restraint since morality itself is *natural*. But this idea of a spontaneous morality constitutes another dubious appeal to nature.

An alternative way of creating order without dependence and domination was advocated by Proudhon—contractualism, or 'mutualism'. *Free* association is not oppressive, he argued, and can be achieved by a multiplicity of contracts governing all social action. The idea of a fair contract, also the linchpin of liberal thought and practice, presupposes equality and good faith between the parties, a paradigm which capitalism belies; capitalist contracts, therefore, produce dependence and injustice rather than mutual benefit for equal contractors. The contracts which Proudhon envisaged would be made after the abolition or equalization of property, and so would be fair. Economic organization would be based on contractual exchange operating through a voucher system which would reflect the value of labour in each product; Proudhon's People's Bank, which never came to fruition, was meant to establish just such a system. As to political organization, he condemned all 'existing' social contracts as unfair, taking more freedom from the citizen than he kept, and he proposed to substitute contracts between citizen, commune, and federal authority which would reserve the majority of powers to the individual: his rights would only be restricted so as to avoid encroaching on the rights of others in the commune. What Proudhon had in mind was, clearly a series of explicit contracts, not the hypothetical social contract by which liberals justified state authority.[23]

Two major criticisms can be made of contractualism. First, it is doubtful that such contracts would be observed in the absence of law or authority: such reasoning led Hobbes to deduce the necessity of a sovereign. Proudhon might reply that in a situation of freedom and equality contracts will be made only when they are so beneficial that the parties are motivated to keep them. But circumstances, and people's wants and needs, change: a beneficial contract made today may be deleterious in a year's time. This leads to the second criticism, which Godwin made long before Proudhon was writing: permanent contracts infringe our liberty.[24] Godwin attacked marriage and similar institutions for this reason. If an anarchist holds that being bound to keep a promise she has voluntarily made infringes her liberty then, logically, she should never make promises: yet contractualism is an important element in some anarchist theory. Can the anarchist who wants to maximize individual freedom consistently hold that people are bound by contracts and promises? According to some accounts of

23. Proudhon, *Selected Writings*, pp. 56–70.
24. Godwin, *Enquiry*, pp. 102–11.

self-identity—for example, Godwin's, where the individual is viewed as an ever-changing entity—a promise freely made by Self 1 at Time 1 would intolerably restrict the freedom of Self 2 at Time 2. But if the Self is instead regarded as a persisting, rational entity, it would be irrational and immoral for it to repudiate promises and contracts unless external conditions had changed dramatically. The extreme position which Godwin advocates, if followed to the letter, would destroy the possibility of society or self-fulfilment since most of the activities which make life worth living rest on explicit or implicit contracts or promises—making friends, joining a club, marrying, and so on. Without such promises, or if they were made but constantly repudiated, life would be chaotic and pointless. The anarchist who rejects all contractual notions is bereft of a constructive basis for society.

ANARCHIST INDIVIDUALISM

The goal of anarchism is to eliminate dependence and oppression. The abolition of authority will bring about freedom which in turn will promote individual happiness. Anarchism, like liberalism, focuses on the individual: how, then, do their concepts differ? First, most anarchists accept the essentially social nature of mankind and would dismiss as unrealistic the abstract individuals who populate orthodox liberal thought—for example, 'rational economic man', whose maximized profits are attributed entirely to his own efforts, rather than to the social network which facilitates his enterprise. Their criticism of liberal individualism parallels Marx's attack on bourgeois rights. Proudhon and Kropotkin both divined that, since capitalism depended on co-operative labour, the liberals' declaration of extreme individualism was false. Kropotkin also condemned the 'narrow-minded' individualism which remains after the absorption of so many previously individual functions by the state, a condition exacerbated by the modern welfare state. Nevertheless, capitalism was a necessary precondition for the development of anarchist ideas of individualism. indeed, Read argued that individualism is only possible in a complex society with an elaborate division of labour.[25] Anarchists conceive of individualism as self-fulfilment within society, not as the withdrawal and self-differentiation which liberals emphasize and which ultimately rests on wealth. While anarchists, like liberals, locate the ultimate value in the individual, they re-define satisfaction in non-economic, non-utilitarian terms and their conception of freedom highlights the inseparability of the individual–society amalgam. Society is analogous to a multiple equation in which each interconnecting variable (each individual's freedom and potential) is to be maximized at a level consistent with equal maximization of all the other variables.

Individual fulfilment is achieved through *creative work*. Godwin's ideal of leisurely craftsmanship is echoed in many other anarchist accounts of work. Proudhon said that 'social communion and human solidarity' are the products of ideal labour. Properly organized work would surpass leisure pursuits in the

25. H. Read, 'The philosophy of anarchism', in *Anarchy and Order*, Faber & Faber, 1954.

pleasure it provided. He considered the division of labour a natural, permanent phenomenon which makes each individual equally useful to society. For Kropotkin it was axiomatic that 'everyone should be pleased with his work' and he, like William Morris, cited the construction of mediaeval cathedrals as examples of co-operative, spiritually uplifting labour. Bakunin was less idealistic: work was, simply, the source of all value and utility, and men must work to live. He also suggested that those unwilling to work should be deprived of political rights for shirking their duties to the community, and left to starve:[26] a severe pronouncement (possibly addressed to future ex-capitalists), but one not altogether antithetical to anarchist ethics. Love for the individual does not entail sympathy for the 'free-rider'. For the more socialistic anarchists, work was the all-important source of social value, individual satisfaction, and moral virtue. They probably underestimated the alienating nature of industrial work: whether satisfying work is possible in the industrial context is a question which neither Bakunin nor Marx debated at sufficient length, since they predicated work satisfaction upon the ending of exploitation.

Godwin and Thoreau sought to reduce labour to a minimum, so as to maximize the time available for intellectual pursuits. Despite his admiration for craftsmanship, Godwin prophesied that machinery would reduce necessary labour time to half-an-hour a day, while Thoreau praised 'fruitful idleness', a concept which seems to presuppose the backdrop of an industrious society which nurtures the fruitfully idle.[27] Admittedly, both were prepared to settle for a more ascetic form of life in exchange for greater leisure, but neither had much understanding of the irreversibility of industrialization. However, many contemporary anarchists would find themselves more in accord with these two than with the anarchists who imagined that industrial work would continue, in an idealized form.

Co-operation, of which capitalist production offers a sad travesty, was to be the basis of anarchist society. This could take various forms. 'Natural' co-operation, seen in the lives of animals, was instanced in the family, an institution which many anarchists upheld, unlike the early socialists, perhaps for the reason invoked by modern pluralists, that it constitutes a defence against the potentially authoritarian state. 'Social' or 'artificial' co-operation is exemplified in the division of labour. Proudhon's contractualism formalizes co-operation between individuals and groups, while other anarchists hoped for spontaneous co-operation based on the moral sense which would pervade all social activity. Obviously, all forms of human life rest on some degree of co-operation, whether conscious, unwilling or unwitting. But the anarchists were not merely stating this as a truism, for they asserted the principle of co-operation against the prevalent ideology of competition which Social Darwinism had reinforced.

Can the co-operative organization of society be reconciled with the anarchist preoccupation with independence and freedom? Not for Godwin, who considered it a violation of individuality. But if the individual is viewed as a being-in-society, and the essentially co-operative nature of society acknowledged, the two can be

26. Bakunin, 'Social and economic bases of anarchism', pp. 137, 141–2.
27. H. D. Thoreau, *Walden* (Ed. J. Krutch), Bantam, 1962.

reconciled, at least in theory. Co-operation is a quasi-moral concept which reconciles altruism and egoism by asserting that the individual enhances her own good by promoting the good of all.

ANARCHIST VALUES

Social justice results necessarily from organizing society on anarchist principles. Most anarchists advocate the abolition of property and inheritance, and egalitarian policies, but there is no general agreement among them on the form which the new distribution should take. Proudhon favoured the personal ownership of land and tools by peasants to safeguard their independence. The Russians, influenced by socialist doctrines, advocated collective ownership of the means of production by each 'productive unit': Kropotkin envisaged these as communities, Bakunin as industrial associations. But by contrast, the maverick Stirner asserted 'What man can obtain belongs to him: the world belongs to *me*. Neither God nor Man ('human society') is proprietor, but the individual'.[28] Few anarchists would have agreed with this solipsistic view of social justice.

The idealization of equality is a necessary consequence of the anarchist view of human nature. Equality is implicit in all propositions about the abolition of authority and property: it is also a precondition of co-operation, which cannot succeed among unequals. Various definitions of equality were proposed to serve as the basis of social justice. For Godwin, justice is the distribution of goods to those who can best benefit from them (equality of satisfaction). Proudhon advocates equality of conditions (equality of opportunity) but not of wellbeing, which is the worker's own responsibility. He also says that anarchy is 'an order where all *relationships* are of equality'. Bakunin espouses distributive justice according to 'deeds', or work, measured in labour time (equality of treatment), whereas Kropotkin, true to the principles of mutual aid, and doubting that anyone would shirk the joys of creative work, proposes distribution according to need (equality of satisfaction). Anarchists tend to ignore the haunting problem of scarce 'positional' goods, which cannot be distributed on an egalitarian basis, and also that of natural inequalities. But it could be argued that most positional goods would disappear altogether—for example, power and prestige—as would the desire for such things. Godwin predicted that the desire for distinction would disappear along with property. If such hopes fail, maybe an authoritative allocation would still be needed, and this could undermine the basis of anarchist society. Or perhaps a non-authoritarian principle of distribution of scarce goods could be agreed, such as a lottery or a rotation system, to preserve the essentially egalitarian nature of anarchist justice.

An important instrumental value in anarchist society is *education*. Enlightenment philosophers such as Condorcet had remarked that the ignorance of the masses made them prey to exploiters and charlatans, a theme taken up by the anarchists, some of whom, like Godwin, advocated education for its spiritually

---

28. M. Stirner, 'The ego and his own', in Horowitz, *The Anarchists*, p. 311.

elevating effect while others, like Proudhon and Bakunin, saw it as an instrument of liberation, since the strength of authority decreases as the level of education increases. The ideal was a 'polytechnical' education: a balanced training in science, the arts, and professional studies. The need for education follows from the view that man is a *tabula rasa*: education can transform him. In the anarchist scheme of things, it has three distinct functions: first, to increase the understanding of workers so that they are able to throw off the yoke of authority and, second, to re-educate those brought up under the old system. The third, continuing, function would be as a device for maintaining order: the process of reasoning would be taught in school, as would the moral principles which formed the basis of the anarchist order. Education is a recurrent theme in modern radical and anarchist thought, with writers such as Illich and Frire rejecting the structures of authority built into education systems and recommending forms of education which emphasize *learning* rather than *teaching*.[29] The belief in education as a pure tool of enlightenment is redolent of the anarchist's basic optimism about human nature.

CONTEMPORARY ANARCHISM

Although many anarchists today still subscribe to the values of Bakunin and Kropotkin, there are two new, divergent currents of anarchist thinking. One is *anarcho-capitalism*, a form of libertarian anarchism which demands that the state should be abolished and that private individuals and firms should control all social and economic affairs. Anarcho-capitalist theory flourished in the 1970s with thinkers such as Murray Rothbard and David Friedman arguing that all the state's functions for which there is a genuine demand (i.e. demand backed by cash) could be assumed by private entrepreneurs, including policing and defence functions, while social evils like pollution could be controlled by charging the pollutors for their activities; a similar case is made by Ayn Rand.[30] Nozick's notion of the minimal-state utopia differs only in detail rather than in principle from such schemes but is more philosophically argued. To support the minimal state thesis, he develops an entitlement theory of justice based on ownership (discussed in Chapter 16) and argues that individual rights should be inviolable. The absolute right to private property, viewed as the mainstay of human liberty, lies at the heart of these pleas for unrestrained capitalism. In *Defending the Undefendable*, Block writes in similar vein, demanding that activities such as drug-pushing and prostitution should be decriminalized, since they represent voluntary transactions in which the state has no right to intervene.[31]

Block's argument highlights the weak point of anarcho-capitalist theory: how can a transaction between a desperate addict and a drug-dealer be seen as a

29. See I. Illich, *Deschooling Society*, Penguin, 1973, and N. Postman and C. Weingartner, *Teaching as a Subversive Activity*, Penguin, 1971.
30. M. Rothbard, *For a New Liberty: The Libertarian Manifesto*, 3rd edn, Libertarian Rev. Foundation, 1985; D. Friedman, *The Machinery of Freedom*, 2nd edn, Open Court, 1989; Rand's works include titles such as *The Virtue of Selfishness* and *Philosophy: Who Needs It?*
31. W. Block, *Defending the Undefendable*, Fleet Press, 1976.

perfectly fair, voluntary 'contract'? These thinkers ignore the many inequalities which *laissez-faire* would reinforce and magnify, and turn a blind eye to the human misery which would result—presumably taking anarchism to be based on the axiom 'I am not my brother's keeper', which almost every earlier anarchist, except Stirner, would have repudiated. They do not inquire into the socially produced injustices of contemporary capitalist society, or indicate any intention to remedy these at the start of their liberationist utopia. They are prepared to sacrifice the many collective goods which enrich our lives (e.g. parks, roads, hospitals) unless these can be financed privately. While condemning absolutely state coercion, they tacitly condone the economic and interpersonal coercion which would prevail in a totally *laissez-faire* society. Most anarchists share the egalitarian ideal with socialists: anarcho-capitalists abhor equality and socialism equally. Their true place is in the group of right-wing libertarians described in Chapter 3.

The other new strain of anarchism is that proposed by thinkers influenced by the radical movements of the 1960s and early 1970s. Anarchism was reformulated in the era of student revolt, hippy and other life-experiments and general 'permissiveness'. Those nurtured on a countercultural diet of Marcuse, Timothy Leary (*The Politics of Ecstasy*, 1968) and their epigones perceived the anarchist ideal largely in terms of personal, spiritual liberation or escape—an aspiration which can hardly form the basis of a *social* theory. The psychological focus of such theories is alienation, while the social focus is the critique of consumer capitalism. Authority is seen as a vicious Hydra, whose heads appear everywhere: individual salvation is the best hope. For some, the anarchist impulse was transformed into self-centred spiritual preoccupation, which offered inner freedom: hence, the popularity of contemplative religions and the regular pilgrimages to India and Tibet. Others sought release through hallucinogenic drugs. Many people of the same generation opted for life in communes of like-minded people, practising self-sufficiency wherever possible. All these choices were inspired by the conviction that the best that could be done was to set a *cordon sanitaire* between oneself and the corruption of advanced capitalist society.

Many who call themselves anarchists today preserve some of the older doctrines, however: a resistance to Marxist-Leninist authoritarianism and a continuing refusal to organize politically, which has caused contemporary anarchists to prefer spontaneous action and 'situationism' to concerted activity. This preference was evident in the student uprisings of 1968 in France and the USA, which were largely anarchist in spirit and with which many of the libertarian left associated themselves. In essays published in the journal *Anarchos* during the late 1960s, Murray Bookchin argued that spontaneous action was part of a wider belief in spontaneous development. Like Tolstoy, who emphasized living in harmony with nature, Bookchin asserted that

> Spontaneity, far from inviting chaos, involves releasing the inner forces of a development to find their authentic order and stability . . . The ecological principles that shaped organic societies re-emerge in the form of social principles to shape utopia.[32]

32. M. Bookchin, *Post-Scarcity Anarchism*, Wildwood House, 1974, p. 21.

Bookchin combined exhortation to popular revolution and support for anarcho-communism with the characteristic critique of orthodox Marxism. His prescient warnings about ecological disaster and speculations about small-scale production and alternative technology made him one of the earliest eco-anarchists.

The tactics of modern anarchism have ranged from sporadic acts of violence (as practised by the Baader–Meinhof group in Germany, for example), through hopeless, heroic conflict with armed police and troops, and 'class war' demonstrations in rich residential areas, to the peaceful symbolism of putting flowers in the barrels of guns and on the security fences surrounding nuclear bases. The plurality of approaches and aims among twentieth-century 'anarchists' makes it hard to codify their thought. Nevertheless, they offer important critiques of contemporary society: Marcuse's *Essay on Liberation*, dealing with the 'false needs' implanted by consumer culture, is one such.[33] A number of feminists would also describe their ideas as anarchist: authority is, for them, a masculine concept. The resistance of women's groups to the emergence of leaders and their insistence on consensual, discursive decision-making is in the spirit of anarchism. Two well-known feminist novels, Ursula LeGuin's *The Dispossessed* (1974) and Marge Piercy's *Woman on the Edge of Time* (1976) describe feminist utopias which are anarchist in organization: these express as well as anything the feminist aspiration for a form of society free from hierarchy, authority and male domination and show that its necessary fulfilment is in a society best described as anarchist. There is, unfortunately, no space here to do more than intimate some of the directions which modern anarchist thinking has taken. However, enough has been said to show that most contemporary anarchists have nothing in common with those libertarians of the far right, the anarcho-capitalists, who wish to see consumer capitalism reign, untrammelled by government.

OBJECTIONS TO ANARCHIST THEORY

The most frequent objection to anarchism is that, nice though it would be, we could never entirely eliminate anti-social acts and crimes by the use of morality. Undoubtedly, some small communities have successfully eliminated deviance on the basis of shared moral or religious codes: the mechanism of self-enforcement and mutual surveillance has been proved very effective while the supposedly deterrent effect of punishment is still a subject of controversy. A combination of morality and incentives to good behaviour could perhaps maintain social order. As for criminals or disruptive elements, Godwin suggested expulsion, while Bakunin suggested starvation for the anti-social individuals who refused to contribute, although later, 'having become exceedingly rare exceptions, those cases of idleness shall be regarded as special maladies to be subjected to clinical treatment'.[34] To be

33. H. Marcuse, *Essay on Liberation*, Penguin, 1971. For accounts of modern anarchist theory and practice of this 'countercultural' genre, see T. Roszak, *The Makings of a Counterculture*, Faber, 1970, D. Apter and J. Joll (Eds), *Anarchism Today*, Macmillan, 1971 and M. Bookchin, *Post-Scarcity Anarchism*.
34. Bakunin, 'Social and economic bases of anarchism', p. 142.

consistent, anarchist society should tolerate 'deviance' (the concept itself is an authoritarian one, according to radical sociologists) but this might threaten social unity. The objection about deviance is a practical one, but is based on a pessimistic view of human nature: if you accept the anarchists' optimistic view, the possibility of a society without deviance follows. A related question is whether the moral principles which anarchist individuals followed would coincide sufficiently to produce social unity without some authoritarian imposition of a moral code. Some anarchists emphasized private judgement in moral matters, but would the result not be a wild diversity of moralities? This seems a risk in these days of moral subjectivism. However, the early anarchists believed that there were discoverable, objective moral *truths*, existing in nature or in human reason, which could be universally known and followed. This was the basis of their optimism, although it appears as their weakness to the modern philosopher.

Another frequent criticism of anarchism is that *leadership* is a 'natural' phenomenon which cannot be abolished. Leadership is not identical to what the anarchists meant by authority which was, for them, an essentially coercive phenomenon. Leadership might therefore exist in the absence of authority. In a society of equals, people could accept the leadership of, say, a scientist on some decision in her field of expertise, without following her on other matters. She would be *an* authority, not *in* authority. The fact that many people today think of leadership as natural and necessary is partly the product of their education and of the structure of society, both of which are tailored to produce two classes, the leaders and the led. But the idea of a leaderless society is not self-contradictory, or inconceivable. There are indeed occasional experiments in decision-making without leadership, or collective leadership: from 1974 to 1985 'consensus management' (by a team of equals) was practised, not very successfully, in the British National Health Service, and women's groups usually favour collective decision-making, as do workers' co-operatives. The major disadvantage is the slowness of decisions taken collectively rather than by executive: the great advantage is that those involved afterwards feel that their views were taken into account, and will adhere to the decisions. It is this sense of control over one's own destiny, which can never be achieved under authority, which anarchist society would promote. And the anarchist analysis is valuable in illuminating the conceptual separation of leadership and authority.

THE ETHICS OF VIOLENCE

The strongest criticism of anarchism concerns its exponents' willingness to use violent methods. In fact, the pervasive caricature of the bomb-throwing anarchist is belied by most anarchist theory. A variety of non-violent means have been proposed for the realization of the anarchist ideal. Godwin believed in the force of moral persuasion, while Proudhon advocated propaganda plus passive resistance to government, both of which he practised himself. Similarly, Thoreau engaged in civil disobedience—for which he was imprisoned—and personal withdrawal from the society which he found so corrupt. The most commonly canvassed tactics were those of propaganda, education, and self-help. In the 1880s the 'narodniki' set out to live with and educate the Russian peasants as the first step towards revolution. Bakunin's preference for violence and conspiracy is usually attributed to his collaboration with the anarchist Nechayev, who was obsessed with assassination and terror; at other times Bakunin also favoured education. Tolstoy was famous for his pacifism and Kropotkin too was essentially pacific, although he argued that violence was justifiable as retaliation against governments using force. This argument was reiterated by modern anarcho-socialists such as Marcuse, who maintained that the covert violence of the modern state justified a violent response; other modern liberationist thinkers advocate withdrawal from the oppressive society and the establishment of communes which have a propagandistic intent as well as offering the free life on a microcosmic scale. Finally, ridicule has also been used as an anarchist tactic, as it was by the American students who nominated a pig for president. It could be more widely used as a powerful, non-violent weapon but its main disadvantage is that it offers no *positive* message to the unconverted. Anarchists, then, cannot and should not be universally identified as advocates of violence and terrorism.

Militant and violent anarchists fall into two main groups: the anarcho-syndicalists, and the many individual anarchists who espoused assassination and 'propaganda by deed', methods which are branded as 'terrorism' by the modern state. Any account of their activities falls into the field of history rather than theory, but the arguments justifying such tactics must be considered. Anarcho-syndicalism flourished in France and Russia (1890–1910) and in Spain in the 1930s. The anarchist syndicates, or unions, used the economic strike weapon for political purposes. Strikes were spontaneous, often violent, and were prolonged even when employers made concessions, for political effect. The movement declined in France and Russia for various reasons—partly because many improvements were gained and employment increased, partly because moderate workers preferred to join different unions as the militant unions antagonized government and public opinion.

The French thinker Sorel attached himself to the cause of anarcho-syndicalism, and his book, *Reflections on Violence* (1908), justified violent means. He maintained that middle-class violence is pervasive but disguised, and legitimized by reference to God and the state, whereas proletarian violence is 'purely and simply an act of war', and is vindicated by the brutal nature of state violence. Sorel glorified the general strike as a 'myth' with which workers could act and terrorize politicians. Although agreeing with some tenets and aims of Marxism, he emphasized the mythical nature of the strike and the 'catastrophic' nature of the transition to socialism to show that the revolution would be a practical, spontaneous, emotional act not capturable in 'scientific' theory. This anti-intellectual, apocalyptic vision was combined with tactical advice to syndicates: bourgeois attempts at conciliation of the strikers must be repulsed by increased violence and higher demands, to intensify the struggle. Violence itself had an expressive and educative function. Sorel presents his advice as a tract on the ethics of violence, distinguishing it from 'brutality' (the middle-class epithet for proletarian violence) and finding in it something pure, a virtue of its own. 'In the total ruin of institutions and morals there remains something which is powerful, new and intact . . . the soul of the revolutionary.'[35] Although today Sorel is associated as much with fascism as with anarchism, owing to the espousal of his views by some Nazis, his arguments widely influenced the anarchists of his time.

What Sorel, the syndicalists and the individual anarchists who committed acts of terror, had in common was a belief in the exemplary nature of action. Propaganda by deed would intensify people's feelings of oppression and initiate the struggle. The individuals who planted bombs, often suicidally, or attempted assassinations were partisans of heroic violence—the logical choice for the anti-political anarchist—whereas the syndicalists had to concede the necessity of organization, since individuals cannot make a strike. However, all forms of violence, including political strikes, which do not necessarily involve physical coercion, meet with the same objections from the state authorities. They are categorized and condemned as criminal, as anti-democratic, as violating the sanctity of human life, and as treating human beings as means to an end—a moral crime in itself, which is exacerbated when the end is only desired by a minority.

It seems that the state, which claims to speak for the people, whatever its political complexion, holds all the moral trumps. So can any defence of violence be offered by anarchists who choose it as a method? Three defences suggest themselves, which may be used in combination, but which sometimes get misleadingly confused. The first is that *violence merits violence*. This principle can be justified in two different ways. First, it could be argued that whoever uses violence deserves, in some absolute moral sense, retaliation—the *lex talionis*. Advocates of violence in a secular era hesitate to use this justification since it invites many challenges: in what sense does the attacker 'deserve' the retaliation? Who shall judge precisely what degree of violence is deserved, and ensure that it will not be excessive? Although the assassination of a despotic ruler sometimes appears as rightful revenge, it is hard to decide when such revenge is proper, and what it achieves. In democratic societies, the power-holders are our own representatives, and if they are held to be guilty of oppression and to merit revenge, then so must we all: their victimization then appears merely arbitrary and, equally, the assassination of any individual elector would logically be justified by her complicity in their actions. (The terrorist violence of the IRA against private individuals is sometimes justified on such grounds, and because 'he who is not with us is against us'.) The consequence of using revenge as a justification is that in a democratic society, with the diffusion of responsibility, all are equally implicated.

In fact, the crude be-done-by-as-you-would-do morality which revenge implies would be eschewed by most anarchists, although the principle of revenge is sometimes cited as a rhetorical justification of violence. Since anarchists believe in the social determination of individuals, and often condemn punishment for this reason, they should, to be consistent, reject the idea of revenge.

The other version of the 'violence merits violence' argument more often invoked today, does not maintain that two wrongs make a right, as the first

---

35. Sorel, *Reflections on Violence*, p. 49.

version seems to, but that violence in self-defence against violent attack, duress or coercion, is permissible. This view condones and limits, rather than justifies, violence. The principle of self-defence is well established in law and was stated by Hobbes and Locke as a consequence of the first 'law of nature', which commands self-preservation. Perhaps the right to self-defence *is* axiomatic and requires no further justification, but the political situations in which it is usually invoked are not analogous to the paradigm case of the directly threatened individual. The revolutionary or terrorist often claims to be acting *on behalf of others* (not always with their consent), whose lives are *not directly threatened* (even if they are made miserable), by attacking those who are *functionaries* of the state (and are not themselves the oppressors). Imagine that an anarchist discovers the whereabouts of a state computer which secretly amasses data with potentially coercive uses; she plants a bomb in the building which destroys the computer but kills several clerks and programmers. The dead individuals scarcely merited this violence (unless one accepts the dangerous principle of guilt by association), which was really aimed at the originators of the system and the state in general, both of which are well out of reach of the bomb. Nor was this a paradigm case of self-defence, unless the term is extended so far as to become meaningless. Similarly, when bombs are planted in expensive metropolitan restaurants, a practice common to past and present anarchists and other revolutionaries, those killed are often not members of 'the Establishment', but are said to be symbolic representatives of state power because of their wealth and status. Again, their 'violence' (as members of the ruling class, even if passive ones) can only be said to justify the violence done to them by a roundabout chain of reasoning, whether self-defence or retaliation is cited as the grounds. The assassination of a repressive monarch or an authoritarian politician seems, *prima facie*, more justifiable (if viewed as the removal of the originator of the oppression), and it should be remembered that most anarchist theory was developed at a time when such individuals were numerous: but the attempted adaptation of the justifications by revenge and self-defence to the modern democratic state causes grave difficulties.

The violent anarchist's predicament is that she wishes to destroy an abstraction—authority, or the state—but can only kill individuals. The state's structure is impregnable and in part intangible, and so the tactics of erosion are used: but these destroy innocent people. The 'reciprocal violence in self-defence' argument seems morally valid as a general justification of violent opposition to a state which is provenly coercive, but it fails to vindicate particular cases of violence against individuals who are in no sense guilty of violence themselves, or whose complicity in an oppressive system does not justify making them suffer for the guilt of all the rest. It is also hard to establish when the case really is one of self-defence and when there is a real threat to individuals' lives or wellbeing. And how many people must be 'under threat' before self-defence can be invoked? In the modern state most social control is now so unobtrusive that it does not manifest itself as coercion or repression—but rather as indoctrination, or manipulation of the rate of employment—and so does not seem to merit a violent response, which would appear excessive.

The second justification of violence offered by some anarchists is that *the ends justify the means*, a necessary precept of revolutionary thought. This implies that violence, even against a symbolic victim, is justified by its consequences, and the ideality of the revolutionary's goal. But both the Christian and humanist moralities prevalent in Western society hold that the preservation of human life is an end in itself—the highest end—and that taking life cannot be justified as a means to an end, except possibly in the controversial cases where this preserves many other lives, as in a war, or the shooting of a terrorist holding several hostages. This stance is reinforced philosophically by Kant's injunction that individuals should be treated as ends in themselves, never as the means to other individuals' ends. The anarchist who advocates violence may provisionally accept the sanctity of life, while arguing that in an oppressive society this has in some instances to be subordinated to the struggle for a better life for all: it cannot therefore be regarded as inviolable. Unfortunately, the terrorist does not pause to consult the victim on this fine moral point. (If the victims are power-holders, the terrorist might also argue that the 'right' to reciprocal violence overrides the sanctity-of-life argument. The implication of this would be that there are two classes of individuals, one whose right to life is forfeit because of their oppression of their fellows.) Ultimately, an anarchist employing this argument has to contend—and believe—that the goal of an anarchist society, with benefits for the many, justifies violence against the few. Violence is thus vindicated by a calculation of the social good. But this argument would be denied by those who maintain the absolute sanctity of life, and in advancing it the anarchist or revolutionary finds herself with strange bedfellows, the utilitarians.

A third defence, which avoids directly sanctioning violence, runs as follows: the state invents a self-justifying moral ideology, which includes the doctrine of the sanctity of life (often extended to the sanctity of property), not through a genuine respect for life, but so that the state can condemn violence or any move towards revolutionary change. This morality is hypocritical and deceptive. The revolutionary should therefore disregard its precepts and create a new revolutionary ethic. Marx, Lenin, and Sorel would all have agreed with this reasoning. This approach, then, justifies violence indirectly by refusing to debate it in terms of the orthodoxy which condemns it.

There is evidently an unbridgeable gap between the individual's desire for self-preservation and respect as an individual (which the precept of the sanctity of life expresses as a moral right), and the moral calculus which justifies violent means by good ends, which benefit society. No advocate of revolutionary violence, including the anarchist, is likely to produce a justification which would satisfy the victim, because of this lacuna. Subjective morality, which puts self-preservation at a premium, is on a different level from the 'objective' social morality to which revolutionaries make appeal. And because the state, including the Church, is the source of moral authority, the revolutionary is unlikely to be able to justify violent actions to the majority of the population which has been inculcated with such ideas, even if the victims are unpopular politicians and not randomly chosen civilians. She must simply accept being treated as a criminal and a moral outlaw, according to their legality and morality, and hope for the triumph of her idea through the enlightenment of the population by her propagandistic deeds. The process is a long one.

Curiously, anarchists have been attacked more fiercely for their sporadic, spontaneous use of violence than have Marxists for their explicitly revolutionary violence—perhaps this is because its random, terroristic aspect makes it so menacing to the mass of the population. The early association of anarchism with the pure destructiveness of nihilism also discredited it. But such associations have distorted the public image of a political ideology which has never ceased to advocate a pacific, moral form of society based on *good will*, free from all violence and oppression. While the virtues of the anarchist ideal can and should be evaluated separately from the question of methods, the anarchists' reflections on the ethics of violence also deserve consideration in a world where political violence is increasingly common. However, anarchism's strength lies not in its occasional advocacy of violent means but in the model which it offers of a free society, which differs from the liberal model, of which it constitutes a criticism. Although some forms of anarchism, such as those of Nozick and Stirner, manifest themselves as extreme forms of right-wing individualism, anarchism in general is a political ideology which seeks to realize the best socialist ideals without the intervention of the potentially authoritarian state.

FURTHER READING

H. Barclay, *People without Government: An Anthropology of Anarchy*, 2nd rev. edn, Kahn & Averill, 1990.
A. Carter, *The Political Theory of Anarchism*, Routledge & Kegan Paul, 1971.
G. Crowder, *Classical Anarchism*, Clarendon Press, 1991.
H. J. Ehrlich *et al.* (Eds.), *Reinventing Anarchism*, Routledge & Kegan Paul, 1979.
T. Honderich, *Violence for Equality*, 3rd rev. edn, Routledge, 1989.
D. Miller, *Anarchism*, Dent, 1984.
J. R. Pennock and J. W. Chapman (Eds.), *Anarchism*, New York U.P., 1978.
A. Ritter, *Anarchism: A Theoretical Analysis*, Cambridge U.P., 1980.
R. P. Wolff, *In Defence of Anarchism*, Harper & Row, 1970.

Chapter 7

Conservatism

Conservative mentality as such has no predisposition towards theorizing. This is in accord with the fact that human beings do not theorize about the actual situations in which they live as long as they are well adjusted to them . . . Conservative mentality as such has no utopia.[1]

(*Karl Mannheim*)

It is with infinite caution that any man ought to venture upon pulling down an edifice which has answered in any tolerable degree for ages the common purposes of society.[2]

(*Edmund Burke*)

As Mannheim suggests, conservatism is not an explicit or self-proclaimed ideology. There are no essential conservative texts, although many texts are conservative. The literal meaning of the term comes from the idea of *conservation*, and conservative ideology is formulated anew in response to each attack made on the existing social order, which conservatives wish to conserve—this is why conservatism is often described as a reactionary doctrine, i.e. a doctrine which evolves as a reaction to (and against) new developments. Thus, conservatives in the last two centuries have taken issue in turn with radicalism, liberalism, and socialism. The French Revolution and the growth of individualistic, *laissez-faire* liberalism were two pivotal events in the development of nineteenth-century conservatism—both challenged the power of the governing classes. In the twentieth-century, the spread of socialism, the rise of communism and the Cold War were formative influences on conservative thinking. There is moreover an enduring hostility among conservatives to utopianism, whatever its complexion, because of its assumed tendency to overthrow established institutions and dispossess people of what is rightly theirs.

---

1. K. Mannheim, *Ideology and Utopia* (trans. E. Shils), Routledge & Kegan Paul, 1960, p. 206.
2. E. Burke, *Reflections on the Revolution in France*, (Ed. C. C. O'Brien), Penguin, 1969, p. 152.

Conservative ideology, as discussed here, is not of course identical to the doctrines of the British Conservative Party. In Britain we conceive of conservatism differently from other Europeans, as a result of our political history. In the nineteenth century, reforming Conservative ministries were not uncommon—those of Peel and Disraeli are famous—while historically the Conservative Party displaced the Liberals, absorbing in the process many liberal beliefs. The acceptance of constitutional government and individual rights distinguishes our tradition of 'liberal conservatism' from that elsewhere in Europe, where conservatism was, and often still is, associated with royalism, catholicism, and other reactionary or authoritarian tendencies—in France, for example, many nineteenth-century conservatives were authoritarian and bonapartist or even ultramontane (an extreme Catholic grouping), rather than liberal. This should be borne in mind, since the conservative outlook described here may seem more illiberal to British readers than the Conservative politics with which they are familiar. In so far as conservatism can be presented as an ideology, it is because it derives from a small number of beliefs and intuitions which form a coherent world-view: the connection between these beliefs and conservative political doctrine will be explored in the sections below. Conservative political principles are more easily enumerated: foremost among them is the maintenance of property rights. Lord Hailsham justifies property as an individual right, a safeguard for the family, a benefit to the community (because it provides incentives to work) and a bulwark of liberty against the state, in that it represents an economic power base which can oppose the state.[3] As a consequence of their belief in property, conservative theories represent the interests of the propertied classes and conservatives therefore tend to support entrenched privilege and a hierarchical organization of society. Other beliefs include strong government, law and order, family, community, nationalism, patriotism and the maintenance of moral standards: all these beliefs can in turn be related to the maintenance of property rights.

AGAINST CHANGE

First, it is a commonplace that conservatives dislike change. The classic critique of political change is that of Plato, who wrote in the fourth century BC, when the democratic city-states in Greece were past their heyday and Athens, where Plato lived, had undergone a series of turbulent political changes in a short time, experiencing tyranny, demagogic democracy and reactionary oligarchy. Plato's political theory developed as a reaction against political uncertainties and abuses. Also his philosophy was in part a rejoinder to the runaway relativism implied in Heraclitus's doctrine, 'all is flux', which suggested that no definite, permanent truths could be established. Plato believed that there existed, in a transcendental or metaphysical dimension, absolute 'Ideas', political and moral truths which constituted the models that men should aspire to imitate in their behaviour and

---

3. Viscount Hailsham, *The Conservative Case*, Penguin, 1959, p. 97.

social organization. His ideal republic was to be ruled by Philosopher Kings, whose wisdom and goodness came from their contemplation and understanding of the Ideas of truth, beauty, justice, and the supreme Idea, the Good. This perfect society would instantiate the Ideas—perfect Justice, absolute Good. A consequence of his absolutist notion of the Good and the ideal state was that Plato regarded any departure from the model republic as being tantamount to imperfection and decay.

Having described the republic, Plato sketched the inferior political forms which would result if various aspects of it were changed.[4] Although some interpret this as a prediction of the decline into decadence, with democracy, then tyranny, marking the final, furthest departures from the ideal, it can also be read not as a historical but a theoretical argument: we can infer from his system of thought that any change in the *perfect system* leads away from the Ideas, towards imperfection. The greater the change, the greater the evil. Since Plato it has been a common conservative conviction that change equals decay or presages dissolution into chaos. A similar belief is manifested in *Leviathan* when Hobbes enjoins us to obey the sovereign in all circumstances, lest the overthrow of authority should lead to a dissolution of society and a return to the savage anarchy of the state of nature. Stability is therefore the dominant conservative ideal, arising from this aversion to change: *peace* and *order* are instrumental ideals which help promote social stability, although they are also valued for their own sake.

Plato's argument, that if a perfect society could be achieved, any alteration to it would lead to imperfection and evil, is logically impeccable. However, problems arise when this 'no change' doctrine is applied to societies which are patently less than perfect, that is, to any real society. Nevertheless, a conservative might still argue the undesirability of change on three different grounds. First, it can be said that any existing, functioning political form, however imperfect, is preferable to the new system which change might bring about. Better the devil you know . . . . All man-made change is risky since the outcome of reform—and, *a fortiori*, of revolution—cannot be accurately predicted and so cannot be proved desirable in advance. This is necessarily true, for just as the problem of induction in empirical science is that future events cannot be predicted with absolute certainty, the problem in social and political science is that we cannot foretell the results of social innovation, especially as, given the unique and historical nature of each political society, we have fewer comparable instances on which to base our generalizations and predictions than the natural scientist. Conservatives rightly hold that the results of a revolution cannot be *known* in advance to be an improvement. By contrast, their own theory draws safely on the knowable past and present and is immune from such uncertainties. However, the would-be reformer might retort that society is so unjust that it is strongly probable, if not certain, that the proposed changes will constitute an improvement. She could also contend that, since unplanned changes will occur in any case, which might be more harmful than planned change, rationally planned reforms should be

---

4. Plato, *Republic* (trans. H. D. P. Lee), Penguin, 1955, Part 9.

implemented. But many conservatives would reject this point too, having, like Hayek, a dislike of artificial or contrived change and a predilection for unplanned change or 'evolution'. It is important to note that the conservative case against change often rests on a distorted account of the available alternatives. A false dichotomy is posed, suggesting that the choice is between: (a) what exists at present; and (b) one particular, undesirable, alternative. 'The House of Lords may be an anachronism, but single-chamber government would give a dangerous monopoly of power to the House of Commons, hence the House of Lords must remain as it is.' Imputing only one, unacceptable, alternative to your political opponent is a well-known sleight of hand.

A second, archetypal argument in favour of 'no change', advanced by Burke, is that existing social and political forms have a special virtue because they are refined and sanctified by *tradition*, and so should be preserved unchanged. The problems involved in the notion of tradition will be considered further below, but as an argument against change it does not have the compelling force which Burke attributed to it. Tradition is itself built up out of a series of historical changes, reforms and evolutions and there is no reason why each new innovation, or even a revolution, should not later be seen as part of a tradition. Historians can speak of France's revolutionary tradition without self-contradiction. The argument from tradition can be seen as a more sophisticated version of the third argument against change, that *whatever is, is good*, however imperfect it may be. Few conservatives would like to express such an overtly reactionary sentiment, but it underlies many conservative arguments. This dictum, 'whatever is, is good', violates the philosophical convention that values cannot be derived from facts: that is, the mere fact that society is as it is cannot entail or prove that it is *good*. Such evaluations are merely the product of our minds. The absurd consequences of this philosophical error were satirized in Voltaire's novel *Candide* where the philosopher Pangloss, says, every time that a grotesque disaster smites him and the hero, Candide, 'All is for the best in the best of all possible worlds'.

In fact, the argument that no changes should be made because what exists is good is not always the result of spurious optimism of the kind which Voltaire satirized. It could be theoretically vindicated by a thinker with the religious conviction that the world is as God made it, and is therefore good, because willed by God. (This is not the place to embark on theological arguments as to how God can will suffering and imperfections.) Alternatively, someone might believe that there was a natural evolutionary process at work in society which meant that the existing form of society, whatever it might be, represented the best achievable at this stage of development—so, whatever is (now) is good (now). Hegel's idea of Absolute Spirit actualizing itself through the historical process, becoming concrete in various societies, led him to a similar optimism and the view that 'the real is the rational', which validated existing social forms. Each stage of historical development is good, therefore, in that it forms a necessary part of the whole dialectical process. The thinkers who consider that a form of society gains a special moral value by virtue, simply, of existing, are usually those who see society as reflecting a fixed order, divine or natural, or as instantiating some metaphysical ideals—the latter view was held by the nineteenth-century idealist thinker (and poet), Coleridge. Such convictions are unlikely to be held by those who consider society a human artefact which can be changed and perfected by human beings, at will—these are the reformers.

The idea of degeneration through change on which many conservative arguments implicitly rest is based on what could be called an 'essentialist' view of the existent, which holds that it is not merely constituted by a series of accidents and contingencies, but has some immutable, and valuable, essence. Conservatives will define certain elements as constituting the essence of a particular political system, then will strive to preserve them. But with an entity as complex as society, there are many differences of opinion as to where the 'essence' lies. In any case, the belief in essences is philosophically dubious.

In resisting change, the conservative resists the theories of human progress which flourished in the Enlightenment and have dominated liberal and, to some extent, socialist thinking ever since. For Enlightenment philosophers, each new historical period marked a higher stage of civilization and human achievement. But the literal meaning of progress is neutral—a moving forward (in time or space)—and many conservatives equate progress in time with decadence in morals. Indeed, there are a number of conservative theories of history as *regression*, from the myths of classical times which located a Golden Age in the distant past and charted the decline of mores through the Silver to the Iron Age, and the revelations of Christian eschatology, which predict the decline of men into bestiality and the reign of anti-Christ before the end of the world, to those eighteenth-century conservative philosophers who considered the culture of the 'moderns' greatly inferior to that of the 'ancients' of classical times. So, if history is the record of change, and change is synonymous with decline, it follows that the best we can do is to resist change, halt mankind's decline and so—by implication—end history.

In political practice conservatives cannot ban change for ever, nor is that a necessary consequence of their ideology in every case. For Plato, it was a consequence of his philosophical system that change in the ideal republic would be evil; religious believers who perceive a divine order in society might take a similar stance. But for most conservatives what matters is how change comes about, and its scope. Burke argued that 'a state without the means of some change is without the means of its conservation' and justified moderate change when this was necessary for the survival of the system.[5] Such change should be organic, building on existing customs and traditions of society. Conservatives often resort to an organic metaphor in defending their society against sudden or radical change—which would be as drastic as amputation or shock treatment to the body—and also employ it to explain how acceptable degrees of change might come about, likening it to 'pruning' or 'healing'. Even before Darwin, a concept of evolution was implicit in conservative thinking: political society was said to evolve gradually, conserving the best in its traditions, which guaranteed its survival and prosperity. Revolution is the precise opposite of evolution and

5. Burke, *Reflections on the Revolution in France*, p. 106.

threatens the whole organism with sudden death, which is why Burke opposed the French Revolution so strenuously. An evolutionary theory of change demands little or no political action for it is seen as a spontaneous process.

Discussions of change and conservation raise a philosophical problem about the meaning of 'change' which potentially challenges conservatism. This is demonstrated by the 'systems theory of politics' pioneered by Easton, which hypothesizes a model of society based on a simple organism or cell.[6] The goal of the political system is said to be 'survival' (like that of the cell), and it tries to preserve itself by processing the people's demands ('inputs') via various policies ('outputs') designed to win their approval. The problem with Easton's functionalist model is that it offers no satisfactory criteria for measuring how much change a system can absorb before it becomes a different system, or 'dies'. To apply his analysis, Easton, like other conservatives, must define the 'essence' of the system, that which must be preserved for it to survive—and such definitions will always be controversial and insubstantial. The upshot of Easton's analysis could be summarized as 'a system is a system is a system', an uncritical conclusion which tends to support the *status quo*. The problem about what counts as damaging change and what is acceptable as evolutionary change is a perennial one for conservative philosophers.

THE VIRTUES OF TRADITION

Despite the conservative pessimism about progress, Burke's celebrated defence of tradition against the iconoclasm of the French Revolution seems implicitly to rest on a conception of human and social progress: if the present is good, in that it incorporates the accumulated wisdom of the past, civilization is, presumably, progressing cumulatively. But Burke would have denied this interpretation. *Reflections on the Revolution in France* (1790), wherein he extolled the virtues of the English political tradition, was equally a rejection of the liberal theory of progress as innovation. For Burke, what is preserved of the past is good, what is new is—often—bad. The present is good because of the residue of the past which it contains. Conservatism is not progress, but the avoidance of regression. The inconsistency of Burke's position is that, while he now vilified the French Revolution, he, as a Whig, had previously justified the English Revolution of 1688 (which had in effect established a constitutional monarchy) as the vital source of England's proudest constitutional traditions, and as a defence of traditional rights.

For Burke, adherence to tradition was essential because it created social continuity and continuity furthered social tranquillity, the ultimate political goal. Tradition signified building on the wisdom of past generations. As Burke said, 'We procure reverence to our civil institutions on the principle which Nature teaches us to revere individual men: on account of their age, and on account of

6. D. Easton, *A Systems Analysis of Political Life*, Wiley, 1965.

those from whom they are descended'.[7] Society is conceived of by Burke as a partnership between living, dead and future generations. A more recent definition by G. K. Chesterton, which reflects the same conviction, runs as follows:

> Tradition means giving votes to the most obscure of all classes: our ancestors. It is a democracy of the dead. Tradition refuses to submit to the arrogant oligarchy of those who merely happen to be walking about.

Oakeshott too praised the role of tradition as the accumulation of experience and it is often cited as a justification of policy by British Conservatives, particularly when defending established institutions against attack—for example, the House of Lords.[8]

The debate about tradition is often depicted as one between the commonsensical conservative, who realizes that wisdom is inherited across generations and that we cannot extirpate the past, and the naive and fanatical utopian who wishes, in Popper's words, to make a blank canvas of society, on which to scrawl his own prejudices.[9] Needless to say, in reality, those who want reform or even revolution accept that some traditions are ineradicable. A revolution may leave traditional ways of life and many institutions untouched. It is often said that the Russian Revolution substituted one authoritarian regime for another, thus preserving the traditional political culture of deference to an omnipotent leader. The quarrel is really between those who want more tradition and less change, and those who want the reverse, not between total preservers and all-out destroyers. So conservatives are, in a sense, right in emphasizing the strength of tradition, but not so in using it to mean something necessarily good.

Three further criticisms can be made of the notion of tradition espoused by Burke and some modern conservatives: first, it assumes that what is preserved over time is what is *best*. Burke believed that time 'refines', but there is no conclusive evidence to support such optimism. Some things are preserved because they are socially useful, like property rights, but others survive by accident and others, though socially undesirable, survive over time because they satisfy certain needs or desires—for example, the use of intoxicants and drugs, and prostitution. Any argument that the preserving and/or weeding out of political institutions, social mores and other behaviour systematically conserves what is best must ultimately make appeal to a hypothesis of social evolution, or some concept of divine purpose, neither of which is verifiable. Second, there is no good reason why past traditions should be binding on the present. Written constitutions are often justified on the grounds that they may prevent rash future generations from committing political follies—but the suspicion that future generations will need such protection already presupposes that history is a process of decline rather than progress, for otherwise it would be reasonable to suppose that they would be wiser (more advanced) than ourselves, and so to avoid binding them. A belief in progress therefore annuls the principle that tradition should be binding. In fact,

---

7. Burke, *Reflections on the Revolution in France*, p. 121.
8. M. Oakeshott, *Rationalism in Politics*, Methuen, 1962, Chaps. 1 and 7.
9. K. Popper, *The Open Society and its Enemies*, Routledge & Kegan Paul, 1962, Vol.1, pp. 157–68.

political institutions do not function on the assumption that we are bound by the decisions of our forefathers. In Britain, no parliament can bind a future parliament, and even in countries where there are written constitutions or higher laws, these can only delay popular changes for a certain time. (It would, of course, be purely sentimental in Western terms to justify the maintenance of traditions on the grounds that we owe it to our ancestors although this sort of duty forms a part of some cultures, e.g. traditional Chinese culture.) Third, once the concept of tradition is invoked, as was suggested earlier, *any* existing institution can claim its protection. Burke's idea of refinement through time is too indefinite to serve as a criterion to demarcate true traditions. How long does it take for a tradition to be constituted? Is the French Fifth Republic a political tradition yet, or should it be seen as the usurper of the Fourth Republic? Are all traditions worth preserving? Some diehard communists in Russia may still be striving to revive the 'Stalinist tradition': what would Burke have said to that? In short, there are no criteria for what counts as a tradition, and so conservatives may find themselves defending the upholding of tradition *per se*, whatever it might be. (Hobbes finds himself in the parallel position of advocating obedience to the sovereign, whoever it may be, for fear of impending chaos.) 'Preserving tradition' is not a substantive doctrine and cannot help the conservative to discriminate between good and bad institutions.

The *invention of tradition* was a common strategy among nineteenth-century romantic conservatives, including writers such as Coleridge, Wordsworth and Carlyle and a number of German philosophers. These romantics deplored the modern phenomena of industrialism, liberal individualism and the market society. They harked back to a (largely mythical) past, to harmonious bucolic communities bound together by shared religious beliefs and customs. The invention of a Golden Age is not confined to conservatives: Tolstoy's pastoralism is usually considered a form of anarchism, while William Morris (a convinced socialist) depicted a bucolic past-future in *News from Nowhere* (1891). Thus, Golden Age-ism is characteristic of the romantic movement in general rather than of conservatism in particular, but it can supply the utopian element which conservatism otherwise lacks because of its natural pessimism, by offering an invented past to be re-created.

HUMAN IMPERFECTION AND INEQUALITY

The pessimistic view of human nature held by many conservatives is another cornerstone of their doctrine. Typically, their assumptions about human nature emphasize its weakness, selfishness, and irrationality. The Judaeo-Christian account of the 'fall of man' and original sin was the foundation of such views which were later presented in secular guise—for example, in Machiavelli's account of man's depravity,[10] and in Hobbes's depiction of the aggressive and selfish

---

10. N. Machiavelli, *The Prince* (trans. G. Bull), Penguin, 1961, p. 96.

behaviour of men in the state of nature which justified the creation of an absolute sovereign.[11] These and similar premises suggest that people are incapable of self-government, or even of moral and sociable behaviour, in the absence of coercion, and so entail the need for authoritarian forms of government. Government is seen primarily as a device for keeping order, and only secondarily as an instrument for satisfying people's needs. If such human inadequacy were genuinely universal (as the hypothesis of innate wickedness deriving from original sin suggests), humankind would certainly be in difficulties, with nobody capable of governing himself or others, but conservatives—inconsistently?—combine this premise with a hypothesis of *natural inequality*, which resolves the problem as follows: since some people are innately 'superior' to others, it is both reasonable and natural that they should govern. Furthermore, an elite group can embody a collective wisdom beyond that of mere individuals. Elite government and hierarchical, class-stratified society are, evidently, necessary consequences of the conservative view of human nature. Plato's ideal republic consisted of three classes (plus the slaves, fourth-class non-citizens), class membership being determined partly by birth, partly by the individual's abilities. If, as Plato expected, every individual is ideally suited to his appointed role in society, as the Philosopher Kings are to ruling and the artisans are to labouring, there could be no discontent at the class system since all would experience equal, though differentiated, satisfaction. But the basis for such rigid classification of individuals is very dubious, theoretically and practically.

However, Plato's justification of inequality (each class in the *Republic* has a different, specialized function) and his insistence on the parallel between the composition of the state and that of the individual inaugurated a metaphor which became of great importance for conservative political theory.[12] Whereas convinced egalitarians may liken society to a complex machine, with interchangeable and equally important parts, those who believe in deep-rooted inequality find it more condign to envisage society as a living organism in which each specialized organ plays a different but crucial part in the wellbeing of the whole, with all the organs acting in harmony and receiving their reward, good health and nourishment. (While Plato likened society to a living human being, Aristotle drew an analogy between the polity and vegetable organisms, and speculated on the natural limits to growth and development which societies, like plants, would experience.[13])

In terms of social organization, the premises of inequality and of natural class distinctions militate against the social mobility which liberals advocate. Burke talked of society as operating according to a '*fixed compact* sanctioned by the inviolable oath which holds all physical and all moral natures each in their *appointed place*'.[14] Knowing your place, and sticking to it, is a virtue prized by orthodox conservatism. There was in Burke's thought an incipient conflict

11.   T. Hobbes, *Leviathan*, Penguin, 1968, Chap.XIII.
12.   Plato, *Republic*, ss.344, 368–75, 429, 520.
13.   Aristotle, *Politics* (trans. T. A. Sinclair), Penguin, 1962, pp. 27–8.
14.   Burke, *Reflections on the Revolution in France*, p.195. Emphasis added.

between this virtue and the 'getting ahead' on which capitalism rests. In retrospect, Burke appears to be trying to accommodate the rising, mobile middle classes in his theory—without much enthusiasm—by demonstrating that they too belong to the natural aristocracy of talent. The meritocratic pretensions of nineteenth-century liberal intellectuals like J. S. Mill were anathema to conservatives. Knowing your place is the basis of life in the traditional societies which conservatives often admire, as Disraeli admired feudalism. This doctrine may rest not only on the premise of inequality but also on the hypothesis that there is a divinely ordained order in society. For example, the *varna* system of Hindu social organization distinguishes four castes. Moral duty, *dharma*, consists in performing the duties of one's caste. (Hence the acute hostility experienced by the *harijans*—the 'untouchable' outcasts—when they try to better their situation.) A Christian hymn, 'All things bright and beautiful', reminds us that 'the rich man in his castle, the poor man at his gate, God made them high and lowly, and ordered their estate'. This docile perspective on life was savagely parodied by Dickens in *The Chimes*:

> O let us love our occupations,
> Bless the squire and his relations,
> Live upon our daily rations,
> And always know our proper stations.

Conservatives often believe that inequality exists not only between classes but between other categories of people, such as men and women: some strongly conservative fundamentalist Christians in the USA opposed the constitutional amendment designed to guarantee equal rights to women on the basis of biblical texts which declared women to be inferior to men.[15] Similarly, some more conservative thinkers believe in inequality between races and even in a natural hierarchy of races which entitles the superior race to govern the others. Conservative thinkers, being convinced of the superiority of some people to others, at least in terms of their abilities, if not of their immortal souls, accept the permanent necessity for hierarchical and inegalitarian social institutions, justifying them on the grounds that class differences will not create social conflict or disorder because all will belong to the classes to which they are naturally suited and organic harmony will reign between the classes. This may seem a plausible social theory, but it must be relinquished when individuals start to manifest discontent at class distinctions or to exhibit the desire and the capacity for upward social mobility—as they surely will. Ironically, despite this predisposition towards class society, many modern conservatives declare themselves 'against class' and against class politics, and plead for social unity. This plea may be partly tactical, given that socialists often take their stand on an assumption of class antagonism: the conservative response is to assert that classes are unimportant and that what is vital to social good health is the unity of the whole. The organic analogy 'proves' that class harmony is natural. There is an unresolved paradox in the conjunction

---

15. See P. Schlafly, 'What the Equal Rights Amendment Means', repr. in L. T. Sargent (Ed.), *Extremism in America*, New York U.P., 1996, pp. 256–264.

of these two ideas, class society and social unity, which conservatives overcome by invoking the organic analogy or by an act of will—for example, Disraeli proposed an alliance between the upper and lower classes against the encroaching middle class, calling for 'one nation'. But the more usual approach is to deny the class problem altogether. In quotidian politics, the denial of class antagonisms may store up trouble and be self-defeating because they are likely to erupt in a disruptive way.

CONSERVATIVE POLITICS

The political consequence of the pessimistic and inegalitarian view of human nature is an acceptance of the need for either *authoritarian government* or, at least, *authoritative leadership*, carried on by an elite, often without the participation of the mass. Such a government need not be oppressive and may well be paternalistic, with wise rulers governing the less able masses in their best interests. Conservatives have typically been associated with royalist movements in Europe, and the French Revolution's attack on the monarchical principle inspired the conservative thinkers Maistre and Tocqueville to criticize democracy for its oppressive populism. Conservatives advocate monarchy on the ground that the hereditary monarch embodies tradition and continuity, rather than on the more dubious ground of his or her inherent superiority, and also because they believe in the leadership principle. In countries where monarchy has been superseded, they may transfer their loyalty to a strong president or some other form of elite government. In Britain where there is a mixed constitution, conservatives express similar predispositions by upholding the supremacy of parliament and, in particular, of the executive against interference by other groups (for example, trades unions) and against excessive interference by the electorate.

The organic analogy, whether animal or vegetable, reinforces the case for specialization of function within society and for elite government, which is justified on the grounds that some are naturally best equipped to rule. Elite government is indeed a perennial theme of conservative thought and is often coupled with criticism of the democratic principle and its assumption of political equality. Burke talked of the 'natural aristocracy' as the repository of virtues.[16] Carlyle asserted that 'the few Wise will have ... to take command of the innumerable Foolish'.[17] The Marquis of Salisbury wrote: 'political equality is not merely a folly,—it is a chimera ... the multitude will always have leaders among them, and those leaders are not selected by themselves'.[18] Even in the semi-egalitarian present, the British Conservative Party has habitually represented itself as '*the* party of government', trading on the same connection. Many conservatives would reject the notion of popular government but would accept democracy as a

---

16. Burke, *An Appeal from the New to the Old Whigs . . .*, in *How Conservatives Think*, P.W. Buck (Ed.), Penguin, 1975, p. 52.
17. T. Carlyle, 'The present time', in *How Conservatives Think*, p. 59.
18. Marquis of Salisbury, 'Difficulty of Combining Government by Numbers with Government by the Best Men' in *How Conservatives Think*, p. 116.

means of validating the rule of the elite—one outcome of this approach is the 'elite theory of democracy', discussed in Chapter 12.

Many past and present conservatives express the desire to eschew adversarial and conflict-based politics (which they often associate with democracy) and to promote *consensus*, as if institutionalized disagreement (even an official opposition) were disruptive and distasteful. Social and political stability is the underlying goal, but there is also a hint of the mediaeval theological view of politics as being occasioned by the fallen nature of man, which entails that political activity can never be a good in itself, only a necessary evil. This view contrasts sharply with the Greek theorists' idealization of political life and citizenship. The chief task of politics, seen in the light of conservative presuppositions, is the maintenance of law and order, the restraining of the unruly. To this end, many conservatives before the democratic era would not even have conceded the propriety of constitutional restraints on government and would have agreed with Hobbes that the scope and powers of government, or of the sovereign, were necessarily unlimited. As Hobbes said of his absolute sovereign, he who wills the end (i.e. order) must will the means. But Burke later indicated how conservative and constitutional politics can blend, advocating a 'mixed government' on the English lines, with a monarch constrained by parliament and parliament restrained by a relatively small and exclusive electorate. While the sovereign, the 'Monarch-in-Parliament', is not subject to supreme laws, she is obliged to obey higher ethical principles, one being that she may not break the law. (Coleridge similarly advocated a balanced constitution with a traditionalist aristocracy in the House of Lords being balanced by a more progressive and commercially minded House of Commons.) Burke also disapproved of conflict during elections which were in his day often violent, not to say corrupt, but thought that parties need not be 'outlawed' if they promoted 'healing coalitions'—that is, social unity. His famous definition of a political party was:

A body of men united for promoting by their joint endeavours the national interest upon some particular principle in which they are all agreed.[19]

Burke's well-known theory of representation by the wise, his rejection of delegation and his advocacy of the independence of representatives follow directly from his belief in a natural aristocracy. The political arrangements which Burke proposes reflect his suspicion of people's baser motives, his desire for moderation and, above all, his hopes for social unity.

The fear of disorder and impending anarchy, and the yearning for stability, are fundamental to conservative psychology and the ideology is, largely, the translation of these fears and desires into political proposals. Social disruption is to be avoided at all costs, and an authoritarian form of government can best ensure this. ('Authoritarian' in this context denotes a government where the people have little or no control, rather than an actual dictatorship.) With regard

19. Burke, *Thoughts on the Cause of the Present Discontents*, in *Edmund Burke on Government, Politics and Society*, B.W. Hill (Ed.), Fontana/Harvester, 1975, p.113.

to the individual's position in relation to government, conservatives reject 'inner freedom' as an ideal (as Mannheim notes) since this could lead to unorthodoxy or anarchism, and they wish to subordinate individual free will to 'objective freedom'—usually in the guise of duty—that is, freedom to do what you ought to do. Except when conservatism is infused with liberal ideas, as in the English tradition, individualism is seen as dangerous and undesirable: conservatism is holistic in its approach to politics. Burke anathematized the abstract 'rights of man' as revolutionary nonsense and defended individual freedoms only as far as they were 'prescriptive' or traditional, like the rights established in the tradition of common law and equity. He viewed political liberties 'as an entailed inheritance derived to us from our forefathers, and to be transmitted to our posterity'.[20] Rights cannot be created in a rationalist vacuum.

Another crucial political ideal common to all conservatives is that of nationalism, which entails the duty of patriotism. For the Greeks, city-states were sacred places and likewise, for many conservatives, the nation is sacrosanct—by contrast with the internationalist doctrines of socialism and, to some extent, of liberalism. While nationalism was a liberal and liberating force at some moments in the nineteenth century (e.g. where Greek independence and Italian liberation were concerned) in many cases it was transformed into a right-wing movement, bound to concepts of blood and race. The conception of the nation is based either on the organic analogy, which suggests that the nation is a natural unit (despite the constant gerrymandering of boundaries throughout world history), or on the supposition that the national entity is the product of evolving tradition, a slow but indestructible accretion of land, culture and institutions. (Some extreme right-wing groups, like fascists, base nationalism on the idea of race, arguing that the 'natural' national unit is one which embraces the whole of a racial group.) Conservatives would maintain that the social cohesion within a nation, reinforced by a common language and shared institutions, were stronger than any internally divisive forces, such as those of class. This preoccupation with the nation was exemplified recently in Britain, where the issue of nationalism caused a schism in the Conservative Party between those who favoured a British presence within the European Union and those 'Euro-sceptics' who feared that deeper involvement in the EU would destroy national sovereignty and threaten our national identity.

Among other conservative political principles are the maintenance and protection of private property, the rule of law and strict punishment for offenders, the strengthening of the family and the promotion of moral values centred on self-restraint and moderation. Duties to the community are emphasized, rather than individual rights. Some recent populist 'communitarian' tracts have railed against individualism and the modern emphasis on rights, especially welfare rights; such tracts are in fact re-statements of the classic conservative view that the civic bond is cemented by absolute duties and that

---

20. Burke, *Reflections on the Revolution in France*, p. 119.

social responsibility and service are fundamental to society.[21] A key 'negative principle' of twentieth-century conservatism has been opposition to socialism with its progressive and rationalist approach, and to the totalitarian excesses of communism. The threats posed by radical creeds reinforce the conservative conviction that traditional social institutions like private property and the family must be upheld. Conservatives do not harbour any utopian expectation that human beings can become perfect, and so their hope for a well-ordered society is based on the control of the darker side of human nature and damage limitation through strong legal controls and a non-permissive moral culture. In Britain in the 1990s the Conservative government became discredited partly because the lax behaviour of some Conservative politicians was so at odds with the basic moral values which the party professed.

THE CONSERVATIVE MENTALITY

The conservative philosophical tradition is diverse. Some thinkers, in their search for *absolute authority*, accept the existence of absolute ideas—unchanging truths which can act as political and moral standards for all time. But modern theorists with conservative leanings such as Oakeshott, Hayek, and Popper (the latter two are best described as liberal-conservative) stand squarely in the tradition of empiricism and advocate a search for political truth through trial and error, accumulated wisdom and modest change. These three thinkers are *anti-rationalist*, and object to reformers who try to impose on society rationalist schemes dreamt up in their heads, an aspiration which they attribute to utopians and totalitarians. Like Burke, they eschew abstract reason and prefer practical principles. In contrast to the rationalist and idealist approach, the conservative approach to politics may seem haphazard, untheoretical and largely pragmatic. Indeed, until the 1980s it was the boast of the British Conservative Party that it was not dogmatic but *pragmatic*, in the sense of not being entangled in rationalist schemes, and *non-ideological*, ideology being condemned as an inflexible, distorted, partial, and non-pragmatic approach to politics. The rejection of ideology in principle (although conservatism cannot fail to be ideological in essence) contrasts sharply with the general conservative predilection for certainty and for authoritative sources of knowledge. But conservatives see ideology as the creation of extremists and fanatics, and a powerful poison. In the search for absolutes, they have preferred to look to religion and even to nature.

Many parallels exist between the orthodox Christian and the conservative ways of thinking and perceiving the world. This is not to say that all conservatives are necessarily Christians, although Lord Hailsham, in *The Case for Conservatism*, made religious belief a central tenet.[22] The connection lies in the coincidence of assumptions. Both Christians and conservatives see mankind as fundamentally

---

21. See A. Etzioni, *The Spirit of Community*, Simon & Schuster, 1994, and D. Selbourne, *The Principle of Duty*, Sinclair-Stevenson, 1994.
22. Hailsham, *The Case for Conservatism*, Chap. 2.

marred and weak, in need of redemption or of a political saviour ('strong leadership'). Both have an eschatological outlook, being obsessed with the fear of chaos, the breakdown of order, and both predict moral decline and decadence. They are willing to defer to absolute values and accept absolute authority as a refuge from social and moral dissolution.

Non-religious conservative thinkers often replace God with Nature and regard inequality, leadership, and evolution as social phenomena justified by nature's own processes. Burke argued that conservation was nature's own pattern. 'By preserving the method of Nature in the conduct of the state, in what we improve we are never wholly new, in what we retain we are never wholly obsolete.'[23] The fallacy of reading natural laws into the artifices of society is self-evident. But many conservative thinkers who would disagree with Rousseau on everything else, agree with him that society corrupts men, and so look to nature as a moral indicator of how we should behave.

It is clear from these observations that conservatives usually have a strong moral sense. Their political theory and social policy revolves round the enforcement of law and order and the maintenance of moral standards in sexual and other matters, so as to control the 'beast within'. Naturally or religiously sanctioned institutions such as the family are to be preserved and politics must operate on the natural basis of the leaders and the led. Political obligation is seen as a moral, not merely a contractual, duty. In the distant past, this was justified on religious grounds, by the 'divine right' of monarchs, but today conservatives are more likely to refer to the organic view of society which views the individual as a small but essential part, owing a duty to society because she benefits from the wellbeing of the whole. Evidently, such doctrines are far removed from the 'amoral' attitude of liberalism, with its emphasis on rational utilitarian calculation and on contractual and prudential obligation.

As to government's responsibility for social welfare, conservatives would prefer individuals to look after their own needs, being suitably rewarded for fulfilling the duties of their stations in society—a reasonable hope in unchanging, traditional societies but one unlikely to be realized in periods of rapid social and economic change. The doctrine of *self-help* taken together with Social Darwinism ('the survival of the fittest'), with its corollary of the weeding out of the inadequate advocated by Spencer, appealed to the liberal conservatives of nineteenth-century England. However, the more customary approach to inequality and poverty has been the idea that the rich should help and protect the poor, this being one of their natural duties—an attitude reminiscent of feudal practice. Hence, the tradition of philanthropic aristocrats in Victorian England. From the conservative viewpoint, a welfare state based on individual taxpayers' contributions is an artificial, impersonal creation which destroys natural relationships and precludes the ancient duty of *charity*. Although mutual dependence and charity may not seem to characterize the policy of the 1980s conservative administrations in Britain and

---

23. Burke, *Reflections on the Revolution in France*, p. 120.

the USA, it must be recalled that they both aligned themselves with classical liberalism, which emphasized self-help and independence.

In terms of the *practice* of politics, the conservative's rejection of ideology, rationalism, and radical reform stems from the perception of society as a natural entity, which cannot be artificially manipulated. Nor can the rich and complex 'tapestry of life' be governed by simplistic theoretical principles: pragmatism is the only valid political method. Conservatives may therefore advocate diverse or even contradictory policies at different times, but the aim of their intervention in politics is always the conservation of what is good in society and the promotion of social cohesion and harmony. These are the highest political ideals of conservatism, ideals which, it should be noted, allocate a minor place to the individual and the foremost place to the social whole. In practice, such politics almost invariably uphold the *status quo*. Conservatism therefore tends to support what Lukács called 'the sterile tyranny of the existent'.

Because of conservatives' reluctance to subscribe to an explicit ideology, the meaning of conservatism can only be pieced together through the excavation of particular beliefs and convictions. In *The Psychology of Conservatism*, Wilson unearthed nine aspects of the 'conservative character' which include a belief in strict rules and punishment, conventionalism, anti-hedonism, militarism, opposition to scientific progress, and intolerance of minorities.[24] Despite the piecemeal nature of many conservatives' understanding of their own ideology, when the fundamental assumptions are examined, they show the essential coherence of the specific beliefs, and suggest that conservatism is indeed a unified doctrine. But, given its pragmatic approach to politics, conservatism is perhaps better classified as a disposition or a world-view than treated as an explicit ideology. Mannheim's exploration of the 'conservative mentality' takes this approach. He notes the conservative's unthinking inclination 'to accept the total environment in the accidental concreteness in which it occurs, as if it were the proper order of the world'. Conservative philosophy is only developed as a result of challenges from other ideologies, in particular, from liberalism, when it takes the form of a counter-utopia, an instrument of self-defence. Hence it is sometimes characterized as positional or situational. 'Intellectual conservatism' is created to defend a social order which is already determined and fixed: Hegel's achievement as a conservative was to raise 'an already present mode of experience to an intellectual level'.[25]

For the conservative, 'the fact of the mere existence of a thing endows it with higher value'. Mannheim also remarks on the conservative propensity to accept or exaggerate the irrational elements of the mind. Mannheim's contention is that conservatism only becomes an ideology *after the event*, justifying a way of life which has already been established. This fits with what has already been suggested, that conservatism is a formal, not a substantive, doctrine, which recommends the preservation of what exists, whatever that may be. The particular doctrines to which conservatives adhere at any time are therefore dependent on

24. G. Wilson (Ed.), *The Psychology of Conservatism*, Academic Press, 1973.
25. For Mannheim's view of conservative thought, see *Ideology and Utopia*, pp. 132, 206–15.

the social context. For these reasons, conservatism can be neither progressive, nor fully determinate in the content of its beliefs. Nevertheless, some radical right-wing movements have boasted of being progressive—for example, fascism.

While a point-by-point comparison of conservative and fascist beliefs discloses a number of shared convictions and assumptions—patriotism, nationalism, an organic view of society, inegalitarianism, appeal to traditional virtues, hatred of socialism, and pragmatism—these do not constitute a good reason for equating them. The fascist idea is one of a revolutionary start, which conservatives would naturally reject, followed by conservative stability. It can be argued that the initial impulse to change and restructure society distinguishes fascism completely from conservatism. Fascists share the 'conservative mentality' to some extent, but lack the moral inhibitions with respect to political behaviour and the fear of tampering with existing social forms, hence the radical and inhumanitarian face of fascism. To take one example, most British Conservative politicians, although they wish to limit or halt immigration, accept the existence of an established ethnic minority population in Britain as a *fait accompli*: it must now be regarded as part of the social whole, and treated accordingly. By contrast, neo-fascist parties such as the British National Party do not accept the accomplished fact and seek to undo it by compulsory repatriation or by harassment leading to 'voluntary' emigration of ethnic minorities. While fascists seek to reverse social developments which they deplore, conservatives try to make the best of them and integrate them into the existing social system.

CONSERVATISM TODAY

An analysis of conservative ideas in contemporary political debate cannot ignore the resurgence of right-wing ideals and policies in the 1980s which coincided—not merely by chance—with a prolonged world recession which has put an end to the postwar decades of affluence in the West. As political psychologists contend, voters become more right-wing when their standard of living is threatened. Thus, the 1980s saw the rise of a new ideological variant of conservatism in the West, the New Right. Right-wing libertarian and New Right Conservative theories developed as a reaction against social democracy and welfare liberalism. In economics, the New Conservatives adopted a Hayekian, *laissez-faire* approach— they became 'neo-liberals'. They favoured privatization of national assets and deregulation of markets (e.g. the reduction of employment protection, building safety regulations, etc.) to encourage business. Social services were cut or abolished: people were to be forced to be self-reliant. Economic freedom was to be maximized, but what of personal freedom? New Right thinkers were often libertarian, especially in the USA, where they advocate minimal government regulation of private life, but in Britain there are many New Right thinkers with more conventional conservative values such as Scruton, who emphasized allegiance, tradition and national identity and advocated stricter laws and fewer safeguards for individual freedom.[26] Extreme libertarian arguments have already been discussed in Chapters 3 and 6, and the more moderate neo-liberal and New Right approach which will occupy us here.

The practical outcome in Britain of this general move to the right was the election in 1979 of a 'radical' and doctrinaire government, headed by Margaret Thatcher, who remained Prime Minister until 1990. The Thatcher approach to policy was clearly ideological from the outset, and thus a departure from the pragmatism of previous Conservative governments. A major plank of the government's programme was the monetarist principle expounded by the economist Friedman, which requires minimum government intervention in the economy, except for a strict control of the money supply to curb inflation. This was, essentially, a neo-liberal policy, founded on the belief that free enterprise, unhindered by state interference, would produce a healthy, efficient economy via the market mechanism. The market was, wherever possible, preferred to the state. A series of Conservative administrations divested the state of many functions which it had previously had, by extensive privatization of public utilities and many functions previously performed by the civil service. These developments were part of an anti-state drive and a deliberate rejection of the Keynesian policies favoured by socialist governments, which advocated intimate state involvement with the economy and an expanding public sector to stimulate growth and employment. Thus, the choice of an economic policy is not politically neutral: both monetarism and the Thatcher government's policy of raising indirect taxes and lowering income tax (a move towards 'regressive' taxation which redistributes money towards the better-off sections of society) reflected ideological choices. The justification of such moves was the orthodox liberal one, that low direct taxes encourage individual responsibility, enterprise, and productivity. The cuts made in public expenditure were also intended to shift the balance of the economy back towards private enterprise and *laissez-faire*. However, the result has been the destruction of part of Britain's industrial base (described as 'streamlining') with no correlative and compensating investment in new industries and with the consequence of increased unemployment.

A paradoxical aspect of New Right Thatcherite policy was that it was anti-state but pro-authority. The state's role as an economic agent and as distributor of welfare was deliberately reduced (by privatization and the curtailing of social services), while simultaneously many of its control functions were extended. The maintenance of law and order was a much-emphasized aspect of government policy, and the state's powers of control were enlarged—over unions and over 'rebel' local councillors who defied government policy and tried to assert their autonomy. The powers of the police were increased and the legal rights of accused individuals were reduced. It seems that, while the benevolent face of the state was being erased, its disciplinary role was deliberately reinforced—from paternalism

---

26. An excellent account of New Right doctrines is given in R. Levitas, 'New Right Utopias', *Radical Philosophy* **39**, Spring 1985; see also R. Levitas (Ed.), *The Ideology of the New Right*, Polity Press, 1986, and D. Wendelken, 'Contemporary conservatism, human nature and identity: the philosophy of Roger Scruton', *Politics* (1996), 16 (1), pp. 17–22.

to patriarchy? These contradictory developments reflected the incongruous mixture of conservative and neo-liberal beliefs which animated the British Conservative Party at the time: state control in the social sphere, free enterprise in the economic sphere. But the extension of centralization and of the state's coercive functions is in turn hard to reconcile with the New Right's declared dislike of the state itself and its attendant bureaucracy. One other, less tangible, goal of government policy was a 'remoralization' of society, a revival of non-permissive morality and the restoration of conservative values such as discipline, thrift, hard work, and the family, in preference to the values of personal freedom and self-development.

What was remarkable about New Right Conservatism in Britain was its ideological approach to policy-making—a radical innovation for a formerly pragmatic party—and the fact that what the government actually chose to conserve was the free enterprise society beloved of classical liberalism. The resulting blend of statist and individualistic, inegalitarian and formally egalitarian, policies illustrates the idiosyncratic nature of British Conservatism which has eschewed the straightforwardly reactionary attitude of many European conservatives. Britain was not alone in undergoing a resurgence of conservative neo-liberalism: the economic aspirations of President Reagan were similar, and 'Thatcherism' found admirers and emulators elsewhere in Europe. Conservatism was, in fact, spurred on to a new ideological self-definition by the failure of social-democratic governments to maintain prosperity in the face of economic crisis. (Adamant anti-socialism and anti-communism was another feature common to all the New Conservative theorists and politicians.) This bears out Mannheim's observation that conservatism manifests itself in a coherent, ideological form as a result of antagonism to other ideologies.

IDEOLOGY OR INTUITION?

The pragmatic nature of political conservatism has been emphasized. It is, in the literal sense of the term, a reactionary ideology, evoked as a reaction against other doctrines. Unlike fascism, it has no fixed goal or purpose. It therefore manifests itself in different political stances according to circumstances. Nevertheless, it is rooted in widely shared intuitions and emotions. Many people who do not vote Conservative are instinctively conservative. Biologically we are *all* 'conservative'—the human organism tries to preserve itself and to avoid violent effort, disruption and change—and Freud held the same to be true of the psyche, with 'Thanatos', the conservative principle, symbolizing the drive to inertia, or the 'death wish' and striving to prevail over 'Eros', the active life instinct. Some conservative instincts are pre-intellectual, and come into play when rationalist ideologies fail us. Typically, conservatism dictates a passive approach to politics, and even a certain fatalism, since conservation and the prevention of change can often best be brought about by *inaction*. Conservatives usually object to planning and major reforms. This is partly because the success of reforms can never be guaranteed, whereas the virtues of existing systems are tried and tested, and partly because of conservatives' pessimism about human nature. Being sceptical of human capacities and intelligence, they are unlikely to trust the reformer or utopian in preference to nature and custom. Reform and social revolution also rest on ideologies or abstract theories of which conservatives are congenitally suspicious, being anti-intellectual at heart, and knowing the ability of the mind to deceive itself, and others. Burke and his French contemporary, Joseph de Maistre, attacked the French revolution vitriolically, because of its abstract principles and utopian dreams. Society is an organism, not a machine, and cannot be refashioned according to human will or purpose. The conservative hostility to utopianism continued in the twentieth century, with Hayek and Oakeshott decrying the presumptuousness of socialist planning and 'rationalism' in politics—indeed, Hayek saw such planning as the road to serfdom and to totalitarianism. In answer to a utopian, the conservative would reply with the adage 'The best is the enemy of the good'. In some circumstances the conservative point against social engineering is certainly well-made. In the colonial era, imperialist powers like Britain attempted to graft their own political institutions on to different cultures, with disastrous results. The imposition of Westminster-style democracies on African countries has been a failure in many instances. Starting in the 1890s, the colonial powers created the modern map of Africa on the basis of their essentially European understanding of nation-states and national boundaries: the new boundaries cut across many tribal and ethnic allegiances and have been a constant source of dispute and conflict in the post-colonial era. So the conservative recommendation that political and social reform or re-construction should build sensitively on existing social phenomena carries conviction—and indeed is sound common sense.

Because conservatism frequently appears as the opponent of change, or as a reaction against more constructive ideologies, we must finally ask whether it truly merits the title of 'ideology'. No doubt conservatism is the chameleon among ideologies, since its guise depends on the context and the nature of its enemy, but certain fundamental convictions have been identified which constitute a distinct political standpoint. The premises on which these convictions rest, that human nature is imperfect and inequality is natural and desirable, are certainly credible, and can perhaps claim more supporting empirical evidence than, say, the premise of human goodness or perfectibility. But conservatism seems an essentially incomplete and somewhat negative ideology because it offers no constructive goals for the future and does not inspire political commitment and activism: the conservative would, however, make no apology for this, seeing activist or utopian movements as dangerous and doomed to fail. Burke's defence of conservatism amounts to the claim that it tempers change with caution and respect for tradition. If we already lived in utopia, this might be the right path to follow, to prevent a fall from grace, a diminution of social perfection. But in real societies, the justification of existing imperfections by conservative arguments can delay or altogether prevent much-needed social improvement.

FURTHER READING

L. Allison, *Right Principles*, Blackwell, 1984.

R. Devigne, *Recasting Conservatism*, Yale U.P., 1995.

S. Hall and M. Jacques (Eds.), *The Politics of Thatcherism*, Lawrence & Wishart, 1983.

A.O. Hirschman, *The Rhetoric of Reaction: Perversity, Futility, Jeopardy*, Belknap Press, 1991.

T. Honderich, *Conservatism*, Hamish Hamilton, 1990.

D. S. King, *The New Right: Politics, Markets and Citizenship*, Macmillan, 1987.

R. Levitas (Ed.), *The Ideology of the New Right*, Polity Press, 1986.

R. Nisbet, *Conservatism*, Open University Press, 1986.

M. Oakeshott, *Rationalism in Politics*, Methuen, 1962.

N. O'Sullivan, *Conservatism*, Dent, 1976.

A. Quinton, *The Politics of Imperfection*, Faber & Faber, 1978.

R. Scruton, *The Meaning of Conservatism*, 2nd edn, Macmillan, 1984.

R. Scruton (Ed.) *Conservative Texts: An Anthology*, Macmillan, 1991.

Chapter 8

Totalitarianism

A system where *technologically advanced instruments* of political power are wielded *without restraint* by *centralized leaderships* of an *elite movement*, to effect *total social revolution*, including the conditioning of man, based on an *arbitrary ideology* proclaimed by the leadership in an atmosphere of *coerced unanimity* of the entire population.

This description of totalitarianism[1] suggests that it is a clearly definable phenomenon. However, the concept of totalitarianism presents many problems to the political theorist, by contrast with such definitive usages by political scientists and the simplistic use of the word in political argument. Although the term 'totalitarian' was used in a laudatory sense by Mussolini to denote his own fascist corporate state, it was later popularized by the opponents of fascist and communist dictatorships, such as Neumann,[2] and is now invariably used in the pejorative sense, often very loosely. It is therefore difficult to distinguish a purely objective meaning of the term. Totalitarianism, although included in the section of this book concerned with ideologies, is not an ideology like the others discussed here: nobody advocates totalitarianism for its own sake, or proclaims herself 'proud to be totalitarian'. And yet the term is used by its critics as if it represented a distinct political anti-ideal, despite the fact that they concoct their definition of the concept on the self-contradictory basis of two mutually opposed ideologies and political systems, fascism and communism. Totalitarianism is included here partly to expose the fallacy of treating it as a distinct, if deplorable, political ideology, and partly because it is methodologically instructive to see how the self-appointed critics of totalitarianism have constructed the idea on shaky theoretical foundations.

---

1. This passage is a compilation of the totalitarian characteristics listed in Z. Brzezinski, 'Totalitarianism and rationality', *American Political Science Review* L, 3, 751–63 (1956).
2. See, e.g., S. Neumann, *Permanent Revolution*, Pall Mall, 1965.

The most influential views on the subject have been propounded by political scientists, historians, and psychologists, rather than by political philosophers, hence the diversity of approaches. Taken together, their works offer much useful information about the activities of absolutist states in this century, but whether they have succeeded in isolating a *sui generis* political form and ideology must be doubted. These various approaches will be summarized and discussed, and then a theoretical critique will be offered.

THE PHENOMENOLOGICAL APPROACH

This approach identifies the phenomena characteristic of totalitarian societies and consists largely of an account of their political methods and institutions. The 'six-point syndrome' of Friedrich and Brzezinski is the best known characterization.[3] They argued that the totalitarian state is constituted by:

(1) An official ideology incorporating a vision of the ideal state, belief in which is compulsory. Unorthodoxy is punishable.
(2) A single party which is bureaucratic and hierarchical, usually led by one man.
(3) A terroristic police.
(4) A monopoly of communications.
(5) A monopoly of weapons.
(6) A centrally directed economy.

These are characteristics which the authors found to be common to Nazi Germany, Russia under Stalin, communist countries in Eastern Europe and Mussolini's Italy. As they pointed out, conditions (3)–(6) are strongly dependent on advanced technology, so that totalitarianism can only emerge in societies at a certain stage of their development. We should note that this definition deliberately discounts the 'illusion' of democracy found in some totalitarian societies and centres on the essential elitism of such systems.

Each of the six points can be elaborated further to convey the repressive nature of totalitarian society. The single party brooks no institutional rivals: despite the official dualism which may exist between state and party (as in the Soviet Union where many institutions were duplicated at state and party level), the state is subjugated by the party and remains an empty form. The independence and impartiality of that traditional watchdog, the judiciary, is subverted, as are other potentially autonomous sources of authority, such as the Church and the family. All popular opposition to the party is eliminated, being branded as anti-social and immoral. In this respect, as in many others, totalitarianism is the antithesis of pluralism, which tolerates heterodoxy, and accepts that there is a multitude of competing political truths; for this reason, Finer calls totalitarianism 'monistic',[4] while others describe it as 'monolithic'. John Gray has argued that

---

3. C. J. Friedrich and Z. Brzezinski, *Totalitarian Dictatorship and Autocracy*, 2nd edn, Harvard U.P., 1965, pp. 21–22 especially. The status of the Friedrich/Brzezinski analysis is usefully criticized in A. James Gregor, *Interpretations of Fascism*, General Learning Press, 1974, Ch. 7.
4. S. Finer, *Comparative Government*, Allen Lane, 1970, p. 77.

[t]he totalitarian project is the project of suppressing civil society—that sphere of autonomous institutions, protected by the rule of law, within which individuals and communities possessing divergent values and beliefs may coexist in peace.[5]

Later elaborations of the totalitarian syndrome give special prominence to the role of the self-proclaimedly infallible and invincible leader, the symbolic figurehead parodied in Orwell's *Nineteen Eighty-Four* (1949) as 'Big Brother'. It is immaterial who the leader is, Orwell implies, or even whether he is alive or dead—he is primarily the emblem of the state, the embodiment of the will of the people. The totalitarian state rests on unlimited, unconstitutional power (critics disregard official constitutions since they are so often abrogated) and effects an enlargement of the public or political sphere so as to include even private life and morality within the reach of political action. (This averts the unorthodoxy and opposition found within the extensive sphere of individual privacy in liberal democracies.) To this end, the people are controlled coercively by the laws, the police and the use of terror, and by the direction of labour in the planned economy. The most powerful means of control is ideology, the instrument of persuasion and indoctrination. All the critics of totalitarianism remark on the 'irrational' nature of totalitarian ideologies, which is apparent even when they purport to be scientific, like Marxism. Cassirer analyses the ritual and mythical aspects of fascist ideology while Marcuse detailed the 'magical' quality which Marxist doctrine assumed in the USSR.[6]

Clearly, the various parts of the totalitarian syndrome are not accidentally combined but are intimately and necessarily connected, each being essential to the reinforcement of the others and to the maintenance of the totalistic nature of such systems. The elements taken together form a coherent, self-perpetuating political system. A further impression of life in such a system can be gained from the celebrated dystopian novels which depict totalitarian societies. Orwell's *Nineteen Eighty-Four* and Zamyatin's *We* (1921) emphasize the elitist and terroristic aspects of such societies, while Huxley's *Brave New World* (1932) and Karp's *One* (1953) suggest how the physical and mental conformity which destroys the identity of the individual can be achieved by ideology, conditioning and even by genetic engineering. These fictions embellish tendencies observable in real totalitarian societies and all focus chiefly on the annihilation of individuality, which seems to Westerners the most abhorrent aspect of such societies. These novels therefore constitute useful appendices to the academic expositions of the phenomenological approach.

However, from a theoretical viewpoint, the chief objection to the approach exemplified by Friedrich and Brzezinski, although it may be factually accurate, is that it assumes what it seeks to prove. First, certain societies are branded as totalitarian presumably on the basis of some intuition or adverse judgement—then, the characteristics which they share are listed, while their dissimilarities are conveniently forgotten. The fact that left-wing and right-wing totalitarian states

---

5. J. Gray, 'Totalitarianism, reform and civil society', in *Totalitarianism at the Crossroads* (Ed. E. F. Paul), Transaction Books, 1990.
6. E. Cassirer, *The Myth of the State*, Oxford U.P., 1946, Chaps II, XVIII; H. Marcuse, *Soviet Marxism*, Columbia U.P., 1958.

rest on antithetical ideologies is glossed over. (This method is similar to that used by some political scientists to 'analyse' democracy. The USA is declared to be democratic, then the characteristics of democracy are enumerated by abstracting from its political institutions. The descriptive approach precludes deeper analysis of the idea, and its critical application.) Another danger of the phenomenological approach is that non-totalitarian states may exhibit some of the six features: indeed, some thinkers claim to see a convergence between totalitarian and advanced industrial states which makes it hard to maintain that totalitarianism is a distinct species of political society, the contrary of liberal democracy. The question of how many of the six features a state must exhibit before it becomes totalitarian is essentially unanswerable. Ultimately it is unsatisfactory to define a political concept purely in terms of appearances and characteristics which may be accidental, as do Friedrich and Brzezinski, since this gives rise to the problems already mentioned and provides no explanation of the nature or motivation of the totalitarian state. Nor does this approach substantiate the view that totalitarianism is a *sui generis* ideology, for a collection of political methods does not constitute an ideology. In essence, the phenomenological approach mistakes a set of political *methods* for a homogeneous political *goal*.

THE SOCIO-HISTORICAL APPROACH

The political theorist and historian Arendt attempted to explain the emergence and the nature of totalitarianism by searching for its roots in historical events and in political culture. She called totalitarianism 'total terror'. She also *assumed* that Nazi Germany and communist Russia were totalitarian and that the concept had a distinct, definable meaning. Using Germany after the First World War as an example, she identified the four conditions essential to the formation of a totalitarian state:[7]

(1) Class and community breakdown has occurred during and after war, because of rapid industrialization and the spread of individualistic liberal doctrines.
(2) The unpoliticized mass is suddenly enfranchised, but its lack of political culture and ignorance of democratic procedure makes it an easy prey to demagogic leaders.
(3) A 'negative solidarity' is artificially generated within the mass of individuals who were sundered by conditions (1) and (2); this has, however, none of the positive connotations of 'class solidarity'. Individuals flee from their isolation and search for personal identity through mass activities, such as vast political rallies. Displaced intellectuals espouse the movement in a similar search for identity, and thereby legitimize it.
(4) The precondition for a totalitarian society is a large population, since such states habitually generate internal cohesion by the creation and persecution of scapegoats on a large scale (e.g. the Jews in Nazi Germany).

---

7. H. Arendt, *The Origins of Totalitarianism*, rev. edn, Allen & Unwin, 1967.

The six characteristics of the totalitarian 'syndrome' are necessary consequences of these objective historical conditions. A powerful and irrational ideology is needed to explain the world to the politically naive masses, while the breakdown of classes and other social groupings and the isolation of individuals makes terror and mutual spying a convenient way of keeping order at low cost, with little risk of mass retaliation. An omnipotent symbolic leader supplies—albeit illusorily— the solidarity which individuals lost when the traditional community vanished.

Arendt gives a powerful insight into the working of Nazi Germany, from which she was a refugee, and her hypothesis that terror in the absence of opposition does not disappear but becomes *total* may prove to be an important and sinister political truth. Nevertheless, her 'theory' of totalitarianism rests largely on the special case of Germany, and the induction of general laws from single instances is a risky procedure, however inspired the theorist. One consequence of Arendt's account is that totalitarianism could only emerge at a certain historical point in a country's development. Therefore, if the problems posed by (1) and (2) could be resolved in other ways the risk might be avoided altogether. The socio-historical approach also offers no evidence that totalitarianism is a homogeneous political phenomenon or a distinct political ideology.

Another historical analysis of right-wing totalitarianism, again based on the German experience, was that of Weiss, who considered fascism a resurgence of an older political phenomenon, the 'radical right', which is often reactivated during periods of rapid social change and modernization when 'upstart' liberals and radicals become the dominant class and other groups suffer anomie.[8] Weiss argued that in the unstable postwar period in Germany an alliance was formed between threatened landowners and the fearful lower-middle class, whose sentiments were vocalized and vulgarized by Hitler. These rightist elements disliked urbanization and the resulting crime and decadence and were attracted by solutions such as the creation of an 'organic' state, and the revival of peasant virtues. In an era when reactionary conservative politics seemed outmoded, fascism provided an answer to the right's deep hatred of both liberalism and communism. Thus, Nazism called itself 'the third way'. Weiss's account of fascism again provides no theoretical analysis of totalitarianism and suggests that fascism itself is not an original ideology, but a negative and pragmatic reaction to prevailing ideologies, which provides a new outlet for those who would otherwise be conservatives. The analyses of Arendt and Weiss show clearly that any attempt to understand fascism or communism as historical movements has the inevitable effect of dissolving the notion of totalitarianism as a general, unified phenomenon.

THE ESSENTIALIST ANALYSIS

Attempts were made to incorporate the concept of totalitarianism into political theory by various writers who sought to show the special and unique nature of the political form through an examination of the assumptions and implicit premises

---

8. H. J. Weiss, *The Fascist Tradition*, Harper & Row, 1967.

of totalitarianism. Foremost among these was Talmon, who found the origins of 'totalitarian democracy' in eighteenth- and nineteenth-century thought dating from Rousseau,[9] and Popper, who traced the advocates of the 'closed society' back to Plato, and also found theoretical antecedents of totalitarianism in Hegel, Marx and Utopian thinkers.[10] The following characteristics were singled out as conditions for totalitarian thinking:

(1) A Utopian Vision

The dominant ideology offers an explicit vision of the ideal society, a goal to which everything must be subordinated, even if it is never achieved. On the basis of this unique political 'truth', all rival ideologies are outlawed: there is no acceptance of a plurality of truths, and no tolerance. Talmon finds the origin of this in Rousseau's General Will—though he might equally have blamed exclusive religions such as Christianity for this mode of thinking—while Popper detects them in Plato's absolute Ideas, and condemns this way of thinking as antithetical to the 'open society'. In institutional terms, the 'utopian' way of thinking leads to one-party states and one-candidate elections—to the 'monolith'.

(2) Despondency about Human Nature

Like other ideologies, totalitarianism rests on a view of human nature: this is Hobbesian in its pessimism and conservative in its condescension and also harks back to the views of mediaeval political theologians about original sin. People are seen as innately wicked, weak, selfish, and hence anti-social. They are childlike, incapable of leading autonomous lives or of taking decisions for themselves, are in need of security, and can only exist as part of the social entity. Because people are irrational and irresponsible, their salvation lies in their leaders: in the Middle Ages, in the King-cum-Shepherd, in modern times, in the state. These premises are diametrically opposed to the liberal view of man as rational and independent, and equally opposed to Marxist assumptions about sociability, but they reflect and elaborate the standard 'pessimistic conservative' view of man's fallen state. Cassirer contends that the rituals and myths of Nazism were devised expressly to make real people resemble this archetype, reducing them to irrational, primitive beings. Since totalitarian theories and other theories resting on similar premises recommend elite rule, the obvious objection is that if human nature is universally blemished, the leaders themselves must be equally blemished and incapable of leadership. But, needless to say, such theorists also—paradoxically?—posit ineradicable inequality and would retort that there are two natural classes, the leaders and the led, a doctrine found in Plato and in Nietzsche's idea of the Superman, and one which critics read into Lenin's account of the role of the Party. This view of human nature, and of the necessity of elitism, is self-evidently opposed to democratic aspirations and gives the lie to the false pretensions of some totalitarian states to democratic institutions.

9. J. L. Talmon, *The Origins of Totalitarian Democracy*, Praegar, 1960.
10. K. Popper, *The Open Society and its Enemies*, Routledge & Kegan Paul, 1962. Vols 1 and 2.

(3) Real Needs

Totalitarian ideologies make a distinction between people's felt and real needs, arguing that their defects make them incapable of knowing their own good. Talmon analyses Rousseau's dictum that man can be 'forced to be free' in being made to conform to the General Will (which is but his own *real* will) in these terms. A benevolent despot, or the Party acting as the 'vanguard of the people', enacts the 'real' needs of the people, often against their will and even coercively. The result is paternalism backed by force. According to liberal-democratic theory, the only possible guide to people's 'real' needs is their democratically expressed preferences. People may not think deeply enough, or with enough foresight, but if we disregard their 'felt' needs or preferences, there is no guarantee that the rulers will not substitute their own selfish interests for those of the people, which is exactly what totalitarian leaders are reputed to do. The liberal argument that each man knows his own interests best contradicts the idea that he can have 'real' needs unknown to him, although most liberals would readily admit that people can be mistaken about their interests and must on occasion be guided by governments.[11]

The liberal critique of the idea of 'real needs' or 'real interests' arises partly from the 'openness' of liberal thinking, the conviction that there is no single political truth but a multiplicity of individual interests and value-judgements, and partly from the more cynical conviction, reinforced by studies of elitism and Michels' 'iron law of oligarchy',[12] that power-holders will invariably pursue their private interests when unrestrained by a free, democratic system, although they may try to disguise these as the 'real' interests of the people or as the state's interest, falsely equating the state and the people. The exclusive vision of the ideal society mentioned above explains and exonerates references to 'real' needs and even, in some cases, the adoption of coercive means to achieve the ideal. Thus, the exclusive vision of truth, plus the notion of 'real' needs, explicates and justifies the arbitrary and repressive nature of totalitarian rule. If the leaders or the party, their eyes fixed on a utopian vision, are acting to realize that vision, why should they be impeded by the superficial preferences of the uneducated, by legality or by other conventional rules of procedure which might delay the attainment of the goal? The Good sweeps all before it.

(4) The Sacrifice of Freedom

In order to attain the ideal, totalitarian states reduce the degree of personal and political freedom, sometimes offering greater material security instead. This strategy results from the view of human nature outlined above. If people are incapable of freedom, freedom cannot realistically be given priority as a political ideal. As is well known, the citizens of the 'totalitarian' communist countries had little political freedom, but a fair degree of economic security; this reflects the relative values allocated to these two ideals. Liberal theorists find the totalitarian

---

11. B. Barry, 'The public interest', in *Political Philosophy* (Ed. A. Quinton), p.116.
12. R. Michels, *Political Parties* (trans. E. Paul and C. Paul), Free Press, 1962, pp. 342–56.

attitude to personal freedom the most abhorrent aspect of such systems and treat it almost as the defining characteristic of totalitarianism.

(5) The Hypertrophy of Politics

In Talmon's words, totalitarianism in operation 'politicizes' the whole of life, extending the public sphere unduly and invading privacy in ways injurious to individual wellbeing. Talmon stresses this politicization phenomenon as evidence of a totalitarian reconceptualization of the role of the public and private spheres, the effect of which is greatly to reduce the latter, by comparison with the prominent place that it occupies in liberal theory. It should be pointed out that this criticism is based on the remarkably attenuated view of the scope and importance of politics and public life held by liberal democrats, and their conviction that it is possible to be politically neutral and objective about major social issues. These views are certainly not shared by other cultures, past or present. For Plato and Aristotle, man was *Homo politicus* and his self-fulfilment was to be found, precisely, in the public sphere and through political participation rather than in economic and private life.

In Britain, we tend to see politics as something which people have the right *not* to participate in, something which is strictly voluntary. As a consequence, we deplored the political education or 'indoctrination' which occurred in Soviet schools as a forcible politicization of children and, by contrast, we eschew political subjects in school. (Yet there is much to be said for not allowing children to grow up ignorant of political matters, believing that politics is 'out there', beyond their control and irrelevant to their personal lives.) Making voting compulsory in Britain would be regarded as a gross violation of privacy. Liberals also look with disfavour on totalitarian states' interventions in 'private' matters such as birth control, although the effects of population explosions are indisputably political. Examples of the liberals' deliberately restricted view of politics and the 'public interest' could be multiplied indefinitely: they reflect an individualistic political culture. But, if totalitarian states extend the scope of political action to include aspects of life which liberals consider private, this is not a contravention of a universal norm, because there is no *natural* limit to political activity or to the scope of legal regulation, even though liberals wish to set such a limit. In South Africa in the days of apartheid, racist laws even extended into the bedroom, forbidding sexual relationships between whites and blacks. In a totalitarian state the law may also try to regulate people's minds. This may be deplorable but it is not *per se* illegitimate. But for the liberal critic, one of totalitarianism's worst crimes is to acknowledge no boundary between the public and the private, and to treat social life as a homogeneous phenomenon, subject to political regulation in all its parts.

(6) State Supremacy

Closely associated with the expansion of the political sphere is the exaltation of the state in totalitarian thinking. The individual is perceived as a subordinate part of the greater whole and not, as by liberals, as the locus of the supreme political value. Individuals are, as a consequence, treated as if they were uniform ciphers, with identical needs and wants—'enforced homogeneity'. The survival of the state at all costs and by all means becomes the dominant political goal. In fascist Germany, the state was viewed as a mystical entity, whose existence was bound up with the purity of the race and the territorial integrity of the nation. By contrast, Marxism is, officially, anti-state, but communist practice strengthened and exalted the state apparatus and also, contrary to the internationalist aspirations of socialism (although understandably in the context of the emergence of the USSR), adopted a highly nationalistic outlook. So, in fact, the two archetypal ideologies which supported totalitarian systems had very different theoretical analyses of the state, even if their practice looked similar. As Barber points out, 'statism' is what most people would identify as the defining characteristic of totalitarianism. As can be seen, this is an inevitable consequence of the assumptions made about human nature and human needs.

The essentialist definition of totalitarianism can therefore be summarized as 'total methods in pursuit of a total goal', which Popper claimed to find originating in Plato, and Talmon in Rousseau. Evidently, the assumptions and ideals imputed to totalitarianism by their critics deny and negate the values cherished by liberal democrats at every point. Four liberal convictions are particularly menaced by totalitarianism:

(1) That social good cannot be precisely defined, so that an open-ended approach should be taken towards the ideal society, and no dogmatic political ideology should be officially adopted.
(2) That people know their own real needs and their best interests, and it is mere presumption for rulers to dictate or gainsay these, which should be expressed through the democratic process. Totalitarian forms of democracy on the Rousseauist or Marxist model are discounted, being defined as not democratic in the liberal way.
(3) That if state power is minimized, under a system of democracy and consent-based laws, people can make the choices which maximize their personal utility.
(4) That the plurality of needs, desires and tastes in political and private matters can only be catered for in a system based on tolerance which also allows legitimate opposition.

The underlying value which gives rise to these convictions is the uniqueness and importance of the individual and her rights. It is a commonplace that 'individuality' is suppressed or extinguished in totalitarian societies: enforced equality and uniformity takes over. Yet it may be said that we in the West have a questionable notion of individuality, resting heavily, as it does, on the individual's ability to distinguish herself from others by means of expenditure and possessions. Totalitarian states have been accused of suppressing individuality by conditioning the minds of their inhabitants—but nowhere, even in the free world, do individuals resemble the rational, autonomous beings of Enlightenment philosophy. All individuals are conditioned one way or another, but we happen to prefer the covert conditioning which takes place in the West. It cannot, of course, be true that totalitarianism eliminates individuality—the existence of individuals is a biological fact, and no society can entirely succeed in curbing self-assertion, although attempts may be made to control its manifestations, via norms and conventions, as in liberal society, or coercively. What is true, on the other hand, is that the ideologies dominant in totalitarian societies allocated a less prominent place than liberals do to the individual in their conception of the social whole. This may justify a more holistic approach to policy, but it cannot abolish real individuals, although it can curb their freedom.

A further point in mitigation of liberal criticism of totalitarianism is that it, like liberal democracy, claims to realize the good of the people, and both may be right in their own sense. Western democracies are slaves to the short-term preferences of electors and realize the people's good in that respect, whereas a one-party democracy could claim to realize the long-term good of the community taken as a whole. Likewise, both forms of democracy might assert that they follow the will of the people: in the case of liberal democracy, this is the immediate subjective will, and in 'totalitarian democracy' it is the real, objective will, similar to Rousseau's General Will. If we accept that both sides make such claims seriously, totalitarianism cannot be summarily dismissed as a cynical contravention of the will, and the good, of the people.

The problem in considering the essentialist definition is that the 'ideology' of totalitarianism has been compiled by its detractors in such a way as to show it to be the antithesis of liberal individualism. Whether such a doctrine exists is therefore highly questionable. The inhabitant of a communist society would call herself a communist, not a totalitarian. And communism and fascism, which are habitually equated with totalitarianism in Western parlance, do not share every one of the assumptions and values said to constitute the essence of the ideology. Popper *et al.* have in effect deduced these unstated assumptions and values from the practices which they consider totalitarian, then pieced them together into a coherent political outlook which, nevertheless, differs fundamentally from the two archetypal ideologies of totalitarianism. Popper and Talmon proceeded to reinterpret the works of earlier theorists in terms of this constructed ideology—retrospectively and anachronistically.[13] This is not the place to enter into the details of such debates as 'Was Rousseau a totalitarian?' which are, in any case, self-evidently futile, but it should be said that the theories of Rousseau and Plato coincide only at some points with what are held to be the main tenets of totalitarian ideology, and that Popper notoriously distorted Plato's views at many points in order to brand him as the first enemy of the open society.[14]

---

13. See Popper and Talmon as cited, and also R. Crossman, *Plato Today*, Allen & Unwin, 1937; A. Cobban, *Rousseau and the Modern State*, Allen & Unwin, 1964, and E. Cassirer, *The Question of Jean-Jacques Rousseau*, Columbia U.P., 1954.
14. Popper's misrepresentations and misquotations are catalogued in R. Levinson, *In Defence of Plato*, Harvard U.P., 1953, Chap. 9.

What can be inferred from the essentialist analysis is that there is a recurrent tendency towards absolutism and elitism in political thought. But these writers wish to establish a stronger thesis, namely, that totalitarianism itself has been implicit in certain works of political theory since classical times. Yet as the six-point syndrome suggests, totalitarian systems could not have existed before advanced industrial society, since so many of their features depend on high technology and efficient communications, so that to suggest that totalitarianism is one of the perpetual themes of political thought must be nonsense. Certainly, we can concede that autocracy and so-called totalitarianism rest on some shared beliefs, particularly that of the need of the populace for strong, even dictatorial, leadership. In that respect, both are the polar opposites of the optimistic views of liberals and socialists about the possibility of self-government and popular sovereignty. Autocracy and totalitarianism both put the nation or state above the individuals who compose it, but not always for the same reasons. Modern autocrats often display transparent self-interest, whereas totalitarian states at least purport to further the good of the people.

The essentialist analysis, then, goes further towards descrying a theoretical element in totalitarianism than the other two analyses, but unfortunately the totalitarian 'ideology' which it concocts has no self-styled adherents and has to be *imputed* to people who would not recognize it as their own ideology. To avoid this incongruity, totalitarianism might be said to be a meta-ideology, belonging to the system itself: a curious and untenable idea, for what can an ideology be which has no individual adherents? These difficulties suggest that the advocates of the essentialist analysis have not discovered a distinct totalitarian political theory, nor a totalitarian ideology, although their approach has been fertile in generating spirited witch hunts for the progenitors of the totalitarian bastard.

A significant by-product of the essentialist approach is that *utopianism* has been categorized as a species of totalitarianism, or as being potentially totalitarian. Schapiro listed the reasons for this, arguing that the utopian:[15]

(a) is preoccupied with ends and indifferent to means;
(b) views man and society as a totality;
(c) makes firm and dogmatic assumptions;
(d) is preoccupied with management (as opposed to democratic politics); and
(e) neglects human variety, and seeks to impose uniformity.

Since the diversity of utopian texts far exceeds the diversity of those states called totalitarian, generalizations about utopianism are even more ill-founded. What utopian thinkers have in common with totalitarian states is a single-minded commitment to a definite social ideal, although their ideal societies differ vastly. Popper says that this entails that they will attempt to realize that ideal in the face of all opposition, by force if necessary,[16] an invalid inference, as most utopians proposed to use rational persuasion to realize their goals and relatively few gained, or even tried to gain, the political influence necessary to pursue their

---

15. L. Schapiro, *Totalitarianism*, Macmillan, 1972, pp. 85–90.
16. Popper, *The Open Society and its Enemies*, Vol. 1, pp. 157–68.

ideals. Totalitarianism and utopianism are both seen by liberals as forms of thought which justify ignoring people's legitimate wishes in order to impose some higher aim, but there is scant evidence for this in the case of the utopian, who promotes her ideal precisely because she believes that it will make people happy and that, when they understand it, they will also pursue it.

Needless to say, few utopias exhibit more than one or two points of the six-point syndrome, nor do they share all the assumptions and values specified in the essentialist view of totalitarianism, except, of course, the first, the utopian vision. It is this commitment which seems to make utopianism antithetical to the liberal-democratic ideal which declares that the good society is whatever the democratic will of the people makes it (in theory at least), so that the 'good society' is a fluid and flexible concept: democracy is an ideal *procedure* rather than a substantive ideal. The rationalist approach to changing society favoured by utopians is contrary to the pragmatic, piecemeal method of social change which Popper sees as appropriate to the open society and he compares it to what he considers a sinister feature of totalitarian societies, *planning*, alias social engineering. Utopianism is a particular method of political *theorizing*, while totalitarianism has been defined by its critics on the basis of political *practice*: these two 'isms' are therefore qualitatively and conceptually different and it is hard to accept that they have anything in common except their arousal of suspicion among liberal democrats.[17]

THE FASCIST EXAMPLE

Fascism is closely related to totalitarianism in most people's minds, and it is discussed here as an example of a doctrine which favours totalitarian methods of government. Kitchen argues that fascism was aimed 'mainly at the destruction of most of the liberties and norms of liberal society'.[18] The 'liberal societies' of Italy and Germany in the 1920s were relatively young, and suffering from the economic and psychological impact of defeat in the 1914–18 war. Liberalism was ailing: fascism and Nazism moved in to administer the *coup de grâce*. Fascism tends to appear when the working class's aspirations to socialism have been defeated, as they were in the failed revolution of 1918 in Germany. The capitalist elite becomes more ready to support non-liberal governments which are strongly anti-socialist— as the captains of industry supported Hitler in the 1930s. Among the people, the supporters of fascism are not industrial workers, but the petty bourgeoisie, artisans and small farmers who fear socialism and bankruptcy. Fascist governments often give little material reward to these supporters, but divert their frustration and anxiety by propaganda and by bellicose foreign adventures to stir up patriotic enthusiasm. Historically, the two most notorious fascist regimes, those of Hitler and Mussolini, despite their railing against liberal norms

17. For further references to the attack on utopianism, see G. Kateb, *Utopia and its Enemies*, Collier-Macmillan, 1963. See also B. Goodwin and K. Taylor, *The Politics of Utopia*, Hutchinson, 1982, Chap. 4.
18. M. Kitchen, *Fascism*, Macmillan, 1976.

and some aspects of capitalism, did little to change existing economic relationships, and protected property and the economic elite.

To the liberal notion of society as a collection of free individuals, fascism opposes a corporatist ideal which is the modern version of the organic conception of society. Diverse social groups are inseparably 'incorporated' in the body politic: their function within it gives them their identity. Individuals, in turn, gain identity through membership of these groups. The Italians viewed corporatism economically: important economic groups were integrated in the state processes. For the Germans, however, corporatism was something more sentimental—a racist, *volkisch* aspiration which was part of Nazi mythology rather than a principle of social or economic organization.

Fascists are instinctively anti-intellectual and emphasize the irrational components of behaviour. Fascism presented itself, especially in Germany, as a myth, a set of beliefs above rational explanation. As a result, fascist 'theory' is scarce and, as theory, painfully inadequate. The majority of the many books on fascism written since 1945 concentrate on the historical causes of the fascist phenomenon, rather than analysing the ideology—because there is so little to analyse.

The best-known aspect of fascism is its racialist basis. The underlying premise is that of natural inequality and fascists hold that this exists between races as well as between individuals. The 'myth of race', and that of Aryan supremacy, was founded on various pseudo-scientific doctrines of the nineteenth century, particularly on those of Chamberlain, who developed the idea of a 'folk nation' destined to triumph.[19] A confused blend of these doctrines was used to justify first imperialism, then the colonization of 'inferior races', then anti-semitism. Volk/ Nation and Blood/Race, with its corollary of racial and sexual purity, were key components of the Nazi myth. Social Darwinism played an important part in fascism, both in justifying the natural selection and triumph of some races at the expense of others (Bernhardi said 'War gives a biologically just decision'), and also in vindicating the elite political leadership which characterizes fascist states, the strong ruling the weak. Needless to say, the doctrine of the survival of the fittest is directly opposed to humanitarian ethics and to welfare policies directed at disadvantaged members of society. Fascists advocated elite and authoritarian government while invoking the support of the masses to validate their dictatorships by popular acclaim, as at the Nuremberg rallies. This ambivalent attitude towards the mass—contempt and invocation—caused Talmon to refer to such states as 'totalitarian democracies'.[20] Mussolini's dictum 'Believe, obey and fight' illustrates the authoritarian aspect of fascism and its reliance on the deference of the masses.

Fascists view society as a totality, an organic unity, and this, conjoined with a belief in elitism, is liable to produce authoritarian politics and a totalitarian state. Furthermore, fascists insist that the state is above morality and can do no wrong—a view in support of which the Nazis invoked Nietzsche's Superman, who

---

19. See, e.g., H. S. Chamberlain, *Ideal und Macht*, Munich, 1916.
20. J. L. Talmon, *The Origins of Totalitarianism*, Praeger, 1960.

was above all moral constraints. Neither individual rights nor tradition and law are allowed to hamper fascist leaders or the actions of a fascist state on the world stage. Fascism could be viewed as pragmatism taken to extremes—the no-holds-barred approach to politics. This explains why, historically, fascist parties were able both to distinguish themselves doctrinally from socialism, and to savagely persecute communists, while simultaneously introducing quasi-socialist welfare measures to alleviate social problems and win support. It is no accident, although it *is* a paradox, that Hitler called his party the National Socialist Party. Given the fascists' elevated notion of the 'Volk' or race, it is quite consistent for fascist governments to improve the wellbeing of the master race as far as possible, while treating other races as sub-human.

Fascism is by no means a danger of the past: during the war in Bosnia, 'ethnic cleansing' by the Serbs revived memories and fears of fascism. There is a resurgence of neo-fascist and neo-Nazi movements in Eastern Europe, in Germany and in Russia. Many nationalist parties in the former communist countries contain racist elements—for example, Vladimir Zhirinovsky's Liberal Democratic Party in Russia. In France, the extreme right-wing anti-immigrant party, Front National, led by Le Pen, has experienced some striking electoral successes. In Britain the British National Party pursues anti-immigration and racist policies and Combat 18, a more extreme neo-Nazi group, has been linked with assaults on property and hate mail. The USA has a long history of racist sub-groups, starting with the Ku Klux Klan, which has continued over the last three decades; groups still use the terms 'Nazi' and 'Aryan' in their titles.[21] Racism and anti-semitism characterize all these movements. The rapid resurgence of such emotions during a period of economic recession suggests that fascist attitudes cannot be totally erased by liberal-democratic culture, and lends some credence to the view that totalitarianism may have an underlying psychological explanation.

THE PSYCHOLOGICAL ROOTS OF TOTALITARIANISM

While Arendt specified the social and historical conditions for totalitarianism, others searched for its roots in the psychology of individuals. Adorno and others produced an influential study on these lines in the aftermath of the Second World War, *The Authoritarian Personality*. Individuals were asked to agree or disagree with long lists of statements, some crudely expressed, designed to elicit anti-semitic and other fascist prejudices. The totality of their answers gave them a ranking on the 'F-scale', said to measure fascist tendencies, and on a scale of ethnocentricity which showed their inclination to adhere to their own in-groups and to be hostile to, or make scapegoats of, outsiders and members of other ethnic groups. What was revealed was that a worryingly high percentage of individuals had deep-rooted fascistic, ethnocentric or anti-semitic prejudices which, along with other attitudes, added up to the 'authoritarian personality'. Also, potentially

---

21. See L. T. Sargent (Ed.), *Extremism in America*, New York U.P., 1995, pp. 115–190.

fascist individuals were found to combine a high degree of aggression towards the groups they hated with a high degree of deference to those in authority, from which Adorno deduced the permanent danger of fascist or other authoritarian forms of government arising.[22] His fear seems to be borne out by the current resurgence of neo-fascist groups in Europe and by the persistence of extreme racist groups in the United States.[23]

The phenomenon of deference was also studied experimentally by the psychologist Milgram, who induced his subjects to give electric shocks of increasingly high voltage to 'victims' (who were in fact actors, placed behind glass screens, simulating pain and anguish as the 'shocks' were given) in the belief that they were participating in an experiment to show the connection between pain and short-term memory. His aim was to study the reaction of those giving the shocks, and to see what percentages refused at the outset on humanitarian grounds, or stopped during the experiment, or went on to the end, giving what they knew to be painful or lethally high-voltage shocks. An important feature was the presence of white-coated 'psychologists' who assured the subjects that no lasting pain or damage would be caused to their victims (contrary to common sense) and encouraged them to go on even if they wanted to stop. In many cases the psychologists' orders outweighed the agonized pleas of the victims and the main experiment showed a 65 per cent rate of obedience. In *Obedience to Authority* Milgram draws out the political implications of his findings, arguing that people low down in a legitimized chain of command will commit atrocities because they are merely obeying the orders of those above, which absolves them of personal responsibility: this, he considers, explains the inhumane behaviour of guards in Nazi death camps and some of the atrocities committed by US troops in Vietnam.[24] The level of pure deference to authority, especially when clad in a white coat and speaking with the voice of Science is, he concludes, a disquieting threat to our democratic political culture.

Both Adorno's and Milgram's work met with highly critical receptions because their conclusions were unpalatable, but also because their research techniques were dubious and, in Milgram's case, unethical, since he had deceived his subjects. But if there is some truth in their results and conclusions, they imply that it is always possible for a totalitarian state to establish itself with the ready acquiescence of the large percentage of 'deferentials', and to use them to coerce or victimize their less acquiescent fellows. This may be so, but what these experiments could not reveal was whether deference and other authoritarian attitudes are innate or acquired: this is crucially relevant to whatever political inferences are drawn. It is unlikely that they are innate: Germans were not born hating Jews, but were socially conditioned to do so. Deference to authority is also more likely to be a conditioned response than to be a genetic trait of the 'weaker' members of society. So such experiments do not finally establish definite unchanging facts about personality and political attitudes. Undoubtedly,

---

22. T. Adorno *et al.*, *The Authoritarian Personality*, Harper & Bros, 1950.
23. For information about the USA, see L. T. Sargent (Ed.), *Extremism in America*.
24. S. Milgram, *Obedience to Authority*, Tavistock, 1974.

appropriate kinds of education and socialization would do much to lower future generations' rating on the fascist and deference scales.

The Freudian psychologists Reich and Fromm also attempted to explain the origins of fascism by 'the fear of freedom'.[25] Reich located the cause of individual acquiescence in the rise of fascism in the strict patriarchal family traditional in Germany at the time. This produced, in the children who suffered an illiberal upbringing, sexual inhibitions, strong deference to authority, and a psychic structure full of contradictions which made conversion to the irrational doctrine of fascism easy and led to a fear of, and flight from, freedom, into the arms of Hitler. Fromm too argued that alienated modern man sought to escape from freedom through authoritarian political structures. Speculative theories like these do not offer empirical evidence, but only hypotheses—which may, nevertheless, be valid.

All the psychological theories cited here offer support for the major assumption pinpointed by the essentialist theory of totalitarianism, namely, the irremediable weakness of human beings, which makes authoritarian governments necessary. Whatever the validity of such theories, it is salutary to be reminded that the potential for totalitarianism is located in men's minds rather than, or as well as, in historical circumstances or in the wickedness of would-be despots. The reaction to such revelations as Milgram's should be a concerted search for techniques of child-rearing and socialization which produce independent, anti-authoritarian adults. (But those who believe that personality is genetically determined are likely to draw more pessimistic conclusions, and to recommend authoritarian institutions.) The psychological approach to totalitarianism does not, of course, constitute a political theory in itself, but provides circumstantial evidence for those analysing it theoretically.

TOTALITARIANISM DISSOLVED

In the 1960s and 1970s, as the spectre of fascism receded and détente quelled some Western fears about communism, political theorists reassessed the work on totalitarianism in a calmer and more sceptical mood and acknowledged the deficiencies of the accounts of totalitarianism described above. Barber contrasted the essentialist or 'traditionalist' approach, which sees totalitarianism as a political condition found potentially in all places at all times, with the phenomenological or 'modernist' view which depicts it as a uniquely twentieth-century phenomenon, particular to high-technology societies. He criticized both approaches for their lack of objectivity and in their place offered a theoretical analysis of a more limited concept, that of 'totalism', the total integration of all parts of society and the fusion of individuals with the whole. Most people think of totalitarianism as necessarily being 'statist totalism', where the state coercively obliterates the boundaries between the public and private spheres and subjugates

25. W. Reich, *The Mass Psychology of Fascism* (trans. V. R. Carfagno), Farrar, Strauss & Giroux, 1970; E. Fromm, *Escape from Freedom*, Farrar & Rinehart, 1941.

individuals, but other forms are equally possible. Indeed, Barber suggested that the USA could become totalist 'by seepage' (by gradually adopting totalitarian methods), despite the pluralists' constant assertion of the distinction between the public and private spheres. A third possibility is 'communitarian totalism', where individuals realize that they can gain the greatest fulfilment by activity in the public sphere, and voluntarily surrender their private selves. Ideally, this is what socialism would achieve. Barber asserted that the standpoint from which totalitarianism was defined and condemned was that of an outmoded liberal individualism, and he criticized the contemporary use of the term as 'conceptually archaic', suggesting that it should be replaced with the more precise concept of 'totalism'.[26]

Even if Western political scientists still consider totalitarianism a unique political form, many theorists would accept the import of Barber's argument, that the concept itself is meaningless because of the contradictions inherent in every approach which seeks to elucidate it. But certainly there are still important distinctions to be drawn between individualist and totalist political systems and between authoritarian and democratic forms of government. A society can be authoritarian with or without the devices and methods found in the states which are called totalitarian, whenever an elite dictates to the majority of the population, in whatever guise—whether as experts, professional politicians or as 'the voice of the people'. Totalitarianism cannot be treated as a political ideology because it is not itself based on a political ideal: rather, it represents a set of methods which some political ideologies have assimilated as a means of realizing their chosen ideals, while other ideologies, like liberalism, repudiate them utterly.

However, another factor which caused political theorists to call into question the established view of totalitarianism was the detectable convergence between the 'free world' and those societies stigmatized as totalitarian, with respect to various aspects of social and political organization. As left-wing critics argued, some of the six points of the syndrome were also instantiated in the West. Marcuse argued that capitalism is based on covert violence and that the tolerance which we vaunt is essentially repressive since it outlaws political views outside the liberal consensus and makes life unpleasant for the advocates of such views—*vide* McCarthyism and the controversial *Berufsverbot* which excluded political 'extremists' from public office in West Germany. Ideology in the West is every bit as strong as it was in the former Eastern Bloc, but is presented as a common-sense, consensual view about the right and proper nature of society, rather than as a quasi-scientific dogma embedded in obscure texts. The media may be free but, by and large, they reinforce this consensus. A cynic might argue that Britain and the USA have virtually one-party systems, disguised as adversary politics. The American President may not be Big Brother, but he has more power of life and death than any other world leader. And from the point of view of the individual, is there much difference between living in a state-planned economy and living in a

---

26. B. Barber, 'Conceptual foundations of totalitarianism', in *Totalitarianism in Perspective* (Eds. C. J. Friedrich, M. Curtis and B. Barber), Pall Mall, 1969.

private enterprise economy directed by uncontrollable, giant corporations hand-in-glove with the military and the politicians? Anyone who thinks that Western countries operate on the free-market, individualistic, and pluralistic basis which liberal-democratic theory extols, should read Mills's *The Power Elite* and the anonymous satire, *Report from Iron Mountain*, two early exposures of the power of the military-industrial complex.[27] In terms of its byzantine structure, the Western elite, viewed objectively, may look much like that of the former USSR, except that the titles of the power-holders are different.

Such analogies between the 'free' and the 'totalitarian' world can be extended endlessly. Because those who operate with an idea of totalitarianism based on the six-point syndrome do so largely in order to distinguish political systems which they dislike from liberal democracy, the appearance of such convergences is sufficient reason to abandon the phenomenological approach, which no longer serves this tendentious purpose. The essentialist approach is defective because it specifies a loose set of political attitudes, assumptions, and ideals, some of which have been shared by a disparate variety of political theorists, thus giving rise to the absurd claim that all sorts of past thinkers were totalitarian. By concentrating on ideas rather than methods it, too, fails to prove that the political forms which are its target are uniquely totalitarian: rather, it suggests a continuum of political ideas and forms stretching from the absolutist to the democratic, with various so-called totalitarian states located at different points on the continuum. This approach would at least distinguish left- and right-wing totalitarianism, since communist states would presumably appear nearer to the democratic pole than fascist states. The historical approach offers a conception of totalitarianism as a political form specific to certain social conditions and does not provide any account of it as a political ideology.

Barber's analysis of the core idea of totalism, an emphasis on the social whole, which can be realized in different ways, is nearer the mark, and suggests that totalism is not itself an ideology, but a value which might be adopted by different ideologies and might even be realized, unwittingly, by seepage, or incremental growth of the state. Barber's account can be used to distinguish between fascist and communist states, both totalist but in different ways—an important theoretical advance, since the two systems are significantly different. Of course, from a restricted viewpoint, fascism and communism can be made to seem the same. Both threaten and oppose liberal democracy, and from the perspective of the repressed individual there may be nothing to choose between them. But from the wider, theoretical perspective, they differ significantly, and any adequate analysis must acknowledge this.

The conclusion of this assessment of the various accounts of totalitarianism is that political theory should eschew the concept on the grounds that it contains contradictions, is too wide (in the essentialist account) or too narrow (in the phenomenological and historical accounts) to operate satisfactorily in political analysis, and conflates widely differing political systems. We might in its place

---

27. C. Wright Mills, *The Power Elite*, Oxford U.P., 1956; *Report from Iron Mountain* (Ed. L. Lewin), Penguin, 1968.

profitably adopt Barber's idea of totalism, or a notion of authoritarianism. The function of such ideas in political ideologies could then be analysed. Jettisoning the concept has a further merit: the term 'totalitarian' has been hopelessly debased by its regular use as a term of abuse. When the USSR (before 1991), China, Cuba, Haiti and the Philippines (before 1986), El Salvador, Argentina and (until the mid-1970s) Greece, Spain, and Portugal are all described by the same epithet, there is no possibility of analysing the differences between their political systems, or passing discriminating judgements on their varying ideologies and goals. All have been condemned as equally bad, because 'totalitarian'. The revulsion induced by the adjective 'totalitarian' in too many cases prevents us from trying to understand and assess the aims of the ideology prevailing in a so-called totalitarian country.

To deny that the idea of totalitarianism has a useful role to play in political theory is not to condone the practices of reputedly totalitarian states, past and present. Dissolving the concept of totalitarianism should have the constructive result of widening awareness of and sensitivity to the potentially totalistic or authoritarian aspects of all societies. If totalitarianism remains a pejorative term, confined by a narrow definition to Hitler's Germany, communist states and a few other unfortunate countries, it will not be conceived of as a possible threat to liberal-democratic societies. If, instead of thinking of totalitarianism like this, we consider the nexus of authoritarian and totalistic features found in the so-called totalitarian countries, we can inquire to what extent they also manifest themselves in capitalist society. As Friedrich and Brzezinski admit, the methods which they characterize as totalitarian are simply the methods available to any government in advanced industrial society. With the increasing degree of state activity in Western countries, the state might well choose to adopt any or all of the methods which constitute points (3) to (6) of the syndrome. Some have already been adopted in part—the inhabitants of many Western countries go in fear of armed and aggressive police forces. Democratic control appears to be ineffective against the momentum of state self-aggrandizement. So liberal democracies, instead of defining their preferred political system as the antithesis of totalitarianism, should contemplate the shared risks. This suggests that, although the classical works on totalitarianism have grave shortcomings viewed as theoretical analyses of the idea, they should still be read, with an eye on our own predicament. The technology for imposing a totalitarian state exists in all modern industrial countries.

FURTHER READING

The classic texts about totalitarianism were written in the 1950s. Since the fall of communism in the USSR, the topic has been relatively ignored by political theorists.

R. Aron, *Democracy and Totalitarianism*, rev. edn (Ed. R. Pierce), Ann Arbor, 1990.
B. Chapman, *Police State*, Macmillan, 1970.
C. J. Friedrich, *Totalitarianism*, Harvard U.P., 1954.
C. J. Friedrich, M. Curtis and B. Barber, *Totalitarianism in Perspective*, Pall Mall, 1969.
F. A. Hayek, *The Road to Serfdom*, Routledge, 1944.

C. Lefort, *The Political Forms of Modern Society: Bureaucracy, Democracy, Totalitarianism* (Ed. J. B. Thompson), Polity Press, 1986, Part 3 especially.
E. F. Paul (Ed.), *Totalitarianism at the Crossroads*, Transaction Books, 1990.
L. Schapiro, *Totalitarianism*, Macmillan, 1972.

Chapter 9

Feminism

If all men are born free, how is it that all women are born slaves?[1]

Feminism is about the oppression of women by men. In Western countries where women have equal legal and political rights, oppression may seem an exaggerated claim. However, women did not gain the vote until in the twentieth century; when John Stuart Mill championed female suffrage in 1869 he did not hesitate to liken the situation of women to that of slaves. The suffragist movements of the nineteenth and early twentieth centuries constituted the 'first wave' of feminism. Once political equality was gained, many activists felt that their cause was achieved and feminism was largely dormant for several decades. But the vote did not serve to right all women's wrongs, and since the 1960s there has been a flood-tide of feminist literature. The early texts of this 'second wave' argued that the vote was only a first step; inequalities and oppression still formed part of the social fabric and had to be eradicated. These resulted from the 'gendered' nature of society and 'patriarchal attitudes'. Feminism as an ideology provides a conceptual framework which can be applied to most aspects of society and culture, and later second-wave theorists analysed political thought, history, psychology and the arts from a feminist perspective.

Western feminism is a broad, eclectic doctrine within which there are a number of different strands. These are (i) liberal feminists, who hold that liberal rights should be fully and equally extended to women, (ii) socialist feminists, who argue that women's liberation is part of the class struggle and will be realized as socialism is achieved, (iii) the 'radical feminists' who contend that sexual oppression requires a radical re-structuring of social organization, extending (for some) to separatism or lesbianism, and (iv) postmodern feminists who use the insights of postmodernism to question gender-based norms, along with all other

---

1. M. Astell, Preface to *Reflections on Marriage* (1700) in *Astell: Political Writings* (Ed. P. Springborg), Cambridge U.P., 1996, p. 18.

norms. Feminism in the Third World often diverges from all these approaches; the overt and widespread oppression of women in many Third-World countries calls for a different analysis and different cultural and political contexts may constrain the terms in which the feminist challenge can be expressed.[2] There are, inevitably, analytical and tactical disagreements between the advocates of these different feminisms, which can only be intimated in a short discussion such as this.

Given the impressive quantity of feminist texts produced in the last three decades, a highly selective approach must be taken here. This chapter focuses on the main social and political issues identified by Western feminists and discusses their views on human nature, gender, patriarchy and oppression. Finally, it examines three important feminist strategies to combat oppression. First, though, I consider some of the enduring, irrational prejudices which have served over time to justify the treatment of women as an inferior part of the human race.

THE DEMONIZATION OF WOMEN, AND OF FEMINISM

Since the biblical tale of the Garden of Eden and the 'Fall of *Man*', women in the Judaeo-Christian world have been viewed with suspicion by men. Eve, it will be remembered, was tempted by Satan in the form of a snake to encourage Adam to eat an apple from the Tree of Knowledge, which God had forbidden, and as a result the pair were evicted from Paradise. From this story comes the idea that women are temptresses and are weaker, more gullible and irrational and less law-abiding than men and prone to be in league with the Devil. The elaboration of the 'temptress' image across the ages occurred in many cultures. Women's sexual passions were thought to be insatiable, their sexual lures were thought to befuddle men and distract them from productive activity and lawful behaviour. A similar perspective is found in the Hindu doctrine which held that a man's semen was a precious life-force: only by female wiles and temptations could he—reluctantly—be persuaded to part with it. The 'gullible and irrational' accusation has often been repeated, with little apparent basis beyond the fact that until the present century women have been denied the education which fosters rationality and the opportunity to operate as rational beings in the political and economic spheres. The idea that women are especially susceptible to the Devil's wiles gave rise to the appalling persecution of so-called witches in the middle ages and beyond. More generally, there was an enduring current in Western thought and literature which asserted (rather than argued) that women were vehicles for the untamable forces of Nature, for carnality and mystery, while men represented reason, culture and a more spiritual force. This idea germinated in ancient mythologies and was fuelled by the fake 'travellers tales' of the seventeenth and eighteenth centuries, which portrayed women in 'primitive' societies as libidinous and promiscuous.[3] You

---

2. See M. J. Alexander (Ed.), *Feminist Genealogies, Colonial Legacies, Democratic Futures*, Routledge, 1997.
3. A famous example is Denis Diderot's *Supplément au voyage de Bougainville*, written 1772, published 1796.

may judge the extent to which these images were projections of the (male) authors' fantasies.

The demonization continued long after the witchhunts ceased: in the nineteenth century, the vilest abuse was heaped upon women campaigners for female suffrage and in the twentieth century 'second wave' feminists were vituperated by male critics—in particular, their (imputed) personal sexual proclivities became the subject of salacious comment. Feminism itself has been criticized and ridiculed to the point where many women say that they believe in women's rights but that they are *not feminists*. This is what I refer to as the 'demonization' of women and of feminism. The association of women *as such* with Nature, irrationality and untamable forces (let alone the Devil!) is a patent absurdity, since both sexes are equally part of animal nature and both equally undergo social conditioning. One must conclude that a fear of the subversion of the male social order, which equality of the sexes would bring about, has been the moving principle of most objections advanced against the 'liberation' of women from oppression and their acceptance as equal members of society. No privileged class surrenders its privileges without a struggle. Demonization is one mode of defence against the threat to male privilege, more covert but more insidiously effective than coercion. For similar reasons, the champions of racial equality have often been vilified and demonized and parallel myths and doctrines have been invented, depicting subject races as irrational, childlike, more in tune with nature than with civilization, to justify their continued subjection, especially in colonial settings.

Just as racism plays upon supposed differences between races, so anti-feminism usually asserts that essential differences between the two sexes make different social roles and treatment appropriate. Demonization is one extreme outcome of this approach: *romanticism* is another version—a vision of womankind as more innocent, natural, virtuous, beautiful and more in need of protection than mankind. As we shall see, feminist theorists must take a stand on this issue, and they divide into those who argue that there are no fundamental differences between the two sexes except the obvious anatomical and reproductive differences, and those who hold a more 'essentialist' view, arguing that women and men differ in fundamental ways and that this 'difference' should be preserved, even celebrated, while maintaining equality of respect for both sexes. We will examine the implications of these two approaches, starting with the familiar topic of human nature.

FEMINISTS AND HUMAN NATURE

Assumptions about human nature are often pivotal in determining the outcome of any political theory. Apart from the questions of whether human nature is universal, malleable, perfectible and so on, feminist theorists need crucially to consider whether 'female human nature' differs significantly from 'male human nature'. If it does not, as Carole Pateman and others contend, we should not acknowledge any distinct and separate spheres of activity for women and men, nor should we argue that a 'sexual division of labour' is natural. We may acknowledge natural, *biological* differences, but any assumption that these inexorably lead to social inequalities between the sexes is overtly or covertly patriarchal. By contrast, Shulamith Firestone, in a 'radical feminist' text, identified biological differences as the origin and source of women's oppression. Firestone declared 'pregnancy is barbaric' and argued that artificial reproduction (using an artificial womb) was essential to achieve women's liberation; such wombs could even be implanted in men.[4] Pateman criticizes Firestone's approach as 'a theoretical dead-end . . . [which] implicitly accepts the patriarchal claim that women's subordination is decreed by nature'.[5] If nature in the form of *biological* differences does not decree different *social* roles for the two sexes, one superior to the other, then the alternative conclusion—and for many feminists the only politically correct conclusion—is that inequalities between the sexes have been socially constructed according to patriarchal norms, from the earliest times.

The view that sexual inequalities do not express essential, natural sexual differences but are socially constructed raises a number of questions. If anatomical and reproductive differences are socially insignificant, *who* then constructed the gendered systems which oppress women?[6] Why did women not construct social norms to their own advantage? If men constructed patriarchal societies out of a *tabula rasa* situation of natural equality, was this because men were naturally more motivated to seek power and domination than women? If so, we must concede at least one, socially significant, *natural* difference between the sexes, which undermines the original 'no natural difference' assumption. At one extreme we could resort to a 'patriarchal conspiracy' theory about the social construction of gender inequalities, or at the other extreme, we could imagine an invisible hand process which constructed larger social differences on minor natural differences. More moderately, we could conjecture that the oppression of women has been created by a process of historical accretion, that one patriarchal society begets another. But how were such historical patterns established if there were no significant differences between the sexes? Many feminists reject such speculations, along with the idea of an original sexual difference, but they may still encounter anti-feminist allegations that women's inferior social position originated in such a difference.

Clarity is needed about biological roles and their consequences, since many arguments—some for and some against feminism—revolve around what the 'natural' sexual division of labour might be. Analogies with the animal world are potentially misleading. In the natural world, biological differences create different patterns of activity for male and female during the breeding process. In some species the male tends the eggs and young (e.g. midwife toads); with many birds the brooding of eggs and the nurture of the young is shared, but where food is abundant and predators few the female does it all; the female tiger raises her young entirely alone. With some more gregarious mammals, like the primates, the

---

4. S. Firestone, *The Dialectic of Sex*, Paladin, 1972, p. 188ff.
5. C. Pateman, *The Disorder of Women*, Polity Press, Cambridge, 1989, p.126.
6. Anarchism poses a parallel conundrum: if human beings in a natural state are equal and good, how did society become corrupt and oppressive?

care of the young—apart from suckling—is shared by members of the group, including the males, although the biological process of suckling binds the infant to the mother and male animals are (as far as we know) ignorant of their paternity of the young. There are also hermaphroditic creatures (e.g. snails) and creatures (e.g. some fish) which can turn from female to male as species survival requires.

So the animal world provides myriad models of sexual roles and parenting and offers no conclusive lessons about what is natural. The viviparous nature of human beings determines a certain role for human mothers from which the midwife toad example cannot free them: gestation must take place within their bodies, unless Firestone's vision can be realized. In an imaginary state of nature, the nurturing of infants would be a task which only natural mothers could perform until the infant was weaned. But in the *social* context, a nursing mother might breast-feed another woman's child if it is orphaned (although this would be exceptional in the natural world) and wealthy women used to put their children out to wet-nurses to avoid the aggravation of breast-feeding. Infants can be fed on milk substitutes so that weaning can in principle take place immediately after birth.[7] So the extent to which a woman's activities are restricted by her biological functions is limited to the later part of pregnancy, during birth and—*to an optional extent*—until the child is weaned.

The biological functions relating to reproduction need occupy only a small part of any woman's life span now that family size can be limited by contraception, and women cannot be said to be disqualified from equal participation in economic and public life by those functions. Even in societies where women have large families by Western standards they are often heavily engaged in agriculture and return to work soon after childbirth, carrying the infant with them to suckle. (This may not be ideal, but it shows that economic activity is compatible with frequent child-bearing in some kinds of economy.) The feminist argument, then, is that the biological differences on which social inequalities have been constructed relate to a temporary period of restricted capacity in women's lives, surrounding the birth of children. These biological differences and brief interludes away from public life are in no way a rational ground for *social* inequalities. Where women and men are equal in all relevant social respects, there is injustice if they are treated unequally.

Challenging this conclusion is the argument that, although biological differences between the sexes do not justify widespread social inequalities, there are innate psychological and physiological differences which *do* justify differential treatment. Glenn Wilson, a psychologist, argues against sexual equality on this basis, citing a study about the early differentiation between small boys and girls:

> At the toddler stage, boys and girls react differently to a physical barrier preventing them from reaching their toys. Girls tend to stand at the barrier and cry, while boys are rather more resourceful, trying to find a way round it.[8]

---

7. But there are social and medical pressures to breast-feed and mothers who do not do so are often made to feel guilty. There are also regular scares about the dangers of milk substitutes. Some feminists view these pressures as male manipulation masquerading as medical science or psychology.

8. G. Wilson, 'Biology, sex roles and work', in *Liberating Women . . . from Modern Feminism*, Ed. C. Quest, Institute of Economic Affairs, London, 1994, p. 65.

Wilson enumerates many other studies of psychological sex differences carried out by psychologists and experts in child development, and concludes:

> In short, men and women are quite different in many respects, including talents, motivation, personality, and social communication, *and these differences are largely innate*.[9]

Wilson's own explanation of how some women succeed in the 'male' sphere of work is that they do so because they have either been masculinized in their upbringing or have inherited some male characteristics; for example, Wilson has claimed that male (long) finger-length in women is associated with assertiveness.[10] He also contends that 'differences in ability are now known to result from differences in brain structure laid down under the influence of hormones during pre-natal development'[11] and his argument is that, if women are disadvantaged when competing with males in the world of work, it is because their abilities are significantly different. Wilson's argument is polemical and, I believe, methodologically flawed, but it is cited here as a modern version of the anti-feminist 'fundamental sexual difference' case.

Can feminists rebut psychological and physiological studies which apparently demonstrate innate sex differences and threaten their own argument that the sexes are relevantly similar and deserve equal treatment? A weak response would be to accept the data but to assert that men and women are still human and so deserve equal respect—but this would not avail against arguments for different treatment. But there are stronger responses: we can reasonably contest the interpretation of the results of such studies, which are often ambiguous. The girl toddler who cries when deprived of her toys by a barrier may have chosen a better means of recapturing her toys than the 'more resourceful' boy—she is summoning her powerful parents directly to her aid, rather than manifesting weakness. (There is also evidence that parents treat baby boys and girls differently which may in turn explain different behaviour patterns.) We can also justifiably contest the validity of these studies and hence their results: in scientific and social-scientific experiments, different research frameworks and methods may produce diametrically opposed results, and commentators, like Wilson, often cite the study which suits their purpose. It is also appropriate to question the motivation of the researcher. As Thomas Kuhn has argued powerfully, disinterested or value-free research is almost impossible;[12] those who set out to look for sex differences are likely to find some. Ultimately, research dedicated to proving or disproving the existence of innate sexual differences is likely to be as inconclusive as research trying to prove that human personality is the result of heredity rather than conditioning, or vice versa. The 'nature or nurture' debate could be rehearsed ad infinitum without being finally resolved. Physiological accounts of brain formation and function may seem more prejudicial to feminist arguments than

---

9. Wilson, 'Biology, sex roles and work', p. 69. Emphasis added.
10. G. Wilson, 'Finger length as an index of assertiveness in women', *Personality and Individual Differences*, **7**, 1986, pp. 111–112.
11. G. Wilson, 'Biology, sex roles and work', p. 60.
12. T. Kuhn, *The Structure of Scientific Revolutions*, 2nd edn, Chicago U.P., Chicago, 1970.

the psychological studies. But our understanding of whether or how brain structure actually affects intellect and ability (except in extreme cases such as brain damage) is not sufficiently advanced for there to be definitive theories about the effects of sexual differences in brain structure: for example, anti-feminists point out that men's brains are larger than those of women, while feminists retort that female brains are larger relative to body size, which is usually a better indicator of intelligence. Overall, it is rash to draw conclusions about socially relevant sex differences from such studies.

Wilson has used modern psychological studies to re-state a much older case about the natural differences of ability between the sexes. Rousseau offered the classic version of this case, which has been challenged by many feminists:

> General differences present themselves to the comparative anatomist and even to the superficial observer; they seem not to be a matter of sex; yet they are really sex differences . . . where man and woman are alike we have to do with the characteristics of the species; where they are unlike, we have to do with the characteristics of sex . . . A perfect man and a perfect woman should no more be alike in mind than in face.[13]

Émile, Book V, deals with the upbringing of an ideal wife, Sophie, for the ideal youth, Émile. Rousseau expands on 'sexual' differences and (invalidly) infers the necessity of different education and different spheres of activity for men and women: 'the man should be strong and active; the woman should be weak and passive'—what is natural is right. By contrast, feminists contend that what may appear natural is neither necessary nor good, and that most 'natural' differences are socially constructed.

GENDERED SOCIETY

The feminist rebuttal of all such appeals to Nature is that sexual (as opposed to biological) differences are not innate but are the products of *gendered* society. Mary Wollstonecraft, an early feminist critic of Rousseau and his spineless Sophie, argued that apparent sexual differences were the result of upbringing and education. Writing of the supposed intellectual inferiority of women, she argued:

> I shall insist only that men have increased that inferiority till women are almost sunk below the standard of rational creatures. Let their faculties have room to unfold, and their virtues to gain strength, and then determine where the whole sex must stand in the intellectual scale.[14]

Mill was still obliged to make a similar point to opponents of women's suffrage seventy-five years later:

> What is now called the nature of women is an eminently artificial thing—the result of forced repression in some directions, unnatural stimulation in others.[15]

---

13. J.-J. Rousseau, *Émile* (trans. B. Foxley), Dent (Everyman), London, 1911, pp. 323–4.
14. M. Wollstonecraft, *A Vindication of the Rights of Woman* (1792) (Eds. S. Mukherjee and S. Ramaswamy), Deep & Deep, Delhi, 1992, p. 38.
15. J. S. Mill, *The Subjection of Women* (1869), Oxford University Press, 1912, p. 451.

Twentieth-century feminists would agree; they argue that the inequalities between the sexes derive from the gendered norms of male-dominated society. 'Masculine' and 'feminine' norms are artificially constructed on the basis of a false biological distinction.[16] Furthermore, gender itself is not a fixed concept and its demarcation lines can be challenged.

> It is true that every society uses biological sex as a criterion for the ascription of gender but . . . no two cultures would agree completely on what distinguishes one gender from the other.[17]

Cross-cultural comparisons bear out Ann Oakley's statement: in some cultures men freely express their emotions and cry openly, while in other cultures women do what we might regard as 'man's work' such as road building in India. But patriarchy consistently devalues feminine characteristics. Oakley details how gender identity is created for girls and boys from their earliest infancy. In the West, masculine and feminine norms are reinforced by dress, hair-length, toys and parental reactions and expectations. 'A multitude of studies agree that by the age of four children have a firm knowledge of sex identity and are well able to perceive distinctions of gender role',[18] even though the defining characteristics of their sex identity are (usually) hidden by clothing. School-teachers then take over the task of socializing children into their future roles. Education in Britain earlier in this century, as in other countries, was more highly gendered than it is today; the move to co-educational schools and the national curriculum make equal education more possible and diminish the likelihood of girls being taught cookery ('home economics') while boys learn woodwork and trigonometry. But girls are often still excluded from 'boys' sports' such as football and rugby, their lesser physical strength being the purported reason.

On the practical plane, what must concern feminists most is that gendered attitudes and stereotypes will have been inculcated long before the child enters school (unless its parents are very enlightened) and that these will be shared and upheld by most of the adults that a child encounters, as well as by its peers. Furthermore, gender identities and attitudes are polarized in a way that embodies power and hostility—boys are glad not to be girls and regard them as an inferior species while girls (if they are lucky in their upbringing) may feel the same in reverse—if not, they may actually feel inferior. (Freud's influential theory of penis envy offers a severely flawed explanation of the origin of this sense of inferiority in young girls and it has been strongly contested by many feminists.[19]) The possibility of achieving feminism's goals must rest ultimately on revolutionizing such *attitudes*, since most feminists hold that gendered concepts of identity, of

---

16. Modern feminists use 'sex' to refer to biological differences between women and men while 'gender' refers to socially constructed differences. Earlier feminists referred to both of these as sex differences or sexual differences, which can be confusing.
17. A. Oakley, *Sex, Gender and Society*, Temple-Smith, London, 1972, p. 158.
18. Oakley, *Sex, Gender and Society*, p. 177.
19. See, e.g., S. de Beauvoir, *The Second Sex* (trans. and ed. H. M. Parshley), Penguin, 1972, p.70ff., and B. Friedan, *The Feminine Mystique*, ch. 5 for two early criticisms. Many other feminist texts also contain critiques of Freud's theory although feminists have also employed psychoanalysis to explain how individuals seek identity through sexual and gendered roles.

masculinity and femininity, are at the root of women's oppression. Although Western feminists usually focus on attitudes to women in Western countries, their accounts of gender construction and the resulting social inequalities are borne out amply by the treatment of women in non-Western societies. The analysis of gender goes beyond personal identity, and feminists argue that most aspects of society, and bodies of knowledge, are gendered—politics, art, medicine, science and work itself are already conceptualized in gender-laden terms.

PATRIARCHAL SOCIETY

Whereas accounts of gender identity are primarily psychological and cultural accounts, the theory of patriarchy projects gender difference into the political domain. A patriarch is by definition the father or ruler of a family or tribe and so 'patriarchy' is the rule of patriarchs: in modern feminist thought the word denotes, more broadly, political rule by men over women or, even more broadly, male-dominated society.

> Patriarchy as a political structure seeks to control and subjugate women so that their possibilities for making choices about their sexuality, childrearing, mothering, loving and laboring are curtailed. Patriarchy, as a system of oppression, recognizes the potential power of women and the actual power of men. Its purpose is to destroy woman's consciousness about her potential power, which derives from the necessity of society to reproduce itself.[20]

In this definition, Zillah Eisenstein grounds women's power too exclusively in their reproductive functions for my own taste. By identifying women so closely with their reproductive capacities, she espouses an 'essential difference' position which can be turned against women and used to justify inequality and discrimination. But she is voicing a common feminist view that women's capacity to abstain from sexual activity and motherhood poses a major threat to men, who are strongly motivated to ensure their own succession and the survival of their blood-line. (The widely popularized 'selfish gene' theory propounded by Richard Dawkins adds weight to this view of men's motivation, although whether as a theory it provides an adequate account of human social behaviour is an open question, which cannot be fully debated here). Equally, women possess the power of denying men sexual satisfaction—the theme of Aristophanes' comedy, *Lysistrata* (411 BC), in which Athenian women went on strike sexually to induce their husbands to end the war with Sparta. Male sexual gratification, male blood-lines and male gene survival would be jeopardized by women's sexual abstinence or infidelity, hence devices and institutions developed throughout the ages to assure the husband's conjugal rights and the paternity of his children.[21] The widespread hostility during this century of male legislators to contraception and abortion might be adduced as circumstantial evidence for Eisenstein's analysis.

---

20. Z. R. Eisenstein, *The Radical Future of Liberal Feminism*, Longman, New York, 1981, p. 14.
21. The situation for women is different, of course, since their genes will pass to their children, no matter who the father is.

Although debate was often couched in religious terms about the sacredness of life and the duty of procreation, the underlying male anxiety was, feminists would hypothesize, that if contraception and abortion were readily available, women would gain control over their own reproductive functions, threatening family structures and patriarchal succession.

Eisenstein suggests the male justification for patriarchy *ex post* as it were: these are reasons why men benefit from and defend patriarchal institutions. But why patriarchy at all? The history of the development of patriarchy is, of necessity, conjectural. If patriarchy originated in the earliest human societies there would have been little understanding of the reproductive process, let alone genes and blood-lines, so the control of women's reproductive faculties could hardly have been the purpose of the system, although the control of women's sexual availability might have been at stake. Matriarchy and matrilineal society would have been more appropriate, given this state of knowledge, and some feminists have argued that this, logically, must have preceded patriarchy, as did Friedrich Engels—'the overthrow of mother right was the *world-historic defeat of the female sex*'.[22] A vulgar hypothesis is that in primitive societies based on hunting and war men's domination naturally resulted from their greater physical strength and the relative weakness of women during frequent pregnancies. But why should the same principle continue to hold sway in more peaceful societies based on agriculture and commerce, and indeed in modern society, where physical strength affords no advantage? The history of religion and mythology offers another perspective on women's situation in early times: Joseph Campbell illustrates the importance and supremacy of the 'great mother goddess' in occidental mythology from the neolithic age (an early agricultural stage) until the start of the Iron Age, when her cult was 'radically transformed, reinterpreted, and in large measure even suppressed by those suddenly intrusive patriarchal warrior tribesmen whose traditions have come down to us chiefly in the Old and New Testaments and in the myths of Greece'.[23] Despite these intrusions, the Greek Pantheon boasted some powerful females, especially Diana the hunter, Athena, goddess of wisdom, and Aphrodite, goddess of love—the relics perhaps of earlier, omnipotent goddesses. Puzzlingly, these deities were still worshipped in patriarchal societies like ancient Athens, where the sexes were largely segregated, women could not be citizens and male homosexual love was probably more respected than heterosexual love.[24] As monotheism advanced the goddesses perished; the 'one god' of patriarchal religions like Christianity and Islam was always male. Whatever the origins of patriarchy, it appears to have been well established in the ancient societies of the Mediterranean of which we have historical knowledge, and male domination has continued and expanded ever since. Even when women are queens or goddesses, they are so within the confines of patriarchy.

22. F. Engels, *The Origin of the Family, Private Property and the State* (1884), in *Karl Marx and Friedrich Engels, Selected Works*, Progress Publishers, Moscow, 1970, vol. 3, p. 233.
23. J. Campbell, *The Masks of God*, Vol. 3 *Occidental Mythology*, Penguin, 1976, p. 7. Part I of the book describes the mother goddess cult; the later parts detail its suppression and transformation.
24. K. J. Dover, 'Classical Greek Attitudes to Sexual Behaviour', *Arethusa*, 6 (1973), pp. 59–73.

The prevalence of patriarchy in Europe since the Roman Empire is better documented; historical records describe laws and institutions which clearly indicate male supremacy in the political, economic and social spheres. The Christian church, whether Catholic, Orthodox or Protestant, has been a bastion of male domination; so was the feudal social system. Later, the new liberal ideas of personal freedom and rights did not extend to women and, as a few examples from recent British history demonstrate, married women were, to all intents and purposes, treated as their husband's property. Divorce was almost impossible except by a costly private act of Parliament until 1857 when the Divorce Court was established; even so, women plaintiffs had to prove adultery *plus* cruelty or desertion whereas a husband could gain a divorce simply on the basis of his wife's adultery. Until the Married Women's Property Acts (1870, 1882 and 1893) a woman's property became her husband's on marriage and she had no control over what he did with capital or income. If her husband died intestate, a woman received only half the estate (or one-third if there were more than two children) while a husband received the whole estate if his wife died intestate. And only in 1891 did a Court of Appeal judgment (*Reg. v. Jackson*) establish that a husband could not legally detain his wife in his house against her will.[25] At this time women could still not vote in parliamentary elections, sit on a borough or county council,[26] study at the older universities or enter any leading profession except medicine or teaching. The Sex Disqualification Removal Act (1919) finally removed barriers to professional life and university education. A 1918 Act gave women over thirty the vote, based on occupancy derived from the husband, an inequity not rectified until 1928 when women gained votes on equal terms. Although Mary Wollstonecraft and other women had argued for the rights of women in the eighteenth century and J. S. Mill had (with some degree of support) proposed women's suffrage in the House of Commons when the 1867 Reform Act was being passed, women's 'emancipation' proceeded at a snail's pace, not because it lacked advocates but because of strong resistance from the majority of men in power.

How could patriarchy so successfully survive the development of liberalism with its values of personal freedom, rights and self-development? Analysis of the writings of political theorists such as Hobbes and Locke suggests an answer. A sustained account of the intermeshing of patriarchy with modern political theory is offered by Carole Pateman in *The Sexual Contract* (1988), a work of detailed textual criticism of the contractarian tradition. She states that, despite differences, 'the classic contract theorists have a crucial feature in common. They all tell patriarchal stories,'[27] and their liberating individualism focuses on the concept of the purely *masculine* 'individual'. Whether relations between men and women are equal in the state of nature (as in Hobbes's *Leviathan*) until women are conquered

25. The theme of the domestic imprisonment of women, especially of daughters, was common in eighteenth- and nineteenth-century novels. See W. Stafford, 'Narratives of women: English feminists of the 1790s', *The Historical Association*, 1997, pp. 24–43, esp. p. 27ff.
26. Women could vote in borough and county elections, which made the refusal of the parliamentary vote even more anomalous.
27. C. Pateman, *The Sexual Contract*, Polity Press, Oxford, 1988, p. 41.

or, as in Locke's theory, women are already subject to the conjugal (not political) power of their husbands which men have had since Eve became subject to Adam, the social contract is a contract between men. A woman's interests are only represented—or not—by her husband as ruler of the household and political actor. Women have no separate political voice and effectively no role in the polity created by the social contract except as the subjects of their patriarchal husbands. Patriarchal right is transformed from a natural right within families (Locke) to a political right, as marriage becomes one of the foundational institutions of patriarchal society. Pateman demonstrates the absence of women from the theories which gave rise to the individualistic liberalism which effectively excluded women from political consideration for several centuries. She also criticizes the rather loose associations made by some feminist commentators between patriarchy as a familial institution and patriarchy as the political rule of men and argues for tighter analysis. Her own rigorous analysis of social contract theory 'reveals that civil society, including the capitalist economy, has a patriarchal structure'.[28] In other words, patriarchy in liberal society is not just another example of perennial, generalized male domination, but is quite specific to that form of society. This conclusion has important consequences for the socialist feminist view of how politics and the economy need to be restructured.

WOMEN AND CAPITALISM

> For equality to exist between men and women, the structure of patriarchy must be destroyed; and for this to happen today, they must also dismantle capitalism.[29]

Socialist feminists link the oppression of women in the industrial society specifically to capitalism, although they would agree that women were also oppressed in different ways in pre-capitalist societies. In *Woman's Estate* (1971) Juliet Mitchell criticized radical feminists such as Firestone, who concentrated too exclusively on 'feminist instinct' and 'undifferentiated male domination' while ignoring the role which capitalist exploitation played in oppressing men and women alike. Early critics of capitalism were also short-sighted in a different way: Mitchell criticized Marx and Engels in particular for treating women's position as a mere aspect of the 'bourgeois' family and considering the family itself as 'merely a precondition of *private property*' which was the real focus of their economic theories.[30] She argued that the family deserved independent analysis. Engels hoped that industrial automation would presage the emancipation of women, since it made physical strength irrelevant and would enable women to enter the (capitalist) economy, giving them economic independence. Mitchell, however, argues that it is the family role which traps women outside the capitalist economy: their family role consists of three functions—reproduction, sexuality and socialization of children. As she points out, these three functions can be

28. Pateman, *The Sexual Contract*, ch. 2, 'Patriarchal Confusions', p. 38.
29. Eisenstein, *The Radical Future of Liberal Feminism*, p. 246.
30. J. Mitchell, *Woman's Estate*, Penguin, Harmondsworth, 1971, p. 80.

separated: the mother need not rear the children, and sexuality can be separated from motherhood when contraception is available. The Marxist cry for the 'abolition of the bourgeois family' is an empty exhortation: Mitchell argues that only when these three functions and the fourth, economic function in which women are sometimes involved (the productive process) have been transformed can women's liberation be achieved.[31] Regarding the family, Mitchell thinks that a plurality of institutional forms is needed, within which women and men can relate and raise children in different ways. Mitchell's more socialist argument is that women need to participate in the workforce in order to develop revolutionary class-consciousness but that they are prevented from this by family duties, which withdraw them from the labour force during the formative working years and condemn them thereafter to part-time or peripheral employment. This absence has allowed socialism itself to develop as a male-centred doctrine:

> feminist consciousness has been inadequately represented in the formation of socialist ideology, [just] as the oppression of women has, so far, been inadequately combated in socialist revolutions.[32]

There is an obvious paradox in Mitchell's proposal that women should be 'liberated' to join an exploited workforce, which is not entirely resolved by the response that *first* women must gain economic independence through working, *then* they must gain revolutionary consciousness by being exploited and *finally* they can liberate themselves by a socialist revolution. More practically, some of Mitchell's arguments have been overtaken by recent economic changes: a far greater percentage of women are now in work than in 1971 and the ratio of employed women to men in employment has increased, partly because the economies of the West have shifted from heavy industry and manufacture towards service industries. But much of the work undertaken by women is part-time or low-paid and women are often 'homeworkers' (for example, making garments at home, or doing telephone sales). This means that they are more exploitable and have much less legal protection than women who work in offices and factories, where their interests can be protected by unions. In these changed circumstances, Mitchell's call for the transformation of women's productive and reproductive capacities as central to a socialist revolution still rings true and many non-socialist feminists also call for such a transformation.

Mitchell attempts to show that women's oppression in modern times is a product of capitalism in the economic sphere and of its corollary, the bourgeois family, in the private sphere. Women's oppression, in other words, is one aspect of class oppression. This account would seem unduly narrow to non-socialist feminists whose chosen targets are domestic oppression and gendered attitudes, rather than economic systems; these hallmarks of subjection are found in both capitalist and non-capitalist countries and must therefore require a less specific and contextual analysis, extending beyond the capitalist economy. Another criticism made of socialist feminists is that (for similar reasons) they cannot prove

31. Mitchell, *Woman's Estate*, ch. 5.
32. Mitchell, *Woman's Estate*, p. 96.

theoretically that a socialist revolution would by definition abolish patriarchy and women's oppression; this is an aspiration but not a certainty. Mitchell herself is highly critical of communist countries which made no serious effort to change the position of women (other than by making them workers as well as mothers) and which manipulated women's reproductive capacities for the state's own ends. But would 'true socialism' do better?

Approaching socialist feminism from another angle, I find an implicit account of women's economic oppression in Marx's theory of exploitation even though Marx (unlike Engels) was uninterested in the position of women. However, Marx asserted that the worker's wages cover not only his own subsistence but also the 'reproduction of labour'—that is, his wage serves to raise his family, the future labourers. Thus, part of the surplus value appropriated by capitalists collectively is, in effect, a new generation of workers delivered free of charge. It is free because the wage of the worker with dependants is no higher than the wage of the single worker and there is certainly no assumed element in the wage for the mother who actually bears and rears the children. She provides entirely unpaid labour and 'future surplus value' for the capitalists and is therefore the *most exploited actor* in the capitalist drama—her name does not even appear on the cast list! (This analysis would need to be modified in the modern context where the state takes considerable responsibility for the next generation, providing education, health-care and social benefits out of taxation. But companies still get their workforces largely free of charge.) This account of exploitation could lead feminists in a revolutionary Marxist direction: with the abolition of private capital and distribution 'to each according to his needs', the economic oppression of women should cease. Alternatively, it could lead to the reformist, but still radical, conclusion that employers should pay a wage direct to any employee's partner who acts as full-time child-rearer and home-maker, as well as to the employee. Thus employers collectively would contribute to the rearing of future employees. Tax allowances for workers with dependants are a gesture in this direction but, in Britain at least, these allowances are reflected in the worker's increased pay-packet and do not directly reach the child-rearer, whose work as such remains unpaid.

The unacknowledged economic contribution of housewives and mothers was the subject of a lively and well-theorized 'wages for housework' debate among left-wing feminists in the 1970s.[33] Apart from the oppressive and repetitive nature of housework in itself, a dual economic oppression was identified: the oppression of housewives as unpaid workers by the capitalist system and the 'private' economic oppression of non-working housewives by husbands who gave them inadequate housekeeping allowances. Estimates of the economic value of the housewife's many functions (as nanny, cleaner, cook, secretary, laundress and provider of sexual services) suggest that few husbands could afford all these services if they had to be purchased at market price, so that housewives are seriously exploited. The fact that many women now work has not radically

---

33. For a useful collection of articles see E. Malos (Ed.), *The Politics of Housework*, Allison & Busby, 1980.

changed their situation; most of them additionally perform the majority of household tasks unpaid—working the so-called 'double day'—and so the housework debate remains an important tributary to mainstream socialist feminist arguments about women's economic oppression.

A different and covert kind of oppression imposed on women by capitalism is the 'burden' of consumption. Betty Friedan (whose views are discussed in detail later) asked 'Why is it never said that the really crucial function, the really important role that women serve as housewives is *to buy more things for the house*?'[34] American women, when Friedan wrote, had 75% of the purchasing power—they were *the* sales target. Friedan's revelations of 'The Sexual Sell' were assisted by her access to the private archive of an 'institute for motivational manipulation' which contained data from in-depth interviews with thousands of women; this was used to formulate products and advertisements which appealed to housewives but were in no way intended to transform the lives of this captive audience.

> No-one . . . denied that housework was endless, and its boring repetition just did not give that much satisfaction . . . But the endlessness of it all was an advantage from the seller's point of view.[35]

Friedan gives evidence of a cynical sales process which manipulated the housewife's guilt or promised her greater satisfaction in her chores, in order to maximize her consumption.

The economist John Kenneth Galbraith also analysed the housewife's role in the age of consumerism: 'rising standards of popular consumption, combined with the disappearance of the menial personal servant, created an urgent need for labor to administer and otherwise manage consumption.' The possession and consumption of goods, Galbraith argues, is not pleasurable unless the management of these processes—shopping, servicing, repairing—can be delegated to some menial. Capitalist societies have gradually converted non-employed wives into a 'crypto-servant class' of administrators who manage household consumption and 'make indefinitely increasing consumption possible'. Paradoxically, the wealthier the household, the harder the woman's role, because more consumption has to be organized.[36] In Friedan's words, 'they were so *busy*—busy shopping, chauffeuring, using their dishwashers and dryers and electric mixers . . . and doing thousands of little chores'.[37]

The irony, then, is that women are exploited under capitalism whether they are employed or not. As employees, they are often more exploited than male workers because of discrimination or low-paid work. As housewives, they are in an oppressive state of economic dependency on their husbands or partners; they are also exploited through their unpaid contribution to maintaining the capitalist workforce and furthermore, as Friedan and Galbraith argue, they are compelled

34. B. Friedan, *The Feminine Mystique*, Penguin, 1965, p. 181.
35. Friedan, *The Feminine Mystique*, p. 191.
36. J. K. Galbraith, *Economics and the Public Purpose*, Deutsch, 1974, ch. IV *passim*.
37. Friedan, *The Feminine Mystique*, p. 208.

willy-nilly to engage in consumerism, which sustains and perpetuates the capitalist system—which is fundamentally a patriarchal system. Of the three kinds of exploitation, the second is the most significant, being specific to women. Feminists of every persuasion would agree that the economic dependence of non-earning women on men is at the root of their personal subjection to men and that such dependence must be eradicated. But proposals for this eradication are not without problems. A 'waged' housewife would still be condemned to unfulfilling work and sequestered in the home. Women in employment may be treated more exploitatively than men and they usually face an additional burden of housework and child-care when they return home. A better solution is needed and for some feminists this is socialism.

OPPRESSION

Bodily Oppression

We have reviewed some of the conditions for oppression identified by feminists: gendered systems, patriarchal society, the patriarchal family and capitalism. It is appropriate, finally, to attend to the realities of the physical oppression which male-dominated societies inflict, or have inflicted, on women; some of these can only be described as atrocities. In *Gyn/Ecology* (1979) Mary Daly recounts practices of physical mutilation, such as female foot-binding, prevalent for centuries in pre-Kuomintang China, and female circumcision—clitoridectomy and infibulation which, unlike male circumcision, often lead to physical deformity and lifelong pain and ill-health, if not death. This is still regularly practised in parts of Africa and the Islamic world and is estimated to affect at least eighty million women and probably many more. These mutilations are almost invariably carried out by other women, usually relatives, and the reason given for the practice is that uncircumcised girls will be unmarriageable. Daly calls these sadistic practices 'Sado-Rituals' and identifies their characteristics: they are obsessed with purity (of the woman involved), the ritual aspect erases responsibility for the atrocities, women are used as 'token torturers' although the mutilations are for men's benefit and in general these 'gynocidal' practices, once established among the upper-classes, spread to the wider society.[38] The mutilations, purportedly designed to enhance a girl's future marriageability, essentially ensure her dependence on her husband—women with bound feet could scarcely move out of the house—and in the case of circumcision her sexual fidelity, by making sex a source of pain for her, rather than pleasure.

Even more drastic were customs such as suttee (the compulsory immolation of Hindu widows, including child-brides, on their husbands' funeral pyres) and, in the West, witch-burning. Daly quotes a Hindu man vindicating the practice of suttee:

---

38. M. Daly, *Gyn/Ecology*, Women's Press, 1991 re-issue, pp. 130–3.

We husbands so often make our wives unhappy that we might well fear they would poison us. Therefore did our wise ancestors make the penalty of widowhood so frightful—in order that the woman may not be tempted.[39]

To Daly's catalogue of oppression could be added the current (although covert) practice of female infanticide in China, a product of the one-child-per-family law; in India female infanticide is also practised and there are many recent authenticated instances of 'bride-burning', to secure the benefit of the dowry without the disadvantage of keeping the wife. There is a growing problem of child prostitution (mainly of girls, but also of boys) and 'sex tourism' in countries like Thailand. But we must not confine the account of bodily oppression to anti-woman practices in non-Western countries: Daly also cites the horrendous 'medical' experiments carried out on women in Nazi concentration camps and she indicts many invasive practices of modern Western (male) gynaecological medicine and surgery as anti-woman, oppression disguised as science or as healing. The rape statistics in Western countries are also indicative of a high incidence of anti-woman behaviour.

Images and Propaganda

Other forms of oppression well-established in Western cultures are less dramatic than mutilation and murder, but equally redolent of male domination. These were explored by second-wave feminists such as Betty Friedan, author of a pioneering book, *The Feminine Mystique* (1963), which is credited with having started the second wave. Friedan had trained as a psychologist and later worked as a journalist and her interviews and encounters with groups of women led her to identify 'the problem that has no name'. Middle-class American women with settled, apparently happy family lives, replete with material comforts, were nevertheless unhappy and discontented—they felt empty and hollow, unfulfilled by domestic life. Friedan accounted for this in terms of their unrealized potential; most had been educated to college or university level, yet they were condemned by 'the feminine mystique' to be housewives and to find their identity in being 'Bob's wife', 'Tom's mother' and the household manager. Marriage and motherhood had become the inevitable destiny of the victims of the feminine mystique. Friedan traces the development of this mystique through the changing role-models offered by women's magazines in the 1950s, the manipulation of women as consumers by advertising and the influence of Freudian psychology, especially as it was disseminated through popularizing books on child-rearing and women's problems. As an example, she quotes Helene Deutsch, a Freudian psychologist writing on women in the 1940s:

---

39. Daly, *Gyn/Ecology*, p. 124, quoting K. Mayo, *Mother India*, Blue Ribbon Books, New York, 1927, pp. 82–3. Suttee was legally abolished by the British in the early nineteenth century, but continued illegally in parts of India for a long time.

> Women's intellectuality is to a large extent paid for by the loss of valuable feminine
> qualities . . . All observations point to the fact that the intellectual woman is
> masculinized; in her, warm, intuitive knowledge has yielded to cold unproductive
> thinking.[40]

Even education had been suborned, Friedan found, with many educationists
concerned that over-education or scientific education would stultify girls'
femininity; some colleges had switched the emphasis of their syllabuses towards
home economics and other domestic topics. The idea of career women, and
educating girls for careers, was denigrated. Friedan elaborates the damaging
effects of the mystique on husbands and children, as well as the self-image and
self-esteem of its women victims. Her solution is education as the road to
fulfilment—serious education for girls and flexible education for older women
who want to recapture missed opportunities.

As a general account of oppression, *The Feminine Mystique* has many
shortcomings. Working-class women have different problems from Friedan's
largely middle-class subjects. Her consideration of economic discrimination was
brief[41], because the women she dealt with were not active in the economic sphere
where such discrimination operates. She also assumed without question that the
search for female identity through a career or other forms of self-realization must
be *compatible with* marriage and motherhood. She did not propose radical
changes in these institutions but rather that they should be gently reformed so as
allow women an identity of their own. And, according to Germaine Greer, she
misunderstood sexuality.

> [Friedan's] whole case rests upon the frustration suffered by the educated woman
> who falls for the Freudian notion that physiology is destiny. For Mrs Friedan
> sexuality seems to mean motherhood . . . [she stresses] non-sexual aspects of a
> woman's destiny at the expense of her libido . . .[42]

By contrast, sexuality was central to Greer's book *The Female Eunuch* (1970),
where she charted the sexual 'castration' of women achieved through the male–
female polarity imposed by patriarchal society. Our understanding of what is
physically desirable in women is formed by male requirements and desires; non-
titillating aspects of women's sexual being, such as menstruation, are to be treated
as secret and shameful unless they can be employed to demonstrate women's
unsuitability for certain kinds of work—a strategy which Greer calls 'the
enlistment of menstruation in the anti-feminist argument'.[43] The stereotype of the
'Eternal Feminine' is created, but this is paradoxically a sex-less image which
requires the denial and negation of true female sexuality, thus thwarting and
deforming women's energy. Greer illustrates how the oppressive feminine image is
imposed on women from infancy onwards and how it upholds the 'middle-class
myth of love and marriage'. Underlying the facade of respect for femininity is

---

40. Friedan, *The Feminine Mystique*, p. 151, quoting H. Deutsch, *The Psychology of Women—A
    Psychoanalytical Interpretation*, New York, 1944, Vol. I, p.290.
41. Friedan, *The Feminine Mystique*, pp. 327–8.
42. G. Greer, *The Female Eunuch*, Flamingo, 1991 reissue, p. 333.
43. G. Greer, *The Female Eunuch*, 1993, p. 59.

male loathing and disgust, reflected in the obscenities by which men refer to women and their sexual organs: 'women have very little idea of how much men hate them',[44] but domestic violence and rape are indicators. The misery and resentment of women trapped in the patriarchal society will, Greer hopes, transmute into revolution—as a start, women should reject consumerism and fashion and refuse to marry.

> Women's liberation, if it abolishes the patriarchal family, will abolish a necessary substructure of the authoritarian state . . . it is time for the demolition to begin.[45]

Friedan's book created a sensation as the first book of second-wave feminism published in the USA. Greer's and Daly's works are stronger stuff and their revolutionary conclusions proved too radical for many, women as well as men. Far more extreme than these was Valerie Solanas's *S.C.U.M. Manifesto* (1967) (S.C.U.M. stood for 'The Society for Cutting up Men'), a sustained and virulent invective against men and an exhortation to exterminate the male sex. Solanas achieved world-wide notoriety in 1968 for shooting the artist Andy Warhol as a demonstration that the men's world had to be physically defeated. Excesses such as this and the outspoken language and uncompromising posture of books like *The Female Eunuch* unfortunately blinded many, both men and women, to the merits of the feminist analysis of gender and patriarchy and contributed to the demonization of feminism. But this reaction does not prove that the books were *wrong* on all points!

More Propaganda—Mothers and Children

Moving beyond the image of the 'Eternal Feminine', it is instructive to examine two other contrived images which serve to keep women securely in their place in the patriarchal family. Feminists have sometimes accepted the received images of mother and child too easily, but these images too are subject to manipulation. *Motherhood* is treated by some feminists as a fixed point in women's lives and in social and family life. But the image of motherhood has often been manipulated to suit the needs of male-dominated society. This happened in the USSR under Stalin, where after a period of liberation and sexual equality in the 1920s contraception became unavailable and abortion was made illegal.[46] In Nazi Germany, false eugenic theories made the propagation of pure Aryan children a priority and suitable mothers were identified for breeding purposes; propaganda emphasized 'children, church, kitchen' as the proper preoccupations of the ideal German woman. Authoritarian regimes like these are frequently conservative and male-chauvinist in their attitude to women—but a similar manipulation of the female image took place during and after the Second World War in Britain and America. At the start of the war women were needed to work in vital industries— after the war it was imperative that they should quit their jobs, to make employment available for returning soldiers. A 1980 feminist documentary film,

44. Greer, *The Female Eunuch*, p. 279.
45. Greer, *The Female Eunuch*, pp. 368–9.
46. See S. Rowbotham, *Women, Resistance and Revolution*, Penguin, 1972, ch. 6.

Rosie the Riveter, shows American government propaganda films encouraging middle-class women to take factory jobs as part of the war effort. Working-class women doing low-paid work were also able to take better jobs at male rates of pay. To encourage mothers to go to work, one such film showed happy children playing in nurseries while their mothers worked, the message being that they were as well looked after there as at home. Postwar propaganda films reversed the image: they emphasized the duties and pleasures of the suburban housewife, cleaning and cooking with all the latest gadgets. Also, warningly, they showed children with working mothers hanging around the street in delinquent gangs. The message was clear—ideal American women should stay at home tending their husbands' and children's needs. Many women fell for it, especially as they were being laid off work to provide jobs for the demobilized men. *Rosie the Riveter* is a startling revelation of how crudely and successfully the image of ideal motherhood was manipulated in the national interest in a liberal-democratic country. To take such an easily manipulated concept as a fixed point in feminism would be unwise.

Nevertheless, some pioneering second-wave feminists later revised their theories to assert the importance of motherhood and women's right to become mothers— thus reversing the earlier feminist argument that women have the right *not to* become mothers. In *The Second Stage* (1981), Friedan criticized the 'extreme' feminist reaction against motherhood and the 'feminist denial of the importance of family, of women's own needs to give and get love and nurture, tender loving care'.[47] Friedan's work was based on discussions with young, professional working women who felt frustrated at having to postpone motherhood, or choose between career and family. She now asserted women's 'need for love and identity, status, security and generation through marriage, children, home, the family', which are as important as the need for power, identity and status through work or social action.[48] American feminists, she thought, were wrong to give up on the family rather than attempting to change it, and perverse in denying the importance of motherhood, thus alienating many women. They had created a dangerous conservative backlash from the so-called 'moral majority', especially evident in the 1980s controversy over the legality of abortion in the USA. Contraception and abortion have been a central demand of twentieth-century feminism, as part of the demand for women's control over their own bodies. But the message of the later Friedan was the equal centrality of the right *to choose to have children*. In a similar recantation, Greer (*Sex and Destiny*, 1984) also changed tack and extolled the virtues of motherhood.

Childhood is also treated by many feminists as a fixed point towards which mothers must orientate themselves. Janet Radcliffe Richards deplores 'the incompatibility of most work with the bearing and raising of children',[49] intimating that work is somehow to blame. Many feminists argue as if the length of childhood and the necessity of round-the-clock child-care were 'givens'. But the

47. B. Friedan, *The Second Stage*, Abacus, 1983, p. 22.
48. Friedan, *The Second Stage*, p. 95.
49. J. Radcliffe Richards, *The Sceptical Feminist*, Penguin, 1994, p. 152.

duration of childhood has been prolonged by compulsory education and regular rises in the school-leaving age plus, recently, severe youth unemployment. In the early stages of the industrial revolution in Britain children worked long hours in factories which, incidentally, meant that their mothers could do so too. Now, the working hours for school-age children are legally limited; children are not seen as economic beings but as the recipients of full-time care at home or at school. It is illegal to leave children alone in the house and parents are prosecuted for doing so; in one recent controversial case a lone mother who had formerly been living on benefit went out to work to improve the household income and was prosecuted for leaving her young child alone—yet the cost of providing child-care would have consumed most of her earnings. The absence of live-in grandparents and extended family networks makes child-care the chief concern of many mothers. The final result of the Victorian 'invention of childhood' for the middle classes is a protracted period of emotional and financial dependence for children, which restricts primarily the mother's activities since servants and nannies are not available (as they were in Victorian times) except to the relatively wealthy. It has also been argued that the mutual mother–child dependence created thereby is unhealthy and emotionally damaging for both parties.[50]

In many non-Western countries children form part of the household economy and work, or care for younger children while their mothers work. The consequent loss of education makes this an undesirable model, but it indicates that images and expectations of childhood are also flexible. Mothers need not be trapped by institutionalized images of childhood. Many liberal feminists address the problem of child–mother dependence by arguing for free or subsidized child-care. Firestone, more radically, argues that the dependence of children is also a form of oppression and that their liberation should be part of the women's liberation struggle. She condemns the segregation of children from adults and complains 'in no case has the concept of childhood itself been questioned, or the apparatus of childhood (the elementary school, special literature, 'toys' etc.) discarded altogether'.[51] Her solution, financial allowances for children and the constitution of 'legal contract short-term households' where groups of adults contract to live together and give children a stable upbringing for ten years is sketchy and might not commend itself to most feminists, whatever their reservations about the nuclear family. But if women are to be liberated, then logically either society should provide accessible, low-cost child-care facilities or the structure of motherhood and childhood should be radically altered. Feminist analysis of the patriarchal family may centre on the subjection of men to women, but a pivotal element in that subjection is the mother–child nexus, which must be re-structured if their project is to succeed.

---

50.   See, for example, Friedan, *The Feminine Mystique*, ch. 12.
51.   S. Firestone, *The Dialectic of Sex*, p. 205.

The Causes of Oppression

Is the oppression of women culture-specific or universal, deliberate or unconscious, personal or institutional? Most feminists would argue that male domination is not culture-specific—it is found in capitalist and non-capitalist societies alike, and in liberal-democracies as well as illiberal societies: the problem is universal. On the aetiology of oppression, feminists are not committed to the strong and probably untenable proposition that men actively conspire to oppress women, just as Marx was not committed to the view that capitalists conspired together to exploit the workers; conspiracies may sometimes occur, but not systematically. It can more simply be argued that men acting rationally in their own interests are bound to oppress women, since the interests of the sexes are polarized: men may be unaware of this opposition of interests since they too are acting out gendered roles, and many women who have 'bought' the old culture and gender system may be similarly unaware. Some feminists also assert that rationality itself is structured around male interests and male privilege, which makes it hard to challenge using the same (male) logic. Feminists do not need to maintain that men are *wilful* oppressors, but merely to establish that the gender system and gendered institutions have already established their domination.

One anti-feminist argument which needs rebutting is that women *want* to be oppressed in some masochistic way. A reasoned response is that women have little chance to resist oppression, as Mill argued:

> Every one of the subjects [of male power] lives under the very eye . . . of one of the masters . . . with no means of combining against him, no power of even locally overmastering him, and . . . with the strongest motives for seeking his favour and avoiding to give him offence . . . In the case of women, each individual of the subject-class is in a chronic state of bribery and intimidation combined.[52]

At the individual, domestic level, there are many reasons for women's acquiescence in male power, such as economic dependence, fear of reprisal or love for the children. Simone de Beauvoir offers a complementary explanation of acquiescence, claiming that girls are brainwashed with lies about love and marriage. As a consequence,

> it must be admitted that the males find in woman more complicity than the oppressor usually finds in the oppressed. And in bad faith they take authorization from this to declare that she has *desired* the destiny that they have imposed on her.[53]

So women's often unwitting complicity in their gendered roles is not tantamount to a request to be treated oppressively. No more, for Marx, would the workers' apparent acceptance of their exploitation amount to a request to the employer to exploit them. Both women and workers appear complicit because they suffer false consciousness about their true interests. It shows 'bad faith', wilful distortion, to argue that women desire oppression.

---

52. Mill, *The Subjection of Women*, p. 439.
53. S. de Beauvoir, *The Second Sex*, p. 730.

Jean Elshtain asserts that 'the innovative and revolutionary thinkers are those who declare politics to exist where politics was not thought to exist before'.[54] Modern feminists are certainly revolutionaries in this respect: they subscribe to the view that individual acts of oppression, such as abuse or violence in the home or harassment at work, are *political* and not just personal acts—they are a domestic or private expression of patriarchal politics. Hence the 1970s slogan, 'the personal is the political', which directed feminist attention to the analysis of family life and male–female relationships. This is why on the personal plane most feminists seek to challenge male domination in their daily lives and personal relationships, as well as advocating institutional changes—and why many have engaged in practical schemes to combat domestic oppression, setting up shelters for battered wives and providing other services for the victims of domestic violence.

As these analyses of the extent and causes of oppression indicate, changing gender definitions and attitudes is as crucial to the feminist struggle against oppression as institutional changes. We now look at three central strategies which feminists have proposed, which might realistically be employed to transform liberal societies. I omit some more revolutionary ideas already mentioned such as artificial reproduction and separatism, since they would require a more radical restructuring of society than we can currently envisage.

FEMINIST STRATEGIES

Eliminating Discrimination

Liberal feminists wish to give women the same rights as men in political, economic and social life, and thus to make human rights work in women's favour; they also favour equality of opportunity. But they would argue that even in liberal societies which promise equal opportunity there is overt or covert discrimination, or else institutions and practices are constructed according to male norms in such a way that women are in practice unequal and discriminated against. Sex discrimination occurs where gender is brought into an appointments process or any other allocation process in an arbitrary or irrelevant way. Because of sex discrimination legislation, Britain has changed from a society in which, thirty years ago, jobs were strongly gendered to a society where it is illegal for job advertisements to express any preference for male or female employees. Critics of this development would say that it is rational and necessary to allocate some jobs on the basis of sexual differences such as physical strength—for example, men may make better miners. To concede that sex or gender differences are sometimes relevant would lead to the endorsement of an 'equal but *in some respects* different' approach; such a move is strongly criticized by the more radical feminists who claim that the concept of difference itself always relates to a male norm, or to the 'normal male', as Mendus argues (see the section below).

---

54. J. B. Elshtain, *Public Man, Private Woman*, Princeton U. P. , 1981, p. 201.

Discrimination in employment is a key issue for liberal feminists since it makes nonsense of equality of opportunity. Despite the existence of sex discrimination laws, the allocation of jobs (or other benefits) according to gender-neutral criteria will not guarantee equality if the nature of the work is already 'gendered', and even gender-neutral criteria may be covertly discriminatory. Suppose an apparently neutral job specification requires that the successful applicant will spend a week every month in America on business and one of the selection criteria is therefore that 'applicants must be free to travel'. Is this indirectly a discriminatory criterion and a gender-biased job, because women with family responsibilities could not take on such work? If so, should such jobs be outlawed because of their inbuilt discrimination, or radically transformed by, say, job-sharing? Similar questions have been asked about parliamentary 'jobs' because MPs' notoriously eccentric hours of work are incompatible with family obligations.

The argument against discriminatory, gender-biased criteria can be extended to call into question the entire idea of qualifying criteria for any kind of work. In the mid-1970s I sat on a university working party to monitor possible discrimination in the employment of women academics, who were severely under-represented among the permanent staff at the time. Among other issues, we considered whether the 'normal' expectation that applicants for lectureships should have a PhD was discriminatory. Some people argued that since fewer women (at that time) took higher degrees, because they had married and had children after their first degree, the requirement of a PhD was indirectly discriminatory—it was not a gender-neutral criterion. Should we then conclude that if women cannot compete on equal terms in a particular arena, we should change the rules of the competition? Liberal feminists would be reluctant to agree to such a radical conclusion, since they believe in merit as well as in equality of opportunity. An alternative to changing the rules of the competition is to adopt a policy of *positive discrimination* (which Americans, less pejoratively, call *affirmative action*). In the above example, this would require a university to inform candidates that 'candidates without PhDs, especially women, will be seriously considered on their merits'. It would also require appointment boards to view an intelligent woman without a PhD as no less appointable than an equally intelligent man (or indeed, another woman) with a PhD. This move is prejudicial to the better-qualified man (or woman); it also threatens to subvert the notion of appropriate job qualifications. Critics argue that positive discrimination in favour of some is always discrimination against others—also, that it is unjust to appoint a woman on the basis of her membership of a group or category (i.e. because she is a woman) rather than on her personal merits. How then can liberal feminists cope with the conundrum that equal opportunities for women in a gendered world may only be achieved through positive discrimination in favour of the less well qualified, which means less than equal opportunities for men? In such a context, implementation of this liberal principle appears self-defeating. These problems are discussed further in Chapter 14 below.

Equal opportunities are not achieved simply by making all jobs equally open to both sexes, because women may be less well qualified, or less free to adapt to the job's requirements because of family ties. Moreover, some feminists argue, work is a male-defined activity, defined so as to make women appear unsuitable for work. Radcliffe Richards puts the case: 'if women had been fully involved in the running of society from the start they would have *found* a way of arranging work and children to fit each other. Men have had no such motivation and we can see the results', and 'there is something radically wrong with a system which forces so many women to choose between caring properly for their children and using their abilities fully'.[55] The modest, reformist demand for liberal equality logically takes liberal feminists beyond equal employment legislation and commits them to advocating either a radical re-structuring of work to fit in with family life or a radical re-structuring of family life, motherhood and childhood.

Celebrating Difference

Susan Mendus states that 'to be different is to deviate from some norm and . . . that norm is invariably a male norm . . . [democratic theory] must recognize not only that difference is sometimes ineliminable, but also that what counts as difference is not value-neutral'.[56] Women are often viewed as different and correspondingly disadvantaged when measured according to male norms—for example, employers often view pregnancy as a disadvantage, even as 'an illness'. Feminists disagree about the role of difference in their theories. Suffragettes (and early feminists like Wollstonecraft) asserted that women and men were equal in terms of reason and capacity, to highlight the injustice of denying women the same vote and the same legal rights as men; they emphasized similarities to gain a limited, political end. But many feminists with the wider brief of ending male domination have been at pains to emphasize some fundamental differences between men and women. They wish to valorize and celebrate the different-ness of women, on the basis that this difference is something which they claim for themselves and not something ascribed to them by men as a mark of inferiority.

Some pro-difference feminists focus on the body processes which relate to women's reproductive role: these are unique to women, something which men cannot share, something of which to be proud. Motherhood and nurturing are likewise celebrated as a special talent of women. This approach, a complete reversal of Firestone's ('pregnancy is barbaric') approach, has strongly conservative implications. Other pro-difference feminists believe that women have different capacities, thought processes and ways of moral reasoning. In male culture, these divergent 'knowledges' are suppressed by masculine logic and ethics and the universalizing (male) approach deriving from the Enlightenment, which excludes plurality and devalues difference. Woman-centred analysis, by contrast, builds on female differences and has been applied to the social sciences, philosophy, history, the arts and language itself, creating alternative perspectives and new bodies of knowledge. In social science, for example the masculine

55. Radcliffe Richards, *The Sceptical Feminist*, pp.152, 219.
56. S. Mendus, 'Feminism and democracy' in J. Dunn (Ed.), *Democracy: The Unfinished Journey*, Oxford U.P., 1993, pp. 218–19.

principle favours objectivity, positivism and value-neutrality as aids to the understanding of society; subjectivism and personal experience are not valued as sources of insight. Feminist social science researchers have favoured qualitative, rather than quantitative, social research. They argue for interview or discussion-based methods, where the researcher and her 'subject' cooperate, the subject's personal experiences are valued and the subject is not treated instrumentally as in some 'male' research. Such an approach would emphasize the social construction of social phenomena and not seek some 'objective reality'.[57] A social science incorporating female modes of thought would give radically different insights into the nature of society.

In the conclusion of her influential book on women's moral development, *In a Different Voice* (1982), Carol Gilligan argues that men and women have different moral 'voices'. By combining their insights

> we arrive at a more complex rendition of human experience which sees the truth of separation and attachment in the lives of women and men and recognizes how these truths are carried by different modes of language and thought.[58]

Gilligan's interview-based research on moral identity and moral views showed significant differences between women and men; in her 'rights and responsibilities' study, she met many women students who had learnt the ethic of self-sacrifice from their mothers. In such an ethic, consulting one's own wellbeing was often stigmatized as selfishness. The students were trying to reconcile the 1970s ethos of personal development and autonomy with these earlier moral precepts which emphasized responsibility to others and not harming others. They had started to grasp 'the essential notion of rights, that the interests of the self can be considered legitimate'.[59] Women, Gilligan found, saw their identity in terms of relationships and attachments and followed an ethic of nurture, responsibility and care; their moral judgements were more contextualized than the men's more objective judgements. In many situations, this approach conflicts with the more 'masculine' ethic of individual rights and justice—for example, following an impartial rule of justice may result in harm to some individual, or insisting on one's rights may jeopardize a relationship. There are, Gilligan concluded 'two different moral ideologies . . . separation [from others, their needs etc.] is justified by an ethic of rights while attachment is supported by an ethic of care'.[60] If Gilligan is right and women's moral reasoning differs from that of men, should one 'moral ideology' prevail over the other? Could they co-exist or will the 'nurturers' always be taken advantage of by the rights theorists' single-minded pursuit of autonomy? Will Kymlicka discusses the 'care v. rights' question sensitively and at length, but finds no definitive answer as to how we might fully reconcile the pursuit of autonomy

---

57. See L. Stanley and S. Wise, *Breaking Out: Feminist Consciousness and Feminist Research*, Routledge& Kegan Paul, 1983.
58. C. Gilligan, *In a Different Voice: Psychological Theory and Women's Development*, Harvard U.P., 1982, pp. 173–4.
59. Gilligan, *In a Different Voice*, p. 149.
60. Gilligan, *In a Different Voice*, p. 164. Note the (unconscious) similarity in her comment to Marx's view that bourgeois rights justified 'the separation of man from man'.

with responsibilities of care to others, especially if the 'others' are not those personally known to us but 'all other human beings'.[61]

Some adherents of the 'different but valid' approach find an ally in Fritzjof Capra's radical approach to science and knowledge. Capra made use of the contrasting models of consciousness which the Chinese associate with the two sexes. While Yang, the masculine principle, is associated with the competitive, the aggressive, the rational and the analytic, the female principle, Yin, is associated with responsiveness, cooperation, intuition and a 'synthesizing' intellectual approach.

> Society has consistently favoured the yang over the yin—rational knowledge over intuitive wisdom, science over religion, competition over co-operation, exploitation of natural resources over conservation . . . . This emphasis [is] supported by the patriarchal system . . .[62]

The Chinese injunction is to balance the two kinds of consciousness so that neither dominates. But some feminists who believe in different male and female modes of thought suggest that the female mode is more valid and valuable than the male mode, that intuition is superior to reason. This seems mistaken: intuition may suggest the solution to a problem, but to gain public acceptance the solution must be justified by rational argument. Claims to a special, privileged feminine mode of reasoning should, I submit, be viewed sceptically.

Postmodernist feminism initially placed the concept of difference on a new plane, drawing on a corpus of psychoanalytic and semiological literature in the French tradition.

> Feminist uses of psychoanalysis that encourage the liberation of the poetic and welcome the traces of the unconscious within their own discourse help us to illuminate 'that vast chamber' of unsaid meaning, the language of our difference.[63]

This approach delved into the construction of language and into female 'silences'—things which must remain unsaid, or cannot even be thought, within male-dominated discourse. Women were exhorted to celebrate their 'otherness' from men and re-discover and rejoice in their own secret language—for example the language of mothers and daughters, 'subliminal, subversive, preverbal'.[64] In fact, by the 1980s postmodern feminists were already challenging the concept of 'difference' because it implied an acceptance of the female/male binary opposition, which consigns women to a set of norms definitionally opposed to the male norms and so limits their potential. The new wave advocated a plurality of norms and identities for women, grounded in their lived experience; differences between women were as important as male–female differences. More radically still, Judith Butler has opposed all attempts to theorize 'woman' as a universal concept and has argued that gender is entirely independent of sex; it is

61. W. Kymlicka, *Contemporary Political Philosophy*, Oxford U.P., 1990, pp. 262–86.
62. F. Capra, *The Turning Point: Science, Society and the Changing Culture*, Wildwood, 1982, pp. 21–2.
63. C. Burke, 'Rethinking the maternal', in H. Eisenstein and A. Jardine (Eds.), *The Future of Difference*, G. K. Hall, 1980, p. 114.
64. C. Burke, 'Rethinking the maternal', p. 113.

a free-floating artifice, with the consequence that *man* and *masculine* might just as easily signify a female body as a male one, and *woman* and *feminine* a male body as easily as a female one.[65]

For Butler, gender identity is created simply by the *performance* of gendered roles; she advocates undermining the heterosexual norm by dissonant, subversive performances such as drag and cross-dressing.[66] The political impact of the heterodox postmodernist analyses has been limited because of their essential relativism, which affords no definitive models or strategies for women's liberation; however, the approach has been important in psychoanalysis, literary criticism and the analysis of gendered language.

The assertion of difference by some feminists raises two problems—one concerning its validity and the other concerning its consequences. Against the difference approach, it can be argued that feminine ways of thinking and the feminine ethic are the products of gendered conditioning and are not essential female characteristics. (Wollstonecraft came near to making such a point when arguing that the apparent irrationality and frivolity of women were the result of their systematic degradation by and dependency on men—but she was not commending irrationality.[67]) If the majority of women have lived 'private' lives, caring for husbands, children and other dependants, their moral views, and those transmitted to their daughters, will inevitably be bounded by the importance of relationships, sympathy and care. Likewise, analytic reason will not be the forte of women who have not been educated in systematic thinking. In short we cannot prove that these differences are innate rather than the result of experience or gendered conditioning. If our ways of thinking arise from our life experiences, then men and women with similar experiences and education will think the same way—difference is not inevitable. But it may still be valid to celebrate 'feminine' ways of thinking because it they reflect different ways of being and offer an alternative to masculine modes.

If, however, the differences are considered innate, certain disquieting consequences follow: it could be asserted that any woman who argues a case analytically, or insists on her rights and autonomy, must have been 'masculinized' and must be untrue to her instincts, a victim of false consciousness. More worryingly, in a culture based on masculine norms, the different feminine mode of thought is likely to be branded as deviant and inferior—this denigration is precisely what feminists seek to anticipate and prevent by asserting the independent validity of the feminine thought processes. Of course, there is no reason why, if there are such differences, the male norm should be privileged, but it is likely to be so in a male-dominated society. (To privilege female norms and declare female thought processes *superior* is a crude reversal of the problem, and no solution. To advocate that men should develop, rather than dismiss, 'feminine' qualities is a more positive approach.) Most worrying is the danger that insisting on innate differences assists the justification of inequalities to the detriment of

---

65. J. Butler, *Gender Trouble: Feminism and the Subversion of Identity*, Routledge, 1990, p. 6.
66. Butler, *Gender Trouble*, p. 137.
67. Wollstonecraft, *A Vindication of the Rights of Woman*, ch. 2.

women. Aristotle's maxim, that it is as unjust to treat unequals equally as to treat equals unequally, can be wielded by anti-feminists (for example, Wilson, cited earlier), who are only too happy to argue that male–female differences are good grounds for different treatment of men and women. In particular, the feminists who emphasize women's maternal and nurturing instincts are God's gift to conservative critics, who will say 'I told you so' and consign them to be nannies and nurses for ever. These are reasons why the 'celebration of difference' is a high-risk feminist strategy, even if its purpose is to create a culture where both male and female ways of thinking, and being, are equally respected and do not give rise to gendered inequalities.

Re-constituting Politics

An important achievement of feminist philosophers has been their exposure of the gendered nature of liberal and democratic political theory and their re-conceptualization of political ideas. Among their targets have been the public–private division of society, the reality of liberal rights and the nature of liberal democracy. We saw in Chapter 3 that liberalism proposes a division between the public or political sphere and the private sphere of economic and social life, often referred to as the division between state and civil society. Some feminist theorists base their challenge to liberalism on this dichotomy while others identify the classical Greek distinction between domestic life and public or social life as more relevant to the oppressed position of women. On either view, women have traditionally been relegated to the domestic sphere, with no political significance or voice. For Eisenstein, 'this division of public and private life is at one and the same time a male/female distinction . . . ideology identifies the realm of female, family, private life, as outside political life and the domain of the state'.[68] The state, although apparently entirely separate from the institution of the patriarchal family in this model, in fact intervenes to uphold patriarchal power by regulating marriage, divorce, family property, contraception and abortion. This is why, Eisenstein argues, feminists must view the bourgeois liberal state not as a neutral arbiter between conflicting interests but as pivotal in maintaining both capitalist power and patriarchal power. Uniting the public and the private, the personal and the political, is neither a practical nor a theoretically sound solution to the problem in Pateman's view, but she argues that the interrelation of the two spheres should be more clearly recognized in any 'future, democratic feminist social order'.[69]

Classical liberal individualism, as noted earlier, is built on a notion of the male individual and, it is argued, buttresses his power over women by granting him privacy in his domestic life. Most of the rights which liberalism guarantees are relevant to the political, economic and social lives of men and do not protect women in the domestic sphere. Although women have political rights in modern

---

68. Eisenstein, *The Radical Future of Liberal Feminism*, p. 223.
69. C. Pateman, *The Disorder of Women*, Polity Press, 1989, p. 134.

democracies, some other liberal rights are worthless in the context of economic and educational inequalities, and women are accordingly deprived of their benefit. Liberal societies boast of the individual right to privacy which distinguishes them from authoritarian societies. Catherine Mackinnon has argued that the *male* right to privacy strengthens the division between public and private: it places private wrongs beyond public redress and thereby 'depoliticizes' the oppression of women in the private sphere[70] (for example, domestic violence may be viewed as a private matter beyond legal intervention). In other words, men can oppress women in private with the state's blessing, although, as noted above, the state is swift to intervene when women demand the right to control their own reproductive functions. Overall, the rights and freedoms offered by liberal society chiefly benefit men. There has been improvement in the rights of women since the 1980s when a number of these feminist critiques were written. For example, in Britain the police are now willing to intervene in violent domestic disputes and have set up a number of Domestic Violence Units since 1987—and, famously, a judgment of the House of Lords in 1991 made marital rape unlawful.[71] Marriage has become less popular and over time the equal rights of co-habiting partners have been legally recognized. These changes are, I believe, evidence that feminism has affected attitudes and practices in this country even if the patriarchal structure remains largely unscathed.

The initial feminist critique of democracy was, of course, that it excluded women. One justification of this exclusion was the argument that citizenship was based on being able to take up arms to defend one's country, which women could not do, while another was that citizens contributed to the country's economy by working—which ruled out most middle-class women. In Britain, during the First World War the contribution of some four million women to the war effort rendered such arguments specious and women gained the vote. This has by no means led to equal representation in parliament or to a 'women's agenda' receiving serious attention. Second-wave feminists have criticized both the principle and the practice of democracy on various grounds—for example (i) women cannot be properly active in the political sphere because of their private (domestic) roles, (ii) the supposedly impartial role of the politician may threaten women's concerns and bolster dominant, male interests, (iii) the system is designed around male norms and gives power to the dominant group and (iv) the failure of democracies, even when women are enfranchised, to remedy women's inequalities is evidence of a gender bias in democracy itself. Feminists would also concur in the more general criticisms of democracy: it is unrepresentative; it is run by (male) elites; adversarial and competitive politics are destructive of negotiation and compromise, and majoritarian democracy disadvantages minorities and

---

70. For Mackinnon's account of privacy see C. Mackinnon, *Feminism Unmodified: Discourses on Life and Law*, Harvard U.P., 1987.

71. *Reg. v. R.* In the earlier Court of Appeal judgment (which the House of Lords upheld) Lord Lane C. J. described the decision as 'the removal of a common law fiction which has become anachronistic and offensive', the fiction being that a wife was deemed to have consented irrevocably to sexual intercourse with her husband. *Weekly Law Reports*, 1991, Vol. 3, p. 777.

militates against difference. One of the less convincing feminist arguments (in my view) is that democracy itself is flawed because it has not 'delivered the goods' for women in particular. Many other groups could complain of non-delivery. Doubtless the elite and patriarchal nature of democratic institutions is partly to blame, but so are faulty systems of representation. Beyond that there is also the fact that democracy cannot perform simultaneous miracles for a plurality of groups with differing and sometimes conflicting interests—democracy is about balancing interests, and particularly about balancing budgets when every interest group demands resources.

Among the practical remedies which feminists have advocated is equalization of political access. In Britain, the 'Three Hundred Group' campaigned (without success) for an equal number of women MPs, while in 1996 the Labour Party experimented controversially with all-women short-lists in the selection of constituency candidates until these were declared illegal. The experiment revived all the arguments against positive discrimination and quotas but nevertheless resulted in the election of 101 women Labour MPs in 1997. A second proposed remedy is that oppressed groups should have special representation in democratic parliaments or be given public funding to organize themselves—ideas which raise questions like 'which groups count?' and 'who decides which groups count?' Anne Phillips has analysed the difficulties posed by feminist proposals, especially the idea of a participatory and discursive democracy. She notes the incompatibility of more active participation with women's domestic roles, and also points out that the extensive participation practised by early women's groups had some adverse effects: there was insistence on consensus and the 'false unities of sisterhood' even to the point of illiberality.[72] Mendus's solution is a democratic practice which recognizes social heterogeneity: 'it must therefore cease to pursue equality by trying to eliminate difference and instead concentrate on pursuing it by recognising difference more adequately'.[73] Most feminist proposals for democratic improvement would be endorsed by many minority groups since they are intended to combat the exclusion of group interests from the political process. They are, essentially, a re-working of the arguments against majority tyranny and elite domination.

A wider political question is whether a gender-neutral society would be possible without obliterating all but the essential differences between the sexes and imposing an artificial uniformity which oppressed everyone equally and which would almost certainly require to be maintained by coercion. Any answer to this must be speculative, but in this connection it is instructive to refer to the many *feminist utopias* written in the last two centuries. These provide radically divergent models for alternative futures without oppression—some in which women and men live on equal terms, some in which women rule over men. There are also separatist utopias which are in effect utopias of despair, suggesting that women and men can never co-exist in harmony and equality. There is sadly no space to

---

72. A. Phillips, *Democracy and Difference*, Polity Press, 1993, ch. 6.
73. Mendus, 'Feminism and democracy', p. 218.

review the feminist utopian tradition here, but these works merit study as a vigorous and imaginative strand in the development of feminist political theory.[74]

FEMINISM AS IDEOLOGY

So potent a movement as feminism has inevitably created a backlash, mainly among right-wing thinkers. Typically, such critics argue that (i) gender differences reflect natural differences in the ability and characteristics of the sexes, (ii) voluntary servitude is not servitude, and women's complicity in domestic and marital 'oppression' proves that they enjoy or benefit from it, and (iii) that women's central role in the family gives them unique status and power.[75] These attacks on feminism usefully illustrate the nature of ideology itself: for any explanation of social phenomena, a contrary and incompatible explanation can be advanced. The two world-views are opposed at every point: where feminists see subjection and oppression, critics see benefit and contentment. A more positive critique not incompatible with feminism has been developed by some male theorists who have been prompted by the feminist movement to re-think the economic and social position of men; some would argue that men are also oppressed by gender and by the patriarchal system—by the expectation that they should be the breadwinners and take economic responsibility for the family.

If ideologies are comprehensive and action-guiding accounts of political and social life, feminism is clearly an ideology, albeit an ideology with many different strands. The first wave of feminists had a limited political aim, which they achieved; second-wave feminists offered a comprehensive critique of society and far-reaching proposals for change. They argued that society is based on a patriarchal order and that women are oppressed by gendered institutions and practices, and even by gendered language. They claimed the equality of women in all socially relevant respects, and radical feminists in addition argued for respect for and valorization of difference, allowing women to have their own voice. There have been fierce internal debates within the movement, and schisms: some black American feminists rejected middle-class feminism because it ignores the double oppression, racial and sexual, of poor, black women. Third-World feminists also consider the Western analysis is only tangentially relevant to the problems which they experience. But whatever its internal differences and complexities, modern feminism offers a subversive social analysis which continues to resonate and may in time see off the opposition.

74. See C. Kessler, *Daring to Dream: Utopian Stories by United States Women: 1836–1919*, Pandora Press, 1984; D. Lewes, *Dream Revisionaries: Gender and Genre in Women's Utopian Fiction, 1870–1920*, University of Alabama Press, 1995, and L. Sargisson, *Contemporary Feminist Utopianism*, Routledge, 1996.
75. See the collection of articles in C. Quest (Ed.), *Liberating Women . . . from Modern Feminism*, Institute of Economic Affairs, London, 1994, for examples of such arguments.

FURTHER READING

Many classic feminist texts have already been mentioned in the chapter, and these amply repay reading. More recent texts include:

V. Bryson, *Feminist Political Theory: an Introduction*, Macmillan, 1992.

J. Evans, *Feminism Today: an Introduction to Second-Wave Feminism*, Sage, 1995.

J. Grant, *Fundamental Feminism: Contesting the Core Concepts of Feminist Theory*, Routledge, 1993.

J. Lovenduski and V. Randall, *Contemporary Feminist Politics: Women and Power in Britain*, Oxford U.P., 1993.

H. S. Mirza, *Black British Feminism: A Reader*, Routledge, 1997.

L. Nicholson (Ed.), *The Second Wave*, Routledge, 1997.

C. Pateman, *The Sexual Contract*, Polity Press, 1988.

A. Phillips, *Democracy and Difference*, Polity Press, 1993.

C. Weedon, *Feminism and the Politics of Difference*, Blackwell, 1997.

Chapter 10

Green Ideologies

In nature, nothing exists alone.[1]
(*Rachel Carson*)

The idea that 'nothing in nature exists alone', that all of nature is interconnected, is a fundamental axiom of Green political thought, an axiom which leads many ecologists to a 'one-earth' theory. Whether this insight commits Greens to a political perspective, and whether that perspective can properly be designated an ideology, is the subject of this chapter. Carson's theme was the undesirable effects of human interference with nature and natural processes. Since Carson wrote *Silent Spring* in 1962 many examples of such damaging effects have been discovered and widely publicized, such as the destruction of rain forests, over-fishing, pollution from acid rain, global warming, and the depletion of the ozone layer. All these are the consequences (often unintended) of human intervention in nature. But it could be argued that, however simply we lived, we would impinge on and interact with the rest of the natural world, if only by building shelter and eating plants and animals. We are ourselves part of nature. Who then is in a position to say which human interventions are bad and which are good? The answer to this is often given from a human perspective—e.g. our interventions are depleting the resources which our children and grandchildren will need—rather than on the basis of concern for other life forms on the planet, and this anthropocentrism is challenged by some Greens. One important moral and political question for Greens is whether we can rise above the human perspective in our evaluation of the effects of human activity; there is also a question of whether a *human* ideology can possibly be eco-centred, rather than human-centred, and still achieve political success. Among the other political problems faced by Greens is the difficulty of transforming the 'Nimby' attitude (Not In *My* Back Yard) to environmental destruction into a more global political outlook,

---

1. R. Carson, *Silent Spring*, Pelican, 1982, p. 60.

which would occupy itself with the consequences of our actions on distant societies; Greens also need to overcome the equally individualistic 'Not in *My* Lifetime' myopia which may prevent us from taking timely action to avert future disasters.

Green ideas were scarcely articulated as part of a general ecological outlook until the 1970s and yet many of the phenomena stressed by Green thinkers and Green activists have become familiar causes of concern to most of us, in the West at least. Few days pass when the quality press does not carry several news items about threats to the environment or ecological disasters. This raised consciousness must in part be attributed to the work of organizations like Greenpeace and Friends of the Earth and to the activities of Green parties—it may also be that such disasters are becoming more frequent because of an accelerating level of human intervention and exploitation. Because of the enhanced level of concern, most conventional political parties have now formulated Green environmental policies, albeit in diluted forms—they remain 'grey' parties by the Greens' reckoning. The environmental pressure groups are, some would say, more preoccupied with nature than with human society and politics. If Green politicians start with similar concerns, how can they develop a *political* agenda, since this must inevitably be more human-centred? This chapter will assess whether the claim that there is a distinctive 'Green politics' is valid and whether Green theory constitutes an ideology as such.

There is as much ecology-related and Green literature as there is feminist literature, and the Green movement encompasses as many controversies and internal differences as the feminist movement. This chapter will therefore deal with the raw materials of the Greens' arguments, rather than the fine details of individual theorists' positions. However, there are broad groupings of Green thinkers and activists which must be distinguished, to set the scene for later arguments.

SHADES OF GREEN

To detail all the political and philosophical differences within the Green camp would require an elaborate taxonomy. Here I shall introduce only the main distinctions. The first is between *environmentalism* and *ecologism*. Environmentalists are concerned with moderating the impact of human activity on the environment and with protecting nature as far as is compatible with human purposes. They do not propose radically to alter these purposes—for example, they might argue for better public transport to reduce the use of cars, but not for major changes in the social and economic structure to obviate the need for personal mobility. Environmentalists, typically, argue for re-cycling, economy in the use of resources and for protection and conservation of wildlife and countryside. Ecology, a science developed in the nineteenth-century, is the study of organisms in their own environment and the mutual interactions between the two. 'Ecologism' is a doctrine which advocates the radical transformation of the relationship between human beings and their environment. Thus, by contrast with environmentalist proposals for better public transport, some Greens would argue for the creation of small self-reliant communities (similar to those envisaged by certain anarchists) so that people need not travel much at all. Green doctrine contains many shades of opinion and a contrast is usually drawn between the 'light Greens' and the 'dark Greens' or, similarly, between 'shallow ecologists' and 'deep ecologists'. The proponents of 'dark' or 'deep' Green principles assert that all species live in 'one world', a world whose fragile balance is jeopardized by human activities. Typically, they argue for an ecocentric view of the world, regarding the planet and its eco-systems as something with intrinsic value beyond any value which the human race may have, or may bestow. 'Light' or 'shallow' Greens are more likely to be anthropocentric in their approach and may argue—at least for political purposes—that the reason for minimizing human intervention in the natural world is to ensure the survival of the human race—in other words, they may use instrumental arguments about conservation of the natural world, even though they would deny that humankind has a right to exploit or dominate that world. In some respects, their position may be very close to that of the environmentalists. The dark/light distinction is very fluid, and Greens of different hues may find themselves in agreement over political tactics and arguments while, philosophically, they are divided. Also, because the Green movement is young and developing, its proponents often modify their arguments and positions—for example, Rudolf Bahro moved from socialism to eco-socialism and the German Green Party but in 1985 left the Party because of ideological differences about vivisection, which he opposed. Green ideas have also been fused with other ideological positions—there are eco-socialists (like Bahro and Gorz), eco-anarchists (e.g. Bookchin), a number of eco-feminists, eco-conservatives and even eco-capitalists. Some of these doctrines will be referred to when we review Green arguments.

A further distinction must be drawn between academic (philosophical), political and scientific ecologists. Those who philosophize about man's relationship to nature may also be politically active—or not. Political Greens may hold philosophical positions but are mainly committed to promoting eco-friendly politics. Both draw on the work of scientific ecologists to support their arguments about how human beings should change their behaviour. But the relationship between scientific and normative ecology is not one of direct entailment. The scientist may analyse how an ecological system, e.g. a watercourse, operates and how it sustains wildlife and may measure the effects of human activity on its operation, but these observations in themselves lead to no normative conclusions. The conclusion that human intervention changes the environment *for the worse* is a value-judgement imposed on, but not derived from, a set of facts. Those who watch wildlife films on television know that, after portraying apparently unspoilt, self-sustaining eco-systems, the films regularly conclude with ominous warnings that human encroachment now threatens such systems. (Wildlife films actually contribute to the preservation of eco-systems and other species by drawing attention to their precarious natural balance and—like zoos, some would argue—because they enable people to enjoy them without travelling to see them in person.) But natural systems are changing continuously—as the evolutionary history of the planet illustrates—and someone might argue against the Greens that human-induced changes are not in themselves worse than any 'natural' changes.

I first consider the Green critique of existing human practices which in turn constitute arguments in favour of their own eco-friendly policies. As will be seen, some of their arguments take an instrumental form (i.e. the despoliation of nature actually runs counter to human purposes) or, similarly, a prudential form (we should avoid making certain interventions because they threaten us with local or global disaster). Such anthropocentric arguments assume human interests to be of central importance. The ecocentric arguments, by contrast, are based on an assumption of the intrinsic value of other life forms and the axiom that human beings have no right to intervene in ways that damage other species, even when such interventions serve human purposes in the short run. The arguments will be dealt with under three headings: economic arguments, arguments against pollution and moral arguments.

ECONOMIC ARGUMENTS

We live on a planet of finite size but we use it as if it were a limitless source of resources and a free dustbin.[2]

Economics is often described as the science of scarcity. In the West we live in an age of relative abundance but Green politics is nonetheless informed by a vision of imminent scarcity. Although Green politics developed in the 1970s and came into prominence in the 1980s, some of its roots lie in the 1960s, when left-wing critics such as Marcuse railed against the materialism of capitalist society and pointed out that capitalism could only grow by depleting the natural resources on which it relied for production: the more rapidly capitalism expanded, the more swiftly would its raw materials be exhausted. Short-term goals such as consumer satisfaction were taking precedence over long-term objectives such as sustainability or the search for renewable energy sources. For many Marxists, in any case, capitalism was not viable in the long term because of this and its other fundamental contradictions (see Chapter 4). Many adherents of the 1960s counter-culture rejected consumerism and sought a more 'natural' way of life as part of their opposition to capitalism, living in communes and preaching self-sufficiency. In the same decade, Establishment politicians and economists were vexed by the decreasing growth rates in some advanced capitalist countries.[3] Much orthodox economic theory had been posited on continued rapid growth—something approaching 10% p.a. rather than the 3% to which Britain was then reduced. (Such growth, postwar, had helped to alleviate social discontent by allowing the working classes to share in an enlarged prosperity without major redistribution—the decline in growth rates was therefore also a cause for social concern.) In 1972, Meadows et al. published *The Limits to Growth* (subtitled 'A

2. *Green Party Manifesto*, The Green Party, 1997, p. 2.
3. See, for example, N. Kaldor, 'Causes of the slow rate of economic growth in the United Kingdom', Inaugural Lecture, Cambridge U.P., 1966.

Report for The Club of Rome's Project on the Predicament of Mankind'). The Meadows study examined five factors which determine and limit growth— 'population, agricultural production, natural resources, industrial production, and pollution'.[4] These factors remain the major concerns of the Greens today. The Report was novel in taking a global, rather than a narrowly national, perspective—an anticipation of the 'one world' position. A simple arithmetical calculation shows that (e.g. for a sum of money on which interest is paid) a growth rate of 2% results in a doubling of the sum in 35 years, while for 10% the 'doubling time' is only seven years: such rapid growth is termed 'exponential'. The researchers' analysis showed that the world population was growing exponentially, as were world industrial production and the economic growth rates of individual nations; they predicted that within 100 years the world would come up against absolute limits to further growth because of its finite natural resources, many of which (such as fossil fuels) are non-renewable. In such circumstances, the outlook must be one of social unrest, wars fought over resources, the immiseration of some populations, a lower standard of living for all and a devastating degree of pollution throughout the world. The authors of the report argued for global economic equilibrium rather than further growth, while acknowledging that such an edict would appear to developing countries as 'a final act of neocolonialism' unless they were compensated for reduced growth (since a reduction of growth levels together with fast-growing populations would otherwise doom them forever to relative impoverishment).[5] Thus was born the 'zero-growth' or equilibrium thesis, which influenced many Green thinkers and some of the more radical economists.

In 1992, Meadows et al. produced a new report, *Beyond the Limits*, which reviewed their earlier predictions in the light of contemporary trends. Between 1970 and 1990, many 'selected human activities' had more than doubled in volume—the consumption of coal, the number of registered automobiles and electricity generating capacity, to cite just a few examples. In the same period, the human population had grown from 3.6 billion to 5.3 billion.[6] Among the problems of such exponential growth is the possibility of sudden catastrophes (e.g. the depletion of the ozone layer, which may also be exponential) as well as the gradual reduction of everyone's living standards as the limits are reached or exceeded. The authors recommended a radical revision in the policies which perpetuate growth of production and consumption. They advocated population control and an increase in efficiency in the use of resources. They concluded that a *sustainable society* may still be possible, but that it would require

> a careful balance between long-term and short-term goals and an emphasis on sufficiency, equity and quality of life rather than on quantity of output. It requires more than productivity and more than technology; it also requires maturity, compassion and wisdom.[7]

---

4. D. Meadows et al., *The Limits to Growth*, Pan, 1974, pp. 11–12.
5. Meadows et al., *The Limits to Growth*, p. 194.
6. D. Meadows et al., *Beyond the Limits*, Earthscan Publications, 1992, p. 7.
7. Meadows et al., *Beyond the Limits*, p. xvi.

They also made an important—but probably over-optimistic—distinction between growth and development arguing that development connotes the realization of potential whereas growth means an increase in size through the use of resources: 'although there are limits to growth, there need be no limits to development'.[8] A similarly optimistic distinction was also made by J. S. Mill, who also favoured a 'stationary state' economy in the context of Malthusian arguments about population and growth.[9]

Green interpretations of the sustainable society differ. Light Greens are more open to the idea of a 'technological fix'—for example, new sources of energy (solar, water and wind energy) might in time replace the non-renewable energy resources, while the problems of pollution could be dealt with by stringent laws requiring anti-pollution devices or (less effectively) taxes on polluters. But it can also be argued that these measures would require expensive technology and the use of more resources which may themselves create further pollution. For example, catalytic convertors for cars require factories to produce such devices while modern wind farms create considerable noise pollution for local residents. Dark Greens are more committed to a revolution in human lifestyle which would make some resource-consuming and pollution-creating processes unnecessary and would reduce our reliance on others. More will be said later of these possible radical solutions.

In this economic debate, a salient question for Greens is whether the depletion of resources and pollution are features of capitalism in particular or industrialism in general. In 1971, Bookchin asserted that 'bourgeois exploitation and manipulation are undermining the very capacity of the earth to sustain advanced forms of life', and maintained that bourgeois society pits man against other men and also against the natural world.[10] Gorz argues that economic rationality should be subordinated to eco-social rationality, which challenges capitalist logic and its paradigms of growth and productivity; the essential components of capitalism—markets, consumption and the continuous creation of needs and desires—are destructive of ecological rationality.[11] He holds that 'eco-capitalism', with its emphasis on re-cycling and other half-measures, does not resolve the problem. The polarization of society between the rich and poor grows apace and unemployment is now a major problem for many industrial countries. Gorz argues that reduced working hours (RWH) combined with increased productivity would allow a reduction in unemployment, given a situation of low growth; RWH would also free people to undertake valuable but non-remunerated activities. (One axiom of Green argument, shared in part by feminists, is that capitalism confines 'work' too narrowly to those activities rewarded by wages, fees or salaries.) The overall effect of RWH should be redistributive, thus achieving socialist objectives in Gorz's view,[12] but it can be argued that his scenario relies

8. Meadows et al., _Beyond the Limits_, p. xix.
9. J. S. Mill, _Principles of Political Economy_, Penguin, 1970, p. 116 (Bk. IV, ch. vi).
10. M. Bookchin, _Post-Scarcity Anarchism_ (1971), Wildwood House, 1974, pp. 36, 63.
11. A. Gorz, _Capitalism, Socialism, Ecology_ (trans. C. Turner), Verso, 1994, p. 12.
12. Gorz, _Capitalism, Socialism, Ecology_, ch. 9.

too heavily on improved technology and enhanced productivity to count as Green.

The argument that socialism is inherently more eco-friendly than capitalism does not withstand scrutiny, unless it refers to certain versions of utopian socialism which emphasized low-technology production and agriculture—those of Fourier or William Morris, for example. Communism has been ecologically disastrous: the USSR and the communist countries of Eastern Europe had even worse records of pollution than advanced capitalist societies. Most socialists have assumed that the industrial system will continue but the ownership of the means of production will change. While a socialist society might distribute resources more equally, this is likely to increase the propensity of the newly enriched 'workers' to consume, since their marginal rate of consumer expenditure is greater than that of more wealthy people. Similarly, the increasing prosperity of Far-Eastern countries like Malaysia and Korea (and even China) creates greater overall demand for goods and resources as people who have lived in relative poverty become able to afford mass-produced consumer goods. The deep Green argument is that, in ecological terms, not only capitalism but the 'super-ideology'[13] of industrialism itself is the culprit. This implies a more radical solution than the mere abolition of capitalism—it implies a radically new mode of production based on lower technology and, correspondingly, total social re-organization. Such solutions are discussed later in this chapter.

Reducing Consumption

The Green analysis cannot be confined to economics alone, because (as Marx would have been the first to point out) this affects all other aspects of society. Whether capitalism produces the desire to consume or whether consumer demand stimulates capitalism may now be a chicken-and-egg question, but all Greens would unite on the need to reduce the consumption of unnecessary goods and deep Greens demand a radical re-evaluation of what exactly *is* necessary to human life. As we have seen in earlier chapters, giving the government or some other group the right to define which needs are real and which are artificial and unnecessary is an invitation to paternalism or, worse, to authoritarianism. Although many adherents of Green ideology practise Green consumption patterns in their own lives (e.g. by becoming vegetarians and refraining from buying cars) their rate of conversion by example is bound to be low and, unless disastrous scarcities should occur naturally, legislation is the most likely method of curtailing consumption—if Green arguments are accepted. In fact, state control of consumption has a long pedigree: in ancient Rome there were 'sumptuary laws' against excessive expenditure and ostentatious consumption by the rich and in the eighteenth century Godwin and Rousseau suggested the re-introduction of such laws to limit consumption. The twentieth-century liberal/libertarian doctrine of freedom of consumer choice make such laws sound oppressive but in fact most governments impose taxes on consumption goods and the rates of tax (e.g. VAT)

---

13.   A. Dobson, *Green Political Thought*, 2nd edn., Routledge, 1995, p. 33.

are regularly manipulated to control consumption patterns in accordance with government policy and to make some goods too expensive to be consumed widely. Countries with adverse trade balances have sometimes levied penal taxes on imports to cut the consumption of foreign goods. So the idea of reducing consumption by taxation is not revolutionary; it can be given a Green twist by taxing resource-depleting goods and those goods whose manufacture creates pollution more heavily than eco-friendly goods.

The world's population will soon reach six billion. Another way of reducing consumption and resource depletion therefore is to limit and then reduce population levels globally. This proposal, although self-evidently a desirable step (as indicated in Meadows' statistics and projections), has provoked internal disputes between Greens and led to charges of 'eco-fascism'. Population reduction involves both practical and moral problems (the practical problems are well-known and need not be reiterated here). The highest population growth is in Third-World countries, in the 'South' rather than the wealthy 'North',[14] and they also have the highest levels of population in absolute numbers: however, consumption is differentially spread across and between populations. An American may (for example) consume more resource-intensive consumer goods in a year than ten Chinese. If that were so, overall consumption could be curtailed either by reducing the future American population by a relatively small percentage or by reducing the Chinese population by a much larger percentage. Reducing populations exclusively in low-consumption countries would leave untouched the problem of excessive consumption in the advanced capitalist countries. In these circumstances, the spectacle of high-consumption countries advocating that poorer countries should reduce their populations is unseemly and inequitable and has led to understandable resentment in Third-World countries (even though many of those countries have devised their own programmes for population control). Furthermore, the injunction from the West to reduce Third-World populations could be perceived as racist.

Similarly, the limitation of population by immigration controls, 'the strictly logical position as far as ecologists are concerned' (Porritt), is potentially racist; Porritt's qualification, that it is also 'part of the logic of ecology that such an approach should *in no way* be discriminatory in terms of race or colour' would be hard to prove.[15] Why should it not be discriminatory—or simply be neutral about discrimination? Indeed, 'ecological logic' (whatever that is) might well dictate that people of the same ethnic and cultural background should live together without the incursion of too many outsiders. Various human-related principles such as egalitarianism and non-discrimination have been grafted on to ecological principles by Green thinkers and politicians, but these ideals do not form a necessary part of ecological logic. Those in favour of immigration might point out that would-be immigrants would be consuming resources wherever they lived:

---

14. The North/South distinction between the rich and poor nations of the world was famously made in the 'Brandt Report'. See W. Brandt et al., *North–South: A Programme for Survival*, Pan, 1980.
15. J. Porritt, *Seeing Green*, Blackwell, 1984, p. 191. See also Andrew Dobson's comments in Dobson, *Green Political Thought*, p. 95.

against that, it can be argued that people usually emigrate for economic betterment, to countries with a higher standard of living, so that high immigration levels into advanced industrial countries would increase overall consumption levels. The immigration issue is fraught with questions of race and justice and therefore highly problematic; also, it is inevitably enunciated in nation-specific terms (i.e. it concerns prevention of over-population in a particular country) which are in contradiction to the global outlook of true 'ecological logic'. It is therefore something of a political red herring rather than part of the world population issue.

Beyond the population-related issues already considered are further moral issues which can only be intimated here: the Chinese one-child policy has been widely criticized as contravening individual freedom to have children or, more precisely, the right (if there is such a right) for people to have as many children as they wish, regardless of whether those children will use a disproportionate share of the world's finite resources. Should population limitation policies be coercive? This is perhaps the only effective solution and even then, as the Chinese have discovered, it is widely flouted and may have unintended side-effects such as female infanticide. Another issue, which is both practical and moral, is how excessive child-bearing is to be prevented. The most effective method of contraception (apart from sexual abstinence) is the Pill—a chemical solution of which Greens may well disapprove, especially since it seems to have the unintended effect of increased oestrogen levels in drinking water and a reduced male sperm count. If abortion is the chosen method of control, as it was latterly in Soviet Russia, moral issues about the unborn child are raised. Coercive solutions may be branded as eco-fascist. The neo-Malthusian solution (that plagues, famine and diseases such as AIDs are welcome and natural methods of population control) is also seen as eco-fascist or as morally unacceptable, not least because it too would affect Third World populations most. The issue of population control is thus fraught with moral and practical difficulties, although as an objective it commands the approval of most governments in the world. The Greens share in these difficulties; furthermore, if they believe in natural processes and non-intervention, should they approve of interference with the natural conception process at all? Greens are often forced to choose between necessary evils (as are we all) and it is hard for them to maintain consistency, especially on the population question. They can hardly assert that a human population of zero, a world without human beings, would be the ideal, or that a human race which consumed as little as possible should be what Green politics should aim at—yet this sometimes seems to be the logical conclusion of their arguments.

Most Green thinkers predict that the standard of living in the advanced industrial countries will soon start to diminish and that in due course this will also be the case worldwide. In the second half of the twentieth century in Britain, the workers' standard of living increased because of the growth of the national income, although they only had the same percentage share of the national income as before—i.e. their situation relative to the rich had not changed. Workers in many industrialized countries, including Third-World countries, have benefited for the same reason. If in the future national income becomes smaller, the poor in any country will get poorer if the national 'cake' continues to be divided in the same proportions as before. The same point applies to poor countries in the global economy. Greens sometimes argue that wealth and income will have therefore be distributed more evenly, as if this were a necessary or logical consequence of diminishing global wealth. Unfortunately, that is not so: many impoverished societies have maintained a sharp division between the rich and the poor and in the envisaged future of falling production and consumption any powerful elite could well condemn the majority to poverty in order to enhance its own wealth. The Green aspiration to greater equality of distribution is, I would suggest, a piece of political realism designed to cope with falling standards of living and prevent social and international instability, rather than something which inheres in ecological logic. Even so, the idea of *global redistribution* is unlikely to be a vote-winning policy for Green parties campaigning in Western countries, for obvious reasons.

ANTI-POLLUTION ARGUMENTS

Many Greens pay tribute to Rachel Carson's *Silent Spring* as the first formative work in the modern ecology movement, although their focus is usually on the more contemporary concerns discussed above which were not directly considered by Carson—the depletion of resources, the 'limits to growth' argument and the possibility of sustainable societies. Carson, a genetic biologist, marshalled evidence about the deadly concentrations of poison building up in the food chain due to extensive chemical spraying in the USA, and its devastating effects on all life forms. By modern Green standards, her approach may seem over-concerned with the effects of these phenomena on human life—the 'human instrumental' approach to ecological issues. But if you read her book, you will probably never spray the greenfly on your favourite rose, or eat an unwashed lettuce, again.

Pollution can be broadly defined as alteration to or destruction of established eco-systems—this might in some cases more properly be referred to as *exploitation* of those systems. It can also be more narrowly defined as the introduction of poisonous or otherwise harmful ingredients into local environments (e.g. traffic fumes in a city or chemical sprays in the countryside) or into the global system (e.g. carbon dioxide emissions which change the balance of the earth's atmosphere). The wider definition of pollution can include both local and global effects: it would include phenomena like the encroachment into wildlife areas by cattle-grazing or agriculture, which is common today in Africa and India, and was also characteristic of the colonization of the great plains of America by cattle ranchers and cereal farmers in the last century. Equally, the destruction of forest habitats in order to introduce profitable monocultures (e.g. rubber and oil palm plantations in substantial tracts of Malaysia) falls under the wider definition but the effects are primarily local. We could call such operations '*pollutive exploitation*'. Some human activities have both local and global effects: the destruction of South American rain forests by logging destroys flora and fauna and traditional human life patterns, and is also said to affect the earth's atmosphere and climate.

Because we are not really 'one world' but two—the North and the South—different arguments may need to be used against these different kinds of pollution, and this illustrates the difficulties of the supposedly universalist Green position. Most pollution (widely or narrowly defined) is the result of industrial activity or of industrial exploitation of natural resources, e.g. mining or logging. A reversion to pre-industrial economies worldwide would clean up the world—but that is hardly on the cards. In the Third World, extended cattle-grazing or cash-cropping represent alterations to traditional ways of life which are, directly or indirectly, brought about by industrial processes or by enmeshment in the world economy (cash-crops being a short-term solution to national debt for Third-World countries). There is an evident irony when Western countries, which have transformed and domesticated their own natural environments in the interests of industry and intensive agriculture, call upon Third-World countries to prevent their people from encroaching on wildlife areas in the course of trying to scratch a living at subsistence level, because of the 'intrinsic value' of those eco-systems. The crusade against industrial pollution in the West (and in industrialized parts of the Third World) is clearly in the interests of local human inhabitants, whereas a Green crusade against *pollutive exploitation* in Third-World appeals to supra-human, abstract values such as the intrinsic value of other species or of eco-systems themselves in defiance of the interests of local inhabitants. But there is also the suspicion that Westerners want such areas to be preserved so that they can enjoy unspoilt beaches and wildlife safaris. A total ban on pollution and pollutive exploitation would affect the inhabitants of different regions of the world differentially, but would almost certainly affect Third-World workers and subsistence farmers most of all—by contrast, Western industry could still clean up its act, at a cost. Green arguments about pollution, exploitation and the economy are therefore inextricably related. Pollution does not just occur by itself but is usually a result of human economic activity—even pollution by tourism and travel is an aspect of economic activity. It is clear that, if the West wants the Third World to become Greener, it must offer compensation for the livelihoods lost, as some Greens advocate. But the mechanics of such compensation, and the level at which it should be set, would be highly contentious, especially in a context where the advanced economies were also in serious decline because of Green policies and falling industrial activity.

Enough has been said to demonstrate that the argument against pollution and pollutive exploitation as an instrumental or prudential argument (i.e. an argument in the human interest) is essentially a light Green argument and subject to moral and practical compromises. It differs from the arguments which deep Greens might use about the rights of other species and the intrinsic value of nature. The instrumental argument contends against active pollution which endangers our own health and the health and wellbeing of future generations and which may also destroy attractive recreational resources by wrecking natural scenery and making some forms of wildlife extinct. More abstractly, the instrumental argument can assert that our industrial and extractive processes may well have unseen or unforeseen anti-human consequences, such as depleting the ozone layer. By contrast, non-instrumental arguments require greater humility on the part of human beings and dwell on the rights or intrinsic value of other species. Such views question the unique moral value of human life—so often taken for granted—and they are discussed in the section below. However, it is clear that in the political sphere the instrumental arguments are liable to prove more potent than any 'rights of nature' arguments, because of the understandable prevalence of human self-interest in political discussion and decision-making. Greens who really believe in 'rights of nature' type arguments may therefore resort to instrumental arguments when canvassing support—and indeed deep Greens may sometimes masquerade as light Greens for this reason.

MORAL ARGUMENTS

Moving beyond the instrumental or prudential arguments for Green politics, there are several different moral positions that Greens may adopt:

(i) The recognition that other species (including plant species) have a right to survive and a right to our respect. Or, more strongly,

(ii) The acknowledgement that other species have *intrinsic value*, beyond human valuation, as do local eco-systems. Or, more strongly still,

(iii) The holistic position that the planet as a whole eco-system has an absolute and intrinsic value.

In evaluating these arguments, we must return to the question of anthropocentrism. It is hard to see how arguments advanced by human beings can be anything other than anthropocentric since they are couched in human language and in terms of human rationality and ultimately of human concerns and interests. If other species are to be taken into account in such arguments, it is because human beings choose to do so. The rights of other species argument has parallels with animal rights arguments and is prone to the same inconsistencies and limitations. If we are obliged to respect and not interfere with other species, it may be because they, like us, have nervous systems and crucially (as Bentham said) can feel pain. But this leaves us with the problem of how to treat species which—as far as we know—do not satisfy these criteria: for example, simple organisms, bacteria and plant life. It is relatively easy to respect mammals and other vertebrates, but what about wasps and viruses? The animal rights arguments—apart from the difficulties of contending that animals could have rights, since rights are essentially a human concept—seem to make an invidious distinction between different kinds of creature, and to leave out plant life entirely. Conflicts between rights are a familiar aspect of rights arguments, and the rights position does not help greatly in answering the question how rights conflicts between human beings and other species should be resolved—e.g. what should the African peasant farmer do about the depredation of his essential crops by protected elephants living on the nearby nature reserve? It is hard, at least for the peasant, to give a non-anthropocentric answer.

The argument which holds that all other species have an intrinsic value is philosophically puzzling, as stated above, because it is humans that bestow value on things. Essentially, the intrinsic value argument requires a non-human value-giver, i.e. a god. (Hinduism and in particular the Jain religion preach the equal importance of all Brahma's creation and the duty to preserve all living creatures, but such arguments are not available to non-believers.) The extinction rates among non-human species due to human interference with natural habitats may be deplored, but extinction was a regular phenomenon in the world long before humans evolved—how can the intrinsic value argument cope with this fact? Can anyone maintain that every species on the planet has equal intrinsic value? The question of whether the last smallpox viruses (kept in laboratories) should now be destroyed is a good test. Beyond the prudential reasons for maintaining small, secure supplies of the virus for medical purposes, in case it should ever recur naturally, can anyone really contend that the virus has an intrinsic value and that the world is a richer place while it survives? Intrinsic value arguments are perhaps useful in causing us to recognize the value of other species and preventing us from privileging the human race in every context, but the philosophical basis of such arguments is inevitably flawed. The 'value' of the human race against the value of other species inevitably presents a problem when *they* pose a threat to, or problem for, *us*. Absolute values are as hard to countenance as absolute rights.

It is the health of the planet that matters, not that of some individual species or organisms.[16]

The strongest and least anthropocentric argument is the holistic argument that the planet as a whole forms a single eco-system which maintains and regulates itself and evolves by processes beyond human understanding[17] in which every species plays a useful part. This approach asserts the interconnectedness of all parts of nature and the symbiotic nature of life on earth. *Biological diversity* and *biospherical egalitarianism* are central values of the holistic position, because a wide variety of species is necessary to maintain the system and no species is (as far as we know) more important than any other in its contribution to the whole. The most prominent proponent of the holistic view is the scientist James Lovelock who advanced the 'Gaia hypothesis'.[18] The earth goddess was worshipped in many ancient cultures and Gaia was her Greek name: she represented creation, fertility, abundance. Lovelock used the name to symbolize the fact that the earth is the source of all life (with some help from the sun and moon)—it is our only resource. Over time the earth 'copes' with environmental and exogenous changes by various feedback and adaptation processes to maintain itself in a stable state—for example, the composition of the atmosphere has changed very little (we think) over millions of years. Ice ages, exploding volcanoes, the arrival of meteorites are all absorbed in the eco-system, as is the

16. J. Lovelock, *The Ages of Gaia*, Oxford U.P., 1989, p. xvii.
17. We may have scientific understanding of parts of the process but not of how the whole maintains itself in equilibrium or evolves—not least because the processes may operate over very long time cycles, unobservable to us.
18. J. Lovelock, *Gaia: A New Look at Life on Earth*, Oxford U.P., 1979.

extinction and evolution of species. The Gaia hypothesis was adopted with enthusiasm by some ecologists and further popularized by religious and New Age thinkers who took a more spiritual view of the earth as:

> a living entity with the equivalent of senses, intelligence, memory and the capacity to act . . . Gaia is non-human. She is the earth spirit, she is life, the ground, the air, the water and the interaction between all their inhabitants. Within the fabric of Gaia, the earth organism or the earth spirit . . . there is an interwoven and intelligently driven web which searches for balance, continuance and stability.[19]

While the scientific hypothesis certainly focuses on balance, continuance, stability and the feedback mechanism, some Gaia acolytes are prone to personify the earth in a way which defies scientific analysis or validation, as the quotation above suggests. Lovelock himself argued that there was no discernible purpose behind the planet's eco-system, and certainly no favouritism to human beings in its operations.

Lovelock's hypothesis has been highly controversial in the scientific community; such a long-term and large-scale hypothesis can hardly be tested by controlled experiments in a scientific way, and it relies heavily on circumstantial evidence and re-interpretation of existing data. However, Lovelock's idea has informed the thinking of many deep ecologists, who use it to point up the dangers of human intervention in the eco-system: for example, our industrial and extractive processes and agriculture and forestry reduce biodiversity by making whole species locally or globally extinct by polluting or destroying their habitats. Whole local eco-systems are being destroyed with frightening rapidity. There are also myriad instances where well-meaning (but anthropocentric) human intervention to control 'pest' species has had highly damaging and unforeseen results—e.g. the introduction of cane toads to Queensland, Australia, to control weevils has resulted in the highly poisonous cane toads becoming a widespread major pest and one which threatens the survival of native species.

The problem for ecologists is that Lovelock's hypothesis does not entail a clear condemnation of human intervention; by contrast, the argument that the earth will adapt and regain equilibrium, *whatever human beings do*, might be seen as licensing any interventions we might make. The extinction of species has occurred throughout the planet's history—why should we worry if rather more have become extinct in the last hundred years, especially if Gaia has such an admirable compensation system? On the other hand, the hypothesis helps the deep Green position in some ways: it emphatically treats human beings merely as part of nature rather than privileging them above other species and it certainly lends itself to the development of ecocentric ethics. It gives moderate although not unequivocal support to the values of diversity and biospherical egalitarianism, mentioned above. Also, in its steadfast opposition to the human

---

19. K. Pedler, *The Quest for Gaia*, Souvenir Press, 1979, p. 13.

exploitation of nature it presents a stark challenge to the instrumental view (found in the Bible, for example) that the natural exists for the purposes of such exploitation.[20]

Having reviewed the Greens' critique of modern society, and indicated some of the shortcomings of the Greens' own arguments, I now turn to the constructive aspect of Green thought—how would a future, Greener society be organized?

GREEN UTOPIAS

> Environmentalism is about conviction—conviction that a better mode of existence is possible.[21]

'Ecotopias', Green images of the Good Society, pre-date the modern Green movement. In particular, models of eco-friendly communities are found in the ideas of the early anarchists. In 1791, defying the progress of the Industrial Revolution, Godwin proposed that human communities should be arranged as a series of small 'parishes', in a loose national (but not nationalistic) federation; their economies would be based on craftsmanship and traditional occupations. Proudhon and Kropotkin also advocated craft-based economies, being convinced that the work of the skilled craftsman harmonized with natural processes rather than exploiting them as industrial production did; to this picture Kropotkin added various principles of human and social interaction ('mutual aid') drawn from his study of co-operation between animals and symbiosis within eco-systems.[22] William Morris (although a Marxist rather than an anarchist) proposed an ecological utopia in *News from Nowhere* (1891): he envisaged a predominantly rural society with no great cities and little industry but much handicraft. The inhabitants were no longer duped into buying 'a never-ending series [of] sham or artificial necessaries' and goods were only produced when needed. 'All work which would be irksome to do by hand is done by immensely improved machinery; and in all work which it is a pleasure to do by hand, machinery is done without.'[23] Morris tried to practise these principles in his own life, creating a community of artists and craftsmen who produced beautiful artefacts. In the early twentieth century a more rationalist and scientific challenge to capitalism was offered by a number of Central European economists such as Popper-Lynkeus, Ballod-Atlanticus and Neurath, who produced blueprints for socialist societies based on ecological economics. They challenged the supremacy of the market, criticised many features of industrial capitalism such as the growth of car manufacture and the consumption of non-renewable resources, and suggested 'practical utopias'. Ballod's ideal society, for example was based on cities of

---

20. In *Genesis*, 1, xxvi–xxviii, God is said to have given man 'dominion' over the natural world; this is often interpreted as an instrumental right, but alternative interpretations suggest that 'dominion' signifies *stewardship*.
21. T. O'Riordan, *Environmentalism*, Pion Ltd., 1981, p. 300.
22. Discussion of the ideas of Godwin, Proudhon and Kropotkin can be found in Chapter 7 above.
23. W. Morris, *News from Nowhere* (Ed. K. Kumar), Cambridge U.P., 1995, pp. 96, 100.

limited size (10 000 inhabitants) and model farms supporting nearby communities and re-using their waste as a fertilizer.[24] These economists' acceptance of industrialism would antagonize some contemporary Greens, but their project of adapting classical economic principles to accommodate ecological principles remains of central importance.

Bookchin, a modern anarchist, bases his ideal society on that fundamental anarchist principle, spontaneity:

> Spontaneity in social life converges with spontaneity in nature to provide the basis for an ecological society. The ecological principles that shaped organic societies re-emerge in the form of social principles to shape utopia.[25]

He criticizes the hierarchical institutions of bourgeois society and the centralized economy of industrial societies, proposing instead 'regional eco-technology—a situation in which the instruments of production are moulded to the resources of an ecosystem'.[26] Food producers and farmers must operate in co-operation with nature rather than in defiance of nature. Industrial units located within 'ecocommunities' should be smaller and should use 'clean' power—solar, wind and water power. De-urbanization and de-centralization would create small, face-to-face human societies and the ideal eco-anarchist community would itself be like an eco-system and would be in harmony with and dependent on its natural environment: this close dependency would increase respect for the environment. Self-sufficiency would be the objective and there would be a variety of communities, each adapted to and formed by its own environment.

Bookchin's themes are reprised in more recent accounts of *bioregionalism*, which recommends decentralized communities living and working according to the natural resources of naturally defined regions, with little trade or interchange. The emphasis would be on labour-intensive, organic agriculture rather than industrial production but the (inevitably) lower standard of living would not prevent a higher, more natural quality of life from developing. It is usually assumed that there would be collective ownership of the natural resources in any bio-community, so that the deprivations suffered in this new form of society would be equally shared and therefore mitigated. The starting point for such arguments is that today's urban communities are incapable of feeding themselves or supplying their other material and energy needs: the only hope for self-sufficiency is small, dispersed communities which can process natural resources at sustainable rates, to satisfy their much reduced needs.

One advocate of the bioregional principle is Kirkpatrick Sale, who criticizes modern 'myths of bigness' and false principles like the 'economies of scale' and argues that communities and institutions, like living organisms, have an optimal size, exceeding which will affect all their components adversely. Sale follows in the tradition of the influential economist Schumacher, who had earlier argued that

---

24. For an interesting discussion, see J. M. Alier, 'Ecological economics and concrete utopias', *Utopian Studies*, Vol. 3, No. 1, 1992, pp. 39–52.
25. Bookchin, *Post-Scarcity Anarchism*, p. 21.
26. Bookchin, *Post-Scarcity Anarchism*, p. 41.

'small is beautiful' and proposed smaller units of production, the use of intermediate technology and communal ownership.[27] Sale's proposed solution to the excessive size and growth of society, which harms us all, is to re-constitute society according to the 'human scale'. He paints an attractive picture of the life of early human beings but anticipates those critics who might condemn him for primitivism by the following qualification:

> It is not the Paleolithic state of affluence that I suggest we all return to, but there is something in the Paleolithic understanding of the limits of material amassment that does seem pertinent. For what made them affluent was, in truth, their self-sufficiency, their ability to satisfy all of their needs within their own means.[28]

Sale argues that modern cities of 50 000 inhabitants could in principle become self-sufficient. He sets out rules for self-sufficiency which include the sharing of facilities and tools within neighbourhoods, recycling and repairing, dependence on handicrafts rather than manufacture, the use of local products and materials rather than imports, using general rather than specialized machines, multipurpose factories and—most important—doing without what is not needed.[29] He argues that historically communities without authority or state institutions tended to be peaceful, harmonious and stable. His proposed utopian communities would 'almost automatically' move towards democracy. Sale contends that, while the modern world is characterized by *simplicity* (e.g. monocultures and standardized products), his system would generate *complexity* and *diversity*, the very characteristics which contribute to stability in the natural world.

For much of modern humanity's short history (currently estimated at under 100 000 years) people have in fact lived in bioregional communities. Barter and trade may have increased the variety of goods available from the earliest times but self-sufficiency had to be the norm when communications were difficult or the weather was inclement. Expanding trade and industrial production were accompanied by specialization between countries and between towns and villages (e.g. the 'wool towns' of East Anglia); trade increased prosperity but also increased inter-dependency. Yet some undeveloped or unexplored parts of the world continued to operate on bioregional principles: native Americans and Inuits were still living in essentially bioregional communities until the expansion of the United States during the nineteenth century, as were 'undiscovered tribes' in remote parts of the world until this century. History shows that bioregional living is feasible. Assuming that industrialization, urbanization and the global division of labour could somehow be reversed, would it be desirable? Deep Greens such as Sale and Tokar think so—others may have doubts. Among the obvious objections is the fact that bioregions are differentially hospitable to human life and

---

27. E. F. Schumacher, *Small is Beautiful: A Study of Economics as if People Mattered*, Blond & Briggs, 1973.
28. K. Sale, *Human Scale*, Secker & Warburg, 1980, p. 393. Sale is uses 'affluent' to denote a society 'in which all the people's material wants are easily satisfied'. In the history of ideas, 'primitivism' is the error of which Rousseau was (wrongly) accused—the desire to return to a state of nature. Most Greens are not primitivists, but may be accused of being so because of their advocacy of simpler ways of living.
29. Sale, *Human Scale*, Ch. 11, *passim*.

differentially endowed with natural resources. People who found themselves in the more arid regions at the inception of bioregionalism would suffer relative deprivation for ever (even if trade were permitted they would have little to exchange) and would have a legitimate complaint about the social injustice of the new arrangement. Presumably anti-emigration and anti-immigration policies would have to be strictly policed—by someone—or populations would again start to concentrate in the more favoured areas, thus re-playing our previous history. The bioregionalists' cavalier injunction that people would become accustomed to doing without things which they could not produce themselves would be a hard lesson for modern human beings to learn. This utopia, in other words, sounds like dystopia to all but deeply committed Green utopians.

Although the anarchist element in Green utopianism may lead to the conclusion that Green communities would be organized on anti-hierarchical, egalitarian principles, the result of a Green revolution could be something very different. To achieve and enforce the reduction of living standards brought about by bioregionalism might require severe policing by an authoritarian global power or by authoritarian local states. Global redistribution would certainly need enforcement. Likewise, the major social restructuring necessary for creating optimal-sized communities would presumably require central planning and directed economies, more reminiscent of Stalin's Russia than Bookchin's dream. The spontaneously formed anarchist community is likely to be the exception rather than the rule. Many Green thinkers and eco-anarchists have debated these possibilities and O'Riordan offers a useful summary and analysis.[30] Implicit in many Green arguments is the need for some form of coercion because the privileged inhabitants of rich countries are unlikely to yield up their privileges or to accept a lower standard of living voluntarily. As we saw earlier, population limitation is unlikely to occur on a voluntary basis. At the individual level, most people would be reluctant to change their consumption habits unless forced to do so (and resentful if *forced* to do so). Even relatively minor policy changes such as anti-pollution measures have to be enforced by law, and the reformist policies proposed by Green parties are often quite coercive—for example 'the implementation of recycling plans should be made a statutory duty [for local authorities]'.[31] The chances of eco-anarchism, eco-socialism or any other ecological utopia being achieved spontaneously are therefore low. Implementation of a Green revolution would require strong government and powerful enforcement agencies.

There are of course many different images of ecotopia—too many to describe here—and Green utopias differ significantly from the light Green policies which appear in party manifestos. Many such policies appear to have no direct or necessary connection with ecological premises and to owe a lot to socialism. For example, Greens regularly advocate a guaranteed basic income as part of the process of redistribution and social restructuring which seriously Green policies

30. O'Riordan, *Environmentalism*, pp. 303–307.
31. *Green Party Manifesto*, p. 9.

would necessitate.³² They are less than convincing about how such a basic income could be afforded, especially in a falling-growth economy. The Green proposals for radically participatory democracy also seem to be borrowed from critics of modern democracy and bolted on to other Green arguments; yet, as we saw above, a Green utopia would not necessarily be democratic and egalitarian. Such are the problems which arise through trying to make what originated as an essentially single-issue movement into a political movement with a comprehensive social programme.

PROBLEMATIC QUESTIONS

This review of Green critical thought and Green utopias has already highlighted a number of practical and philosophical difficulties and some hiatuses in Green argument. I now turn to some other areas where Green theory risks inconsistency, indeterminacy or self-contradiction, and to some practical questions.

'Nothing Exists Alone'

Green campaigners would like us to subscribe to the doctrine of the interconnectedness of nature as a safeguard for other life forms: it warns us that human interventions may have unforeseen, harmful consequences. The problem is that such an all-encompassing principle obliterates any possibility of selectivity in our understanding of our own relationship with nature and of the processes of eco-systems. Discrimination becomes impossible: it might (in principle) be as damaging if I kill a fly as if a mining company destroys a whole eco-system. Taken to extremes, this leaves us no option but the unfeasible one of not interfering with nature at all. But other species interfere with and compete with each other—what is different about human interventions? The extreme position would deter us from apparently benign interventions such as creating wildlife reserves, as well as from apparently destructive ones. The problem is, of course, that although we might acknowledge the interconnected-ness of all the parts of the natural world, some are more closely or more remotely connected with others and our scientific knowledge about the nature and proximity of such connections is still incomplete and limited.

There are, however, indicative data collected by ecologists and natural scientists which suggest that vigorous eco-systems are those inhabited by a diversity of plant, animal and insect species. Deep Greens therefore propose that the ecocentric principles of diversity and complexity should govern human interventions in the natural world. Such values have not proved very potent when local environments are threatened by human development—hence the mass protests by Green activists in Britain against various motorway projects (most famously, the pioneering Twyford Down protest in 1993 which has been emulated since in many campaigns). Human interests do not invariably prevail: in most

32. See, e.g., *A Green Manifesto for the 1990s*, Eds. P. Kemp and D. Wall, Penguin, 1990, p. 92. The same promise appears in the 1997 *Green Party Manifesto*, p. 3.

countries some areas with unique eco-systems and wildlife are protected, but they are often threatened by human development or encroachment. Those arguing against such developments are in effect demanding that people should give priority to non-human interests, which is a difficult case to argue politically. In principle the interconnectedness doctrine and the values of biodiversity and complexity could constitute useful constraints on human activity but we do not always understand how to apply them in particular cases because they are somewhat indeterminate.

Individuals and Species

The preservation of species is another area of Green thought fraught with difficulty. Should one species take precedence over another species in the preservation stakes? What view should we take when one species is the predator of the other? In an environment free from human intervention, nature decides such questions. Should human beings play God in environments where they have the power to intervene, and an interest in intervening, to preserve one species at the expense of another? Is it justifiable to exterminate foxes to preserve lambs and chickens? The imperative to 'preserve species' for the sake of biodiversity could be interpreted as an imperative to strive to preserve every individual member of a species or alternatively to preserve the whole species, without worrying about particular individuals. The latter interpretation suggests that we need not concern ourselves about individual deaths or local 'extinctions' (e.g. if frogs in one part of Britain were dying out because of local pollution, they would remain in abundance elsewhere) whereas the first position suggests that we should concern ourselves with maintaining local eco-systems (e.g. the garden pond) and even with trying to save individual frogs (e.g. by keeping cats out of the garden). We cannot, of course, preserve a species without preserving some of its individual members, but any injunction to try to preserve every member of every species would be an exigent moral imperative. It becomes even more demanding when applied to species which prey upon human beings, e.g. head lice and tapeworms. Another dilemma arises about domesticated animals. Many Greens advocate vegetarianism and the non-exploitation of animals: if these principles were universally adopted, whole species—sheep, cattle and pigs—would have to be eliminated, having no further use for human purposes, since we would certainly not want enormous numbers of wild cattle eating our soya-bean crops. Arguments about the value of species and the problems of competing species (including human beings) raise highly complex questions which cannot be answered here. Nor can Green theorists give determinate answers to such questions.

The Rights of Future Generations

Preserving the world's resources for future generations has been a theme not only of light Green thought but of recent social justice theories such as that of Rawls, discussed in more detail in Chapter 16. Rawls makes the assumption that each individual in the Original Position would be a 'head of family' and would desire to further the welfare of his nearest descendants.[33] Thus, whatever an individual's position in time, he is 'forced to choose for everyone', i.e. to take into account future generations, since he cannot choose principles of justice which would favour his own children exclusively, being behind the 'veil of ignorance'. These assumptions led Rawls to conclude that the contractors would adopt a *'just savings principle'* which would determine the social minimum for the present generation and set a rate at which it should save for posterity. Rawls covertly assumes that to preserve the human race is morally good, and that to guarantee our descendants a standard of living no worse than our own (and, ideally, better) is also a moral imperative. 'The life of a people is conceived as a scheme of co-operation spread out in historical time.'[34] Avner de-Shalit has also argued, from a more communitarian stance, that our obligation to future generations is one of justice, especially where environmental policies are concerned.[35]

These and similar arguments about our obligations to future generations, which give philosophical support to the light Green position, are unavoidably anthropocentric. The just savings principle enjoins us to conserve resources and eco-systems for the enjoyment of future generations on the assumptions that (a) resources are non-renewable or non-replaceable, (b) future generations will live in a similar way to us so that we should preserve for them the means to a similar lifestyle and (c) the human race is worth preserving. These assumptions, even (c), might be challenged from the non-anthropocentric position which some deep Greens might take. The deep Green perspective would in turn be criticized by those who see the wellbeing of human race as the only possible source of values in human ethics. Either way, such arguments lead to teleological questions about the purpose of humanity, of nature and of the planet itself, questions which Greens are in no better position to answer definitively than other philosophers. However, the 'future generations' argument is fundamentally important to the Green cause as it directs attention beyond our present concerns as a matter of justice.

Green Ambivalence about Science

Ecologism as a political doctrine has emerged from scientific ecology, a science which has grown into an academic discipline since the Darwinian biologist Haeckel first coined the term in the nineteenth century. The dangers to which Greens alert us are based on their interpretation of scientific data about changes and trends in the natural world. This scientific base is crucial in preventing ecologism from being seen as merely another romantic, back-to-nature doctrine. The paradox for contemporary Greens is that they criticize the instrumentalism of conventional science while relying on its discoveries to develop or validate the norms which they are promoting. This ambivalence creates certain difficulties. As I argued earlier,

---

33. J. Rawls, *A Theory of Justice*, Harvard U.P., 1971, p. 128.
34. Rawls, *A Theory of Justice*, p. 289.
35. A. de-Shalit, *Why Posterity Matters: Environmental Policies and Future Generations*, Routledge, 1995.

scientific data do not generate norms—human interpretations and value-judgements alone can create moral prescriptions. Furthermore, scientific data may frequently give rise to different interpretations and competing value judgements. Ultimately, norms and science (and indeed norms and nature) do not mix.

A second problem is that much of the scientific data on which Greens must rely is so incomplete or so time-limited that interpretations of what it portends may be gravely mistaken. The increasing hole in the ozone layer appears bad, but the planetary eco-system may have the capacity to repair it over time—we simply do not know. In any case, the shortness of our lives and the panic about skin cancer make it difficult to take a longer-term, ecocentric view of the ozone hole. There have been cases where Green activists misinterpret or mis-use scientific methods and data. The well-publicized Greenpeace campaign (1995–1996) against Shell's proposal to dump the obsolete Brent Spar oil platform in deep water was remarkably successful, but later it was revealed that the scientific evidence mustered by Greenpeace about the potential pollution effects of deep-sea disposal was radically erroneous and that the deep-sea solution would have been the best and most ecological. This fiasco has made many people sceptical of the Greens' other 'scientific' claims and warnings—including many scientists who are, in any case, aware of the limitations of their own data.

While many Greens oppose the scientific, rationalist world-view on the grounds that it goes hand-in-hand with an instrumental and exploitative approach to the world's resources and the global eco-system, they cannot do without scientific evidence to support their arguments. At the same time they cannot afford to acknowledge that such evidence is often dubious or incomplete, or that it admits of other interpretations. The role of science in Green theory is therefore highly problematic.

Collective Action and Free Riders

A more practical problem which afflicts light Greens is how they can achieve a Greener world, given the obstacles to successful collective action and people's tendency to free-ride. Even if most individuals in a society personally favour Green policies, such as the recycling of waste, it may still be difficult to mobilize them to endorse compulsory recycling measures. For each individual, it is easier to put all her rubbish into one dustbin rather than sort it into separate bins or take it to the local recycling centre, which often means a car journey. Most of us are would-be free-riders, hoping that others will recycle their waste without giving ourselves the trouble of doing so. In general, the only cure for self-interested free-riding is an authoritative, legal remedy. To prevent cars polluting a city centre, the most effective solution is to make it pedestrian-only, otherwise each car owner will regularly find it essential for one reason or another to break the voluntary code which enjoins people not to drive into the city centre unless they really must. Each individual driver will be inclined to think, with some justification, 'If I don't use my car, someone else will use hers, so why should I refrain?' Public goods such as a clean and pleasant environment will rarely be provided by spontaneous collective action and must be obtained by 'coercion' as Olson concluded.[36] The only secure defence against free-riders for Green measures is a coercive one.

The idea of voluntary collective action on which light Greens would like to rely is a non-starter where day-to-day convenience is concerned. For example, any drive to save energy or water on a voluntary basis is almost certainly doomed. The exhortation to switch off unnecessary electrical apparatus or to save water will be ignored by many people. A possible solution is to meter all water supplies and to charge penal rates for water and electricity—but super-charging clearly penalizes the poor most heavily and would therefore be socially unjust (as well as contributing to excessive profits for the utility companies). These everyday examples illustrate the difficulty of achieving any saving or resources on a voluntary basis in societies which promote consumer choice and individual freedom. If people cannot even be motivated to save resources for which they have to pay, the incentive to save resources for future generations is certainly not compelling for any individual resource-consumer. Any light Green solution of encouraging voluntary economies in the use of resources is likely to fail and so light Greens must logically espouse compulsory measures: the dark Green solution would in any case be far more radical and less voluntary. This in turn points up the importance of achieving political power.

Human Ambivalence about Nature

Finally, I turn to a wider question—how do human beings view the natural world. Do Green campaigners need to convert us to a different perspective on nature? Western thought since Plato has abounded with dualistic contrasts between the human world and the natural world, contrasts reinforced by the Judaeo–Christian tradition. Nature represents 'dark forces', the untamable, the irrational, the amoral and even the immoral. Eastern philosophy and religion are not so polarized; instead they view humankind as part of the cosmos. However, as capitalism spread across the globe it carried with it the Western rational, scientific perspective (sometimes characterized as 'Prometheanism'[37]) and an instrumental attitude to the natural world; this has been adopted in part even by societies with a very different view of nature. In this account, human beings are set apart from Nature and are destined to use it for their own purposes and to 'master' it. Bookchin analyses the dualism between 'a misconceived nature' and 'a domineering humanity':

> Nature, in effect, emerges as an affliction that must be removed by the technology and domination that excuse human domination in the name of 'human freedom'.[38]

36. M. Olson, *The Logic of Collective Action*, Shocken, 1971.
37. Prometheus was the character in Greek mythology who made men out of clay and taught them the arts and sciences. He stole fire from the Gods and gave it to men. He represents the active, achieving side of human nature and also, some would say, the spirit of *hubris* (insolence and overweening pride).
38. M. Bookchin, *The Modern Crisis*, Black Rose Books, 1987, p. 52.

Even the contrasts frequently made between nature and nurture or heredity and environment implicitly refer to this dualistic outlook and to the supposed superiority of the social over the natural world. As a species we are nevertheless divided in our attitudes to nature—some people are all for it, others dead against it. 'Instrumental subjective reason either eulogizes nature as pure vitality or disparages it as brute force.'[39] Rousseau was on the side of vitality; he reversed the usual polarities by contrasting *nature* and *artifice*, the natural world and the artificial social world which he despised. His distinction was influential in the development of a pro-nature perspective which is sometimes (misleadingly) referred to as 'pastoralism' or (even more misleadingly) as 'primitivism'. This positive valuation of nature has taken many forms—for example it includes the romantic movement of the nineteenth century (Wordsworth, Coleridge et al.), naturism (nudism), eco-conservatism, Green Nazism and eco-feminism.

It is worth considering briefly why the last three movements mentioned above appear to share a pro-nature position when their politics are so different. Traditionally, in Britain and elsewhere, the 'old conservatives' were landowners, accustomed to living with and on nature and used to practising stewardship of the land which was their own livelihood: conservation was necessarily part of their lives. Also, conservative thought (as noted in Chapter 7) is often based on the organic analogy between society and living organisms or eco-systems. The 'Green Nazis' built on an earlier German tradition of the *Wandervögeln* ('roving birds') who were students who rejected urban life and spent time hiking in the countryside. Darré, the Nazi Minister of Agriculture (1933–42) advocated organic farming and the preservation of rural communities; he believed that peasant life was morally superior to town life and industrial production.[40] Peasants represented the earth's vitality. Many critics would say that both the conservative and the Nazi approach to nature were reactionary and anti-progressive, harking back to some lost Arcadia, but Darré considered it progressive and optimistic.

Women have often been identified with nature and demonized on that account, as we saw in Chapter 9. Man's vocation of mastering (and exploiting) nature is paralleled by men's activities of taming and mastering women. Eco-feminism capitalizes on the more natural, intuitive characteristics of women and rejoices in their proximity to nature and their part in natural processes such as child-bearing. Just as Darré thought that peasants were morally superior because of their affinity to nature, eco-feminists may consider that woman are superior to men because they represent natural forces. This perspective, which clearly emphasizes *difference,* has been criticized by feminists like Plumwood,[41] for the sort of reasons outlined in Chapter 9—like other kinds of 'difference feminism' it runs certain risks. If nature is treated instrumentally and exploitatively, women may receive similar treatment. Women's alliance with nature is a liability, not a strength, in a world where nature is devalued.

---

39. M. Horkheimer, *Eclipse of Reason*, Seabury Press, 1974, p. 126.
40. A. Bramwell, *Blood and Soil*, Kensal Press, 1985, p. 8. The book is a biography of Darré.
41. See, e.g., V. Plumwood, *Feminism and the Mastery of Nature*, Routledge, 1993.

'Nature' clearly means something rather different to old conservatives, to Green Nazis and to eco-feminists, but their shared hostility to the prevalent instrumental approach to nature constitutes an area of common interest between these very different doctrines, and this hostility is also shared with most other Greens. All this suggests that a pro-nature, pro-environment perspective can form a part of many different ideologies or belief systems although it is incompatible with, for example, raw capitalism or raw communism (as practised in the former Soviet Union) because of their emphasis on industrialization and expansion at all costs. It would be unwise, I think, for Greens to try to enforce a uniform view of nature and equally unwise to argue that eco-friendliness entails one particular kind of politics when there are clearly many forms of social and political life which could serve Green purposes.

GREEN SUCCESSES

If success were measured only in electoral terms, the verdict on the Greens would have to be 'not proven'. Although Green parties have enjoyed some successes, especially in Germany where they achieved 7.3% of the vote in 1994, they remain on the fringes of conventional democratic politics. But they have been strikingly successful in raising consciousness about environmental issues, so that today many social and political issues are evaluated in Green terms as well as in conventional right–left terms. Most large businesses have voluntarily adopted pro-environment policies; they highlight their recycling programmes and the steps that they are taking to reduce pollution. McDonald's were the plaintiffs in the longest trial in English legal history (1994–1997), successfully suing two Green activists who had published libellous pamphlets accusing the company of destroying rain forests, cruelty to animals, causing Third-World starvation, exploiting staff and various other bad practices. Such is the contemporary awareness of Green issues in the West that no modern company can afford to be viewed as eco-hostile. Big business today is reformist Green (environmentalist) rather than deep Green, of course, but this marks a remarkable transition over the last decade and a remarkable achievement for the Green lobby.

Whether the Greens have been successful in promulgating Green ideology as such is also doubtful. The problems inherent in some of their arguments are an obstacle to a coherent ideology as are the different doctrines advanced by thinkers of various shades of Green. Most of us would concur in some of the reformist or environmentalist arguments, which do not threaten our lifestyles unduly. Various deep Green arguments *do* pose such a threat and therefore they appear more 'ideological' than the reformist versions. If an ideology must offer an action-guiding set of beliefs, then deep Green doctrines do so: the central belief is that human beings should interfere with nature as little as possible and should respect and preserve all eco-systems. But no single or clear vision of the Good Life emerges from deep Green assumptions about nature: indeed, how could it, since these are assumptions about other species rather than about human beings? To maintain that we are part of nature does not entail that we should base our social arrangements on—say—those of baboons, any more than that baboons should live like ants. So even the deepest Green doctrine falls short of being an ideology, since ideologies are inevitably anthropocentric and concerned with human society. The fact that Green ideas are so readily absorbed into other ideologies differently positioned on the political spectrum suggests that 'ecologism' is not a free-standing ideology—if it were, such assimilation would be difficult or impossible.

Because light Green ideas and prescriptions are simply assimilated by 'grey' political parties, it is the deep Greens who are more likely eventually to develop a distinctive, ecocentric ideology. They face two major problems. The first, political problem is the major redistribution and social upheaval that would follow any thoroughgoing implementation of radical Green ideas, both of which would militate against the self-interest of a significant section of the world's population. To create a political doctrine which demands personal sacrifice—whether for the sake of other species or for the sake of the human inhabitants of distant countries—is to court rejection. The second, philosophical problem is to create an ideology which is free from all the inconsistencies mentioned earlier—for example, an ideology which does not privilege humankind above all other species, yet does not reduce its 'rights' below those of all other species. To decide on the proper place of the human species in the world is no easy matter.

FURTHER READING

A. Dobson, *Green Political Thought*, 2nd edn., Routledge, 1995.
A. Dobson and P. Lucardie (Eds.), *The Politics of Nature*, Routledge, 1995.
R. Eckersley, *Environmentalism and Political Theory*, UCL Press, 1992.
R. Goodin, *Green Political Theory*, Polity Press, 1992.
T. Hayward, *Ecological Thought, An Introduction*, Polity, 1995.
A. Leopold, *A Sand County Almanac*, Ballantine Books, 1970.
T. O'Riordan, *Environmentalism*, Pion Ltd., 1981.
J. Porritt, *Seeing Green*, Blackwell, 1984.
C. Spretnak and F. Capra, *Green Politics: The Global Promise*, Paladin, 1986.
E. O. Wilson (Ed.), *Biodiversity*, National Academy Press, 1988.
D. Worster, *Nature's Economy: A History of Ecological Ideas*, 2nd edn., Cambridge U.P., 1994.

Chapter 11

Beyond Ideology: Nationalism

Nationalism is primarily a political principle, which holds that the political and the national unit should be congruent.[1]

(Ernest Gellner)

Today the world is full of conflict, as perhaps it always has been. The major superpower confrontation, which dominated the world for forty years, has been superseded by a series of internecine conflicts within and between societies, in which each warring faction claims *nationalism* as its rationale and goal. From the British perspective, we need look no further than Northern Ireland for an example. Further east, there have been violent conflicts between ethnic groups within the Eastern European countries—most recently the war between Serbs and Croats in what was formerly Yugoslavia, which resulted in a complex re-drawing of the map, and which may still explode into renewed violence. Beyond that, there have been conflicts between the republics of the former USSR including a violent dispute between Armenistan and Azerbaijan over border territories and areas inhabited by a mixture of their two peoples. Further east still, India is racked by what the Indians refer to as 'communalist' struggles, in Kashmir (between Hindus and Muslims, where loyalties are divided between India, Pakistan and Kashmir itself), and in the Punjab, where Sikh activists demand a separate state. Sri Lanka is torn by strife between the Tamil minority and the Sinhalese. In the Middle East, there are continuing territorial disputes between Arab countries, as instanced by the Iraqis' 1990 invasion of what they claimed as their 'historic' territory, the independent state of Kuwait, which precipitated the Gulf War. The long-running Arab–Israeli dispute continues despite the precarious 'peace process'. The Kurds in Turkey, Iraq and Iran demand an independent Kurdistan. Afghanistan is riven by internecine conflict between the Islamic Taleban and the so-called 'warlords' who represent different ethnic minorities. Africa too is frequently smitten by civil

---

1. E. Gellner, *Nations and Nationalism*, Blackwell, 1983, p. 1.

wars and conflicts which arise from the hostility of different tribes which were grouped together when the colonial powers drew up the boundaries of Africa before independence. All these disputes can be described as nationalist, and the list seems endless.

When we speak of nationalism as a movement or an ideology today, we are not referring to the sort of nationalism or 'patriotism' which people feel for a country to which they are contented to belong—a feeling which includes a sense of community and which is important to the maintenance of a society. I am not addressing that kind of nationalism in this chapter, except incidentally; rather, the subject is the activist nationalism which advances demands that, if accepted, would radically change society. The nationalist chameleon takes on different forms, depending on the circumstances in which it appears. In a colonized country, it appears as a liberationist pro-independence movement. In an established federal country with a multiplicity of regions and ethnic differences, such as India, it takes the form of 'communalism' and separatism. In Africa, nationalist movements are often described as 'tribalism', which seems the most accurate description of the civil war in Rwanda between the Hutus and the Tutsis which started in 1994 and led to massive bloodshed. In those parts of the former Yugoslavia inhabited by a mixture of Serbs and Croats, it might even be described as racism. The ultimate desire of a nationalist movement (except in the colonial situation, where independence is the aim) is secession from the larger community or, if the nationalists are in the majority, the expulsion of minorities from the community and the establishment of a homogeneous nation. Another form of nationalism is *irredentism*, the aim of which is to bring together all the members of a particular ethnic group in a united territory under self-government. Examples are the movement for Italian unification in the nineteenth century and the Kurds' demand for an independent Kurdistan.

The ideologies described in Part II of this book are, in the main, doctrines with internationalist aspirations. Whether we look at liberalism, Marxism, socialism or anarchism, they are posited on explicitly internationalist and humanitarian assumptions; that is to say, on assumptions which do not distinguish between the rights, needs and aspirations of people according to their ethnic origins or geographical location. (Ecologists, too, do not distinguish between peoples or races but see us all as inhabitants of one earth.) The human rights proclaimed by liberals purport to be 'universal'. Socialism and Marxism also make no distinctions between people on the basis of national identity or domicile. By contrast, nationalism invites us to make such distinctions. But the bases on which these are to be made are, as we shall see, both shifting and analytically suspect.

WHAT IS A NATION?

Can nationalism as a doctrine be defined so as to clarify the basis of the conflicts mentioned at the start of this chapter, with all their different contexts and origins? We need first of all to consider what a nation is, and what constitutes national identity. J. S. Mill offered an analytical definition based partly on *will* and partly on natural sympathies:

> A portion of mankind may be said to constitute a Nationality, if they are united among themselves by common sympathies, which do not exist between themselves and any others—which make them co-operate with each other more willingly than with other people, desire to be under the same government, and desire that it should be government by themselves or a portion of themselves, exclusively.[2]

What are the 'common sympathies' to which Mill refers? They can be as diverse as the reasons for choosing our friends. Shared religion has often been claimed by nationalists to be the foundation of national identity. But since religious allegiance usually cuts across other criteria of identity (for example, language, culture and geography) it is hard to see that religion could be the sole basis of nationhood in the modern world, especially as religions are often subject to schisms which divide rather than unite individuals—Catholic and Protestant, Shia and Sunni Muslim.

The idea that nationhood should be based on racial identity has been condemned by many Western thinkers this century because of the appalling consequences of racism, demonstrated by the Holocaust in Nazi Germany and more recently by 'ethnic cleansing' in the former Yugoslavia and the bloody war between Hutus and Tutsis in Rwanda. Hannaford argues that the idea of race is a uniquely modern invention; he traces its development as a functioning *political* concept in the last two centuries and contrasts this with an earlier view that citizenship was what made someone a member of a community. As Darwinism became widely accepted,

> the tests of true belonging were no longer decided on action as a citizen but upon the purity of language, colour and shape. And since none of these tests could ever be fully satisfied, all that was left in place of political settlement were ideas of assimilation, naturalisation, evacuation, exclusion, expulsion, and finally liquidation . . . None of these later philosophical, historical and scientific hypotheses of race offered a fit, or useful, conception upon which to base an understanding of either past or present civil association, except in terms of perpetual war.[3]

Terms like 'race' and 'nation' can also be used in a wider sense which embraces shared history and customs. A recent industrial tribunal reasoned that 'the English and Scots are separate racial groups defined by reference to national origins'[4], and the following—somewhat impressionistic—definition of 'nation' was offered during a 1972 court case about race discrimination:

> The Scots are a nation because of Bannockburn and Flodden, Culloden and the pipes at Lucknow, because of Jenny Geddes and Flora Macdonald, because of frugal living and respect for learning, because of Robert Burns and Walter Scott. So, too, the English are a nation—because Norman, Angevin and Tudor monarchs forged them together, because their land is mostly sea-girt, because of the common law and of gifts for poetry and parliamentary government . . .[5]

_____

2. J. S. Mill, *Considerations on Representative Government*, Oxford U.P., 1912, p. 380.
3. I. Hannaford, *Race: The History of an Idea in the West*, Woodrow Wilson Centre Press and Johns Hopkins U.P., 1996, pp. 14–15, p. 9.
4. 'Scots and English are different races, tribunal decides', G. Bowditch, *The Times*, 28.4.1997, p. 4.
5. Ealing v Race Relations Board, 1972, 2, *Weekly Law Reports*, 71 at p. 85.

But even if racial identity could be objectively established by reference to genes or origins, why should it have any bearing on citizenship, political rights and national self-determination? The supposed relationship between race and other 'common sympathies' and self-government is challenged by Anthony Smith in *National Identity*. He defines a nation as follows:

> a named human population sharing an historic territory, common myths and historical memories, a mass, public culture, a common economy and common legal rights and duties for all members.[6]

Smith enumerates the various components which might constitute a sense of identity between individuals, ranging from kinship, regional loyalty, class membership, religion, shared culture, shared territory and shared language to common ethnic origins. As a sociologist, he is sensitive to the important function of the sense of identity as 'a powerful means of defining and locating individual selves in the world' and as a means of creating social cohesion, and he believes that national identity may serve that purpose.[7] But he argues that national identity, and hence nationhood, is a cultural concept. As such, it has no immediate conceptual relationship with *the state*, a conglomerate of political institutions.

What constitutes a 'national unit' is inevitably determined by 'arbitrary judgements': so Breuilly argues in *Nationalism and the State*. In different circumstances, skin colour, religion, location, language or culture might be perceived as the 'natural' method of classification. In some parts of the world, application of these different taxonomies would produce contradictory results, dividing those who feel themselves to have a united identity, or amalgamating those who do not. Breuilly also argues that nationalism operates with three mutually incompatible notions: (1) the idea of a unique national (i.e. cultural) community, (2) the idea of a nation as a society which should have its own state, and (3) the idea of a nation as a body of citizens (i.e. a political conception) whose self-determination is justified in terms of universal political principles. He argues that there is no necessary, logical connection between the cultural conception (1) and the political conceptions (2) and (3), because they are different in kind. In fact, the meaning of 'nation' has changed between the three definitions.[8] To take the argument to an absurd extreme, it is as if I were to argue that all red-haired people should be entitled to live together and govern themselves. Having red hair has nothing to do with the right, or otherwise, to self-government. Breuilly's analysis leads him to conclude that nationalism is a characteristically modern device for resolving the eternal conflict between *the state*, viewed as political institutions and domination, and *society*, viewed as groups and individuals. 'Nationalist ideology is a pseudo-solution to the problem of the relationship between state and society.'[9] He concludes that nationalism arises chiefly when it is

---

6. A. D. Smith, *National Identity*, Penguin, 1991, p. 14.
7. Smith, *National Identity*, p. 17.
8. J. Breuilly, *Nationalism and the State*, Manchester U.P., 1983, pp. 341–2.
9. Breuilly, *Nationalism and the State*, p. 349.

the most convenient form for opposition to the state to adopt, and he offers historical examples to show when and why such opposition did or did not manifest itself in a nationalist guise. Often, it seems, ethnic identity has been redescribed as nationalism and then exploited by a leading oppositional group for the purposes of political gain. This is especially true of anti-colonial struggles, where populations were induced to support the liberators by appeals to their ethnic or cultural identity but soon found themselves the victims of a new exploiting class, the 'national bourgeoisie'.

THE INCOHERENCE OF NATIONALISM

The doctrine of nationalism, when scrutinized, can be seen to suffer from conceptual incoherence and indeterminacy. This can best be illustrated by looking at some 'hard cases', and the absurd or problematic conclusions to which they can lead.

(1) Multiple and Conflicting Bases for 'National Identity'

There are, as was mentioned earlier, multiple possible bases for national identity, some of which come into conflict. The inhabitants of Switzerland speak French, German or Italian, depending on the canton. Thus, if language were taken as the basis of cultural identity, the Swiss would constitute three different 'nations', each of which would presumably gravitate towards its homophonous neighbour— France, Germany or Italy. But the 'Swiss' identity of the Swiss overrides any potential language-based identification with the people of neighbouring countries, and the possible aggravations of living in a multilingual society are alleviated by the federal political system of Switzerland, which allows the cantons a degree of independence, and the carefully cultivated linguistic skills of the Swiss themselves, which make communication possible. This helps to explain why Switzerland did not support the Axis powers during the second World War but remained neutral, despite the fact that about 40% of Swiss are German and 20% Italian. Thus, shared history and territory have prevailed over linguistic identity in the reinforcement of Swiss nationality.

It is quite conceivable that a country most of whose inhabitants are culturally 'identical' in terms of language will be ethnically non-identical (as in the United States), or religiously differentiated (Northern Ireland), or that a diasporic group with ethnic and linguistic identity (the Jews, the Greeks) will be integrated into many different societies as citizens. The question of what is the 'natural' basis of national identity is infinitely debatable, and any view about which particular set of people should be grouped in which national unit will be inherently controversial.

(2) A Licence for Fragmentation

There is no inbuilt limitation on the fragmentation to which nationalism based on a sense of cultural or ethnic identity could lead. The Welsh might have sound reasons for claiming independence; if that were achieved, could the majority in the newly independent Wales reasonably prevent the inhabitants of Aberystwyth seceding to form a new 'nation' if the latter discovered a national identity separate from that of the rest of the Welsh? What if the Liverpudlians announce that they feel more culturally identical to the Irish than to the British? What if the 'Muslim Parliament' in Bradford or the Polish community in West London decide to declare unilateral independence? Is there a natural minimum size which a breakaway 'national' unit must attain before its claims are valid? Viability is one limiting factor, a factor which often hampers the aspirations of ethnic minorities, but it is only a practical consideration, not one which bears upon the rights and wrongs of nationalism based on identity.

These apparently preposterous examples seem less so when you consider that all Eastern European countries have pockets of ethnic minorities from neighbouring countries—Rumanians in Hungary, Hungarians in Rumania, Serbs in Croatia and Croatians in Serbia. These 'outsiders' often live not on the borders but in enclaves deep inside the country or intermingled with the majority population, so that a simple redrawing of boundaries could never suffice to satisfy the nationalist aspirations of the minorities. This practical difficulty which thwarts nationalist impulses in some places is important; more important theoretically is the fact that, according to nationalist logic, any group anywhere which decides to assert a sense of identity on some ground or another, would be legitimately entitled to declare independence. This would often be self-defeating, as the Welsh example given above suggests, because it is a necessary consequence of a successful nationalist movement that it should try to maintain the position of 'top nation' in the country in which it has triumphed, which will often mean that it has to thwart the desires of other nationalistic minorities within its territories. But should not nationalists support nationalism everywhere, if it is truly an ideology?

(3) The Problem of Multiple Loyalties

Individuals feel multiple loyalties—to friends, family, political associates, religion, locality, ethnic groups, linguistic groups and the state—simultaneously. If a nationalist movement is posited on one of these bases alone, many individuals will be divided in their loyalties. Where there are what political scientists refer to as 'cleavages' in society, such as cleavages of class, race or religion, and where these are 'cross-cutting' or non-coincident (for example, as where members of different races belong to the same class or share the same religion), social stability tends to be promoted. Conversely, where the cleavages coincide, as when the poorest group is racially distinct and practises a different religion from other groups, the chances of social conflict—and of nationalist or communalist movements—are at their highest. However, in most societies, it is likely that individuals' multiple loyalties will render any nationalist movement based on one vector of national identity unsatisfactory to substantial parts of the community. It may be a question of a trade-off—e.g. you forgo your loyalty to your former political associates in order to immerse yourself in ethnic identity because that seems to be most beneficial. But a nation built on a single basis of loyalty and identity, such as ethnic or religious identity, loses some of the social solidarity generated by the other loyalties which have been submerged in the process of national identification, and this may in turn be damaging.

(4) Circularity

There is an essential circularity in the conception of how a nation is constituted. Gellner says '*nations maketh man*', but also 'nations are the artefacts of men's convictions and loyalties and solidarities'. It is, he states, the *recognition* of these bonds which makes people into a nation, rather than some objectively establishable common attribute such as language or race.[10] Breuilly describes this as the 'voluntarist' view of nationalism, which makes the existence of the nation rest on people's subjective identification with it, but he also argues that individuals' subjective choices can be based on something more objective, such as the idea of 'What it means to be French'.[11] Hobsbawm argues that neither the subjective nor the objective view of what constitutes a nation holds water. The objective definitions of nationhood are open to factual objections (he enumerates factual objections to the Tamil's claim to nationhood in Sri Lanka as an example), while the subjective criterion of members' consciousness of belonging to a nation is 'tautological and provides only an *a posteriori* guide to what a nation is'.[12] So it seems that a nation only becomes such when people feel themselves to be members of it: this certainly sounds circular. The basis of that feeling might be some 'objective' attribute (such as race) or shared characteristic (such as a common language or culture), but these are essentially chosen or 'willed' by the people who wish to create a nationalist culture—usually, by some leadership group wishing to create nationalist feeling among the masses.

(5) Logistical Limitations

If some definition of identity other than citizenship of the existing society is accepted as a valid basis for nationalist movements in a multi-ethnic or multicultural country, the difficulty of achieving separation or secession may be immense. People are mobile, land is not, and territory is a prerequisite for setting up a nationalist state. But people become attached to their locality and are understandably reluctant to vacate it for the convenience of another group. Cyprus (whose whole history is one of conquest and colonization) was effectively partitioned in 1974 by the invasion of the Turkish army; Greek and Turkish Cypriots, who had previously lived intermingled in reasonable harmony throughout the island, were forced to flee to the south and north sectors respectively. The expulsion/repatriation solution, which left lasting embitterment and hostility between the two communities, is undesirable, but perhaps feasible for a small island community; it was also tried when India and Pakistan were divided in 1947, and bloody atrocities ensued on an enormous scale. But even

---

10. Gellner, *Nations and Nationalism*, p. 7.
11. Breuilly, *Nationalism and the State*, p. 8.
12. E. Hobsbawm, *Nations and Nationalism since 1780*, Cambridge U.P., 1990, p. 8.

where self-contained cultural or ethnic ghettos of limited size exist, secession is often virtually impossible for economic and social, as well as logistical, reasons: there would not be much support in the United States generally for an 'independent Harlem' in New York—nor, I suspect, in Harlem. The revolutionary appeals for a 'Black State' to be created within the USA would run into appalling logistical difficulties if they were to be implemented.

Summarizing the position, we can see that:

(1) it is hard to distinguish legitimate and illegitimate bases of 'national identity'. This can be based on many different characteristics (race, language, location, culture); there is no *natural* basis for national identity, and so every proposed basis is disputable, and may indeed be disputed by those adversely affected by it. No-one is in a position to determine what is or is not a legitimate nationalist aspiration, in my view.

(2) There is no necessary relationship between the idea of an ethnic or cultural community and the concept of political sovereignty. The demand that such a community should be self-determining is a demand, not an absolute truth.

(3) We are accustomed to nationalist movements based on ethnicity, religion, language and culture, but that does not mean that these are the only grounds for demanding independence, nor indeed, as Breuilly says, that they are legitimate grounds for entitlement to self-government. Other grounds might come into favour, such as gender (we already have radical feminist separatism), wealth (many of the wealthy have already 'seceded' to tax havens), or intelligence. Could movements based on such claims be properly denied? The fact that this question of principle cannot be answered (except according to personal taste) indicates the indeterminacy and incoherence of the concept of nationalism.

(4) Nationalism practised universally is bound to be self-destructive, as the discussion of fragmentation indicated.

(5) The idea of nationhood cannot be defined solely in objective or subjective terms, and the use of an admixture of both leads to a circular definition.

(6) The concept of national identity also rests on the false premise that each human being has one determining 'identity', rather than multiple loyalties.

In addition to these philosophical failings of nationalism, the practical consequences of thoroughgoing global nationalism would be disastrously fissiparous, for reasons already illustrated, and not in the end conducive to human wellbeing.

THE ORIGINS OF NATIONALISM

Historians and analysts of nationalism are in dispute as to when the idea was invented. But the majority of writers believe that nationalism is essentially a phenomenon of the nineteenth and twentieth centuries. It seems that the demise of the monarchical principle in Europe paved the way for nationalism based on linguistic identity. Once people had been liberated from the notion that their status was that of *subjects*, usually the subjects of a feudal baron and ultimately of the monarch (who frequently belonged to a different 'nation' anyway), other possible bases for social and political unity came under consideration, and linguistic identity combined with location eventually emerged as the most acceptable basis for nationality and self-determination. Linguistic identity proved important in the late nineteenth century in the Balkans and after the First World War, when old empires were dismantled and new nations created. Later, the presence of German-speaking minorities in Czechoslovakia and Poland was Hitler's ostensible reason for invading those countries in 1938 and 1939; the Second World War resulted.

Modern nationalism developed between 1800 and 1950 when Europe was still the major force in the world, and had colonized most of it. In the second part of the twentieth century the colonized countries, having been thoroughly imbued with European notions of nationalism, claimed national identity and the right to self-determination as the basis of their liberation struggles and subsequent community-building, although their idea of what constituted a nation often shifted from language to culture and ethnic identity. The term 'nationalism' is still used but with different connotations.

Gellner applies historical and sociological analysis to the nationalist phenomenon, and argues that there is a necessary connection between nationalism and *modernity*. The modern economy objectively requires a powerful, centralized state and the state in turn requires 'the homogeneous cultural branding of its flock', for greater efficiency and cohesion.[13] This requirement coincides in part with people's subjective needs; the rapid social changes which industrialization, mobility, high technology and rapid communications bring about leave individuals deracinated and lacking in identity; the promulgation of a national identity via nationalist doctrines and movements can help them 'locate' themselves. Thus nationalism (promoted through mass education, political movements or armed struggle) is both psychologically and socially functional; it aids individual fulfilment and social solidarity. The argument is questionable: as Breuilly suggests, there are usually more convincing explanations for a particular nationalist movement than its social or psychological functions; the latter normally appear as incidental benefits.[14] But if those who link nationalism and modernity are right, it must necessarily be a doctrine of limited duration and application, since, when the problems of modernization are overcome and individuals have relocated themselves in the world through establishing their chosen national identity, it will have served its purpose.

Another view of nationalism is that it was a perverse invention of European thinkers, a doctrinal disease which later, regrettably, infected other parts of the world. Those who criticize nationalism on these lines are often motivated by abhorrence of the many wars to which nationalism has given rise. In his influential critique of nationalism, Kedourie advanced this view, arguing that the doctrine of self-determination had its origins in Kant's idea of the free,

---

13. Gellner, *Nations and Nationalism*, p. 140. See p. 111ff for the general argument about modernity.
14. Breuilly, *Nationalism and the State*, pp. 32–6.

autonomous, moral, self-determining individual; the 'nation' was envisaged as such an individual writ large. Kedourie insists that 'far from being a universal phenomenon, [nationalism] is a product of European thought in the last 150 years'.[15] McNeill also acknowledges the European authorship of the idea and argues that the European idea of a homogeneous national identity is distinctly idiosyncratic; in his view, the societies of the Middle East in ancient times and Europe in the Middle Ages were based on *polyethnicity*. Conquest, enslavement, trade and disease (which necessitated the importation of outside labour into large urban centres) produced civilized, polyethnic societies at those periods of history and cultural homogeneity was then seen, by contrast, as being characteristic of remote and barbarous peoples.[16] McNeill believes that the enthusiasm of the eighteenth-century European intelligentsia for the civilized values of ancient Greece and Rome, including the ideal of a city-state composed of a free and homogeneous citizenry, led to the peculiarly European view of the nation as a homogeneous entity. (His view is borne out by the public anxiety about 'racial tension' in multicultural European societies; underlying this is the assumption that homogeneity is the safe and civilized norm.) McNeill is suggesting that there are other, heterogeneous forms of nationhood. Certainly, the nationalist movements for decolonization often resulted in the creation of nations composed of many different cultural groups, such as India and various African states; this might be viewed as a deliberate repudiation of the European norm of homogeneity. But these polyethnic nations have, in turn, been threatened internally by separatist movements which the state brands as 'tribalist' or 'communalist'. Nationalism, then, takes on different forms according to historical circumstance. In this case, is any generalization about its nature as a doctrine possible?

IS NATIONALISM AN IDEOLOGY?

Most books on ideologies include a chapter on nationalism.[17] Conversely, many books on nationalism deny that it can be viewed as an ideology. Hobsbawm, a left-wing historian, offers a sustained critique of the concept of nationalism. He, like other analysts, argues that 'no satisfactory criterion can be discovered for deciding which of the many human collectivities should be labelled [as a nation]'; the criteria are fuzzy and shifting, and mainly employed by propagandists.[18] He too notes the potentially contradictory elements of nationalism:

> the apparent universal ideological domination of nationalism today is a sort of optical illusion. A world of nations cannot exist, only a world where some potentially national groups, in claiming this status, exclude others from making similar claims.[19]

15. E. Kedourie, *Nationalism*, 3rd edn, Hutchinson, 1966, p. 74.
16. W. H. McNeill, *Polyethnicity and National Unity in World History*, University of Toronto Press, 1986.
17. See, for example, L. T. Sargent, *Contemporary Political Ideologies*, Brooks/Cole, 1990, Chap. 2.
18. Hobsbawm, *Nations and Nationalism since 1780*, p. 6.
19. Hobsbawm, *Nations and Nationalism since 1780*, p. 78.

In other words, successful nationalists do not regard *all* nationalist aspirations as equally valid, as they should if their beliefs were ideological. Hobsbawm does not classify the doctrine as an ideology because, in his view, nationalism does not provide a sound basis for restructuring the world or creating stable political systems. It is also being overtaken by events; the internationalization of the world economy is effectively depriving individual nations and national governments of power. What price nationalism then? Hobsbawm is in sympathy with Breuilly's view, mentioned earlier, that the cultural assertions and the political demands of nationalism are essentially unconnected.

Minogue, a right-wing critic of nationalism, writing in 1967 when nationalist anti-colonial movements were prevalent, stated that '[n]ationalism is a set of ideas, but as they travel from continent to continent, these ideas add up less to a theory than a rhetoric . . . by which a certain kind of political excitement can be communicated from an elite to the masses'. His argument was that the core of nationalism is a paradox—the paradox that, whereas nationalism describes itself as representing the political and historical consciousness of the nation, it actually *invents* the nation. He concludes that nationalism 'has contributed little more than a new vocabulary to the history of political evil'.[20] Anderson also argues that nationhood and nationalism are 'cultural artefacts', and he proposes a definition of the nation which emphasizes this: 'an imagined political community . . . imagined as both inherently limited and sovereign'. He notes that nationalism has inspired few great thinkers, compared with other 'isms', and draws a contrast between the political power of nationalist doctrines and their 'philosophical poverty and even incoherence'.[21] None of these writers, then, would consider nationalism to be an ideology.

If we now attempt to determine whether nationalism is indeed a political ideology by reference to the analysis offered in Chapter 2, it fails. Nationalist doctrine holds that a nation has a unique national identity (whether this is constituted by ethnic similarities, language, shared history or something else) and that this entitles it to self-government—that is, not to be subject to an 'alien' power. Some versions of nationalism, such as Nazism, also add that this entitles the nation to exclude or expel—or, at worst, exterminate—all ethnically or culturally distinct groups who happen to live in the territory but do not share the prevailing national identity. The usual definitions of *ideology* emphasize its comprehensive nature: it is 'a life-guiding system of beliefs' or 'a coherent value-laden mode of understanding the totality of phenomena'.[22] Thus, nationalism appears to lack the encompassing quality which distinguishes an ideology from other, partial beliefs. Nationalism may dictate that culturally identical people should not be ruled by outsiders, or should not have to live cheek-by-jowl with other ethnic groups, but it does not, for example, inform us about what kind of

---

20. K. Minogue, *Nationalism*, Methuen, 1967, pp. 153–5.
21. B. Anderson, *Imagined Communities*, Verso, 1983, pp. 13–15. Anderson rightly points out that any community larger than the primitive village in which face-to-face contact between all the inhabitants is possible, is in one sense an imagined community. But nationalist movements invent the community *de novo*.
22. See Chapter 2 above, footnotes 5 and 6.

political system should be set up, or what form social justice, liberty and rights should take within the new nation. Nationalism lacks political content in this respect; it also lacks the utopian content which—*pace* Mannheim—lies at the heart of ideologies. Although in Mannheim's sense of the term, separatist or liberationist nationalist movements could be described as utopian, since they tend to overthrow the existing order, they lack the central core of social and political values which form a necessary part of utopian thinking. In this respect, nationalism is like conservatism, an essentially reactive doctrine, although in other respects it is radical.

In fact, the conservative view of the 'organic society' certainly has strong links with some forms of nationalism, as does Hegel's theory of the nation-state. Conservatives like Burke emphasized the identity engendered in a society by shared history and tradition, as we saw in Chapter 7. Contemporary conservatives such as Scruton have also revived neo-Burkean arguments about the importance of identity, adding that this identity may be based on ethnic as well as cultural origins.[23] It need hardly be stated that, in the wrong hands and the wrong circumstances, such arguments can nourish racism. Nationalism is, in most contexts, including those mentioned at the start of this chapter, a manifestation of *ethnocentrism*; this is an attachment to one's own 'group', accompanied by hostility to (and resentment of) outsiders. The drive to identify oneself with an 'in-group' is certainly a powerful human motive, which most of us experience even as schoolchildren, and one that need not necessarily be based on ethnic identity; if ethnic distinctions are lacking, other features such as class, neighbourhood, religion or language will serve just as well. But ethnocentrism is not far removed from race prejudice, and can readily be transformed into racism or used to support fascism. However, like racism, ethnocentrism is an attitude, an instinct perhaps, and a motivating force certainly, but not an intellectually developed ideology.

Our understanding of the status of nationalism as a doctrine can be enlarged if we consider its relationship to religion. Religions (I would argue) are not in themselves ideologies, but they can provide prescriptions for daily living and prescriptions for social, economic and political arrangements. (The judicial decision in Pakistan in 1992 to prevent banks from charging interest, in accordance with the Islamic law forbidding usury, is one example.) In that respect, they have something in common with the utopian ideas at the heart of ideology. By contrast, although nationalism may share the mythic qualities of religion, it offers no prescription for social arrangements beyond the axiom that the national (cultural) unit and the political unit should be co-terminous and self-governing. Hobsbawm makes a similar point when comparing nationalism with religious fundamentalism. He argues that, although we might see 'ethnic exclusiveness, xenophobia and fundamentalism as aspects of the same general phenomenon', they differ radically because fundamentalism provides 'a detailed and concrete programme' whereas 'the call of ethnicity or language [i.e. nationalism] provides

---

23. For a liberal commentary on Roger Scruton's view see M. Canovan, 'On being economical with the truth: some liberal reflections', *Political Studies*, XXXVIII, 1 (1990).

no guidance for the future at all. It is merely a protest against the status quo'.[24] So, although we might detect similarities between religion and nationalism, viewed as politically powerful doctrines and as potent sources of conflict and cleavage, and although religion has often formed the basis of the 'cultural identity' which gives rise to nationalism, the two kinds of doctrine are distinct: by comparison with religion, nationalism has a hollow centre.

There is, then, a wide measure of agreement between historians and political philosophers that nationalism is not an ideology, even though some commentators describe it as such in a loose sense. Nationalism is best viewed as a myth, whose intrinsic vagueness makes it valuable to propagandists and opponents of the state; like a chameleon, it changes to suit the context. Nationalism lacks the utopian element which inspires ideologies. It can make no concrete proposals, other than the demand for the independence of the national unit, until it is united with a political ideology.

NATIONALISM, LIBERALISM AND DEMOCRACY

The relationship of nationalism to liberalism is complex. In some respects they are mutually supportive, in others they undermine each other. Although the right of self-determination of nations may seem like a more global version of the individual's right to freedom and autonomy, there are obvious differences between the individual and the group, and especially between the individual and a group constituted on some arbitrary basis. The history of nationalism suggests that, whereas sometimes successful nationalism allies itself to liberal ideals on the domestic front, often it does not. Plamenatz makes a distinction between two types of nationalism which he calls 'Western' and 'Eastern'. The first type, exemplified by the nationalist movements in nineteenth-century Europe is liberal, the second illiberal. Illiberal nationalism is said to be the nationalism characteristic of people who have come to be viewed as 'backward' by the more advanced nations, and who feel the need to transform themselves, usually by state-directed economic development; Plamenatz cites as examples China, India and some African nations.[25] Nationalism, then, does not necessarily culminate in liberalism and nationalist doctrines and practices are often contrary to both liberal and democratic beliefs, except in the cases where the nationalist cause adopts one or both of these ideologies as part of its creed.

The issues of ethnic identity and national separatism pose two particularly difficult problems for liberals. Ethnocentrism—and by extension, I believe, nationalism—is antithetical to the universalist liberal ideal of human rights and freedom (and equally opposed to the socialist ideal of universal equality and fraternity). The notion that people are equal and rights are universal, regardless of colour, creed or class, forms the basis of the liberal myth that society is, ideally,

---

24. Hobsbawm, *Nations and Nationalism since 1780*, p. 168.
25. J. P. Plamenatz, 'Two types of nationalism', in E. Kamenka (Ed.), *Nationalism, The Nature and Evolution of an Idea*, Edward Arnold, 1976, p. 27ff.

composed of free and rational individuals who have in some sense chosen to be there and who relate to their fellow-citizens in a spirit of legal and political equality; their social bonds or commitments are voluntarily assumed. The sociological revelation is that in real societies there exist bonds of community based on racial affinity and cultural identity, which run deeper than, and threaten, the liberal social contract; such bonds are involuntary, being constituted by birth or upbringing, and cannot be eradicated by exposure to liberal doctrines of universal rights and human equality. This is a revelation which endangers the liberal myth itself, for it suggests that the liberal edifice is built on sand.[26]

The 'principle of the self-determination of peoples' has been endorsed by many UN resolutions, but this does not decide the question of which 'peoples' are entitled to self-determination. Michael Freeden proposes that self-determination should apply to communities which are *already* actors on the international scene: 'self-determination is the exercise of each [actor's] right to independence in relation to external rule or influence', i.e. right to sovereignty.[27] Others apply the term to *emergent nations or communities*, which means that separatist movements can claim self-determination as a right.

Mill offered a classical liberal argument for national self-determination, arguing in favour of 'free institutions'. If people are bound by common sympathies there is a prima facie case for uniting them all under the same, separate, government. 'This is merely saying that the question of government ought to be decided by the governed.'[28] Since free institutions are under threat in countries composed of different nationalities it is desirable that national and state should coincide. If, when a country becomes democratic, it contains two antagonistic nationalities, Mill said 'there is not only an obvious propriety, but . . . a necessity for breaking the connection [between the two] altogether'.[29] For Mill, then, nationality and the right to secede are strongly bound up with *free institutions* and the right to self-government and hence with individual freedom and non-tyranny. The fact that he wrote in a period when most European countries were not democratic allowed him to imagine, mistakenly, that the development of democracy could solve the problem of nationalities in a rational way.

RIGHTS OF SECESSION

If the minority will not acquiesce, the majority must, or the government must cease . . . If a minority, in such case, will secede rather than acquiesce, they make a precedent which, in turn, will divide and ruin them; for a minority of their own will secede from them, whenever a majority refuses to be controlled by such a minority.[30]

26. This point is explored in Canovan, 'On being economical with the truth: some liberal reflections' and at more length in M. Canovan, *Nationhood and Political Theory*, Edward Elgar, 1996.
27. M. Freeden, *Rights*, Open University Press, 1991, p. 75.
28. Mill, *Considerations on Representative Government*, p. 381.
29. Mill, *Considerations on Representative Government*, p. 388. Ch. XVI is worth reading in its entirety as a liberal statement of the right to secede.
30. A. Lincoln, 'First Inaugural Address, Final Text', 4.3.1861.

In ancient Rome, 'secession' meant the migration of the plebeians outside the city walls, to compel patricians to grant redress of their grievances. In modern times, it refers to withdrawal from an alliance or federation or from a political or religious association. The idea suggests a certain formality but today the demand for secession is often adopted by a separatist minority within a nation which seeks independence and claims an independent territory. Often the 'secessionists' are peoples who were formerly subjugated by invading peoples (e.g. the Welsh), and often the minority is regionally based—the demand becomes more problematic if it is not. Secessionists usually wish to form a sovereign state, although they may sometimes wish to join another state. But essentially, they wish to re-draw boundaries and not merely to emigrate to a country which they favour more than their current country. Secession involves questions of individual rights and minority or group rights.

The best known case of secession occurred in the United States, when the eleven Southern slave-owning states seceded from the Union in 1861. Two issues were involved: could the individual States secede from the Union, and were the States sovereign or was the (federal) nation? After the Civil War, in the Supreme Court (Texas v. White 1869) the Union was described as an 'indestructible Union'[31]—an example of 'victor's justice'. Secession in this case was not based on nationalism or race as such but on ideology and the question of whether slave-owning was acceptable. Although the northern States were more of a racial mix because of immigration from Europe and the southern States had more WASPs (White Anglo-Saxon Protestants) and black slaves, the difference was really one of culture. Europe differs from the United States in the nineteenth century in that national identity *is* an issue, and debates and anxieties over national sovereignty among EU members are by no means confined to Britain. But in the future we might face similar issues of separatism in Europe: can a country secede from the European Union (EU), given that the Treaty of Rome is 'perpetual'? Does sovereignty ultimately lie with the member states or with the institutions of the EU?

The question of *separatism* and *secession* threatens to hoist liberal democrats with their own petard. The liberal values freedom, the democrat values popular sovereignty, and the liberal-democrat is concerned about 'suppressed' minorities whom the majority permits to be neither free nor self-governing. Beran comments that the unity of a liberal society should be based on consent, not force. 'The consequent moral right of individual citizens to leave their state permanently is not contested by liberal democrats in theory or practice, nor should the consequent right of a community of citizens who wish to leave a state with the land they occupy [be contested]'.[32] Beran argues that any group is *entitled* to secede from a state, since no 'social contract' can be irrevocable; on the other hand, the state may be 'justified' in resisting secession under certain conditions (for example, if the group is too small to be a viable independent state, if it refuses to allow sub-groups the same rights of secession or tries to exploit them, or if it

31. A. M. Potter, *American Government and Politics*, Faber, 1962, p. 48.
32. H. Beran, 'More theory of secession; a response to Birch', *Political Studies*, XXXVI, 2 (1988), p. 317.

occupies an area with a disproportionate share of the state's resources, or a militarily strategic area).[33] In many cases, including those of Scotland and Quebec, Beran concludes, secession would be justified; it is indeed an *entitlement* of the Scots and Québecois in liberal-democratic terms. It appears, then, that the logic of liberal democracy, if applied globally, would lead to a rash of secessions and a vast multiplication of small nations, many of which might be illiberal and aggressive. As the quotation from Abraham Lincoln at the head of this section implies, there is no logical limit to the secessionist principle. But perhaps it is illiberally paternalistic to worry about such an outcome of applied liberal principles.

Buchanan also argues the compatibility of secession with liberal ideals: 'the right to secede is the logical extension of a principle of toleration thought to be central to the liberal point of view'.[34] He concludes that there is a *moral right to secede* and that liberals should take secession seriously, as a way of affirming their commitment to liberal institutions while acknowledging that some communities cannot flourish within the liberal state and that it would be wrong to force them to conform. The moral right to secede can be asserted when the state perpetrates serious injustices against a group; such injustices include not only the violation of basic rights, but also 'the injustice of discriminatory redistribution', where a group of 'haves' is taxed exploitatively to benefit the 'have-nots' in another region of the country (as were the Ibos in Nigeria before they seceded to form Biafra, and the Serbs, according to Buchanan, in the former Yugoslavia). The preservation of an indigenous culture can also be a ground for secession under certain limiting conditions. Buchanan deals in detail with the difficult questions of whether injustices against a group by the state can generate a claim to *territory* (he rejects the 'historical grievance' basis for territorial claims by any seceding group), and whether a prosperous group within a nation has a duty to compensate the poorer groups left behind if it secedes taking with it an area rich in natural resources. What Buchanan's discussion makes clear is that although secession is a moral right, every claim to secede must be examined in context and pass a series of practical and moral tests before it can be (morally) approved.

The 'democratic' case for secession has been argued by Birch:'the right to get out is a shorthand label for the right of ethnic or cultural minorities concentrated *in viable territorial areas* to secede from their existing state and become completely self governing.'[35] Where a separatist movement has substantial support in a disputed region, Birch suggests four (alternative) conditions, any of which alone would justify secession:

1. The region was included in the state by force and its people continued to refuse consent to the union.
2. The national government had seriously failed to protect the rights and security of the citizens of the region.

---

33. Beran, 'More theory of secession: A response to Birch', p. 319.
34. A.Buchanan, *Secession*, Westview Press, 1991, p. 31.
35. A. H. Birch, *The Concepts and Theories of Modern Democracy*, Routledge, 1993, p. 131. My emphasis.

3. The political system had failed to safeguard the legitimate political and economic interests of the region, creating serious relative deprivation.
4. The national government had ignored an explicit or implicit bargain which preserved the essential interests of a particular region that might be outvoted by a national majority.[36]

Limiting conditions such as those proposed by Buchanan and Birch hold out some hope of moral order in an area of politics where chaos threatens but, as Birch himself concedes, the contexts and contingencies of nationalist movements differ so widely that 'the question of abstract rights has only a minor role to play'. The parties in nationalist conflicts are unlikely to put their claims to philosophical arbitration.

Liberalism itself was engendered in societies where deep cleavages existed; Locke's famous *Letter Concerning Toleration* reflected the need to keep the English community 'whole' in the face of strongly felt religious divisions. Liberalism is, in a sense, committed to creating an artificial community in the midst of diversity and potential conflict. Little wonder, then, that liberals in particular deplore the spectacle of a world where communities are being torn apart by racism, sectarianism, separatism, communalism, tribalism and similar conflicts, which may all be described under the general heading of nationalism. But liberals, as Beran argues, are committed by their own principles to accepting the moral right of nationalists to succeed in their aims. The fact that the consequences of a doctrine may be damaging or disastrous is not *per se* a good reason for rejecting it. For liberals, today's strident nationalism offends universalist beliefs which rest on three centuries of Enlightenment and post-Enlightenment rationalist beliefs. However, it is pointless for liberal theorists politicians to act like King Canute, trying to hold back the waves. Nationalism has some valuable aspects; it has helped abolish imperialism (although it scarcely presents a defence against neo-imperialism), created new nations, liberated minorities, given people identity and pride. What weight should these facts be given against the fact that it also leads to wars, separatism, secession and racism?

Democracy and nationalism, like liberalism and nationalism, are sometimes mutually supportive and sometimes mutually destructive. Although the nationalist ideal is based on self-government by a homogeneous group, this does not entail in logic or in practice that political power must be shared equally *within* the group, as democracy would prescribe. Often it is not. Kedourie takes the view that successful nationalism may achieve nothing more than a change of despot. 'To welcome or deplore a change in government because some now enjoy power and others are deprived of it is not enough. The only criterion capable of public defence is whether the new rulers are less corrupt and grasping, or more just and merciful'.[37]

From another perspective, we can see that some sense of nationhood is crucial to the survival of democracies; the absence of a uniting sense of community may destroy a democracy, as may the activities of disenchanted minorities who express

---

36. Birch, *The Concepts and Theories of Modern Democracy*, pp. 131–2.
37. Kedourie, *Nationalism*, p. 140.

their opposition through nationalist separatism. A democracy which, by whatever means, manages to exclude (or to avoid acquiring) minorities which might become dissident and so achieves cultural homogeneity, is better equipped to resolve internal conflicts on the basis of a general consensus of values—which is the essence of democracy. So the questions of democracy and nationalism are deeply entangled. However, the uniting sense of community which democracy requires might equally be built on cultural diversity, given the right social and educational systems, and does not require as a necessary condition cultural or ethnic identity and nationalism of an exclusivist kind.

OBJECTIONS TO NATIONALISM

There is a surprising consensus among Western thinkers that nationalism is an undesirable phenomenon and it is especially unpopular among those writing in the late twentieth century. There are historical reasons for this: the experience of Hitler's expansionist nationalism, with its corollary of genocidal racism, has left a deep scar. The fear that 'She who says nationalism today, says racism tomorrow' is a potent one. The existence of Israel, a state created on the nationalist principles of ethnic, religious and cultural identity, has led to a permanent state of conflict in the Middle East, which centres on the suppressed nationalist claims of the Palestinians who used to occupy the territory that is now Israel. That situation is not a good advertisement for nationalism. A factor particularly relevant to the attitude of American writers is that the United States is a polyethnic community, and if it were to admit the right of minorities in democracies to separation or secession, wholesale disruption of the American state could ensue. Such factors constitute explanations why these thinkers are hostile to nationalism, rather than reasons why they should be so.

Unrestrained nationalism would make for a bleak future. Imagine a world where each nation-state asserted its independence and autonomy and adopted an combative attitude to other nations and a repressive attitude to its own minorities. But the foreseeable practical consequences of universal nationalism—the break-up of communities, the fragmentation of the world political and economic scene and the proliferation of illiberal and intolerant regimes and wars—are not theoretical, but practical, reasons against the nationalist principle. The theoretical reason is that that principle, as was argued above, can be shown to be conceptually incoherent and lacking in content.

If nationalism is regarded as a negative and divisive force in the world, there are possible strategies to counteract its effects. One is to persuade nationalist movements to settle for less than secession and independence: within the European Union some regions which were militantly nationalist have been pacified by being granted the status of autonomous regions. This may be more in their interest than total secession, as Barry argues:

> a nationalist movement that settles for a high degree of political autonomy (including control of the educational system and the cultural apparatus), combined with

economic concessions from the rest of the country to its region, is not the less a nationalist movement for that.[38]

Another strategy is to adopt the European Union's 'principle of subsidiarity', which states that decisions should be taken at appropriate levels in the political and administrative structure, so that those with the greatest interest in the results, and those who have to pay for the decisions, should have a voice in making them. This would dictate that the decision to built a cottage hospital (for example) should be taken at the local level and funded locally, whereas the decision about a large specialist hospital should be taken and funded regionally, or even nationally. The subsidiarity principle, which encourages participation and responsibility at different levels, would benefit cultural minorities located in a particular area, as they could then influence the policies affecting them and gain a measure of autonomy.

A third strategy is to attempt to create a sense of community in a society that is multiracial or contains diverse cultures or creeds, so long as the larger community has logically defensible boundaries, a shared history and some *raison d'être*. Evidently, the sense of identity with people 'of one's own kind', whatever that kind may be, is a fundamental and instinctive feeling which can be a source of support and loyalty to the community, or a terrible destructive force. It may sometimes be possible to create new, homogeneous societies in which the sense of identity has a positive and cohesive effect; but more often we are faced with established societies with new minority problems, societies which would be destroyed if those minorities resorted to nationalist separatism, with damaging effects for all those concerned. There, the answer must surely be to attempt to generate a sense of community through diversity. This is why contemporary political theorists have been increasingly engaged with the idea of multi-culturalism and collective rights for minority cultures.[39]

FURTHER READING

J. Breuilly, *Nationalism and the State*, Manchester U.P., 1982.
A. Buchanan, *Secession*, Westview Press, 1991.
M. Canovan, *Nationhood and Political Theory*, Edward Elgar, 1996.
E. Gellner, *Nations and Nationalism*, Blackwell, 1983.
I. Hannaford, *Race: the History of an Idea in the West*, Woodrow Wilson Centre Press and Johns Hopkins U.P., 1996.
E. Hobsbawm, *Nations and Nationalism since 1780*, Cambridge U.P., 1990.
E. Kedourie, *Nationalism*, 4th edn, Blackwell, 1993.
D. Miller, *On Nationality*, Oxford U.P., 1995.
A. D. Smith, *National Identity*, Penguin, 1991.

---

38. B. Barry, 'Nationalism' in D. Miller (Ed.), *The Blackwell Encyclopaedia of Political Thought*, Blackwell, 1987, p. 353.
39. See, for example, W. Kymlicka, *Multicultural Citizenship: A Liberal Theory of Minority Rights*, Oxford U.P., 1995.

Part III

Ideas

Chapter 12

Democracy

One fundamental task of political theory is to offer justifications for the disposition of power in political systems. Such justifications are usually moral since, if people can be induced to adopt and internalize moral principles, it is more conducive to social order than if they have to be coerced into obeying the political authority. As Chapter 2 suggested, these justifications are invariably and inescapably ideological and reflect the 'total ideology', the wider culture within which they are formulated. In the past, many different philosophies of power were advanced: Plato argued that political power was the province of the wise, the Philosopher Kings, who were in intimate contact with the world of Ideas from which they could infer correct political decisions. In the Christian mediaeval period, many thinkers held that the king was the vicegerent of God on earth, so that obedience to him was the first duty of the Christian citizen. Other theorists, including Nietzsche, have argued, in effect, that 'might is right' although many would condemn this as immoral. What these justifications have in common is that they make no appeal to law, laying stress instead on Absolute Truth, the divine will, or tradition, custom or force.

By contrast, the democratic justification of political power is essentially *legalistic*, being based on the legal idea of a contract. Modern democrats have discarded the fallible idea of the social contract and argue instead that democracy is based on the consent of the people which, once given through the voting process, obliges them to obey the chosen government.[1] Behind the democratic viewpoint lies the hypothesis that power and the right to exercise power belongs to the people, although in some theories, 'the people' refers to an aggregate of individuals, in some, to a collective entity. Democratic theory not only specifies that people should govern themselves, but also that the purpose of government is

---

1. See, e.g., J. P. Plamenatz, *Consent, Freedom and Political Obligation*, 2nd edn, Oxford U.P., 1968.

the good of the people. The following ideas are central to what may be called 'classical' democratic theory:

(1) Supremacy of the people.
(2) The consent of the governed as the basis of legitimacy.
(3) The rule of law: peaceful methods of conflict resolution.
(4) The existence of a common good or public interest.
(5) The value of the individual as a rational, moral active citizen.
(6) Equal civil rights for all individuals.

Not all these ideas are logically connected, but as democratic theory developed historically they were moulded into a unified theory. Before discussing the problems of democratic theory and practice, an account of the theory itself is necessary. This is not the place for a history of the democratic ideal, but it is important to appreciate the movement from elitist conceptions of democracy with a limited franchise to the egalitarian ideals of the nineteenth century, and the swing back in the present century to restricted, elitist views which cast doubt on the capacity of the people to participate in politics. The term 'democracy' is by no means unproblematic. It has been used to describe political systems as widely different as those of the USA, communist countries and the one-party states of Africa. The reasons for this will become clear when we consider the diverse theories of democracy. Each ideology which proclaims the virtue of democracy borrows elements from the democratic theory most compatible with its other ideals and incorporates them—hence, each ideology views democracy in a different way.

THE CLASSICAL IDEAL

The Greek notion of democracy influenced modern views, but differed from them substantially. Contrary to popular mythology, Greek democracy was far from ideal. Etymologically, the word means 'the rule of the *demos*, the mass of people', and it denoted a form of government distinct from aristocracy and from oligarchy, the rule of the few. Nevertheless, democracy was still a *partial* form of government, since the 'mass' would naturally pursue its own interests at the expense of other sections of the population, penalizing the wealthy by taxation. In modern times, fear of the 'populist' aspect of democracy—mob rule and vendettas—was reawakened by the French Revolution. Plato considered democracy a decadent form of government, an 'imperfect society', three removes from the perfect republic and only one notch better than tyranny. He called it 'an agreeable, anarchic form of society, with plenty of variety, which treats all men as equal, whether they are equal or not'.[2] Plato emphasized the degree of individual freedom under democracy, of which he disapproved, because it weakened society as a whole. Aristotle was also disenchanted with this form of government, but he

---

2. Plato, *Republic* (trans. H. D. P. Lee), Penguin, 1955, pp. 330–1.

offered an analysis of the ethical principles of democracy.[3] Liberty is its aim, which means 'ruling and being ruled in turn', and implies a 'live as you like' principle from which spring various problems because, in conjunction with equality, it entails being ruled as little as possible, ideally by nobody.[4] Justice in such a democracy is based on numerical equality, and the rich and poor exercise exactly the same influence, but the danger here is that justice will be decided by the numerical majority and will be unjust towards minorities, such as the rich.[5] Aristotle's analysis exposed the social dangers entailed by realizing the concepts of liberty and equality.

In the middle ages, doctrines of the mystical unity of all believers in the Church and their equal subordination to God's will as expressed by kings, made democratic ideas irrelevant. But the rise of the secular monarch called forth new, embryonically democratic ideas which at first aimed at curtailing the king's power over the people—or rather, over their elected representatives. Social contract theory, discussed in Chapter 3 above, was crucial in establishing a foundation for democracy, since the idea of a contract made when all men could be assumed to be equal led to the conclusion that the present power-holders only hold power in trust for the people. Locke's second *Essay* sets out the principles for the composition and overthrow of governments. Government is set up to protect 'life, liberty, and estate' and emerges from a quasi-civilized state of nature via the social contract. From the original postulate that men are naturally rational, capable, and self-interested, he deduces that government must be by the people and aimed solely at their own good. They may elect representatives, delegate powers, and agree to abide by majority decisions, but ultimately the representatives and officials hold their powers on trust and are responsible to the people.[6]

The other details of Locke's version of democracy follow naturally from his original assumptions. Given that consent is the only legitimate basis for authority, we can only be subjected to laws by our own consent. Those who do not explicitly consent to a government are said to consent tacitly by living under its laws and accepting its protection.[7] The principle of consent is the theoretical basis and justification of democratic rule, and the foremost characteristic of government is the rule of law, which Locke describes as 'not so much the limitation as the direction of a free and intelligent agent to his proper interest'.[8] Law does not infringe, but supports, individual liberty—an important liberal tenet. 'For liberty is to be free from restraint and violence from others, which cannot be where there is not law; and is not . . . "a liberty for every man to do what he lists".'[9] Locke envisaged the law as mainly being concerned with the protection of property: indeed, his democracy was an association of property-owners. Despite this bias, Locke also propagated an idea of equality among citizens. All preserved their

3. Aristotle, *Politics* (trans. T. A. Sinclair), Penguin, 1962, Bk VI, Chaps. 2–3.
4. Aristotle, *Politics*, pp. 236–7.
5. Aristotle, *Politics*, p. 239.
6. Locke, *Essay*, Chap. IX.
7. Locke, *Essay*, s. 119.
8. Locke, *Essay*, s. 57.
9. Locke, *Essay*, pp. 143–4.

equal natural rights, which the government was bound to protect, and all were equal in their subordination to government. At the same time, citizens are independent, equal members of the sovereign people.

At the heart of Locke's idea of democracy is the conviction that individuals know their own interests best, so that paternalistic government is inappropriate and oppressive. The government's only duty is the protection of those interests. The fiduciary nature of government leads to the radical conclusion that the people are entitled to overthrow a government which breaches their trust, for example, by taking away their property or enslaving them. This invitation to popular revolution is less open than it seems, for Locke was wary of specifying the conditions under which it would be justified.[10] The ultimate sovereignty of the people constitutes an important safeguard in the democratic tradition, at least in theory. Much of Locke's *Essay* is devoted to the checks and balances which would prevent the organs of government from exceeding their powers, although these are of interest to the constitutionalist rather than to the theorist. (Montesquieu's *Spirit of the Laws* (1748) echoed some of Locke's sentiments, and praised the then English system of government for its admirable separation of powers.)

Almost a century after Locke, Paine wrote vindications of both the American and French Revolutions—*Common Sense* (1776) and *The Rights of Man* (1791–92). Although he was not a systematic philosopher, the now familiar ideas of Locke appeared in his writings with new additions. 'Every citizen is a member of the sovereignty, and, as such, can acknowledge no personal subjection: his obedience can only be to the laws'. Government is properly based on a social compact, but the English government of the time had arisen out of conquest, '*over the people*'.[11] Having thrown off the yoke of absolute monarchy, the individual's only duty is to laws which, in effect, he has himself made. Paine quoted the French *Declaration*: 'The law is an expression of the will of the community. All citizens have a right to concur, either personally or through their representatives, in its formation.'[12] The corollary of such a requirement was elected, representative government with universal suffrage. Paine emphasized the equality of all men in respect of their rights and, above all, their extensive right to liberty, which 'consists in the power of doing whatever does not injure another'. The emphasis of democratic theory was thus already shifting from the assertion of the people's collective rights against the king to the individual's rights, which would protect his independence against the government or state. Indicative of this shift was the addition of a Bill of Rights to the American constitution, which had originally weighted the odds heavily against the individual.

The drawing up of the American constitution provided the first chance for the pragmatic development of democratic theory, by trial and error. *The Federalist*,[13] a paper produced by the Constitution's 'founding fathers', debated the theoretical

10. Locke, *Essay*, Chap. XIX.
11. T. Paine, *The Rights of Man*, Penguin, 1969, pp. 92–4.
12. Paine, *The Rights of Man*, p. 133.
13. A. Hamilton, J. Madison and J. Jay, *The Federalist* (Ed. M. Beloff), Blackwell, 1948, Paper X especially.

issues. Hamilton's fear of mob rule, a democratic bogey since the time of Plato, was reflected in provisions for indirect elections to the Senate and Presidency, and for allowing state legislatures to set restrictive qualifications for the franchise. (Of course, logically, democratic theory should not acknowledge the danger of mob rule, because the basis of the theory is the ideal of the active, intelligent citizen.) Madison feared the creation of a permanent, tyrannical majority in a homogeneous democracy such as Rousseau had described, but hoped that the size of the USA and the people's diversity of origins and interests would itself be a safeguard—he advocated *pluralism*, a system of group representation not dominated by parties. He wished to forestall the formation of political parties which might lead to factionalism and majority tyranny. In practice American political parties have rarely espoused dogmatic policies or threatened to become permanent majorities, except in the aftermath of the Civil War, because of the wide interests which they represented. It was once said that 'the two great parties were like two bottles. Each bore a label denoting the kind of liquor it contained, but each was empty'. As Dahl has argued, 'the majority never rules, consequently it can never tyrannize'.[14] The constantly changing composition of the political majority in the USA thus fortuitously prevents a permanent majority developing—a fact which underlines the importance of social conditions for the achievement of democracy.

The writers of *The Federalist* favoured co-operation, deliberation, and bargaining as methods of decision-making, by contrast with the straight majority voting practised in the English parliament. The American approach is reminiscent of Rousseau's idea that members of the community should know and understand each others' points of view and interests. Implicit in the arguments of the *Federalist* was the justification for what Americans have often idealized as consensus politics and bipartisan policies—although it could be said that these are simply a manifestation of the domination of a permanent centrist majority, and that factions, disputes, and decisions by voting might be preferable. From the inception of the US Constitution, British and American versions of the democratic ideal began to diverge, despite the common influence of Locke, so that the differences today between revised Madisonian democracy or 'pluralism' and the populist democracy of Britain are considerable. The latter accepts that permanent, opposed interests should be represented through adversary politics, and that policies should be imposed by a majority vote without attempts at co-operation and conciliation. The federal nature of the USA necessitates a pluralist system, while the British conception of democracy favours strong, majority government without mediation. (Membership of a federal Europe could threaten this—hence the controversy in Britain over the European Union.)

The classical democratic theory of the eighteenth century was revamped by J. S. Mill to emphasize its idealistic and individualistic nature. *Representative Government* (1861) discusses the practical organization of government which would achieve democratic ideals yet avoid evils such as the dominance of the

14. R. Dahl, *A Preface to Democratic Theory*, Chicago U.P., 1956, pp. 132–3.

working classes, while _On Liberty_ (1859) sets out the background of individual rights required for a proper democracy. Democracy itself no longer needed justifying, for democratic republics and constitutional monarchies were more common by the time Mill wrote, so that he abandoned any preamble about contract and consent and merely asserted that the ideal form of government 'is that in which the sovereignty . . . is vested in the entire aggregate of the community'.[15] This is conducive to order, progress, and permanence. Mill's account of representative democracy is strongly individualistic: the most important feature of a democracy is the calibre of the individuals who compose it, who should be rational, educated, and active. Taking part in political debate and voting would, Mill supposed, educate people, and the prime aim of government is their mental advancement. Underlying such claims is a vision of the individual as an independent creative and moral agent, capable of development. Hence, Mill's emphasis on freedom and the right to self-determination. 'No intention, however sincere, of protecting the interests of others can make it safe or salutary to tie up their hands'.[16] Clearly, Mill views political activity as a good in itself, and this proposition is central to the defence of democracy, which is a less than ideal form of government in some respects—for instance, with regard to efficiency.

Writing in support of universal suffrage before it was attained in Britain, Mill put forward a theory of representation to justify his demand. He argued that the representative system produced government by intelligent men, whose wisdom outreaches that of their constituents and safeguards the government from 'popular clamour', since elected representatives must act on their own judgement and not be mere delegates. This 'theory', an idealized account of the workings of the British parliament, recalls the claim of James Mill (Mill's father) that the middle-classes were the repository of wisdom and should supply moral leadership.[17] J. S. Mill's stress on representation and his proposal for plural votes for the educated or, failing that, for the wealthy, reintroduced an elitist element into democratic theory which, by its own logic, should be strictly egalitarian. In Tocqueville there is a parallel admission of the moral rightness of democracy, coupled with a revulsion from its implications; Tocqueville described the majority principle as absurd because it extended the theory of equality to men's intellects.[18]

The problem of minorities greatly exercised Mill, who foresaw his own class, the intelligentsia, being swamped when the franchise was enlarged. For such an individualist, the question of minorities is really the question of oppressed individuals writ large. He advocated proportional voting as an institutional safeguard for permanent minorities, but also argued that their best defence was to consolidate themselves as interest groups and to remain informed and active.[19] _On_

---

15. J. S. Mill, _Considerations on Representative Government_, Oxford U.P., 1912, p. 186.
16. Mill, _Considerations on Representative Government_, pp. 188–9.
17. James Mill, _Essay on Government_, Cambridge U.P., 1937, pp. 63–73.
18. A. Tocqueville, _Democracy in America_, H. Commager (Ed.), Oxford U.P., 1946, p. 183.
19. Mill, _Considerations on Representative Government_, Chap. VII.

Liberty states the need for the individual to protect himself from public opinion, and Mill's support of minorities reiterates this at the political level. Both Tocqueville, who made a study of American democracy in the early nineteenth century, and Mill acclaimed the theoretical virtues of democracy in producing active, public-spirited citizens, but both issued practical warnings about its social consequences, fearing pressures to conformity and the tyranny of majority opinion.[20] Mill's advocacy of democracy must be seen in this light, and also in the light of his argument that the scope and activities of the state should be limited as narrowly as possible, to prevent oppression and preserve the independent initiative of the citizens.[21] Even 'the ideally best polity' has its limitations.

ELITISTS AND PLURALISTS

The twentieth century has seen an explosion of writing about the nature of democracy. The approach taken has often been critical, deploring the fact that the democratic ideal, now widespread, has not created world peace and prosperity. Bryce bemoaned the absence of goodwill, public spirit, and cooperation among democratic citizens, and he and Schumpeter both consider that democracy has been degraded to a *means* for procuring material benefits for the people and is no longer an end in itself. Schumpeter proposed a realistic, procedural account of democracy as competition among leaders for the people's votes. But these critiques, which are discussed later, did not really impinge on the individualistic ideals of democracy, citizenship, and participation, although they showed them to be inadequately realized in reality. However, more recent American political science produced political data which have given rise to two rival theories of modern democracy, the *elitist* and the *pluralist*.

The term 'elite' connotes exclusiveness in combination with special skills or resources; not every minority or interest group can be described as an elite.[22] The sociologist Pareto distinguished governing from non-governing elites and contrasted both with 'the mass'. There has been extensive investigation of the role of elites in politics since Pareto's classic study, and the parallel analysis by Michels of the 'iron law of oligarchy' at work in every political organization, but these discoveries were viewed as ominous for democracy, except by those such as Ortega y Gasset who deplored the mass mediocrity of democratic society and praised elitism.[23] To test the truth of these hypotheses, empirical studies were devised to identify the supposed political elites by looking at the stratification of power and the positions and the reputations of 'notables' of local communities. Such studies flourished in the 1950s and 1960s, mainly in the USA, and were based on the *behaviouralist* method, an investigative approach which focuses on

20. Tocqueville, *Democracy in America*, Chap. XV; J. S. Mill, *On Liberty*, Collins, 1962, Chap. III.
21. Mill, *On Liberty*, pp. 243–4.
22. For an introduction to the subject, see T. Bottomore, *Elites and Society*, C. A. Watts, 1964. Also, J. P. Plamenatz, *Democracy and Illusion*, Longman, 1973, Chap. 3 gives an account of the relevance of early elite theorists to democratic theory.
23. J. Ortega y Gasset. *The Revolt of the Masses*, Unwin, 1961.

the behaviour of individuals in political situations. Much criticism was directed at the methods used, but this did not prevent the general political conclusion being drawn, that local politics was dominated by elite groups. A particularly influential work was Wright Mills' *The Power Elite* (1956), which exposed the workings of an industrial–military–political complex in American national politics. Miliband produced a similar but more critical exposure of the British elite in *The State in Capitalist Society* (1969). A combination of distaste for 'mass society' and disillusionment with the 'ideal' democratic voter, whose extensive apathy was revealed in Berelson's study, *Voting* (1954), conduced to the development of an empirically based theory about the compatibility of elite rule with democracy, now known as 'democratic elitism'.

The politically active elites in a modern democracy are, of course, an iceberg, only the tip of which appears in national parliaments, although the political leadership itself constitutes an elite which develops special interests which are not typical of the people it represents. The Burkean theory of representation is often invoked to prove that the political elite is necessarily wise and chooses what is best for the electorate, but this justification contradicts the definition of an elite as a group pursuing its own interests. Another defence of elites states that their power is not a threat to democratic procedure because, with a multitude of elites which can freely 'circulate' in and out of power, each is kept within bounds. Indeed, to achieve anything, they must negotiate and co-operate so that no one elite is wholly autonomous or in control of the others. The average voter is assumed to have little or no control over these elites, but Key, Truman and other political scientists have taken the view that the elites share a consensus on the rules of the democratic game, which they observe. This is small comfort to the democratic citizen since it is conceivable that one or several elites will one day find themselves in consensual agreement to break the rules and destroy the democratic system. Wright Mills considered that other elite groups were not powerful enough to withstand the combined 'power elite'—hence the promotion of the armaments industry and arms race. He argued that the power elite should be submitted to the control of intellectuals, while Schumpeter thought that it could be made periodically responsible to the people through elections. But in all democratic theory, responsibility is a poor second to control since the leadership presents *faits accomplis* to the electorate: responsibility as a concept has a built-in time-lag, which may be fatal, and similarly the now fashionable idea of accountability is one of being called to account after the event.

Advocates of 'elite democracy' enumerate the various political virtues of elites in the political arena. It is argued that elites are the educated, active, and dynamic force in modern democracy, a necessary replacement for the mythical ideal citizen. Keller believes that the elite's set of articulated beliefs, or its ideology, gives it moral and social leadership (a disturbing suggestion from the viewpoint of tolerance and freedom of opinion). Truman argues that the consensus of elites prevents a demagogic rising of the masses, referring critically to Hitler's meteoric rise to power in a country which lacked a leadership elite. Wright Mills praises the ability of elites to centralize power and so to control decisions of national consequence. Tussman, in his account of political obligation, emphasizes the role that the intelligent elite plays in forming the duties and opinions of 'the clods' (i.e. the rest of the population). But many of the arguments for accepting elites as part of the democratic system are mere apologies resting on the weakest form of functionalist argument: the political system works, and we think it good, elites form part of this system, therefore elites perform a function in the system and hence are good.[24]

From the viewpoint of individualistic, liberal-democratic theory, there are strong objections to accepting democratic elitism as an ideal form of government. The elite outlook treats the majority of people as passive consumers, incapable of exercising power or judgement, and totally apathetic. But, as Bachrach pointed out, the 20% of 'apathetic voters' (non-voters) identified in the USA of the 1950s and 1960s significantly coincided with the poorest stratum of the population.[25] Perhaps we should reform social conditions rather than revise the democratic ideal. Elite theory treats democracy as a mere *means*, not as an end in itself—an ethical process, participation in which will educate and develop people. It denies the ideal of political equality, readily accepting the fact that some have more power than others and making no attempt to redress the balance. The typical elitist formulation of political equality is 'equal eligibility to power status' which, like 'equality of opportunity', leaves much to be desired. Elite theory also falls foul of Madison's and Rousseau's interdiction of factions. It capitalizes on studies of voter ignorance and apathy to vindicate itself. As Bachrach points out,[26] the definitions used in the theory are tailored to show that the existing system meets the requirements of democratic elitism, and its American proponents support the existing system as being a comfortable equilibrium, not far from ideal. Of course, many people believe elite leadership to be a natural and necessary phenomenon, and a number of utopias have featured elite ruling groups—Plato's Guardians, Saint-Simon's technocrats—and many societies have prospered under elite government, but this is hardly the point. Democracy is on principle antithetical to all elite or oligarchic forms of government, and puts its faith in the political capability of the ordinary person. A theory which tries to join elite rule and democracy seeks to reconcile the theoretically irreconcilable.

In the heyday of elite studies, Dahl published *Who Governs?* (1961), a study of community power in New Haven, which found there was no identifiable, dominant elite among a whole galaxy of 'influentials', i.e. prominent members of the community. Dahl concluded that New Haven was a *pluralist democracy* and went on to develop his theory of pluralism, or 'polyarchy', the rule of the many, which he claims to be the form that modern American democracy takes, deriving from the original Madisonian ideal.[27] Polyarchy is rule by a series of minorities, some self-interested, some public-spirited, all of whom accept the established form

---

24. For citations and summaries of the major literature in the elite theory debate, see P. Bachrach, *The Theory of Democratic Elitism*, London U.P., 1968; S. Lukes, *Power: A Radical View*, Macmillan, 1974; and B. Holden, *The Nature of Democracy*, Nelson, 1975, Chap. 6 especially.
25. Bachrach, *The Theory of Democratic Elitism*, p. 34.
26. Bachrach, *The Theory of Democratic Elitism*, p. 98.
27. Dahl, *A Preface to Democratic Theory*, Chap. 1.

of politics; their policy proposals lie within boundaries prescribed by consensus. Everyone in an interest group is represented in this political process, although Dahl's theory has been criticized for ignoring 'political marginals' such as the very poor who have no resources and belong to no pressure groups. The pluralist system is decentralized and advances in policy depend heavily on bargaining.

One could say of such a political system that it aims to reach compromises, rather than to discover political truth or the 'right' policy. This is borne out by Dahl's emphasis on the 'instrumental goals' of the pluralist system, which are the conditions for the sort of government which will maximize the 'primary goods' which people want. The theory of polyarchy is, it appears, about the *process* of government rather than about the ideal political system. But this limitation has not stopped it from being presented as if it described an ideal which is instantiated by American democracy today.

The advantage of pluralist over elitist theory is that it suggests that the political system is all-inclusive, and operates on the basis of consensus, which ensures that everyone's interests are taken into account, and everyone attains satisfaction, while elite theory entails the possibility of a dangerous divergence of interests between rulers and ruled. Dahl's account of polyarchy answers Madison's fear of the permanent majority: the multiplication of minorities and the endless negotiations between them forestall any possibilities of tyranny. However, elite and pluralist theories are not far apart: it is perfectly feasible that in a pluralist system some elites would become dominant, and indeed Dahl has often been branded an elite theorist, although he denies it and asserts the polarity between the theories. Controversy about research methods was rife among the adherents of the two theories for two decades, with each group accusing the other of choosing the method which suited its prejudices; in the late 1970s, as Waste illustrates, 'a general climate of peace was attained among the community power researchers'.[28] Meanwhile, critics of behaviouralism such as Lukes have called into question the methods used by both groups of researchers.[29] However, these disputes need not concern us here, except to suggest that political theorists should always be wary of the claims of political science to establish factual truth.

The debate must be seen in the light of increasing scepticism about the validity of orthodox democratic theory. Berelson's voting study concluded with the paradox that incompetent citizens produced competent government; political scientists then began to speculate that apathy and passivity were actually 'functional' to democracy and that the system was best maintained by having active elites make choices for the passive masses.[30] Thus, political scientists produced an account of democracy in operation and endowed it with normative value, claiming both that it factually refuted the classical democratic ideal and that it replaced that ideal, becoming a new norm of good government. One

28. R. J. Waste (Ed.), *Community Power*, Sage, 1986. The introductory essay by Waste gives a succinct summary of the pluralist–elitist debate and a useful bibliography of the major works on community power over four decades. See also the Introduction in G. W. Domhoff and T. R. Dye (Eds.), *Power Elites and Organizations*, Sage, 1987.
29. S. Lukes, *Power: A Radical View*, Macmillan, 1974.
30. B. Berelson *et al.*, *Voting*, Chicago U.P., Chap. 14.

objection to this claim is that elite and pluralist theories of democracy merely idealize what exists and disguise the imperfections of the system; another is that classical democratic theory never pretended to be factually true, but was intended as a yardstick by which real democracies could assess themselves and strive for improvement.[31] But one might also defend the new theories against the accusation that they are merely descriptions of the present disguised as ideals; although classic theories such as Locke's now appear to have a timeless ideality, they too emerged from the existing political situation, just as elite theories do. The main objection, though, to elite and pluralist theories is that they have no critical purchase on the present system, since they are devised to justify it. This must arouse our suspicions.

One other modern theory of democracy deserves a mention. Downs analysed the democratic process in terms of economic concepts. He hypothesized that citizens behave rationally, aiming to maximize their personal utilities through political participation, while parties act to maximize their votes. Self-interest is the dynamic of the system, which also has affinities with utilitarianism. Voting is seen as a short-term sacrifice which will only be undertaken if the potential rewards are adequate and if the voter's 'party differential' is high, i.e. if she cares who wins. The parties are therefore induced to offer high rewards for the voter's vote.[32] The voter gets satisfaction (if the party keeps its promises) and the party gets power. This 'descriptive definition' of democracy omits the ethical ideals found in classical theory, but it has a normative component, for it implies that the system will spontaneously maximize everyone's utilities. It echoes Adam Smith's hope that an invisible hand would aggregate the self-interested acts of economic individuals into a general prosperity. Similar to Down's theory are the exchange and transactionist theories of politics which view each political act as a profitable exchange between individuals or groups.[33] As with the elite theories, Down's theory has a descriptive basis: its normative element lies especially in its validation of the existing form of politics and its implication that all is for the best in this world.

The group of democratic theories just described share certain traits which distinguish them from classical theory. They deliberately omit the idealistic aspects and describe political activity in realistic, factual terms, reducing political motivation to self-interest. Consequently, democracy is seen purely as procedure, a procedure justified as the best method of maximizing utility. This justification has the disadvantage that, once the ethical reasons for preferring democracy have been abandoned, if it can be shown to be inefficient (as it can), a *more* efficient form of government should, logically, be chosen to replace it. The new theories often emphasize the maintenance and stability of the democratic system itself as its systemic goals, rather than its instrumental role in satisfying or educating citizens; as Davis says, such theory 'vindicates the main features of the *status quo*

---

31. G. Duncan and S. Lukes, 'The new democracy', *Political Studies*, **XI**, No. 2, 156–77 (1963).

32. A. Downs, *An Economic Theory of Democracy*, Harper, 1957.

33. For an account of exchange and transaction theories see S. Waldman, *The Foundations of Political Action*, Little, Brown & Co., 1972.

and provides a model for tying up loose ends'.[34] By restricting the scope of theorizing to the narrowly political sphere of action, these modern theories ignore imminent threats to democracy from outside the political system: large corporations and the bureaucracy tend to promote non-democratic ideals and exercise a good deal of control over the political process, with no accountability to the electorate. Nearly all these theories commit what Holden calls 'the definitional fallacy':[35] because the American political system is *called* a democracy, they deduce the characteristics of democracy from what they observe there. This is particularly true of Lipset's account of democracy in terms of the material and social conditions he observes in Western societies.[36] A theory constructed like this has no critical force and is inherently conservative.

This is why the comparison of modern and classical democratic theory is not merely an academic issue, an artificial confrontation between Dahl *et al.* and the long-dead J. S. Mill. Arguments which 'prove' that the USA (or Britain) is a democratic country give important support to the prevalent liberal ideology, and counter any radical critique of political institutions. Hence, an understanding of modern democratic theory and its methodological and idealistic failings is important. The table which follows makes a schematic comparison of the classical and modern theories of liberal democracy.

'RADICAL' DEMOCRACY

In the period of the Enlightenment, while Locke's idea of democracy was becoming more and more closely associated with the liberal ideal, another version of democracy was developed by Rousseau which, in the present century, has become closely associated with Marxism. Rousseau was born in Geneva, then an independent city ruled at that time by the Calvinist Fathers but small enough to be a direct democracy. Although he spent most of his life in France, this greatly influenced his ideas. Rousseau has been called 'timidity personified' but his theory constituted a strong attack on the corrupt despotisms of continental Europe. Also, unlike other French philosophers who admired the English system, Rousseau argued that its representative nature made the citizens no better than slaves.

> The people of England regards itself as free; but it is grossly mistaken; it is free only during the election of members of parliament. As soon as they are elected, slavery overtakes it, and it is nothing.[37]

The solution was a direct democracy in which everyone could represent himself and Rousseau looked admiringly to the democracies of classical antiquity for this ideal. Such a democracy solves the problem of political obligation and other

34. L. Davis, 'The cost of realism: contemporary restatements of democracy', in *Apolitical Parties* (Eds. C. A. McCoy and J. Playford), T. Crowell, 1967, p. 198.
35. Holden, *The Nature of Democracy*, p. 6.
36. S. Lipset, *Political Man*, Heinemann, 1960, Chap. 2.
37. Rousseau, *The Social Contract*, Dent, 1913, p. 78.

Classical and modern democratic theory compared

Classical democratic theory	Modern democratic theory
(1) From Locke onwards, enshrines supremacy of people.	(1) Tends to emphasize supremacy of *the system*; one goal is maintenance of the system.
(2) Makes consent of governed a prerequisite for legitimate government, which makes periods of defeat acceptable to minorities.	(2) Dismisses idea of consent (with good reason) but replaces it with weaker notion of consensus, giving citizens at most a retrospective control over government.
(3) Often postulates a common good (cf. the 'right answer').	(3) Argues there can never be *one* good; the conflict–consensus balance will produce a selection of policies, a variety of goods.
(4) Emphasizes individual freedom; individual to pursue his/her own best interests with minimum interference; commitment to minimum law.	(4) Emphasis on system detracts from notion of minimum law—a discarded ideal. National security, welfare legislation require the law to be more extensive.
(5) Takes individual as basic unit of democratic model; assumes he/she is rational, ethical, active, and self-interested. His/her political actions have importance since the majoriy is composed of individuals.	(5) Sees interest group as fundamental, politically active unit. Disregards all individual characteristics except self-interest. Makes mass-apathy functional and necessary. 'Political man' plays many roles, has multiple loyalties—classical democrat considered him single minded and one dimensional.
(6) Stipulates that political equality is a fundamental ideal—although this can lead to injustice in a simple majoritarian democracy, when permanent minorities are submerged. Solutions to 'the intensity problem' would undermine political equality.	(6) Transforms idea of political equality from one-man-one-vote into equal access to interest groups etc. Would argue that pluralist theory gives minority bargaining power and therefore greater equality. Can cope with 'intensity problem' in this way.
(7) Early democratic theory emphasized the possibility of radical, though controlled, change.	(7) Modern democratic theory, idealizing stability, equilibrium, system-maintenance, implicitly denies possibility/usefulness of change.

paradoxes, for when the individual confronts the law, he is confronting laws which he himself freely made. To obey oneself is to be free. Hence, Rousseau's own paradox, which has invited so many unfavourable interpretations, that in being forced to obey the law man is 'forced to be free'.[38] Rousseau's *Social Contract* (1762) begins with an account of an original contract in which each individual renounces his natural liberty in exchange for the equality and formal or 'conventional' liberty which society offers. He forgoes some of his power over himself and gains power or influence over his fellows in exchange—a mutual assurance scheme.

The ideas of the common good and the General Will are central to Rousseau's analysis. Locke's theory began with an individual who best knows his own interests, and for Locke the common good is merely the aggregate of all private interests. But for Rousseau, the common good is something which benefits all individuals equally, but may not coincide with their personal interests, subjectively viewed. The General Will, the dynamic, decision-making element in Rousseau's democracy, is defined as that which promotes the common good.[39] The concept is a baffling one, since Rousseau makes it clear what it is *not* but not what it *is*. It is not the will of all individuals added together and averaged out (this he calls the *volonté de tous*) nor is it the will of the majority. Anyone, or any group, might serve as the mouthpiece of the General Will: 'this does not mean that the commands of rulers cannot pass for general wills, so long as the sovereign [i.e. the people] offers no opposition'.[40] In other words, the General Will is not essentially a democratic notion, although Rousseau thought it could best be realized through a direct democracy where the people's sovereignty would act as a safeguard against the imposition of any 'particular wills'. It may help our understanding of the General Will if it is thought of as the 'right answer' to some question, the answer which most effectively promotes the common good. For some questions, e.g. for a mathematical problem, we cannot predict which person in a group will get the right answer, nor is there any reason to think that individuals collectively could find the solution better than singly, but as long as the answer is right, the method of finding it (i.e. which people were asked) is relatively unimportant. The problem with this analogy is that 'What is the common good?' may not be a question with a unique right answer.

The democratic process envisaged by Rousseau consisted of deliberation, then voting. During discussion, individuals were entitled to put forward their private interests, but in the voting process, they should vote for what they considered to be the common good: ideally this would produce a unanimous vote. This seems less hopelessly optimistic when one remembers that Rousseau assumed certain specific social conditions: a small, homogeneous community of craftsmen, whose education and background would be similar and whose interests would therefore tend to coincide. However, he also proposes the expedient of a Legislator, who would promulgate laws for the common good which the sovereign people could

---

38. Rousseau, *The Social Contract*, p. 15.
39. Rousseau, *The Social Contract*, Bk II, Chaps. I–III.
40. Rousseau, *The Social Contract*, p. 20.

accept or reject.[41] Critics view this as an invitation to dictatorship, but it is more likely a realistic acknowledgement that a collective body is usually unable to initiate proposals without effective leadership or guidance.

Another important element in the theory is Rousseau's condemnation of 'partial societies'—that is, groups with vested interests which may prove divisive, and stop the General Will from forming. Rousseau probably had in mind the economic monopolies and small privileged groups which manipulated French politics to their own advantage at the time. His fear of factions clearly influenced Madison, and the French revolutionaries. When the Jacobins suppressed the Girondins (1793–95), they cited Rousseau in justification. Thus, Rousseau's position has been condemned as being authoritarian and inimical to free speech. It shocks those who see adversary politics as the watchdog of freedom and the spice of life, and it is certainly anathema to the pluralist, yet, in terms of Rousseau's own logic and his belief in the possibility of a common good, it is sound. In stripping the citizen of self-interest and making him merely a spokesman for the common good, Rousseau foreshadows the worse excesses of totalitarianism, it is argued.[42] But he thought that on entering society the individual gave up selfish pleasures to attain the more fulfilling role of moral agent and citizen and it is on this elevated plane that he forms part of the General Will, which in turn creates the conditions for private pleasure.

To many, Rousseau's 'democracy' seems to enhance the authority of the state and to pave the way for a totalitarian society, because of his readiness to submerge the individual in the General Will and his denial that private interests should be paramount in politics. This debate has already been discussed in Chapter 8. But it is certain that Rousseau admired and advocated democracy: his idea of the General Will was obscure, perhaps confused, but not malevolent. However, he has been further discredited in the West because of the use of a number of his ideas in Marxism. The classless society achieved after a communist revolution would, it is said, achieve such a homogeneity of interests that there should be no political opposition or factions. Direct democracy was supposed to operate in post-revolutionary Russia through the workers' Soviets, although this quickly turned into 'democratic centralism', where commands were transmitted *downwards* from the top. Many have seen echoes of the General Will in Lenin's notion of the dictatorship of the vanguard party, acting on behalf of the proletariat: it could claim to be the spokesman for the true common good of those workers deluded by bourgeois ideas and suffering false consciousness. Ultimately, the common ideal of Rousseau and Marx is unmediated *popular sovereignty*, an idea which horrifies the champions of representative democracy, who fear the untutored instincts of 'the mass' erupting into politics because the people may be wayward and fickle. Holden notes another danger of popular sovereignty, namely, that it admits no justification (such as Locke saw) for the limitation of powers:

---

41. Rousseau, *The Social Contract*, Bk II, Chap. VII.
42. See footnote 13 to Chapter 8 for citations of typical literature on this.

Once government is postulated as the complete servant of the people, it is sometimes hard to retain the view of it as a hostile force that has to be kept within strict limits.[43]

So popular sovereignty, paradoxically, unleashes the leviathan of the state. But liberal democrats cannot criticize direct democracy and popular sovereignty for this without a degree of hypocrisy. The average citizen is assumed by such liberals to be sufficiently rational and educated to vote, but nothing more, and they themselves are thus committed to an elitist view of political ability which could just as well form the basis of an oligarchical theory as of a theory of representative democracy. The fear of the 'mob' dies hard, and the more that theorists separate the roles of citizen and politician, the more they condemn the masses to political passivity, ignorance, and alienation—the very preconditions for a mob! The early liberal-democratic premise that each has rights and interests which merit representation and the later premise that each has a political capacity both entail a form of government based on popular sovereignty; only elitist convictions can prevent us from admitting this. Our theoretical repugnance for the Rousseauist–Marxist, radical-democratic ideal embroils us in certain inescapable inconsistencies. Of course, the difference between representative and direct democracy is not merely one of procedure: representation qualitatively changes the nature of the system, and promotes a different ideal from that of popular sovereignty, an ideal more compatible with liberal values.

To summarize, the argument for democracy runs as follows: the postulate that the individual has the right to and the capacity for self-rule entails popular self-government, with consent as the basis of the government's legitimacy. Related ideals are freedom under law, equality of political rights, and the value of individuals *qua* citizens. Representative democracy adds to these the necessary virtue of government accountability and responsibility to the electorate. Radical- and liberal-democratic theories differ over the possibility of a common good, the scope of government, the desirability of plural interests and factions, and the role of the state, but both treat democracy as an ideal, not just a government apparatus, and so neither theory should be taken as primarily offering an empirical account. In each case the ideal must be distinguished from the associated conditions and the mechanisms of democracy such as the secret ballot, which may reflect the spirit of democracy but are really cultural details, separable from the ideal.

Following this survey of the main elements of various democratic theories I shall discuss the conceptual weaknesses of the ideal and offer a critique of some of its presuppositions. Foremost among these is the so-called paradox of democracy.

DEMOCRACY'S PARADOX

The democratic citizen frequently finds herself in the position of wanting one law to be enacted, but having to obey a contrary law chosen by the majority; even

---

43. Holden rehearses all the typical liberal arguments against popular sovereignty in *The Nature of Democracy*, Chap. 2 and its Appendix.

worse, she votes for the losing party and has to obey laws passed by its rival. Such events are more than a passing annoyance, and it is essential for the stability of democracy that the citizen should not disobey, revolt or secede whenever this happens. Yet democracy constantly puts the citizen in the dilemma of believing one thing and having to do another. Her dilemma can be represented as the irrational state of holding two contradictory moral beliefs: 'X is wrong' and 'X is right if the majority thinks it right' entail that if the majority enacts policy X, it is simultaneously right and wrong for that citizen. The problem is usually expressed as follows: how can the individual follow her own will, yet conform to that of the majority? A number of solutions have been proposed. In general, the citizen who voted for the losing party can console herself that her party may win next time, a consolation that will only be effective in a society with a fair degree of consensus and a low level of inter-party conflict. But the moral dilemma arises more acutely with regard to particular policies, where two principles come into conflict. Wollheim's solution is to say that individuals hold both direct moral principles, such as 'murder is wrong' and oblique, or second-order, moral principles, such as 'what the majority decides is right'. He argues that there cannot be a contradiction between these two kinds of principles (whereas two direct principles could be contradictory), because direct and oblique principles are not 'immediately' incompatible. So the citizen who believes that X is wrong, but is right if the majority wants it, is not irrational or self-contradictory.[44] Wollheim has been criticized for this sleight of hand: the idea of 'immediacy' is alien to logic—either there is a contradiction or there is not. In any case, the postulate of two different sorts of moral principles is unacceptable to many philosophers.

Another proposed solution was offered by Schiller:[45] majority rule is a convenient form of decision procedure, he argues. In subscribing to it, we accept it as the best procedure available; this is a *rational* commitment. The obligation which follows from such commitment is not an overriding imperative but a rational or prudential obligation, which cannot override moral principles. Of course, if our moral belief that X is wrong leads us into disobedience, we are endangering the majority principle practically, but we are not in self-contradiction. Equally, we can retain our moral belief that X is wrong and obey the law enjoining us to do X without suffering a moral crisis: the prudential commitment has overridden the moral principle, simply. Schiller argues that universal rational (non-moral) acceptance of democratic procedure is a sufficient condition for democratic government, which does not demand moral commitment, but his view tends to undermine the idea of democracy as an ethical ideal to which we should commit ourselves morally.

Rousseau's solution to the problem has already been intimated. He asks 'How can a man be both free and forced to conform to wills that are not his own?' Part of his solution deals with the lawmaking process: men can promote their own beliefs in debate but should ignore these when it comes to voting and vote for

---

44. R. Wollheim, 'A paradox in the theory of democracy', in *Philosophy, Politics and Society*, 2nd Series (Eds. P. Laslett and W. G. Runciman), Blackwell, 1972. See also B. Barry, *Political Argument*, Harvester, 1990, pp. 58–66.
45. M. Schiller, 'On the logic of being a democrat', *Philosophy*, **XLIV**, 46–56 (1969).

what appears to be the common good. For this to be a satisfactory solution, we must first believe, as Rousseau did, that the common good can be unambiguously identified. Rousseau's proposal splits the individual into two selves—the private person and the citizenly self—and so evades the psychological problem which arises when someone has two contradictory desires. Rousseau's case for why we should obey laws of which we disapprove is that it would be self-contradictory to disobey laws which we ourselves had taken part in enacting.[46] This may carry some weight in a direct democracy, but the representative system interposes so many mediating levels between the citizen and legislation that she could easily undertake civil disobedience (or indeed criminal activity) without feeling the contradiction which Rousseau foresees.

The paradox of democracy can be viewed as a special case of the permanent tension between individual freedom and authority. This is sharply emphasized under the liberal-democratic form of government, which claims to promote freedom. In a society like Britain, where consensus on the political system is reasonably strong and political conflicts and controversies fairly muted, the so-called paradox may seem an academic irrelevance. Our society is a tolerant one: doctors who think abortion wrong are not obliged to perform the operation, and people rarely come face to face with the paradox in its acutest moral form. But in a situation of ideological or minority conflict, Wollheim's solution (if the direct moral principle prevails and determines people's behaviour) might cause a breakdown of democracy, whereas Rousseau's would probably preserve it. The whole debate is therefore crucial for the legitimization of government and the laws, for establishing political obligation and for upholding the majority principle. Which solution to the paradox you prefer depends on how certain you are of your beliefs and whether you value them more than political stability. Those adhering to some system of moral absolutes, such as a religion offers, may decide to defy the majority, buoyed up by their moral infallibility, while those with a more subjectivist view of ethics may be swayed by the majority's view of what is right, or allow their prudential commitment to democracy to outweigh their moral principles. This suggests why democracy is more at risk and harder to establish in a country with a strong and absolutist religion.

Karl Popper identifies another paradox of democracy, which might also be called a paradox of freedom. He notes that Plato implicitly raised the question of what the position would be if people in a democratic society voted to be ruled by a tyrant. This would be like using your free will to enslave yourself. This paradox, in Popper's view, confounds

> all those democrats who adopt, as the ultimate basis of their political creed, the principle of the majority rule or a similar form of the principle of sovereignty. On the one hand, the principle they have adopted demands from them that they should oppose any but the majority rule, and therefore the new tyranny; on the other hand, the same principle demands from them that they should accept any decision reached by the majority, and thus the rule of the new tyrant.[47]

---

46. Rousseau, *The Social Contract*, pp. 30–1.
47. K. Popper, *The Open Society and its Enemies*, 5th edn, Routledge, 1974, Vol. I, p. 123.

Popper, the great exponent of 'the open [liberal] society', used the paradox to reinforce his attack on the theory of unchecked sovereignty which he considered a necessary consequence of some kinds of democratic thought. However, the paradox is brought into prominence whenever an authoritarian party stands for democratic election, as the Nazi party did in Germany, or the Islamic Salvation Front in Algeria in 1992, which campaigned on the basis that it would 'depluralize' the state—that is, institute non-democratic Islamic fundamentalist rule. There may be no elegant theoretical solution to this paradox, but its practical consequences present a problem: what can we do if people wish to throw away their freedom?

THE PROBLEM OF MINORITIES

The paradox of democracy describes the position of those individual citizens who in normal circumstances find themselves in agreement with the majority and with democratic procedure. But what of groups who, because of their race, religion, geographical or economic situation, or moral beliefs (or a combination of these) find themselves permanently in the minority? They are unlikely to agree that majority opinion is right and that its laws are just: more likely, they will begin to question the validity and value of democracy itself. Given the heterogeneity of people in most modern societies, democratic theory has sought various ways of safeguarding the position of minorities, to prevent oppression and foster greater justice. In fact, the problem of minorities is the greatest threat to any established democracy, as experience has shown: the Basques in Spain, the Catholics in Ulster and, currently, ethnic minorities in many Eastern European countries and in the former Soviet Republics. The individualistic axiom of political equality, 'one man one vote' which is built into democratic theory as a fundamental ethical principle, upholds majority rule, which is widely accepted as the only practicable method of decision-making, even though it is less ideal than unanimity. A unanimity requirement would, of course, be the ultimate protection for all minorities, even minorities of one, but it would also lead to endless political impasses.

In practice, the position of minorities varies with the political system. The American system, a plurality of minorities, with its emphasis on wheeling-dealing, compromise and consensus, affords some protection, whereas the British 'populist', first-past-the-post electoral system, and the strength of party discipline in parliament, tends to submerge minorities unless they are aggressive and vocal. The easiest case to solve theoretically is that of the 'intense' minority and the indifferent majority. People have preferences of varying intensities, and it would surely be unjust to allow an intense and committed minority to be constantly outvoted by an indifferent majority, if the minority's preference concerned only itself, and threatened no harm to the majority.[48] Thus, most people in Britain are indifferent as to whether the Welsh language is used in Welsh schools and

---

48. W. Kendall and G. W. Carey, 'The "intensity" problem in democratic theory', *American Political Science Review*, **LXII**, No.1, 5–4 (1968).

courtrooms, but the Welsh-speaking population feels passionately about this, so its wishes should prevail. Utilitarians solve the problem in the contrary direction, however. They hold that interpersonal comparisons of preference (with regard to intensity) cannot be made, and that everyone should 'count as one' in utility calculations, i.e. each vote should have equal weight. This would mean that minorities were permanently submerged, however just their cause. So the utilitarian approach leads to evident injustices, but, on the other hand, so would the weighting of votes to benefit minorities, which would undermine the political equality which is the basis of consent and of the legitimacy of democratic government. (Mill's proposal of extra votes for the intelligent and/or wealthy, for example, seems manifestly unjust.) To institutionalize the position of minorities goes against democratic equality, while to leave their cause to the good nature of the majority will in many cases mean that they suffer injustice, or even oppression.

It seems that no theoretical solution to the problem can be proposed that does not threaten basic democratic principles: maybe we can only introduce *ad hoc* constitutional and conventional safeguards as such cases arise. Proportional representation (PR) is the most easily institutionalized way of guaranteeing protection to minorities, as Britain's acceptance of PR in Northern Ireland (while it was rejected for the rest of the United Kingdom) indicated. In some parliaments, minorities are guaranteed a certain member of seats, as were the whites in Zimbabwe initially, after independence. Elsewhere, it might be appropriate to give an identifiable minority or interest group a veto over legislation specifically affecting them. It might, for example, be thought appropriate to give women, or women MPs, a veto on legislation concerning abortion, as the people most closely affected. The problem with vetoes in general, as shown by problems in the UN Security Council and the European Union, is that they tend to prevent any decisions. Sometimes it is possible to remove minority matters from majority control altogether, as when Welsh or Scottish matters are referred to the appropriate Grand Committees which have statutory powers. In the original US Constitution, the slave-owning Southern states were given a veto over legislation concerning slaves, and thus protected at the most fundamental level. This raises the question of which minorities should be considered legitimate, and protected. I can, presumably, choose whether or not to be a slave-owner, but not whether to be a Welsh-speaker, black or a Catholic. If minority interests are to be institutionally protected, they should be 'permanent' interests, arising from some unalterable characteristic of the individual and not, for example, economic interests which she has voluntarily adopted. But then, the members of a traditional mining community did not, on the whole, freely choose to become miners. All this goes to show that if the principle of protection is conceded, the practical problems involved in deciding which minorities legitimately deserve protection will be extensive. As a rule, such decisions are taken *ad hoc* in emergencies, which adds to the confusion and does not suggest any general rule which democracies might adhere to.

The case of minorities is a special problem for liberal democracy because it is based on individual interests and political equality and prefers to overlook the existence of interest groups acknowledging which would detract from the individualistic approach. The citizen is primarily seen as a voter, whose major interests exist in another (private) sphere, so that no conflict of a citizen's political and economic roles appears in the abstract theory. However, liberal democracy's individualistic concerns demand that it should attempt to solve the problem of minorities since a minority, after all, consists of a large number of individuals. Commentators from Tocqueville onwards have deplored the dangers of majority tyranny in practice, but this does not mean that minorities are just an *empirical* blot on an otherwise satisfactory theory. In so far as democratic theory assumes that individual interests are independent, homogeneous, and compatible, it falsifies reality, for all modern, multicultural societies are composed of groups of unequal size with various, potentially conflicting, interests. Democratic theory, whether liberal or radical, is essentially a theory about the peaceful reconciliation of differing interests and so the existence of minorities should be one of its original premises, a problem to be dealt with theoretically as well as institutionally. Pluralist democratic theory moves in this direction by making minorities the *sine qua non* of democratic government. The institutional protection of genuine minorities is something which the majority owes them, in all justice. But informal safeguards are equally important: minorities should not forget Mill's injunction to them to be informed, active, and articulate in the protection of their own interests. In a society which practices the kind of tolerance of others' beliefs and habits that Mill recommends, minorities would rarely need to seek redress of their grievances in the political arena. So tolerance is one of the most important safeguards.

The problem of minorities seems to call into question the 'one man one vote' principle, which implies that the majority has the right to dictate to the minority. The principle was asserted, particularly by Bentham, at a time when only a section of the population had political power, when it constituted a radical claim. But this simple maxim cannot constitute the full basis of democracy, for it does not solve the problem of how votes should be aggregated. A complicated voting system— some kind of PR—is needed to make 'one man one vote' true in a representative democracy. Even with PR, minorities may suffer because much more than voting rights is needed to ensure the adequate representation of their views: they also need access to MPs, to the media, and to information. 'One man one vote' implies equal capacity and equal desert on the part of all voters, an idealistic assumption, but ignores the differential weighting which particular electoral systems may give to different votes. Nor does it specify whether the elected representative is to act as a delegate, reflecting the voters' views, or as a true representative. It also treats the limited political sphere as all-important, and ignores the political significance of other factors: economic and social standing lead to inequalities of influence even in the best designed electoral system. In Britain today, the realization of 'one man one vote' through PR would presumably dissolve existing majorities into minorities and radicalize the political system, but even that dramatic change would ignore the other factors which detract from political equality. The conclusion must be that while 'one man one vote' provides a useful safeguard for individuals and emphasizes their ultimate importance in liberal democracy, considerably more factors than the vote must be taken into account in order to guarantee political justice for everybody.

DEMOCRACY AND LIBERALISM

Despite the frequent yoking together of these two ideas, a number of writers point out the potential incompatibility of the individualistic aspirations of liberalism and the collectivist democratic notion, 'the will of the people'. Analysis shows a number of theoretical conflicts which may become flashpoints in the daily politics of liberal democracy. The first problem is that of representation. Liberal ideology assumes the separation of the political and private spheres, and representative institutions achieve this *par excellence*; politics becomes an elite profession, with obvious concomitant disadvantages, but this also leaves ordinary individuals free to pursue their private interests most of the time, except on election day. This is practically convenient, but it complicates and dilutes democracy.

According to Locke, men pursue their own interests through elected governments; according to Rousseau, one person cannot represent another, and democracy should be direct and participatory. Rousseau's view seems philosophically sound. If you could represent me ideally, you would need so much understanding and knowledge of me and my interests that you would virtually be identical with me, in which case I may as well represent myself. However, given the size of nation-states, representation has long been inevitable and various theories have been developed to justify the institution by proving that the individual is in fact properly represented. First, the representative can be viewed as a delegate, who reiterates the views of constituents and expresses no independent opinion. The view expressed in *The Federalist*[49] was that the representative should be a mere spokesman, made accountable by frequent elections. Marx, in praising the democratic arrangements of the Paris Commune, emphasized the delegate role of the representatives, and the electors' power of instant dismissal.[50] The practical difficulties of a delegate system are plain: unless a single issue is at stake, how could the delegate fully represent, or even know, the wide variety of the opinions and interests of the electors? Only where electors had overwhelming common interests as perhaps they had in the Paris Commune, could this begin to work. Even the advocates of the delegate role do not suggest that electors should *instruct* their delegates in detail: the device adopted is rather that of recall, so that the 'spokesman' role really reduces to a system of strict responsibility to the electors.

A different theory of representation is the 'microcosmic' theory, which sees parliament as a microcosm of the nation. Each representative is taken to be typical of a class of persons, whose interests she will automatically promote. This would not be easy to organize, since some criteria would be needed to decide which interests are worthy of representation, but some countries have succeeded in composing second chambers on this sort of basis. Theorists have tried to solve the problem similarly: Saint-Simon's ideal parliament was to be composed of scientists, industrialists, and men of letters, these being the most important

---

49. *The Federalist*, Paper LII.
50. *The Civil War in France* in Marx and Engels, *Selected Works*, Vol. 2, Progress, 1969, pp. 220–2.

interest groups in his utopia. In the past, this 'typical' representation occurred haphazardly in Britain: a miner might be elected by a mining community—but it is less frequent as politics becomes more professionalized. In any case, elections are not vital to this form of representation: a 'typical trade unionist' could equally well be *nominated*, and a system of co-option of those who typify certain interest groups is used by some government bodies. It would also be possible, by using a random selection process, to compose a parliament of representatives typical of the population at large; some thinkers have argued that such a body would be more responsive and less elitist than an elected parliament.[51] Typical or microcosmic representation, then, is not essentially a democratic idea if democracy is equated with the electoral process: indeed, it was cited as a justification for not reforming the English Parliament in 1832 since MPs, although corruptly elected, were said to typify the interests of various groups. Certainly, in any elected body a degree of typical representation will emerge spontaneously, since those elected will have certain interests which are representative of those of a larger group in society.

The third theory, always popular in Britain, is that representatives should be accountable but independent, acting on behalf of their electors but using their own judgement. This tradition can perhaps be traced to Hobbes's assertion that the authorization of a representative binds the 'author' (elector) to follow his decisions, but gives him no control over these decisions, and in Hobbes's view does not even make the representative accountable.[52] The case for independent representatives was stated in its classic form by Burke; he admitted the MPs' ultimate responsibility to the electors, but thought that infrequent elections would preserve their independence and ability to act for the public good, and help them to avoid embroilment with the private interests of electors.[53] Behind Burke's reflections lay a faith in the wisdom of the 'natural aristocracy' from whom representatives would be drawn, and a fear of the demagogy and mob rule which might result from anything approaching popular sovereignty. Later Mill asked, 'Ought pledges to be required from members of parliament?', and decided that they should not. The voters' perception of the 'mental superiority' of the candidate should make them tolerant of his acting independently, except on the fundamental issues on which he was elected.[54] Today, British MPs jealously guard their independence, in line with such arguments, and parliament's usual reluctance to hold referenda, except in special, constitutional cases, is an assertion of parliamentary sovereignty—a doctrine which comes as something of a surprise for those who think that democracy means the sovereignty of *the people*.

Behind the notion of the independent representative lies a number of ideas; the paternalistic aspect is clear in Burke's and Mill's emphasis on the intelligence and wisdom of the representative. The view that representatives should be able to

---

51. A random selection process is recommended by E. Callenbach and M. Phillips in *A Citizen Legislature*, Banyan Tree Books, 1985, and by B. Goodwin, *Justice by Lottery*, Harvester, 1992.
52. Hobbes, *Leviathan*, Chap.16.
53. E. Burke, *Reflections on the Revolution in France*, Penguin, 1969, p. 303ff.
54. Mill, *Considerations on Representative Government*, p. 333.

promote the national interest, free of selfish interests, suggests an underlying conception of a common good, more appropriate to 'radical' democracy, and contradicting the Lockean view that a government's duty is the preservation and pursuit of individual interests. In Britain, the strength of party discipline and the theory of independent representatives means that the government may only enact the will of the people in the remotest sense, or not at all. At a fundamental level, representation conflicts with liberal individualism and makes elite government likely, with all its correlative dangers. Only by ensuring maximum accountability of the representatives to the electorate can we avoid such representation leading to a government divorced from the people. (Even if the problem of representation were solved, the British system of adversary, majoritarian politics means that 49% or more people may be unrepresented by each government—and in fact governments are often elected on the votes of 38% or less of the people. In 1997, the Labour Party received only 44% of the vote yet won nearly two-thirds of the available parliamentary seats. Thus, the mechanics of the electoral system can further dilute the democratic elements in a representative system.)

The incompatibilities between democracy and liberalism rest on the clash of two basic principles: the will of the people, and individual freedom. Berlin argues that democracy facilitates the 'positive liberty' of self-government, and, if popular sovereignty is interpreted literally, no limitation on the government's activities is theoretically allowable.[55] In other words, if the people are the sovereign, they can do anything—which would include oppressing individuals. Berlin feared that the paternalistic element in democracy was antagonistic to the liberal ideals of non-interference and minimum government. He argued that the liberal ideal might, in theory, prosper under a non-interventionist dictator: there is no necessary affinity of liberalism with democracy. The ideal for liberalism is 'every man his own legislator', but when Rousseau, Hegel, and Marx attempted to reconcile this theoretically with democracy, liberals labelled them 'authoritarian'. Whether the two political ideals are seen as compatible depends partly on the assumptions made: the postulate that people are homogeneous or classless validates the popular sovereignty of Rousseau or Marx, whereas the belief that they are irreducibly different requires a pluralist democracy with liberal safeguards in the form of individual rights. Democracy proper also requires more individual participation than liberals, who put such a high value on privacy, would countenance. The general opposition in Britain to compulsory voting (a very minimal citizen's duty) is indicative of the way in which the liberal focus on private life undermines the participatory spirit of democracy, as does the representative system.

An indirect incompatibility between the two ideals occurs through the mediating idea of equality. Democracy creates limited, *artificial* equality for everyone in the political sphere, viewed as voters, while the liberal value 'equality of opportunity' in the socio-economic sphere sanctions the development of *real* inequalities which effectively destroy the equality of the vote and of other political

---

55. I. Berlin, 'Two concepts of liberty', in *Political Philosophy* (Ed. A. Quinton), Oxford U.P., 1967.

rights. So, while democracy threatens liberalism, liberalism undermines democracy. Usually it is the radical and popular elements of democracy that are perceived as potentially threatening to liberalism; liberals are happy with the representative system which makes parliament an autonomous elite body. But it is not surprising that, despite these theoretical divergences, liberalism and democracy have blended so well historically. Both oppose older, autocratic forms of rule and claim to destroy old social hierarchies. The ideal of tolerance is common to liberalism and representative democracy, although radical democracy is criticized for its potential intolerance. Ultimately, the liberal values life above everything, and so considers peace essential, and democracy is clearly the most promising device for peaceful conflict solution. It is therefore worth suffering the occasional tensions between the two ideals, from the liberal's viewpoint.

DEMOCRACY AND TRUTH

The long-standing controversy over what form of democracy is ideal rests ultimately on conflicting perceptions of the relation of democracy to truth. An important axiom of formal logic is the 'law' of the excluded middle, which states that a proposition is either true or false. This impeccable, dichotomous reasoning cannot be transferred directly to the real world, where it is often fallacious to propose two alternatives as if these exhausted the available possibilities. 'Either he is a Marxist or he is not' is logically correct, a matter of definition, but 'Those who are not with us are against us' fallaciously excludes various alternatives or 'middles'. The exclusion of intermediate possibilities entails a choice between two propositions which, by implication, encompass between them all the possibilities. This is false in the contingent real world.

The relevance of this to British politics is that our populist democracy has long operated on the covert assumption that there are only two sides to every question, a further implication being that one side is necessarily right. This dichotomous approach to politics has sometimes even been blamed on the rectangular shape of the House of Commons, which supposedly encourages the two-party system. The 'winner takes all' electoral system also certainly plays its part. Much parliamentary procedure seems to stem from a misapplication of the law of the excluded middle. In voting, MPs are forced to choose between policies presented as dichotomies which exclude other viable alternatives—although these are sometimes dealt with as amendments. 'Either–or' logic, in conjunction with the two-party system, moulds the form in which policy issues are perceived, and presented to the public. It also influences our perception of voter rationality: 'Don't knows' are treated as just that, and never as a group of people who might adhere to options which they cannot express through voting. The dichotomous approach has beguiled us into a system of adversary politics, whose shortcomings Johnson exposed in *In Search of the Constitution*:[56] it also causes us to believe that one-party systems, where only one side of any question is—supposedly—put, are

_____

56. N. Johnson, *In Search of the Constitution*, Pergamon, 1977.

undemocratic. Even the increasing strength of a third party, the Liberal Democrats, has scarcely changed the 'either–or' manner in which political issues are presented to the British public.

In order to criticize or validate this approach to politics, we have to decide whether democracy deals in truth, opinion or the representation of material interests. If it deals in truth, and if we could be sure of being right, only one side of the question would need to be put, the right side, and a one-party system would be adequate. British democracy actually represents opinions and interests in parliament but, deceptively, the rhetoric of our politics is about truth. Are there in fact objectively right solutions to political questions, or only *preferred* solutions (opinions)? Depending on how we answer this, we can decide what organizational form is best for ascertaining the truth, or for reflecting preferences. A caveat is needed about truth. The difficulty of determining objective truths even in science has been discussed, and this book has emphasized the permeation of all political thought and activity by ideological elements. Truth must be established with implicit reference to some epistemology, or theory of knowledge; but rival epistemologies abound. However, some past political philosophers dealt with truth as if it were unproblematic, and realizable in politics, notably Plato and Rousseau.

During the Enlightenment, Rousseau and Condorcet based political theories on the assumption that political truths 'exist' and await discovery. Rousseau's analysis of the common good is typical: for any political problem, there is one solution which would conduce to the good of all members of society, the 'true' solution. This depends on his assumption that people's interests are similar. If reality *is* structured like this, one-party democracies are justified and so is enlightened despotism or the rule of Plato's Guardians. For both Rousseau and Condorcet, political truth was fused with moral right. The idea of the common good was also adopted by the liberal T. H. Green, who made it the basis of political obligation. Plamenatz has argued that the idea is fallacious or nonsensical: the idea that two non-identical individuals could share a common good is suspect, and in a self-proclaimedly pluralistic society the notion is evidently false.[57] This discovery is not fatal to the idea, however: in every case there must be an optimal policy which would benefit as many people as possible— if only this could be infallibly calculated. But we might not label merely optimal politics as 'true' or 'right'. Condorcet and, in our own time, Black, have mathematically shown that if each individual has a 51% chance of being right in a decision, the majority has a more than equal chance of being right, which approaches 100% the more nearly the majority approaches unanimity.[58] However, 'being right' suggests that politics is a matter of deciding what is true, which may not be the case.

Some political questions *can* be posed so that there is an objectively true answer. Will a reduction in public expenditure increase unemployment? We know

---

57. Plamenatz, *Consent, Freedom and Political Obligation*, Chap. 3.
58. B. Barry, 'The public interest', in *Political Philosophy* (Ed. A. Quinton), Oxford U.P., 1967, p. 122.

that it will. The role of politicians is not to discover or verify this but to decide whether it is a good thing. Ultimately, major political questions turn on judgements of value, rather than truth. But can there be a *right* choice between values (in which case Rousseau's system is still appropriate) or are we merely forced to accept majority opinion on such matters? Modern liberal-democratic theorists have imbibed the logical positivists' view that value judgements are unverifiable, so that no rational method can exist for choosing between them. In the absence of such standards, opinion is the only guide. Liberal-democratic theory makes the simplifying assumption that the vote reflects such opinion, the political consumer's preference. This stipulation is probably untrue in the absence of the conditions built into an abstract model of political choice (i.e. voting), which state that the voter should have perfect knowledge of all the alternatives, and be offered a full range of choices. In voting conditions of restricted choice, it is mere deception to argue that an expressed preference is anything more than a suboptimal choice, the best of non-ideal alternatives. However, in the absence of divinable political truths and in the realm of unverifiable values, opinion is omnipotent. Most modern theories of democracy assume that opinion and interests are the stuff of politics, and they prescribe maximizing strategies, rather than procedures for determining what is true and right.

The suboptimal conditions under which the voter expresses her opinions must be emphasized, in view of the interpretation of election results in democratic countries as a mandate, and as 'the will of the people'. Perhaps, if the presuppositions of the various theoretical models were fulfilled, such an interpretation would be valid. And if, as Rousseau assumed, we lived in a small, close-knit society, what we chose might always be for the common good. Again, if in Britain we had equal constituencies, proportional representation, a range of parties reflecting all shades of political opinion and MPs who acted as delegates, our elections might indicate the will of the people and so realize the representative democratic ideal. But, given imperfect conditions, what value or interpretation are we entitled to put on election results?

Asking whether democratic politics is, ideally, about truth, values, opinions or interests, helps us to highlight the assumptions underlying our own political system. If MPs are regarded as representatives who apply their superior knowledge and intelligence to make correct decisions, the inference is that the purpose of the political system is to discover truth and right. On the other hand, a system of delegation or typical representation suggests that politics is a matter of expressing opinions and interests. It is not surprising to find that recent theories of voting—elitist, cynical but doubtless realistic—argue that voting has a largely *expressive* or therapeutic function, which allows people to express their views and let off steam while politicians and civil servants go about their business of taking decisions, with very little accountability to the electorate. The British government of the day justifies its measures by whichever theory of politics fits best: sometimes MPs are enlightened representatives, deciding what is right (as when they abolished capital punishment despite the fact that majority public opinion was against this), more often they seek to reflect their electors' interests. Because we are all, by and large, moralists, government decisions are usually clothed in the language of 'truth' and 'right' which is, in fact, inappropriate to liberal democracy. The liberal outlook emphasizes the importance of individual interests, the variety of possible truths, and the need for tolerance, so that the claim of a democratic system to decide on truth and right is in principle antithetical to the liberal ideal.

Another way of expressing the difference between liberals and other democrats on this matter is that, for someone like Rousseau, the right solution still exists even if politicians fail to discover it, whereas the liberal may consider even a second-best solution as optimal, in that it is the expression of public opinion. Marxists, like Rousseau, look to politics for the discovery of truth and the establishment of right, arousing deep suspicion among liberals. An idealistic answer to the question of what politics is about is that it *should be* about truth and right while, pragmatically, it still has to take some account of individuals' interests. The conclusion must be that your view of the nature and the goal of politics determines the theory of democracy which you opt for.

THE WILL OF THE PEOPLE

This chapter has shown the empirical obstacles which stand in the way of the democratic realization of 'the will of the people'; it also points to the conclusion that the idea itself is theoretically problematic, as Riley has demonstrated, for the same reasons that 'the common good' is problematic.[59] Whereas a Marxist government, modelling itself on Rousseau's theory, might proclaim that it represents the will of the people, a liberal democracy has to solve the problem of how a general will could be reached by the aggregation of individual wills, a task made even harder by the work of Arrow, which shows that individuals' wishes cannot be satisfactorily aggregated into socially beneficial choices.[60] Schumpeter attempts a theoretical solution in his 'neoclassical' theory of democracy, which aims to revise the classical democratic ideal, which he defines as:

> That institutional arrangement for arriving at political decisions which realizes the common good by making the people itself decide issues through the election of individuals who are to assemble in order to carry out its will.

He shows that this definition embodies four fallacious assumptions concerning the common good, the will of the people, rationality, and the existence of definite answers to political questions. He then sets out to substitute a theory free from such questionable assumptions, which centres on *leadership*. Democracy is:

> That institutional arrangement for arriving at political decisions in which individuals acquire the power to decide by means of a competitive struggle for the people's vote.[61]

---

59. P. Riley, *Will and Political Legitimacy*, Harvard U.P., 1982.
60. K. Arrow, *Social Choice and Individual Values*, 2nd edn, Yale U.P., 1963, Chap. 5 especially.
61. J. Schumpeter, *Capitalism, Socialism and Democracy*, Allen & Unwin, 1943, pp. 250, 269 especially.

The essence of democratic procedure becomes the choosing of a 'national executive', or government—a practical conclusion which Schumpeter reached by observing the American political scene, rather than a theoretical insight. The idea of a *manufactured will* is central to his theory; this 'artificial will' is created by the leaders and by 'the persuaders', so that it becomes widely accepted as the will of the people. Other theorists have also accepted the need to create an artificial will where people are passive or ill-informed: Rousseau's legislator, and Bentham's, and Mill's informed minorities execute such a task.

The virtue of such a system is that the leaders can take into account the long-term interests which individuals might ignore, opting for immediate gains; its vice is the lack of protection against the self-interest of such leaders. Schumpeter believes he has taken care of this by emphasizing the accountability of leaders through elections, but if the leaders can manufacture a will, they can certainly achieve acceptance of policies furthering their personal interests. Neoclassical theory reintroduces the risk of manipulative leaders, against which the democratic tradition always struggled by advocating 'the will of the people' as the final arbiter. Schumpeter seems to have abandoned the concept of democracy as a *good in itself*, and dedicated himself to describing what is a reasonably workable form of government, given the size of modern nation-states and our sentimental attachment to democratic formulae; however, he concedes that democracy upholds certain values, which is why it deserves support. But Schumpeter's theory seems, like that of Dahl, to endow a descriptive account of Western (more precisely, American) government with a normative value.

Much has been written about the role of 'public opinion' in controlling seemingly intractable political institutions and making them bow to the will of the people. Bryce, in *Modern Democracies* (1921), a comparative study of various democracies, asked, 'How is the people to exercise its power?'. 'By voting' is the usual answer, but Bryce argued that 'what purports to be the will of the people is largely a factitious product, not really their will' because of the representative system, corruption, and the reduction of all men's opinions, wise and foolish, to the same weight (an anti-democratic point).[62] He argued that public opinion should be an independent factor in the governmental process, operating to control and influence elected representatives. The current ubiquity of opinion polls suggests that this is the one of the rare cases where the will of a political theorist was realized. However, the addition of public opinion as a separate factor adds little to democratic theory, in which it was always implicit, although we are now able to quantify such opinion, which may make it more influential.

One attempt to amend the practice of liberal democracy so as to realize the will of the people was the widespread movement for participation of the 1960s and 1970s in the West, which fought against centralization, bureaucracy and the increasing elitism of politics. The continuing participation movement can be viewed as an attempt to persuade individuals to become in reality the active, rational, informed citizens of Mill's democratic theory, operating not primarily in

62. J. Bryce, *Modern Democracies*, Macmillan, 1926, 2 vols.

the narrow political sphere, but within the plethora of groups and organizations in society. (In Britain, the Liberal Democrats' long-standing demand for decentralization and regionalism is symptomatic of the participatory ideal, as is the Labour Party's policy on Scottish and Welsh devolution.) Participation does not merely denote a higher level of political activity, through established political channels, but the intervention of citizens in areas formerly thought to be the province of politicians, civil servants or experts: experiments with worker participation and Community Health Councils are examples of forms of participation inaugurated from above, while the formation of tenants' and neighbourhood associations and other self-help groups such as those for women and ethnic minorities are participation initiated from below. The idea of widespread participation challenges various preconceptions of liberal democratic ideology—the primacy of the representative system, and the separation of politics from other parts of life and the desirability of 'apathy'—and might eventually bring about a revision of the theory, although in empirical analysis the phenomenon of participation can comfortably be accommodated within an account of pluralist democracy. Liberalism has always been ambivalent about participation: the individual is paramount, she wishes to protect her interests, she is politically rational and capable, but ultimately she prefers to spend time on other things, while retaining a notional ultimate control over the politicians. Any growth in the theory and practice of participation could help to make that control more than just notional.[63] A further contribution to the participation debate is made by recent literature on accountability in education, health, science and other areas subject to government intervention. However, the principle of account-ability is a second-best principle—an attempt to exert some retrospective control over policies and institutions which are, by and large, not democratically constituted. Accountability is no substitute for participation. There have also been various proposals for reconstituting democratic institutions by introducing elements of randomness or rotation into the selection of representatives, to create more 'typical' and responsive governments and to counteract corruption and elitism.[64]

NEW FORMS OF DEMOCRACY

Proposals for transforming democracy in the 1990s have also emphasized citizen involvement in the political process. *Deliberative democracy* is a new, flexible version of the more institutionalized participation theories of the 1970s which turns on the quality of the debate of political participants rather on the mechanics

---

63. For interesting discussions of participation see G. Duncan (Ed.), *Democratic Theory and Practice*, Cambridge U.P., 1983; D. Held and C. Pollitt (Eds.), *New Forms of Democracy*, Sage, 1986. On participation, see also C. Pateman, *Participation and Democratic Theory*, Cambridge U.P., 1970, P. Green, *Retrieving Democracy*, Methuen, 1985, and J. H. Nagel, *Participation*, Prentice-Hall, 1987.
64. See B. Goodwin, *Justice by Lottery*, Chap.7, for a summary of recent proposals for random selection and rotation.

of participation. It challenges recent views that (i) democracy is the expression of private interests and a resolution of conflicts between them; (ii) it is the wise choices of elite representatives; (iii) it is mere competition between parties for votes and (iv) it serves a merely 'expressive' function. Deliberative theories seek to reinstate the role of reason and logic in democracy, without reverting to the Enlightenment view that there is a right answer to any political question which democracy should strive to reach. In these new theories we can see the influence of Habermas's idea of 'communicative action' which rests on individuals in a political situation trying to reach understanding through dialogue. In such situations truth, normative legitimacy and sincerity should characterize the 'discourse' and the better argument should prevail.

James Fishkin has master-minded experimental debates on the 'deliberative opinion poll' model. Election candidates meet a sample of 'delegates' selected to be representative of the entire electorate and over several days they discuss policy issues with candidates and with each other and express preferences on issues and candidates. Their conclusions provide a guide to how the whole electorate would think if all voters had the same opportunities for deliberation, a guide which politicians should regard as 'prescriptive'. In Fishkin's view,

> Deliberative opinion polls offer a new kind of democracy, one that combines deliberation and political equality . . . [it] gives to a microcosm of the entire nation the opportunities for thoughtful interaction and opinion formation . . . it brings the face-to-face democracy of the Athenian Assembly or the New England town meeting to the large-scale nation state.[65]

There are three conditions for democracy, Fishkin argues: (1) there must be political equality, (2) decisions must embody deliberation and (3) the system must avoid tyranny of the majority. He considers the USA is moving towards a 'plebiscitary model' of democracy, where policies are formulated in accordance with the views expressed in opinion polls, but argues that this approach achieves political equality at the expense of deliberation. He also believes that information technology could make deliberative democracy a reality, and suggests 'the electronic town meeting' where the citizens network by computer and can express their views—an idea canvassed as long ago as 1970 by Wolff, who imagined an 'in-the-home voting machine' which would enable citizens to vote on policy issues after watching a television debate.[66] The idea that technology can overcome politicians' lack of responsiveness to the electorate is now a common one, but one obstacle to the realization of electronic democracy is the cost of wiring everyone up. Major objections are that non-literate citizens would be marginalized or excluded and that the resulting system would almost certainly privilege self-selected activists and interest groups.

While deliberative democracy seeks to overcome some of the failings of representative democracy, 'associative democracy' seeks to re-structure the

---

65. J. Fishkin, *Democracy and Deliberation*, Yale U.P., 1991, p. 4. See also Fishkin, *The Dialogue of Justice: Towards a Self-Reflective Society*, Yale U.P., 1992 and D. Miller, 'Deliberative Democracy and Social Choice', *Political Studies*, Special Issue 1992, pp. 54–67.
66. R. P. Wolff, *In Defense of Anarchism*, Harper & Row, 1970, pp. 34–35.

political process itself. Paul Hirst argues for the transfer of many state functions to 'voluntary and democratically self-governing associations'.[67] The state would be decentralized and the political structure would become more pluralistic through power-sharing between such associations. Thirdly, he proposes an economy organized on the basis of mutualism, with co-operative-style firms where workers participate in the management and governance. Hirst's associationalism is an unusual blend of New Right ideas (rolling back the state), nineteenth-century socialist and anarchist ideas (mutualism and co-operativism), guild socialism and contemporary beliefs about the virtues of pluralism and multi-culturalism. As with deliberative democracy, we may wonder what chance it has of being realized.

This account of democratic theories has shown the fallacy of distinguishing too strictly between means and ends, although such a distinction must be attempted in principle. The idealistic spirit of democracy is constantly modified in the attempt to realize it institutionally, as is shown by the imperfections of democracies all the world over. The analysis has touched on practical problems such as the irresponsibility of institutions, the anomalies of voting behaviour and the problems of representation, which may seem to be procedural matters, because such factors colour and modify our perception of the ideal. None of the ideal versions of democracy is likely to be fully realized because of such practical obstacles. The theory of democracy which we adopt depends ultimately on other ideological beliefs that we hold. In *The Real World of Democracy* (1966), Macpherson challenged the Western conviction of the superiority and uniquely democratic nature of liberal democracy. He distinguished the narrow sense of democracy (which entails certain rights and institutions) from a broader sense, conceived in terms of the equality achievable in a classless society. This distinction makes it possible to evaluate the democracies of communist and developing countries. The 'communist democracies' failed to implement the narrower sense of democracy, but had some claim to be democratic in the broader sense, while one-party states in the developing countries may, under certain conditions, achieve 'narrow' democracy and are usually dedicated to implementing the 'broad' democratic goal of an equal society. Macpherson thus showed that the democratic ideal can be put into practice in different ways: liberals do not have a monopoly of democratic virtue. Indeed, Macpherson himself argued that liberal democracy has not lived up to its claim to maximize satisfaction and that important changes are needed.

There is a considerable literature on the relevance of democracy to developing countries. Democracy is clearly a culture-specific system and ideal and its claims to universal application have been disputed. Prominent non-Western politicians, such as Lee Kuan Yew of Singapore, have argued that democracy is inappropriate to non-Western cultures and 'tiger economies'. Many Islamic revivalists would take a similar view. African leaders have also argued for the democratic validity of their one-party systems. Space constraints prevent me from exploring these arguments here but, as Parekh argues, beyond liberal democracy stand more

---

67. P. Hirst, 'Associative Democracy', *Dissent*, Spring 1994, pp. 243–4. See also P. Hirst, *Associative Democracy*, Polity Press, 1993.

universal principles of good government which may license different kinds of democracy and may even validate non-democratic systems.[68]

In conclusion it must be emphasized that democracy, in any of its ideal versions, is concerned with the maintenance and extension of human liberty through self-government. However, the ideal needs the support of other ideological beliefs to gain substance, and the fusing of democracy with ideology often seems to transform democratic theory and practice out of recognition. Ultimately, and ideally, every theory of democracy seeks to uphold the political equality of human beings, the value of deliberation, and the exchange of ideas and the resolution of conflict by peaceful means.

FURTHER READING

A. H. Birch, *The Concepts and Theories of Modern Democracy*, Routledge, 1993.
I. Budge, *The New Challenge of Direct Democracy*, Polity Press, 1996.
D. Copp, J. Roemer, J. Hampton (Eds.), *The Idea of Democracy*, Cambridge U.P., 1995.
R. Dahl, *Democracy and its Critics*, Yale U.P., 1989.
G. Duncan (Ed.), *Democratic Theory and Practice*, Cambridge U.P., 1983.
P. Green, *Retrieving Democracy*, Methuen, 1985.
R. Harrison, *Democracy*, Routledge, 1995.
D. Held, *Models of Democracy*, 2nd edn., Polity Press, 1996.
D. Held (Ed.) *Prospects for Democracy*, *Political Studies*, (1992) **XL**, Special Issue.
P. Hirst, *Associative Democracy*, Polity Press, 1993.
B. Holden, *Understanding Liberal Democracy*, Philip Allan, 1988.
C. B. Macpherson, *The Real World of Democracy*, Oxford U.P., 1966.
C. B. Macpherson, *The Life and Times of Liberal Democracy*, Oxford U.P., 1977.
A. Phillips, *Democracy and Difference*, Polity Press, 1993.
A. Weale, *Democracy*, Macmillan, 1997.

---

68. B. Parekh, 'The cultural particularity of liberal democracy', *Political Studies*, **XL**, Special Issue, 1992, pp. 160–75.

Chapter 13

Power, Authority and the State

This chapter deals with one side of the most important polarity of modern political society, the polarity between the state and the individual. In liberal thought, individual freedom and rights are given primacy: they are seen as necessary attributes of human beings. The powers and rights of the state are held in trust and are limited by people's natural rights. This view would also be professed by social-democratic parties and by some conservative parties operating within liberal-democratic systems. Some ideologies accord primacy to the state, however—fascism and other doctrines based on an organic conception of society, and communism in its practice. Individual rights are then perceived as something granted to individuals by the state, which is the locus of all powers and rights, and strictly limited by the state's interests. The polarity between the rights of the people and the authority of the state thus disappears, or is only detectable if there is dissent or protest.

Before broaching the topic of the state and its role, it is important to review the concepts of power and authority: without these, the state could not exist. In particular, authority and political obligation (discussed in Chapter 15) are concepts with an important subjective component which determine our attitude to that contemporary reality, the state—although the state itself is, of course, also a social construct, whose operations depend on the people's attitude.

WHAT IS POWER?

Questions of power have been much discussed in the last hundred years by political scientists and sociologists; the exercise of power, and power relationships, are also of interest to psychologists. There is, unfortunately, no space here to enter into the fascinating question of motivation: why do people wish to exert power over each other? Is there an instinct which impels us to try and impose our wishes on others—the 'will to power', as Nietzsche called it—or is it, as Hobbes suggested, merely the scarcity of resources which precipitates power struggles? Modern political thinkers usually avoid these difficult questions by considering the phenomenon of power in institutionalized contexts and archetypal situations. They take it for granted that people are power-seekers, for whatever reasons. Thinkers adhering to ideologies other than liberalism—most notably the anarchists—would question this assumption and argue that power struggles and the thirst for power were symptoms of sick societies which had infected their members: in an anarchist society, the concept of power would be unknown. However, in most other ideologies the issue of power, and how it can be regulated, is an important debate, one to which political philosophers have much to contribute. The distinction between power and authority has exercised many philosophers, who feel that there should be a sharp demarcation between the two rather than the blurring and merging which typifies them in political life. The approach recommended by linguistic philosophers, that we should study the everyday uses of such terms, leads to endless confusion since people, even philosophers, use them interchangeably. If we eschew everyday usage, six separate archetypes can be distinguished which run the gamut of the exercise of power in politics:

(1) *Authority*. This attaches to offices and requires a subjectively deferential attitude on the part of citizens to be fully established. Those in authority may also have recourse to (2)–(5), however.
(2) *Power*. The general ability to influence others which a politician, office-holder or other politically active individual has, and to cause them to do what he/she wants.
(3) *Powers*. Particular rights of office-holders, e.g. the police power to search for drugs, the tax inspector's power to examine bank accounts.
(4) *Coercive power*. The power to make people do things and to punish them if they refuse. This operates according to *rules*, unlike (5).
(5) *Force*. This most accurately describes the use of (4) in an unstructured situation (e.g. during a war or revolution) by a group with a recognizable political identity—the army, a guerrilla band.
(6) *Violence*. As suggested in Chapter 6, this is an emotive and pejorative term. But physically coercive and destructive acts by unauthorized people in orderly situations are usually termed 'violence'. This differs from (4) and (5) in that violence does not usually coerce people to do particular things, but forces the authorities to take notice—e.g. terrorist acts.

The guiding principles determining which of these methods a political operator chooses are effectiveness, economy and acceptability. In the case of a government in a 'normal' situation, (1) will be preferred over (2) as embodying all three criteria, and (2) over (3), and so on. In a revolutionary situation, the order may be reversed, to achieve greater effectiveness. There are many societies where effectiveness and economy are subordinated to other goals such as revenge, or where those in power choose to substitute violence for regulated coercive power— hence the length of Amnesty International's list of torture and other atrocities. With the boundaries between these various concepts provisionally drawn, it is possible to analyse the concept of power. The German sociologist, Max Weber, defined power as '[t]he chance of a man or of a number of men to realize their own will in a communal action even against the resistance of others who are participating in the action'.[1] Power, then, is the ability to cause someone to act in a way which she would not choose, left to herself, in other words, to force someone to do something against her will, by some means. At the personal level, we control others by persuading, threatening, provoking, frustrating them: at the political level, the threat of some sanction, the use of propaganda, the invocation of particular powers, are all operations of power. The different kinds of behaviour which constitutes the exercise of power fall into two categories, 'power over' and 'power to'. Dowding makes an analytical distinction between these two types of political power, defining them as *outcome power*, 'the ability of an actor to bring about or help to bring about outcomes' and *social power*, 'the ability of an actor deliberately to change the incentive structure of another actor or actors to bring about . . . outcomes'.[2] To change someone's preferences ('incentive structure') to achieve your own ends may seem a more innocuous use of power than coercion, but the process still restricts that person's freedom. (Coercion also changes preferences structures: you may prefer to hand over your money to a mugger to being beaten up.) It may be easier to blame someone who visibly has outcome power—and to react against it—than to detect someone's social power.

Political theory asks questions about what power is, where it lies and where it should lie; the answers are interdependent. The second question has caused much controversy among political scientists and is at the heart of the debates on community power (see Chapter 12, the section on 'Elitists and pluralists'). The question whether power lies with individuals (as exchange and transactionist theorists would argue, seeing each exercise of power as part of an individual exchange) or with groups whose members would have no influence alone, is important, as is the analysis of the kind of power created by institutions with rules and norms, such as Weber describes. But what *is* power? Russell defined it as the production of *intended* results: the unforeseen effects of our influence on others cannot be called power.[3] This suggests that power is an *activity*, judged to exist by its consequences, so that power cannot 'lie' somewhere, dormant. Other theorists speak of power as if it were *possessed* by people or groups, which suggests that it *is* possible to have power without always using it. This led elite theorists to invent the mystifying concept of 'latent power', power which lies dormant. On this view, power is an attribute rather than a political activity. The question whether power is a possession/attribute or an activity seems to be something of a verbal wrangle. Someone exercising power must be described as having power (at that moment): someone who formally has, but is not at present exercising, power must also be said to have power. The distinction may be useful for political science

1. M. Weber, *From Max Weber* (Eds. H. H. Gerth and C. Wright Mills), Routledge & Kegan Paul, 1948, p. 180.
2. K. Dowding, *Rational Choice and Political Power*, Edward Elgar, 1991, p. 48.
3. B. Russell, *Power*, Allen & Unwin, 1938.

investigations, and for constitutional theorists but is not especially important for political theorists considering where power *should* lie.

Those who have power (of types 2, 3 and 4) on the political scene are usually office-holders, and also people with special resources which give them political 'muscle'. Power-relevant resources, such as the ability to withdraw labour, may create powerful groups who even rival the government or become engaged in conflict with it, as did the large unions in Britain in the 1970s. Without subscribing to the idea of latent power as a sort of permanent possession, one may say that groups with substantial resources (of money, manpower, etc.) are *potentially powerful*, meaning that they are in a position to exercise power if they choose to intervene. For example, the established Church in England is potentially powerful, but normally stays out of politics. In some countries the Church exercises considerable political power—the influential Catholic Church in Poland does so and therefore it is actually, as well as potentially, powerful. Thus, power seems to be a function both of the possession of power-relevant resources, and of activity, so that either criterion taken alone would not adequately account for the variety of power phenomena, or adequately describe the distribution of power in a particular society.

Why, in a normal political situation, can some people freely exert power over others? The organization of the state establishes certain channels for the enforcement of decisions, and discourages or forbids the exercise of power outside these. Political institutions give powers and other resources to office-holders. In what Weber defines as legal–rational–bureaucratic societies, a description which includes most modern societies, laws and conventions attach both authority and power to *offices*, not to their incumbents. 'The throne is not an empty chair' signifies that the powers and responsibilities of monarchy attach to the throne itself, and to individuals only by virtue of their temporary occupation of the throne. Likewise, the chain of command in the armed forces exists irrespective of which individuals fill the positions, or of their personal merits. In the modern state, the individual's exercise of power has little to do with physical strength, but everything to do with role. In the case of those operating outside the formal power structure, it is probably determined by their economic resources: trades unions may have no formal place in political decision-making but their economic strength may enable them to exercise power and influence decisions. In self-defence against such informal—and threatening—manifestations of power, the state reasserts vigorously its 'right' to the monopoly of power in society, and may pass laws to reduce the scope of such groups for exercising power—as the Conservative government did in the 1980s, to decrease the power of unions in Britain.

Although the powers attached to office come close to authority, political theorists have traditionally distinguished between the two, and separated them conceptually, as a safeguard against tyranny. They also recommend a separation in practice: Plato's Guardians formed a distinct class from the law-enforcing auxiliaries, and Locke advocated a 'balance of powers' between the legislature and the executive (the government), with a view to curtailing the latter's exercise of power by the former's authority as sovereign. But in another tradition, the two are fused: for Hobbes, any such division of labour within the sovereign would have been fatal—'divide and fall'. In reality, the possession of executive power by an organ of the state usually gives it a certain authority, by accidental or deliberate transference—as in the case of the police. The reason why theorists distinguish so sharply between power and authority and try to show the latter to be supreme is that they see *coercion* as the archetype of political power, a form of power which can easily get out of control and must be resisted on humanitarian grounds. Plamenatz writes

> It is a mistake to suppose that power is prior to right and obligation. No man has power unless his right to command is acknowledged by some at least of those who obey him; it is only because they obey him that he has power. All exercise of power is *subject to rules*; it is in principle regular and *cannot last long or be effective if it is often arbitrary*.[4]

Plamenatz's argument is that there is a sense in which we always acquiesce in someone else's exercise of power, and obey their commands of our own free will, even if under duress: you can *drag* the horse to the water, but you can't make it drink. Coercive power alone 'cannot last long or be effective'. Unfortunately, this last remark expresses optimism rather than a necessary truth, for there is no logical or practical reason why a regime based on arbitrary and coercive power should not maintain itself for a long time if it is willing to pay the extra cost of such an uneconomic form of rule. Lukes has distinguished between power based on acquiescence or co-operation and power based on coercion: the former is more common in a stable society, although it is clearly important to have a philosophical analysis of the latter, which will enable us to identify and combat abuses of coercive power, and the use of force. Lukes also argues that a thorough investigation of power would take into account the latent conflict of the interests of the powerful with the *real* interests of the non-powerful, who are deluded or manipulated by a system which works against their real interests. The powerful exercise their power preventively, to stop the interests of the have-nots from reaching the political agenda and the powerless may accede to this, because they suffer from false consciousness.[5]

WHAT CREATES AUTHORITY?

Whether power based on co-operation should instead count as authority can best be answered by analysing the latter concept. Today's authority is the site of yesterday's struggle for power. Experts in jurisprudence describe power as a *de facto* concept, concerning fact or actions, while authority is a *de jure* concept, concerning right. The primary aim of any regime which displaces another by force is to transmute its coercive power into authority, by invoking legal and moral concepts on its behalf, to achieve the deference and co-operation of the people, and to establish its legitimacy in their minds. A government's authority rests both

---

4. J. P. Plamenatz, *German Marxism and Russian Communism*, Longmans, Green & Co., 1954.
5. S. Lukes, *Power: A Radical View*, Macmillan, 1975.

on its legal validity, and on the people's acknowledgement of political obligation, which in turn commands their loyalty to government and the laws. Hence authority has an objective aspect and an internal, subjective aspect and is incomplete and precarious unless both of these are achieved. Where coercion creates obedience at a high cost in manpower and equipment, authority can control both the minds and behaviour of individuals at a very low cost, once it is established and accepted.

Authority's objective basis is usually the law. In a democratic country, it emanates from the constitution which expresses the sovereignty of the people and guarantees the legality of the laws, whereas in, say, an Islamic republic it rests ultimately on the divine will as expressed in the Koran. (We cannot ask that this higher law should be validated by further laws without risk of an infinite regression. As Hart has said, the justification of higher law takes the form of a value judgement—reference to a moral code, for example.[6]) In a post-revolutionary situation, the new regime seeks to create authority by enacting a new constitution. This is not difficult, since the law is ultimately self-validating, according to the positivist view of law,[7] but the regime may have difficulty in persuading people accustomed to an earlier constitution and political tradition to adopt a suitably deferential attitude to its new creation. Probably no usurping or revolutionary regime can exist for long where a widely established democratic tradition emphasizes the people's part in bestowing authority, and given that the exercise of coercive power is so much more costly and less effective than the invocation of authority. But authority is hard to achieve if the people fiercely oppose the new regime, and it takes time to create deference. The English Revolution of 1688 was an example of a popular revolution where enough elements of the previous system were wisely preserved—in particular, parliament—for the majority of the people to transfer their loyalty to the new regime and accept the constitutional laws which it passed.[8] In other situations, a new regime may have to be on its best behaviour for a long time before it gains legitimacy in the eyes of the people.

The interaction between power and authority, fact and right, engrossed all the classical political theorists. Machiavelli is notorious for arguing in *The Prince* that a new ruler, perhaps a usurper, who cannot claim a hereditary or religious basis for his position, must become an expert in the exercise of power and the manipulation of the people to survive, using opportunistic tactics and an 'economy of violence'. Authority is thus not essential in the short run although the prince seeks to acquire it in the long term. Hobbes's sovereign is appointed to enforce obedience to the covenant. In so far as the original contractors authorized him, he is in authority over them. But later generations obey the sovereign for prudential reasons, fearing a return to anarchy, so he could be said to be in power

6. H. L. A. Hart, *The Concept of Law*, Oxford U.P., 1961, Chap. VI, s.1.
7. Austin's famous positivist account of law as the commands of the sovereign backed by force means that no further justification need be sought if there is a determinate, supreme sovereign in a polity. For a modern positivist account of law, see Hart, *The Concept of Law*, Chap. II.
8. The Bill of Rights (1689) placed the monarchy firmly under the law and ensured free elections and free debate in Parliament.

over them, rather than in authority. This is particularly true if one ruler is replaced by another, perhaps by force. The new ruler now fills the role of the sovereign who can alone prevent a reversion to the state of nature, and so is still owed prudential obedience. Hobbes's model has the possibly unintended consequence of legitimizing any successful coup and the *de facto* power thereby established. Only if the original contractors' obligation could somehow be transmitted across generations could new sovereigns be proved to have authority as well as power. Doubtless Hobbes realized that legitimacy was an important attribute of any sovereign, but it is not logically required in his theory, because of the emphasis on prudential obedience.

Locke, by contrast, locates authority in the people as the supreme sovereign. Authority and power are delegated in limited amounts to the government, which remains subordinate to the sovereign people. Individuals are, however, bound to accept the authority and obey the laws of a properly constituted government because these are laws to which they have consented. The contract theories especially make it clear that nothing except coercive power exists in a pre-social situation, where men seek to dominate each other and each individual is fully 'the author' of his own actions, and that authority comes about with the creation of society and a division of labour between the rulers and the ruled. We can be fairly sure that a state based purely on coercive power would be less pleasant for the inhabitants, and less efficient, than one based on authority, so that theories about the nature and creation of authority are important: authority may rest on people's subjective attitudes, but it is a concept with a recognizable counterpart in real life, unlike obligation.

Weber's famous analysis of power is, in fact, a sociological account of authority. Weber was a radical individualist, but also a strong upholder of the primacy of the nation-state, which he considered the final measure of value. Weber himself set little store by the idea of government by the people, but he viewed democracy as a means of selecting the dynamic leadership which he believed Germany needed after the 1918 defeat. He saw different political organizations as 'power structures', each with a 'specific internal dynamic'; on the basis of their power, members claimed specific types of prestige. Three 'ideal types' of organization were distinguished by Weber:[9]

(1) Patriarchal or traditional power supported by traditions and myths.
(2) Bureaucratic power, resting on a rational legal structure and characterized by impersonal rules and regularities, and authority attached to offices.
(3) Charismatic power, which rests on the leader's personality and is the antithesis of permanent, rule-bound authority.

Most interesting is the analysis of charismatic power, also referred to by Weber as charismatic authority. This concept disturbs many political theorists, especially since the rise of Hitler, because it connotes an unpredictable, uncontrollable factor which may threaten or supersede the bureaucratic-democratic form of

---

9. Weber, *From Max Weber*, Part II. 'Ideal types' was Weber's term for archetypes or models in sociological theory.

authority which typifies modern Western society. Although it constitutes a negation of *legally based* authority, charismatic authority essentially relies on the deference of the leader's disciples, for without them she is nothing. Unlike the impersonal authority which characterizes institutions, such authority is entirely personal, and its loss entails immediate loss of the power to influence her followers. Early charismatic leaders were war heroes and divine prophets— today's are demagogues and, occasionally, the leaders of religious cults. Weber sees charisma as ephemeral, but thinks that it can be routinized 'into a suitable source for the acquisition of sovereign power by the successors of the charismatic hero'. He notes that most charismatic kings had regular recourse to a permanent scapegoat to protect themselves from blame for failures, something recommended by Machiavelli; this suggests that charisma is incompatible with responsibility, whereas legally constituted authority and accountability are inseparable. Weber actually considered democratic leadership as a form of charismatic authority, disguised as consent-based legitimacy. The scope for charismatic leaders in a stable, pluralist democracy may seem small, but we can predict that they will emerge in times of crisis. Whether they are successful, and whether they are a blessing or a danger to society, depends largely on how representative of the people is the government at the time. Weber's concept is useful for the analysis of 'abnormal' or unstable situations, so the concept is not fundamental to 'normal' political theory. The importance of the idea of charismatic authority is that it helps us to see 'normal' authority in perspective. But although Weber's sociological approach is useful in classifying the possible varieties of power, political theory, with its normative concern about where power *should* lie, must deal more with varieties of legal–rational authority—at least in the present legal-rational epoch.

Winch's analysis of authority emphasizes its quasi-legal and rational elements. The *de jure* authority to which we are accustomed rests on a system of rules, usually legal rules, which direct people's feelings of deference to appropriate objects. According to Winch, all social activity is participation in rule-governed activities which 'involve a reference to an *established* way of doing things'. This feature of society gives rise to notions of authority, which Winch defines as 'not a kind of *causal* relation between individual wills but an *internal* relation'. He would consider *power* a causal relation, evidently. He also argues that authority is not a curtailment of liberty since 'to follow an authority is a voluntary act'.[10] This conclusion needs some qualification. Even supposing that you freely and rationally decide to acknowledge a government's authority, in choosing to defer to its laws and commands you limit your own future freedom, albeit voluntarily, thus ending up in a state of what has been called 'imperfect rationality', where one chooses rationally *not* to make a future choice.[11] Political authority based on law

---

10. P. Winch, 'Authority' in *Political Philosophy* (Ed. A. Quinton), Oxford U.P., 1967, p. 38.
11. See J. Elster, *Ulysses and the Sirens*, Cambridge U.P., 1979, pp. 88–103. Imperfect rationality occurs in a situation where one makes a subsidiary choice which commits one to a future major choice. Thus, voting can be seen by theorists who use the notion of obligation as committing us to certain future actions which we do not yet know and might not choose freely.

is crucial to the existence of society, and preferable to the use of coercive power, but we cannot pretend that it leaves the individual perfectly free.

This leads to certain problems in evaluating the relative merits of authority and power. The individual may feel more contented when she defers to authority than when she yields to power, whether power appears as the exercise of 'powers' or sanctions, or as coercion. Even if she feels that authority does not rest on her full consent, it is pleasanter to accept its ruling, since her actions then seem partially voluntary, than to be forced by the exercise of power to act against her will. Most people accept authority unquestioningly in their daily lives, having internalized the legitimacy of parents, teachers, government and the state from an early age. However, it could be argued that a state which inscribes the minds of citizens with ideas of authority and obligation disguises their lack of freedom and that this threatens human liberty more than a state which rules by the use of coercion or force. In the latter case, individuals can at least perceive the state's illegitimacy and the threat to their liberty, and can protest and resist. (Some philosophers argue that captivity of the body is preferable to enslavement of the mind for this reason.) This is why critics of the modern capitalist state, who consider it illegitimate, regret its transformation into a benign welfare state which gains authority in the eyes of the people by its dispensation of social justice and its democratic appendages. Marcuse's proclamation that such benign capitalism is based on disguised violence was intended to remove the blindfold of authority and legitimacy from our eyes and encourage us to protect our threatened liberties.[12] His argument imputed false consciousness to the large percentage of the population which genuinely believes the state to be legitimate. A typical strategy for those who believe that the modern capitalist state is based on force, not authority, is to provoke it into showing its hand, so as to expose its true repressive nature. Left-wing thinkers in Britain would argue that what they consider to be police violence at demonstrations (for example, at Anti-Nazi League demonstrations or anti-motorway protests) is symptomatic of the force on which the state is based; the more frequently such events occur, the more people will understand how illusory is their liberty in liberal society. One reply to such arguments is that if the people *think* that the state has authority and legitimacy, then it *has*, since these are constituted largely by the people's attitude to it. Nevertheless, people may be deceived into according approval to a government or system not really in their interests. If they can be persuaded to rescind that approval, the state ceases to have authority (except in the legal sense) although it may retain power for a time. Legal authority without deference is not much use, since it has to be backed up constantly by punishment and coercion. It would, of course, be ideal if just states were always founded on authority while unjust states always revealed themselves to be based on force and so alerted the people who would then overthrow them, but a state's authority in the eyes of the people is not necessarily an indication of its justice. Propaganda is a powerful device for creating authority and is used by both just and unjust governments. However, each political ideology

---

12.   H. Marcuse, *One Dimensional Man*, Sphere, 1968.

gives rise to a theory of when authority is justly accorded, by which the authority of existing states can be evaluated. Needless to say, such theories differ: for a Marxist, the vanguard of the proletariat may justly exercise authority, while for a liberal democrat, authority resides in a parliamentary government, elected under fair conditions. As can be seen, the theory of justified authority is the obverse of the theory of obligation in any ideology.

POWER AND AUTHORITY

The attempt to distinguish rigorously between these two concepts is ultimately doomed to failure. In any normal political situation, and in every state institution, they co-exist and support each other, and between them condition the behaviour of citizens. In most situations, several types of authority and power can be seen to operate, which correspond to those listed in the first section above. Mr White pays his taxes because he voted for the government, approves of its programme and believes in its authority (1); Ms Grey is reluctant but pays, being in awe of the general power of the Inland Revenue (2); Mr Brown tries to evade payment but finds particular powers invoked against him, so conforms (3), and Ms Black defrauds the Inland Revenue and is prosecuted and punished (4). It is clear that the use of force and violence, (5) and (6), indicate abnormal circumstances where authority has broken down. In this example, in the first three cases the same end result is produced, but each taxpayer is influenced by different aspects of the power-authority nexus; the combination of both power and authority in a government is essential, to minimize disobedience. Authority alone might cut little ice with people where their financial interests were concerned: the tax inspector needs both executive powers and legal sanctions.

To the citizen, the power and authority of an institution may seem inseparable. People commonly regard an institution or an individual as having authority because they know that it, or she, has certain powers. Thus it, or she, gains authority in their eyes. This interactive process, with its element of feedback, which underlies the bestowal of authority on institutions and individuals, gives the lie to theorists' attempts to root all authority in voluntary consent. Political scientists proceed more in accordance with the layman's perception. They ask who takes the decisions on particular issues, and whose wishes prevail when conflicts of goals or values arise. This analysis omits all reference to authority and to powers as rights. In a typical study, *Power and Poverty*, the authors wrote, 'To regard authority as a form of power is not operationally useful'.[13] The analysis of power has a tendency, as does much political science, to validate whatever it discovers. This is where the theorist's emphasis on authority is vital: assuming that there *are* methods for validly bestowing authority on a just government, the concept is useful for highlighting areas where part of the state has assumed unwarranted powers, and for detecting other usurpations of power. Plamenatz's observation that the rule of power is necessarily short-lived suggests that

13. P. Bachrach and M. Baratz, *Power and Poverty*, Oxford U.P., 1970, p.33.

whenever a divergence of power from authority occurs, the power-holders will seek to legitimize their position by devising mechanisms for establishing their authority. Hence, it is the cases where power and authority diverge that most interest the theorist, and where the normative and critical force of analysis can come into play.

Much English and American theory about the nature of power is permeated by a conviction of the relative stability of our own political systems, in which power is usually comfortably legitimized and contained by authority. A situation where this reassuring partnership would cease is that which might occur after the devastation of a nuclear war or disaster. Many different scenarios for this have been envisaged in books, films and governments' emergency plans, but most concur in the inevitability of strict martial law, emanating from regional centres of government, keeping the relatively few survivors from rioting and looting, and putting them to work. Would the regional governors and their troops have authority in such a situation? Whether authority is based on consent, justice or the interests of the people, the answer is surely 'No', whatever the emergency laws may prescribe. The democratic apparatus would have disappeared, and the governors could hardly invoke the consent of the deceased population, given in a pre-war election where issues were very different. Nor would the predicted attempts to restore order by force, and communications by directed labour, be much in the interests of those trying to survive from day to day, or earn their gratitude. This hypothetical example suggests that in abnormal situations where authority and power diverge, force will prevail. Without the constraining influence that authority provides, the use of force (unregulated coercive power) is unrestrained, and may be used to promote the interests of the powerful. This illustrates the two-edged nature of authority, which revolutionaries may see only as a means of deluding the population, but which equally acts as a brake on the coercive elements that necessarily underlie government. The retention of an active role in our political thinking for the concept of authority is therefore crucial, although theorists should be more ready to admit and examine its ideological role. To complement our understanding of the importance and interrelation of power, authority and obligation, we must consider the institution to which all three chiefly refer, the state.

THE STATE LEVIATHAN

The term 'state' is a relative newcomer to political debate. Until the nineteenth century political thinkers preferred terms such as 'commonwealth', 'political society', 'sovereign power' and 'government' to denote what would today be called the state. 'Nation-state' is a nineteenth-century term, which embraces the whole of a society as well as its political apparatus. The subject here, however, is the state as the major locus of power and authority in every modern society. The state consists of the legislative, executive and judicial branches of government, along with all the institutions to which they delegate powers (including the civil service, army, police, the media, if these are state-owned, and so on). According to democratic theory, the powers of the separate parts of the state are delegated from the supreme sovereign, the legislature, and subject to its control. If this were ideally realized, the state in a democratic society would be the servant of the sovereign people, but various factors prevent this being so. The shortcomings of the representative system, already discussed, prevent the elected government from being a sensitive barometer of the people's opinions and desires. Secondly, most state institutions are of longer duration than elected governments, so that they form their own long-term policies and acquire vested interests, which new governments may be obliged to accommodate—the tail wags the dog. Thirdly, delegated powers give some state agencies a high degree of autonomy, not always matched by accountability. The persisting nature of state institutions and the transitory nature of governments means that a newly-elected government tends to merge into and be identified with the apparatus of the state, unless it makes special efforts to remain aloof and control the latter. This conceptual and technical separation of government and state and the theoretical subordination of the latter to the former is important when we are trying to gauge how democratic a country is, how accountable its institutions, and whether the state presents a threat to individual freedom.

What is the nature of the state? Four alternative views, embedded in different ideological or theoretical frameworks, are briefly summarized here:

(1) *The contractual view.* The state derives from the voluntary agreement of men, via the social contract, and its task is to promote the interests of the people as individuals (Locke) or as a collectivity (Rousseau). The state's (or sovereign's) power is unlimited (Hobbes), or limited by men's natural rights (Locke), or is constrained to realize the General Will (Rousseau). The hypothesis of the contract thus leads to no *general* conclusions about the nature and powers of the state, as these are deduced from the different original premises of the various theories. However, it does, in Locke's version, lead to a marked distinction between the institutions of the state and civil society, the 'public' and the 'private', and entails a natural demarcation between these spheres.

(2) *The state as arbiter and nightwatchman.* This view derives from the minimal role assigned to the state by classical economists, liberals and libertarians. The state is minimal because state intervention impedes individuals' pursuit of their own interests. The utilitarians in particular emphasized the neutrality of the state. All individuals were considered equal, *qua* individuals, so the state could and should take nobody's part, but should harmonize everyone's interests. The state's origin is unimportant, for its justification lies in the satisfactory performance of its role of negotiator, arbiter and minimizer of conflict. The state is obliged to care equally for all its members, as utilitarianism enjoins, and to ensure this, the state is best subjected to a constitution which enforces its impartiality. On this view, the state is merely the sum of its individual parts, no more, and is seen only as one element, albeit important, in the wider civil society.

(3) *The state as organism.* Conservative romantics like Coleridge, but also the anti-romantic Hegel, conceived of the state as an integrated organism, set

above individuals, a whole greater than its component parts. Hegel was anxious to oust the contract view and the liberalism based on it. The organic ideal denies the possibility of conflicting interests: it offers a 'natural' foundation for the state. Hegel characterized the state as 'abstract mind' which acknowledges no other absolute principles, such as morality, and is an absolute itself. Hence the omnipotence of the state in his theory. On this organic account there can be no balance of powers and no neutrality in the state, for the state has its own holistic interest, far above the interests of individuals.[14] According to this analysis the state represents and embodies the whole society or nation.

(4) *The state as oppressor.* The Marxist analysis, to which most anarchists would also adhere in principle if not in detail. This sees the state as the instrument of the ruling class, and explicitly contradicts the other three views. The state was not built on a contract but on force and usurpation, and cannot be neutral. The modern state is 'a committee for managing the common affairs of the bourgeoisie' and it cannot be an organic unity because society is an imbroglio of class conflict, of which the state's very existence is symptomatic. 'The state is a product and a manifestation of the irreconcilability of class antagonisms'. Marx also notes that the state is an embodiment of individual interest which is opposed to the interest of the whole community. Marx therefore predicted the withering away of the state in a classless, socialist society. This analysis is adapted by contemporary Marxists *mutatis mutandis* to the advanced capitalist state.[15]

Mention must also be made of the concept of the *corporatist state*, which is a form of organization in which interest groups based on function (e.g. producers, trades unions) occupy a privileged position between the state itself and civil society. These groups or organizations have a semi-official status and collaborate with the state in the formation of policy in exchange for favourable terms for their members. The earliest detectably corporatist state was Italy under Mussolini, and the concept of such a state has affinities with the organic concept described at (3) above, with each functional group forming part of the social organism. But in the 1980s a number of theorists adapted the concept of corporatism to describe contemporary capitalist societies so as to challenge the pluralists' optimistic model of an open-textured society with a multiplicity of competing interest groups. However, there is an ongoing debate as to whether corporatist theory represents a theory of a new kind of state, or simply describes a liberal state with a novel form of mediation between interests.[16]

Evidently, ideological convictions condition our understanding of the state, its origins, and its limitations. Despite the Marxist dismissal of the state as a class instrument and given the general suspicion of potentially totalitarian 'organic'

---

14. G. Hegel, *Philosophy of Right* (trans. M. Knox), Oxford U.P., 1952.
15. V. I. Lenin, *The State and Revolution*, Progress Publishers, 1974, p. 10. In Chapter 1, Lenin gives a succinct account of the Marxist view of the state.
16. See A. Cawson, *Corporatism and Political Theory*, Blackwell, 1986 and P. J. Williamson, *Corporatism in Perspective*, Sage, 1989.

views, many Western theorists still wish to regard the state as—ideally—a neutral arbiter with no interests of its own, true to the liberal-democratic tradition, despite the fact that such an ideal is difficult to achieve.[17] Particularly curious is the neutral tone which some such analyses adopt. They seek to define the precise functions of the state, and what distinguishes it from other associations (as if there were a risk of confusion!) but do not question its scope and purposes, perhaps because it is assumed that democratic institutions automatically keep the state within bounds.

A typical approach of this kind defines the state as a system of rules, procedures, and roles, operated by individuals using various methods including coercion. Since this might describe almost *any* system or association, Raphael goes on to list its five special characteristics:[18]

(a) The state has universal jurisdiction.
(b) The state has compulsory jurisdiction.
(c) Its ends are broader than those of other associations which pursue 'privately conceived ends'.
(d) The state has legal supremacy or sovereignty over other associations.
(e) The state ranks as equal with other nation-states, being 'self-sovereign'.

Clearly, all except (c) are defining properties of the state with which even a Marxist would agree. These criteria identify the state as unique among associations, and this proves its clear, indisputable supremacy and directs citizens' basic loyalty towards the state rather than to other sectional associations in society. (Walzer, clarifies this when, discussing obligation, he designates the state a 'primary association', distinct from secondary associations such as the church, firms, and interest groups, membership of which also generates duty and loyalty.)[19]

Having characterized the state thus, can its existence and powers be justified? We could, after all, imagine societies existing without such an overbearing 'association', societies such as the anarchists proposed. One justification for the state's supremacy is its claim to promote the common good, a claim regarded sceptically by liberals and Marxists; the other is the 'arbitral' role of the state which judges between competing claims, considering everyone impartially. Implicit in both these justifications is the claim that the same ends could not be achieved by looser or narrower associations, a claim disputed, for instance, by Nozick who suggests that a market society, with free entry to and exit from a multiplicity of small communities, could spontaneously fulfil both these functions.[20] For all except those who hold an organic, or similar, view of the state, it must justify its existence in terms of the good which it does to the members of the society. We may ask whether these benefits might not be achieved

17. See the chapters by Goodin and Reeve and Jones in R. E. Goodin and A. Reeve (Eds.), *Liberal Neutrality*, Routledge, 1989.
18. D. D. Raphael, *Problems of Political Philosophy*, 2nd edn, Macmillan, 1990, pp. 43–55.
19. M. Walzer, *Obligations*, Harvard U.P., 1970, Chap. 1.
20. R. Nozick, *Anarchy, State and Utopia*, Blackwell, 1974.

in other ways, but for those with a view such as Hegel's, the state is a good in itself and an end in itself, and needs no further justification.

For the legal or the political theorist searching for a definition of the state and its rights, the most important question is where *sovereignty* lies, a question complicated by the fact that some talk of *de facto* sovereignty, a seeming contradiction since the idea of sovereignty rests heavily on *right*. Weber, for example, defined the state's sovereignty in terms of its monopoly of the legitimate use of physical force, and Raphael accuses modern power theorists too of equating sovereignty with 'supremacy of coercive power rather than of legal authority'.[21] The *de facto* approach makes it impossible to establish or dispute the state's *right* to such powers, although it makes sovereignty easier to identify empirically. However, this approach is not adopted by theorists, for whom the normative or *de jure* elements of sovereignty are all-important. In most modern theory, the democratic ideal of the sovereign people is put aside (as an irrelevant truism) then the theorist tries to determine to which of the state's organs sovereignty attaches. Law-making is seen as the essence of the sovereign role but this is not always an unambiguous criterion because the lawmaking function can be, and often is, divided. The 'problem of sovereignty' in political theory now seems an exceptionally sterile academic debate, since sovereignty is clearly diffused in practice, and delegated for operational convenience. Only in a crisis is it important that sovereignty should be concentrated in one part of society—and crises usually arise over conflicting claims to sovereignty. The theorist's role cannot be to determine where sovereignty lies in particular societies—this is a matter for legal philosophers and constitutionalists—but to decide where it should lie, given her analysis of the nature of political society. The democratic theorist, for example, knows that sovereignty should reside in the people or their chosen representatives, and the focus of her analysis would be to consider how it can be ensured that the supreme law-making body is responsible and accountable to the people and not subject to undue influence by non-democratic organizations.

In popular usage, the concept of sovereignty is mainly invoked when other sovereign states seem to threaten a state's supremacy within its own boundaries. Early opponents of Britain's membership of the European Community (EC) argued against the threat to Parliament's legislative supremacy which it posed: one might note that their case could equally have been based on democratic theory alone since the EC was not then, and the European Union (EU) is not now, a democratic organization. Once in the EC, British citizens had to submit to legislation to which they had not consented—a point which still applies as EU regulations are not made by the elected European Parliament. The exclusive emphasis placed on *parliamentary* sovereignty in such cases by British politicians is symptomatic of their tendency to forget the final sovereignty of the people. Sovereignty is also much debated here when a high court judge makes an

---

21. Raphael, *Problems of Political Philosophy*, p.158.

interpretative ruling on some point of law which is contrary to the spirit in which Parliament intended the law to be enforced. Lord Denning consistently did this, 'upholding justice against the law', he said. In such cases politicians would argue that the balance of power between legislature and judiciary is being tilted to the detriment of parliamentary legislative supremacy. In constitutional matters like this, the employment of the concept of sovereignty is appropriate, although the political theorist might again better describe the event in terms of the damage caused to the democratic principle when non-elected, non-accountable judges start to make law.

In daily life, of course, the state is an objective reality to which individuals must accommodate themselves as best they can, but political theory need not endorse this subjection of the moveable to the immoveable. If a legalistic approach is adopted to the state and its sovereignty, there can be no question but that it is supreme according to positive and/or constitutional law. However, the law only goes a certain way towards establishing a state's authority, and laws can be changed, or overthrown. An equally important factor, as was argued above, is the attitude of the people towards the state—their acknowledgement of its authority, and acceptance of their own political obligation. Although these concepts have often been used propagandistically to justify the supremacy of the state over the individual, new conceptions of them could be devised with a contrary, restraining effect on the state. If our notions of authority and obligation could be refashioned on a thoroughly democratic basis, we would tip the balance which so strongly favours the state back a little towards the individual. Of course, this is a long-term process: even if missionary political theorists could popularize their reinterpretation of the individual's duty to the state, and this were widely accepted, the state would continue to hold the monopoly of coercive power, which it could activate against any threatening effects of the conceptual revolution.

For anarchists and Marxists 'state' was always a dirty word, and now a similar attitude is partly pervading liberal-democratic societies, although its cause is different: the modern interventionist state threatens personal liberty in innumerable ways. 'Convergence theory' argued that liberal and Marxist states were converging towards a common pattern of state socialism, alias state capitalism. The details may differ, but the spectacle of a constantly growing state leviathan has been common to both liberal and communist societies. This is ironic both for liberals who remember Mill's injunctions against state intervention and for Marxists who recall Marx's prediction of the 'withering away'. The shared failure of their analyses and ideals should give rise to a different analysis of the nature of the state in advanced industrial society, which will provide different prescriptions from those now available concerning how we can assert the will of the people or the rights of individuals against the state. We have lost control of the modern state theoretically, just as, practically, we are no longer able to enforce its accountability. Wright Mills' account of the power elite and Galbraith's analysis of the technostructure, were pioneering steps towards a new theory of the state, but perhaps Orwell's account, in *Nineteen Eighty-Four* (1949), of the three permanently warring superstates with their terrorized subject populations cannot be bettered by theory.

A number of factors contribute to the distinctive nature of the modern interventionist state. A major factor is the massive advances made in technology which have several consequences. To follow up such advances commercially requires such heavy investment that governments are called upon to finance them, and so become deeply involved in economic enterprise. Where government intervenes, it will also attempt to regulate, hence the need for an increased number of experts called in as aides to government bodies, whose criteria for policy-making may differ from what the people may wish. In particular, the development of nuclear weapons and the arms race, itself an important stimulus to postwar economies, necessarily increased the power and scope of government as the military section of the economy under its control became even larger.[22] (During the Cold War Orwell's predictions were borne out at the ideological level, as each superpower incited its citizens to greater fear and dislike of the opposing power, and to greater loyalty to itself, to justify arms expenditure.) Third, the output of legal regulations necessitated by advanced technology and welfare measures, and by membership of superstates such as the EU, has created and subsequently overloaded large bureaucracies which are only marginally accountable to the people via the democratic process. The heavy involvement of each country's economy in the world economy is another, external, factor which diminishes the controllability of the state: the world economy is not controlled by individual states but it partly controls them, often in ways antithetical to democracy within the countries. Infra-state organizations may have similar effects: the stringent conditions concerning domestic policy attached to IMF loans are an example of such control and it is foreseen that countries which join the single European currency will lose control over their domestic economies.

These are hardly original observations—nor, unfortunately, have they yet become commonplace enough in democratic politics to warrant action to curb these developments. These factors are added to, and enhance, the increasing elitism and isolation of the political process in liberal democracies. Some parts of the state have escaped the control of the governors, other parts are controlled by them, but the governors themselves are largely uncontrolled. It is a poor lookout for democracy, and one which calls for a re-thinking of our old concepts. Since the possession of authority is essential for the maintenance of the state, which cannot afford to operate in the long term by the exercise of power and the use of force, the way in which authority is conceptualized is important. If political theorists could develop and disseminate a more critical concept of authority, resting on stronger forms of consent and accountability, and a more selective, less deferential account of political obligation which emphasized the right to dissent, they could make a useful contribution to controlling the new leviathan.

To this end, the doctrines of freedom and human rights are also crucial. In a society where the rights of individuals are constitutionally safeguarded, the scope of operation of the state is correspondingly restricted. Even if some branches of

---

22. See *Report from Iron Mountain* (Ed. L. Lewin), Penguin, 1968, an anonymous 'hoax' document which nonetheless exposed the truth about the dependence of the US economy on arms production. See also J. K. Galbraith, *The New Industrial State*, Penguin, 1969.

the state habitually violate individuals' rights (as do the 'security services' in many countries), public outcry is certain to follow when such violations come to light, and governments are often forced to reform the errant organ of state. The next chapter therefore discusses the all-important question of individual freedom.

FURTHER READING

K. Dowding, *Rational Choice and Political Power*, Edward Elgar, 1991.
P. Dunleavy and B. O'Leary, *Theories of the State*, Macmillan, 1987.
L. Green, *The Authority of the State*, Clarendon Press, 1988.
D. Held, *Political Theory and the Modern State*, Polity Press, 1989.
B. Hindess, *Discourses of Power: from Hobbes to Foucault*, Blackwell, 1995.
J. Hoffman, *Beyond the State*, Polity Press, 1995.
B. Jessop, *The Capitalist State: Marxist Theories and Methods*, Martin Robertson, 1982.
B. Jordan, *The State*, Blackwell, 1985.
A. Levine (Ed.), *The State and its Critics*, Edward Elgar, 1992.
S. Lukes, *Power: A Radical View*, Macmillan, 1974.
M. Neocleous, *Administering Civil Society: Towards a Theory of State Power*, Macmillan, 1997.
J. Raz (Ed.), *Authority*, Blackwell, 1990.

Chapter 14

Freedom and Rights

The following discussion will take place largely within the framework of liberal-democratic thought, since this is where most theoretical debate takes place on the nature of freedom and rights. The history of the concepts is, in effect, the three-hundred-year history of liberal thought and the 'individual versus the state' antagonism is, effectively, a liberal invention, so that thinkers in other ideological climates often adopt liberal terminology in addressing themselves to the issue.

It is an accident of the English language that we have two words for the same concept, 'freedom' and 'liberty'. They are treated as synonyms in the discussion which follows.

THE MEANING OF FREEDOM

> To renounce liberty is to renounce being a man, to surrender the rights of humanity and even its duties.[1]

The idea of individual liberty is inseparably fused with the theological doctrine that man has free will, with which to choose good or evil, and that this is the defining characteristic of his God-given nature. The philosophical debate as to whether man is indeed free, or determined, in his actions may be more germane to moral than to political philosophy but whichever viewpoint is taken has consequences for the adoption of political ideals. From the eighteenth century onwards, rationalist philosophers insisted that causal explanations could in principle be given of human behaviour, as of events in the natural world, and determinism became a widespread doctrine. The related precept, that human character is formed by social environment, gave rise to a new generation of utopias in which people were to be made perfect by the perfection of social institutions. Marx's materialist analysis stemmed from the same insight.

---

1. J.-J. Rousseau, *The Social Contract*, Dent, 1913, p. 8.

Darwinism and, in this century, the behavioural sciences continued to foster the determinist view of human nature despite which liberty remains our most vaunted political ideal in the West. Many philosophers have contended that a crucial element in social life is the assumption that we are all responsible for our actions, an assumption only possible in conjunction with a theory of free will.[2] How could a liberal system of justice reward people for their merits, if they were not responsible for their achievements? Many liberal thinkers, like Rousseau (quoted above) make freedom man's defining attribute. The democratic ideal too is posited on people's capacity for free (and rational) choice, and one major quarrel which liberals have with Marxists is the latter's 'deterministic' view of human nature. Thus, questions of free will and freedom are at the basis of Western philosophy and Western political society.

We are unlikely ever to prove the case for free will or that for determinism; in any case, most philosophers do not hold that we are totally *determined* or totally *undetermined*. Many hold a 'compatibilist' position, which states that we can be both free and, in part, determined. Certainly, it is possible to specify the determining factors such as conditioning, which limit our *choices*, yet to hold that we still have a degree of *choice*. The degree of free will or causation attributed to human action in a political theory is clearly all-important in deciding how political behaviour is explained and what political values are pursued. Thus, the philosophical assumptions made about free will (although this is not primarily a political question) will set the parameters for an ideology. But when liberty is discussed in political philosophy what is referred to is not so much the individual's capacity for freedom as her 'objective' freedom, defined as freedom from coercion or restraints and freedom in terms of opportunities.

With all due respect to anarchists and libertarians, it must be said that the idea of *absolute freedom* is a chimera, unattainable by individuals in society, which is essentially a system of shared norms and mutual restraints. Most of the activities which make life worthwhile—friendship, marriage, belonging to a group— depend, as was said earlier, on self-imposed obligations or promises which restrict our freedom but enrich our experience. So the concept of the absolutely free individual, untrammelled by laws or morals and unimpeded by the actions of others, cannot function in political argument, even as an unrealizable goal. The focus of argument must instead be whether particular ideologies or political systems *extend* the range of choice and *diminish* interference: that is, the concept must be viewed relatively. Berlin, discussing J. S. Mill, distinguishes between *negative liberty*, freedom from interference, and *positive liberty*, 'the freedom which consists in being one's own master',[3] which he connects analytically with self-government. The potential conflict between the two which Berlin claims to find has been disputed, but his distinction reflects an obvious truth, namely, that there is a category difference between my *rights*, which prevent my being

---

2. See P. Strawson, 'Freedom and resentment', in Strawson, *Studies in the Philosophy of Thought and Action*, Oxford U.P., 1968, and I. Berlin, 'Historical inevitability', in Berlin, *Four Essays on Liberty*, Oxford U.P., 1969.
3. Berlin, 'Two concepts of liberty' in *Political Philosophy* (Ed. A. Quinton), Oxford U.P., p. 149.

interfered with in specific areas, and my *opportunities* (including the greatest opportunity, that of controlling my fate through self-government), which may vary according to social context—even if the negative and positive forms of liberty constantly interact. Both must be considered in answering the question 'How free am I?'

The accounts of liberty given by liberal political theorists have changed over time, according to the source of threats to individual freedom. In the seventeenth century, freedom of religious belief was very important and dominated discussion. In the eighteenth, freedom from the arbitrary will of despots was crucial, and freedom was often viewed in political and constitutional terms. In the next century, J. S. Mill argued for freedom from the tyranny of public opinion and the moral conformism of Victorian society, while in this century freedom for nations ('self-determination') and freedom *from* 'the system' have been among the demands. Positive freedom is even more dependent on context than negative freedom, for each social and technological innovation creates possibilities which people may then claim as rightful opportunities necessary to their self-fulfilment. A government today which restricted the use of cars would be said to be curtailing people's positive freedom, whatever the ecological arguments in favour of such a restriction. A similar argument could be used about expensive medical equipment such as body scanners; these could save lives, but the National Health Service has insufficient funds to make them widely available. Underfunding can thus be presented as a denial of opportunities for good health care. In a progressive, stable society, then, positive liberty is cumulatively extended: a hundred years ago in Britain, primary education was the norm, now free higher education is (supposedly) available for all those suitably qualified and it is proposed that one in three young people should benefit from this opportunity in the near future. Whatever its spiritual drawbacks, affluence increases positive liberty in such ways.

VARIETIES OF FREEDOM

Just as ideas of liberty depend on social context, the accounts of liberty elaborated within different ideologies vary considerably, as Part II has shown. These will now be briefly recapitulated. According to liberals, liberty is intimately connected with law. All are subordinate to laws to which they have freely consented, and so are equally free. As Locke said, 'freedom of men under government is to have a standing rule to live by, common to every one'. Locke's conception also had an economic dimension, for he emphasized man's natural right to appropriate property and to sell his labour; according to Macpherson's interpretation, such early liberal freedom was, effectively, the power to enter into contracts in a system of market relations. With regard to government, Locke said that men's lives are owed to God, and they are not free to enslave or kill themselves: therefore they cannot logically consent to arbitrary governments, which might enslave them. His definition of the task of government as the preservation of natural rights emphasized the limited role of government and the extent of personal liberty in liberal society. Later, when the broad principles recommended by Locke had been constitutionally established in some countries, liberal theory focused on specific political liberties. Mill advocated freedom of thought, discussion, religion, and assembly against contemporary laws which threatened such rights. He also asserted that society had no right to force its moral views on the individual. His famous principle, that society is only entitled to interfere with the individual to protect its members from direct material harm, set a parameter for liberal thinking which still operates to some degree in liberal societies. Mill also defined freedom in the positive sense as the freedom to develop as an autonomous individual through political self-determination and education, although Berlin argues that this may conflict with the non-interference principle. 'Both are ends in themselves. These ends may clash irreconcilably'.[4] Berlin is clearly right: each new government power which theoretically extends self-government may curtail individual liberty. Likewise, each new policy to improve the quality of life and the range of opportunities entails further interference. The *right* to education has been associated with *compulsory education* (even if for the best of reasons, as advanced by Mill, i.e. that it helps a child's development): the right to welfare benefits is accompanied by a duty for claimants to provide information about their private lives. This is a continuing problem for liberals, but most would prefer to exchange some privacy and independence for security and opportunities rather than return to the reign of market forces.

The socialist view of freedom has also been discussed: freedom is seen as self-realization through creative work and leisure, which need not entail a wide range of choice, if individuals are given opportunities suited to their talents and needs. The early socialists' criticism of 'bourgeois' political rights, that they were useless to the majority of the people who had no economic freedom, still holds good for the Third-World countries which maintain some form of democracy in conditions of acute poverty (India springs to mind): might not a dictatorship improve their economic position? Economic freedom is basic for socialists. But many Western socialists insist that political freedoms such as Mill advocated are valuable, and should be retained alongside socialist welfare measures. The classic socialist and Marxist conceptions of liberty rest on a more deterministic view of human nature than that of liberals, and deny the direct correlation of choice and freedom: they do not entail that state power should be minimized, but they do entail the abolition of economic exploitation, the outstanding obstacle to creative self-realization and material sufficiency.

There is another approach to freedom, which appeals to authoritarian thinkers of both right and left, the paradoxical conception of *freedom as obedience*. The doctrine that freedom is doing what you ought to do, or are told to do, is foreshadowed in Christian accounts of God, 'whose service is perfect freedom'. Rousseau is associated by his critics with this way of thinking because he defines freedom as obedience to the General Will. 'Each, while uniting himself with all, may still obey himself alone, and remain as free as before'.[5] Each individual in a society of n people submits to the wills of $(n-1)$ individuals and in return has a

---

4. Berlin, *Four Essays on Liberty*, p. xlix.
5. Rousseau, *The Social Contract*, p. 12.

fraction of power ($1/n$) over the same number—although this is hardly the same as obeying only oneself. The problem is glossed over by the idea of the General Will, which Rousseau defines as what each individual would really will if he could divest himself of his selfish interests. The deviant who is coerced into obeying the law is 'forced to be free', therefore. Freedom is also characterized as obedience to self-prescribed laws by Hegel, for whom the state's political power is the 'externalization' of the individual's will. The individual identifies with the state and thus reconciles outer submission with inner freedom.[6] Such 'mystical' views of freedom arouse the strong suspicion of liberals: although they share the formal assumption that freedom is obedience to self-prescribed laws, since freedom without law is inconceivable, liberals repudiate intangible entities such as the General Will, and describe the visible mechanics of freedom in terms of submission to the will of the majority, where everyone has previously agreed to majority rule. The doctrine of freedom as obedience is most often espoused by thinkers who believe that there can be certainty about what is right or who is to be obeyed. Rousseau defined the General Will as political truth, while Hegel saw the state as the realization of Spirit; the Christian view of obedience rests on similar certitude. The organic view of society leads to parallel conclusions: the whole is greater and wiser than the parts, which must subordinate themselves to it. But those who doubt the possibility of such certainties consider it dangerous to define freedom as the submission to absolutes. Liberals would detect the doctrine of 'freedom as obedience' at work in left-wing societies, on Rousseau's model, and in right-wing states, influenced by the Hegelian view.

It could be said that the liberals' conception of freedom is chiefly concerned with the individual's intellect and conscience, that of socialists, with her material wellbeing and that of 'authoritarians' with her soul. But in this century, developments in psychology have given rise to different conceptions of human nature and of freedom. For example, the behaviourist psychologist Skinner developed a controversial critique of freedom based on determinism.[7] He argued that all living organisms are constantly acted on by the environment, including human beings. Behaviour patterns are established according to whether the (social) environment responds with positive (pleasurable) or negative (aversive) 'reinforcement' to their actions. Although he drew his conclusions from experiments on rats and pigeons, he applied the theory of reinforcement to human beings in society, arguing that the 'contingencies of reinforcement' are manipulated by various controlling institutions such as the state. In earlier times, the forms of control used were 'aversive and conspicuous'—coercion and brutal repression—and in response individuals developed 'countercontrol' devices. (Countercontrol is, in Skinner's terms, the self-defence mechanism by which an organism tries to reduce the control of the environment.) One such device was the doctrine of freedom. However, in modern society the controls employed are *inconspicuous* and *non-aversive*—persuasive ideology, inducement, and covert

---

6. G. W. F. Hegel, *The Philosophy of Right* (trans. M. Knox), Part 3 (iii) and *The Phenomenology of Spirit* (trans. A. V. Miller), Clarendon Press, 1977, s. 371.
7. B. F. Skinner, *Beyond Freedom and Dignity*, Cape, 1972.

manipulation. The result is that, in the absence of visible coercion, people feel themselves, illusorily, to be free. 'The feeling of freedom becomes an unreliable guide to action as soon as would-be controllers turn to nonaversive measures'. Skinner recommended that we abandon the notions of human autonomy, freedom, and dignity, since these are deceptive political ideals, given our status as determined organisms, and that we substitute another value, 'the survival of cultures'. The upshot of Skinner's analysis is that freedom is a chimera: we will always be controlled, and the most we can hope for is non-aversive, inconspicuous controls.

Skinner's method of generalizing from the laboratory to society, from animal to man, and his conclusions, have been strongly criticized,[8] but his arguments are in some ways revealing. He rightly shows that we do not use 'freedom' consistently but employ it to emphasize our likes and dislikes, depending on whether or not we perceive the controlling mechanisms. His analysis makes clear the difference between the subjective and objective aspects of freedom: we may feel ourselves to be free because the controls are hidden and yet, objectively, be unfree. But it is hard to accept this totally deterministic view of human nature or to agree with the Darwinian ideal of the survival of cultures, which seems to brook no distinction between good or bad cultures. An unresolved problem in Skinner's analysis is that of who controls—or reinforces—the controllers, who are equally determined.

The fear of 'hidden persuaders', implicit in Skinner's work, is typical of modern social thought, stemming from our sophisticated understanding of human psychology and from understanding the new, subtle means of communication, persuasion and control which high technology generates. One consequence of these developments has been more subtle analyses of freedom. Marcuse's theory (developed in the radical 1960s and 1970s) serves to illustrate these. He argued that _toleration_ is a form of assimilation which produces 'threatening homo-geneity'. By permitting protest within a given orthodoxy, the liberal establishment removes the capacity for protest. Following Freud, Marcuse analysed the repression of the sexual instinct, Eros, which Freud had seen as essential to the maintenance of civilization. Capitalism rests on the 'performance principle' (the opposite of the 'pleasure principle') which imposes delayed gratification, and transforms libidinal energy into productive labour. In the past, sublimated sexual energy could at least be diverted into protest, but in a sexually permissive society 'repressive de-sublimation' occurs, and sexual gratification can be achieved directly. What seems to be the substance of freedom is thus inimical to it, for a state of relative sexual permissiveness provides 'satisfaction in a way which generates submission and weakens the rationality of protest'. Also, by making people work longer than is necessary, although automation could reduce working hours, capitalism enforces 'surplus repression' of people's energies, leaving them no leisure to act politically. The other threat to freedom identified by Marcuse is 'the closing of the universe of discourse', the manipulation of language by the media and the system to foreclose the possibility of radical thought and protest,

---

8. See, e.g., Noam Chomsky's attack on Skinner's theory in the _New York Review of Books_ Dec/Jan., 1971/2. See too H. Wheeler (Ed.), _Beyond the Punitive Society_, W. H. Freeman, 1973.

and prevent people understanding their true alienation. Theoretical language is gradually ousted and people are obliged to express their grievances in a concrete, factual vocabulary: this makes complaints easier to remedy superficially, and masks a fundamental social malaise. Marcuse was concerned about the all-embracing nature of tolerant, pluralist society, with its bribes of affluence which remove the will to attack the system as a whole. His recommended solution was *liberation from the system*, the destruction of repressive institutions and the achievement of private autonomy. Although Marcuse is usually considered a Marxist, his utopia of personal and sexual freedom is closer to the anarchist ideal.

The barrage of eclectic, often incompatible arguments which Marcuse directed against the system are highly contentious and take us far from the philosophical analysis of liberty, but they constitute an important warning. Freedom is not confined to the sphere of personal and civil rights, and today it is threatened from many quarters, especially by the economic system and by the control and manipulation of information. Knowledge, as the German philosopher Habermas contends, is power. Yet contemporary liberal society is clearly not based on the extensive, direct repression of a police state. The diffuseness of the controlling devices makes it hard to argue that we are the victims of a conspiracy of rulers acting in their own interests. In the 1960s, Marcuse, Illich, Galbraith, and other radical thinkers went beyond crude conspiracy theory to analyse and criticize the complex, all-embracing, supra-individual *system* which pervades and dominates Western societies, despite their appearance of loosely woven pluralism. Their analysis grows more pertinent as time passes.

The modern state system develops its own momentum towards expansion and self-perpetuation irrespective of the individuals operating it, who become subordinate to its goals. Weber analysed this phenomenon in the narrower context of bureaucracy: he argued that over time bureaucracies substitute instrumental goals and their own self-perpetuation for the goal which the institution was originally set up to pursue. Whereas the terms 'liberty' and 'rights' suggest something institutionalized, permitted within the system, Marcuse's prescription for freedom, 'protest', 'the Great Refusal' and 'liberation', connote the rejection of the system itself.[9] How he thought this could be achieved remains obscure, but thanks to Marcuse the idea of liberation became a key idea in radical thought: it connotes both the act of gaining freedom from hidden oppression *and* the subsequent experience of self-realization outside the system. Thus it is a wider and more evocative concept than that of rights, which are necessarily given *within* the system, and a more inspiring one in an age of disillusion.

FREEDOM AND ILLUSION

Common to the modern critiques is the belief that we can be deluded about the extent of our freedom. Can I think that I am free, yet not be free? As we have seen, Marcuse and Skinner would say 'Yes', because people can be tricked by the

---

9. H. Marcuse, *One Dimensional Man*, Sphere, 1968; *Essay on Liberation*, Penguin, 1971.

possession of formal rights and the language of liberty into ignoring the multiplicity of devices, including ideology, which predetermine their choices and ways of thinking. Certainly, feeling free can be an illusion, though a pleasant one, and philosophers have often pondered the case of the 'happy slave' who believes himself to be free. Should he be disabused, and made wretched, so that he can struggle against his enslavement? Philosophers like Godwin think he should, so central to their idea of human life are the notions of freedom and rational knowledge. Marcuse's warning was, precisely, a re-statement of this view, intended to undeceive the happy slaves of capitalism, and it evoked the hostility which the slaves might feel towards the 'benefactors' who propose to release them. A common response to those who seek to liberate the unwittingly oppressed is 'I *feel* free—so leave me alone.' Whether Marcuse's analysis of our illusion of freedom in capitalist society is accurate remains a matter for personal and, inevitably, ideological judgement. If he is right and we are unfree but happy, does it matter? Aldous Huxley, in *Brave New World* (1932), maintained that happiness without freedom was an evil, but this view could be considered too puritanical.

Of course, I may believe that I am free because of the absence of apparent restrictions, and not realize that every 'free' choice that I make is (a) causally determined by my personality and environment, and (b) restricts my future choices. Political theory cannot do much about this aspect of the human predicament, but recognition of it makes us aware that the idea of freedom as an absolute possession is an illusion. Relative freedom is, however, possible, and policy may be directed towards minimizing the restraints on individuals and maximizing their opportunities, but it still cannot make them free in themselves if they do not know how to utilize freedom for self-fulfilment. Potential freedom and opportunities for free action do not constitute *actual* freedom.

Freedom itself is not an illusory concept, but it embraces such a tangle of subjective and objective, personal and public elements that a search for a final definition is doomed. In the political sphere, latterly, freedom has been equated with particular liberties to act or think. In some countries these rights are enshrined in a constitution while in Britain they mainly exist in the spaces between the laws—which are shrinking. Again, the possession of specific liberties cannot *make* us free as individuals, but they help us to exercise our freedom, and their absence would render us more susceptible to oppression. Such liberties operate as elaborations of the generally accepted principle of freedom in changing social circumstances. New rights are constantly demanded in the context of new exigencies. The freedom not to have one's telephone tapped, not to have one's personal data on a police computer, and a woman's right to choose whether to bear children, are all freedoms demanded or established as a result of technological or medical innovations. Although particular freedoms may be changing and precarious, and are often abrogated in emergencies, they offer a rudimentary yardstick for measuring freedom in a society: other criteria, such as the calibre and intellect of the people, which Mill proposed, are too vague.

The major debates about the nature of freedom have taken place within liberal thought, where it remains the highest political ideal. Liberty as an ideal is inseparable from an individualistic ethos: the concept of 'collective' freedom (espoused by some anarchists, socialists and even some right-wing thinkers) is different from, although parasitic upon, the idea of individual freedom. A people may have the right to self-determination, but this collective freedom may actually impose a rigid obligation on individuals to subordinate themselves to the whole. In liberal terms, a free society is one where each individual is equally free, and this is achieved by giving identical rights to all, although some may be materially unequal and, hence, less free despite these rights. Both liberals and anarchists emphasize that freedom for each is bound up with freedom for all, and would argue (for different reasons) that freedom entails equal freedom. Unfortunately, experience does not bear this out. I can often make myself freer at the expense of others; societies have existed with remarkably free rulers and oppressed masses. I think we cannot say that it is part of the meaning of 'freedom' that it should be equal for all, but it *is* a requirement of social justice that if some are free, all should be equally free: political freedoms and other rights must be equally distributed. So what seems to be an individualistic ideal has an inbuilt social dimension.

Freedom as the individual's right to non-interference is a weapon directed both against the state and against her fellow citizens. A vexed question is whether paternalistic intervention by the state or other individuals is ever permissible. Mill stated unequivocally that a government may not interfere to prevent someone harming himself: no compulsory cure for the alcoholic, no law against suicide. However, he admitted that 'self-regarding actions' which also harm others could be restrained. The habitually violent drunkard could be punished for drinking, and a man who 'through idleness' neglected to care for his family could be forced to carry out his obligations—though presumably he could not be made to work for his own good.[10] But since *all* our self-regarding actions may harm someone indirectly, if not directly, there must be a cut-off point to limit state interference in such cases. This line is not drawn consistently in Britain today. Possession of illegal drugs for personal use is a crime, not because the use of drugs is not self-regarding, but largely for paternalistic and moral reasons. In the case of some self-regarding actions outside the scope of morality, the operative criterion seems to be whether they cause a nuisance to the state. When crash helmets were made compulsory for motor-cyclists, and safety-belts for motorists, the major reason cited for state interference was the cost to the state of serious accidents or deaths, in terms of medical care and sickness benefit (for which the injured presumably paid their insurance contributions) and 'lost production': the latter phrase suggests an implicit assumption that each individual has a duty to contribute to national income. Mill would hardly have approved of such reasons. By contrast, the legalization of private homosexual acts between consenting adults constituted an acknowledgement that such acts were purely self-regarding and not the state's concern. (However, judgments of the British courts [1990] and the European Court of Human Rights [1997] upheld that homosexuals engaging in sado-masochist practices, including mutilation, were acting illegally—i.e. that such

10. J. S. Mill, *On Liberty*, Collins, 1962, p. 230.

private behaviour *was* the state's concern, because of its interest in 'the protection of health'.) Although it is unlikely that any general principle restricting state action will be agreed upon, we can analyse—and oppose—interventionist legislation according to whether it is proposed for paternalistic reasons, for moral reasons, or to prevent harm to others: only the latter seems to justify interference in private actions.

The question about paternalism also arises when there are questions of long-term good. May a government because it 'knows best' contravene the people's immediate, expressed preferences in order to promote their future good? Despite his repugnance for state interference, Mill thought it acceptable for education to be made compulsory on these grounds, and for 'advanced' countries to colonize 'savage' peoples in order to civilize them. Many government actions override people's short-term preferences to promote the general and long-term good—that is, there are inevitably both collectivist and paternalistic elements inimical to freedom in all government action, whether in embarking on a defence programme or in engineering short-term economic recessions for long-term prosperity, or in making people pay for a pension scheme. If this is not legitimate, then the case for government disappears altogether.[11] Philosophical accounts of liberty sometimes proceed as if all decisions and actions were simultaneous and all considerations short-lived, but politics is necessarily a long-term enterprise and necessarily involves some paternalistic actions. The best that people in a democracy can do to preserve their liberty against excessive paternalistic incursions is to hold frequent elections and vocalize their discontent with such policies.

The problem with the liberal idea of freedom is the sharp distinctions drawn between public and private, government and people (inappropriate in a truly representative democracy?) and the self and others (as if the individual could exist in society autonomously). The realm of action is less clear-cut than these philosophical categories suggest, and all but the most trivial actions bring us into contact with others, or with the state, or society at large. An action innocent in one context is harmful in another. Since laws cannot cover all eventualities, the best way to guarantee personal freedom of action is the establishment of rights which the individual can invoke if the government or other individuals interfere unduly. The analysis of rights is thus a necessary part of any discussion of liberty.

THE 'RIGHTS OF MAN'

The 'rights of man' rest on the fundamental premise of the right to life, stated as the right not to be deprived of life by other individuals or governments, and as the right of those living to reasonable conditions for life. Traditional liberal accounts of rights rest on the idea of a pre-social state of nature and the myth of a social contract. 'Natural rights' are the rights which some philosophers assumed people

---

11. Libertarians recommend the abolition of nearly all taxes and State services, since they reject the case for paternalism and that for collectivism. Nozick could be taken as their theoretical representative: see *Anarchy, State and Utopia*, Blackwell, 1974.

had even in a state of nature, rights which regulated their interaction according to rationality and/or God's wishes for humankind. Locke said that the task of government was the protection of man's natural rights to 'life, liberty and estate (property)', a view restated in the American *Declaration of Independence*. Paine's classic text, *The Rights of Man*, draws on this and on the claims of the French revolutionaries. He argues that government could only have arisen originally through a contract between men so that theoretically constitutions (based hypothetically on an original contract) have priority over governments. Every civil right is a natural right exchanged. Equal rights attach to each individual by virtue of his existence. Discussing the French *Declaration of Rights*, Paine says that the first three points are fundamental:[12]

(1) Men are born and always continue free, and equal in respect of their rights. Civil distinctions, therefore, can be founded only on public utility.
(2) The end of all political associations is the preservation of the natural and imprescriptible rights of man . . . liberty, property, security, and resistance of oppression.
(3) The Nation is essentially the source of all sovereignty; nor can any INDIVIDUAL, or ANY BODY OF MEN, be entitled to any authority which is not expressly derived from it.

All other rights proceed from these, including political liberty, the limitation of law, the minimization of government, freedom of speech, justice in taxation and everyone's right to choose their government.

Natural rights theory rested on the hypothesis of a pre-social code of natural law, and was widely challenged in the eighteenth century. The critics of natural rights theory came from all parts of the political spectrum. Burke maintained that such absolute and inviolable rights were impossible in society, which is organic, evolving, and hierarchical. Only the rights prescribed by custom could be admitted as antecedent to society.[13] Bentham attacked natural rights both as a legal positivist and as a utilitarian. Such rights were 'nonsense upon stilts' and 'anarchical fallacies'—metaphysical entities which threatened to supplant the authority of law. Nothing not established in positive law could claim to have a higher status than the law itself: the only real rights were positive, *legal* rights, established after the creation of the social and legal systems. Such rights could therefore not be natural.[14] Utilitarianism also could not accede to the existence of such rights as absolutes or ends in themselves, lest they should claim priority over the supreme principle of utility. (Mill later modified utilitarian theory to accommodate the existence of rights and reconcile them with utility.) A further widely accepted criticism of natural rights, voiced by T. H. Green among others, was that they paradoxically impute a quasi-legal system to the supposed state of

---

12. T. Paine, *The Rights of Man*, Penguin, 1969, p. 166.
13. E. Burke, *Reflections on the Revolution in France*, Penguin, 1969, pp. 149–52.
14. B. Parekh (Ed.), *Bentham's Political Thought*, Croom Helm, 1973, p.269. For an account of Bentham's views on rights, see J.Waldron, *Nonsense upon Stilts: Bentham, Burke and Marx on the Rights of Man*, Methuen, 1987.

nature, since rights themselves are a legal concept. But Green believed something could be rescued from the doctrine of natural rights.

> Such a doctrine is generally admitted to be untenable; but it does not follow from this that there is not a true and important sense in which . . . rights and obligations exist . . . which may properly be called 'natural' . . . because necessary to the end which it is the vocation of human society to realize. [15]

Marx attacked the *Declaration* 'of the so-called rights of man' on the ground of its bourgeois content. 'None of the supposed rights of man . . . go beyond the egoistic man . . . an individual separated from the community . . . wholly preoccupied with his private interest'.[16] He argued that the bourgeois state abolished inequalities of wealth, class, and birth 'in its own manner'— deceptively—by giving each man the vote, an abstract right, while outside this narrow political sphere inequalities abounded. As to the *Declaration*, Marx said that *liberty* separates man from man, making him an 'isolated monad', limiting his responsibility to his fellows. *Property* is 'the right of selfishness', *equality* is man's right to be treated, without discrimination, as a self-sufficient monad, while *security* 'guarantees egoism'. Bourgeois man has in theory no communal existence or duties as a citizen: these rights all facilitate his 'withdrawal' from society, allowing him to exploit his fellows without guilt. Most dangerously, these political rights establish an illusion of equality amidst genuine inequality and oppression, just as democracy disguises the repressive and partisan nature of the state. Hence the irony of the liberal claim that government's task is to preserve rights: the state abrogates them by its very nature. Human rights are therefore part of the ruling ideology, part of universal false consciousness. Although the French Revolution had produced the *Declaration*, it was drawn up by members of the bourgeoisie, the ultimate beneficiaries of that revolution. While there is some truth in Marx's view that political rights create a formal, illusory equality which disguises the true state of society, this is hardly a sufficient reason for trying to abolish those rights so that the state can be seen as the source of oppression. But revolutionary strategists have often advocated tactics to provoke repressive state action and the rescinding of rights, to hasten the cataclysm. However, Marxists in the West have usually accepted such rights as instrumentally useful in the pursuit of their goals, and would defend them, with the qualification that they do not constitute *real* equality or freedom.

HUMAN RIGHTS

In the twentieth century, as the conception of rights based on natural law and social contract was no longer tenable, 'natural rights' gave way to 'human rights', which are said to attach to every being by virtue of his or her humanity and right to dignity, independence, and equality of respect. Such assertions are justified by Kantian forms of morality which enjoin equal respect for all human beings as an

---

15. T.H. Green, *Principles of Political Obligation*, Longmans, Green & Co., 1901, pp. 33–34.
16. K. Marx, 'The Jewish Question', in *Early Texts* (Ed. D. McLellan), Blackwell, 1971, pp. 101–4.

absolute. Like the idea of liberty, that of rights evolves according to contemporary events and exigencies. Among the root causes of the First World War were nationalism and the problem of national minorities in large states. After that war, countries joining the League of Nations, whose territory or population had been changed by the war, were obliged to sign treaties or declarations protecting their minorities with respect to freedom of religion, the use of their own languages, the right to education, and similar matters. These provisions particularly affected the countries of Eastern Europe and the Balkans. Contraventions could be brought to the League, although this procedure and the guarantees were not very successful. The principle of self-determination of nations, which dictated no interference in a nation's internal affairs, was also accepted—a collective equivalent of the individual's right to non-interference. But the Second World War proved how poor a protection against powerful predators were national and individual rights, and how impotent was the League to enforce them.

Nevertheless, a further attempt was made to get worldwide acknowledgement of human dignity and rights under the aegis of the United Nations in the 1948 *Universal Declaration of Human Rights*. This reasserted the now familiar rights and some new ones—the right to life, liberty, property, equality before the law, privacy, fair trial, religious freedom, free speech and assembly, to participate in government, to political asylum, and the absolute right not to be tortured. Also, largely at the insistence of the Soviet bloc, various economic and social rights were included: the right to education, to work, to equal pay, to an adequate standard of living, and paid holidays. Cranston states that this 'represented a considerable diplomatic gain for the Communist members of the United Nations', since they could then claim that a number of rights in the Declaration were upheld in their countries.[17] But Western negotiators regarded the economic and social rights as qualitatively different from the other rights, being *ideals* rather than moral claims. This ideological division of opinion reflected the distance between the liberal and the communist view of liberty. In practice, communist states tended to ignore many of the first set of rights but guarantee social and economic rights, while capitalist countries do the reverse. This raises the question whether the *Universal Declaration* has any significant moral or legal status in the signatory countries. Some countries wished it to be incorporated in the positive law of each nation and so be enforceable in the normal way, but the former USSR and other countries opposed this, and doubtless few states would have been willing to accept the wide responsibilities which incorporation implied. It was also asked whether the *Declaration* might not be accorded the status of international law, but this was problematic as the latter deals with nations, not individuals. At present, the European Court of Human Rights may hear individual cases, but governments can still ignore its judgements, contrary to their treaty obligations. Likewise, the 1975 Helsinki agreement on rights, reaffirmed in 1985, is only enforceable 'morally' (a contradiction in terms), by states bringing pressure on each other to

_____

17. M. Cranston, *What Are Human Rights?*, Bodley Head, 1973, p. 54.

observe it—typically, this has meant by pressure from the West on communist countries and Third-World dictatorships. A recent development is the European Union's promotion of a Social Chapter (to which Britain finally subscribed in 1997), which elaborates a number of work- and welfare-related rights binding on member states.

These brief details of the recent history of human rights serve as a background to consideration of the questions raised by philosophers about such rights, such as 'Who should count as human?', 'What are the *basic* human rights?' and 'What is the status of such rights?'. Human rights derive from our nature as human beings, so their content depends on our definition of humanity. Because we are corporeal beings, we have a right to life, freedom from pain and torture, and to sustenance. Because we are rational and thinking, we have the right to freedom of thought and conscience, and so on. As Cranston observes, such rights can only be minimal because they are generalized so as to apply to all. The point of this universality is, of course, to prevent victimization of supposedly inferior races or individuals. But it has recently been asked whether the restriction of rights to the human race is not human chauvinism. Animals too have bodily needs and feel pain (and may, for all we know, think in some way) and so could be said to deserve the same treatment as human beings in many respects. Moral philosophers, most notably Peter Singer, have increasingly advanced the case for animal rights, partly as a protest against the experimental use of animals, partly as a philosophical demonstration that we cannot complacently draw such a clear line between ourselves and other species.[18] It has even been argued (seriously) that sophisticated computers fulfil the criteria for thinking beings, and may have certain rights. These examples are often contested because the notion of human rights seems to rest on an intuitive recognition of others as, approximately, our equals, a condition not fulfilled with respect to animals, but there is a good case for arguing that some of the rights which we attribute to ourselves should be accorded to *all* living things. Science fiction often speculates on how we would treat intelligent beings landing here from elsewhere in space. The more interesting question with regard to rights and morality is how they, the superior form of life, would treat us.

In principle, a catalogue of human rights should not be too long, nor determined by a particular cultural outlook, for human rights specify the minimum conditions for human dignity and a tolerable life anywhere, at any time. However, as the length of the Declarations grows, they contain more and more political rights, most of which reflect liberal-democratic ideology. It could be argued that these are really *civil* rights established in certain societies but not sharing the universal qualities of human rights and not obligatory for all societies. Alternatively, the very idea of a decent human life may include the right to participate in choosing a government and so to control one's destiny. If this is so, human rights do not stop at the satisfaction of our corporeal and intellectual needs, but are a seamless web, covering the political, social, and economic life of

---

18.   T. Regan and P. Singer, *Animal Rights and Human Obligation*, Prentice-Hall, 1976; P. Singer, *Animal Liberation*, rev. ed., Cape, 1990. For an opposing view on animal rights, see R. G. Frey, *Interests and Rights: The Case Against Animals*, Oxford U.P., 1980.

human beings. It is hard to choose between these arguments: the liberal desire to fuse political and human rights suggests an element of moral imperialism, but the acknowledgement, implicit in this, of our political nature is an important assertion. Certainly, if all the political, economic and social rights in the 1948 *Declaration* were realized in one country, utopia would be achieved.

The question of the *status* of human rights is closely linked with that of their enforceability. Such rights are not established in law in many countries, so they cannot be regarded as legal entities or 'possessions' in a legal sense. Human rights are, essentially, *moral claims* to certain kinds of treatment for all human beings, and such claims are only enforceable through conscience, unless they are made law. The issue is obscured because rights are sometimes spoken of as if they were *facts*, to give them greater rhetorical force: 'men are free and equal'. They are presented as analytical truths about human nature for the same reason: man, defined as a free being, necessarily has the right to be free. The philosophical status of human rights is sometimes likened to the status which Kant gave to moral propositions: they are 'synthetic *a priori*' statements. That is, they have an *a priori*, absolute application to all human beings because they derive from the definition of a human being but, paradoxically, they are also 'synthetic' because they refer to the contingent, real world and are not mere tautologies about human beings. Whatever their precise analytical status, which is controversial, statements about rights are normative and prescriptive and empirically unverifiable, hence Bentham's dismissal of them as nonsense, and the suspicion of their status among logical positivists who regard moral and other unverifiable statements as being outside the realm of fact, mere statements of preference.

Rights, then, are essentially part of morality, but are often referred to in quasi-legal terms, to make them seem more authoritative. Plamenatz defined them as follows:

> a right is a power in the exercise of which all rational beings ought to protect a creature, either because its exercise by him is itself good or else because it is a means to what is good.[19]

He later added that someone has a right when no-one ought to prevent him from doing something, or refuse him some service that he needs. His definition, quite properly, links rights to a notion of *human good*; it also brings into prominence the obvious truth that every individual right also creates a duty for other individuals and/or for the state. My rights impose an obligation on everyone else to respect them, and vice versa. There can be no objection to this limitation of freedom as long as rights are acknowledged to be equal and universal. The interplay of reciprocal rights and duties is the basis of most moralities although some moral codes said to emanate from higher sources, such as the Ten Commandments, seem to create only duties: how could man claim rights from God? According to Plamenatz, a right may even justify demanding a service from someone else. If we claim human rights for ourselves, then, we are logically bound to accept our duty to observe similar rights for others, without considering this an

---

19.   J. P. Plamenatz, *Consent, Freedom and Political Obligation*, 2nd edn, Oxford U.P., 1968, p. 82.

infringement of our personal freedom. Only the solipsist could want a world in which she had rights but no reciprocal duties.

Philosophers argue that moral injunctions must observe the axiom that ' "ought" implies "can" ': that is, I cannot be morally required to do something that I am unable to do. Similarly, rights should not, they say, impose duties which are beyond individuals or states in practical terms. Some would argue on these grounds that the economic and social rights advocated by socialists and Marxists countries are illegitimate or vacuous since the preconditions for realizing the right to work, or the right to an adequate standard of living simply do not exist in many countries. The answer is that rights differ from moral imperatives in the following respect: when we say that the unemployed in an impoverished country have the 'right' to a living wage, we are stating a political recommendation, not an imperative but an ideal, in the form of a right. Like other rights claims, this refers implicitly to an idea of the Good Life. However, because such ideals are conditioned by ideology, rights claims of this kind are often highly controversial and open to dispute by the states against whom they are asserted.

Can a hierarchy of rights be identified, showing that certain rights are more basic and less ideological than others, and therefore merit universal application? Hart's argument that the fundamental right is the equal right to be free might be used as the basis of such a hierarchy. But this vague liberal formula would need to be translated into more concrete terms before it could form the basis of a code of rights, and the translation would be controversial. The rights which Amnesty International demands—the right to a fair trial, the right not to be inhumanely treated or executed—seem to be the most basic rights pertaining to social life, although even these reflect certain recent cultural and moral developments and so might not properly be called basic and universal. *If* we could clearly distinguish basic, universal rights from secondary rights (defined as 'ideological' or 'cultural' rights) it would follow that countries could exhort each other to observe the basic rights but should not interfere in the matter of secondary rights which are culture-specific, a matter of choice. But this distinction, which is hard to make philosophically (some of our most basic rights would have been disputed by slave-owning societies), would probably be rejected by countries eager to export their own values. The West habitually strove to make communist countries implement certain rights which are really cultural, but which liberal ideology holds to be universal, such as the rights of free speech and protest. And with the revival of Islamic fundamentalism in many Muslim countries, Westerners have been quick to pass judgement not only on the revival of traditional punishments such as death by stoning (which contravenes the 'basic' injunction against cruel punishments) but also on the restrictive treatment of women. The Islamic countries would say that this is an internal matter bound up with religion, morality, and culture, while we consider it a violation of a basic, universal right, the right of women to be treated with dignity, as free beings, and to have the same rights as men. In short, even if the worst evils such as torture and coercion could be eradicated by the enforcement of basic rights worldwide, while such cultural differences persisted disputes about what other rights should be observed would still continue, with countries taking a missionary stance in favour of the rights favoured by their own ideology and culture.

Some right-wing thinkers are given to speaking of rights as 'privileges'. Since rights are a major defensive weapon against autocratic governments and the hypertrophy of states, it is important to repudiate this conception, which deprives rights of their political force. The connotations of 'privilege' are as follows: first, that it is something which a limited number of people have, second, that it can be taken away, third, that it is given from above and fourth, that it is somehow earned or deserved. By contrast, human rights, first of all, attach equally to all human beings. Second, rights cannot be 'taken away': even when they are contravened, they remain valid moral claims. Third, such rights are, in principle, affirmed by the people through democratically made laws. Fourth, such rights are not earned because they are *a priori* rights—even if elitist governments have sometimes extended legal rights to the people as a reward for 'good behaviour'. Rights, unlike privileges, are not scarce goods, since they can be created easily and often costlessly, so that the element of competition implied in the term 'privilege' is not present in rights. Nor should we feel beholden to a state which allows us extensive rights, for the reasons just mentioned. In fact, the language of rights and their function in political practice both necessitate that they should always be asserted as *rights*, not petitioned for as privileges given from above, which might be rescinded. This sometimes involves the anomaly of asserting as facts what we really know to be moral claims, or ideological preferences, but this tactical rhetoric is necessary in the endeavour of individuals to extract humane treatment from states.

SPECIAL RIGHTS FOR WOMEN?

Before leaving the topic of rights, I shall discuss briefly the question of women's rights, both because of its current importance and as a way of considering more generally the status of the special rights claimed by particular groups or minorities on the basis of their own special characteristics. Claims for women's rights, rights for ethnic minorities, gay rights, and rights for people with disabilities are all current demands. Because human rights belong to all individuals by reason of their humanity, there are no grounds for denying them to people placed in a particular category by certain, 'permanent' characteristics such as race, sex or disability. Nevertheless, in the past women were denied the political and property rights basic to liberal society because they were considered unequal, being supposedly inferior to men in terms of intelligence and judgement. The case for equal civil rights rested, naturally, on the contention that women were equal to men in all relevant aspects. I speak of 'civil rights' here because, although some civil rights such as the right to property were counted as *basic* human rights by liberals, they were simultaneously—and inconsistently—viewed as resting on certain criteria, which women did not fulfil. The extension of such rights to women was an admission of their equality in all relevant respects. Undoubtedly, the achievement of 'bourgeois' rights by women was crucially important, even if some feminists now denigrate it because such rights did not alter other fundamental inequalities.

However, the terrain of the debate on women's rights has now shifted.[20] A group of individuals with full human and civil rights may nevertheless consider that its members have special characteristics which entitle them to additional, special rights. The Women's Movement today concerns itself with such needs. Opponents of the movement may criticize this as a search for what they consider special privileges, since women now have equal basic rights in most Western countries. But the claim to special rights because of special needs or disadvantages should not be viewed as a demand for privileges. Rather, it is a demand for compensating measures to overcome these disadvantages and bring the members of the group up to full equality with other people. Thus, a woman's right to maternity leave (which some men regard as an unwarranted privilege) is intended to put her in the same position as men with regard to security of employment. The childbearing capacity gives women special needs. It may also be that women's lesser physical strength is a reason for giving them special rights: perhaps, to protect themselves against sexual and other attacks, women should be permitted to carry defensive weapons (which, if carried by men, might be termed 'offensive') which allowed them to feel as free to go about the streets as men do. In fact, this special need is not acknowledged, and women in Britain and the USA have been prosecuted for carrying such 'weapons' of self-defence as pepper-pots and dye-sprays. But such a right is not an unreasonable demand in view of women's vulnerability to attack. Special rights, then, are not privileges, but rights which ensure that all members of the community can enjoy their basic rights fully and equally. Special rights are the elaboration of the spirit of human rights in special circumstances.

Nobody disputes the rights of the disabled to disability allowances and other special treatment according to their manifest needs. But the criteria for special rights are widely disputed in the case of women and various minority groups, even when their distinguishing characteristics are just as permanent as those of handicap. 'Special rights for blue-eyed brunettes, next?' is the *reductio ad absurdum* of special rights: but this objection is invalid, for special rights are not the thin end of the wedge. The kinds of characteristics and the needs and disabilities which make special rights appropriate are, by and large, intuitively obvious to any reasonable person, even if there is disagreement on the degree of compensation which they warrant. Special rights are justifiable on the grounds that they are necessary for the enjoyment of basic rights for a certain group, and that without the compensation which they provide human equality would be meaningless.

More contentious than special rights is 'positive discrimination', which Americans call 'reverse discrimination' or 'affirmative action': the giving of 'privileges' to certain groups to correct their particular disadvantages *or* to compensate for unfair discrimination against them in the past. While special

20. See A. Carter, *The Politics of Women's Rights*, Longman, 1988.

rights are also a form of compensation, we could attempt to draw a line—with difficulty—between bringing people up to the same level as others, and giving them unfair advantages. It may seem acceptable that a firm should make crèche facilities available to encourage working mothers to apply for jobs there, whereas many people would find it unacceptable if the firm earmarked a percentage of jobs for women and turned away better qualified male candidates. In this case, men might fairly claim that the quota system detracted from their chances of getting a job, and hence contravened their rights. To this objection, it could be replied that, given the greater difficulty experienced by women in finding jobs because of various prejudices, the quota was justified for egalitarian reasons. The firm might, alternatively, claim that the quota system is positive discrimination to rectify historical injustices experienced by women in the past. (Some US universities reserve places for blacks partly on these grounds.) Needless to say, the generations of past women who have been treated unjustly can never be compensated and, as we have seen in other examples, the principle of correcting *past* injustices leads to both conceptual and practical problems, and is best avoided. It could be said that the first measure (crèches) established equality of opportunity to compete for jobs while the second (the quota) established a more substantive equality of treatment. Liberals object to the latter because it undermines competition and equal opportunity. So the disagreement is ultimately ideological: what does equality mean? Given the hostility to positive discrimination in liberal society, it is only likely to be considered in cases of long-term grave injustice, perhaps as a temporary measure or a gesture of goodwill, in the expectation that in the long run women will get positions on their own merits, when prejudices against appointing them are broken down. But the antagonism created by such measures may sometimes outweigh their benefits (as we see even with the legislation prohibiting racial discrimination in employment). In most cases, the righting of historical injustices across generations is best not attempted—justice and equal rights for the living is the best that can be hoped for in an imperfect world.

A campaign for pay equity for American women in the 1980s provides an example of how righting a wrong for one unfairly treated group can disadvantage other groups. The enforcement of pay equity in San Jose, California, made the position of low-paid men, especially black men, relatively worse, it was said. Similar arguments have been used about positive discrimination. The important point here, surely, is that not all wrongs can be righted simultaneously. If measures to undo the disadvantages which women suffer, or to enforce their rights, are detrimental to other groups, then the rights of these groups must, in turn, be brought to the public's attention. The fact that the rights, status and income of one group are relative to those of other groups must not be used as an argument for maintaining existing relativities when these are themselves unjust.

The arguments valid for women can be extended to all groups who are genuinely disadvantaged by some generally agreed criterion. The principle which should direct policy in a just society is that basic human rights (although, as we saw, this concept involves problems) should be given to all, special rights should be allocated to those with special needs and temporary, 'extra' rights may be given in the form of positive discrimination in exceptional situations.

RIGHTS AND LIBERTY

A final question is whether rights are, or should be, inviolable. It would be nice if they were. But nearly all rights theorists agree that 'reasons of state' and emergencies take priority over rights. Habeas corpus, the most fundamental individual right in the British legal system, has regularly been suspended in wartime and other emergencies—e.g. in Northern Ireland to facilitate the internment of republican supporters (1971). The UN Declaration conceded that some rights are subject to limitations prescribed by law which are 'necessary to protect public safety, order, health, or morals, or the fundamental rights and freedom of others'. Even Bills of Rights can be amended. The usual justification for the abrogation of rights is that the state is acting for the immediate or long-term good of the community. The validity of such claims, especially claims citing the 'national interest' in peace time, is often hard to establish, or dubious. Of course, cases are conceivable where some individuals' rights must give way in the interests of justice for others—for example, the limitation of property rights to ensure a fairer distribution—but in such cases the good envisaged is more demonstrable than in cases where 'reasons of state' are cited. The legal philosopher Dworkin argues for the inviolability of rights,[21] but even if all rights were established in positive law, they would be no more inviolable than the law itself. But, as moral claims should be viewed in principle as inviolable, the violation of rights must always form the basis for a serious moral and political challenge to any state.

Rights are the guarantors of liberty, specific freedoms which, when legally enforced, institutionalize humane morality and tolerance. The language of rights also has an international dimension which legal principles do not, and can be used to propagate humanitarian ideals beyond national boundaries. Rights establish a minimum degree of liberty in society, although personal liberty extends beyond formal rights, of course. Because of these advantages, it is often asked whether Britain should follow other countries in having a Bill of Rights. Given that all laws, including constitutional laws, can be repealed, this could not guarantee absolutely the security of such rights. Nor, *in extremis*, would it prevent a government from contravening those laws. But the purpose of a Bill of Rights is to give governments pause when they are tempted to take coercive measures, and also to ensure automatically that new legislation does not contravene established rights. In both respects a Bill of Rights would seem to be an improvement on our present position, notwithstanding the arguments of those who think that our unwritten constitution is the acme of perfection. On the other hand, it has been argued that the result of enacting such a Bill would effectively empower the judges (who would decide whether legislation was in harmony with the Bill or not, as in

---

21. R. Dworkin, *Taking Rights Seriously*, Duckworth, 1977, Chaps. 6–7.

the USA), thus giving an elite and unelected body too powerful a role in constitutional and policy matters.[22] The debate continues.

In order to assess the degree of freedom in society, we should consider the following factors:

(1) The negative and positive liberties generally available to citizens, and the balance between them.
(2) The extensiveness and intrusiveness, actual and potential, of the laws. (In Britain, laws against obstruction and conspiracy can be extended almost *ad hoc* to cover nearly any behaviour, so the wording of the statute book is not the only relevant factor: implementation must also be examined.)
(3) The role which the people play in promulgating laws; that is, the extent to which the laws are based on democratic consent, and the responsiveness of the government to the people's wishes.
(4) The existence of specific legal rights, such as those listed in Bills of Rights, which represent semi-immovable bulwarks of liberty for the people against the state.
(5) The degree to which the people *feel* free, and understand and discuss freedom, and defend it when under attack. Though feelings of freedom can be illusory, such feelings in conjunction with real freedoms are an important part of the subjective and objective components which together constitute freedom in society.

Finally, something must be said about *tolerance* which, where it exists, regulates the behaviour of individuals to each other, and the state's behaviour towards individuals, in the way most conducive to freedom. In Chapter 3 above, the views of Locke and Mill on tolerance were described, and its special link with liberal values was elaborated. A climate of tolerance, according to liberals, is one in which rights can best be exercised, provided that the violation of rights is not tolerated. Tolerance may be expressed in the form of particular, legally established rights, e.g. the right to freedom of speech, but it must also constitute one of the conventional ground-rules of a society if it is to protect individuals successfully from undue interference.

THE CLIMATE OF TOLERANCE

To tolerate is to endure something of which one disapproves, *voluntarily*, that is, when one has the power to change it. A paradigm case is that of a democracy where the majority tolerates irritating, maybe offensive, behaviour by a minority, which it could easily outlaw, in the interests of social harmony. Also, of course, tolerance is exercised in interpersonal and non-political situations. Society may adopt tolerance as a *value* for several reasons. First, because in particular cases tolerance is less objectionable than the alternatives: we tolerate political extremists

22. 'Democracy or a Bill of Rights', K.D. Ewing and C.A. Gearty, *Society of Labour Lawyers Pamphlet*, 1991.

because we are not willing to condone their persecution, or the suppression of a political viewpoint.[23] Second, tolerance is a necessary consequence of any morality which enjoins us not to use human beings as means to our ends. If I seek to prohibit someone's behaviour merely because it offends me, I am treating her instrumentally, ignoring her right to equality of respect, whereas if her behaviour violates my rights I am justified in putting an end to it. Third, we may tolerate those who hold and express different beliefs and ideas as a consequence of being unsure that our own beliefs or knowledge are infallibly true.

The doctrine of toleration first developed with respect to religion and was later applied to political belief. Religious toleration may be based on the view that no sect has a monopoly of truth, since there is no known method for proving one particular conception of God to be right: therefore all must be tolerated. (It may also be practised for a reason like that mentioned above, that one morally objects to the forcible conversion or punishment of heretics, even though one hates heresy: tolerance is then accepted as the lesser evil, not as a principle in its own right.) Political tolerance rests on the similar view that there can be no conclusive proof or disproof of the truth of political ideas. Since values and ideologies are unverifiable, we cannot choose between them officially, although we may espouse them personally. Political tolerance could also be asserted on the egalitarian basis that, if all individuals are assumed to be of equal worth and dignity, their opinions are also of equal worth, and must not be suppressed: liberalism admits this in assuming each person to be an authority on her own interests. Evidently, tolerance is a political ideal well suited to liberal ideology and the pluralist form of society which fosters a variety of beliefs and values. On the other hand, a totalitarian state, committed to certain political *truths*, would be inconsistent if it tolerated rival doctrines, since these would necessarily be false. Tolerance is therefore usually found in conjunction with liberal democracy, pluralism, and an empiricist theory of knowledge, which concedes that we can never establish truths conclusively, and must admit an element of doubt.[24]

Tolerance in politics is mainly linked with freedom of thought and expression, but in social life the toleration of *behaviour* is also important. Directly harmful behaviour is prohibited by law—which can be said to tolerate everything which it does not prohibit—but some actions which people find offensive are permitted by law, such as 'deviant' sexual behaviour. Mill argued passionately that people should not inflict their moral beliefs on others by legal means, or seek to prevent them from acting 'immorally', since being morally offended does not constitute material harm. In practice, the law has often come down on the side of 'public decency' (the side of the morally offended), especially in sexual matters, despite the fact that passers-by can avert their eyes from the windows of sex-shops or other unseemly sights, so that moral offence is often a self-inflicted injury.

Cases of moral and political intolerance are often parallel because both rest partly on outrage, partly on a paternalistic impulse. (It was presumably as a result of outrage at the violence of the IRA that in 1988 the government prohibited

---

23. P. King, *Toleration*, Allen & Unwin, 1976, pp. 23, 35.
24. Mill, *On Liberty*, Chap. 2. Mill's justifications for toleration were discussed in Chapter 3 above.

television and radio networks from broadcasting the voices of members of the IRA and other proscribed organizations.) In a democracy which tolerates all ideologies in theory, political groups are sometimes banned or denied free expression because their doctrines are inimical to democracy. When this is justified on the grounds that they might convert the foolish and so threaten the democratic system, the reasoning is paternalistic, like that behind banning pornography in case it corrupts the unwary, or 'public morals'. Political intolerance for such a reason is clearly anomalous in democratic systems, which assume political acumen and rationality on the part of their citizens. An alternative justification for banning such groups is that their own ideologies would, in practice, abolish tolerance: by being intolerant themselves, they forfeit the right to tolerance. (Rawls argues on these lines, but concludes that this does not give tolerant people the *right* to be intolerant towards intolerant people, unless their own security requires it.[25]) This be-done-by-as-you-do reasoning is supported by more sophisticated moral theories about the necessary universaliz-ability and reciprocity of moral principles. But to decide when to apply the principle that the intolerant must not be tolerated involves making judgements about people's beliefs, which may be mistaken. Should Marxists or neo-fascists be refused academic jobs, which allow them to propagate their ideas, because such ideas, if realized, might—it is not certain—be intolerant? The virtue of tolerance is, precisely, that it saves us from having to make such judgements. The application of 'reciprocal logic' against the intolerant produces a discriminatory situation in which some people's rights and views are suppressed, and this cannot easily be squared with the liberal support of individual rights, however much poetic justice there may be in it. For this reason, most liberals would probably advocate that we *should* tolerate the intolerant unless they attempt to put their views into practice and threaten the freedom of others.

A different, consequentialist justification for banning certain ideas or ideologies is that they are *harmful*, though not necessarily intolerant or antithetical to democracy. We might decide that ideologies claiming that women, blacks, Jews or other groups were inferior were directly or indirectly harmful to those groups and should be suppressed. The 1965 and 1976 Race Relations Acts in Britain banned 'threatening or insulting words' intended to 'stir up hatred' against any race on the grounds that such words were likely to cause material harm to individuals or social disturbance. In this case, priorities are reversed: tolerance is suspended because its consequences would predictably be worse than those of intolerance. A problem here is that predictions of harm are uncertain: also, that people differ over what counts as harmful. Many champions of the freedom of speech complained about the restriction of rights by the Race Relations Acts, but this is surely a paradigm case of restricting some people's rights to preserve even more important rights for others. Different reasons for intolerance or censorship will usually be given according to one's ideology. A right-wing thinker might give the

25. J. Rawls, *A Theory of Justice*, Harvard U.P., 1971, pp. 216–21.

paternalistic justification, while liberals are more likely to choose the second or third reasons mentioned in the previous paragraph.

Tolerance as a political doctrine is an important part of liberal thought but in any but the most stable and consensual situation it presents liberal-democratic society with dilemmas which are theoretically insoluble, there being no *right* answer to questions such as 'Should we tolerate the intolerant?'. Mendus sees the duty to tolerate the morally intolerable as a paradox of toleration and argues that the self-contradictory nature of such a duty reflects the flaws in liberal theory.[26] But perhaps the theoretical solution lies in treating tolerance strictly as a subordinate and instrumental value, in contrast with the approach of those liberals who view it as good in itself and therefore find themselves with clashes of ideals. On the instrumental view, tolerance would have to give way when primary values such as social justice were at risk (although tolerance is, normally, conducive to justice) and where individuals' lives were threatened.

The diverse practical solutions attempted often result in the erosion of tolerance. The British way has normally been to tolerate the *existence* of political parties hostile to the system—except, because its aims are 'treasonable', the IRA—but to deny them the facilities for assemblies and demonstrations, by means of the local authorities or the police, when material harm is feared. Rumour also has it that life is, informally, made difficult for members of such groups. This compromise vitiates our ideal of tolerance and gives those concerned a rightful grievance: it might be preferable if the grounds for *not* tolerating groups or doctrines were made clear, then applied consistently.

The fragility of an ideal is not a good reason for abandoning it, but rather one for strengthening our understanding of what it entails. The enforcement of human rights is partly an enforcement of tolerance—the tolerance of some for others' non-conformist actions within certain limits, or tolerance by the state of such actions. As was said earlier, tolerance is in principle *voluntary* forbearance, but there are instances of enlightened (and paternalistic) parliaments causing people to become tolerant by means of legislation: the liberalization of the law on homosexuality in the 1960s in Britain has had that effect to some extent. Tolerance is not, alas, instinctive, but it rests on attitudes, and these may sometimes be altered by means of law. It is, despite the problems discussed here, an important instrument in maintaining liberal-democratic society and freedoms.

In conclusion, it may be said that, whatever the power of the modern state, and however fast it may be growing, there is a formidable array of freedom-related concepts which can be used, in liberal societies at least, to combat that growth. But state encroachments are often covert and the task of combating them, once they become manifest, is protracted. The stronger the culture of freedom and tolerance, the better the chance of limiting state power. In this endeavour, democracy is crucial. Only public outrage and unpopularity can force a government to retract measures inimical to individual liberty: the less healthy a democracy and the more apathetic an electorate, the less responsive the

---

26. S. Mendus, *Toleration and the Limits of Liberalism*, Macmillan, 1989, 'Introduction'.

government. Democracy, freedom, rights and tolerance form an important chain of political concepts. Unless they form part of the political culture too, modern states are likely to increase in power and size, whatever their ideological colour.

FURTHER READING

D. Beetham (Ed.), *Politics and Human Rights*, Blackwell, 1995.
S. Benn, *A Theory of Freedom*, Cambridge U.P., 1988.
R. Dworkin, *Taking Rights Seriously*, Duckworth, 1977.
J. Gray, *Mill on Liberty: A Defence*, Routledge & Kegan Paul, 1983.
T. Gray, *Freedom*, Macmillan, 1991.
F. A. Hayek, *The Constitution of Liberty*, Routledge & Kegan Paul, 1960.
P. Jones, *Rights*, Macmillan, 1994.
S. Mendus (Ed.), *Justifying Toleration*, Cambridge U.P., 1988.
S. Mendus, *Toleration and the Limits of Liberalism*, Macmillan, 1989
D. Miller (Ed.), *Liberty*, Oxford U.P., 1991.
J. Raz, *The Morality of Freedom*, Clarendon Press, 1986.
H. Steiner, *An Essay on Rights*, Blackwell, 1985.
J. Waldron (Ed.), *Theories of Rights*, Oxford U.P., 1984.

Chapter 15

Obligation and Protest

I now turn to a concept which is the obverse of the concept of authority, political obligation, and to the question of where such obligation ends—in other words, at what point we are justified in disobeying a law or a government as a legitimate means of protest. The problem of political obligation is sometimes paraphrased as the question, 'Why should I obey the law?' Perhaps the single most remarkable fact about society is that most people, most of the time, acknowledge and obey political authority, however remote it is from their lives, and however much it is against their inclinations or short-term interests. Political scientists explain this phenomenon in terms of our political socialization from an early age,[1] while the theorists explain it in terms of political obligation. But the two explanations are compatible, for the process of socialization contains arguments to convince the individual of the wisdom, morality or necessity of obeying the rulers. Such arguments merit close and critical examination, and this will involve discussion of how political obligation is said to arise. Questions of obligation, Ayer said, are likely to occur only to the members of individualistic societies like those of Ancient Athens or seventeenth-century England. This is because only in a society where the individual has a lively impression of her own autonomy and personal interests does an inevitable tension arise between her will and the commands of the state. In a strongly hierarchical or religious society, with an ideology which binds the individual parts to the whole, such a divergence rarely occurs.

It might be thought that 'political obligation' is a political philosopher's genie, unrelated to everyday politics and meaningless to the man in the street, yet the notion is crucial both to political theory and to state propaganda. Theory needs to explain how we are integrated in society and why we accommodate ourselves to the pressures and demands of our fellow-citizens, even when this is against our interests, or avoidable. Political obligation provides the theorist with a premise of

---

1. R. E. Dawson and K. Prewitt, *Political Socialization*, Little, Brown & Co., 1969.

consistent, law-abiding behaviour applicable to any 'normal' situation; for the state, it is useful to be able to assert the general duty of citizens to obey the laws and respect the government, using one of the accounts of obligation provided by the theorists.

Political and moral obligation are closely linked, and some theorists assert that political obligation is always moral. Obligation operates internally, via the conscience, to procure compliance, yet it must also exist externally, objectively, so that others can remind us of it if we neglect it. Moral obligation used to be seen as emanating from absolute moral codes (often religious codes established by God) which had objective existence yet were internalized and acted upon by individuals. Kant's categorical imperative likewise takes an unconditional form which rests on our nature as moral beings. Such moral absolutes confront us as external forces to which we must adapt our thinking and actions. But since the Enlightenment it has been more usual to regard morality as *self-imposed*, which makes it more acceptable to individuals, although none the less binding; promising is sometimes used as an analogy for how moral obligation is self-imposed, although it is a poor analogy in the case of political obligation, as we shall see.[2] With the emergence of the view of the individual as a rational and independent actor, a contractual model of self-assumed political obligation came into fashion, and this was a watershed in political theory, which had previously ignored the political role of the people. The major contract theories will be stated briefly, and contrasted with the modern account of consent.

CONTRACTUAL OBLIGATION

Hobbes responded to the need for a secular theory of obligation to replace the unconditional obligation which 'divine right' had been thought to impose on the king's subjects. He imagines a pre-social state of nature far from the Garden of Eden, where men are in constant uncertainty, under the threat of violence or sudden death from others. He hypothesizes that to escape from this state of war they would form a society via a 'covenant' to ensure peace and their own survival. But, distrusting each other to keep the pact, they would have to set up a 'common power' above themselves to enforce obedience to it. This power is Hobbes's *sovereign*, authorized to act on behalf of the original contractors. As we saw earlier, Hobbes so defines 'authorization' that the author gives the actor complete power and forgoes the right to instruct him, yet remains responsible for all his actions. Hobbes allocates the sovereign wide, absolute powers necessary for preserving peace and men's lives, and goes on to deduce that, whatever it does, the sovereign cannot injure the subject because this would be equivalent to the subject's injuring himself, and hence absurd. Not surprisingly, Hobbes has been

---

2. The nature of self-imposed obligation is described in R. M. Hare, *Freedom and Reason*, Oxford U.P., 1963.

accused of advocating an absolutist state where citizens have no rights except the ultimate right to try to avoid death if the sovereign seeks to kill them.[3]

From the conditions which Hobbes postulates, a twofold obligation to the sovereign arises. First, the third law of nature is 'That men perform their covenants made',[4] and this *morally* obliges men to obey the original covenant and abide by its consequences. This means that the obligation to obey is partly externally imposed and partly self-imposed, since the laws of nature exist independently of man's will, but the covenant is a self-assumed obligation. Second, *prudence* or *expediency* commands men to obey because any disobedience will threaten the sovereign's existence and could precipitate a return to the warring state of nature. It is often asked whether Hobbes sees obligation as moral or prudential. Both sorts of obligation appear in his theory, but expediency alone would establish political obligation: since *any* regime is preferable to the infernal state of nature, we are obliged by prudence to obey the sovereign, however tyrannical. But what Hobbes intends to create is *unconditional moral obligation in perpetuity.* Most moral philosophers would repudiate such an extreme conception of obligation—even promises can be broken in some situations—and its political consequences would certainly be disastrous, since it gives *carte blanche* to tyrants.

The position from which Locke challenged Hobbes is that a man cannot give away more power over himself than he himself has: this denies the theoretical possibility of *any* absolute sovereign. Locke also located the origin of government in a state of nature, but for him this was a peaceful, semi-civilized state. For greater security of their 'life, liberty, and estate', men consented to form a political community. The result of this contract was a government whose duty was to protect and further their interests, but the people still remained sovereign. Anyone with 'possession or enjoyment of any part of the dominions of any government' gives *tacit* consent to the government and must observe its laws; by this provision Locke answered more satisfactorily than Hobbes (although not convincingly) the question why the descendants of the original contractors should owe loyalty to the government. But tacit consent itself raises many problems because it entails the imputation of obligation to those who have not expressly consented, contrary to the model of self-imposed obligation.[5] Importantly, Locke limits the extent of obligation. The community remains supreme and the people can resume power if the government is generally judged to have betrayed its trust. Obligation is thus conditional and is largely prudential, being tied up with the protection of individual interests, although there is the implication that it also rests on our gratitude to the government for protecting our 'estates', so again there are moral elements in the idea. Locke is also emphatic that men must acquiesce in the laws which they will have to obey: 'the supreme power cannot take from any man any part of his property *without his consent*'.[6] It must be remembered that Locke, like

---

3. Hobbes, *Leviathan*, Penguin, 1968, Chaps XIII–XIX.
4. Hobbes, *Leviathan*, p. 201.
5. J. Locke, *Essay*, Chaps VII–VIII. See also H. Pitkin, 'Obligation and consent', in *Philosophy, Politics and Society*, 4th Series (Eds. P. Laslett, W. G. Runciman and Q. Skinner), Blackwell 1972.
6. Locke, *Essay*, s. 138.

other contract theorists, was not describing a historical contract, but hypothesizing about the minimum conditions under which men would have sacrificed their natural liberty, conditions which should logically limit the scope and activities of real governments.

A number of theorists in the eighteenth century pointed out that the real basis of government was not contractual. Hume, Rousseau, and Paine saw existing governments as founded on force or deception,[7] but while Hume saw this as a reason to reject contract theory altogether, Paine and Rousseau contended that real governments should act *as if* they were based on egalitarian contracts. Rousseau considered that society and government would ideally come about through contract when the risks and inconveniences of the state of nature threatened men's survival. The individual would 'alienate' his natural liberty to the community, receiving in exchange 'conventional' liberty. 'Each man, in giving himself to all, gives himself to nobody . . . he gains an equivalent for everything he loses.'[8] That equivalent is power over others. Each individual is doubly bound, both as a member of the sovereign power to other individuals and, as a member of the state, to the sovereign. While adherence to the terms of the original contract which creates the sovereign appears partly prudential ('violation of the act by which it exists would be self-annihilation'[9]), the obligation to obey the laws made by the General Will can be characterized in several ways. This obligation is implied in the original undertaking, so it would be imprudent to repudiate it; it would also be irrational, and perhaps immoral, to disobey laws which one had oneself made as a member of the sovereign. Day-to-day political obligation for Rousseau clearly stands or falls with the General Will.

The attempt to determine whether obligation, as viewed by the contract theorists, is moral or prudential is more than a philosophical nicety, for it can be argued that we are entitled to reject prudential obligation when it is to our advantage to disobey, whereas moral obligation is more strongly binding and is usually unconditional. This is one of the obstacles encountered by a utilitarian view of obligation, which suggests that someone can disobey the law when this is conducive to his personal utility, a point discussed further below. Contract and consent theory emphasizes the voluntary nature of obligation and thus appeals to cultures which emphasize individuality and free will, but it meets with the difficulty that what has been voluntarily made can also be voluntarily broken: hence, presumably, the introduction of various resistances into the circuit of obligation, such as 'natural laws' enjoining us to keep our promises, which make obligation moral (and externally imposed) in part, and so unconditional. Contract theory, although widely regarded as obsolete now, is interesting because it describes how *authority* is created out of a situation in which there is only naked *power*, the state of nature. This mirrors the philosophical problem of whether

---

7. D. Hume, 'Of the origin of government', in *Essays, Moral, Political and Literary*, Longmans, Green & Co., 1875, Vol. I, pp. 113–17. See also Rousseau, *A Discourse on . . . Inequality*, Dent, 1913, p. 205 and Paine, *The Rights of Man*, Penguin, 1969, pp. 94, 194.
8. Rousseau, *The Social Contract*, Dent, 1913, p. 12.
9. Rousseau, *The Social Contract*, p. 14.

'ought' can be derived from 'is', and is subject to the same objections. The contract theories rest heavily on the original act of promising, a paradigm way of imposing obligation on oneself, but the contract must logically have taken place via an established institution of promising, which is itself a social institution and could not have existed before society, or have been invoked to create society. Similarly, the terms of the contracts turn on men's equal surrender of their natural rights, yet the concepts of rights is itself created by society, and could not therefore be instrumental in the making of the original contract.[10] So there is an insoluble contradiction at the heart of contract theory. Also, as Riley shows, while contract theorists wished to show government as resulting from a free act of will by the people, they were unclear what was meant by 'will'; this explains some of the inconsistencies of their arguments.[11]

The more modern doctrine of consent avoids many of these pitfalls, since it does not concern itself with the origin of government, but with the ongoing process, and allows us to pass continuous judgement on the justice of governments by giving or withholding consent—in theory at least. The theory is tailored to democratic systems of government where there are established procedures for obtaining consent. A modern version of consent theory was offered by Plamenatz, who argued that in voting we consent to obey *whoever* is elected—that is, we really consent to the rules of the democratic game—and that a vote constitutes a 'promise' of obedience to the next government.[12] Any theory of obligation in a democracy must rest on some such argument, yet this is a very strong theory of obligation resting on a very weak act of consent. The elaborate structure of politics means that, although we merely vote for a name or for a short-term programme, we are interpreted as consenting in advance to a multitude of particular acts, many of which do not even appear in the manifesto of the winning party (which in any case, we may have voted against), and also to the system in general. On this theory, to vote is to sign a blank cheque in favour of the democratic system and whatever consequences follow from it in the current election.

Consenting is, of course, an intentional and personal process, yet modern consent theorists take a deliberately objective, standardized view of it: the vote is an act which, no matter what intention underlay it, creates an obligation. Many objections can be made to this wide interpretation of the vote as consent. First, it would scarcely be rational to consent in advance to whatever a government might do, unless it were strictly specified in a manifesto whose terms would not be exceeded. In Britain, protest sometimes arises when governments enact unpredicted measures which are not within its mandate, but doctrines of the mandate equally often present it as a blank cheque which justifies any measures.

---

10. T. H. Green, *Lectures on the Principles of Political Obligation*, Longmans, Green & Co., 1901, p. 66.
11. P. Riley, *Will and Political Legitimacy*, Harvard U.P., 1982.
12. J. P. Plamenatz, *Consent, Freedom and Political Obligation*, 2nd edn, Oxford U.P., 1968, p. 154.

Should we really be said to consent to long-term aims or to express approval of the whole system when we are only invited to express a view on a short-term programme? For consent to create political obligation, an immense weight of interpretation must be laid on the relatively simple act of voting: the average voter might well reject this interpretation of her action and deny that her vote constituted consent. Furthermore, the institutions of liberal democracy, such as the representative system and party machines, exclude the voter from real political power and choice and so distance the act of voting from meaningful consent. More frequent elections and a delegate system might remove this distance. But ultimately voting in a modern democracy is a passive, acquiescent process and only a strong, positive choice really qualifies as consent. Since we are unlikely to attain the ideal conditions for strong consent, it would be more logical to revise the theory and accept a much reduced concept of political obligation—or abandon it.

Several other objections can be made to consent theory. First, if governments make policy by inaction or 'non-decision-making', the people cannot democratically register their consent to, or dissent from, such imperceptible decisions. A case in point is the 'non-decision' by many successive British governments not to undertake the renewal of the sewerage system which is by now well over one hundred years old in Britain's largest cities, and deteriorating rapidly. If this problem does not reach the political agenda (as it probably will not until people start to die of cholera), how can we consent to or dissent from government policy on the subject? (The privatization of water authorities, of course, now provides future governments with an alibi.) To assume that the people have consented to the government's inaction in such cases stretches the already elastic concept of consent out of all recognition. Secondly, a theory which bases political obligation on voluntary consent should logically provide an account of what counts as *dissent*, and how people can reject the political system. Plamenatz's account deprives us of any institutionalized way of expressing dissent from the system: abstention is a weak, ambivalent act which will always be interpreted by governors and psephologists as ignorance or apathy, rather than as a principled rejection of all the alternatives. In reality, the dissenter can embark on direct action and other forms of protest if her dissatisfaction is extensive, but consent theorists would say that she is then breaking her obligation. The fact that consent is defined, but not non-consent, weights the theory in favour of authority.

Clearly there are inconsistencies in consent theory. Our consent is said to create a political obligation which is self-assumed and so should not be repudiated. Yet people who spend their lives without casting a vote are *also* said to have political obligation, presumably on the grounds of tacit consent, which is really an argument based on gratitude for protection by the laws. So there are two different kinds of consent running in tandem which, between them, put everybody under some obligation. Tussman actually makes this explicit: he defects from the idea of active consent altogether (in the light of the facts) but says that 'tacit consent' must be knowing and conscious, a standard only lived up to by a small, aware elite. Nevertheless, *all* are obliged to obey the government since the non-consenting 'clods' are obligated, like children, by the tacit consent of the elite.[13] Plamenatz also confronts the problem—tangentially—by arguing that there must be another basis for obligation as well as consent, for otherwise there would be

> in every state, however democratic, a large number of persons (i.e. non-voters) under no obligation to obey its laws . . . no state could perform its proper functions if it contained a large number of citizens exempt from obedience to its laws.[14]

There is a radical error in this argument, since my feeling no obligation *subjectively* does not mean that I am not under obligation *objectively* to obey the laws, nor does it prevent my obeying them out of prudence. But the conclusion is sound, that consent cannot be the sole basis of 'the duty of the governed to obey their rulers'. Most consent theorists therefore reinforce their arguments by citing other sorts of obligation.

The inadequacy of consent theory turns on two problems. The first is that consent theory, like contract theory, rests on a legal or contractual account of obligation which it tries to amalgamate, unconvincingly, with the older tradition that makes political obligation a moral duty. On the latter view, it is binding, perhaps unconditional, while on the former view, the rational citizen would withdraw his consent and repudiate his obligation when it was to his advantage. To this is added the difficulty that not everyone actively consents by voting, so that alternative accounts of obligation have to be invoked to cover non-consenters and dissenters. A theory of political behaviour can accommodate the fact that some people vote while others abstain, but a theory of obligation with universal import cannot be so open. Someone who argues that some people are obliged because they consent and others because they enjoy the protection of the law, can be accused of over-determining the case of the first group, who also enjoy protection and so must be doubly bound—or else of being bent on laying obligation on everybody, no matter how. In effect, as Tussman argues, there are two classes of citizens, the active and the passive, but to say that the former are more 'obligated' because of their political activity and acumen is a moral, not a contractual, stipulation, with no obvious justification in fact or logic. Perhaps if theorists cannot establish obligation for every citizen on the same basis, consent, they would do better to look for a different, universal source of obligation.

An important question for consent theory is whether we consent to, and have political obligation to, the political system as a whole, to the law in general, to a particular government, or to particular laws, or to a combination of these. Locke provided a tidy answer to this: our contractual obligation is to the political community as a whole, 'society', but we can overthrow a government without endangering society itself, or rejecting our basic obligation, if the government breaks its trust. Otherwise, we are obliged to obey governments and laws to which we have consented. The clarity of this solution diminishes when practical questions are raised about who judges the government to have betrayed the

---

13. J. Tussman, *Obligation and the Body Politic*, Oxford U.P., 1960.
14. Plamenatz, *Consent, Freedom and Political Obligation*, p. 13. The appendix to the second edition modifies Plamenatz's position.

people, and whether objectors to a law are still bound by it. Such questions are theoretically insoluble on this account. Plamenatz's account seems to imply that in voting we assume obligation towards the system, the government *and* the particular laws which it passes. It might be reasonable to interpret the vote as an endorsement of the system, though this would not hold for societies where voting was compulsory. But if you accept the democratic system, Plamenatz says, you also undertake an obligation even to a government you do not vote for—and hence, presumably, are committed to obey its laws. At this rate it would be better not to vote, and have a free conscience. Surely we should be sceptical of these multiple, simultaneous levels of meaning accorded to the vote. Consent theory purports to make political obligation a result of our free choice, then over-interprets our modest act as voters to saddle us with extensive moral obligations. Since, except in rare cases, we never consent to particular measures by voting, it could be concluded that we consent to the general system, and owe it respect, but that our obedience to particular laws is purely prudential, not conditioned by obligation (except for those people who believe that we have a moral duty to obey laws, for reasons other than consent). But this interpretation also fragments consent theory, which must clearly be modified or replaced by some more unified, universal explanation. We now turn to some alternatives.

THE JUST GOVERNMENT

A number of theorists avoid the problem of political obligation by arguing that it exists self-evidently. MacDonald asserts that since political society is essentially a group organized according to rules enforced by some members, society without obligation is impossible. By virtue of being social animals, we are politically obliged. But this makes the concept strongly asymmetrical: we can never deny, or be discharged from, political obligation. This view is reminiscent of that of Bentham, Austin, and other legal positivists who argued that obligatoriness is the essential quality of law. The question 'Why should I obey the law?' is answered tautologously by a definition of law as 'that which must be obeyed'.[15] Arguments of this form would oblige us to obey a cruel despot just as much as a democratic government, and would suggest that the latter is no more legitimate than the former, an implication unacceptable to most people. However, an improved argument on the same lines has been developed to show that we are self-evidently obliged to obey a *just* government, whether or not we consent to it. Pitkin has developed a 'nature of government' theory based on 'hypothetical consent'. If a government is just, you *should* (hypothetically) consent to it, and are therefore (actually) committed to obedience. A legitimate government is 'one which

15. M. MacDonald, 'The language of political theory' in *Logic and Language*, 1st series (Ed. A. Flew), Blackwell, 1960. See also J. Bentham, *A Fragment on Government* (Ed. W. Wharrison), Blackwell, 1967, Chaps IV–V. The circularity of the account is indicated by Bentham's positivist definition of 'duty': 'that which I am punished by law if I do not do'. The Benthamite view of law was restated more famously in J. Austin, *The Province of Jurisprudence Determined*, London, 1832.

deserves consent'. There are two general criteria for determining the justice of a government: the justice of political institutions and procedures, and the justice of the government's measures.

Pitkin believes that this formula answers most questions about obligation adequately, although she thinks no definitive answer can be given to the more philosophical question 'Why should I *ever* be obliged?' As she notes, a determined dissenter can reject such pleas as 'It is for the good of the greatest number' or 'Most of your fellow-citizens have consented to it' by saying 'What have these to do with me?', even if she repudiates morality and her own social nature in so doing. Pitkin's account would show that she was, even so, under obligation.[16] But the 'just government' theory actually transfers the difficulties to the meaning of 'justice'. Is the just government self-evidently just? In *A Theory of Justice*, Rawls takes a similar view of obligation, basing it on the somewhat different idea of hypothetical consent which underlies his theory. Fairness requires someone to accept her obligations, Rawls says, when: (a) the institution is just; and (b) one has voluntarily accepted its benefits to further one's interests.[17] Condition (b), a version of the gratitude argument, seems an unnecessary addition to condition (a). As to (a), Rawls stipulates that when the constitution and social structure are 'reasonably just' we are obliged to comply even with unjust laws.[18] He specifies that we should only tolerate injustice if it is fairly distributed between groups 'in the long run' and that we need not comply with laws denying our basic liberties.[19] In his derivation of obligation from fairness and justice, Rawls mingles moral obligation (gratitude) and consent, for the definition of a just government is one to which we *would have* consented in the ideally impersonal and neutral 'original position'. Hypothetical consent is, of course, several degrees weaker than real consent, for it does not constitute an actual promise, but a promise *imputed to* someone, and so the main weight of Rawls's case rests on this weak link. The injunction to obey unjust laws if the government is 'reasonably' just seems inadequate as a prescriptive principle.

The 'just government' argument avoids some of the conceptual problems of consent theory, and avoids the problem of non-consenters because it holds that our obligation to pursue justice is moral and unconditional (unless a government departs seriously from the path of justice). The theory also helps us to distinguish between the general obligation to a just regime and a modified—or annulled— obligation to particular unjust laws, and allows a theory of disobedience to be formulated without too much inconsistency. The problem of Pitkin's account is that it implies that a just but non-democratic government is still legitimate, although Rawls avoids this pitfall by building a notion of democracy into the idea of the just government. Both theories fail to confront the fact that in a heterogeneous society, ideas of justice will differ (though in Rawls's case, he has

16.   H. Pitkin, 'Obligation and consent'.
17.   J. Rawls, *A Theory of Justice*, Harvard U.P., 1971, pp. 111–12.
18.   Rawls, *A Theory of Justice*, p. 351.
19.   Rawls, *A Theory of Justice*, p. 355.

already stipulated what justice is): in practice, such differences would be important, and attitudes to the same government could vary.

Among other moral theories of political obligation is that of T. H. Green who, despite his liberalism, sought to make obligation strongly binding. He says that our common humanity and rational nature lead us to recognize a common good, which creates moral and political obligation towards our fellows;[20] to deny this would be to deny our humanity. The state promotes the common good and, hence, is owed obedience. Disobedience is only permissible 'in the interests of the state'. So Green's theory rests on our social nature, which creates an *a priori* moral obligation, rather as the justice of a government in Pitkin's theory creates an external imperative to obey: both theories depart from the voluntariness of consent theory, the idea of self-assumed obligation. Green's position resembles that of Rousseau. For Rousseau, the law consisted of self-prescribed rules, but he differs from the consent theorists since, like Green, he sees society as an association of moral beings who are by their very social nature strongly bound to conformity with the laws.[21] But neither Rousseau's nor Green's theory provides satisfactory conditions for the rejection of obligation.

SELF-INTEREST AND GRATITUDE

The utilitarians approached the topic of obligation armed with the felicific calculus. In principle, 'act utilitarianism' simply enjoins us to obey the state when it is beneficial to us: there can, logically, be no continuing obligation as each case must be considered on its merits. Problems arise depending on whether an individual or a social calculus are used. If individuals merely maximized their own utilities, this would frequently absolve them from obligation and justify them in disobedience, or free-riding, in their own interests. As Pitkin remarks, this would imply that at any time, some individuals would be obliged to obey and others would not—an inadmissibly contradictory situation. On the other hand, the 'greatest happiness' principle would often oblige individuals to obey laws which were contrary to their own interests, to benefit the community. The problematic nature of both these alternatives reflects the permanent difficulty of applying an egoistic moral theory to social matters, including the problem of obligation, a problem explored by Nagel.[22] Pitkin points out that utilitarianism, which judges according to the consequences of actions, cannot provide a sound basis for future obligation and obedience.[23] No doubt a utilitarian trying to construct a theory of obligation would have recourse to some form of 'rule utilitarianism', which recommends that we should obey general rules conducive to happiness, even in a particular instance where they run counter to our individual interest; political obligation could be one such rule.

20. Green, *Lectures*, pp. 124–7. See Plamenatz's criticisms in *Consent, Freedom and Political Obligation*, Chap. III.
21. Rousseau, *The Social Contract*, pp. 26, 31.
22. T. Nagel, *Equality and Partiality*, Oxford U.P., 1991.
23. H. Pitkin, 'Obligation and consent', pp. 49–50.

Undoubtedly a survey which asked the question 'Why should we obey the law?', when it did not meet with blank incomprehension on the part of those questioned, would evoke the reply 'Because the law/the state protects and looks after us'. The argument from gratitude is a profoundly commonsense one. It appears in Locke's and Rawls's theory to reinforce the contractual form of obligation, and it may become increasingly popular with theorists as the state intervenes more in our lives and provides us with more benefits. However, the idea of gratitude in the relations of the individual to the state is misapplied. First, as tax payers we pay for all the services and benefits that we receive from the state: gratitude is not owed in such circumstances. Second, the argument extends the interpersonal moral relation of gratitude to the state as if it were a moral agent and our benefactor, which is inappropriate, for the state is not a super-person, and exercises no personal kindness in distributing services and benefits to us, so there is no reason to react morally to its bounty. Gratitude, in any case, leaves too many loose ends: it cannot account for the *origin* of the state's legitimacy because prior to the existence of the state there were no grounds for gratitude, nor can it advise us exactly when our obligation ceases, if the state reduces protection or benefits. It would also justify any form of government, however undemocratic, which protected and nurtured the people. Nor can the problem of individual disaffection be answered by the gratitude argument: what reason for gratitude have disenchanted, unemployed young people? As with the 'just government' theory, there will always be some elements of benefit (or justice) which could be used to justify a generally bad regime, and neither theory indicates how much benefit or justice constitutes obligation, or how little annuls our duty to the state. Both theories suffer another basic weakness: justice and gratitude are, largely, matters of individual judgement, and those who feel unjustly treated would merely be following the recommendation of the theories if they withdrew their allegiance. But a theorist cannot allow that the theory of obligation is selectively binding, like this, for she wants to posit consistent and universal obligation. Despite its commonsense appeal, then, gratitude alone cannot give rise to an adequate theory of obligation, nor, because of its inconsistencies, should it feature in any more eclectic account of obligation.

A number of other theories could also be cited here such as those resting on natural leadership (our duty to follow the wise) or divine right (our duty to obey God); each political ideology has its own preferred account of political obligation. Only anarchists absolve us from it entirely, but they would commend to us a strong sense of moral obligation to our fellows. (This, however, seems more acceptable than the injunction that we should feel a moral duty towards state or government but may be vulnerable to similar objections.) As we have seen, most arguments make obligation partly moral, which is conducive to subjective, internalized feelings of duty which are virtually self-policing, and is therefore a highly efficient, economical way of maintaining public order and keeping down the crime and protest rate. Externally imposed moral imperatives, such as 'the law is that which must be obeyed', are more likely to provoke resentment and resistance than self-assumed obligations—hence consent theory. But consent theories also rely on the general conviction that it is self-contradictory to break a contract, or promise, that you have freely and voluntarily made, so they appeal to personal rationality while invoking moral duty as well. Theorists and ideologists naturally wish to develop theories of obligation which will show everyone to be obliged all the time (except when good reasons exonerate them, such as gross injustice), since they cannot build an account of authority or the state on the basis of partial, non-universal obligation. Hence the search for a single, universal source of obligation, and the problems with theories which produce inconsistent or selective obligation. All such theories seem to overlook the obvious prudential reason, the fear of punishment, which usually motivates obedience to law, perhaps because they wish to maintain that political obligation extends beyond mere obedience and connotes feelings of respect for government, and for the system.

WHY *DO* I OBEY THE LAW?

The objectionable feature of theories of obligation is that they seek to establish that we are all obliged unless we can prove ourselves exempted: the odds are heavily weighted against the individual, in favour of obedience and conformity. This may result from a persistent, Hobbesian fear of social disorder breaking out unless obligation and authority are strictly maintained. However, life would probably go on much the same, even if *all* theories of obligation were suddenly proved fallacious. I shall now discuss some of the reasons for limiting the idea of obligation, or rejecting it altogether. First, obedience to the law is adequately explained without recourse to obligation. Habit, fear, incapacity to disobey (the non-motorist can hardly disobey motoring laws) and inclination to obey (if one approves of the law) are major reasons.[24] Ordinary citizens only infrequently find themselves in a position where it would be convenient to disobey the law: even then, obedience is probably still the rational and prudent course of action. Criminals are people who think they can benefit from lawbreaking, not those who have conceptually rejected their obligation. The inference of some theorists that obedience is tantamount to an admission of obligation is clearly false. The fact that the average citizen has no conception of political obligations casts further doubt on the idea. Explaining the maintenance of political systems, Easton invokes the concept of a 'reservoir of support', built up over time, for a system or a regime. This behaviouralist concept alone would adequately explain continued obedience and the legitimacy of governments, without the need to explore subjective feelings of obligation.[25]

Secondly, as the foregoing arguments suggest, theorizing on the subject is confused, with no general agreement over the basis or extent of obligation. Our duties to the system, the government, the law in general and particular laws are

---

24. For a classic sociological study which suggests the *practical* reasons why people obey the law see A. Podgorecki *et al.*, *Knowledge and Opinion about Law*, Martin Robertson, 1973. Legal theorists such as Austin and Hart recognize this routine obedience to law when they base law in part on the 'habit of obedience'.

25. D. Easton, 'A reassessment of the concept of political support', *British Journal of Political Science*, **5**, 435–58 (1975).

not clearly differentiated, and the relation between these entities is unclear, so that some theorists would consider disobedience of one law an acceptable act of protest, while others would interpret it as threatening the whole structure of society, as did Socrates. Such confusions make the theory an unhelpful guide to action. Thirdly, most people today in our individualistic society, with its emphasis on free will, would deny that obligation can be unconditional, yet the classic theories are heavily weighted in favour of government and offer no philosophical account of justified dissent, in most cases. Thus, they are asymmetrical, yet any theory which seeks to establish obligation should surely offer a corresponding account of when it can rightly be repudiated. Such one-sided theories may be suitable for societies composed of 'deferentials' but they are unacceptable to members of an active, participatory democracy.

But the idea of obligation is important for political propaganda. It appears in the political socialization of children and in governments' justifications of controversial measures. Obligation itself may not be cited, but consent, justice and gratitude are mentioned as reasons for obedience. Devlin's idea that law is co-extensive with morality is also sometimes invoked to persuade us that our moral duty is to obey the laws.[26] Alternatively, people's natural resistance to the imposition of obligation is overcome by pointing out that they have consented to the law through the democratic process. The aim of such arguments is to promote deference to governments which may not always be just, based on consent, or worthy of gratitude. Hence the need for a re-examination of the theory of obligation to help us to assess the familiar political rhetoric more critically.

Because of the propagandistic power of the notion, obligation is more than an academic issue, even if most people 'just do' obey governments. Although theorists often infer a mental acknowledgement of obligation from the fact of obedience, the inner rebel can be an outward conformist, since there are overwhelming prudential reasons for obeying the law. As has been suggested, the hypothesis of obligation over-determines the explanation of obedience, which can adequately be accounted for by prudence. By contrast, Milgram's *Obedience to Authority* (discussed in Chapter 8) also suggests that non-rational, psychological causes determine deference and obedience. Yet the theorist working within the paradigm of free and rational human action is often unwilling to accept such theses; also, he may wish to introduce a normative element which the behavioural concept of *obedience* cannot support. The process is similar to the complex interpretations of the act of voting in democratic theory: obedience to the law is the tip of a conceptual iceberg which the theorist conjectures must consist of consent, moral duty and other intangibles.

I have dealt with obligation at length because of its important role in binding the individual—theoretically—to the government. The acknowledgement of obligation by the people is said to bestow legitimacy on a government, and the 'fact' of legitimacy is then used to encourage obedience. The puzzle is how *subjective* attitudes (on which obligation would rest, if it existed) can ever confer

---

26. P. Devlin, *The Enforcement of Morals*, Oxford U.P., 1965.

the *objective* property of legitimacy on a government. It may be that they cannot, and that legitimacy is a figment of the imagination. But Pitkin would argue that the 'just government' is objectively legitimate, by reason of its just and benevolent procedures and policies. This makes legitimacy independent of obligation, which then derives, objectively, from the justice of the government itself, a reversal of the consent argument. Yet consent theory is clearly of major importance in democracies, for it provides the main justification of government. Marxists may use the consent argument, but they are also likely to argue that the will of the people creates a just socialist government, which is self-legitimizing. With regard to capitalist society, they would argue that class rule and oppression absolves the exploited classes from any obligation; the theory of obligation is a form of false consciousness. Clearly, the notion of obligation is no less ideological than other concepts. The idea is mainly invoked when the legitimacy of governments or laws is challenged, or an abnormal situation arises, to increase obedience and deference. But also, some conception of obligation is vital for any theorist wishing to assert the right to protest, or the 'obligation to disobey', since she can only properly account for these by contrast with some general obligation.

The concept of obligation has been criticized partly because it is habitually invoked to protect governments and the *status quo*, and deprived of any critical content, and partly because of the inconsistencies it embodies. In this controversy, we are forced to choose between individual-based justifications which cannot guarantee universal obligation, and state-centred justifications which make obligation well-nigh unconditional. If the concept is to be retained, the best approach would be to develop a more eclectic theory which showed the various possible sources of obligation and concentrated on people's subjective attitudes to government and law, rather than on the objective existence, in some world of intangibles, of obligation. In fact, the concept of authority could assume many of the burdens now carried by the concept of obligation. Finally, the critical drift of this discussion is not intended as a vindication of the ultra-egoist, who considers that she owes nothing to anyone, nor of her friend the free-rider. Indisputably, we have a duty to our fellow-citizens—some would say, to the citizens of the whole world—a duty to make life tolerable for them, in exchange for similar services. Robinson Crusoe, or Rousseau's noble savage, would not have such a duty, but the objective fact of social life creates it. If you prefer to avoid moral terminology, it can be based, ultimately, on self-preservation. However, theories of political obligation have transformed this wide, humanitarian duty into specific duties to particular regimes which we may feel do not deserve our loyalty, or to laws of which we often disapprove. Hence the need to examine the justness of a government, *and* whether it represents your fellow-citizens before according it the legitimacy which your acknowledgement of obligation is said to create.

The solution offered to the problem of political obligation necessarily determines the answer given to the question 'Have I the right to protest?' If obligation is thought to be absolute and unconditional, as Hobbes believed it to be, the answer to this is clearly 'No'. But other theories of obligation seem to allow us to circumscribe political obligation in a way which leaves space for justifiable protest. In practice, the more tolerant a society which contains diverse opinions and cultures, the fewer the grounds for protest. And, presumably, the more leeway protestors have for voicing their grievances, the more moderate will be the forms of protest which they choose. A tolerant society, then, is committed to tolerate forms of protest not prohibited by law and those established as rights. But is such a society bound to be tolerant towards illegal forms of protest? This will be debated in the following sections.

THE RIGHT TO PROTEST

> To say that there is a right to civil disobedience is to allow the legitimacy of resorting to this form of political action to one's opponents. It is to allow that the legitimacy of civil disobedience does not depend on the rightness of one's cause.[27]
>
> *(Joseph Raz)*

The question at issue is to what extent the individual in a democratic society may rightly protest against laws and policies with which she disagrees. May one embark, as an individual, or as a member of a minority group, on acts of civil disobedience ('direct action') to change such laws, to which one has, in theory, consented, or should one wait to express such protest in the next election, since these laws are, again in theory, the expressed will of the majority? In liberal-democratic societies, the awareness that majoritarianism is an imperfect system and that discontented minorities do exist, has created a fairly lenient attitude to protestors, who are not usually treated as mere common criminals when they break the law. Political theory has an important contribution to make in the establishment of the right to protest, since it can define the limits of permissible direct action.

Civil disobedience may be defined as a principled, purposeful, and public disobedience of the law: *principled*, because it does not result in selfish gain (looting shops is not an acceptable form of protest), *purposeful*, because it is undertaken in order to change particular laws or policies (but not the system in general), and *public* because publicity for the cause is the aim of protestors, and clandestine action cannot achieve this. Fourthly, the protestor must accept the *punishment*, if any, for lawbreaking. Clandestine law-breaking for selfish ends can only be viewed as criminal, while direct action aimed at overthrowing the system (discussed later) must be classified as revolutionary, and its perpetrators usually try to avoid punishment. Protest which takes institutionalized forms—peaceful demonstrations, lobbying MPs—does not enter this discussion as individuals have an established right to take these forms of 'indirect' action in Britain and in the other liberal countries.

Civil disobedience can either take the form of breaking the law being challenged—refusal to fill in census forms by those who object to censuses, for example—or breaking unrelated laws to gain publicity for the protest— occupations actually infringe trespass laws, but call attention to other grievances.

---

27. J. Raz, 'Civil disobedience', in H. A. Bedau (Ed.), *Civil Disobedience in Focus*, Routledge, 1991, p. 161.

So comprehensive is the network of laws that most protestors find no difficulty in infringing them, even unintentionally. Civil disobedience need not cause a public nuisance, but the greater the nuisance, the greater the publicity. At present, I shall consider cases where no-one is harmed by the protest, and only legal or state supremacy is slighted.

Civil disobedience occurs for moral or political reasons. *Moral protest* results when a citizen's moral and political values come into conflict and she gives a higher priority to her moral beliefs. The pacifist who prefers prison to fighting does this. Moral protest is usually an individual activity, often undertaken without missionary intent, even if many individuals protest simultaneously in the same way. (If pacifists united to persuade others not to fight they would doubtless be tried for a treasonable conspiracy.) *Political protest* is usually concerted action, sometimes undertaken because a particular law or policy is seen as unjust, sometimes because the government's decisions are disputed. If such protestors are not to be regarded as common criminals, under a normal application of the law, their position needs explicating theoretically. How protest is regarded depends very much on how the citizen's political obligation is conceived.

Hobbes's view of obligation as unconditional leaves no room for the right to protest. But Locke argued that 'the people' had the right to resist a regime if its measures threatened them, contravening the rights which it was appointed to protect. Locke's theory deals with the 'dissolution' of governments and gives little guidance about resistance to particular laws. In the nineteenth century the American, Thoreau, argued that where unjust laws exist men should not wait to persuade the majority to alter them, but should disobey them individually. He was himself imprisoned for non-payment of taxes which he withheld because he disapproved of the United States' war against Mexico.[28] In such cases, *right* action is revolutionary, he said. While democracy has merely increased 'true respect' for the individual, civilization will finally acknowledge him as a 'higher and independent power'. Thoreau's argument for disobedience was thus primarily moral.

Probably the most important justification of the right to disobey is that of 'Mahatma' Gandhi. Although he was seeking to oust the British from India, his theory of *Satyagraha*, 'holding on to truth', can also justify more limited protest in democratic countries. Satyagraha enjoins us to disobey evil laws, as a moral duty, 'hence Satyagraha largely appears to the public as Civil Disobedience or Civil Resistance'. Gandhi offered a political as well as a moral justification for protest. 'I wish I could persuade everybody that civil disobedience is the inherent right of every citizen. He does not give it up without ceasing to be a man.'[29] Gandhi, once a prosperous lawyer, argued that resisters are 'the real constitutionalists' for, in disobeying and accepting punishment they are, in a sense, *obeying* the law. He recommended that resistance should be active, since

---

28. H. D. Thoreau, 'Civil disobedience', in *Walden* (Ed. J. Krutch), Bantam, 1962, pp. 85–104.
29. W. Reys and P. Rao, 'Gandhi's synthesis of Indian spirituality and Western politics', in *Political and Legal Obligation* (Eds. J. R. Pennock and J. W. Chapman), Atherton Press, 1970, p. 449. See too B. Parekh, *Gandhi's Political Philosophy: A Critical Examination*, Macmillan, 1989.

passive protest appeared as a sign of weakness; it should be civil not criminal, 'sincere, respectful, restrained, never defiant', overt, and should be undertaken by otherwise law-abiding citizens. The anti-imperialist Non-Co-operation movement (1920–22) and the Civil Disobedience movement (1930–33) were both influenced by Gandhi's ideas; in 1947 India and Pakistan finally gained national independence. But, for Gandhi, the right to resist did not end there: he defined self-government as a state where the whole population had gained the capacity to resist a government abusing its powers. Gandhi's theory, then, asserts that injustice always justifies resistance, so that political protest is fundamentally moral, and should take place equally in a non-democratic or democratic state.

Walzer contends that the right to resist is inherent in the pluralistic nature of democratic society.[30] Society consists of 'primary institutions', in particular, the state, and 'secondary institutions' such as the Church, trade unions, and political parties, of which membership is voluntary or 'wilful', unlike membership of the state. Because we opt into these, our commitment is greater than that to the state. Our adherence to the secondary institutions may clash with duty to the state, laying on us an *obligation to disobey*. If a revolutionary party wishes to supplant the state, its members are, because of their voluntary commitment, 'obliged' to support the revolution. Walzer has thus turned consent (on which democratic government is said to rest) against the state by showing that in pluralist democracy our consent and commitment to other institutions is stronger and more active, and justifies disobedience. It is doubtful if any state would accept Walzer's theory, but he provides a respectable justification for the use of protestors. He also argues that in a democratic society, citizens have the right to protest against injurious, anti-democratic institutions *with all necessary force*, and justifies a notorious strike against General Motors in these terms, the latter being at the time an anomalously authoritarian organization within a democracy.

The most famous argument *against* civil disobedience is that attributed by Plato to Socrates in the *Crito*. Socrates, unjustly convicted, and awaiting execution, argued that if he were to escape it would harm the laws and the constitution of Athens; also, that one incurs a debt of gratitude for being nurtured and protected by one's country so that violence against it is a sin. Furthermore, the citizen who does not deliberately leave his own country thereby makes an undertaking to observe the laws. A disobedient individual thus defies the laws trebly—as his parents and as his guardians, and by breaking his own promise. Socrates did not admit even the right to disobey unjust laws, for he equated a single act of disobedience with, potentially, the destruction of the law itself—a common argument against protest, although not a sound one, like most 'thin end of the wedge' arguments. Implicit in his position is the view that we are obliged to obey the laws on three grounds: gratitude, consent and morality.[31] In modern democracies, the arguments against protest are simplified to two: first, that the individual has consented to the democratic system and should obey laws made by

30. M. Walzer, *Obligations*, Harvard U.P., 1970, Chap.1, *passim*. Chap.2, 'Civil Disobedience and Corporate Authority' deals with the strike at General Motors.
31. Plato, *Crito* in *The Last Days of Socrates* (trans. H. Tredennick), Penguin, 1969, p.89ff.

the majority, and second (more pragmatically), that democracy provides the means for peaceful change and for persuading the majority to share one's views so that direct action is never justified.

The philosophical justifications for protest *qua* disobedience are most controversial where there is a clear *prima facie* obligation to obey because the government is democratic or because its laws are just, or both. In a country with an unpopular, unjust, undemocratic government, such arguments would not be needed to convince others that the protestors were right. Some theorists argue that we are always obliged to obey just laws, even when passed by non-democratic governments, but both liberal and radical democrats would doubtless reply that the absence of democracy was itself a sufficient injustice to warrant protest. The stronger one's conception of political obligation, the less likely one is to concede a right to protest. If political obligation is thought to rest on consent *and* justice *and* gratitude, the chance of justifying protest is small, since it is unlikely that a government could violate all three conditions simultaneously. But theories of the state and obligation which allow no scope for protest are incompatible with the view of people as rational, moral, political beings and can be criticized as authoritarian. A theory of obligation resting on consent is probably most accommodating of a right to protest.

THE SCOPE OF PROTEST

The main purpose of a theory of protest is to convince non-protesting citizens that the protestors' behaviour is justifiable, and not merely criminally or socially destructive; it can also help the discontented to decide whether their grievances merit disobedience, or whether they should be pursued through the 'proper channels'. The general justifications for protest have been set out above, but the scope and form of protest permissible in democratic society, and the cases where protest is appropriate, must be carefully specified.

Macfarlane suggests four criteria which should govern political disobedience. He writes from a liberal standpoint and assumes that we have a general obligation to obey the law.[32] He argues that justifiable disobedience must successfully answer four questions:

(1) *What cause does the disobedience serve?* This must be shown not to be purely selfish, but reasonable and just.
(2) *Why does this cause demand 'rejection of one's obligation to the state and its laws'?* Here the protestors must show that other means have been exhausted, or are for some reason inadequate.
(3) *Do the means chosen further the cause?* This question is to rule out 'overkill' and inappropriate forms of action. Some relevance between the means of protest chosen, and the cause, must be demonstrated.

---

32. L. J. Macfarlane, *Political Disobedience*, Macmillan, 1971.

(4) *Do the consequences justify the protest?* The protest should not aggravate the situation. It is impossible to give an answer to this question, since it involves prophecy. Governments may react in a hostile or conciliatory fashion to protest: success is never guaranteed. Perhaps this is a question for the protestor's own conscience. We can construe it as asking 'Do the ends justify the means?'

It is doubtful if Macfarlane's questions would deter 'fanatics', but they could act as a guide for would-be protestors, or as a yardstick by which citizens and governments can judge whether protest is reasonable and deserves sympathy.

If we assume with Thoreau, Gandhi, and others that everyone has *the right to protest*, when is it *right* to protest? What conditions should obtain? To answer this will, indirectly, involve giving general answers to the questions above. In a democratic system, the right to protest clearly does not justify protest designed to favour oneself exclusively, protest aimed at destroying the system, or protest which seeks to circumvent the majority's will because one happens to disagree with the election result. The protests made by individuals on moral grounds, justified by commitment to higher principles, stand on their own and do not require further consideration here. The form which protest usually takes in democracy, given that the majority's will can be enacted by legitimate, parliamentary means, is protest by minorities. These minorities can be classified as *permanent minorities*, marked out by some fixed characteristics such as race, creed or language, and *opinion minorities* who come together because their members share some opinion. Permanent minorities may feel that their special needs are not being catered for (for example, British Muslims who want funding for Muslim schools equal to that for Church of England schools) or that they are being victimized because of their special characteristics. Because they are outnumbered, and because their special needs are unlikely ever to gain sufficient attention or support among the majority, they may conclude that civil disobedience is the only way left to get their cause recognized and remedied.

In the USA, such minorities may gain satisfaction within the system, since policies are passed in Congress by coalitions of minorities who trade reciprocal support. This does not help the marginal groups who have no formal representation. In some countries permanent minorities have constitutional protection, but in Britain no such protection exists and the electoral system militates against anything but majority concerns becoming election issues or reaching party platforms. The majoritarian system can literally *oppress* permanent minorities, who therefore, having failed to get attention in Parliament, feel that they are justified in taking direct action. Their vindication is that they will never win over the majority, which is probably apathetic, or even actively hostile to their cause. Opinion minorities are usually formed to challenge particular laws or policies and are not permanent in composition, nor are their members personally oppressed in many cases (e.g. animal rights protestors). Failing to recruit adequate support from the majority by conventional recruiting methods, or to get parliamentary attention, they may resort to direct action to publicize their cause and attract support: for example, those who contest blood sports have sabotaged hunts, and anti-vivisectionists have stolen laboratory animals and defaced the houses of well-known scientists. In such cases it is often argued that they are abusing the right to protest, since they should try to convert the majority to their opinion, and so enact their policies: they are not in a fixed or permanent minority, and should abide by the democratic rules. (A non-permanent minority consisting of those whose party simply lost the election would certainly not be justified in resorting to direct action for that reason, as this would be breaking the democratic rules.)

However, political circumstances are infinitely variable, and any generalization about when protest is right or wrong is vulnerable to endless counter-examples. In the pure theory of democracy, a non-oppressed, non-permanent minority would be wrong to take direct action against the will of the majority expressed through the government. But in real, imperfect democracy, opinion minorities are not usually in confrontation with the majority, who may even tend to favour their views, but with the government itself, the Establishment, and the system— especially given the shortage of parliamentary time for dealing with non-government business. Civil disobedience may thus be a fitting form of challenge to a government which has little claim to embody the will of the majority in any case. Many protesters are better viewed as a section of the people acting against a government which protects its own interests, rather than as a minority acting against the majority of their fellows. The direct action taken by protestors in 1990 in demonstrating (sometimes violently) against the widely unpopular poll tax in Britain, and by those who refused to pay the tax, could be viewed in this light.

The examples given so far have been of minorities wishing for policies to be enacted or altered and undertaking direct action for publicity purposes. Protest equally encompasses direct disobedience of laws which seem to victimize a minority, or contravene the moral beliefs of a group. In Britain when the law making crash-helmets compulsory for motor-cyclists was passed, the Sikh community, whose members could not fit helmets over the turbans which their religion obliges them to wear, complained that the law discriminated against them because of their religion. They refused to wear helmets, and some Sikhs were arrested frequently and even imprisoned for breaking this law, until Sikhs were made exempt. This was a paradigm case of disobedience—breaking the law and paying the penalty—and also an interesting illustration of the problems of making acceptable laws in a multicultural community. Law has to be made to fit Mr or Ms Average Citizen, but the more heterogeneous a community becomes, the more exemptions there must be, or the more protest.

The most famous cases of civil disobedience have involved groups deprived of civil or legal rights, such as blacks in the South of the USA and in South Africa. Such cases are clear-cut (as far as anything can be in politics) and wholly justifiable. I would also say that a permanent minority with full political rights is still justified in civil disobedience if the majority oppresses it in other ways or denies it the satisfaction of its special needs, when these can reasonably be met. (It would have been unreasonable for the Welsh to demand Welsh-language TV if this would bankrupt all the other television networks. In most cases where financial resources are involved, some compromise which shows willing should probably be accepted as reasonable.) As to opinion minorities, it would be most in keeping with the spirit of democracy if they sought to persuade without direct action. However, the imperfections of the system make the use of other methods understandable. Many other permutations of protest could be discussed, some justifiable, others not, but these examples at least suggest that theories of protest must be considerably elaborated to cover each individual case. One further important case is that where an informed opinion minority tries to change a major government policy between elections by disobedience. Tussman argues that consent is in fact an act of the conscious minority, with the majority, the 'clods' merely acquiescing. On this basis he concludes that if the aware, consenting elite dissents, its wishes should prevail over those of the unthinking clods and be acceded to by the government. Hence he justifies elite protest, in effect, on the basis of superior wisdom—a view that majoritarian democrats would reject.

The right to protest is said to derive partly from the injustice or immorality of the laws or policies in question. But 'unjust' and 'immoral' are themselves disputable categories, and some groups will always consider unjust or wrong what the majority finds just or right, because of ideological or moral differences. Theories of protest cannot solve this problem: they can only state that the *bona fide* protestor is one who believes that injustice is being done or that her moral principles are being violated, and so has the right to protest, whatever her principles.

It might be thought that the use of the phrase 'the right to protest' is ironic, since all the theories insist on the duty to accept punishment for disobedience. If the protestor disobeys and pays the price, where does *right* come into it? The protestor's right is really that her law-breaking actions are justifiable in her own conscience, and that they will be interpreted by her fellows and the government as principled political activity and not as crime or sedition—by contrast with the treatment of dissidents in communist countries, for example, where such a right was not acknowledged and dissidents were treated like criminals, traitors or lunatics. Raz argues that people have a right to political participation and that if this is denied in an illiberal state, they have a right to civil disobedience; conversely, he argues, in a liberal society, where people have the right to participate, they have no right to civil disobedience. In a liberal society, then, disobedients can only hope for forbearance from their fellows and the state: they have no right to tolerance. 'The only moral claim for support [from other citizens] or non-interference must be based on the rightness of the political goal of the disobedient.'[33] The case against admitting a right to protest in a democracy also rests partly on the vulnerability of the theories of protest, which encompass certain contradictions and cannot give absolute guidance as to when protest is, or is not, right. A number of pragmatic reasons are also cited for denying such a right: 'law-breaking endangers the democratically elected government', 'some protestors are just criminals, acting out of self-interest', 'protest disrupts the fabric of society' and 'breaking one law brings the law itself into disrepute'. The truth of

---

33.   J. Raz, 'Civil Disobedience', pp. 166–167.

such generalizations can be debated *ad infinitum*, but the 'practical' case for accepting the right to protest rests on the view that a democratic society is strong enough to absorb dissent, that the majority can be mistaken and that the government often does not represent the will of the majority in any case. More deviously, governments may think that by allowing moderate, if inconvenient, protest, they defuse wider, more fundamental discontent.

The theories of protest reviewed do not condone violence because the individual's right to protest must in a democracy be circumscribed by others' rights. The condemnation of violence is based on a separate value-judgement from that which condemns civil disobedience on the grounds of social disruption, but the two forms of action are often conflated because in practice civil disobedience can lead to violence. Some condemn *all* direct action as being potentially violent, especially those who consider that damage to property is a form of violence. Others argue that threats are a kind of violence, and that disobedience, which is a threat, is therefore violent. To avoid outlawing protest entirely, the first step towards authoritarianism, we need to make a sharp distinction between potential, implied, and covert violence and *real* violence, which actually hurts people. Protest involving real violence is not admissible in a democratic society because it offends the spirit of democracy, which is decision by debate and persuasion and the peaceful resolution of conflict. In liberal democracies it is doubly condemned because of the transgression of the liberal values concerning individual life and human rights. However, violence is not a special, unique form of political action (contrary to common usage); it is a *mode* which political activity may take. Law-breaking and revolution may be violent, or not. But for most people violence is strongly associated with those who seek to overthrow the political system, and all consideration of revolution is complicated by the fact that a revolution whose aims seem reasonable, even just, will be widely viewed as evil if its methods are violent. The arguments about violence were discussed in Chapter 6, and here I shall merely consider whether the right of protest can be said to extend to a 'right of revolution'.

THE RIGHT OF REVOLUTION

The possibilities for political action lie on a continuum which stretches from obedience through tolerated non-conformity, conventional protest, direct action, non-revolutionary terrorism to revolution, a decisive rupture of the existing system. A system based on a democratic ideology can usually survive all forms of behaviour except the directly revolutionary. Within such a system, therefore, there cannot be a 'right of revolution' for individuals or groups by definition. Since each ideology supports a particular political system, there can be no way of justifying a total social revolution in terms of the ideology and the system which it would destroy. When Locke asserted the right to resist a government, the grounds were that the government had transgressed the principles justifying its existence—in other words, the government itself was destroying the political system and the people were entitled to act to preserve the political form based on their previous consent.[34] Locke justified a change of regime, rather than a revolution, a change which would take place *within* the dominant ideology. For liberal democrats a true revolution is an unjustifiable breach of democratic procedure, condemned both for that and for the violence and coercion it entails. But whether the dominant ideology in a country is liberal democratic, communist or right-wing authoritarian, revolutionaries will not be able to establish their right to act in terms of that ideology, or to justify their revolution to the part of the population which adheres to it. It is not unknown for a group to oust a regime in order to pursue established political doctrines more vigorously—this is similar to the situation Locke envisaged—and changes of regime in countries ruled by military juntas are sometimes justified in this way, but this is not a revolution in the usual sense, which connotes the destruction of the system.

The reasons for revolution advanced by Marxists and anarchists have already been discussed, but these related to particular contexts. If a general right to revolution is to be asserted, we must step outside the major ideologies and look for general justifications derived from justice and morality, although these too will not be free from ideology. A justification of revolution must vindicate the violence, dispossession, and coercion which it entails: if a constitutional revolution takes place in a democracy by the majority of the population voting for a different political system, no norms have been violated and no justification is needed. The justification of a general right to revolution in defiance of the ballot box might run as follows: revolution is justifiable when carried out by the majority against a regime (even an elected regime) or a political system which exploits and oppresses the majority. This principle may be extended to include revolution by the minority in the interests of the majority, provided that the majority lends its support to the minority during or soon after the event, thus validating the claim that it is in their interests. (This formula assumes that the majority is fairly large: the rights and wrongs of a revolution in a country divided 50:50 or 49:51 would be infinitely debatable.) This proposed justification evidently countenances the suppression of the interests of the former minority. This is admissible because, since judgements about the relative worth of individuals are invidious and impossible, individuals must be assumed equally worthy, so that the only operable criterion is the numerical one, the wellbeing of the majority. Against such a revolution, supporters of the minority group could argue that they deserve their privileges because of special merit, virtue or wisdom, or that they were, in fact, ruling the majority better than it could rule itself—the paternalistic argument. The arguments for and against popular revolution typically rest on different doctrines—egalitarianism and elitism—and the choice between them is an assertion of fundamental values. But if the majoritarian or popular view is accepted, it could be used as the basis of a general right to revolution. The contexts in which it applies are, of course, far less black-and-white, since most regimes justify themselves in terms of some imagined majority interest. But no assertion of the right of revolution is likely to satisfy those who

---

34. Locke, *Essay*, Chap. XIX.

hold the sanctity of life or the inviolability of property as the highest good, for to them no revolution could ever be validly justified. But the inconsistency of such absolutes has been suggested elsewhere.

It can be objected that real revolutions actually take place without the blessing of such theoretical justification: rights and actions in such a case are unrelated, theory is irrelevant to practice. However, for a revolutionary regime it is crucial to justify its takeover theoretically and so to legitimize itself in the eyes of the population—unless it wishes to keep order by force in the long term. Also, in gaining acceptance by other states, the rightness of its revolution can be an important factor. Mendacious justifications are not uncommon, and new regimes, like old regimes, invariably explain their actions in terms of the interests of the people—even out-and-out dictatorships. However, informed citizens and observers can usually judge such claims to be approximately true or false: if true, the rightness of the revolution according to the general principle should hasten the acceptance of the regime abroad, and loyalty to the system at home.

Those who condemn all revolutions *a priori* because of the violence involved are relatively few. More often, particular revolutions will be condemned or condoned according to whether one approved of the displaced rulers or approves of the new regime ideologically. Terrorism is often judged by the same lights. But there is another standpoint for judging revolutions, that of the disembodied observer with a theory of history. To thinkers such as Machiavelli and Hegel, social change, disruptive or disastrous as it may be for individuals, is a recurrent and necessary event in world history, the necessary condition of progress or of the realization of the World Spirit. Such views are best expressed at a comfortable distance in time and space from the revolutions in question, and could hardly be used to vindicate revolution to its victims. And, although some revolutionaries justified their work rhetorically in holistic terms as the purging of social impurities and the march of civilization, the reasons they offer to their future citizens are grounded not on metaphysics but on the concrete benefits which the revolution will achieve. The 'march of progress' justification of revolution makes no reference to individual or collective wellbeing, and is suspect for this reason and because, as a principle, it has only particular application and is subject to the same criticisms as non-universalizable moral rules. Commentators and politicians often interpret revolutions far away in time or space as progressive while staunchly opposing similar movements in their own back-yards.

It seems, then, that the right to revolution is one which belongs to individuals collectively, but not one which can be established in the constitution of a country—although democrats might say that the right to vote was a right to make minor revolutions. The right to revolution is a moral claim, based on the right to self-defence and on an ideal of human good, 'the wellbeing of the people'. Revolution is undoubtedly the most difficult moral and political problem with which political thinkers must grapple: it is also guaranteed that one theorist's solution will displease most other thinkers. But I would argue that the general principle set out above would offer some guidance for assessing revolutions in whatever kind of society they arose. If space permitted, much more could be said on the subject of liberty, obligation and protest. These topics and the general subject, the position of the individual *vis-à-vis* the state and other individuals, have been discussed largely from the viewpoint of liberal theory and the problems of a liberal-democratic society, because such subjects dominate the writings of political theorists within the liberal ideology. Today, arguments about obligation, freedom and the right to protest have a double function to perform: they must try to convert non-liberal societies to the liberal scale of values and also they should be revived within liberal societies to check the rise of state power and elitist institutions which flourish within democracy and to accommodate the divisions which may arise in multicultural societies. Awareness of such arguments and of our rights as inhabitants of liberal society is therefore essential not only for thinking about, but for living in modern Western society.

FURTHER READING

Most classic modern books on civil disobedience were written during the late 1960s and 1970s, when the Civil Rights movement was active in the United States and protests against the Vietnam war were common both there and in Europe.

H. A. Bedau (Ed.), *Civil Disobedience: Theory and Practice*, Pegasus, 1969.
H. A. Bedau (Ed.), *Civil Disobedience in Focus*, Routledge, 1991.
H. Beran, *The Consent Theory of Political Obligation*, Croom Helm, 1987.
A. Carter, *Direct Action and Liberal Democracy*, Routledge & Kegan Paul, 1973.
P. Harris (Ed.), *On Political Obligation*, Routledge, 1989.
T. Honderich, *Violence for Equality*, rev. edn, Routledge, 1989.
J. Horton, *Political Obligation*, Macmillan, 1992.
G. Klosko, 'Reformist consent and political obligation', *Political Studies*, 1991, **XXXIX**, 4.
A. J. M. Milne, *The Right to Dissent*, Avebury, 1983.
C. Pateman, *The Problem of Political Obligation*, Wiley, 1979.
P. Singer, *Democracy and Disobedience*, Clarendon Press, 1973.
M. Walzer, *Obligations*, Harvard U.P., 1970.

CHAPTER 16

Social Justice and Equality

Justice is the highest goal of political life, yet it is *injustice* which dominates political debate. The reason is that it is easier to identify and to deplore injustices than to define precisely what is lacking in an unjust situation, or what an ideally just situation might be like. Injustice often appears as a departure from an equilibrium of which we approve. In political argument, justice is usually said to be the property of a *distribution* of something—of goods, but also of 'evils'. Some form of social justice is the ultimate aim of political ideologies. But many people associate the term primarily with justice in the legal system, the punishment of malefactors. Here, legal justice will be treated as a concept parallel to that of social justice, concerning the distribution of pains and penalties to the guilty: what both concepts have in common are the ideas of due process, impartiality, and distribution according to appropriate criteria. Additionally, social justice operates in the context of *scarce goods* which have to be appropriately distributed. What economists call 'free goods', such as air and sunshine, do not have to be distributed according to just principles.

Different ideologies produce radically different theories of justice. For Plato, justice was not based on desert, nor on 'giving every man his due', but signified a 'just proportion' between the various parts of society, whereas Aristotle proposed a definition which rested on individual desert and departed from Plato's more holistic view. Many conservatives would regard a hierarchical distribution of goods and privileges as just, or even as divinely ordained. For liberals, distribution according to merit, based on equality of opportunity, is the ideal, while socialists strive for justice based on need and fundamental equality. While Bentham and James Mill defined justice as the impartial application of rules, they and other utilitarians considered that, in principle, justice should be treated as a secondary rule, and subordinated to utility: many other theorists, including 'rule utilitarians' (who, like J. S. Mill, believe that general rules conducive to utility should be followed) see justice as an end in itself. As this wide variety of definitions suggests, justice is a flexible term, which is stretched to fit almost any idea of the

Good. Any analysis intended to produce an authoritative definition of the idea is therefore doomed to fail, or to be challenged or superseded. The intention here is to assess the merits of various theories of justice and to examine the conceptual problems which surround the ideal itself, no matter what content we give to it.

Most modern works of political philosophy start by asserting that justice is a property of *situations* or outcomes, thus avoiding the questions which vex moral philosophers, such as 'Who is the just man?' and 'Can I have a just intention if the outcome of my act is unjust?'. These are questions of private, not political, virtue. But when we treat justice as a property of situations, we must also remember that situations are brought about by human *actions*, which cannot be exempted from questions of justice. Indeed, some philosophers consider that justice is located in the actions or procedures which bring about outcomes, and therefore define it as the impartial application of rules. Ultimately, the two stages are inseparable. First of all, we need to examine the possible methods of distribution which might operate. Logically, any distribution must either be equal or unequal. *Equal distribution* is a simple, numerical form of allocation under which each person gets an equal quantity of a good, irrespective of her personal characteristics. In the case of replicable goods, such as vote, everyone gets one unit and more units are created costlessly as more people qualify to vote. The outcome of an equal distribution can therefore be specified in advance. This is the least problematic method of distribution but, unfortunately, it is not applicable to some situations—for example, where there are scarce and indivisible goods. *Unequal distribution* implies that some individuals are favoured or privileged: an extreme case would be where one individual monopolized the whole of a commodity, and others got none. Unequal, or selective, distribution takes place according to some criterion which relates the goods distributed to special characteristics of their recipients. But a sub-species of unequal distribution is random distribution, where no special criteria are involved, and the outcome is not predictable in advance—for example, a lottery. Both selective and random methods produce unequal distributions which can be justified if appropriate criteria or proper procedures have been observed. Unequal distributions are in many cases intuitively more just than equal distributions. Nobody would dispute that health care should go to the sick rather than the healthy. But if the wrong criteria are chosen, the outcome will be unjust. Our society holds that nepotism is an irrelevant and wrong criterion for the distribution of top jobs, just as social status or wealth are irrelevant criteria for the allocation of medical care or university degrees. Random distribution is the most equitable method in some cases, however. It may be the fairest way of apportioning risk between individuals, and has traditionally been used to select people for dangerous missions. It might also be seen as a fair basis for distributing a limited number of luxuries after everyone's basic needs have been satisfied on an egalitarian basis.

THE CRITERIA FOR JUSTICE

From these preliminary observations, it is clear that what is all-important in constructing a theory of justice is the criterion chosen as appropriate for determining a distribution. Three major criteria are usually offered, *equality*, *merit*, and *need*. Since the eighteenth century at least, when the doctrines of human equality and the 'rights of man' were firmly established in political thought, *equality* has been a fundamental presumption in theories of justice. All individuals are equally deserving unless, or until, proved otherwise. Equality before the law gradually became a tenet of legal systems, replacing the feudal system in which different grades of citizen were tried in different courts and had different legal rights. However, a belief in equality does not necessarily lead to an egalitarian theory of social justice, since the conviction that people are in some basic and abstract sense equal can co-exist with the principle that because people also differ in certain ways they merit different treatment. Fairness requires that equal cases should be treated equally: but, as Aristotle maintained, it is as unjust to treat unequals equally as to treat equals unequally.[1] Certainly, some notion of equal treatment must reside in every theory of justice: a god who strikes down one sinner while another prospers is rightly regarded as unjust. It may be that we have an intuitive perception of equality—young children rapidly learn to call unequal treatment 'unfair', although perhaps this is the result of early conditioning rather than any innate idea of respect for equals. Equality, then, may play a part in a substantive theory of justice, requiring as egalitarian a distribution of goods as possible, as Babeuf demanded in his *Manifesto of the Equals* (1796), or it may operate as an ordering principle at the secondary level, requiring that, as a matter of 'due process', equal cases should be treated alike, in law and in the distribution of goods, according to the other criteria chosen. More will be said of equality as an ideal in its own right at the end of this chapter.

While a thoroughgoing egalitarian theory of justice would hold that each individual deserves as much as the next because of her equal humanity, theories of justice based on *merit* or *desert* distinguish between people and justify differential rewards. (Although 'merit' may suggest present contribution to society and 'desert' may suggest credit accumulated over time, the two criteria function similarly and are sometimes used interchangeably.) Such theories fall into two broad categories, those which hold that moral worth or intrinsic virtues and talents deserve reward, and those which argue that reward should be linked to an individual's contribution to society. In either case a non-natural connection has to be postulated between the individual's merit and the reward, and this in itself is philosophically dubious and practically questionable. Philosophically dubious because there is no *necessary* or *a priori* link between my moral virtue and, say, the amount of wealth which I should be given—the two are incommensurable—and practically questionable because my reward must, surely, be modified according to circumstance: if others already have less than enough, I cannot justly claim a reward commensurate with my own outstanding contribution to society. But the idea that social justice is based on merit, measured by contribution, is the mainstay of the liberal theory of justice, based on the assumption of equality of

---

1. Aristotle, *Politics* (trans. T. A. Sinclair), Penguin, 1962, pp. 73–7, 236–40.

opportunity, the assumption that everyone in the first place should have an equal chance to make a contribution and so to deserve a reward.

Historically, the idea of merit played a progressive role, challenging and superseding the idea that people were entitled absolutely to whatever they happened to inherit or acquire—the rich to their wealth, the poor to their poverty—and when merit, interpreted as contribution, becomes the major criterion of justice, a social element is introduced, the idea that those who contribute most to society deserve most. On this criterion, those who allow their talents to lie fallow deserve no more than those who have no talents. Although a liberal-democratic system of income distribution rests in theory on this criterion, it is in practice very hard to determine exactly what someone's contribution to society has been. The 'self-made man's' wealth rests partly on the labour of his employees, partly on technology and social conditions to which many others have contributed and partly on the fluctuations of the market. His own real contribution may have been minimal compared with these factors. Again, those in high positions who are said to make key contributions to society and so to deserve the highest rewards, presumably gain immeasurable satisfaction from their work and their power and this should be, but normally is not, taken into account in deciding their just reward.

It is usually considered that the criteria of merit and need are diametrically opposed and give rise to antithetical theories of justice,[2] namely liberal and socialist theories. A theory of justice based on *need* presupposes everyone's humanity and equal right to have his/her needs satisfied irrespective of his/her merits, as is suggested by the socialist maxim, 'From each according to his ability, to each according to his needs'. Again, philosophically, it is hard to *prove* that the very fact of being alive and living in a particular society entitles one to help and succour from one's fellows in the satisfaction of one's needs. However, it might be agreed by theorists of most persuasions that human beings have, a priori, equal rights to respect, dignity, and freedom, and it can further be argued that they cannot enjoy these if their basic needs remain unsatisfied. The practical problem in delineating a theory of social justice based on need is to decide what shall count as needs. The minimal income needed to keep a British citizen above the poverty line would make an Indian or Vietnamese relatively rich. While we would accept that good health is a universal need, the standards of medical care considered adequate vary considerably from country to country and the definition of a decent standard of living is even more nation- and culture-specific. It may be possible for a society with socialist aspirations to define and achieve a certain level of need-satisfaction, but this does not remedy the great injustices in a world where many people's most basic needs remain permanently unfulfilled. A system of payment according to need has the disadvantage that outstanding individual contributions may go unrewarded—the bad worker with several dependants would earn more than the productive single worker—but it would be possible to devise a system of distribution which took into account people's needs and, when these were met,

---

2. But William Galston argues that need and desert *are* compatible in *Justice and the Human Good*, Chicago U.P., 1980.

reflected their individual contributions—providing, of course, that resources were more than adequate to meet everyone's basic needs.

A theory of justice based on need reflects a fundamental idea of human equality and happiness, whereas one based on merit rests on a premise of the differential worth of individuals. Both are metaphysical notions not open to empirical proof, and our acceptance of one or the other must rest on a value judgement. And although the ideas of need and merit have supplanted the idea of intrinsic moral worth as a criterion for justice, there are still those who would answer 'No' to the question 'Does the evil man deserve to be happy?'. The theory implied in the latter position poses insuperable problems for any system of social justice, since there is no foolproof way of sorting out the sheep from the goats which could serve as the basis of social policy. This is no doubt why the just man traditionally gets his reward in heaven and the unjust man, in hell.

None of the criteria proposed, equality, merit or need, is problem-free. Desert in the sense of moral worth is hard to measure, merit *qua* contribution may be unintentional or accidental and both criteria may run counter to people's basic needs. Need itself is hard to define, and it is also debatable whether a system of social justice should or should not try to abolish *relative deprivation*, which is the sense of deprivation we get when we see others who are better off than ourselves, even if our own basic needs are met. Furthermore, even when we agree about the criteria for distribution, we may well disagree over the nature of a particular case. For example, having decided that women deserve equal pay with men for equal work, we may dispute whether their work *is* equal in particular cases, as has frequently happened. How a particular criterion should be applied is often hard to decide. The difficulty of choosing between the criteria or deciding a permanent order of priority between them has led some theorists to adopt the 'intuitionist' approach to justice. The intuitionist, in Rawls's words, 'maintains that there exist no higher order constructive criteria for determining the proper emphasis for the competing principles of justice',[3] and holds that there is a plurality of first principles. The intuitionist would therefore contend that the relevance of need, merit, and equality had to be weighed afresh in each case where justice was at stake. But in social policy this approach could lead to confusion and to injustice, in that like cases would not always be treated alike. So it is practically and politically necessary to decide on a dominant criterion, or on constant priorities between the criteria.

Although the criteria for distribution play an important part in any conception of justice, it is clear that justice cannot be said to be *identical* to its criteria. Justice is not solely the satisfaction of need or the reward of merit. But if justice is said instead to be a second-order principle such as due process or fairness in the application of the appropriate criteria in the appropriate case, it is reduced to an insubstantial, ordering principle which cannot give us any advice on how the ideally just society should be organized. There have been many attempts to produce substantive theories of justice (the most important in recent years being

---

3. J. Rawls, *A Theory of Justice*, Harvard U.P., 1971, p. 34.

that of Rawls, which is discussed below) but these differ considerably, according to the other values and ideology to which the theorist adheres. Justice has always been, as democracy is today, a hurrah-word, so there is a risk that the term will be reduced to mean anything of which the speaker or writer approves. While people are quick to point to particular abuses in society as unjust, they are slower to say what form of just organization should replace them. In so far as it is possible to attempt a general definition of justice on which all would agree, we have to stick to the secondary level and define it as an ordering principle which enjoins us to treat like cases alike and, as that implies, with due process, or non-arbitrarily, according to the agreed rules, whatever they may be. Thus we arrive at the paradox that, according to this formal definition, it is possible to administer unjust laws justly: although the fact that due process is used does not make the laws or the society just, it is a shade more just than if those laws were themselves unjustly administered. The ideal is, of course, to have just laws justly administered, but in order to see what such a just society might be like we need a substantive, first-order conception of justice which will in turn rest on value-judgements and ideological convictions. A consideration of the particular conceptions of justice developed within various ideologies will demonstrate what such a substantive view might be like.

LIBERAL, SOCIALIST, AND 'NATURAL' JUSTICE

Liberalism classically takes social justice to consist in distribution according to merit or contribution in a society where there exists a basic equality of opportunity. Given the natural inequalities of talent and inherited and otherwise constituted inequalities of wealth and power, the latter requirement has caused liberals to accept the need for modest state intervention to produce equality of opportunity by means of universal health care and education and other welfare measures. Some non-monetary goods such as rights are distributed equally in liberal society, on the supposition that people are broadly equal in certain respects. Thus, the vote is distributed to each citizen and the duty of jury service is distributed randomly (which in itself is an egalitarian form of distribution) on the assumption that all have an equal sense of fairness and an equal capacity for judgement. The liberal adherence to the idea of the 'just meritocracy' is therefore modified in important respects by more egalitarian considerations, but the dominant idea is that in liberal society the meritorious will be justly rewarded. In this respect it is interesting that the most famous champion of the free market, Hayek (who describes himself as a liberal) admits that the interplay of market forces does not lead to a just outcome.[4] To achieve a merit-based system of justice would therefore, presumably, require a measure of government intervention and economic regulation as well as the welfare measures needed to achieve equality of opportunity. In reality, the absence of equality of opportunity means that the

---

4. F. A. Hayek, *Law, Legislation and Liberty*, Routledge & Kegan Paul, 1982 (one-volume edn), II. pp. 70, 126–8.

system based on merit tends to reinforce the underlying inequalities of liberal society.

In *A Theory of Justice* (1971) Rawls propounds a covertly liberal conception of justice based on a contractual view of society which harks back to Hobbes and Locke. He imagines a hypothetical pre-social or a-social 'original position' in which a number of people are trying to decide consensually on the form of society in which they would all agree to live—they are 'the contracting parties'. The presumption is that they would choose, and agree to maintain, an ideally just society, under the sterile conditions for impartial choice which Rawls posits. Rawls makes various assumptions about these individuals: they are 'mutually indifferent' (neither hostile nor friendly to each other), they do not suffer from 'envy' (feelings of relative deprivation) as long as they are satisfied in their own terms and they are risk-averse. In agreeing on a form of society they all seek to maximize their own interests—interests which Rawls defines as 'primary goods', namely 'rights and liberties, opportunities and powers, income and wealth'.[5] Apart from these assumed propensities, which Rawls takes to be value-free and uncontentious, these people are ciphers. They exist behind a 'Veil of Ignorance' which prevents them from knowing particular details about their own talents, ideals or what their place in the future society might be. The purpose of this device is to get behind people's vested interests, to see what sort of society we would choose if we had no idea of our future place in it. The society chosen in these impartial circumstances would, by Rawls's definition, be just. In earlier versions of his theory, he referred to it as 'justice as fairness' because he argued that the conditions of choice depicted in the original position were ideally fair and would necessarily lead to just choices.

Rawls concludes that in these circumstances each man will choose a kind of society which minimizes his possible losses, making sure that even the worst-off person in that society is not too destitute, in case *he* should turn out to be that person. He calls this the 'maximin' principle, since it maximizes the minimum welfare. The choice of this strategy reflects the assumption that people are not risk-takers, and will therefore choose the safest option. On such a principle, no-one would choose to live in a slave-owning society since he would not risk being a slave despite the gamble that he might end up as the slave-owner living in luxury. Taking the maximin principle into account, plus his definition of primary goods, Rawls asserts that such individuals would logically choose the following two principles of justice:

(1) Each person is to have an equal right to the most extensive basic liberty compatible with a similar liberty for others.
(2) Social and economic inequalities are to be arranged so that they are both: (a) reasonably expected to be to everyone's advantage, and (b) attached to positions and offices open to all.[6]

---

5. Rawls, *A Theory of Justice*, p. 92.
6. Rawls, *A Theory of Justice*, p. 60.

Clarifying the second principle, Rawls says that 'equally open' must mean that equality of opportunity reigns, levelling out natural differences of talent as far as possible. Although Rawls denies that he is justifying meritocracy, this is potentially a merit-based system. He defines 'to everyone's advantage' (2a) in terms of the 'difference principle' which stipulates that a gain for anyone in society must contribute to the expectations of the worst-off person in society (and hence, presumably, to the expectations of all those above him too). He argues that redistribution from the better-off to the worse-off is justified because individuals do not 'deserve' the talents they are born with, and so do not deserve to profit greatly by those talents; similarly, people born without talents or with disabilities do not deserve to suffer or be worse off. Rawls himself regards the difference principle as an egalitarian principle which would prevent the growth of a wide gap between the welfare of the better-off and worse-off members of society but, as critics point out, it is a slim safeguard.[7] The rich can always claim that in increasing their own wealth considerably they are contributing marginally to the welfare of the poorer members of society, for example by increasing their chances of employment and by generating a demand for goods—but this will not produce an egalitarian, but an increasingly stratified society. The first principle of justice has priority over the second, Rawls states: 'people will only agree to limit liberty for the sake of liberty, not for the sake of economic advantage'. However, he concedes that this condition only holds for societies where a certain basic level of material satisfaction has been reached: in very poor countries liberty might justifiably be restricted to further the wellbeing of the people. The economic level at which the first principle gains priority is not, however, made clear, although clearly the West has reached it. The rest of Rawls's long work elaborates the consequences of his conception of justice for social and political organization, and the result looks very like a Western, liberal-democratic society.

Since Rawls's *magnum opus*, there has been a lively debate about social justice, and many attempts to apply his theory to real distributive problems. However, the intellectual tide seems to be turning against 'grand theories' like that of Rawls, which seek to resolve all social questions on the basis of universal principles. Walzer has argued that there exists a diversity of social goods, each of which requires a different distributive criterion, which may vary between societies according to the social meaning or significance of the good. The criteria are, in a sense, intrinsic to the goods. Thus, security and welfare should be distributed according to need, while public positions should go to those with the proper credentials. No general principle will produce just results in every sphere of distribution.[8] If Walzer's analysis is valid, Rawls's whole method is called into question.

More specifically, Rawls has been criticized from the right for being too egalitarian and from the left for being insufficiently so. But his is a typically liberal model of justice. By taking individual preferences as the motivating force of the

---

7. For an early and sustained criticism of Rawls from the left, see R. P. Wolff, *Understanding Rawls*, Princeton U.P. 1977.
8. M. Walzer, *Spheres of Justice*, Martin Robertson, 1983.

model, and asserting that liberty is a primary good, he biases the outcome towards a liberal, *laissez-faire* society, and although he claims that the two principles of justice merely chance to be liberal and follow necessarily from his original, ideologically impartial premises, these premises are themselves those of liberal ideology. In this respect the assumption of lack of envy is crucial, for if the people in the original position knew themselves to be envious, they would surely take steps to minimize the differentials of wealth and wellbeing with something stronger than the difference principle, to avoid the risk of relative deprivation. Rawls proposes that any society or institution can be tested for justice by asking if it lives up to the two principles, but their abstractness makes such testing difficult. It is invariably possible to demonstrate that a social arrangement is to everyone's advantage by taking a limited field of alternatives for comparison. It is better in capitalist society to have businessmen investing and increasing employment prospects while they enrich themselves than to have businessmen taxed so heavily that they have no incentive to invest—but this presupposes that there have to be investors, that capitalism is the only conceivable economic order. In other words, the phrase 'to everyone's advantage' does not specify what comparisons are to be invoked: if the test is made on the basis of an underlying acceptance of a given form of society, the status quo is most likely to be found to be to everyone's advantage.[9]

I have cited Rawls's theory as an exemplar of the liberal view of justice, yet his two principles are not *substantive* in the sense that they state that justice is one thing or another. Rawls himself calls it a *procedural* theory of justice, arguing that:

> pure procedural justice obtains when there is no independent criterion for the right result; instead there is a correct or fair procedure such that the outcome is likewise correct or fair, *whatever it is.*[10]

If the two operational principles of justice are followed, then, the outcome will necessarily be just, and good, although the contours of the just society cannot be specified in advance. There is certainly some justification for taking a procedural approach to justice in the complex real world, where the size of populations and variability of relevant factors make it impossible to specify what each individual should justly have. But in calling his theory of justice 'procedural', Rawls seems to bestow on it an aura of impartiality, although the procedures he specifies are contrived to further a particular form of society, implicit in the original assumptions, which conceal liberal ideals. Although he claims to build a theory of what is good on his account of what is just, or right, he in fact starts out with a definition of primary goods which determines his view of justice—as indeed do most theorists, since it is scarcely possible to separate our conception of what is good for human beings from what we think is right and just for them. Where Rawls is at fault is in presenting his theory as a purely objective and universally applicable argument, when the presuppositions are largely those of liberalism.

---

9. This is shown by W. G. Runciman's application of Rawls's test in *Relative Deprivation and Social Justice*, Routledge & Kegan Paul, 1966, Part I.
10. Rawls, *A Theory of Justice* p. 86. Emphasis added.

The socialist principle of distribution, 'to each according to his needs', is no less 'procedural' than that of Rawls, but the value judgement which it embodies is patently visible. The socialist conception underwent some transformations before it fixed on need as the dominant criterion for justice. The early socialist disciples of Saint-Simon advocated the principle 'from each according to his capacity, to each according to his works', which seems nearer to the merit-based liberal conception. Marx deplored the fact that the capitalist system of justice—reward for contribution—systematically over-rewarded capitalists and exploited workers. He condemned its effect on the worker, whose humanity, dignity and self-respect were threatened and who could scarcely satisfy his own material needs. When Marx claimed that under socialism labourers would be paid the full value of their product he seemed to suggest that socialist societies would adopt a merit-based ideal of justice. In fact, he believed that the merit/contribution principle would prevail only in the first stage of the transition to socialism and that under true socialism *need* would become the criterion for distribution.

Although, as was argued in Chapter 5, socialists hold equality to be the major political ideal, the other criteria also play a part in socialist justice. A socialist ordering of the criteria which determine social justice might be as follows: *need* should prevail as the dominant criterion for ordering the distribution of necessary goods, and allocating opportunities appropriate to talents, with the proviso that equal needs and talents must be treated equally. *Equality* would be invoked in the many areas of life where need is not paramount, and also where the equality of needs and capacities can be assumed, as in the field of political and personal rights. Thirdly, *merit* may determine the distribution of any surplus of goods when basic needs are satisfied—for example, a bonus or incentive scheme might operate once all workers had achieved a satisfactory standard of living. Merit could also properly operate when goods which are irrelevant to needs are to be distributed: the utopian socialist Fourier proposed a complex scheme for the award of honours, worthless but gratifying, to the inhabitants of his utopia. No doubt merit would also prevail in the distribution of *jobs* in any socialist society with a highly specialized industrial economy, so that the most skilled workers got the jobs to which they were best suited, for efficiency's sake. (However, some socialists have envisaged reversion to less complex economies, and even the abolition of the division of labour, which would mean that anyone could pursue any occupation, or indeed several at once; this would eliminate merit in the distribution of work.)

Finally, a socialist society might justly use a random or a rota method of distributing extra goods or positions when all needs were met. This method would also be appropriate for recurring duties. Owen thought that the governing positions would be allocated by rota in his ideal communities, which would have the desirable result of de-professionalizing politics and putting each individual in command and under someone else's command on a regular basis, thus preventing despotic behaviour by the rulers. I have argued elsewhere that a radical form of socialist justice might be achieved by the regular distribution by lottery of jobs, housing, necessary burdens and, most importantly, political power; such a lottery would be impartial between individuals and would be based on the socialist assumption that individuals should be treated as equals. The dynamic of such a system would be that democratic representatives chosen by lottery for a limited and non-renewable term would be highly motivated to legislate to eradicate inequalities in society, lest they themselves should in the future draw a 'losing' ticket in some other distributive sphere.[11]

Evidently, any socialist theory of social justice will, like that of liberals, be a blend of the major criteria which are commonly thought to bear on justice. A socialist who insisted upon distribution solely on the basis of equality would encounter anomalies, as would one who insisted that jobs should be allocated purely on the basis of need or preference. It is the rank ordering of the criteria which is crucial.

One more, limiting criterion might be added to the socialist view of justice, a stipulation that the differentials between the amounts of goods given to individuals should be as small as possible, or should at least be confined within a given range. In other words, having established a welfare minimum via the concept of need, a welfare maximum should also be set, to prevent large differentials of wealth growing and breeding resentment when those at the lower end of the scale perceive that they are relatively deprived. This sort of limitation is hinted at in Rawls's difference principle, but only half-heartedly, as he does not acknowledge in his model that individuals feel envy, or compare themselves with others. Since he does not stipulate that the wellbeing of the better-off and the worse-off should grow in the same proportions, the difference principle would not have the effect of minimizing differentials, and could encourage them. It might be thought deplorable that even a socialist society should have to consider the factor of human envy and the socio-psychological problem of relative deprivation, but presumably until the utopia arrives in which everyone is satiated with personal satisfaction, interpersonal comparisons will be made. (The former USSR failed to check the growth of considerable differentials of income and privilege—this was one of the many reasons why it was not truly socialist, and an important reason for the rejection of the Soviet system by the people. China still suffers similar disparities of wealth.) Many writers outside the socialist school have also condemned wide gaps between wealth and poverty as sources of social divisiveness and injustice. Rousseau stipulated that no man should be poor enough to have to sell himself or rich enough to buy another in the ideal community, while Godwin proposed regulation in an anarchist society to prevent the growth of vast wealth, similar to the 'sumptuary laws' which regulated expenditure and restrained excess and ostentation in earlier societies. So the concern with vast differences of wealth and the danger of relative deprivation is not purely a socialist obsession, although the elimination of such dangers must be a major concern in the delineation of a socialist theory of justice.

Finally, a third category of theories of justice must be mentioned, the conservative theories of justice. An ingenious argument about justice as entitlement based on property rights has been advanced, against Rawls, by

---

11. B. Goodwin, *Justice by Lottery*, Harvester, 1992.

Nozick. It is based on the premise that 'a person who acquires a holding in accordance with the principle of justice in acquisition is entitled to that holding'.[12] This makes entitlement theory 'historical': that is, it takes into account acquisition by accepted methods in the past. Nozick couples this with the assumptions (1) that people are entitled to the benefits derived from their own natural assets (talents, etc.) if these do not harm others, (2) that differential contribution creates differential entitlement, and (3) that rights should not be violated. He believes that entitlement justice could be adequately upheld by the minimal state which he advocates. Although Nozick's assumptions are broadly liberal, the entitlement theory would in practice tend to be conservative, since it leaves little room for questioning or condemning how people came to hold their present resources or for criticizing whatever distributive principle procured those resources for them in the past. (Some prosperous estates in Britain today were granted by monarchs to their current owners' ancestors as a reward for highly suspect activities.)

Less philosophically sound than Nozick's account, although based on similar premises, is the idea of 'natural justice', discussed in Chapter 1, which is firmly rooted in the minds of many people who would have no interest in discussions of equality, need or merit. As has been said, there is no justice in nature, nor injustice, the concept being one which we have invented in an attempt to regulate each others' social activities. The justice which right-wing thinkers regard as natural is usually an existing set of distributions which maintains—or constitutes—a hierarchy or some elitist form of socio-political organization. The argument is that this came about naturally, i.e. in accordance with natural social principles, and is sanctioned by existing laws, and that it must therefore be just. When challenged, such thinkers would probably produce further justifications for such a distribution—tradition, the natural superiority of the favoured classes, God's will. In more vulgar political argument, natural justice is invariably invoked to exclude a group of people from something to which the others feel themselves exclusively entitled. But belonging to a country which happens to find offshore oil off its coast does not in fact make it naturally just that you should have the exclusive use of that oil—as members of the EU once tried to convince Britain—although the ease of access ('possession is nine points of the law') means that in most cases countries will benefit from such resources and, *a fortiori*, from the resources *within* their own territory. Presumably, on the same grounds, the fact that I am born in a country does not give me a greater moral right to live there and enjoy its amenities than someone who may wish to emigrate to that country—although it invariably gives me greater *formal* rights in the form of a passport and citizenship. Likewise, the fact that I am lucky enough to live in a materially affluent society does not make it *just* that I should prosper while others, elsewhere, starve, even if this state of affairs is 'natural' (in the sense of 'unplanned'). Accidents of birth and location are not a proper foundation for justice which is a social, artificial concept, as Hume argued, but while the world is divided into so many rival units, the possibility of any universal, humanitarian

---

12. R. Nozick, *Anarchy, State and Utopia*, Blackwell, 1974, p. 151.

principle of justice operating globally is excluded, and many privileged people will continue to think of the accidents of their birth as their birthright, sanctioned by natural justice.

I have called the dogma of natural justice 'conservative' because it appeals to the innate conservatism in most of us, the desire to keep things as they are. It can hardly be called a theory because it has no clear abstract principles or justification, and so no defence against counterclaims posed by those with other views of nature's intentions. It appeals to us to maintain the *status quo* and rests on *faits accomplis* such as the possession of inherited wealth. If an advocate of natural justice is reminded of the fact that there is now a large 'immigrant' population which was actually *born* in Britain, a fact with the same 'natural' status as the fact that she herself was born in Britain, she will have no second criterion by which to distinguish between the naturalness of the first and the second case. She may, of course, argue that the two facts have a different historical basis and that her historical entitlement to live here is greater than that of a second-generation immigrant: but recent legislation on British citizenship which tried to make precisely such a distinction has been shown to be conceptually confused, and radically unjust. The notion of historical entitlement is a mainstay of the doctrine of natural justice, and has sometimes led to the compulsory expulsion of whole groups from their adopted homes, sometimes to the repatriation of others in 'historic' homelands to the detriment of those already settled there—hence the longstanding Israeli/Palestinian dispute. (The Iraqi invasion of Kuwait in 1990 was based on the contestable claim that Kuwait was 'historically' part of Iraq.) A just social policy simply cannot take into account historical events outside a relatively short time-span—say, one or two generations—without doing grave injury to the living.

Natural justice cannot be admitted as a theory of justice, then, because it suffers such convolutions and self-contradictions in order to prove that what the propounder approves of is naturally just. There is no obviously correct way in which the criteria of naturalness or historical entitlement should be applied. In addition, the doctrine of natural justice is usually propounded self-interestedly by the 'haves' against the 'have-nots' (although when the 'have-nots' use it against the 'haves', it is no better founded), and so it could hardly gain any general credibility as a theory of justice, since *impartiality* is an important element of any such theory. Although natural justice is a fundamentally fallacious account of justice, it is interesting to see that Locke's view of how property came about in the state of nature is akin to the idea of natural justice. According to Locke, God gave the world to men in common but they, by 'mixing their labour' with the raw materials of the natural world, could appropriate it, in particular by tilling and enclosing land. The object appropriated was then justly theirs, according to natural laws, provided that they observed nature's injunction not to appropriate more of anything than they could use—a natural limitation which disappeared when money was invented.[13] The difference between Locke's theory and the

---

13. J. Locke, *Essay*, Chap.V.

version of natural justice discussed above is that the latter entirely omits the idea of *earning the right* to appropriate something, and argues as if mere birth or geographical proximity created certain rights. Locke's argument rested on common assumptions of his time about natural (divine) law, which was contrasted with the transient and often partial secular laws of particular societies. If a well-founded theory of natural law could be formulated, there would be room for a conception of natural justice (which would probably be radical, rather than conservative, in its effects), but this remains an area for speculation. However, in the modern context, where it is utterly divorced from any theory of natural law, the idea of natural justice is an anachronism and a prejudice which should be challenged whenever it is proposed as a justification for some privilege or act of expropriation.

RETRIBUTIVE JUSTICE

Before returning to the general consideration of justice, something must be said about retributive justice, which operates in penal systems. Just as social justice is, according to some, the distribution of goods in proportion to merit, legal justice can be thought of as the distribution of harm in proportion to demerit. The criminal is said to deserve her punishment: some theorists even speak of the criminal's 'right' to punishment. In some theories of retribution, punishment is proportionate to the criminal's moral iniquity, in others, to her infliction of harm on society (a negative contribution). These two rival accounts parallel those which emphasize moral worth and merit, respectively, in social justice. Both theories resolve the problem that misdemeanours and punishments are, by and large, separate and incommensurable, by imputing responsibility and hence guilt to the individual. This responsibility for her moral character and/or for her actions is said to form the bridge between the crime and the punishment, and a necessary condition for retribution. Retribution has close associations with revenge and mere retaliation, but is distinguished from them by the necessity of firmly establishing guilt, and by the fact that legal justice is dispensed according to due process and, in a democratic country, by laws to which everyone has supposedly consented.

During the last century or so, the idea that people's characters and actions are determined by social conditions has pervaded our penal system and modified the concept of responsibility. Such a theory can broadly be referred to as 'deterministic'. During the Enlightenment, theorists like Beccaria and Godwin argued that it was not the criminal who was responsible for the crime but society collectively,[14] and utopias were invented on the supposition that in

---

14. W. Godwin, *Enquiry Concerning Political Justice* (Ed. K. C. Carter), Clarendon Press, 1971, Bk VI. Godwin also cited the earlier humanitarian arguments of C. Beccaria, *Dei Delitti e delle Pene*, 1764.

ideal social circumstances crime would be entirely eliminated. According to the determinist view, whether criminality is caused by environmental factors, or, as theorists like Eysenck argue, by hereditary factors, it is unjust to punish the criminal *retributively*, as if she had committed her crime of her own free will and deserved to suffer accordingly. The most that can be justified is to punish her: (a) to protect society by segregating her; (b) to deter her from committing the crime again; (c) to reform her; or (d) to make an example of her which will deter others from similar crimes. These four, qualitatively different justifications have given rise to four separate accounts of punishment, all of which are challengeable on both philosophical and practical grounds (which there is no space to discuss here) but which at least avoid the two problems inherent in retribution, that of moral responsibility and that of whether society has the right to pass judgement on an individual, let alone to treat her inhumanely because of such a judgement and deprive her of freedom and dignity.

The dispensation and vindication of criminal justice cannot therefore be separated from the general conception of social justice which prevails. A liberal society which holds that the successful woman is responsible for her success and so deserves her reward is also likely to hold that the criminal is responsible for her crime and merits her punishment. A conservative society which believes that intrinsic moral worth should be rewarded will also seek to punish moral iniquity for its own sake, even beyond the degree merited by the crime committed. By contrast, a socialist society ought to acknowledge fully the environmental causes of crime and only punish criminals as far as prevention requires it. (But from what we know of judicial processes in communist countries such as China, a retributive element persists, incongruously, with individuals being blamed rather than social circumstances.) However, it is perhaps as unlikely that any society could forgo some notions of responsibility, guilt and retribution in its penal system as that it could entirely forgo the idea of merit in social justice, for ultimately most political ideologies, and systems, operate on an inconsistent mixture of free will and determinist assumptions.

The institutions of criminal justice have contributed something to theories of social justice, namely, the ideas of due process and of equity in the dispensation of justice, which are equally applicable and relevant to the allocation of goods and opportunities in society as a whole. The Rawlsian idea of justice as a procedure rather than an outcome is also analogous in its form to the judicial process where the outcome, or verdict, of a trial is not specifiable in advance, but the proper and fair procedures for reaching a verdict can be specified. But as with any distribution, the procedure and outcome may differ in their degree of justice: perfectly fair trials have resulted in verdicts which were later found to be unjust, and the same can occur in procedural social justice. When considering distributive justice, we need to bear in mind the legal model but not to over-emphasize the parallel since the persistent emphasis on guilt and retribution, despite the efforts of penal reformers, makes it an unsuitable model for the allocation of social goods where other considerations have also to be borne in mind.

WHAT IS JUSTICE?

Justice is a moral as well as a political concept, which, according to the moral philosopher, can be applied to any or all of the three stages of action—to the intention, the act, and the result. Justice at one stage rarely guarantees justice at another, hence we have problem cases like that of Robin Hood, whose intention of increasing the happiness of the poor (by robbing the rich) was doubtless just and benevolent. Some would say that the *outcome* of his action was just, some would not, but most would agree that his favourite *procedure* was unjust. Only in the simplest case can a just procedure be specified which is sure to lead to a just and predictable outcome, the case which Rawls calls 'perfect procedural justice'.[15] This is exemplified in the division of a cake between two (or more) people. If the principle '*I* cut, *you* choose' is followed, the outcome will always be a fair, equal division of the cake. However much the cutter's intention might be to take the largest share herself, she is obliged to divide the cake equally to avoid the certainty that an unequal division will mean that the smallest slice is for her, the last to choose. In the seventeenth century, this principle was put forward in Harrington's *Oceana* (1656), and gained the name of 'Harrington's Law', and it remains of great interest, being relevant to political and other decisions and the making of contracts. But unfortunately this simple principle of social justice cannot be the foundation of social policy, for those who cut the cake are not those who eat it, and vice versa, owing to the elite nature of governments. But a society where government was by rota, as Owen suggested, might to some extent realize the virtues and the safeguards embodied in Harrington's Law.

One's choice of a theory of justice depends on one's ideological and moral outlook: this in turn also determines whether one locates justice in intentions, acts or outcomes. A moralist concerned with individual responsibility and virtue might emphasize justice in intention and action and tend to disregard *results*, which are never entirely predictable, as long as the two former components were just. But intention is notoriously difficult to establish. In any case, nobody would seriously justify a bad political system or an unjust society on the grounds that the ruler's intentions were good, even if that were cited as a mitigating consideration. Orthodox utilitarians took account primarily of the *outcome* of action and thus avoided these problems: if the outcome maximized social utility it was said to be just. But this ignored the fact that social utility could be increased overall by actions which were, by conventional criteria, unjust, as in the case of Robin Hood. The example regularly used to challenge utilitarians is that, in the case where social utility would be increased by the killing of an innocent scapegoat, their theory would permit this gross injustice. To avoid this and other contradictions, J. S. Mill and others, known as 'rule utilitarians', proposed action-guiding rules to be followed in pursuit of utility: foremost among them was the rule of justice.[16] This avoided various discrepancies but diluted Bentham's

15. Rawls, *A Theory of Justice*, p. 85.
16. J. S. Mill, *Utilitarianism*, Collins, 1962, Chap. V.

injunction that utility was the absolute principle by which everything should be judged. Mill's amendment shifted the emphasis from the outcome to the act, which would be assessed according to whether it followed the justice rule.

Any application of a theory of justice to existing situations (outcomes) implicitly passes judgements on the results of past *actions*, viewing them in the light of their results. When new reforms are proposed to rectify an unjust situation, the theory must scrutinize the justice or otherwise of the proposed action as well as that of the intended outcome: that is, in assessing politics, policy and other activities with respect to justice we have to take into account both means and ends. The question often arises whether a *prima facie* unjust means may be employed to achieve a just end, particularly with reference to redistribution, violence, and revolution. Can injustice be committed for justice's sake? To avoid the censure of those who would say it cannot, because justice, like rights, is to be viewed as inviolable, the reformer or revolutionary will usually allude to the injustices of the existing situation—the wealth to be redistributed has been gained by exploitation of the poor, or those who propose political violence are themselves being unjustly repressed and coerced. Ultimately, in such cases one has to make a calculation of where the greater justice lies but, since outcomes are unpredictable, there is always the risk that taking unjust action will still not result in greater justice. Consciousness of this fact should not, however, turn into a general justification for political quiescence or inaction. Rawls offers an alternative solution to this dilemma which is tempting because it avoids the necessity of weighing means against ends and calculating the incalculable: he suggests that if we cannot be sure of the outcome we should specify a just procedure, and keep to it. But this assumes that the existing situations to which the procedure will be applied are not themselves grossly unjust: and, as was suggested above, Rawls actually builds his own preferred outcome into his two procedural principles. Those who advocate viewing justice procedurally (and therefore limiting the scope of proposed reforms by the procedure) usually do so because they have already attained a state of society which they regard as just, and have specified procedures which perpetuate it. In other words, procedures tend to grow out of an established social system which they reflect and support. The second-order components of justice, fairness and due process, cannot alone create a just society if it does not already exist, and they may even reinforce existing injustices, although they can prevent certain other injustices being perpetrated.

Many important debates arise in connection with social justice, which form the stuff of contemporary political argument. Can justice exist without freedom? Rawls's theory suggests that it certainly cannot, as does liberalism in general, for the liberal theory of justice is said to be 'commutative', based on free exchange.[17] But there is no reason to think that justice differently defined could not exist in a society which was unfree by liberal standards. Everyone could be equally subordinated to the whole by due process in the interests of greater material and moral wellbeing for all, as Rousseau suggests. Justice implies a comparison

---

17. W. B. Gallie, 'Liberal morality and socialist morality', in *Philosophy, Politics and Society*, 1st Series (Ed. P. Laslett), Blackwell, 1956.

between equals, but if in some society equals were equally unfree it could not be said to be unjust on those grounds alone. The charge of injustice is only appropriate when some equals are less free for no good reason. It is really when 'justice' is treated as synonymous with 'good' that there is said to be an essential link between freedom and justice by those who consider freedom a vital part of the Good Life. Certainly, in an ideal society people would be free *and* justly treated, but in imperfect society freedom must sometimes be curtailed for the sake of greater justice, and justice as a distributive and ordering principle can still operate in the absence of a high degree of personal freedom.

Ever since the Industrial Revolution made material affluence seem imminently possible, philosophers have wondered whether problems of social justice might not disappear altogether if a state of superabundance were achieved. If everyone had more than enough, what grounds for complaint could there be, even if some still had more than others? From the utopian socialists to quasi-utopians such as Marcuse, the prospect of abundance has provided a convenient hypothetical solution to problems of distribution—even if that prospect is now receding in the West, and has never existed for most of the world. But, although social justice mainly concerns itself with the distribution of *scarce* goods, in any society, however abundant, there will always be 'positional goods', which remain scarce and will have to be distributed justly. Not everyone can win a race, or be Prime Minister, or live in a secluded country cottage, even in utopia. Ideally, such positional goods might be distributed to those who volunteered to forego some amount of material goods instead of (as so often) to those who are already well supplied. Certainly, a principle for distributing positional goods would be needed even in a situation of abundance, where feelings of envy or deprivation might well shift to the possession or lack of positional goods. It seems, then, that the concept of justice will be with us as long as society lasts, however cornucopian society becomes.

NATIONS AND GENERATIONS

Parallel to questions about the nature of justice *within* a society, is the question whether there should be justice in the allocation of goods between nations. In the second half of the twentieth century, decolonization and the emergence of many new and impoverished nations burdened by debt and threatened by famine has made it an urgent question. According to Singer's 'humanitarian' theory of moral responsibility, the individual has an unlimited duty to help other human beings if it is within his power so to do, even to the extent of reducing himself to bare subsistence level, in order to give to them.[18] (Many would repudiate this logic, being unable to endure the consequences of such a theory, which suggests that we should either reduce ourselves to poverty or suffer constant, overwhelming guilt.) Likewise, if the same principle of moral obligation were applied to nations, most

18. P. Singer, 'Famine, Affluence and Morality', in *Philosophy, Politics and Society*, 5th Series (Eds. P. Laslett and J. Fishkin), Blackwell, 1979, p. 23.

nations would repudiate it, for it would require the depletion of their own resources and the reduction of their citizens' standard of living for the benefit of distant peoples with no well-established claim on their goodwill. Nevertheless, even if the unlimited obligation of Singer's theory is rejected and some concept of limited altruism replaces it, we cannot regard any particular country as an enclave where justice reigns when that country exists in a world where, generally, justice is constantly denied. Justice, however it is conceived, can logically take no account of nationality but enjoins equal treatment of all equal human beings, everywhere. The enormity of the redistributive task which this proposition entails baffles even philosophers, let alone politicians, but the focus on aid to the developing countries indicates some acknowledgement of the industrialized countries' responsibility to share the world's resources more justly. The Brandt report (1980) made this duty quite clear, although little action was taken on its basis. The case for international redistribution has been complicated, and not always strengthened, by the argument that the colonizing countries owe restitution and reparations to their ex-colonies. Questions of historical guilt across generations and between nations are as contentious as those of historical entitlement, but to base the case for international redistribution on the fact that it is grotesque for some to live in luxury while others die of malnutrition gives it an inexorable and persuasive logic—except perhaps to those who think that this, too, is natural justice.

The question of 'justice between generations' has also been widely debated since Rawls's assertion that men in the 'original position' would agree to a 'just savings principle' to cater for and improve the lives of their descendants. Many philosophers, such as Barry, have joined in the discussion of whether we could have *duties* towards future, as yet non-existent generations, and whether we should allocate goods justly between ourselves and them.[19] This is not merely an intriguing puzzle for philosophers, however, since some practical dilemmas of social policy must be resolved by assumptions (albeit covert ones) about the nature of our duties to posterity. For example, whether we should endeavour to reinvest in and renew our industrial base, or go on a prolonged and terminal spending spree is a vital question for the present and future inhabitants of Britain. Whether we have a duty to preserve the world's exhaustible resources for our descendants or a right to exhaust them over the next generation or two—as it is predicted we shall—is a question of global importance, rightly brought into political prominence by the Greens in Germany, and ecology parties in many other European countries. How we should treat the elderly in society (who impoverished themselves to some extent to provide a brighter future for us, and to pay for their own pensions) is another vexed question, becoming more prominent as demography changes, the population ages and inflation erodes life-savings. All these are problems of cross-generational justice.

---

19. B. Barry, *Theories of Justice*, Harvester, 1989, pp. 189–202; see also B. Barry and R. I. Sikora (Eds.), *Obligations to Future Generations*, Temple U.P., 1978.

Laslett argues that we have duties to near-future but not to distant-future generations, and no duties to past generations, except, of course, to those still living.[20] How could such a cut-off point between the near and the distant future rationally operate? The gaps in Laslett's argument show up the complexity of the issue. His case is based on the view, mentioned above, that justice requires us to further the wellbeing of any human being '*actual or potential*' (i.e. including future beings). Does this mean that we actually have a duty to produce as many children as possible so that we can further their wellbeing? The concept of a potential human being is problematic in theory and in practice, as the controversy over abortion has shown. Rawls is nearer the mark than Laslett, perhaps, when he says that men in the original position would see themselves as possible parents in the future society and would therefore choose to provide for the welfare of *all* children under the rubric of justice by choosing a just rate of saving.[21] This argument for cross-generational justice clearly rests on a very different basis from Laslett's view of unlimited moral responsibility—a basis of natural affection. In summary (although the debate is far too complex, and too emotive, to summarize) it can be said that while our duty to living generations, older and younger, can be clearly delineated on the basis of conventional theories of justice, our duties to unborn generations cannot rest on justice defined via equality, need or merit (for all we know, they may be undeserving, or inferior to ourselves, and if we are too careless with nuclear weapons they may not exist at all). Such a duty must rest on a conception of society and humanity as continuing entities, whose preservation has an absolute value. This judgement about the intrinsic value of the human race has no special connection with the idea of justice and is one which not everyone would make. To avoid getting into a debate about life, the universe and everything at this point, we might say that justice can only, practically, concern itself with existing situations and with the living, and also with the marginal overlap between them, the recently dead and the soon-to-be-born. We cannot be required to act morally towards people who will not be born for another hundred years, but we might reasonably be enjoined to act justly and morally towards the next two generations.

The strong moral element in the concept of justice that makes it such a powerful political ideal also creates the danger that anything viewed as morally bad will also be described as 'unjust', as if the words were mere synonyms. Perhaps nothing which is morally bad can fail to be unjust, since bad conduct usually consists of treating others as less than equal or as means to our own ends, and thus ignoring the injunction to treat equals equally which justice makes. But the political concept of social justice has a more limited application than morality, and what is unjust in society as a whole is not necessarily the result of morally bad actions by individuals. The *ordering and regulatory* nature of justice was stated by Plato, for whom justice denoted a due proportion and harmony within society, or a healthy balance between the various faculties of the individual: the just society is

20. P. Laslett, 'The conversation between the generations', in *Philosophy, Politics and Society* (Eds. P. Laslett and J. Fishkin), Blackwell, 1979.
21. Rawls, *A Theory of Justice*, s. 44.

the internally harmonious society and the same is true of individual men.[22] This view is significantly wider than the modern, individualistic and consumption orientated view of justice, which concentrates on who gets what. Plato emphasizes the interrelations of individuals and society, which is largely ignored by the liberal theory of justice, although implicit in the socialist and conservative views. Perhaps future speculation on the subject should take account of the social dimensions which Plato extols.

A fable by J. L. Borges, *The Lottery in Babylon*,[23] helps to clarify a common conviction about the nature of justice. In the mythical Babylon of which he writes, the citizens cast lots every sixty days to decide what their role in society shall be for the next two months. One may draw the lot of a convicted murderer, and be executed, another may be in command of the army, another a slave, and so on. After two months the lots are cast again, and the shuffling recommences. In describing the origins of the custom, Borges says that it started in a small way, but then people became so addicted to the stimulating uncertainty and variety that they demanded the extension of the lottery to all aspects of life. Formally, the Babylonian system is reminiscent of Rawls's procedural model, but the people in the 'original position' in Babylon are *inveterate risk-takers* and ask for no future safeguards for themselves. The justice of the system lies in the *process* of the lottery alone, since of the institutions of Babylon are clearly cruel or unjust and cannot, Borges implies, be reformed. (In this respect Babylon differs greatly from the socialist lottery society which I proposed earlier; that would *create* justice, whereas Borges's lottery merely tempers injustice.) Most people would not willingly live in this Babylon, nor would they consider it the epitome of a just society although, procedurally, it is so. This suggests the extent to which our desire for justice is linked to a desire for the regularity, orderliness, and security, which due process and equity bring into our lives. Likewise, social justice is valued for its importation of these same qualities into the distribution of goods. This is why the best antonym of 'just' is 'arbitrary' and why, while ideologists of various persuasions disagree about the criteria for dispensing social justice—and such disputes are important for political life—none seriously questions the place of justice among our political ideals. No other political ideal remains similarly unchallenged.

JUSTICE AND EQUALITY

Cursory observation of society shows us inequalities of age, ability, sex, intelligence, education and social and economic positions. Why then, when it seems already to be a lost cause, is equality so important and controversial a part of political theory and ideology? From what has been said already, it is clear that justice is intimately connected with equality in the sense of 'fair and non-arbitrary treatment of equals', although it does not necessarily require a substantive

22. Plato, *Republic* (trans. H. D. P. Lee), Penguin, 1955, Part 5.
23. J. L. Borges, *Labyrinths*, Penguin, 1970. For a justification of the lottery principle, see B. Goodwin, *Justice by Lottery*.

equality between individuals. Equality is also the first assumption of morality: we act morally towards others because we assume that they are equally sensitive, equally vulnerable and equally worthy of respect in some formal or abstract sense, even when there are visible differences in the sensitivity and worth of particular individuals. If the people in a certain group are defined as inferior, the requirement to act morally towards them is, some would say, annulled. Genocide, and the oppression of particular groups or races, has usually been justified by redefining such groups as sub-human, unworthy of moral respect. Such a re-definition of the Jews and various other East European peoples was promulgated to justify the murderous activities of the Nazis. The assertion of the ultimate equality of all human beings operates as a defence against such treatment. The equality of humankind, and policies based on it, have sometimes been justified on the empirical grounds that people resemble each other in more ways than they differ, yet it could be said that everyday experience defeats this assertion—what do we notice if not the differences between individuals? However, from the point of view of a dog or a mosquito no doubt the similarities between people are far more striking than the differences. The abstract models which political philosophers sometimes construct, in which all individuals are identical and equally wise, moral and autonomous, obviously dictate that justice should consist in the substantively equal treatment of all. But the natural and artificial inequalities which exist outside philosopher's models demand a justice based on carefully structured *unequal* treatment, devised so as to remove injustices and to compensate for natural disadvantages. Theories of justice, as we saw, need to stipulate the kinds of inequality which make equal treatment inappropriate— inequalities of ability, need and merit, for example. Therefore, although we know intuitively that it would be wrong for any judge to treat similar cases differently, and that a just distribution should be an equal one in the absence of other considerations, numerically equal treatment is not in itself a *sufficient* condition for justice and may even run counter to justice.

An examination of the supposed causes of inequality should precede any discussion of whether equality should itself count as an independent political ideal, and how it should function in a theory of justice. Hobbes imagined a pre-social state of nature in which men had a natural equality of experience and 'prudence' (reason) and an approximate equality of strength. 'From this equality of ability ariseth equality of hope in the attaining of our ends.'[24] The serpent enters this paradise via the scarcity of resources: if two men both want the same thing, and have 'equality of hope' of attaining it, they become enemies. They also, said Hobbes, try to preserve themselves by anticipatory violence against others; furthermore, they desire distinction, the estimation of others, and will extort it 'by damage' if necessary. Thus, approximate natural equality leads, paradoxically, to a war of all against all and the subjection of some by others. Rousseau also sought to explain how the equality existing between happy savages in his mythical state of nature disappeared as societies were formed. He too pinpointed the desire for

---

24.   T. Hobbes, *Leviathan*, Penguin, 1968, p. 184.

distinction as a major cause, along with the inequality of talents which created inequalities of property. Worst of all, social distinction became attached to the possession of property, producing rivalry, ambition, and greed. 'All these evils were the first effect of property, and the inseparable attendants of growing inequality.'[25] So Rousseau too suggests that inequality is not natural, but is imposed by circumstance and, more precisely, by society. 'Man is born equal but everywhere he is in chains.'

Rousseau's hypothesis that men are equal in a pre-social state, or at birth, is tantamount to asserting the abstract equality of humankind, which other eighteenth-century writers such as Paine did more prosaically. However, one need not believe that equality is humankind's original state to believe that it should be a political goal, and today most writers avoid speculating about man's natural state. It is, of course, possible to acknowledge the presence of inequality in society without condemning it: indeed, many conservatives applaud it. Why, then, did Rousseau, the socialists, and the anarchists abominate it? The first, practical reason was the *overt social misery* resulting from inequality in combination with scarcity, which they condemned on humanitarian grounds. Second, inequalities of wealth and privilege lead to *inequalities of power* and to *dependence* and the subordination of some to the will of others, which deprive them of dignity and autonomy. Rousseau thought that such dependence had come about through the need for joint economic activity. Godwin argued that an unequal accumulation of property leads to 'servility, dependency and domination', while Condorcet noted that educational inequalities lead to the dependency and helplessness of the individual. Post-Enlightenment philosophers elaborated these basic criticisms. The list could be extended, but enough has been said to show that social inequalities are not condemned *a priori* by such philosophers, but because they violate other ideals—the enjoyment of a happy, independent, worthwhile life, to which all individuals are equally entitled by virtue of being human.

The champions of inequality defend it not by denying the latter assertion, for this would run counter to the dictates of most religions and moralities, but by emphasizing the functional usefulness of inequality in society, which supposedly benefits everyone. Mandeville argued in *The Fable of the Bees* that inequality produced talent, endeavour and art and Hume concurred. Later, Kant argued against Rousseau that 'inequality is a rich source of much that is evil, but also of everything that is good'. Social Darwinism, which asserted that the 'survival of the fittest' principle should operate unimpeded in society as in nature, gave a new impulse to the inegalitarian cause, with its postulate that some individuals are inferior and that to protect them or compensate for their deficiencies weakens the calibre of society as a whole. Nature abhors equality: 'progress through inequality' was the message. Finally, modern pluralist theories which rejoice in social differences may easily be converted into a defence of inequality. The defenders of inequality usually justify it by reference to holistic criteria such as 'the quality of life', 'the survival of cultures' or 'the advance of civilization',

---

25. J.-J. Rousseau, *A Discourse . . . On Inequality*, Dent, 1913, p. 203.

perhaps because it cannot be satisfactorily justified on individualistic grounds, given that it implies the oppression or even sacrifice of some individuals for others, or for the social whole. Other inegalitarians simply defend social inequality as the just reflection of the genetic differences between individuals, thus implicitly abandoning any conception of their equal worth or equal right to a satisfying life. Sociobiology, taken up by some New Right thinkers, justifies the machinations of the 'selfish gene', and hence inequality, in a way reminiscent of the biological and racial 'theories' produced by Nazism. The assumption that inequality is a natural, permanent phenomenon leads to political theories vindicating hierarchical or elitist forms of society, or justifying unalloyed meritocracy. With the move towards conservative politics during the 1980s, there was a spate of books directed against equality and egalitarians: some of their titles are listed in the notes to this chapter.[26] Most of these works were based on the sort of suppositions mentioned above and/or on dubious arguments such as those which will now be described.

Apart from the argument that inequality strengthens and embellishes the social whole, which seems always to be directed *de haut en bas* (would Spencer have agreed to be weeded out if he was discovered to be genetically inferior?), there are several arguments which attempt to refute egalitarianism by pointing out its shortcomings—these, indeed, are more commonly employed than outright defences of inequality. The first is that we shall never achieve real equality because of the prevalence of natural inequalities and of other human factors such as social envy and greed. This is like saying 'You'll never get 100% in this examination, so don't bother to enter for it'—the fallacy is self-evident. Second, it is argued that egalitarian policies always mean 'levelling down, not up'. This is factually misleading because in any redistribution process some are levelled down, others up. Historically, some socialist revolutions have reduced everyone's living standards for a time: on the other hand the Chinese population is clearly much better-off today than before 1949. To answer this argument in the factual terms in which it is proposed, the egalitarian can argue that in most cases those levelled down are a small minority, so that on any majoritarian principle the levelling up more than compensates in society as a whole. A third argument misdirected against equality was termed the 'tadpole argument' by Tawney. Although many tadpoles are hatched and few survive to become toads, the fact that a few survive is said to justify nature's enterprise. Similarly, some people justify our unequal society (Tawney was writing a study of Britain in the late 1920s[27]) by the fact that exceptional individuals can rise above it. In India, the 'Bombay-beggar-turned-millionaire' myth may comfort or even inspire the poor and alleviate the consciences of the rich, but it is scarcely a *justification* of the

26. Typical of the recent anti-egalitarian school are A. Flew, *The Politics of Procrustes* (Temple Smith, 1981), K. Joseph and J. Sumption, *Equality* (John Murray, 1979), W. Letwin (Ed.) *Against Equality* (Macmillan, 1983). Egalitarianism is defended against such critics in P. Green, *The Pursuit of Inequality* (Blackwell, 1981).
27. R. H. Tawney, *Equality*, 4th edn, Allen & Unwin, 1931.

hierarchical system there. The argument that equality conflicts with freedom has already been discussed in Chapter 5, and shown to be untenable. In short, the arguments offered against egalitarian policies are essentially weak or fallacious, and usually quite tangential to the basic justification of egalitarianism. This tangentiality is not accidental—for to challenge directly the moral tenet of human equality of worth is to open a Pandora's box of amoral and immoral arguments.

Tawney said that to postulate equality as a *fact* about men's characters and intelligence is untenable, but as a value-judgement it is acceptable. Socially, politics should operate to produce equality of circumstance and of quality of life, and although complete equality is not attainable it should be—he said—the aim. This is as good a statement of the egalitarian position as any, and neatly demonstrates that when an egalitarian proclaims 'All men and women are equal' she does not delude herself that this is a fact, but proclaims it as an aspiration. Egalitarian policies in the West have usually been associated with left-wing ideology and the critique of property, but other cultures provide different good reasons for aspiring to a more equal society. In *Coming of Age in Samoa* (1928), Mead described how the Samoan community discouraged precocity and outstanding enterprise or achievement, and was more charitable towards the lazy and the stupid than to over-achievers. This 'levelling down' attitude produced social peace and harmony and in many respects a happy and satisfying way of life, it would appear. Westerners should ask themselves how far the naturalness and inevitability of inequality may have been magnified by an ideology which upholds an economic system whose very essence is division of labour, specialization of function, and large disparities of wealth.

Equality, then, is an ambiguous term. It can be invoked as a substantive or absolute principle which specifically determines the outcome of a distribution, e.g. one-person-one-vote, a uniform distribution. But most political debate focuses on more sophisticated versions of equality: equality of opportunity, equality of treatment or equality of resources. These are second-order, procedural principles which determine strategies and methods of distribution, but not particular outcomes. They are flexible enough to avoid being procrustean, to encompass individual human differences, and are therefore more powerful than the idea of simple, numerical equality—although this too has its place in the distribution of goods such as rights. In one form or another equality is invoked by every theory of justice, if only *qua* equity and due process, for only thus can anyone be sure that their case will be treated on a par with others. An account of equality is thus central to any theory of social justice, but whether equality is valued as an end in itself depends on one's ideological standpoint.

Theoretical analysis can only take us to the threshold of justice, which it analyses as a second-order, formal (insubstantial) principle. At that point, we need the values which ideology supplies to make the ideal substantive, and to step across into the Just Society. In this respect justice illustrates, best of all the ideas discussed in this book, the intimate relation between political ideas and ideologies, and the impossibility of understanding either in isolation.

FURTHER READING

J. Baker, *Arguing for Equality*, Verso, 1987.

B. Barry, *Justice as Impartiality*, Clarendon Press, 1995.

A. Beteille, *The Idea of Natural Inequality*, Oxford U.P., 1984.

D. Boucher and P. Kelly (Eds.), *Social Justice: From Hume to Hayek*, Routledge, 1997.

T. Campbell, *Justice*, Macmillan, 1988.

B. Goodwin, *Justice by Lottery*, Harvester, 1992.

C. Kukathas and P. Pettit, *Rawls: 'A Theory of Justice' and its Critics*, Polity Press, 1990.

W. Kymlicka (Ed.), *Justice in Political Philosophy*, Edward Elgar, 1992.

D. Miller, *Social Justice*, Clarendon Press, 1976.

P. Pettit, *Judging Justice*, Routledge & Kegan Paul, 1980.

L. P. Pojman and R. Westmoreland, *Equality: Selected Readings*, Oxford U.P., 1996.

J. Rawls, *A Theory of Justice*, Harvard U.P., 1971.

M. Walzer, *Spheres of Justice*, Martin Robertson, 1983.

Index of Concepts and Proper Names

Italics refer to main entries